D1384904

HMH | into Reading™

Teacher's Guide

GRADE 3 • VOLUME 2

Authors and Advisors

Alma Flor Ada • Kylene Beers • F. Isabel Campoy
Joyce Armstrong Carroll • Nathan Clemens
Anne Cunningham • Martha C. Hougen
Elena Izquierdo • Carol Jago • Erik Palmer
Robert E. Probst • Shane Templeton • Julie Washington

Contributing Consultants

David Dockterman • Mindset Works®
Jill Eggleton

Printed in the U.S.A.

ISBN 978-0-544-46125-3

2 3 4 5 6 7 8 9 10 0029 27 26 25 24 23 22 21 20 19

4500751544 B C D E F G

Welcome to
HMH Into Reading™

Houghton Mifflin Harcourt is delighted to welcome you to our brand-new literacy program. *HMH Into Reading*™ combines the best practices of balanced literacy with comprehensive coverage of **English Language Arts curriculum standards**.

The authors and consultants who contributed to *Into Reading* share a deep commitment to education and a passion for learning. We look forward to sharing the story of our program with you—and to helping all of your students get *Into Reading* and become lifelong learners.

CONTENTS

PROGRAM OVERVIEW

HMH Into Reading™ Authors and Advisors

Kylene Beers, Ed.D.
Nationally known lecturer and author on reading and literacy; national and international consultant dedicated to improving literacy, particularly for striving readers; coauthor of *Disruptive Thinking*, *Notice & Note: Strategies for Close Reading*, and *Reading Nonfiction: Notice & Note Stances, Signposts, and Strategies*

Joyce Armstrong Carroll, Ed.D., H.L.D.
Nationally known consultant on the teaching of writing, with classroom experience in every grade from primary through graduate school; codirector of Abydos Literacy Learning, which trains teachers in writing instruction; coauthor of *Acts of Teaching: How to Teach Writing*

Nathan Clemens, Ph.D.
Associate Professor, University of Texas, Austin; researcher and educator with a focus on improving instruction, assessment, and intervention for students with reading difficulties in kindergarten through adolescence

Anne Cunningham, Ph.D.
Professor, University of California, Berkeley; nationally recognized researcher on literacy and development across the life span; coauthor of *Book Smart: How to Develop and Support Successful, Motivated Readers*

Martha C. Hougen, Ph.D.
Teacher educator focused on reforming educator preparation to better address the diverse needs of students; coeditor and contributing author of *Fundamentals of Literacy Instruction & Assessment Pre-K–6*

Carol Jago, M.A.
Nationally known author and lecturer on reading and writing with 32 years of classroom experience; author of *With Rigor for All* and the forthcoming *The Book in Question: How and Why Reading Is in Crisis*; national consultant who focuses on text complexity, genre instruction, and the use of appropriate literature in the K–12 classroom

Erik Palmer, M.A.
Veteran teacher and consultant whose work focuses on how to teach oral communication and good thinking (argument, persuasion, and reasoning), and how to use technology in the classroom to improve instruction; author of *Well Spoken* and *Good Thinking*

Robert E. Probst, Ph.D.
Professor Emeritus, Georgia State University; nationally known literacy consultant to national and international schools; author of *Response & Analysis* and coauthor of *Disruptive Thinking*, *Notice & Note: Strategies for Close Reading*, and *Reading Nonfiction: Notice & Note Stances, Signposts, and Strategies*

Shane Templeton, Ph.D.
Foundation Professor Emeritus of Literacy Studies at the University of Nevada, Reno; researcher and practitioner with a focus on developmental word knowledge; author of *Words Their Way*

Julie Washington, Ph.D.
Professor, Georgia State University; researcher with an emphasis on the intersection of cultural dialect use, literacy attainment, and academic performance; author of numerous articles on language and reading development, and on language disorders in urban children growing up in poverty; consultant for *iRead*, *System 44*, and *READ 180* Universal

Into Reading and *¡Arriba la lectura!*

Alma Flor Ada, Ph.D.
Professor Emerita, University of San Francisco; internationally renowned expert in bilingual literature and literacy; author of over 200 award-winning books, both academic and for young readers; a leading mentor in transformative education

F. Isabel Campoy
Award-winning bilingual author of over 150 children's books of poetry, theater, stories, biographies, art, and culture; internationally recognized scholar, educator, and translator; a member of the North American Academy of Spanish Language

Elena Izquierdo, Ph.D.
Associate Professor of teacher education at the University of Texas, El Paso; researcher and practitioner with a focus on dual-language education, biliteracy, and educational equity for English learners

Contributing Consultants

David Dockterman, Ed.D.
Lecturer at Harvard University Graduate School of Education whose work focuses on turning research into effective, innovative practice to meet the variable needs of all learners; advisor on *MATH 180* and *READ 180* Universal

Jill Eggleton, QSO (Queen's Service Order in Literacy and Education), Ed.D.
Leading balanced-literacy expert, international consultant, and teacher with over 35 years of teaching and administration experience; trains and inspires educators in how to incorporate balanced-literacy methods in the classroom; Adjunct Professor, Sioux Falls University; Margaret Mahy Literacy Medal award winner; author of over 1,000 children's books, poetry, and teacher resources

Develop Collaborative, Self-Directed Learners

Into Reading's **Workshop Model** utilizes a gradual release of responsibility that sets students on a path to mastery and success.

Reading Workshop

A quick whole-group minilesson is followed by small-group and independent application time, during which students practice collaboratively and on their own.

WHOLE-GROUP
MINILESSON

Learn Together 15–20 minutes

Whole-Group Minilesson

Students are introduced to skills via **Anchor Charts** and the shared reading of a common text.

Online Ed

ANCHOR CHART 17:
Central Idea

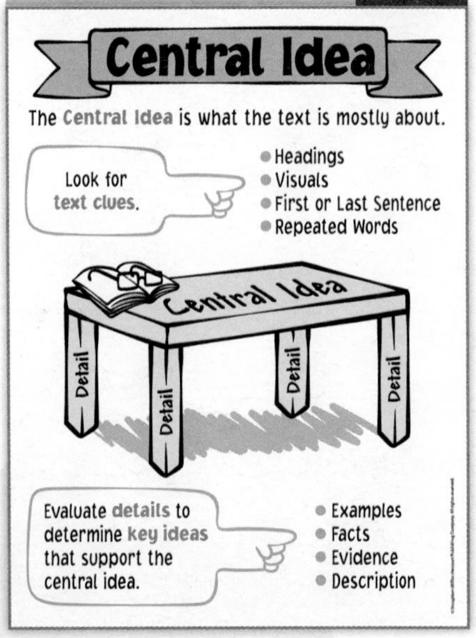
Central Idea
The Central Idea is what the text is mostly about.
Look for text clues.
Headings
Visuals
First or Last Sentence
Repeated Words
Central Idea
Detail
Detail
Detail
Detail
Evaluate details to determine key ideas that support the central idea.
Examples
Facts
Evidence
Description

Small-Group Instruction

Multiple options for small-group instruction allow teachers to meet the needs of diverse learners.

GUIDED READING WITH LEVELED LIBRARY

Advance student ability with texts that engage and challenge readers at their instructional level.

FOUNDATIONAL SKILLS DEVELOPMENT

Build students' reading fluency through application of decoding and spelling skills and other support activities based on need.

SKILL AND STRATEGY LESSONS

Provide targeted support in specific skills and strategies based on individual student needs.

SUPPORT FOR ENGLISH LEARNERS

Provide instruction and practice in a safe, risk-free setting, allowing English learners to experiment with language.

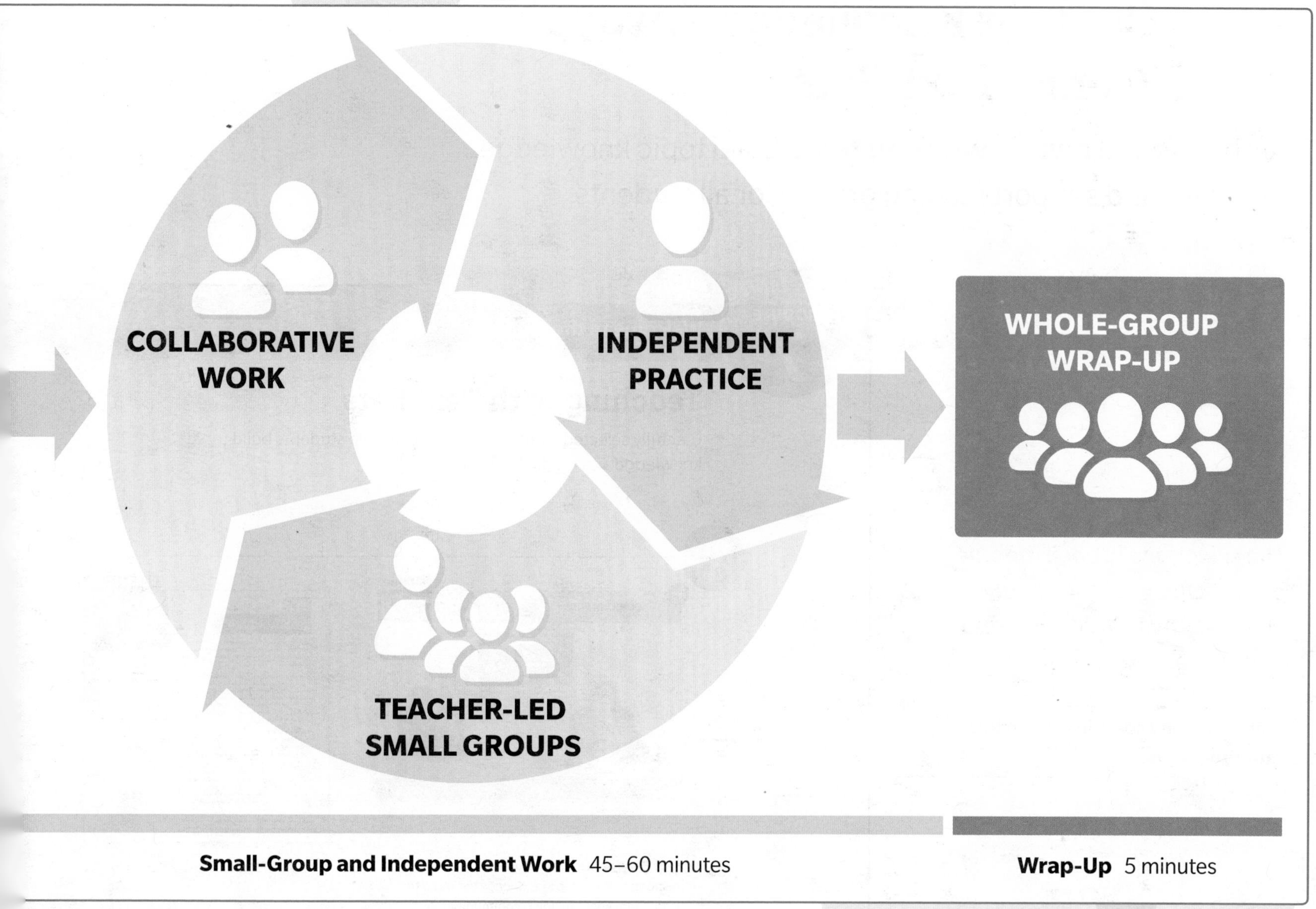

Independent and Collaborative Work

Opportunities for independent work allow students to practice and apply targeted knowledge and skills.

LITERACY CENTERS

Engaging activities across a variety of instructional contexts allow students to synthesize information and solidify their understanding.

- READING CENTER
- VOCABULARY CENTER
- DIGITAL STATION
- WRITING CENTER
- PROJECT CENTER

*my*BOOK

Write-in student text offers opportunities to read, write, and respond to complex texts.

GENRE STUDY BOOK CLUBS

Conversation about books fosters excitement about reading and writing.

STUDENT CHOICE LIBRARY BOOKS

Self-selected reading creates an authentic opportunity for students to practice new skills and heighten reading engagement.

INQUIRY AND RESEARCH PROJECT

Research- and inquiry-based activities are consistent with project-based learning.

Build Content Knowledge Through Multi-Genre Text Sets

Authentic and **award-winning texts** build topic knowledge expertise and support reading growth for all students.

The selections in each module purposefully contribute to students' overall content and genre knowledge.

Introduce and spark interest in the **module topic**.

Model fluent reading and promote listening comprehension.

Build and **activate background knowledge** about the module topic.

Guide students to **interact with complex texts by annotating**, taking notes, and marking text evidence in *my*Book.

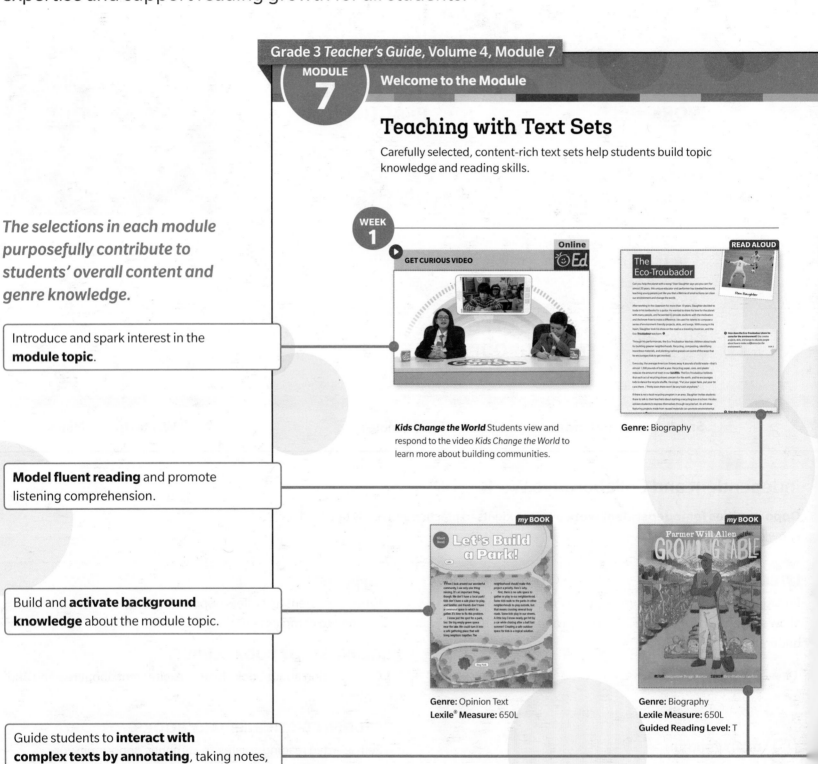

Grade 3 *Teacher's Guide*, Volume 4, Module 7

MODULE 7

Welcome to the Module

Teaching with Text Sets

Carefully selected, content-rich text sets help students build topic knowledge and reading skills.

WEEK 1

Online

GET CURIOUS VIDEO

Kids Change the World Students view and respond to the video *Kids Change the World* to learn more about building communities.

READ ALOUD

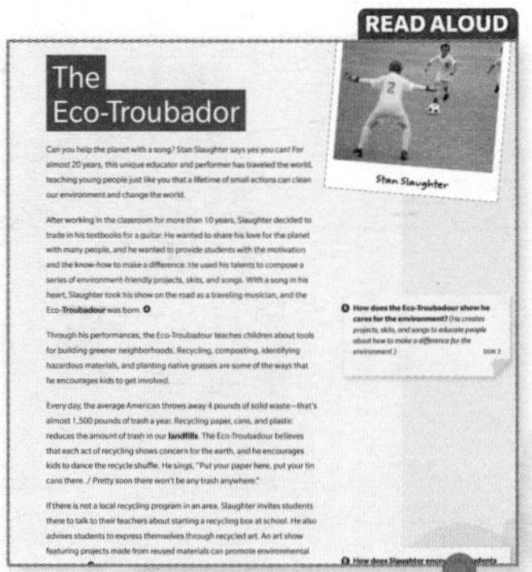

Genre: Biography

*my*BOOK

Genre: Opinion Text
Lexile® Measure: 650L

*my*BOOK

Genre: Biography
Lexile Measure: 650L
Guided Reading Level: T

T6 **Module 7** • Make a Difference

Make a Difference

Essential Question
How can one person make a meaningful difference in their local or global community?

Inspire inquiry and set a purpose for reading.

WEEK 2

my BOOK

ONE PLASTIC BAG
ISATOU CEESAY AND THE RECYCLING WOMEN OF THE GAMBIA

Genre: Biography/Memoir
Lexile® Measure: 570L
Guided Reading Level: P

my BOOK

Genre: Narrative Nonfiction
Lexile® Measure: 770L
Guided Reading Level: P

WEEK 3

my BOOK

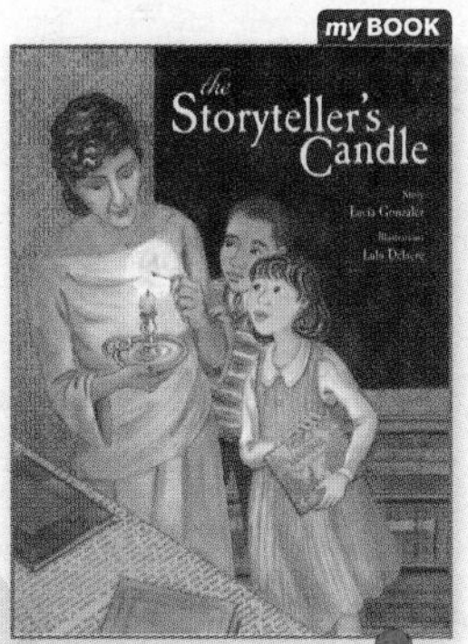

Genre: Historical Fiction
Lexile® Measure: 810L
Guided Reading Level: Q

WRITING FOCAL TEXT

Genre: Argument/Opinion Essay
Lexile® Measure: 450L
Guided Reading Level: J

Launch **Writing Workshop** with high-interest trade books.

Foster Critical Thinking and Deep Analysis of Text

myBook is a student component that provides opportunities for write-in text interactions, such as note-taking, annotating, and responding.

The companion **Teaching Pal** offers point-of-use teacher-directed instructional questions and prompts that encourage critical thinking and deep analysis of the *my*Book student texts.

Grade 3 *my*Book, Book 1, Module 1

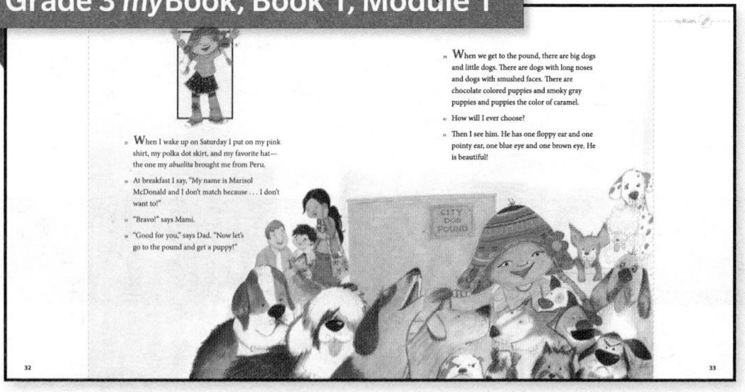

When I wake up on Saturday I put on my pink shirt, my polka dot skirt, and my favorite hat—the one my *abuelita* brought me from Peru.

At breakfast I say, "My name is Marisol McDonald and I don't match because . . . I don't want to!"

"Bravo!" says Mami.

"Good for you," says Dad. "Now let's go to the pound and get a puppy!"

When we get to the pound, there are big dogs and little dogs. There are dogs with long noses and dogs with smushed faces. There are chocolate colored puppies and smoky gray puppies and puppies the color of caramel.

How will I ever choose?

Then I see him. He has one floppy ear and one pointy ear, one blue eye and one brown eye. He is beautiful!

Grade 3 *Teaching Pal*, Book 1, Module 1

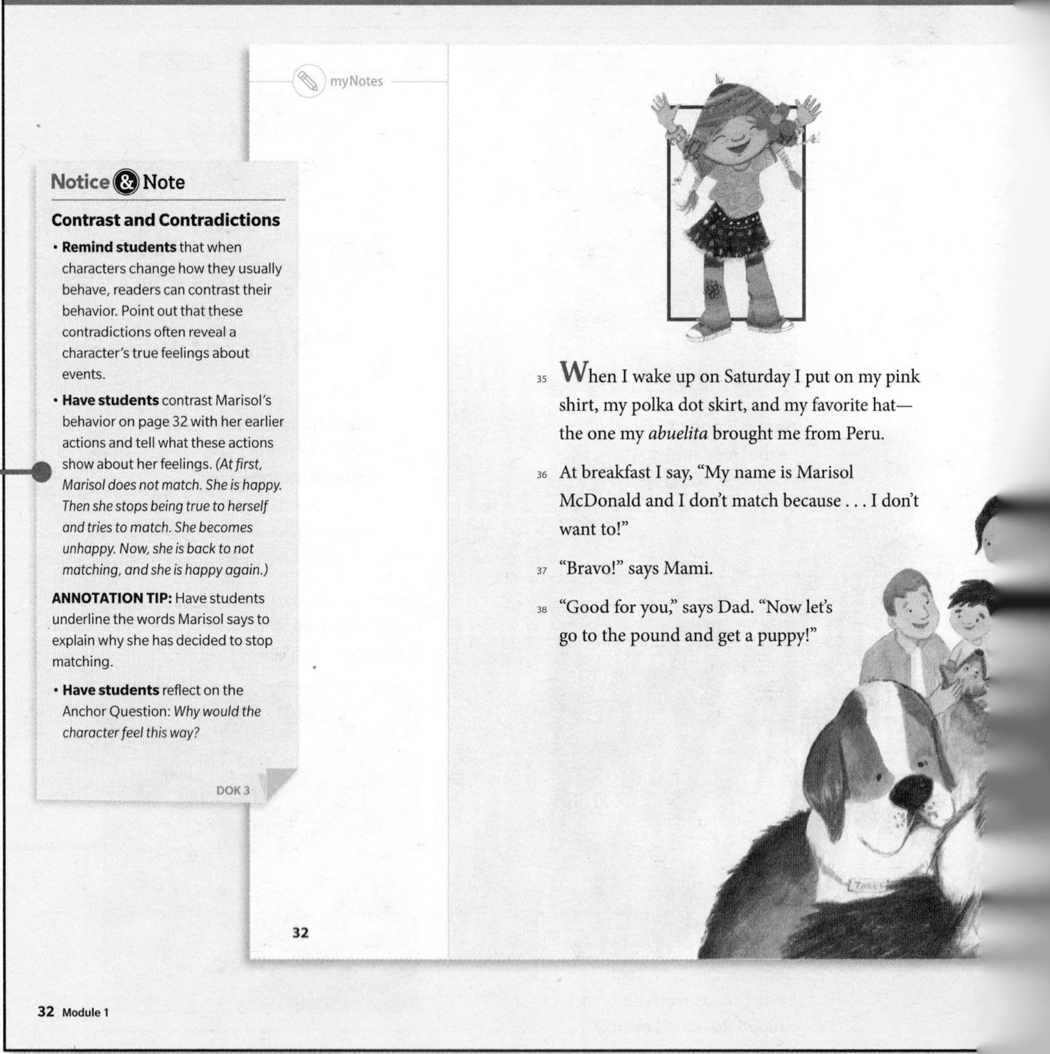

myNotes

Notice & Note

Contrast and Contradictions

- **Remind students** that when characters change how they usually behave, readers can contrast their behavior. Point out that these contradictions often reveal a character's true feelings about events.
- **Have students** contrast Marisol's behavior on page 32 with her earlier actions and tell what these actions show about her feelings. *(At first, Marisol does not match. She is happy. Then she stops being true to herself and tries to match. She becomes unhappy. Now, she is back to not matching, and she is happy again.)*

ANNOTATION TIP: Have students underline the words Marisol says to explain why she has decided to stop matching.

- **Have students** reflect on the Anchor Question: *Why would the character feel this way?*

DOK 3

35 When I wake up on Saturday I put on my pink shirt, my polka dot skirt, and my favorite hat—the one my *abuelita* brought me from Peru.

36 At breakfast I say, "My name is Marisol McDonald and I don't match because . . . I don't want to!"

37 "Bravo!" says Mami.

38 "Good for you," says Dad. "Now let's go to the pound and get a puppy!"

32

32 Module 1

Notice & Note

Use these notes to help students **deepen their understanding** as they learn to look for signposts in the text in order to create meaning.

Notice & Note

Strategies for Close Reading

Develop attentive, critical readers using the powerful work of Kylene Beers and Robert E. Probst. Notice & Note introduces Signposts and Anchor Questions that help readers understand and respond to critical aspects of both fiction and nonfiction texts.

SIGNPOSTS

Signposts alert readers to significant moments in a text and encourage students to read closely.

Fiction

- Contrasts & Contradictions
- Words of the Wiser
- Aha Moment
- Again & Again
- Memory Moment
- Tough Questions

Nonfiction

- Contrasts & Contradictions
- Extreme or Absolute Language
- Numbers and Stats
- Quoted Words
- Word Gaps
- 3 Big Questions

Kylene Beers and Robert E. Probst

READ FOR UNDERSTANDING

During a first reading of the text, guide students to respond to questions, prompts, and annotation tips designed to help them **arrive at the gist of the text**.

myNotes

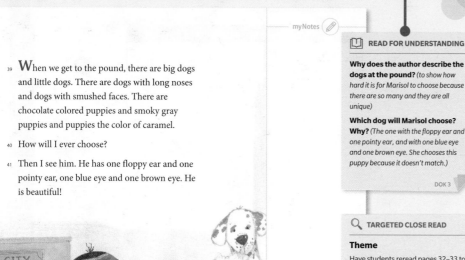

39 When we get to the pound, there are big dogs and little dogs. There are dogs with long noses and dogs with smushed faces. There are chocolate colored puppies and smoky gray puppies and puppies the color of caramel.

40 How will I ever choose?

41 Then I see him. He has one floppy ear and one pointy ear, one blue eye and one brown eye. He is beautiful!

33

READ FOR UNDERSTANDING

Why does the author describe the dogs at the pound? *(to show how hard it is for Marisol to choose because there are so many and they are all unique)*

Which dog will Marisol choose? Why? *(The one with the floppy ear and one pointy ear, and with one blue eye and one brown eye. She chooses this puppy because it doesn't match.)*

DOK 3

TARGETED CLOSE READ

Theme

Have students reread pages 32–33 to analyze the theme.

What is the theme of this story? *(It is more important to be yourself than to try to be like others.)*

How is this theme different from the topic? *(The topic is what the story is about—how Marisol tried to change from not matching to matching. The theme is the lesson readers can get from the plot events.)*

ANNOTATION TIP: Have students write a note that summarizes the lesson Marisol learned in the story.

DOK 3

Marisol McDonald Doesn't Match 33

TARGETED CLOSE READ

During subsequent readings, students **closely analyze the text** to apply skills and demonstrate knowledge.

Make Meaningful Connections Between Reading and Writing

During **close reading of the *myBook***, students identify and annotate literary elements, genre characteristics, and evidence of author's purpose and craft. This analysis **supports their own development as writers** across multiple forms and genres.

Writing in Response to Reading

Students engage in deep analysis of literary and informational texts as well as media selections.

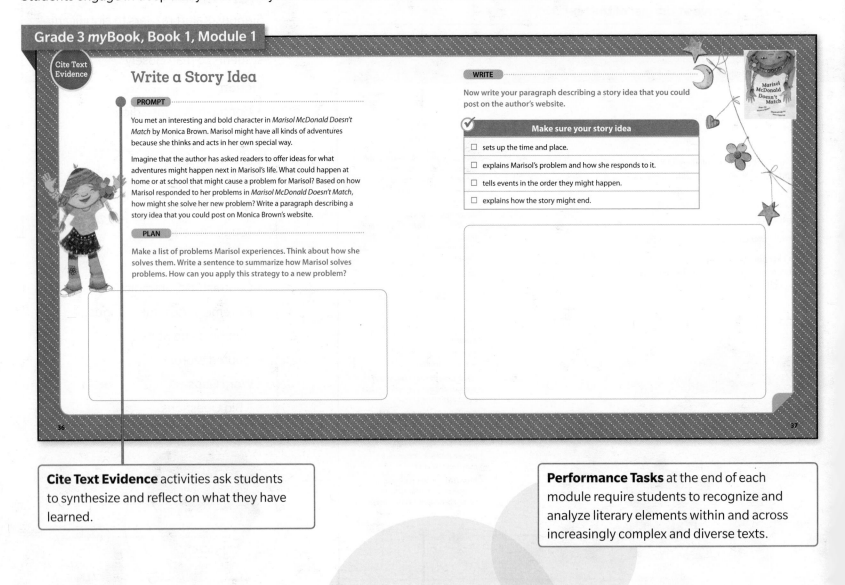

Grade 3 *myBook*, Book 1, Module 1

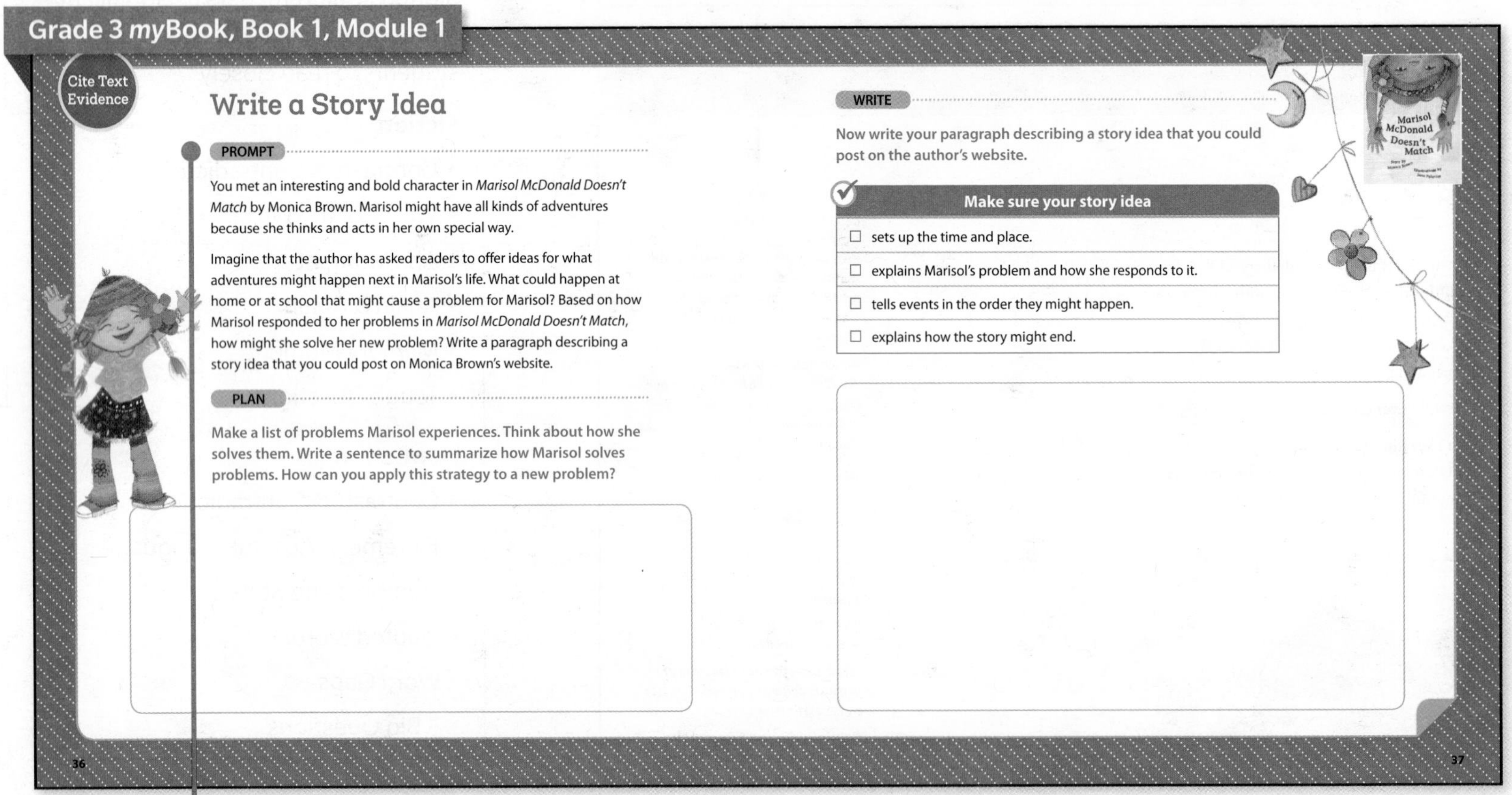

Cite Text Evidence

Write a Story Idea

PROMPT

You met an interesting and bold character in *Marisol McDonald Doesn't Match* by Monica Brown. Marisol might have all kinds of adventures because she thinks and acts in her own special way.

Imagine that the author has asked readers to offer ideas for what adventures might happen next in Marisol's life. What could happen at home or at school that might cause a problem for Marisol? Based on how Marisol responded to her problems in *Marisol McDonald Doesn't Match,* how might she solve her new problem? Write a paragraph describing a story idea that you could post on Monica Brown's website.

PLAN

Make a list of problems Marisol experiences. Think about how she solves them. Write a sentence to summarize how Marisol solves problems. How can you apply this strategy to a new problem?

36

WRITE

Now write your paragraph describing a story idea that you could post on the author's website.

Make sure your story idea

- ☐ sets up the time and place.
- ☐ explains Marisol's problem and how she responds to it.
- ☐ tells events in the order they might happen.
- ☐ explains how the story might end.

37

Cite Text Evidence activities ask students to synthesize and reflect on what they have learned.

Performance Tasks at the end of each module require students to recognize and analyze literary elements within and across increasingly complex and diverse texts.

"Writing as a process means giving students time to prewrite, write, postwrite, proofread, and edit their papers. It means teaching writing, not just assigning it. It means teaching the various forms of writing so students think through their meaning, their purpose, the needs of their audience to determine the most appropriate genre."

—*Dr. Joyce Armstrong Carroll*

Writing Workshop

Into Reading employs a Writing Workshop method of instruction that is student-centered, process-driven, and collaborative.

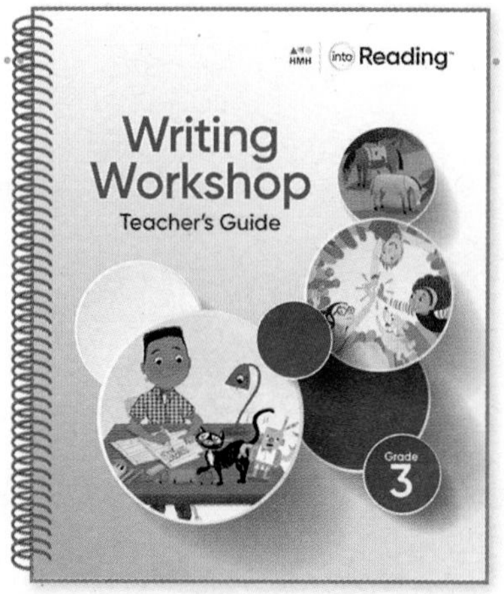

Writing Workshop made explicit:

- Instruction, activities, and routines for every stage of the writing process
- Extensive teacher modeling and tips
- Digitally projectable instruction at point of use

The **Writer's Notebook** directly supports the act of writing by allowing students to set and evaluate personal goals, interact with writing models, use a variety of prewriting strategies, and confer with peers.

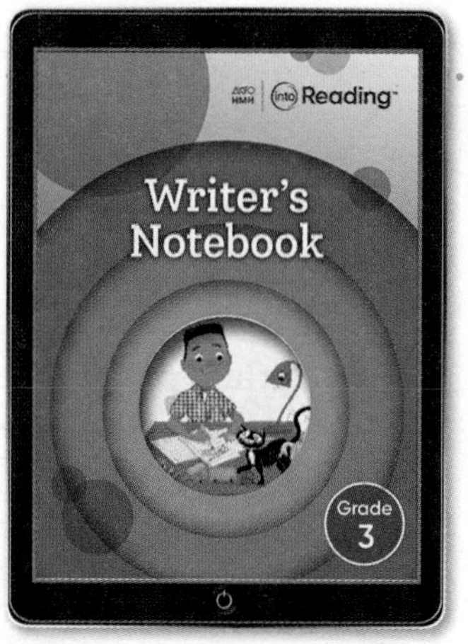

Focal Texts connect to module topics and serve as a springboard for discussion around the module topic and writing prompt.

Support Vocabulary and Language Development

Explicit vocabulary instruction that **builds in depth and rigor** supports students in gaining **academic language skills**.

Build Vocabulary Networks

Use known vocabulary words as springboards to new, unknown words with **morphological or semantic relationships** (generative vocabulary), exposing students to word networks that will expand their vocabulary.

Grade 3 *myBook*, Book 1, Module 1

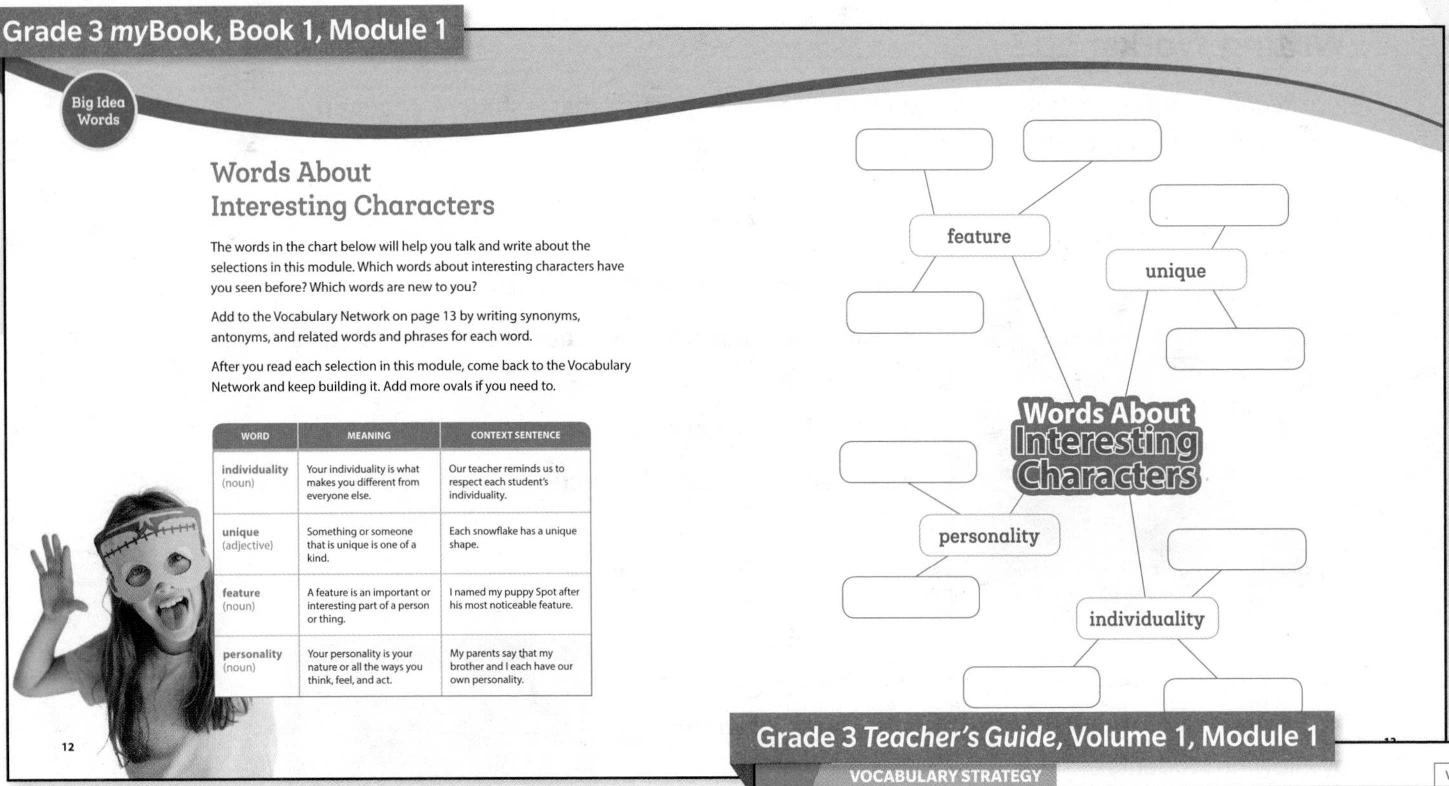

Big Idea Words

Words About Interesting Characters

The words in the chart below will help you talk and write about the selections in this module. Which words about interesting characters have you seen before? Which words are new to you?

Add to the Vocabulary Network on page 13 by writing synonyms, antonyms, and related words and phrases for each word.

After you read each selection in this module, come back to the Vocabulary Network and keep building it. Add more ovals if you need to.

WORD	MEANING	CONTEXT SENTENCE
individuality (noun)	Your individuality is what makes you different from everyone else.	Our teacher reminds us to respect each student's individuality.
unique (adjective)	Something or someone that is unique is one of a kind.	Each snowflake has a unique shape.
feature (noun)	A feature is an important or interesting part of a person or thing.	I named my puppy Spot after his most noticeable feature.
personality (noun)	Your personality is your nature or all the ways you think, feel, and act.	My parents say that my brother and I each have our own personality.

12

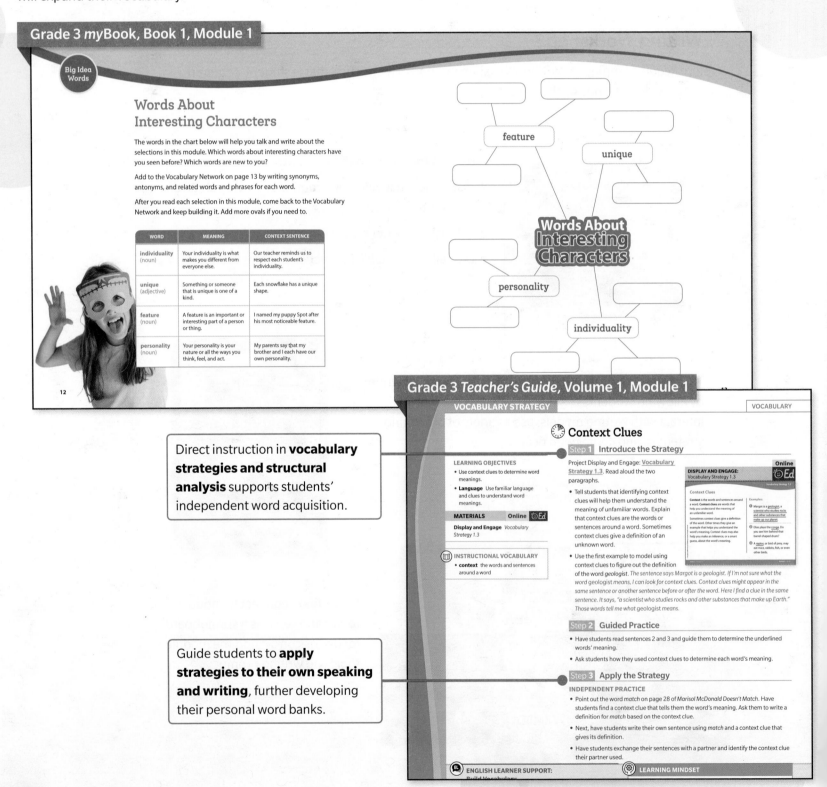

Direct instruction in **vocabulary strategies and structural analysis** supports students' independent word acquisition.

Guide students to **apply strategies to their own speaking and writing**, further developing their personal word banks.

Grade 3 *Teacher's Guide*, Volume 1, Module 1

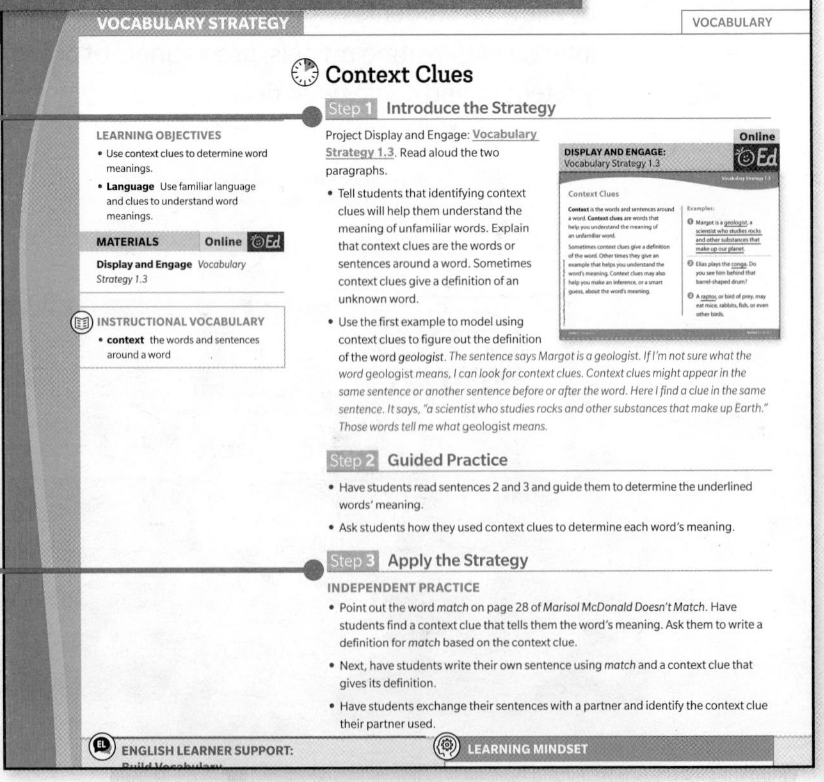

VOCABULARY STRATEGY

VOCABULARY

Context Clues

Step 1 Introduce the Strategy

LEARNING OBJECTIVES
- Use context clues to determine word meanings.
- **Language** Use familiar language and clues to understand word meanings.

MATERIALS Online Ed

Display and Engage *Vocabulary Strategy 1.3*

INSTRUCTIONAL VOCABULARY
- **context** the words and sentences around a word

Project Display and Engage: Vocabulary Strategy 1.3. Read aloud the two paragraphs.

- Tell students that identifying context clues will help them understand the meaning of unfamiliar words. Explain that context clues are the words or sentences around a word. Sometimes context clues give a definition of an unknown word.
- Use the first example to model using context clues to figure out the definition of the word *geologist*. *The sentence says Margot is a geologist. If I'm not sure what the word* geologist *means, I can look for context clues. Context clues might appear in the same sentence or another sentence before or after the word. Here I find a clue in the same sentence. It says, "a scientist who studies rocks and other substances that make up Earth." Those words tell me what* geologist *means.*

Online
DISPLAY AND ENGAGE: Vocabulary Strategy 1.3

Context Clues

Context is the words and sentences around a word. **Context clues** are words that help you understand the meaning of an unfamiliar word.

Sometimes context clues give a definition of the word. Other times they give an example that helps you understand the word's meaning. Context clues may also help you make an inference, or a smart guess, about the word's meaning.

Examples:
1. Margot is a geologist, a scientist who studies rocks and other substances that make up our planet.
2. Elias plays the conga. Do you see him behind that barrel-shaped drum?
3. A raptor, or bird of prey, may eat mice, rabbits, fish, or even other birds.

Step 2 Guided Practice

- Have students read sentences 2 and 3 and guide them to determine the underlined words' meaning.
- Ask students how they used context clues to determine each word's meaning.

Step 3 Apply the Strategy

INDEPENDENT PRACTICE
- Point out the word *match* on page 28 of *Marisol McDonald Doesn't Match*. Have students find a context clue that tells them the word's meaning. Ask them to write a definition for *match* based on the context clue.
- Next, have students write their own sentence using *match* and a context clue that gives its definition.
- Have students exchange their sentences with a partner and identify the context clue their partner used.

ENGLISH LEARNER SUPPORT:

LEARNING MINDSET

Develop Research and Communication Skills

Opportunities to engage in **multimodal literacies**, **inquiry and research**, and **oral presentations** build the communication skills that are critical to college and career readiness.

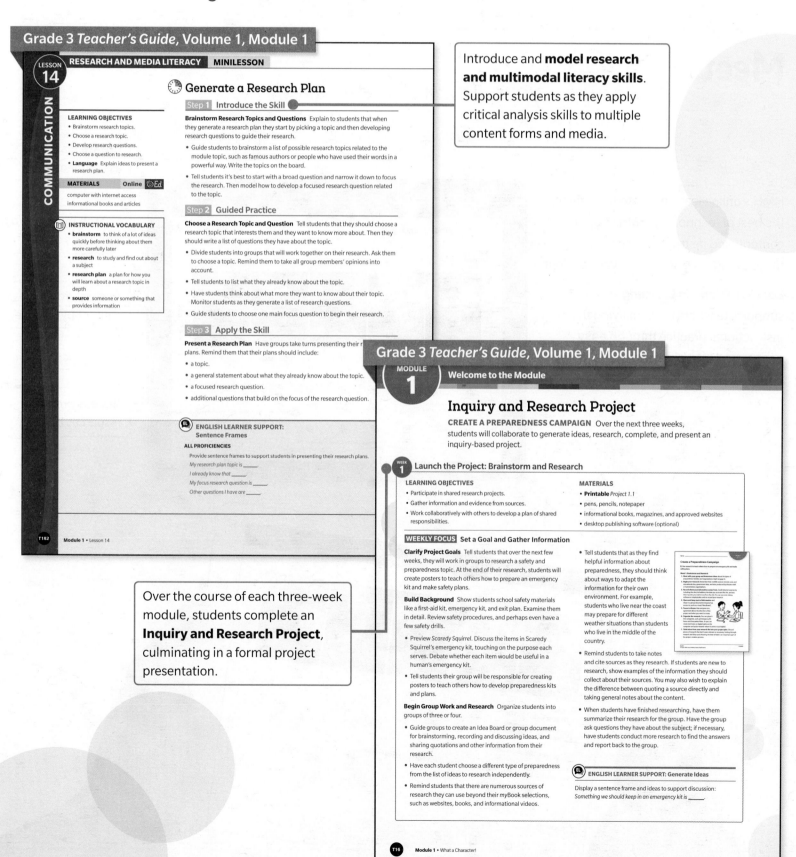

Grade 3 *Teacher's Guide*, Volume 1, Module 1

LESSON 14

COMMUNICATION

RESEARCH AND MEDIA LITERACY | MINILESSON

Generate a Research Plan

LEARNING OBJECTIVES
- Brainstorm research topics.
- Choose a research topic.
- Develop research questions.
- Choose a question to research.
- **Language** Explain ideas to present a research plan.

MATERIALS Online Ed

computer with internet access
informational books and articles

INSTRUCTIONAL VOCABULARY
- **brainstorm** to think of a lot of ideas quickly before thinking about them more carefully later
- **research** to study and find out about a subject
- **research plan** a plan for how you will learn about a research topic in depth
- **source** someone or something that provides information

Step 1 Introduce the Skill

Brainstorm Research Topics and Questions Explain to students that when they generate a research plan they start by picking a topic and then developing research questions to guide their research.

- Guide students to brainstorm a list of possible research topics related to the module topic, such as famous authors or people who have used their words in a powerful way. Write the topics on the board.
- Tell students it's best to start with a broad question and narrow it down to focus the research. Then model how to develop a focused research question related to the topic.

Step 2 Guided Practice

Choose a Research Topic and Question Tell students that they should choose a research topic that interests them and they want to know more about. Then they should write a list of questions they have about the topic.

- Divide students into groups that will work together on their research. Ask them to choose a topic. Remind them to take all group members' opinions into account.
- Tell students to list what they already know about the topic.
- Have students think about what more they want to know about their topic. Monitor students as they generate a list of research questions.
- Guide students to choose one main focus question to begin their research.

Step 3 Apply the Skill

Present a Research Plan Have groups take turns presenting their r[…] plans. Remind them that their plans should include:

- a topic.
- a general statement about what they already know about the topic.
- a focused research question.
- additional questions that build on the focus of the research question.

ENGLISH LEARNER SUPPORT: Sentence Frames

ALL PROFICIENCIES

Provide sentence frames to support students in presenting their research plans.

My research plan topic is ____.
I already know that ____.
My focus research question is ____.
Other questions I have are ____.

T182 Module 1 • Lesson 14

Introduce and **model research and multimodal literacy skills**. Support students as they apply critical analysis skills to multiple content forms and media.

Grade 3 *Teacher's Guide*, Volume 1, Module 1

MODULE 1

Welcome to the Module

Inquiry and Research Project

CREATE A PREPAREDNESS CAMPAIGN Over the next three weeks, students will collaborate to generate ideas, research, complete, and present an inquiry-based project.

WEEK 1 Launch the Project: Brainstorm and Research

LEARNING OBJECTIVES
- Participate in shared research projects.
- Gather information and evidence from sources.
- Work collaboratively with others to develop a plan of shared responsibilities.

MATERIALS
- **Printable** *Project 1.1*
- pens, pencils, notepaper
- informational books, magazines, and approved websites
- desktop publishing software (optional)

WEEKLY FOCUS Set a Goal and Gather Information

Clarify Project Goals Tell students that over the next few weeks, they will work in groups to research a safety and preparedness topic. At the end of their research, students will create posters to teach others how to prepare an emergency kit and make safety plans.

Build Background Show students school safety materials like a first-aid kit, emergency kit, and exit plan. Examine them in detail. Review safety procedures, and perhaps even have a few safety drills.

- Preview *Scaredy Squirrel*. Discuss the items in Scaredy Squirrel's emergency kit, touching on the purpose each serves. Debate whether each item would be useful in a human's emergency kit.
- Tell students their group will be responsible for creating posters to teach others how to develop preparedness kits and plans.

Begin Group Work and Research Organize students into groups of three or four.

- Guide groups to create an Idea Board or group document for brainstorming, recording and discussing ideas, and sharing quotations and other information from their research.
- Have each student choose a different type of preparedness from the list of ideas to research independently.
- Remind students that there are numerous sources of research they can use beyond their myBook selections, such as websites, books, and informational videos.

- Tell students that as they find helpful information about preparedness, they should think about ways to adapt the information for their own environment. For example, students who live near the coast may prepare for different weather situations than students who live in the middle of the country.

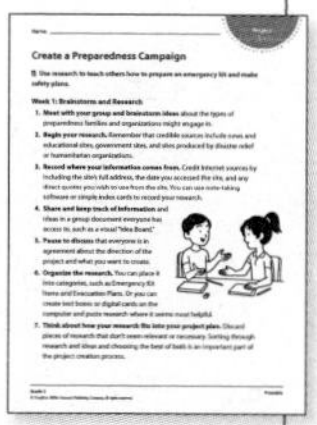

- Remind students to take notes and cite sources as they research. If students are new to research, show examples of the information they should collect about their sources. You may also wish to explain the difference between quoting a source directly and taking general notes about the content.
- When students have finished researching, have them summarize their research for the group. Have the group ask questions they have about the subject; if necessary, have students conduct more research to find the answers and report back to the group.

ENGLISH LEARNER SUPPORT: Generate Ideas

Display a sentence frame and ideas to support discussion: *Something we should keep in an emergency kit is ____.*

T16 Module 1 • What a Character!

Over the course of each three-week module, students complete an **Inquiry and Research Project**, culminating in a formal project presentation.

Use Technology to Enhance Instruction

Use the *Ed* online learning system to **access digital tools and instructional supports** and to **manage student work** easily and efficiently.

Meet Ed *your friend in learning*

HMH's online learning system combines the best of technology, *HMH Into Reading* content, and instruction to personalize the learning experience for every student.

Ed: Your Friend in Learning® also supports teachers by simplifying their instructional practice through **easy access** and **intuitive pathways** to **key content**, **assignments**, and **data**.

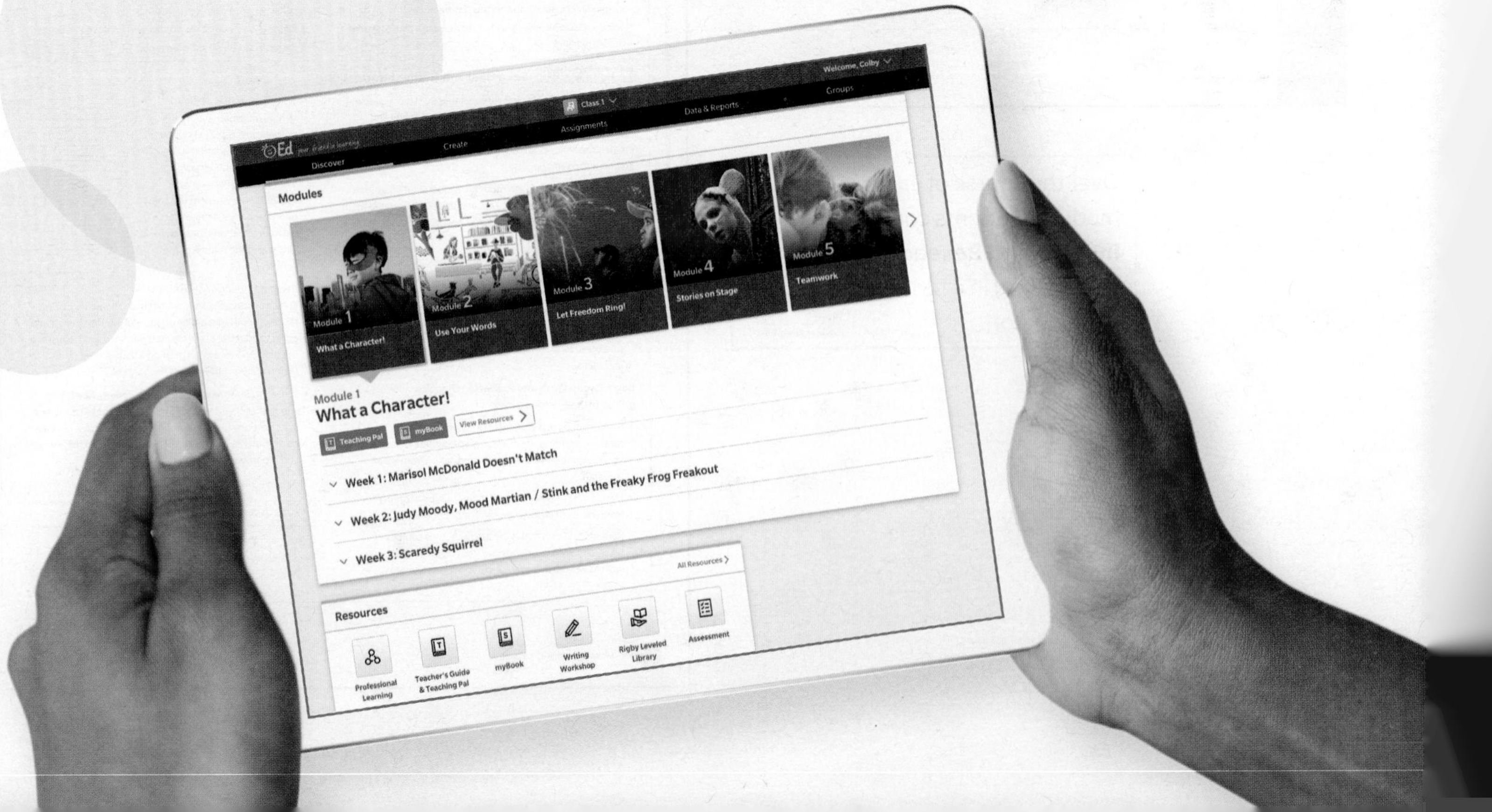

View Data and Reports.

Use data to

- Monitor progress
- Assign resources
- Form flexible groups

Ed: Your Friend in Learning® is a registered trademark of Houghton Mifflin Harcourt.

Maximize Growth Through Data-Driven Differentiation and Assessment

Meaningful data insights help teachers determine a daily skills focus for minilessons and small-group needs.

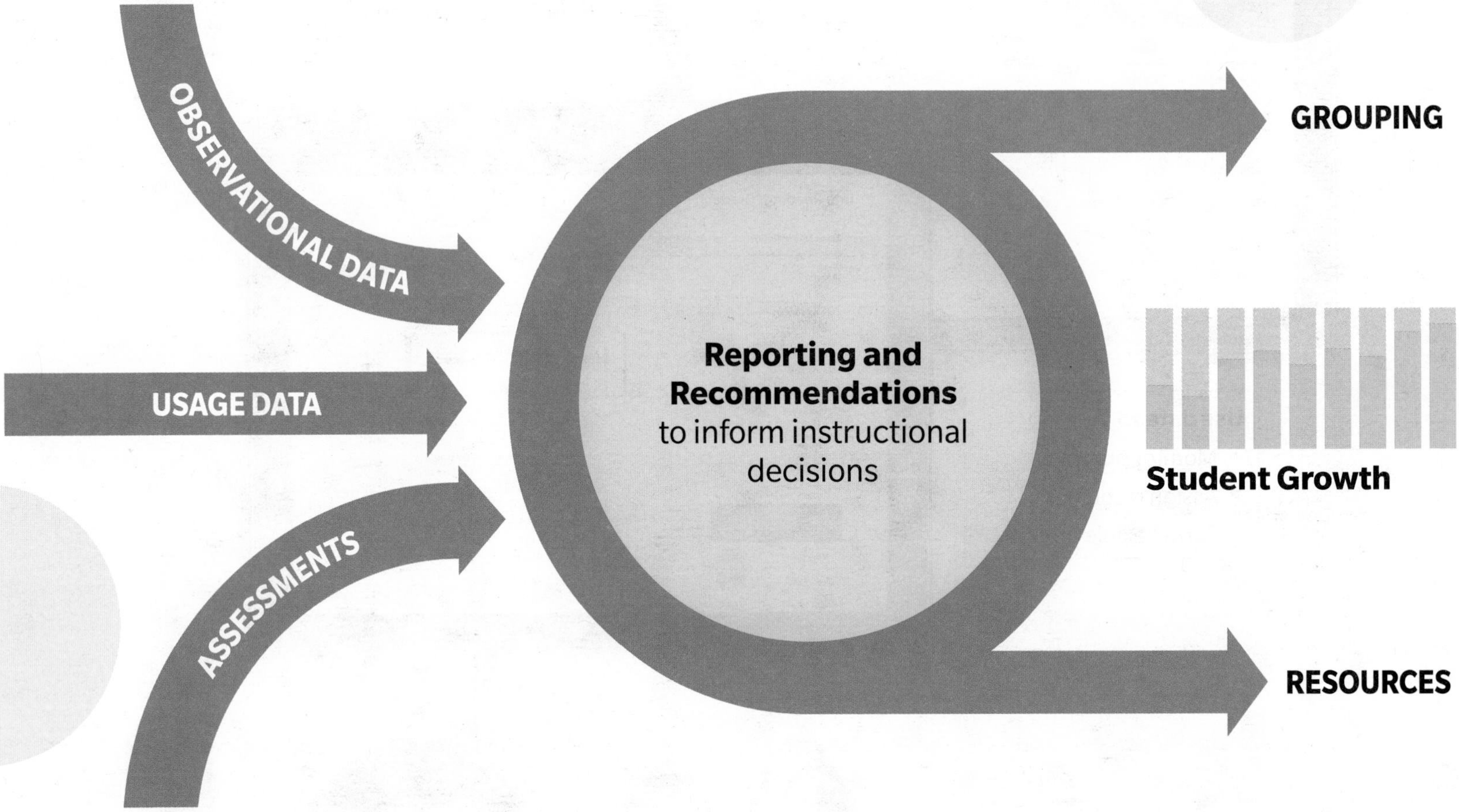

Actionable reports drive grouping, reading, and instructional recommendations appropriate for each learner.

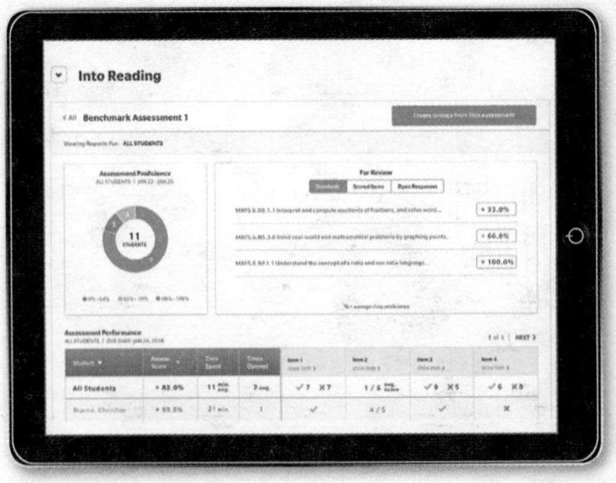

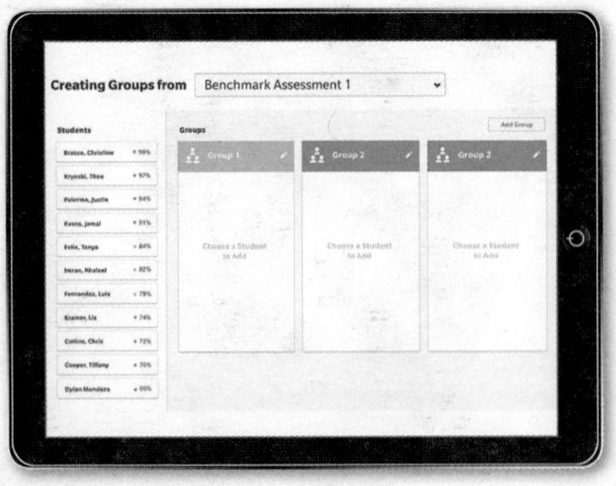

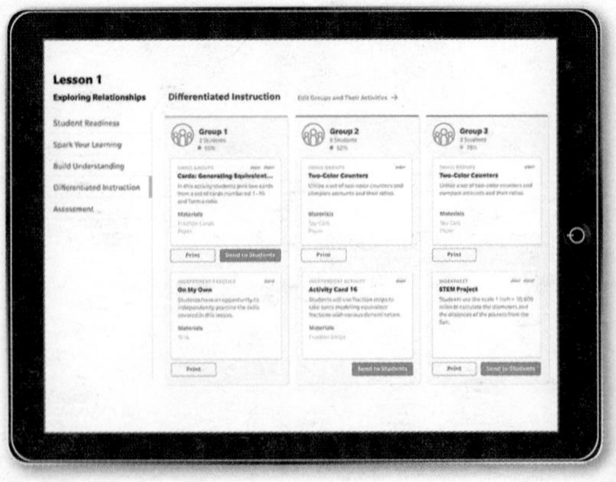

REPORTS

Multiple report views allow teachers to **see the gaps and gains** of the class at any moment throughout the school year.

GROUPING

Data-driven recommendations dynamically assign students to groups, allowing teachers to target learning needs and differentiate instruction.

RESOURCE RECOMMENDATIONS

Based on data, resources are recommended to **target students' individual learning needs**.

ASSESSMENTS AND PROGRESS MONITORING

Adaptive Growth Measure and Guided Reading Benchmark

3 times per year

Adaptive Growth Measure and Guided Reading Benchmark allow teachers to gain an understanding of where students are on the learning continuum and identify students in need of intervention or enrichment.

Module Assessment

12 times per year

Module Assessments, given every three weeks, assess mastery of skills covered during the course of the module across all literacy strands.

Ongoing Feedback from Daily Classroom Activities

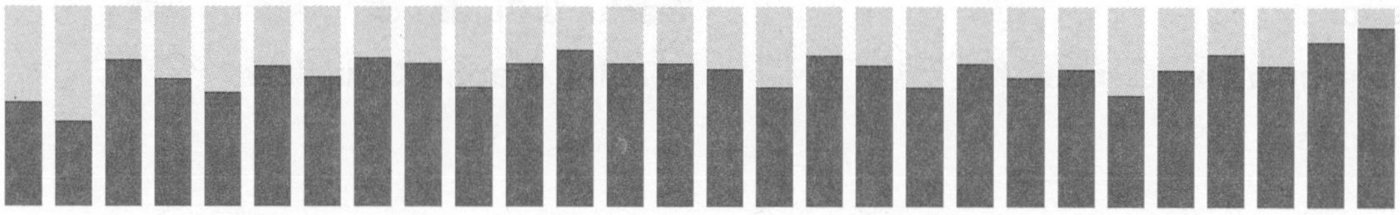

Formative Assessment data, collected across a variety of student activities, help teachers to make informed instructional decisions. Data sources include:

- Weekly Assessment
- Selection and Leveled Reader Quizzes
- Performance Tasks
- Independent Reading
- Skills Practice
- Usage Data
- Teacher Observations
- Running Records
- Inquiry and Research Projects

Flexible Resources for Responsive Teaching

Into Reading offers daily options to **reinforce**, **extend**, and **intervene** in teacher-led small groups in order to meet the needs of all learners.

GUIDED READING GROUPS

KEY RESOURCES

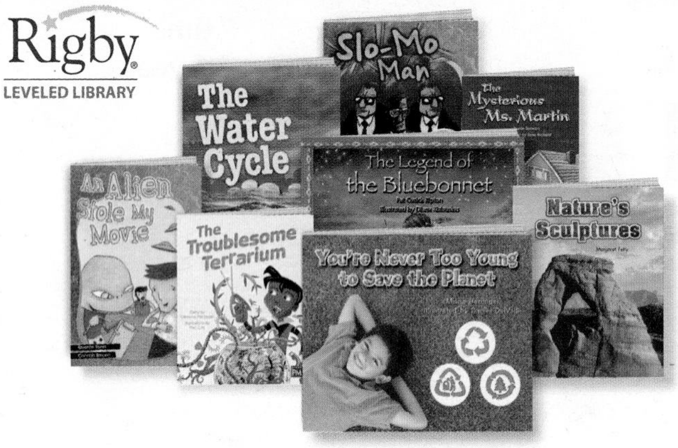

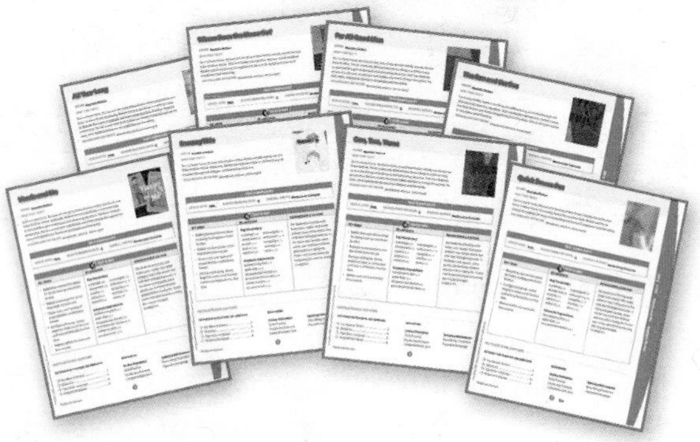

- **Rigby Leveled Library***
- **Take and Teach Lessons**
- **Guided Reading Benchmark Assessment Kit**
- **Leveled Reader Quizzes**

**Access to the full K–6 library available online.*

HOW TO USE

- Use the Guided Reading Benchmark Assessment to determine students' instructional level for **guided reading groups**.
- **Reinforce**, **extend**, or **intervene** by choosing just-right books from 570 unique Leveled Readers from across the spectrum of guided reading levels.
- Select from the **flexible teaching sessions** on the Take and Teach Lessons to deliver scaffolded instruction while meeting with guided reading groups.
- **Assess** students' comprehension of each text using the Leveled Reader Quizzes.

READING SKILL & STRATEGY SUPPORT

KEY RESOURCES

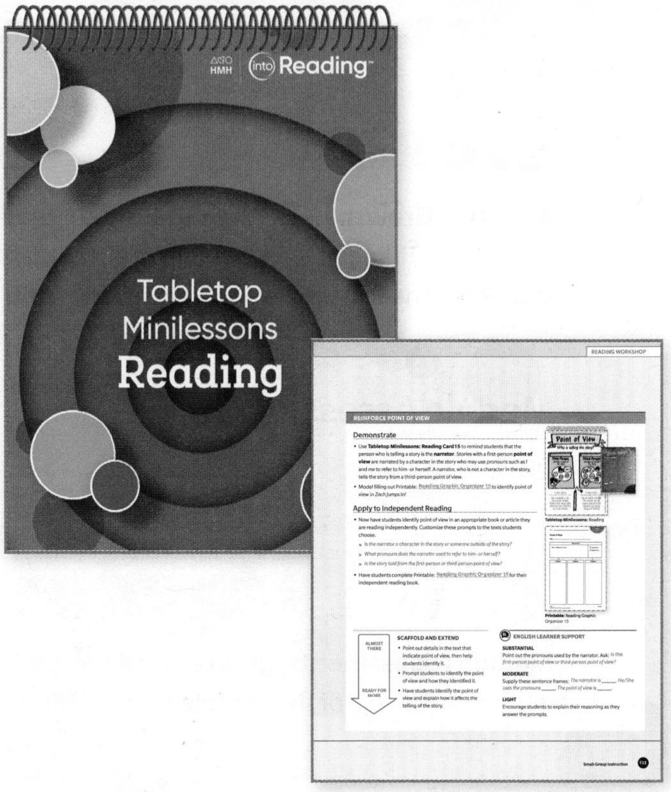

- **Tabletop Minilessons: Reading**
- **Teacher's Guide**
- **Reading Graphic Organizers**

HOW TO USE

- **Reinforce** Using your Teacher's Guide and the differentiated instruction on Tabletop Minilessons: Reading, review the skill or strategy from whole-group Reading Workshop and connect it to any text.
- **Extend** Deepen understanding of the skill or strategy from whole-group Reading Workshop by using the Ready for More prompts in your Teacher's Guide or on Tabletop Minilessons: Reading with texts that will challenge students.
- **Intervene** Use data to inform which grade-level skills or strategies to reteach. Use the Almost There prompts in your Teacher's Guide or on Tabletop Minilessons: Reading with accessible texts.

FOUNDATIONAL SKILLS SUPPORT

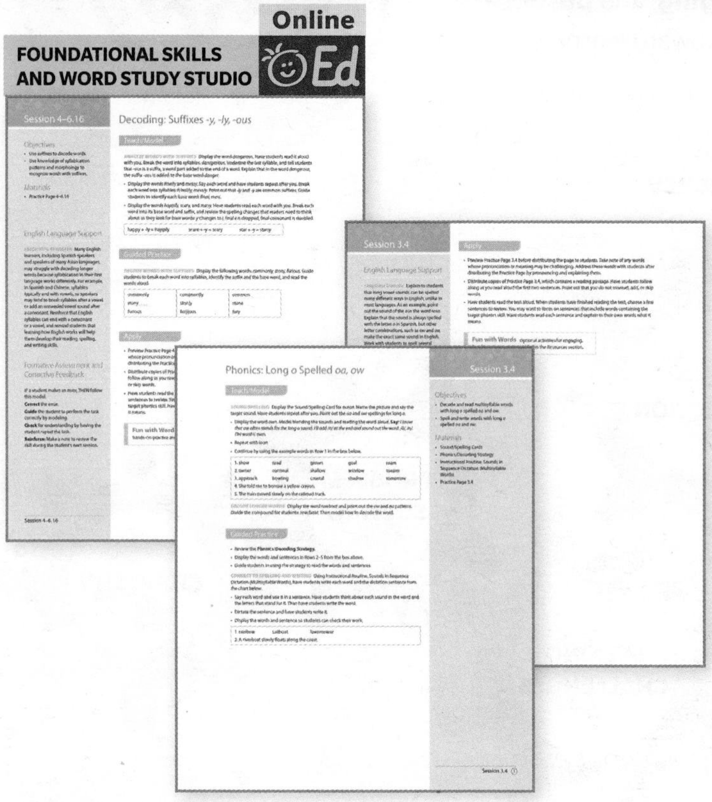

- **Teacher's Guide**
- **Foundational Skills and Word Study Studio**

- **Reinforce** Guide students to practice the Foundational Skills, using support in the Teacher's Guide.
- **Extend** Use data to inform which Foundational Skills a student is ready to learn beyond where the rest of the class is learning. Select appropriate lessons from the Foundational Skills and Word Study Studio.
- **Intervene** Use data to inform which prerequisite Foundational Skills a student needs. Then select appropriate lessons from the Foundational Skills and Word Study Studio.

ENGLISH LANGUAGE DEVELOPMENT

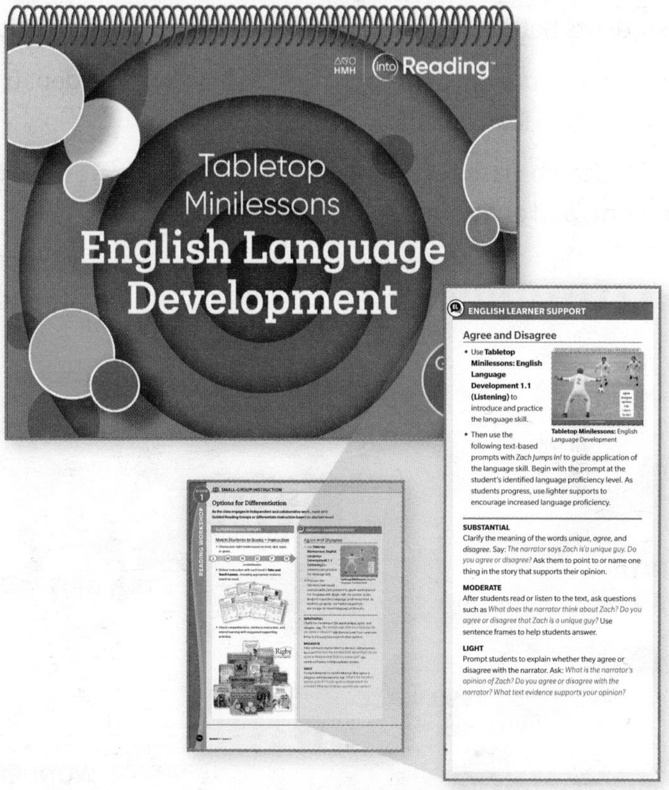

- **Tabletop Minilessons: English Language Development**
- **Teacher's Guide**
- **Language Graphic Organizers**

- **Deliver** daily instruction at students' **language proficiency level**, using the prompts in your Teacher's Guide or on Tabletop Minilessons: English Language Development. Each week's instruction focuses on a particular language function across one of these literacy domains: listening, speaking, reading, writing, collaborative problem-solving.
- **Use language supports** such as sentence frames and phrase banks to guide effective expression and empower students' language development.

Foster a Mindset for Learning

Through a partnership with **Mindset Works®**, *Into Reading* incorporates the latest research, strategies, and practices to build a community of resilient, curious learners.

- Introduce the learning mindsets: **growth mindset**, **relevance**, **belonging**, and **purpose** to help students better understand their self-perception and attitudes toward learning.
- Establish the **tenets of growth mindset**, so that each student understands that he or she has the capacity to learn and grow.
- Target the research-based stances and skills that are key to **student agency**, **engagement**, and **academic success**.

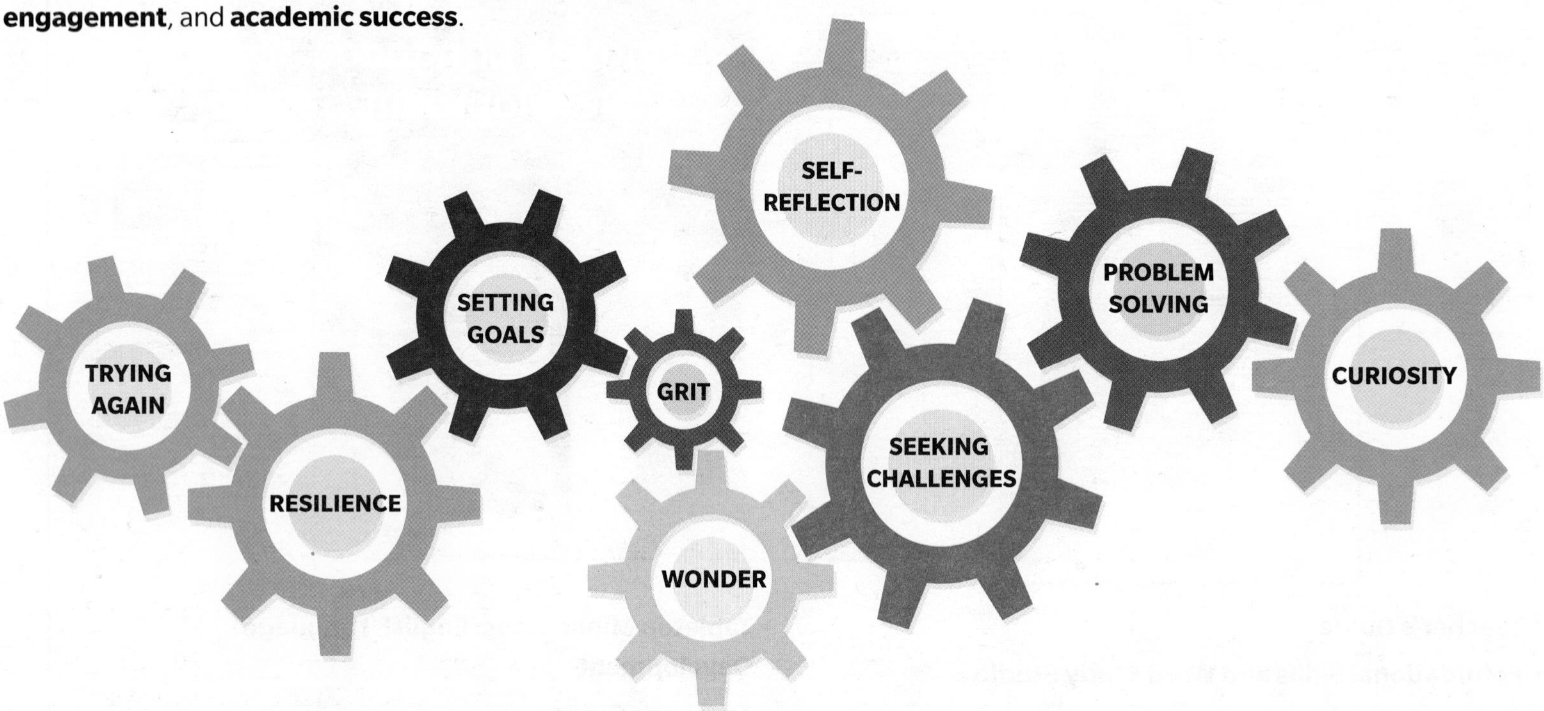

Connect with Families and Community

Engaging with families and the community is critical to student success in school. *Into Reading* provides resources to help teachers interact with families throughout the school year.

- **The write-in format of *my*Book** gives families a front-row seat to their child's thinking and progress over time. Upon completion of each *my*Book volume, children can take home and share literature, encouraging a strong home-school connection.
- **Family Letters** inform families about the skills, strategies, and topics students are encountering at school, extending rich dialogue beyond the classroom.

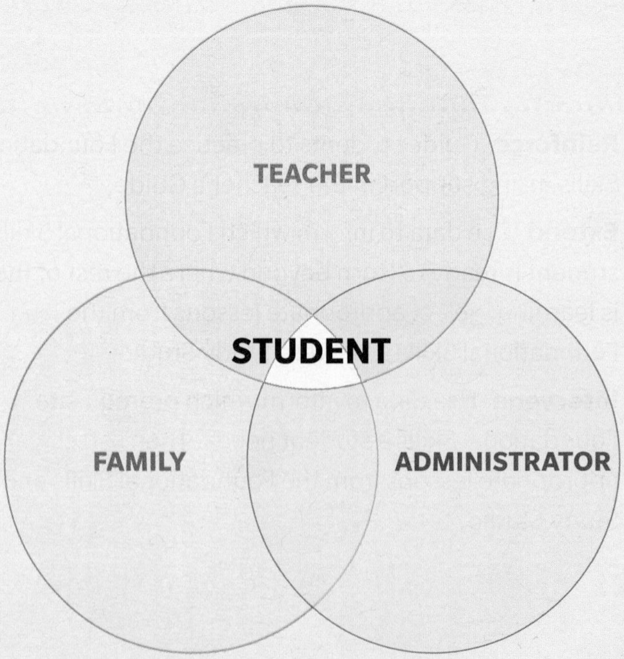

Build a Culture of Professional Growth

Embedded and ongoing **Professional Learning** empowers and supports teachers to be developers of high-impact learning experiences that provide all students with opportunities for reading and writing success.

Build Agency with Purposeful, Embedded Support

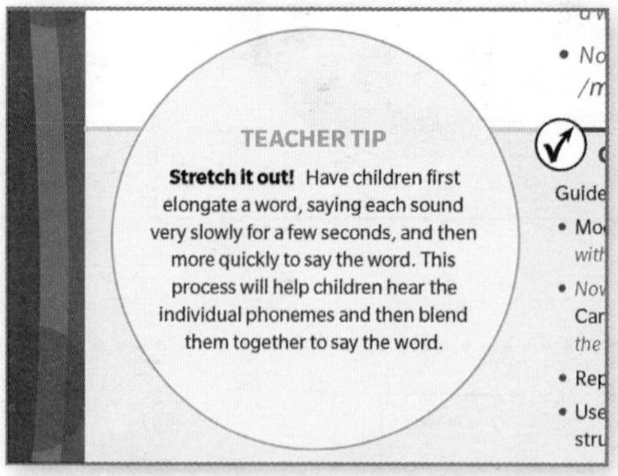

TEACHER TIPS

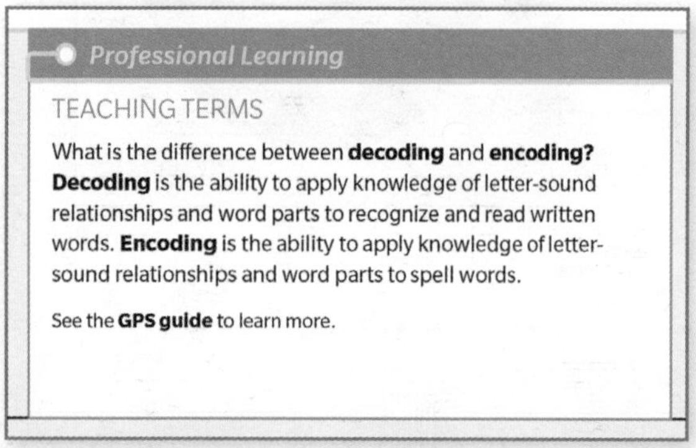

PROFESSIONAL LEARNING REFERENCES

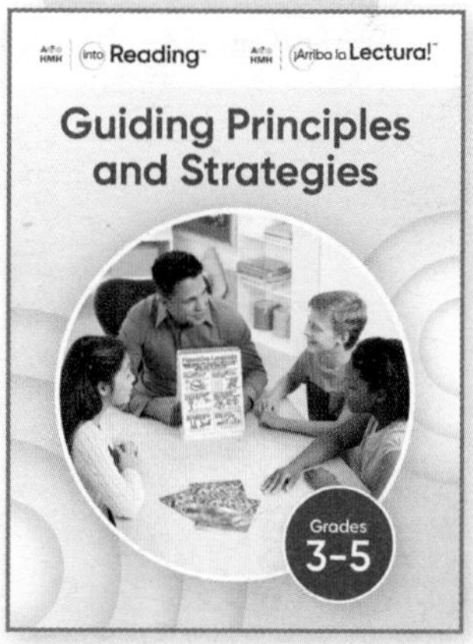

CLASSROOM VIDEOS

ON-DEMAND PROFESSIONAL LEARNING MODULES

Grow Your Practice with Personalized Blended Professional Learning

- **Getting Started and Professional Learning Guide:** Learn the program components, pedagogy, and digital resources to successfully teach with *Into Reading*.
- **Follow-Up:** Choose from a variety of instructional topics to design a personalized in-person or live online Follow-Up experience to deepen program mastery and enhance teaching practices.
- **Coaching and Modeling:** Experience just-in-time support to ensure continuous professional learning that is student-centered and grounded in data.
- **askHMH:** Get on-demand access to program experts who will answer questions and provide personalized conferencing and digital demonstrations to support implementation.
- **Technical Services:** Plan, prepare, implement, and operate technology with ease.
- **International Center for Leadership in Education (ICLE):** Partner with ICLE to strengthen rigor and relevance in the literacy classroom.

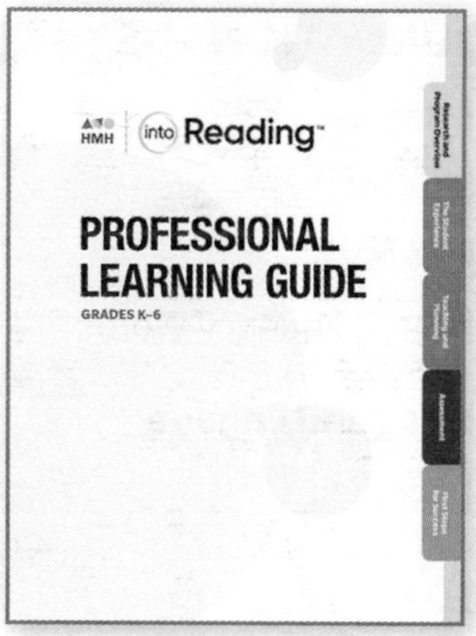

Student and Teacher Materials

WHOLE GROUP

Student Materials

Online

ONLINE STUDENT MANAGEMENT CENTER

- Access all program materials
- Complete and submit assignments and assessments
- Track progress

***my*Book:** 2 Books

Teacher Materials

Online

ONLINE STUDENT MANAGEMENT CENTER

- Access all program materials
- Plan lessons
- Assign materials
- View reports
- Group students

Teacher's Guide
6 Volumes

Writing Workshop Teacher's Guide:
1 Volume

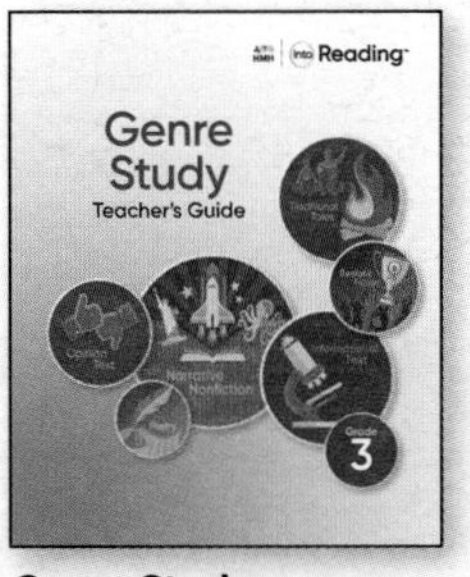

Genre Study Teacher's Guide

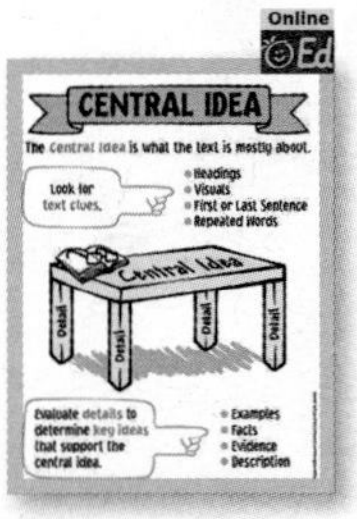

Anchor Charts

Teaching Pal
2 Books

Teacher Resource Book

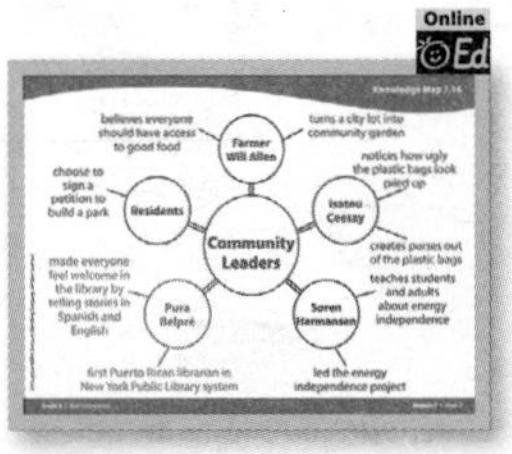

Display and Engage

FOUNDATIONAL SKILLS

Printables:

- Spelling
- Fluency
- High-Frequency Words

Display and Engage

- Decoding

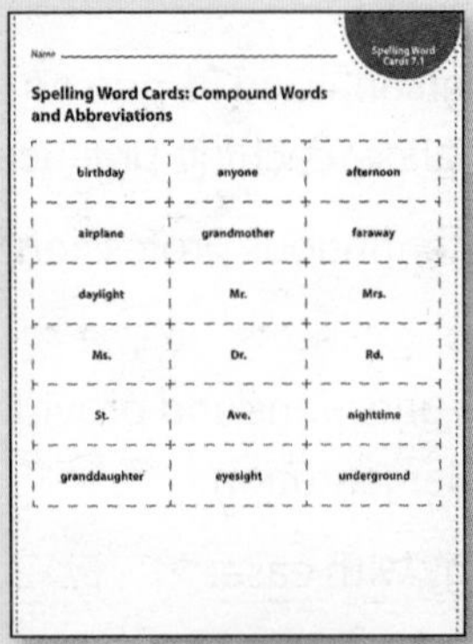

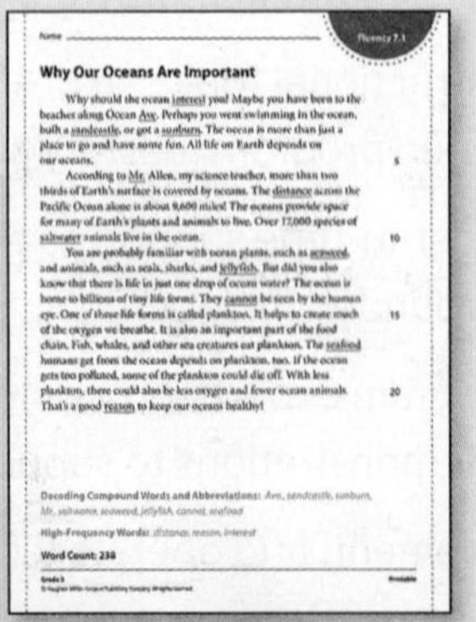

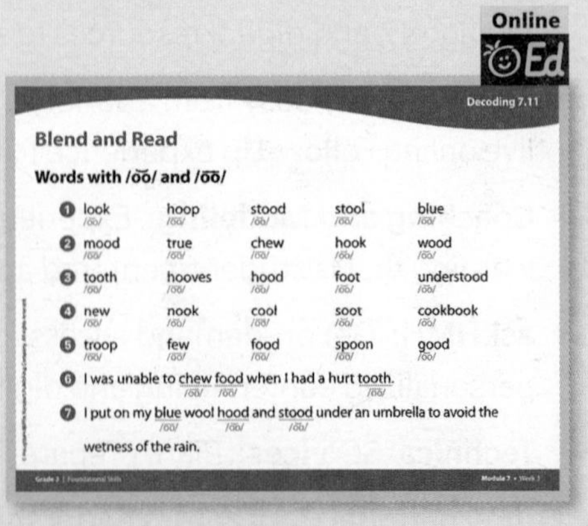

SMALL-GROUP AND INDEPENDENT APPLICATION

Student Choice Library:
6 copies of each title

Rigby
LEVELED LIBRARY

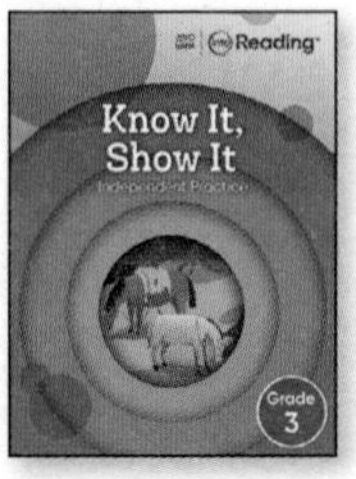

Know It, Show It

Writer's Notebook

Printables include:
- Readers' Theater
- Reading Remake
- Graphic Organizers
- Projects
- Keyboarding
- Reading Log
- Listening Log
- Anchor Charts

Take and Teach Lessons:
Leveled Readers

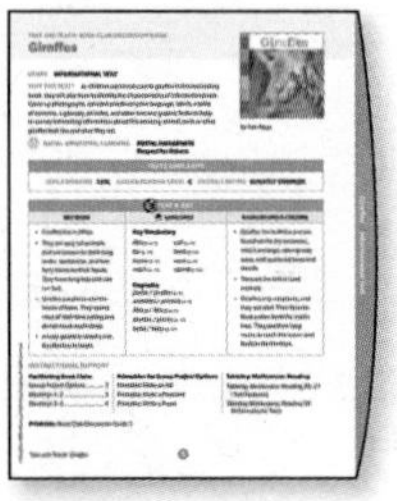

Take and Teach Lessons:
Book Club Discussion Guide

Tabletop Minilessons:
Reading

Tabletop Minilessons:
English Language Development

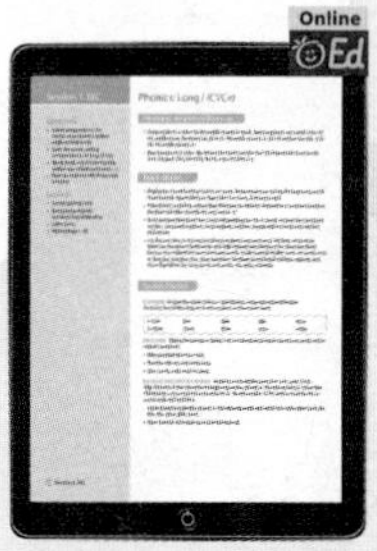

Foundational Skills and Word Study Studio

ASSESSMENTS

Data & Reporting:
- Adaptive Growth Measure
- Guided Reading Benchmark Assessment Kit

Program Assessments:
- Leveled Reader Quizzes
- Weekly Assessments
- Module Assessments

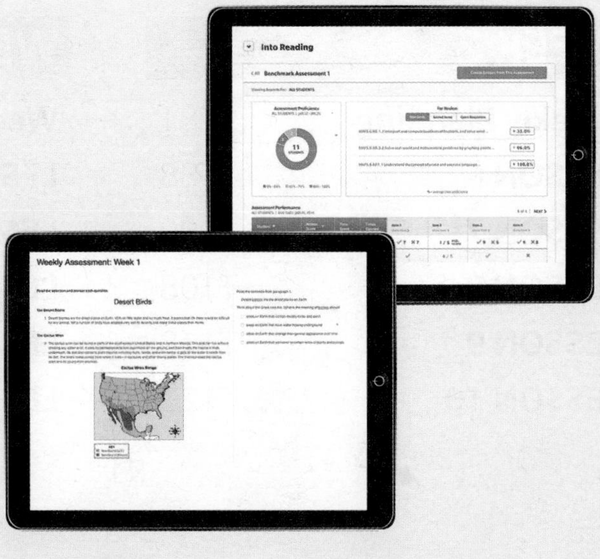

PROFESSIONAL LEARNING & IMPLEMENTATION SUPPORT

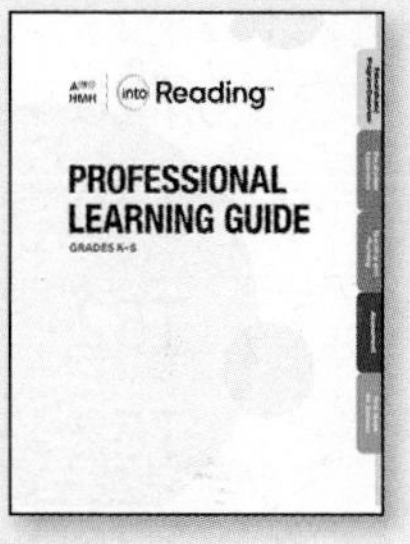

Professional Learning Guide

Guiding Principles and Strategies

VOLUME 1 TABLE OF CONTENTS

MODULE 1 What a Character!

***my*Book, Book 1**

MODULE 1 What a Character!

5

WEEK 1

WEEK 2

WEEK 3

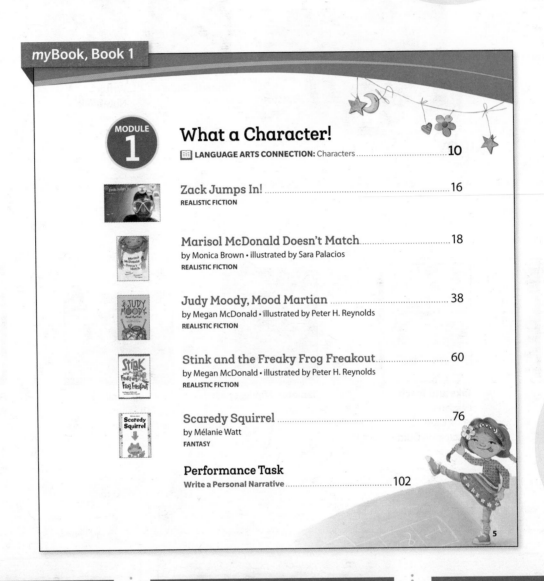

MODULE 2

Use Your Words

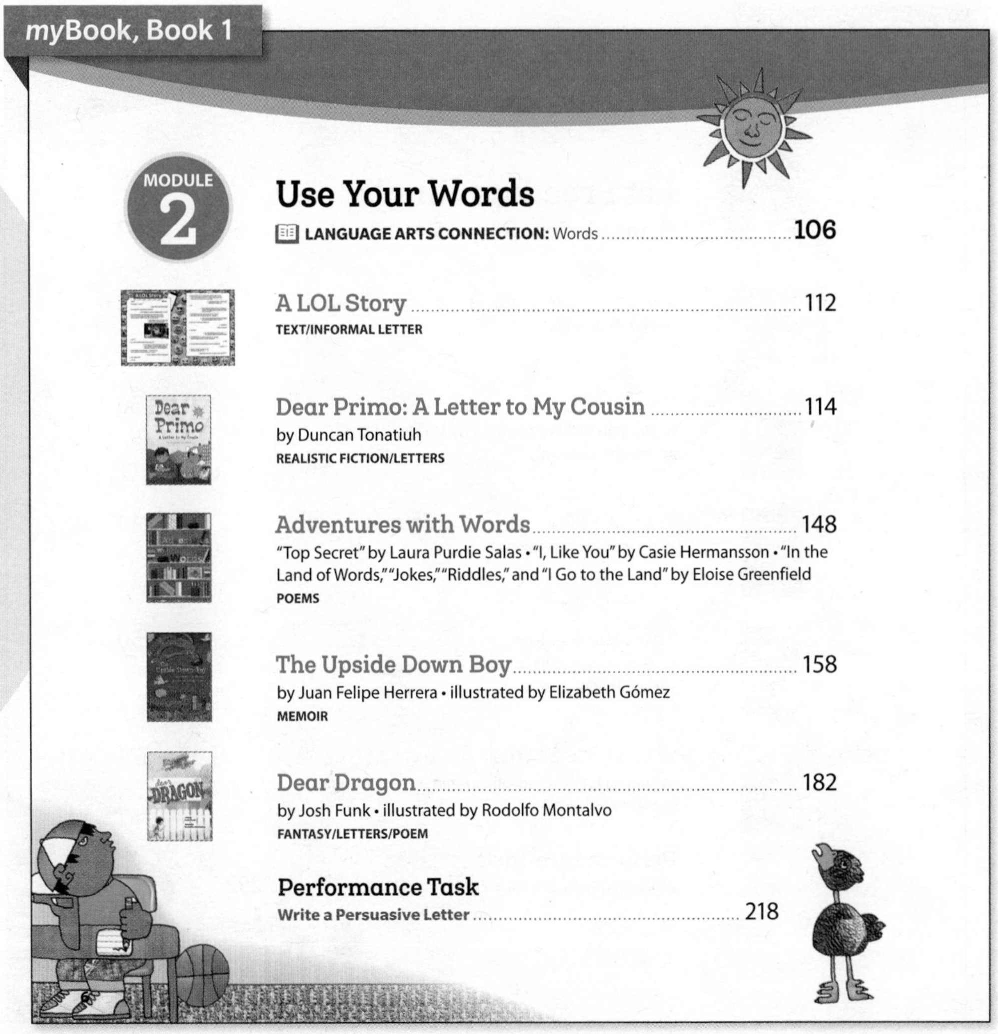

*my*Book, Book 1

WEEK 1

WEEK 2

WEEK 3

VOLUME 2 TABLE OF CONTENTS

MODULE 3

Let Freedom Ring!

MODULE 4

Stories on Stage

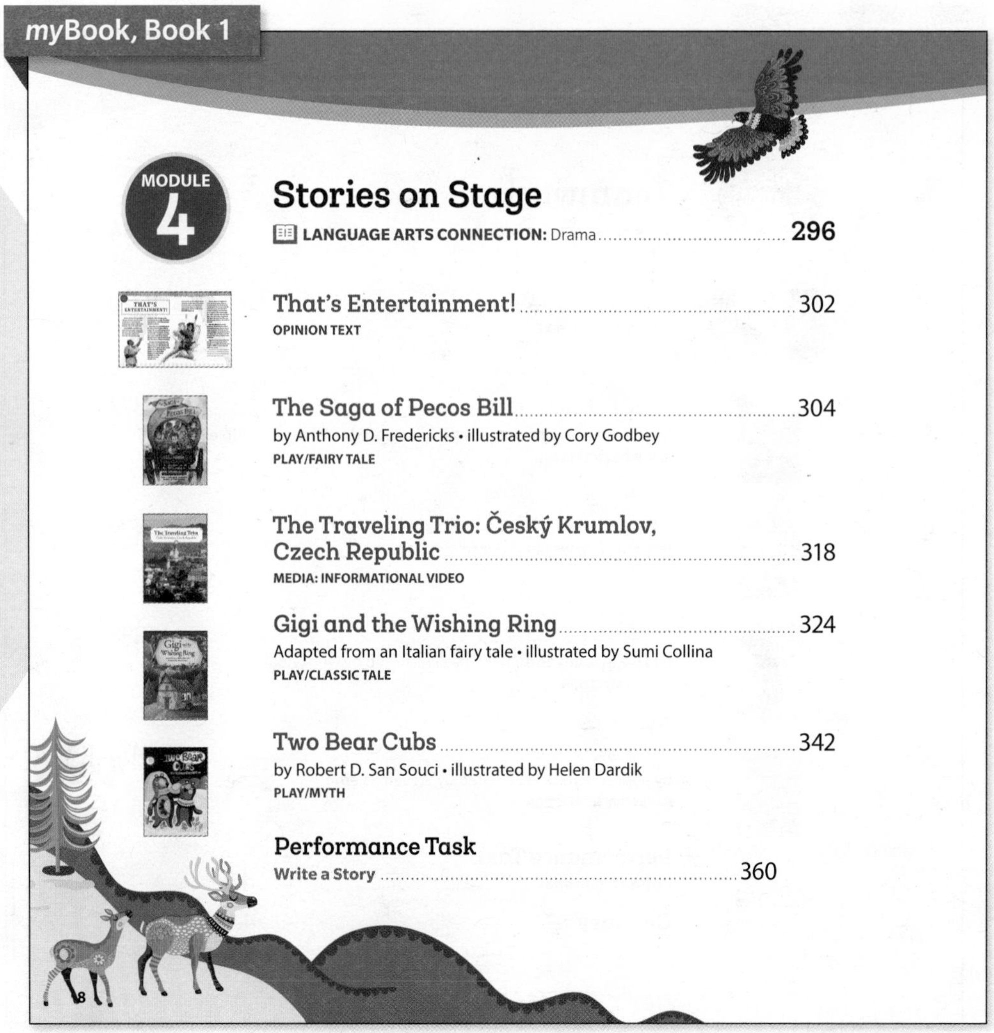

*my*Book, Book 1

MODULE 4

Stories on Stage

WEEK 1

WEEK 2

WEEK 3

TABLE OF CONTENTS

MODULE 5

Teamwork

*my*Book, Book 1

MODULE 5

Teamwork

WEEK 1

WEEK 2

WEEK 3

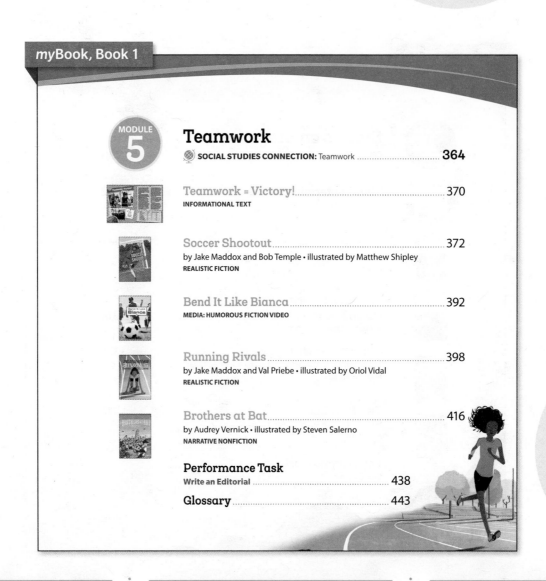

MODULE 6

Animal Behaviors

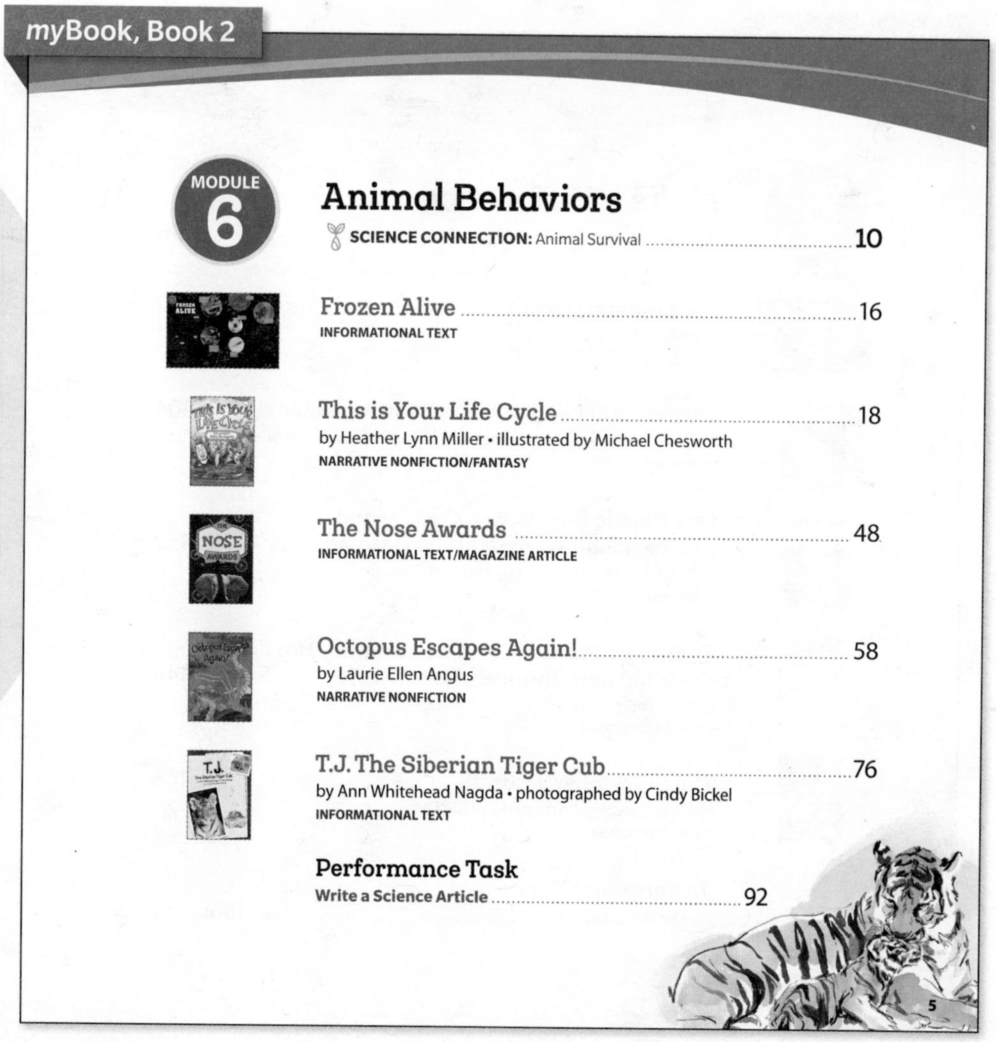
myBook, Book 2

MODULE 6

Animal Behaviors

5

WEEK 1

WEEK 2

WEEK 3

VOLUME 4 TABLE OF CONTENTS

MODULE 7

Make a Difference

*my*Book, Book 2

MODULE 7 Make a Difference

6

MODULE 8

Imagine! Invent!

*my*Book, Book 2

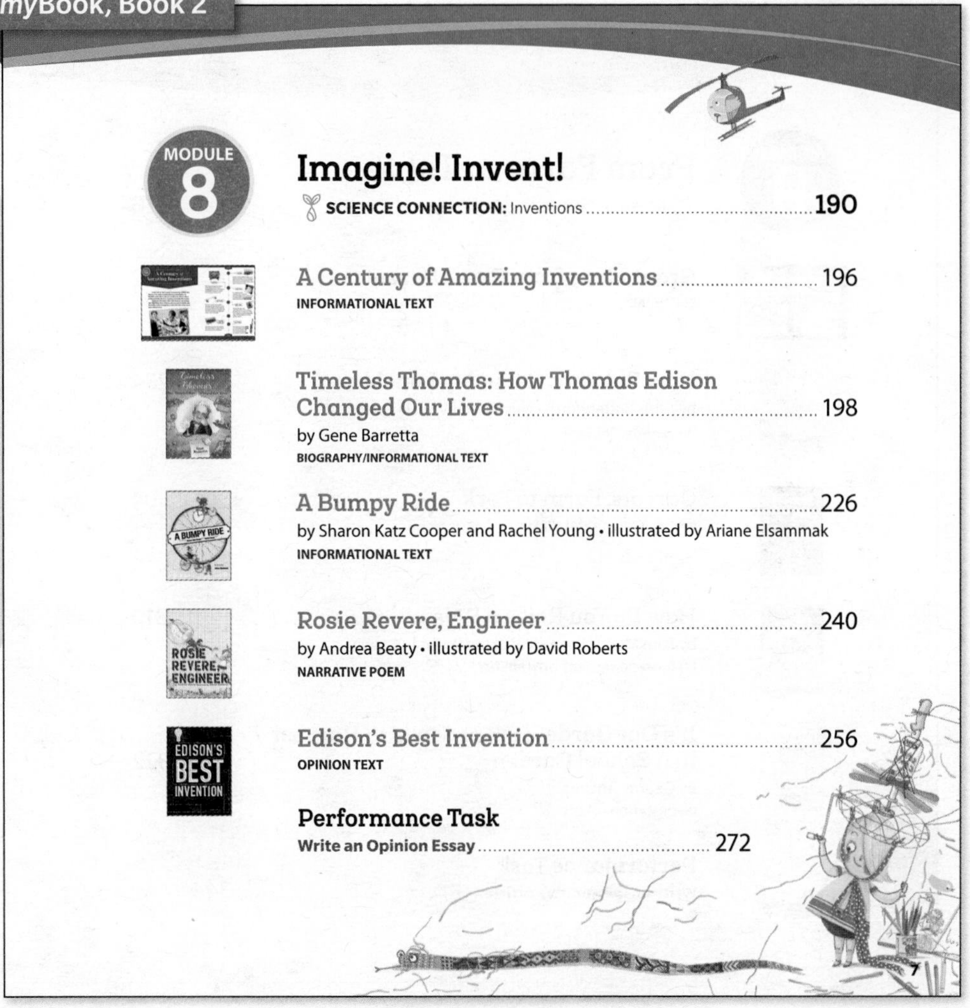

WEEK 1

WEEK 2

WEEK 3

VOLUME 5 TABLE OF CONTENTS

MODULE 9

From Farm to Table

MODULE 10

Tell a Tale

*my*Book, Book 2

WEEK 1

WEEK 2

WEEK 3

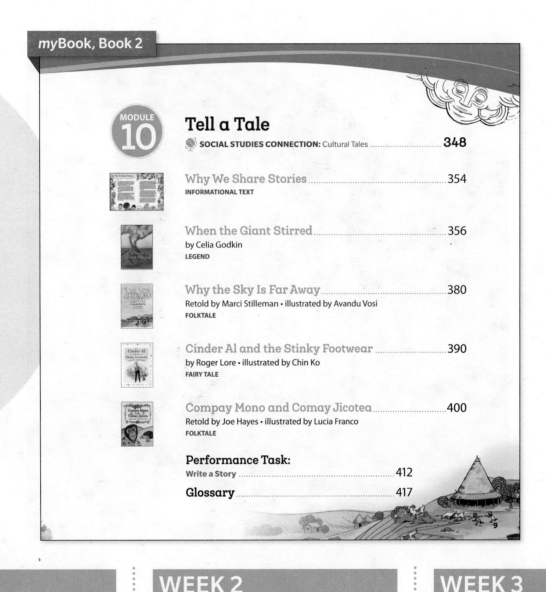

VOLUME 6 TABLE OF CONTENTS

MODULE 11

Genre Study: Nonfiction

MODULE 12

Genre Study: Literary Texts

Small-Group Reading

Rigby®
LEVELED LIBRARY

The Rigby Leveled Library offers a carefully controlled continuum of texts, spanning a range of levels, topics, and genres.

GUIDED READING LEVEL	L	M	N	O	P	Q
	15 TITLES PER LEVEL					

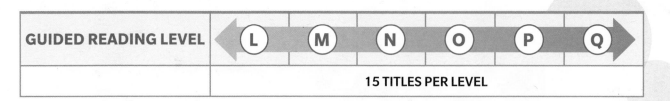

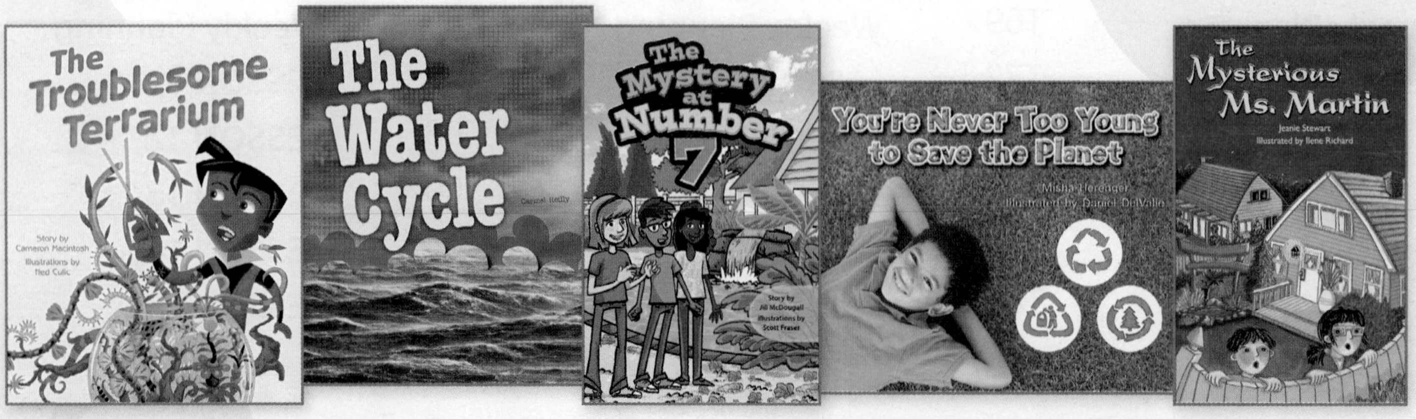

Let Freedom Ring!

MODULE 3

Essential Question

How do historic places, documents, and symbols represent our nation?

SOCIAL STUDIES CONNECTION:
U.S. History

In this module, students will listen to, read, and view a variety of texts and media that present them with information about important U.S. documents and symbols.

A genre focus on nonfiction provides students with opportunities to identify central idea, text structure, and media techniques in order to better understand unfamiliar texts. Students will also encounter video to build knowledge across genres.

As students build their vocabulary and synthesize topic knowledge, they will learn more about our country's history and how various symbols came to represent the values and ideals of the United States.

Building Knowledge Networks

As students read, view, and interact with the texts and media in this module, they build deep topic knowledge about important U.S. documents and symbols, and how this information connects to their lives

Online Ed

DISPLAY AND ENGAGE: Knowledge Map 3.14

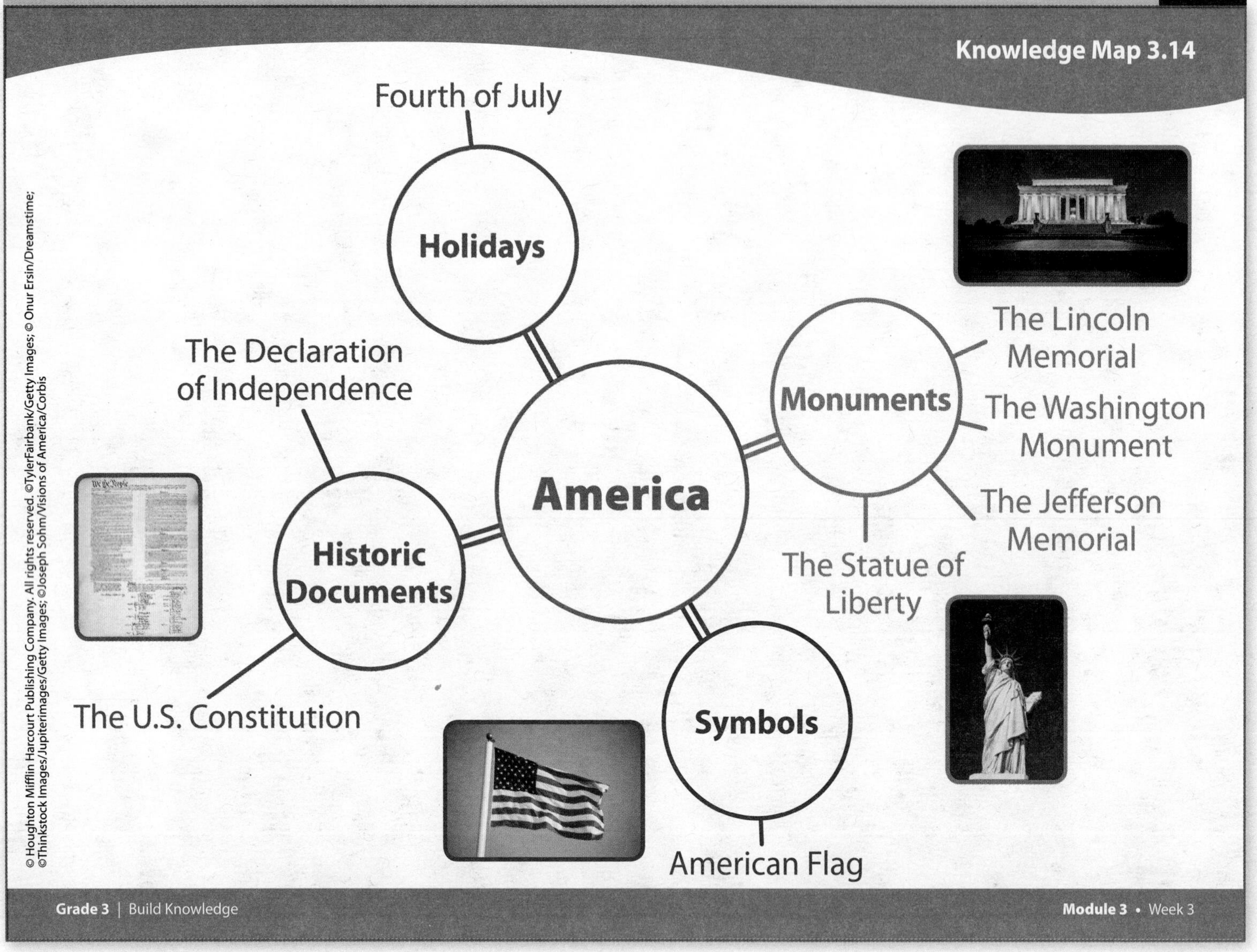

Synthesizing Knowledge

1. At the beginning of the module, introduce the module topic. Point students to *my*Book, Book 1, page 226, and use Display and Engage: **Knowledge Map 3.1** to give students the first step in building their Knowledge Maps throughout the module.
2. After reading each text, have students add to the Knowledge Map in their *my*Book. At the end of each week, use Display and Engage: **Knowledge Map 3.5**, **3.10**, or **3.14** and discuss the added information.
3. At the end of the module, students will synthesize what they have learned about the topic and make connections to self, society, and other texts.

Fostering a Learning Mindset

Throughout this module, look for the Learning Mindset feature to introduce the Learning Mindset focus—**grit**—and use the suggestions to weave it throughout students' literacy instruction as they encounter new texts and practice new skills.

Key Messages

- Our brains are like muscles, the more we work them the stronger they become. Hard work leads to success.
- We rarely get things right the first time we try. We have to keep trying!
- Display Anchor Chart 31: My Learning Mindset throughout the year. Refer to it to introduce grit and to reinforce the skills you introduced in previous modules.
- Recognize when students consistently exhibit a Learning Mindset focus.

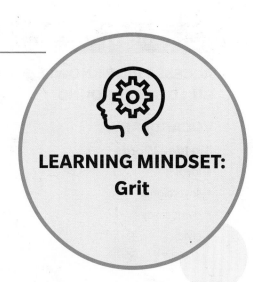

LEARNING MINDSET:
Grit

Online Ed

ANCHOR CHART 31: My Learning Mindset

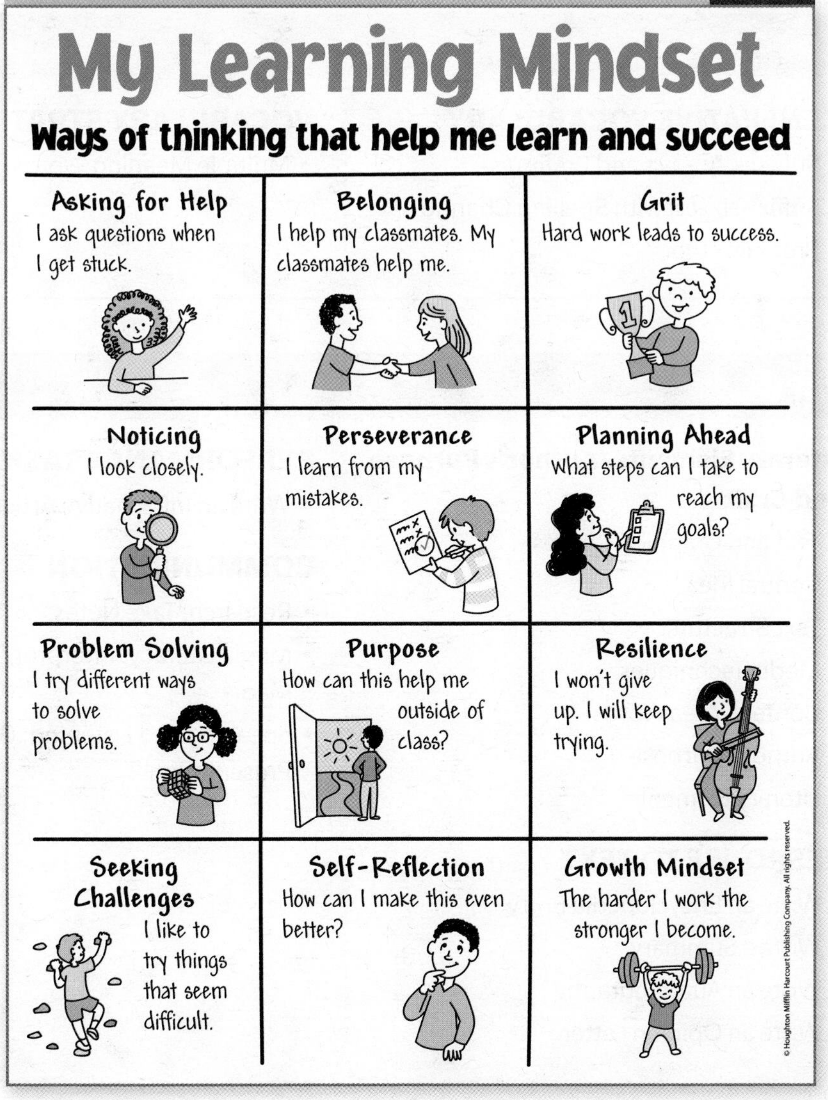

My Learning Mindset
Ways of thinking that help me learn and succeed
Asking for Help
I ask questions when I get stuck.
Belonging
I help my classmates. My classmates help me.
Grit
Hard work leads to success.
Noticing
I look closely.
Perseverance
I learn from my mistakes.
Planning Ahead
What steps can I take to reach my goals?
Problem Solving
I try different ways to solve problems.
Purpose
How can this help me outside of class?
Resilience
I won't give up. I will keep trying.
Seeking Challenges
I like to try things that seem difficult.
Self-Reflection
How can I make this even better?
Growth Mindset
The harder I work the stronger I become.
© Houghton Mifflin Harcourt Publishing Company. All rights reserved.

Developing Knowledge and Skills

Students build topic knowledge and develop academic vocabulary, reading, communication, and writing skills through daily whole- and small-group instruction.

LEARNING MINDSET: Grit

Build Knowledge and Language

ACCESS PRIOR KNOWLEDGE/ BUILD BACKGROUND

VOCABULARY

Big Idea Words

- *loyal*
- *sovereignty*
- *democracy*
- *civic*

MULTIMEDIA

Active Listening and Viewing

- Get Curious Video: American Landmarks

Vocabulary

ACADEMIC VOCABULARY

- Critical Vocabulary
- Instructional Vocabulary

GENERATIVE VOCABULARY

- Suffixes *–y, –less* and Prefix *dis–*
- Suffix *–er/–est* with Spelling Change
- Prefix *im–* (*not*)

VOCABULARY STRATEGY

- Multiple Meaning Words

Reading Workshop & Vocabulary

MULTIPLE GENRES

Genre Focus: Nonfiction

- Informational Text
- Informational Video
- Narrative Nonfiction

COMPREHENSION

Use Metacognitive Skills

- Synthesize
- Retell/Summarize
- Ask and Answer Questions

Literary Elements/Author's Purpose and Craft

- Text and Graphic Features
- Central Idea
- Text Structure
- Media Techniques
- Content-Area Words
- Author's Purpose
- Literary Elements

RESPONSE TO TEXT

- Write an Encyclopedia Entry
- Write a Summary
- Write an Autobiography
- Write an Opinion Letter

PERFORMANCE TASK

- Write an Informative Article

COMMUNICATION

- Research: Take Notes
- Media Literacy: Interpret/Analyze Media
- Speaking and Listening: Give a Presentation

Essential Question
How do historic places, documents, and symbols represent our nation?

Foundational Skills

DECODING
- Three-Letter Blends *(spl, scr, spr, str)*
- Words with /j/, /k/, and /kw/
- Silent Letters *(kn, wr, gn, mb, rh)*

SPELLING
- Three-Letter Blends *(spl, scr, spr, str)*
- Words with /j/, /k/, and /kw/
- Silent Consonants

FLUENCY
- Reading Rate
- Phrasing
- Expression

Writing Workshop

WRITING PROCESS
Informational Text
- Plan and Generate Ideas
- Organize
- Draft
- Revise and Edit
- Publish and Present

WRITING FORM
Descriptive Essay

GRAMMAR
Conventions
- Verb Tense I
- Abstract Nouns

Demonstrate Knowledge

INQUIRY & RESEARCH PROJECT
- Create a National Symbols Pamphlet

ASSESS LEARNING
Formative Assessments
- Selection Quizzes
- Weekly Assessments
- Module Assessments

Performance-Based Assessments
- Informative Writing
- Inquiry and Research Project

Teaching with Text Sets

Carefully selected, content-rich text sets help students build topic knowledge and reading skills.

WEEK 1

Online

GET CURIOUS VIDEO

American Landmarks
Students view and respond to the video *American Landmarks* to learn more about our nation's symbols.

READ ALOUD

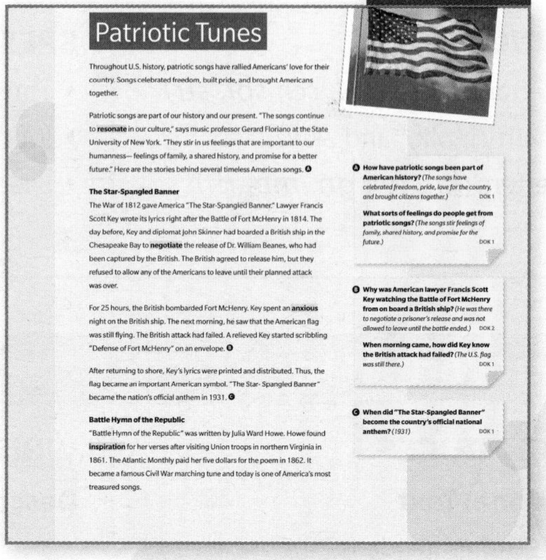

Patriotic Tunes

Throughout U.S. history, patriotic songs have rallied Americans' love for their country. Songs celebrated freedom, built pride, and brought Americans together.

Patriotic songs are part of our history and our present. "The songs continue to **resonate** in our culture," says music professor Gerard Floriano at the State University of New York. "They stir in us feelings that are important to our humanness— feelings of family, a shared history, and promise for a better future." Here are the stories behind several timeless American songs. A

The Star-Spangled Banner
The War of 1812 gave America "The Star-Spangled Banner." Lawyer Francis Scott Key wrote its lyrics right after the Battle of Fort McHenry in 1814. The day before, Key and diplomat John Skinner had boarded a British ship in the Chesapeake Bay to **negotiate** the release of Dr. William Beanes, who had been captured by the British. The British agreed to release him, but they refused to allow any of the Americans to leave until their planned attack was over.

For 25 hours, the British bombarded Fort McHenry. Key spent an **anxious** night on the British ship. The next morning, he saw that the American flag was still flying. The British attack had failed. A relieved Key started scribbling "Defense of Fort McHenry" on an envelope. B

After returning to shore, Key's lyrics were printed and distributed. Thus, the flag became an important American symbol. "The Star- Spangled Banner" became the nation's official anthem in 1931. C

Battle Hymn of the Republic
"Battle Hymn of the Republic" was written by Julia Ward Howe. Howe found **inspiration** for her verses after visiting Union troops in northern Virginia in 1861. The Atlantic Monthly paid her five dollars for the poem in 1862. It became a famous Civil War marching tune and today is one of America's most treasured songs.

A **How have patriotic songs been part of American history?** *(The songs have celebrated freedom, pride, love for the country, and brought citizens together.)* DOK 1

What sorts of feelings do people get from patriotic songs? *(The songs stir feelings of family, shared history, and promise for the future.)* DOK 1

B **Why was American lawyer Francis Scott Key watching the Battle of Fort McHenry from on board a British ship?** *(He was there to negotiate a prisoner's release and was not allowed to leave until the battle ended.)* DOK 2

When morning came, how did Key know the British attack had failed? *(The U.S. flag was still there.)* DOK 1

C **When did "The Star-Spangled Banner" become the country's official national anthem?** *(1931)* DOK 1

Genre: Informational Text

my BOOK

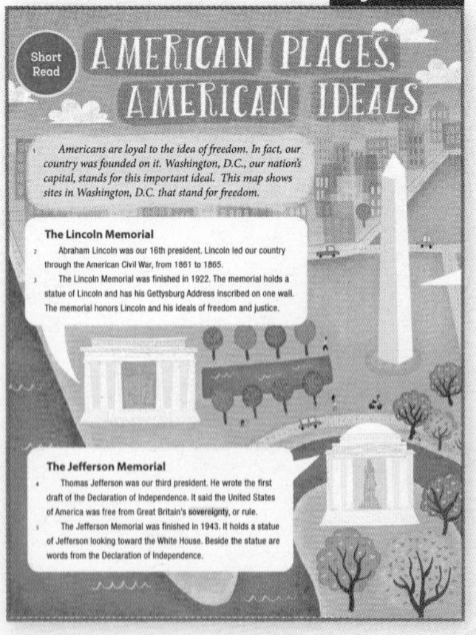

Short Read

AMERICAN PLACES, AMERICAN IDEALS

1 *Americans are loyal to the idea of freedom. In fact, our country was founded on it. Washington, D.C., our nation's capital, stands for this important ideal. This map shows sites in Washington, D.C. that stand for freedom.*

The Lincoln Memorial

2 Abraham Lincoln was our 16th president. Lincoln led our country through the American Civil War, from 1861 to 1865.

3 The Lincoln Memorial was finished in 1922. The memorial holds a statue of Lincoln and has his Gettysburg Address inscribed on one wall. The memorial honors Lincoln and his ideals of freedom and justice.

The Jefferson Memorial

4 Thomas Jefferson was our third president. He wrote the first draft of the Declaration of Independence. It said the United States of America was free from Great Britain's **sovereignty**, or rule.

5 The Jefferson Memorial was finished in 1943. It holds a statue of Jefferson looking toward the White House. Beside the statue are words from the Declaration of Independence.

Genre: Informational Text
Lexile® Measure: 670L

my BOOK

Genre: Informational Text
Lexile® Measure: 650L
Guided Reading Level: P

Essential Question

How do historic places, documents, and symbols represent our nation?

WEEK 2

my BOOK

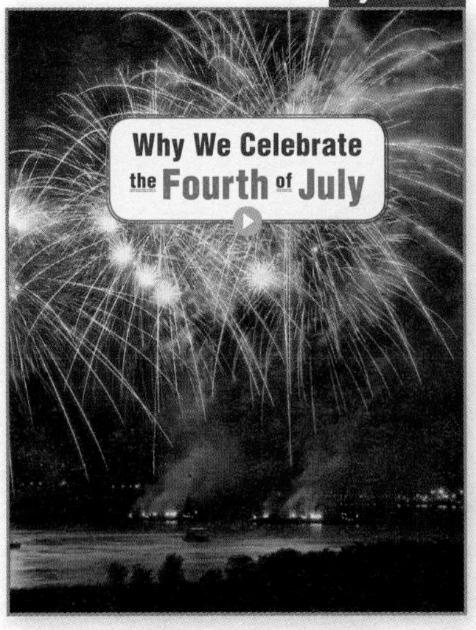

Genre: Educational Video

my BOOK

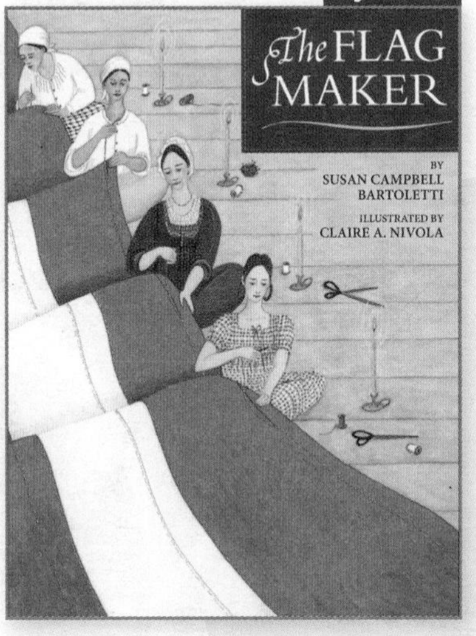

Genre: Narrative Nonfiction
Lexile® Measure: 620L
Guided Reading Level: R

WEEK 3

my BOOK

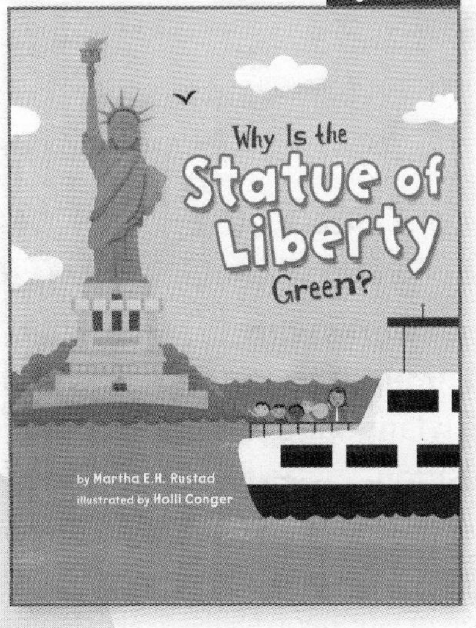

Genre: Narrative Nonfiction
Lexile® Measure: 560L
Guided Reading Level: N

WRITING FOCAL TEXT

Genre: Fiction
Lexile® Measure: 920L
Guided Reading Level: M

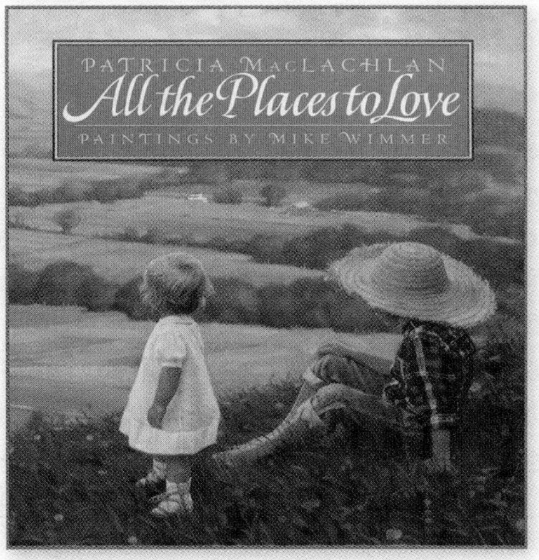

Reading Workshop

During Reading Workshop, students will engage daily in a variety of whole-group, small-group, and independent literacy activities. Multiple options for differentiated instruction allow teachers to tailor instruction based on student need.

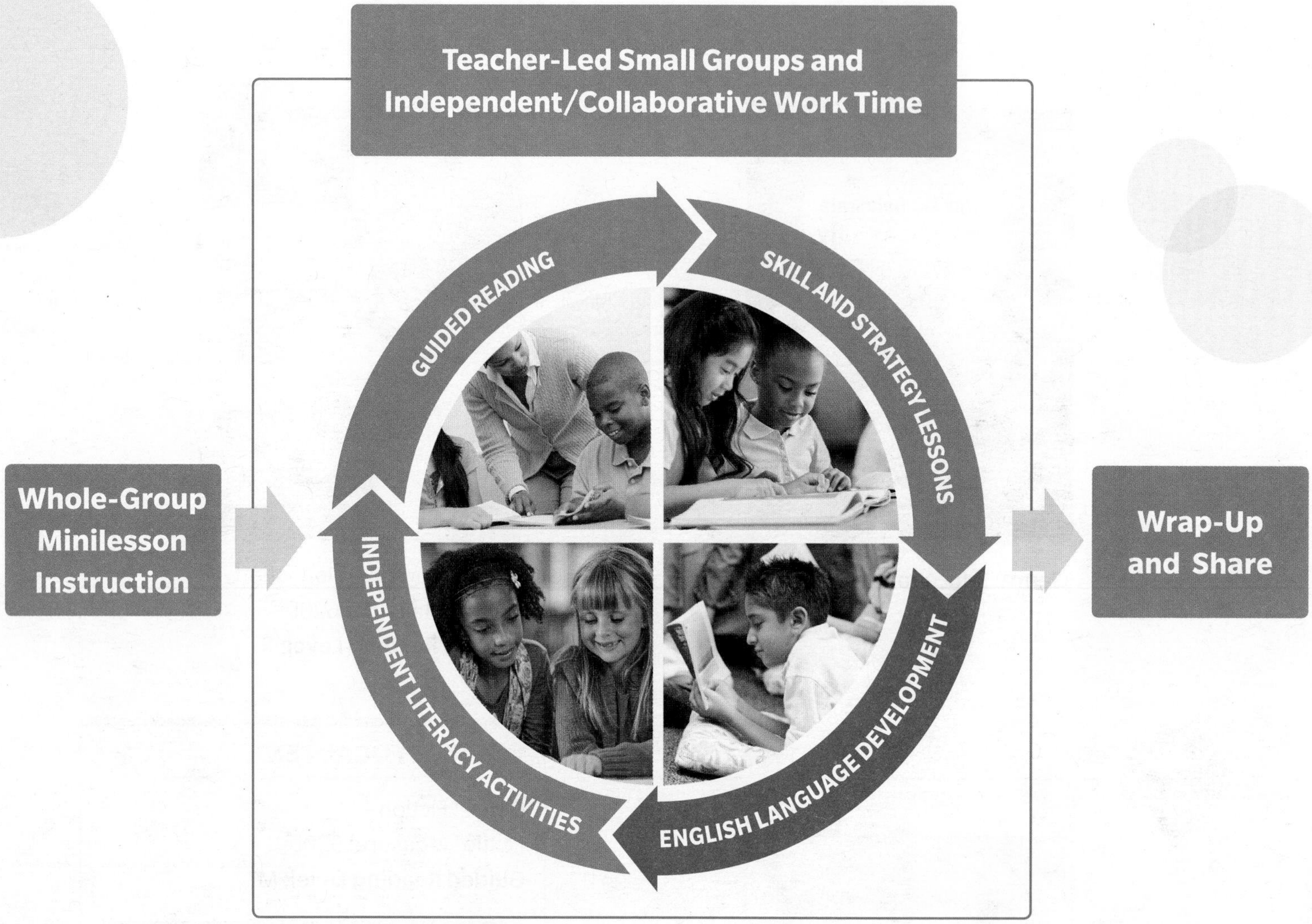

GUIDED READING

Teacher works with students at their instructional guided reading level.
Using the Rigby Leveled Library, pull just-right books to facilitate guided reading lessons.

SKILL AND STRATEGY LESSONS

Teacher works with small groups to reinforce reading skills and strategies.
Group students for targeted support. Lessons may be connected to the daily whole-group minilesson or based on student need.

ENGLISH LANGUAGE DEVELOPMENT

Teacher works with small groups to support English language acquisition.
Lessons provide students with opportunities to engage in language skills across all the literacy domains in a safe small-group environment.

INDEPENDENT LITERACY ACTIVITIES

While teacher works with small groups, other students work independently.
Students engage in literacy activities that reinforce the lesson's learning objectives.

Forming Small Groups

Guided Reading Groups

- Assess students periodically, using running records or other diagnostic assessments to determine each student's guided reading level.
- Choose books from the Rigby Leveled Library based on reading level or choose strategies that you plan to teach or practice with each group.
- Use assessment data and information from conferences to frequently regroup students based on reading level.
- Refer to Take & Teach lessons to guide reading instruction, check comprehension, and extend learning.
- Access online Printables, comprehension quizzes, and additional resources that promote revisiting the Leveled Readers for multiple purposes.

Skill and Strategy Groups

- Observe students during whole-group minilessons to determine who may benefit from targeted support or extension of the day's reading skill. Use assessment data and information to group students according to need.
- Use Tabletop Minilessons: Reading to scaffold students' understanding of the skill through an Anchor Chart and supporting lesson.
- Access online Printables for students to apply their understanding of the skill to an independent reading book.

English Language Development

- Use Tabletop Minilessons: English Language Development to teach and practice language skills. Guide students to apply them to each lesson's text at their identified language proficiency level.
- Access online Printables for students to apply the skill to an independent reading book.

SETTING READING GOALS AND CONFERRING

- Talk to students about their strengths and areas for growth during conferences.
- Work with students to set realistic reading goals that will support them in reaching the next guided reading level.
- Teach strategies that will help students achieve their goals and remind them to use the strategies when they read. Review strategies frequently with different books.

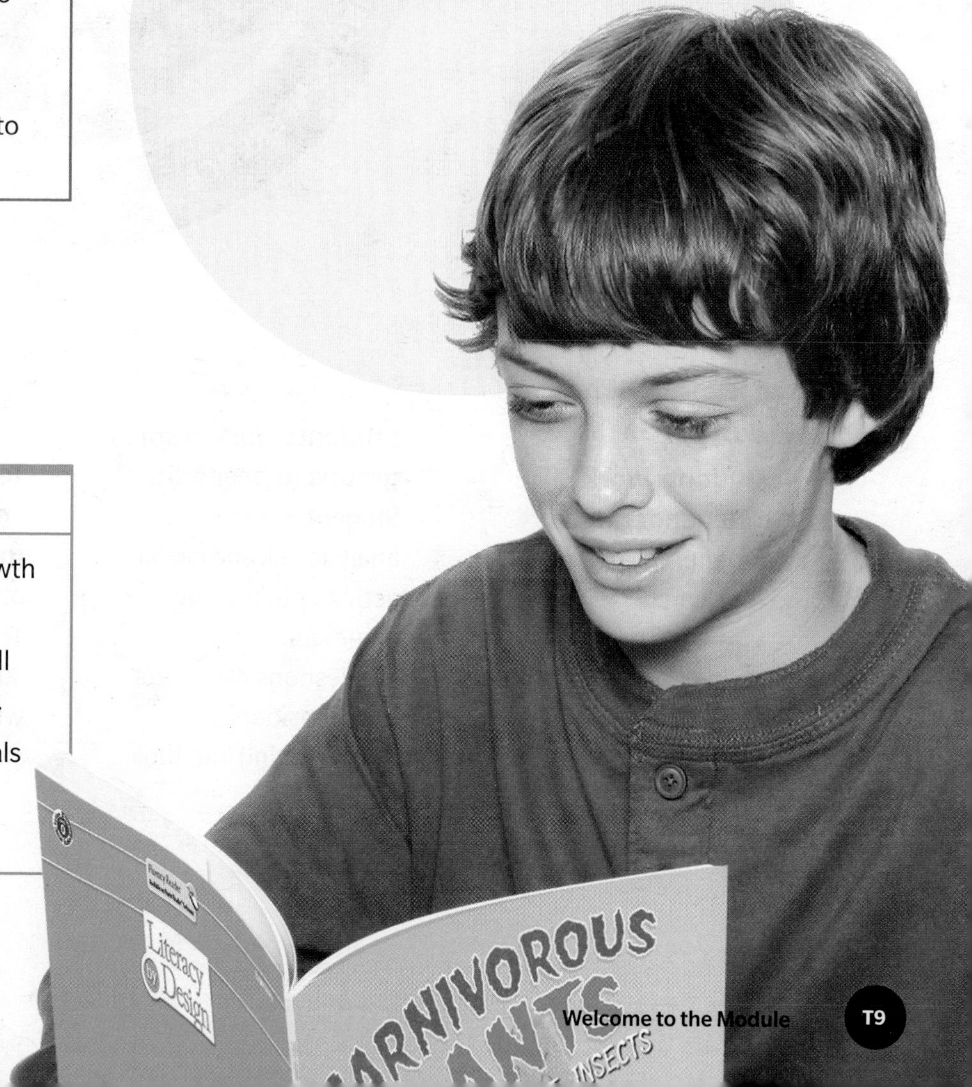

Writing Workshop

Students will engage in the full writing process to produce a description during this three-week module. The Writing Workshop Teacher's Guide provides explicit instruction and ample opportunity for students to write daily.

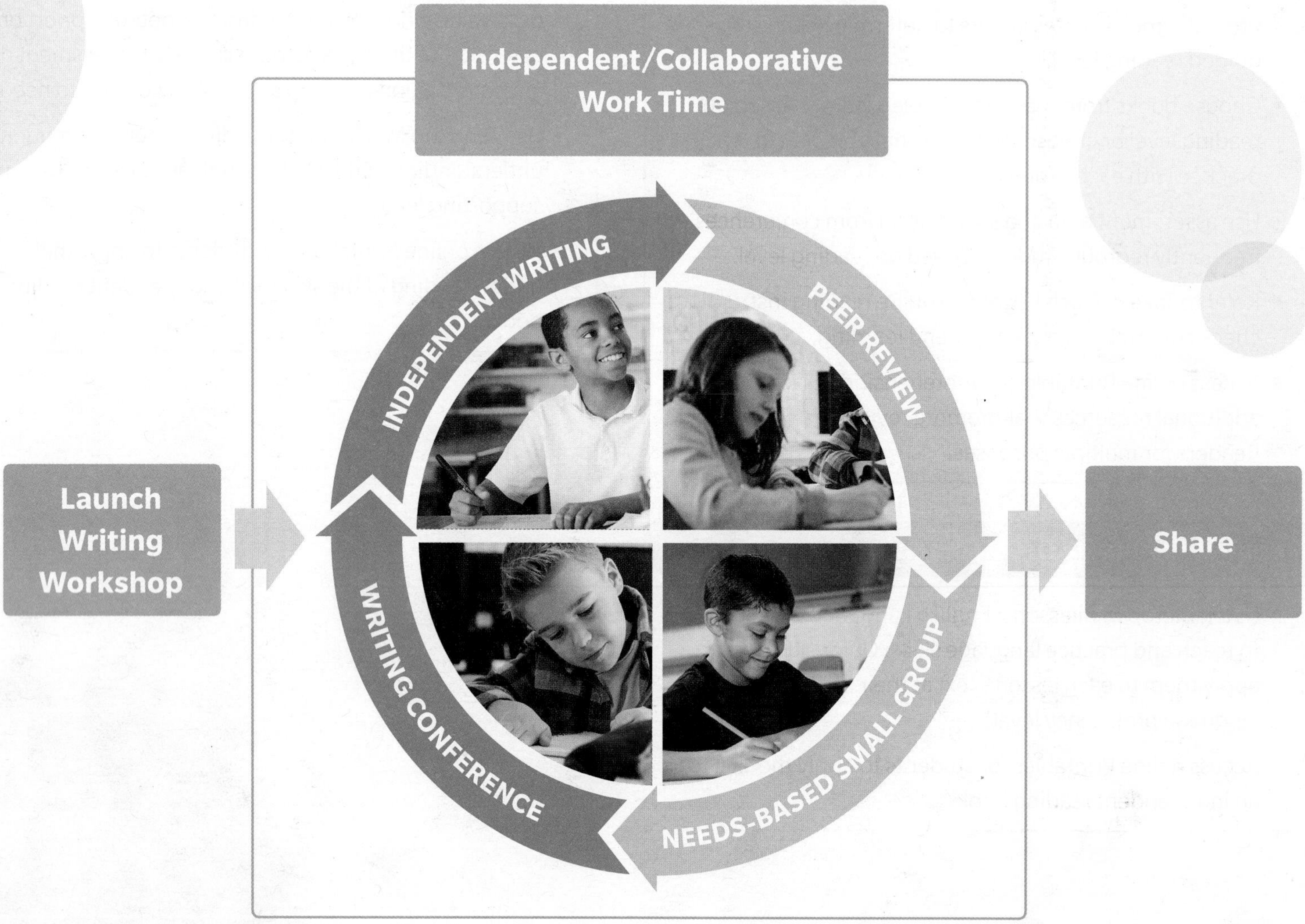

INDEPENDENT WRITING

Students work independently to:

- generate ideas/ research
- prewrite
- draft
- write
- revise and edit
- publish

PEER REVIEW

Students work in small groups to peer edit. Students engage in analytic talk and clocking activities to provide comments and suggestions that peers may consider incorporating into their writing.

NEEDS-BASED SMALL GROUP

Teacher works with small needs-based groups on grammar and writing skills. Targeted minilessons support development of writing and grammar skills in areas of need.

WRITING CONFERENCE

One-on-One Conferring Teachers meet with students one-on-one to set writing goals and to provide feedback throughout the writing process.

Descriptive Essay Writing Module Overview

Writing Workshop Teacher's Guide, pp. W33–W50

WEEK 1

- Introducing the Focal Text
- Vocabulary
- Prewriting I: Preparing to Write
- Prewriting II: Choosing Descriptive Words
- Drafting I: The Central Idea

WEEK 2

- Drafting II: Organizing a Description
- Drafting III: Moving into the Draft
- Drafting IV: Completing the Draft
- Revising I: Sentence Variety
- Revising II: Conferencing

WEEK 3

- Revising III: Descriptive Words and Phrases
- Editing I: Spelling and Mechanics
- Editing II: Peer Proofreading
- Publishing
- Sharing

FOCAL TEXT

All the Places to Love by Patricia MacLachlin

WRITING MODE Informational Text

WRITING FORM Descriptive Essay

FOCAL STATEMENT Places leave impressions.

Writing Prompt

- **READ** this sentence: Places leave impressions.
- **THINK** about a description of a place you are familiar with.
- **WRITE** a descriptive essay about that place. Give plenty of details, descriptions, examples, and facts to explain why it is memorable.

Assessment and Progress Monitoring

Ongoing formative assessment guides daily instruction, while performance-based assessments demonstrate student progress toward mastery of module skills and standards.

FORMATIVE ASSESSMENT

Selection Quizzes

Assess comprehension of the *my*Book text selections:

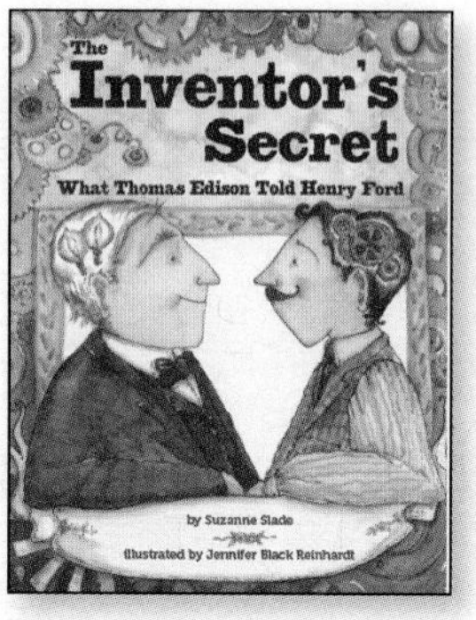

Weekly Assessments

Assess students' understanding of the key Reading and Writing skills, covered during each week of instruction.

Ongoing Formative Assessment Tools

- Leveled Readers Cards
- Selection Quizzes
- Running Records
- 1:1 Observation Records
- Daily Lesson Checks and Correct & Redirect opportunities in the Teacher's Guide

Module Assessment

Measure student's proficiency in the critical skills covered in this module:

- Generative Vocabulary
- Vocabulary Strategies
- Comprehension
- Grammar
- Writing

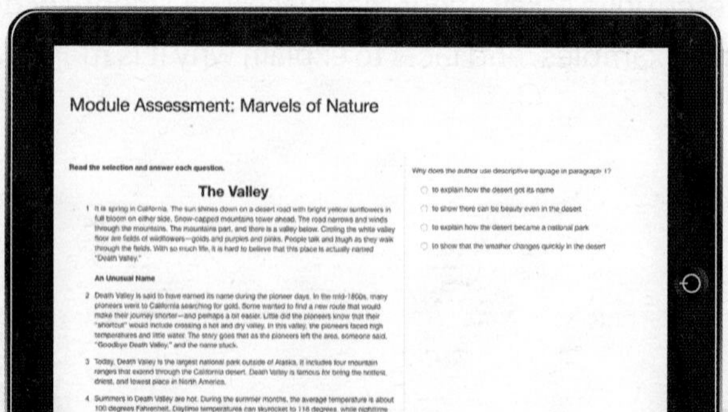

PERFORMANCE-BASED ASSESSMENTS

Performance Task

Students synthesize what they have learned from the module's text set and demonstrate their genre and topic knowledge by completing a Performance Task in response to the Essential Question.

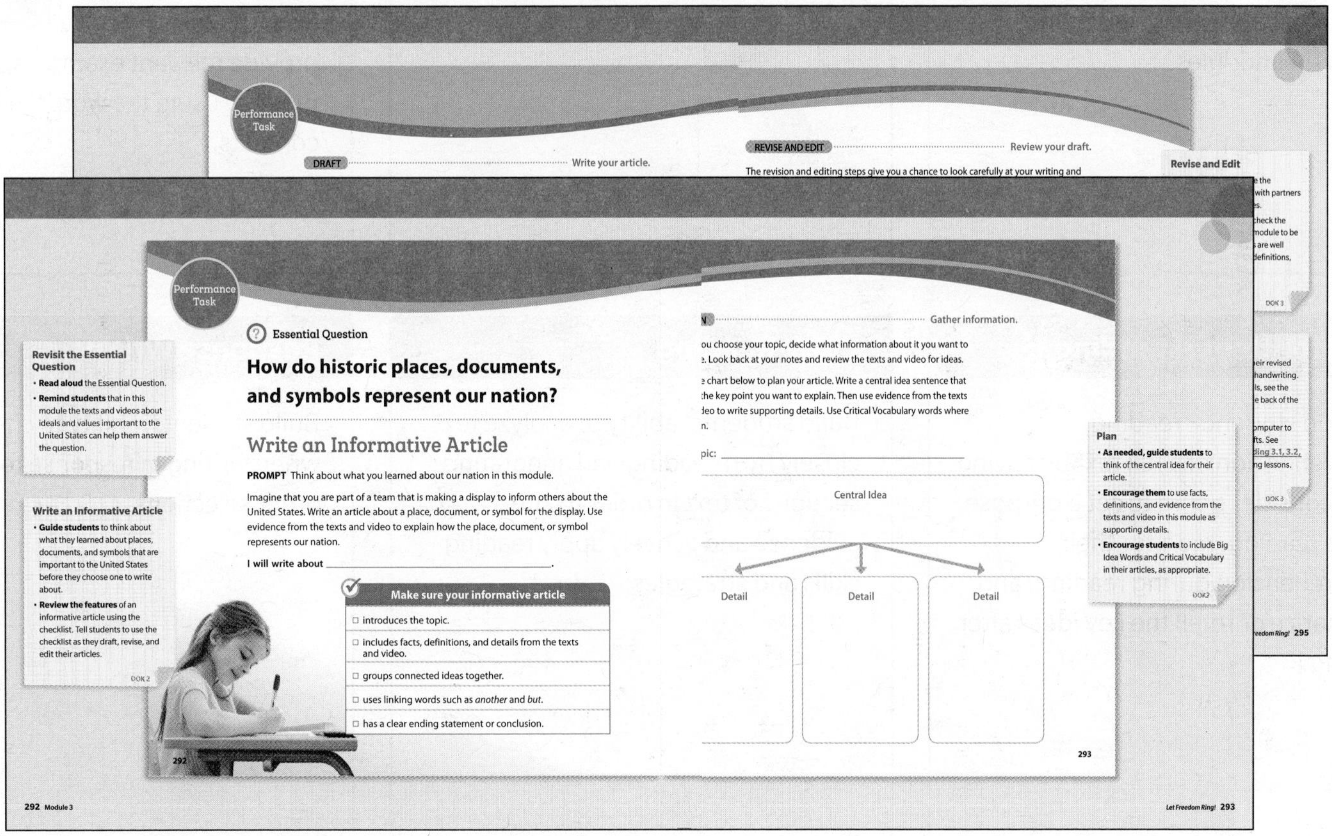
Performance Task

Revisit the Essential Question
- **Read aloud** the Essential Question.
- **Remind students** that in this module the texts and videos about ideals and values important to the United States can help them answer the question.

Write an Informative Article
- **Guide students** to think about what they learned about places, documents, and symbols that are important to the United States before they choose one to write about.
- **Review the features** of an informative article using the checklist. Tell students to use the checklist as they draft, revise, and edit their articles.

DOK 2

Essential Question

How do historic places, documents, and symbols represent our nation?

Write an Informative Article

PROMPT Think about what you learned about our nation in this module.

Imagine that you are part of a team that is making a display to inform others about the United States. Write an article about a place, document, or symbol for the display. Use evidence from the texts and video to explain how the place, document, or symbol represents our nation.

I will write about ________________.

Make sure your informative article
- introduces the topic.
- includes facts, definitions, and details from the texts and video.
- groups connected ideas together.
- uses linking words such as *another* and *but*.
- has a clear ending statement or conclusion.

Gather information.

Central Idea

Detail | Detail | Detail

Plan
- **As needed, guide students** to think of the central idea for their article.
- **Encourage them** to use facts, definitions, and evidence from the texts and video in this module as supporting details.
- **Encourage students** to include Big Idea Words and Critical Vocabulary in their articles, as appropriate.

DOK 2

292 Module 3

Let Freedom Ring! 293

Tailor Instruction to Meet Student Needs

Throughout the course of the module, in Writing Workshop, students work through the stages of the writing process. Student writing can be evaluated according to the rubric provided for the module's writing form, located in the Teacher Resource Book.

Teaching with Instructional Routines

Use recursive, research-informed instructional routines to support lesson planning and maximize students' learning.

Active Viewing

Build and extend students' knowledge about a topic by having them actively view and respond to both the Get Curious Videos at the beginning of each module and the videos that appear as selections within the modules.

FOCUS ROUTINE

Active Listening

Increase students' familiarity with fluent reading and develop their listening comprehension by having them actively listen and respond to a text on the module topic read aloud.

Vocabulary

Explicitly teach the meaning of topic-related and academic vocabulary words from the texts, provide relevant examples, and practice using the words in familiar contexts.

Read for Understanding

Develop students' reading comprehension of a full text by having them consider genre to set a purpose before reading, monitor their comprehension during reading, and summarize or retell the key ideas after reading.

Close Reading

Build students' ability to analyze text closely by rereading and annotating sections of text in order to cite evidence and actively apply reading skills and strategies.

Response Writing

Build students' ability to cite evidence when writing in response to texts and other selections.

Additional Routines

ENGAGEMENT ROUTINES

- Choral Reading
- Partner Reading
- Echo Reading
- Turn and Talk
- Think-Pair-Share
- Solo Chair
- Collaborative Discussion

Refer to the **GPS guide** for support with using the routines embedded throughout the lessons.

FOCUS ROUTINE

Active Listening

Use the **ACTIVE LISTENING** routine to

- engage students with the topic and build excitement to learn more.
- provide exposure to target content-area and general academic vocabulary words.
- model fluent reading.
- practice listening comprehension skills through discussion.

ACTIVE LISTENING ROUTINE MATERIALS

Use the **Teacher Read-Aloud** text to engage students in listening to and responding to text read aloud.

- Ensure that students needing support for unfamiliar vocabulary understand the meanings of the Quick Teach Words.
- Encourage students to review the Essential Question and Lesson 1 text to make comparisons to the Read-Aloud Text after it has been read.

ACTIVE LISTENING ROUTINE IN ACTION

ROUTINE STEP	MODEL LANGUAGE
1 **Set a purpose for listening.** Connect to the module topic.	*As you listen to this text, think about the genre and the topic. Then, decide on your purpose for listening. Ask yourself what you want to learn from the text.*
2 **Read aloud the text.** Tell students to listen carefully and be prepared to answer questions about the text.	*Listen carefully to the text I'm about to read and be prepared to answer some questions about it. Note the expression I use and the rate at which I read.*
3 **Respond to the text.** Ask students to participate in **THINK-PAIR-SHARE** as they compare the information in the Read-Aloud Text to what they have already learned about the module topic.	*Think about what you have learned from this text. Did you meet your purpose for listening? How does what you learned from this text add to your knowledge of the module topic? How does it connect to the Essential Question?*

Inquiry and Research Project

CREATE A NATIONAL SYMBOLS PAMPHLET Over the next three weeks, students will collaborate to generate ideas, research, complete, and present an inquiry-based project.

WEEK 1 Launch the Project: Brainstorm and Research

LEARNING OBJECTIVES

- Participate in shared research projects.
- Gather information and evidence from sources.
- Work collaboratively with others to develop a plan of shared responsibilities.

MATERIALS

- **Printable** *Project 3.1*
- pens, pencils, notepaper
- informational books, magazines, and approved websites
- desktop publishing software (optional)

WEEKLY FOCUS Set a Goal and Gather Information

Clarify Project Goals Tell students that over the next few weeks, they will work in groups to research the official United States symbols, such as the bald eagle, the national anthem, the United States seal, and the national motto. They will summarize their research in a pamphlet that showcases these symbols.

Build Background Help children understand what a *symbol* is by discussing your school mascot or those of local sports teams. Ask volunteers to name symbols of the United States, prompting with hints as necessary. List these on the board.

- Use a discussion of your state symbols to help students realize that some symbols are well known and others might be more obscure. Also use the discussion to point out that not all symbols are visual (for example, play a recording of your state song or the national anthem).
- Tell students that their group will be responsible for researching other symbols of the United States and designing a pamphlet that shows and explains these symbols.
- Before the lesson, collect samples of pamphlets to display and discuss. Show children how pamphlets are laid out in a tri-fold format. Have them unfold the sample pamphlets and examine where the "front" of the pamphlet is actually located on the page. Have each child practice folding a pamphlet with a piece of notebook paper. Then have them add some simple content (perhaps some information about the school) so they can practice laying out content properly in the tri-fold format.

Begin Group Work and Research Organize students into groups of three or four.

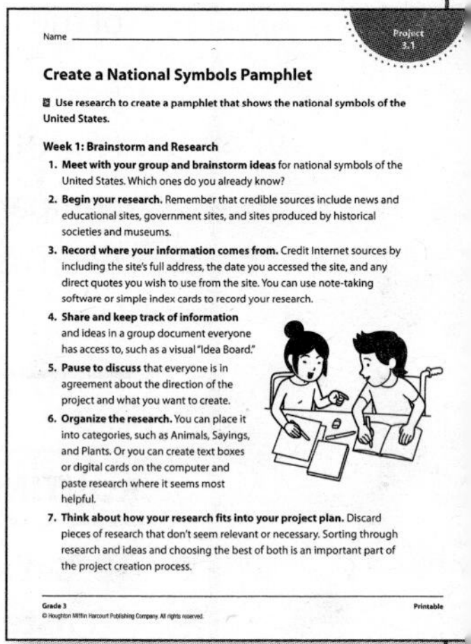
Name ______

Project 3.1

Create a National Symbols Pamphlet

Use research to create a pamphlet that shows the national symbols of the United States.

Week 1: Brainstorm and Research

1. **Meet with your group and brainstorm ideas** for national symbols of the United States. Which ones do you already know?
2. **Begin your research.** Remember that credible sources include news and educational sites, government sites, and sites produced by historical societies and museums.
3. **Record where your information comes from.** Credit Internet sources by including the site's full address, the date you accessed the site, and any direct quotes you wish to use from the site. You can use note-taking software or simple index cards to record your research.
4. **Share and keep track of information** and ideas in a group document everyone has access to, such as a visual "Idea Board."
5. **Pause to discuss** that everyone is in agreement about the direction of the project and what you want to create.
6. **Organize the research.** You can place it into categories, such as Animals, Sayings, and Plants. Or you can create text boxes or digital cards on the computer and paste research where it seems most helpful.
7. **Think about how your research fits into your project plan.** Discard pieces of research that don't seem relevant or necessary. Sorting through research and ideas and choosing the best of both is an important part of the project creation process.

Grade 3 Printable
© Houghton Mifflin Harcourt Publishing Company. All rights reserved.

- Guide groups to create an Idea Board or group document for brainstorming, recording and discussing ideas, and sharing quotations and other information from their research.
- Remind students that there are numerous sources of research they can use beyond their *my*Book selections, such as websites, encyclopedias, and other reference books.
- Have students research American symbols independently, collecting facts and details about each symbol when possible.
- Tell students that as they find helpful information, they should record it and cite their sources.
- After individual research is complete, have groups meet to share what they learned. Encourage them to ask each other questions to stimulate further research.

EL ENGLISH LEARNER SUPPORT: Generate Ideas

Display a sentence frame and ideas to support discussion: *Things that remind me of the United States are ______.*

WEEK 2 Write and Create

LEARNING OBJECTIVE

- Record notes and use them to make a comprehensive list of national symbols.

MATERIALS

- **Printable** *Project 3.2*
- note cards, paper, pencils
- desktop publishing software

WEEKLY FOCUS Develop Ideas

Plan and Draft Guide groups to create a comprehensive list of American symbols they studied.

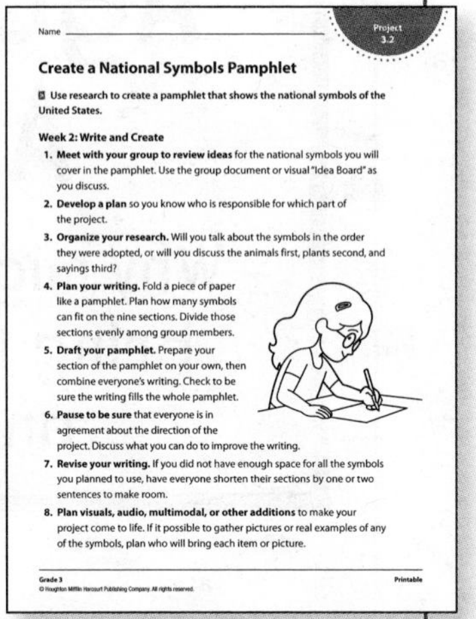

Name ______

Project 3.2

Create a National Symbols Pamphlet

Use research to create a pamphlet that shows the national symbols of the United States.

Week 2: Write and Create

1. **Meet with your group to review ideas** for the national symbols you will cover in the pamphlet. Use the group document or visual "Idea Board" as you discuss.
2. **Develop a plan** so you know who is responsible for which part of the project.
3. **Organize your research.** Will you talk about the symbols in the order they were adopted, or will you discuss the animals first, plants second, and sayings third?
4. **Plan your writing.** Fold a piece of paper like a pamphlet. Plan how many symbols can fit on the nine sections. Divide those sections evenly among group members.
5. **Draft your pamphlet.** Prepare your section of the pamphlet on your own, then combine everyone's writing. Check to be sure the writing fills the whole pamphlet.
6. **Pause to be sure** that everyone is in agreement about the direction of the project. Discuss what you can do to improve the writing.
7. **Revise your writing.** If you did not have enough space for all the symbols you planned to use, have everyone shorten their sections by one or two sentences to make room.
8. **Plan visuals, audio, multimodal, or other additions** to make your project come to life. If it possible to gather pictures or real examples of any of the symbols, plan who will bring each item or picture.

Grade 3 Printable
© Houghton Mifflin Harcourt Publishing Company. All rights reserved.

- As students compile their lists, remind them to take notes about the meaning or history of the symbols.
- Put each student in charge of compiling all the group research about one or more specific symbols.
- Instruct groups to narrow their list of symbols to the ones that interest them most or that they think would most interest their audience.

Revise Writing Have students read what they wrote about their symbol to the group. Ask group members to make suggestions about what other information they might like to know about the symbol. Allow time for additional research.

Create and Integrate Visuals Show students several pamphlets so they understand the way information is organized. Guide them through the process of laying out their information in the tri-fold format.

EL ENGLISH LEARNER SUPPORT: Share Ideas

Have students complete this sentence frame: *The symbol I am writing about is* ______.

WEEK 3 Present and Reflect

LEARNING OBJECTIVE

- Participate in a presentation about United States symbols.

MATERIALS

- **Printable** *Project 3.3*
- handwritten note cards
- copies of group's pamphlet

WEEKLY FOCUS Present and Reflect

Practice and Present Have students practice presenting with a small group. See Lesson 15, p. T190.

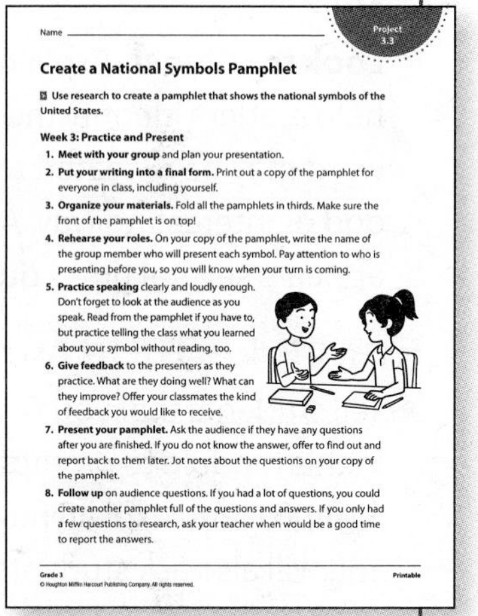

Name ______

Project 3.3

Create a National Symbols Pamphlet

Use research to create a pamphlet that shows the national symbols of the United States.

Week 3: Practice and Present

1. **Meet with your group** and plan your presentation.
2. **Put your writing into a final form.** Print out a copy of the pamphlet for everyone in class, including yourself.
3. **Organize your materials.** Fold all the pamphlets in thirds. Make sure the front of the pamphlet is on top!
4. **Rehearse your roles.** On your copy of the pamphlet, write the name of the group member who will present each symbol. Pay attention to who is presenting before you, so you will know when your turn is coming.
5. **Practice speaking** clearly and loudly enough. Don't forget to look at the audience as you speak. Read from the pamphlet if you have to, but practice telling the class what you learned about your symbol without reading, too.
6. **Give feedback** to the presenters as they practice. What are they doing well? What can they improve? Offer your classmates the kind of feedback you would like to receive.
7. **Present your pamphlet.** Ask the audience if they have any questions after you are finished. If you do not know the answer, offer to find out and report back to them later. Jot notes about the questions on your copy of the pamphlet.
8. **Follow up** on audience questions. If you had a lot of questions, you could create another pamphlet full of the questions and answers. If you only had a few questions to research, ask your teacher when would be a good time to report the answers.

Grade 3 Printable
© Houghton Mifflin Harcourt Publishing Company. All rights reserved.

- As students present, remind them to speak clearly and at a comfortable pace, to use gestures, and to make eye contact with their audience.
- Remind listeners to be attentive and polite, and to take notes.

Reflect and Celebrate Establish a time for students to reflect on the project and what they've learned, and to celebrate their achievements.

- After the groups have presented, have students discuss what they learned from other presentations. Have them tell about their favorite part of the project.

ASSESS LEARNING Online Ed

See the Inquiry and Research Project Rubric in the Resources section of the Teacher's Guide.

EL ENGLISH LEARNER SUPPORT: Present Ideas

Work with students to rehearse their presentations. Coach them as necessary to monitor their oral language and self-correct, and to use more formal instead of informal English.

Notice & Note

Introduce this module's Signposts, using these lessons. Revisit the Anchor Charts, as needed, as you encounter the Signposts during Shared Reading.

NARRATIVE Again and Again

INTRODUCE THE SIGNPOST

- Tell students they might notice that in some stories, the author repeats certain things, such as events, images, or words. Recognizing repetition is important because it might give the reader a better understanding of the setting or a character, or it might reveal a big idea about a story. Repetition could also be an important symbol.
- **Look for Clues!** Explain that there are usually clues in the story that help readers identify the Again and Again Signpost. For example, a word may be repeated several times, and sometimes it is used in an odd or interesting way. Another clue is when the same image appears several times during the story.

NOTICE & NOTE IN ACTION!

- Tell students that you will pause as you read certain *my*Book stories in this module to prompt them to notice the Again and Again Signpost and explain how they would apply it to that page or pages. You will also ask students to note in their books things in the text or visuals that will help them remember the Signpost and why it is important to the story.

ANCHOR QUESTION

- Display Anchor Chart 40: Again and Again and discuss the Anchor Question. Tell students that they will ask themselves this question after noticing the Again and Again Signpost. Answering this question will help them understand something special about the story that the author wants them to notice.

Online Ed

ANCHOR CHART 40: Again and Again

Again and Again
Why might the author bring this up again and again?

This module's Signposts are featured with the texts below, which contain strong examples of the Signposts as well as complementary comprehension skills. Encourage students to use their growing bank of known Signposts as they read different texts.

LESSON	TEXT	GENRE	COMPREHENSION SKILL	SIGNPOST
2	The U.S. Constitution	narrative nonfiction	Synthesize Information	3 Big Questions
8	The Flag Maker	narrative nonfiction	Retell Important Ideas	Again and Again
11	Why Is the Statue of Liberty Green?	narrative nonfiction	Ask and Answer Questions	3 Big Questions

Professional Learning

RESEARCH FOUNDATIONS

"The compassionate and open-minded reader should be able to discuss and negotiate, collaborate and compromise, and so use language to work things out."

—Beers & Probst (2017)

See the **GPS guide** to learn more.

NONFICTION 3 Big Questions

INTRODUCE THE SIGNPOST

- Explain to students that when they read nonfiction texts, it is important to remember that the author is saying something about a certain topic. Readers cannot assume that everything the author says is true or correct. The author might include his or her opinions. Readers should question what the author says and how it relates to what they already know.

NOTICE & NOTE IN ACTION!

- Tell students that you will pause as you read certain *my*Book selections in this module to prompt them to ask themselves the 3 Big Questions about a page or pages. You will also ask students to note in their books things in the text or visuals that will help them remember the questions, help them answer the questions, or tell why the questions are important to the text.

ANCHOR QUESTION

- Display Anchor Chart 49: 3 Big Questions, and discuss the Anchor Questions. Share that students will ask themselves these questions when they see new, confusing, or challenging information in a nonfiction text.

Online Ed

ANCHOR CHART 49: 3 Big Questions

3 Big Questions
• What surprised me?
• What did the author think I already knew?
• What challenged, changed, or confirmed what I already knew?

Kicking Off the Module!

Get started with Module 3 by setting goals with students and connecting with families.

Set Goals with Students

Tell students that over the next few weeks, they will build and strengthen their reading, writing, listening, speaking, and thinking skills as they explore U.S. symbols:

- Encourage students to reflect on their prior learning and to set personal goals for the upcoming module.
- Share a K-W-L Chart like the one at the right to support students in setting goals. Model examples and record goals for each student.
- Revisit students' goals throughout the module to help them track progress and reflect on their learning.

What I Know	What I Want to Know	What I Learned

Connect with Families

Share Printable: Family Letter 3 to support students' learning at home:

- Offer support to help families discuss the module topic and the module's Big Idea Words.
- Encourage students to read at home with their families, and provide ideas for families to talk about books together.
- Suggest vocabulary activities to support literacy.

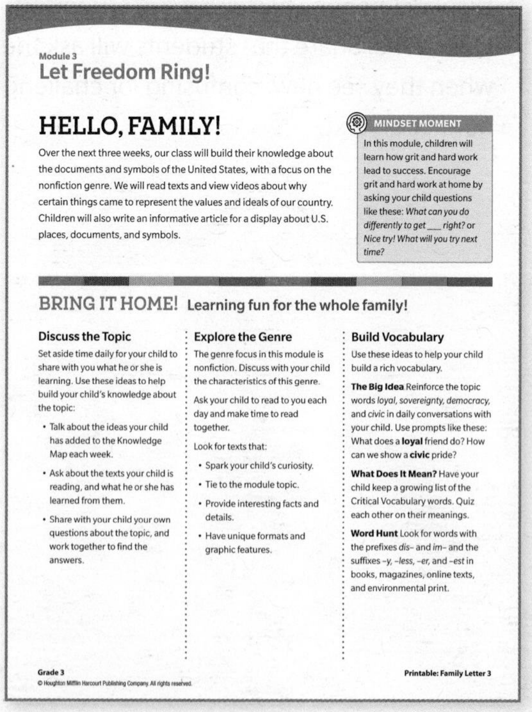

Module 3
Let Freedom Ring!

HELLO, FAMILY!

Over the next three weeks, our class will build their knowledge about the documents and symbols of the United States, with a focus on the nonfiction genre. We will read texts and view videos about why certain things came to represent the values and ideals of our country. Children will also write an informative article for a display about U.S. places, documents, and symbols.

MINDSET MOMENT

In this module, children will learn how grit and hard work lead to success. Encourage grit and hard work at home by asking your child questions like these: *What can you do differently to get ___ right?* or *Nice try! What will you try next time?*

BRING IT HOME! Learning fun for the whole family!

Discuss the Topic

Set aside time daily for your child to share with you what he or she is learning. Use these ideas to help build your child's knowledge about the topic:

- Talk about the ideas your child has added to the Knowledge Map each week.
- Ask about the texts your child is reading, and what he or she has learned from them.
- Share with your child your own questions about the topic, and work together to find the answers.

Explore the Genre

The genre focus in this module is nonfiction. Discuss with your child the characteristics of this genre.

Ask your child to read to you each day and make time to read together.

Look for texts that:

- Spark your child's curiosity.
- Tie to the module topic.
- Provide interesting facts and details.
- Have unique formats and graphic features.

Build Vocabulary

Use these ideas to help your child build a rich vocabulary.

The Big Idea Reinforce the topic words *loyal, sovereignty, democracy,* and *civic* in daily conversations with your child. Use prompts like these: What does a **loyal** friend do? How can we show a **civic** pride?

What Does It Mean? Have your child keep a growing list of the Critical Vocabulary words. Quiz each other on their meanings.

Word Hunt Look for words with the prefixes *dis–* and *im–* and the suffixes *–y, –less, –er,* and *–est* in books, magazines, online texts, and environmental print.

Grade 3

Printable: Family Letter 3

Printable: Family Letter 3

SOCIAL STUDIES CONNECTION:
U.S. History

Let Freedom Ring!

Essential Question How do historic places, documents, and symbols represent our nation?

Essential Skills

VOCABULARY

- Critical Vocabulary: *loyal, sovereignty, democracy, civic, delegates, convention, domestic, tranquility, welfare, posterity*
- Vocabulary Strategy: Multiple Meaning Words
- Generative Vocabulary: Suffixes *–y, –less*; Prefix *–dis*; Spiral Review: Suffixes *–y, –ly*

READING WORKSHOP

- Text and Graphic Features
- Synthesize
- Central Idea
- Text Structure
- Text and Graphic Features

FOUNDATIONAL SKILLS

- Decoding: Three-Letter Blends (*spl, scr, spr, squ, str*)
- Spelling: Three-Letter Blends
- Fluency: Reading Rate

COMMUNICATION

- Listening Comprehension
- Research: Take Notes
- Make Connections

WRITING WORKSHOP

- Informational Writing
- Verb Tenses

LEARNING MINDSET: Grit

THIS WEEK'S SELECTIONS

Teacher Read-Aloud

INFORMATIONAL TEXT
Patriotic Tunes

myBOOK

INFORMATIONAL TEXT
American Places, American Ideals

myBOOK

INFORMATIONAL TEXT
The U.S. Constitution

Rigby
LEVELED LIBRARY

WEEK 1

Week at a Glance

Suggested Daily Times

- **BUILD KNOWLEDGE & LANGUAGE/ VOCABULARY** 10–15 minutes
- **READING WORKSHOP** 60–85 minutes
- **FOUNDATIONAL SKILLS** 15–30 minutes
- **COMMUNICATION** 15–30 minutes
- **WRITING WORKSHOP** 30–45 minutes

This Week's Words

BIG IDEA WORDS

loyal *sovereignty* *democracy* *civic*

CRITICAL VOCABULARY WORDS

delegates	*convention*	*domestic*
tranquility	*welfare*	*posterity*

HIGH-FREQUENCY WORDS

region	*Europe*	*moon*
village		

INSTRUCTIONAL VOCABULARY

heading	*map*	*symbol*
synthesize	*central idea*	*detail*
evidence	*organization*	*text structure*
label	*sidebar*	*subsection*
text feature		

Assessment Options

Online Ed

- **Selection Quiz: *The U.S. Constitution***
- **Weekly Assessment**
  - Comprehension: Central Idea, Text Structure, Text and Graphic Features
  - Generative Vocabulary: Suffixes *–y, –less;* Prefix *dis-*
  - Vocabulary Strategy: Multiple Meaning Words
  - Grammar: Verb Tenses

Intervention

For students needing strategic intervention, choose from daily small-group options for differentiation. Access online Foundational Skills and Word Study Studio for additional support.

LESSON 1

BUILD KNOWLEDGE & LANGUAGE

Teaching Pal

Module Launch, pp. T28–T29
- **Introduce the Topic:** Let Freedom Ring!
- Big Idea Words: *loyal, sovereignty, democracy, civic*

READING WORKSHOP

Teaching Pal

American Places, American Ideals
GENRE Informational Text
Shared Reading: MINILESSON, pp. T30–T31
- Connect and Teach: Text and Graphic Features
- Apply to Text: ***American Places, American Ideals***
- Engage and Respond: Speaking and Listening

SMALL-GROUP INSTRUCTION

Options for Differentiation
- Guided Reading Groups, p. T32
- English Learner Support: Synthesize, p. T32
- Reinforce Text and Graphic Features, p. T33

Options for Independent and Collaborative Work, pp. T34–T35

FOUNDATIONAL SKILLS

Decoding, pp. T36–T37
- Three-Letter Blends (*spl, scr, spr, squ, str*)

Spelling, p. T38
- Three-Letter Blends

Fluency, p. T39
- Reading Rate

WRITING WORKSHOP

Descriptive Essay, p. W34–36
- Introducing the Focal Text

Grammar, p. W270
- Past and Present Tense

LESSON 2

VOCABULARY

Academic Vocabulary, pp. T40–T41
- Introduce Critical Vocabulary: *delegates, convention, domestic, tranquility, welfare, posterity*

READING WORKSHOP

Teaching Pal

The U.S. Constitution
GENRE Informational Text
Shared Reading: MINILESSON, pp. T42–T43
- Connect and Teach: Synthesize
- Apply to Text: ***The U.S. Constitution***
- Engage and Respond: Speaking and Listening

SMALL-GROUP INSTRUCTION

Options for Differentiation
- Guided Reading Groups, p. T44
- English Learner Support: Synthesize, p. T44
- Reinforce Synthesize, p. T45

Options for Independent and Collaborative Work, pp. T46–T47

COMMUNICATION

Listening Comprehension, pp. T48–T51
- Teacher Read-Aloud: *Patriotic Tunes*
- Focus on Fluency: Reading Rate
- Engage and Respond: Speaking and Listening

WRITING WORKSHOP

Descriptive Essay, p. W37
- Vocabulary

Grammar, p. W271
- Present, Past, and Future Tense

LESSON 3

VOCABULARY

Academic Vocabulary, p. T52
- Review Critical Vocabulary: *delegates, convention, domestic, tranquility, welfare, posterity*

Vocabulary Strategy, p. T53
- Multiple Meaning Words

READING WORKSHOP

The U.S. Constitution
GENRE Informational Text
Shared Reading: MINILESSON, pp. T54–T55
- Connect and Teach: Central Idea
- Apply to Text: ***The U.S. Constitution***
- Engage and Respond: Close Read Screencast
- Engage and Respond: Write an Encyclopedia Entry

Teaching Pal

SMALL-GROUP INSTRUCTION

Options for Differentiation
- Guided Reading Groups, p. T56
- English Learner Support: Synthesize, p. T56
- Reinforce Central Idea, p. T57

Options for Independent and Collaborative Work, pp. T25–T59

FOUNDATIONAL SKILLS

Decoding, pp. T60–T61
- Three-Letter Blends

WRITING WORKSHOP

Descriptive Essay, p. W38
- Pre-Writing I: Prepare to Write

Grammar, p. W272
- Identifying Present, Past, and Future Tense

LESSON 4

VOCABULARY

Generative Vocabulary, pp. T62–T63
- Suffixes *-y, -less*; Prefix *dis-*
- Spiral Review: Suffixes *-y, -ly*

READING WORKSHOP

The U.S. Constitution
GENRE Informational Text
Shared Reading: MINILESSON, pp. T64–T65
- Connect and Teach: Text Structure
- Apply to Text: ***The U.S. Constitution***
- Engage and Respond: Writing

Teaching Pal

SMALL-GROUP INSTRUCTION

Options for Differentiation
- Guided Reading Groups, p. T66
- English Learner Support: Synthesize, p. T66
- Reinforce Text Structure, p. T67

Options for Independent and Collaborative Work, pp. T68–T69

COMMUNICATION

Project Checkpoint: Brainstorm and Research, pp. T16, T25

WRITING WORKSHOP

Descriptive Essay, p. W39
- Pre-Writing II: Choosing Descriptive Words

Grammar, p. W323
- Review Commas

LESSON 5

VOCABULARY

Academic Vocabulary, pp. T70–T71
- Vocabulary Spiral Review

READING WORKSHOP

The U.S. Constitution
GENRE Informational Text
Shared Reading: MINILESSON, pp. T72–T73
- Connect and Teach: Text and Graphic Features
- Apply to Text: ***The U.S. Constitution***
- Engage and Respond: Reading

Teaching Pal

SMALL-GROUP INSTRUCTION

Options for Differentiation
- Guided Reading Groups, p. T74
- English Learner Support: Synthesize, p. T74
- Reinforce Text and Graphic Features, p. T75

Options for Independent and Collaborative Work, pp. T76–T77

COMMUNICATION

Research, p. T78
- Take Notes

Make Connections, p. T79
- Synthesize Topic Knowledge

WRITING WORKSHOP

Descriptive Essay, p. W40
- Drafting I: The Central Idea

Grammar, p. W274
- Connect to Writing: Using Past, Present, and Future Tense

Literacy Centers

- **While you meet with small groups, have students work independently in Literacy Centers. Familiarize students with the week's activities and post a daily rotation schedule.**
- **Have students complete Printable: Exit Ticket for each activity so you can monitor their work.**

READING CENTER

Readers' Theater

- Preview Printable: **Readers' Theater 3**, "Ring the Bell," and assign parts to mixed-ability groups of five students.
- The part of Max is ideal for struggling readers, and the part of Mr. Franklin can be read by a proficient reader.

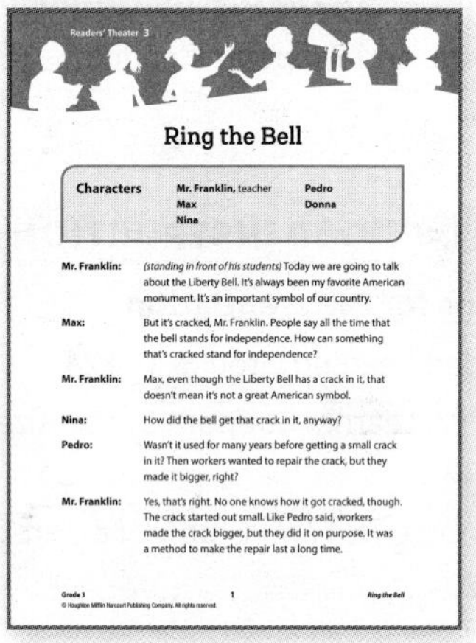
Readers' Theater 3

Ring the Bell

Characters	Mr. Franklin, teacher	Pedro
	Max	Donna
	Nina	

Mr. Franklin:	*(standing in front of his students)* Today we are going to talk about the Liberty Bell. It's always been my favorite American monument. It's an important symbol of our country.
Max:	But it's cracked, Mr. Franklin. People say all the time that the bell stands for independence. How can something that's cracked stand for independence?
Mr. Franklin:	Max, even though the Liberty Bell has a crack in it, that doesn't mean it's not a great American symbol.
Nina:	How did the bell get that crack in it, anyway?
Pedro:	Wasn't it used for many years before getting a small crack in it? Then workers wanted to repair the crack, but they made it bigger, right?
Mr. Franklin:	Yes, that's right. No one knows how it got cracked, though. The crack started out small. Like Pedro said, workers made the crack bigger, but they did it on purpose. It was a method to make the repair last a long time.

Grade 3 1 Ring the Bell

Printable: Readers' Theater 3

Independent Reading

- Display and review Anchor Chart 35: **Choosing a Book**.
- Have students self-select or continue reading an independent reading book.
- Remind students to set a purpose for reading and to record their progress on their Printable: **Reading Log**.
- Have students use Printable: **Independent Reading** for fiction or nonfiction to note key ideas as they read.
- You may want to choose from these additional options to have students interact with their books:
  - » **Mixed-Ability Groups** Students discuss their self-selected books, using the questions on the Reading Log.
  - » **Word Puzzle** Students expand their use of the vocabulary words by creating a word puzzle and having a classmate try to solve it.

Name ______ Centers

Reading Log

Title ______

Author ______ Genre ______

Independent Reading Record

Date ______ Time Spent ______ Pages Read ______

Date ______ Time Spent ______ Pages Read ______

Date ______ Time Spent ______ Pages Read ______

Date ______ Time Spent ______ Pages Read ______

Summary This text is about ______

Questions for Discussion

What was your favorite part of the text? ______

What did you enjoy about the author's writing? ______

Was there something that you did not understand? What was it? ______

Would you recommend this text to a friend? Why or why not? ______

Grade 3 Printable

Printable: Reading Log

VOCABULARY

Super Six Words *(Use in Lessons 2–5.)*

- Have students use Printable: **Super Six Words** to list Big Idea Words and this week's Critical Vocabulary words that relate to the module topic.
- Then have students select six words from their lists that they think are most important, interesting, or new to them.
- Tell students to write a sentence for each selected word.
- Explain to students that they will come back to this list at the end of each week in the module.

Name ______ Centers

Super Six Words

1. Take a clean sheet of paper. Write your name at the top. Then write the module title.
2. Create four columns labeled Week 1, Week 2, Week 3, and Super Six.
3. Each week, list words about the topic from the texts you read in that week's column.
4. At the end of each week, choose and circle six words on your weekly list that you think are most important to the topic.
5. Write a sentence for each of those six words. Make sure your sentences show the meanings of the words.
6. At the end of the module, you will have eighteen words and sentences.
7. Now, choose six words from those eighteen words you think are most important to the topic. Write them in the Super Six column.
8. Use your Super Six words to write a summary of what you have learned about the module topic.

Grade 3 Printable

Printable: Super Six Words

DIGITAL STATION

Listener's Choice

Online Ed

- Have students listen to one of this week's selections, *The U.S. Constitution*, or a Leveled Reader of their choice.
- Tell them to add the title to their Printable: Listening Log, as well as list the listening skills they used, a summary of the selection, and questions they have about the selection or book.

Keyboarding

- Have students practice keyboarding using Printable: Keyboarding 3.1.

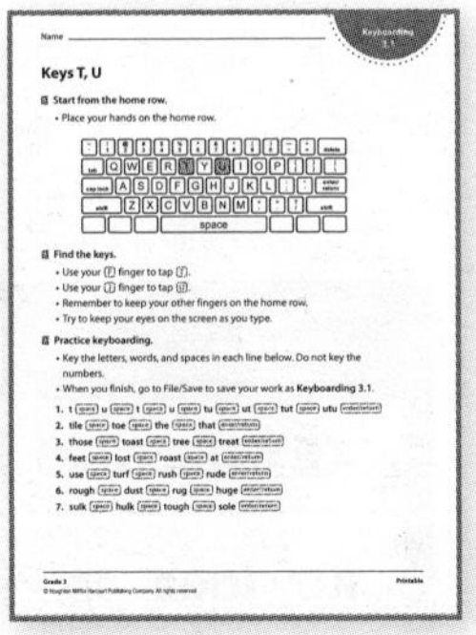
Name

Keyboarding 3.1

Keys T, U

Start from the home row.
- Place your hands on the home row.

Find the keys.
- Use your F finger to tap T.
- Use your J finger to tap U.
- Remember to keep your other fingers on the home row.
- Try to keep your eyes on the screen as you type.

Practice keyboarding.
- Key the letters, words, and spaces in each line below. Do not key the numbers.
- When you finish, go to File/Save to save your work as **Keyboarding 3.1**.

1. t space u space t space u space tu space ut space tut space utu enter/return
2. tile space toe space the space that enter/return
3. those space toast space tree space treat enter/return
4. feet space lost space roast space at enter/return
5. use space turf space rush space rude enter/return
6. rough space dust space rug space huge enter/return
7. sulk space hulk space tough space sole enter/return

Grade 3 Printable

Printable: Keyboarding 3.1

WRITING CENTER

Write an Encyclopedia Entry *(Use in Lessons 3–5.)*

- Have students use Printable: Peer Conferencing Routine to discuss their writing.
- Tell peers to use the tips on *my*Book page 243 as they review the work of others and offer feedback.

Writing Workshop

- Have students work on a piece of writing. They may use the time to prewrite, draft, revise, edit, or publish.
- Students may choose from among tasks such as:
  - » Free-write on your topic and then have a partner check the verb tenses in your writing.
- Display Anchor Chart 37: Cursive Handwriting.

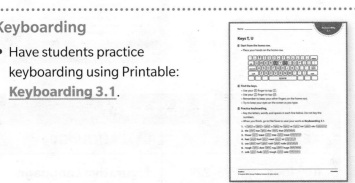

PROJECT CENTER

Project Checkpoint:Brainstorm and Research

- Have students work in groups, using Printable: Project 3.1 to guide them as they begin the project. Groups should complete the following over the course of the week:

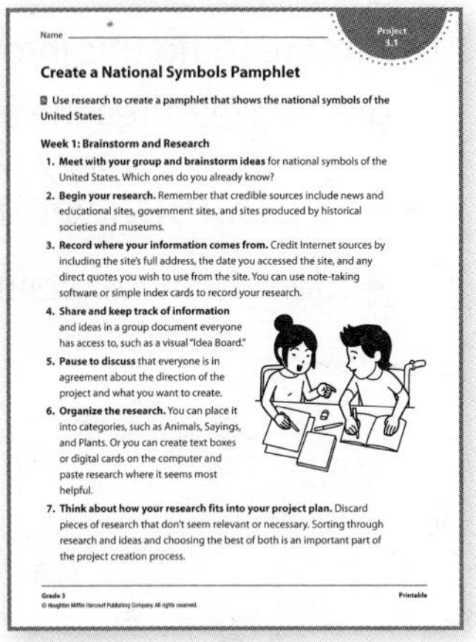
Name

Project 3.1

Create a National Symbols Pamphlet

Use research to create a pamphlet that shows the national symbols of the United States.

Week 1: Brainstorm and Research

1. **Meet with your group and brainstorm ideas** for national symbols of the United States. Which ones do you already know?
2. **Begin your research.** Remember that credible sources include news and educational sites, government sites, and sites produced by historical societies and museums.
3. **Record where your information comes from.** Credit Internet sources by including the site's full address, the date you accessed the site, and any direct quotes you wish to use from the site. You can use note-taking software or simple index cards to record your research.
4. **Share and keep track of information** and ideas in a group document everyone has access to, such as a visual "Idea Board."
5. **Pause to discuss** that everyone is in agreement about the direction of the project and what you want to create.
6. **Organize the research.** You can place it into categories, such as Animals, Sayings, and Plants. Or you can create text boxes or digital cards on the computer and paste research where it seems most helpful.
7. **Think about how your research fits into your project plan.** Discard pieces of research that don't seem relevant or necessary. Sorting through research and ideas and choosing the best of both is an important part of the project creation process.

Grade 3 Printable

Printable: Project 3.1

- ☑ Brainstorm ideas and conduct research into American symbols.
- ☑ Discuss which symbols to include in the pamphlet.
- ☑ Determine how they will share and keep track of their information and ideas.
- ☑ Think about how their research fits into the project plan.
- ☑ Pause during research to confirm that everyone is in agreement about the direction of the project.

Reading Remake

(Use in Lessons 2–5.)

- Have students complete the Write a News Story activity on Printable: Reading Remake 1.
- Ask partners to explain to one another how their news story shows their understanding of the selection.

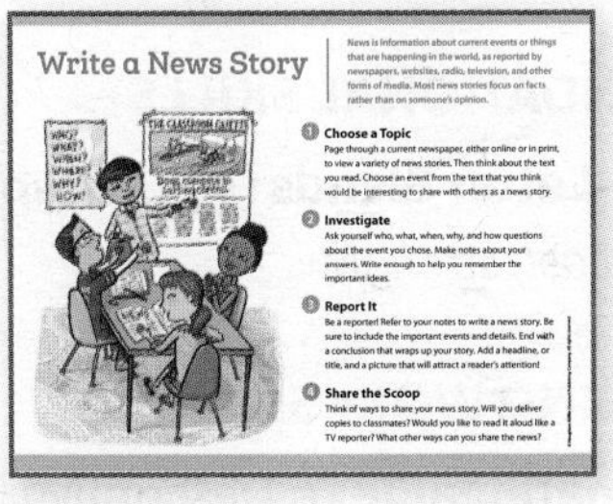
Write a News Story

News is information about current events or things that are happening in the world, as reported by newspapers, websites, radio, television, and other forms of media. Most news stories focus on facts rather than on someone's opinion.

1. **Choose a Topic** Page through a current newspaper, either online or in print, to view a variety of news stories. Then think about the text you read. Choose an event from the text that you think would be interesting to share with others as a news story.
2. **Investigate** Ask yourself who, what, when, why, and how questions about the event you chose. Make notes about your answers. Write enough to help you remember the important ideas.
3. **Report It** Be a reporter! Refer to your notes to write a news story. Be sure to include the important events and details. End with a conclusion that wraps up your story. Add a headline, or title, and a picture that will attract a reader's attention!
4. **Share the Scoop** Think of ways to share your news story. Will you deliver copies to classmates? Would you like to read it aloud like a TV reporter? What other ways can you share the news?

Printable: Reading Remake 1

WEEK 1

Preview Lesson Texts

Build understanding of this week's texts so that you can best support students in making connections, understanding key ideas, and becoming lifelong readers.

American Places, American Ideals

myBOOK

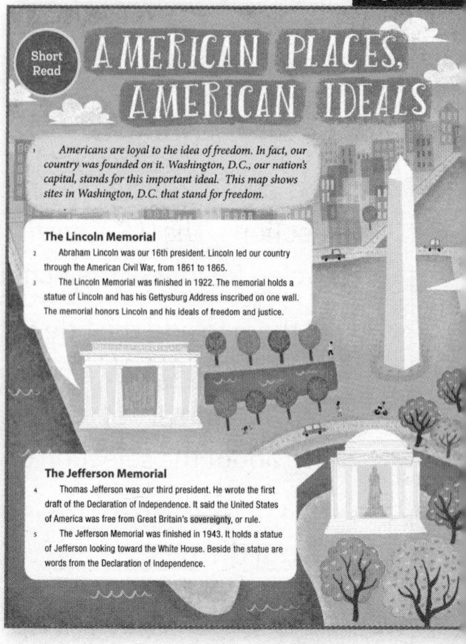

GENRE Informational Text with a Map

WHY THIS TEXT?

After reading this informational text, students should be able to identify the text and graphic features the author uses (map, symbols) and explain the purpose they achieve.

KEY LEARNING OBJECTIVES

- Identify and explain the purpose of text and graphic features

TEXT COMPLEXITY

LEXILE® MEASURE 670L

OVERALL RATING Complex

This selection has complex civics concepts and domain-specific language.

MAKE CONNECTIONS

BUILD KNOWLEDGE AND LANGUAGE

- **Social Studies Connection:** U.S. History

VOCABULARY

- **Suffixes -y, -less:** *sovereignty, democracy;*

FOUNDATIONAL SKILLS

- **Three-Letter Blends (*spl, scr, spr, squ, str*):** *screencast, strongly*

WRITING WORKSHOP

- **Informational Text:** Descriptive Essay
- **Verb Tenses**

TEXT X-RAY

KEY IDEAS	LANGUAGE
Key Idea *pp. 228–229* Our country was founded on the ideas of freedom and equality.	**Figurative Language** **to stand (for something)** *pp. 228–229* Explain that "stand" in this case does not mean to physically stand up. It represents a strong belief in something. In many cases, abstract terms, such as *rights* and *freedom* are used with "to stand (for something)."
Key Idea *pp. 228–229* Some monuments in Washington, DC, honor past presidents and are symbolic of their beliefs. (Jefferson: all people are created equal; Lincoln: freedom for all; Washington: the fight for freedom from Great Britain)	**Idiom** **shape our country's future** *pp. 228–229* Explain that when you shape something with your hands, you change its physical structure, such as when you shape clay. However, "to shape" can also mean to change how things will work, such as the government, which will affect future citizens of this country.
Key Idea *pp. 228–229* Some buildings in Washington, DC represent our country's ideals: civic responsibility/democracy (The Capitol); the White House (democracy)	

The U.S. Constitution by Norman Pearl

GENRE Informational Text

WHY THIS TEXT?
In this civics-based selection, students will learn to synthesize what they have read and identify words that signal a sequence of events (e.g., dates and transitions). Students should be able to determine the main/central idea, as well as identify the text and graphic features the author uses and explain their purpose.

Online
CLOSE-READ SCREENCAST

The U.S. Constitution Have students tap the Closer Look icons to access a screencast in which readers discuss and annotate the key passage. As a class, view and discuss the video.

myBOOK

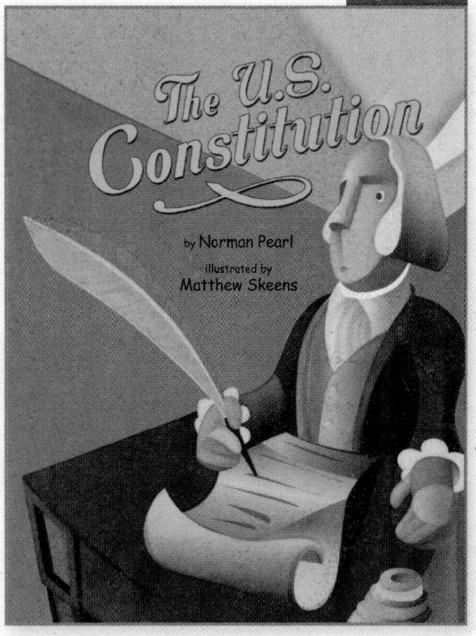

KEY LEARNING OBJECTIVES

- Synthesize
- Text Structure: Sequence
- Central Idea
- Identify text and graphic features

TEXT COMPLEXITY

LEXILE® MEASURE 650L • **GUIDED READING LEVEL** P

OVERALL RATING Moderately Complex

This selection has somewhat complex civics concepts and some unfamiliar language.

MAKE CONNECTIONS

BUILD KNOWLEDGE AND LANGUAGE
- **Social Studies Connection:** U.S. History

VOCABULARY
- **Suffixes *–y, –less:*** *easy, many, any, way, story;*

FOUNDATIONAL SKILLS
- **Three-Letter Blends (*spl, scr, spr, squ, str*):** *strong, stronger*

WRITING WORKSHOP
- **Informational Text:** Descriptive Essay
- **Verb Tenses**

TEXT X-RAY

KEY IDEAS	LANGUAGE
Key Idea *p. 233* The U.S. Constitution is a plan for how government works. **Key Idea** *p. 234* Delegates from the 13 colonies met to write a new set of rules for government. **Key Idea** *p. 236* The U.S. Constitution has three parts: the preamble, the articles, and the amendments. **Key Idea** *p. 240* The U.S. Constitution gives the government power to make laws to protect citizens' rights.	**Content-Area Word** ***headquarter(s)*** *p. 238* English learners may be confused by this term. Explain that when something is "headquartered," it is a place from which something is controlled or directed, such as a business, or in this case, a government (The White House). **Graphic Features** *pp. 231–240* The selection is rich in illustrations, many of which are powerful symbols. Ask students to identify symbols of: freedom (Liberty bell; *pp. 236–237*), the right to vote (ballot; *p. 235, 239*), justice (gavel; *p. 237*), the branches of government (*p. 238*), anti-slavery (open shackles; *p. 239*)

Introduce the Topic: Let Freedom Ring!

LEARNING OBJECTIVES

- Share information and ideas about a topic under discussion.
- Ask relevant questions to clarify information.
- Recognize characteristics of informational texts.
- **Language** Answer questions related to the theme using module vocabulary.

MATERIALS Online Ed

Display and Engage *Knowledge Map 3.1*

Teaching Pal *pp. 222–227*

***my*Book** *Book 1, pp. 222–227*

Get Curious Video *American Landmarks*

Vocabulary Cards *3.1–3.4*

Access Prior Knowledge

- Tell students that in this module they will read texts and view media related to documents and symbols that represent the values and ideals of the United States.
- Have students turn to *my*Book pages 222–223. Read aloud the title *Let Freedom Ring!* and begin a discussion about what it means.
- Have students share ideas about symbols of freedom in the United States.

Build Background

In your Teaching Pal, pages 222–225, use the prompts to guide students through an introduction to the module as they follow along in their *my*Book.

- **Discuss the Quotation** Lead a discussion about the quotation from "Our Flag."
- **Essential Question** Introduce the Essential Question. Then use the **ACTIVE VIEWING** routine with the Get Curious Video: American Landmarks Tell students that the video is informational, so they should expect to see and hear facts about the topic.
- **Big Idea Words** Use the **VOCABULARY** routine and Vocabulary Cards 3.1–3.4 to introduce the topic vocabulary: *loyal, sovereignty, democracy,* and *civic*. Then have students begin the vocabulary network on page 225. Encourage them to add to it throughout the module.

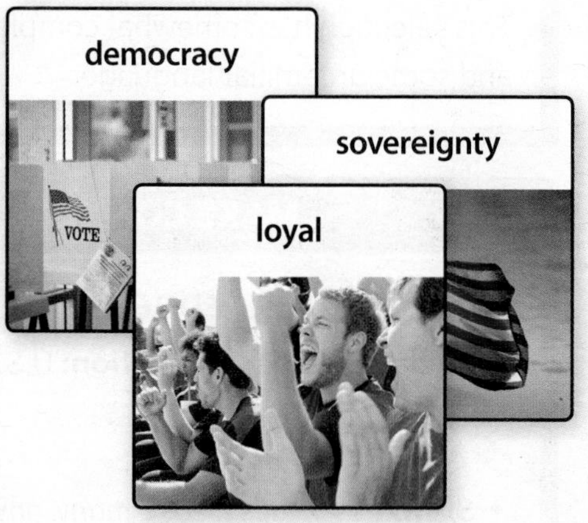

Vocabulary Cards

LEARNING MINDSET

Grit

Introduce Explain the meaning of grit and point out examples and opportunities as students encounter them in the module. *When you have grit, you have courage and determination to keep going, even when things are difficult. Sometimes learning requires grit. We might not get it right on the first try, but we keep going no matter what!*

Go to Your
Teaching Pal

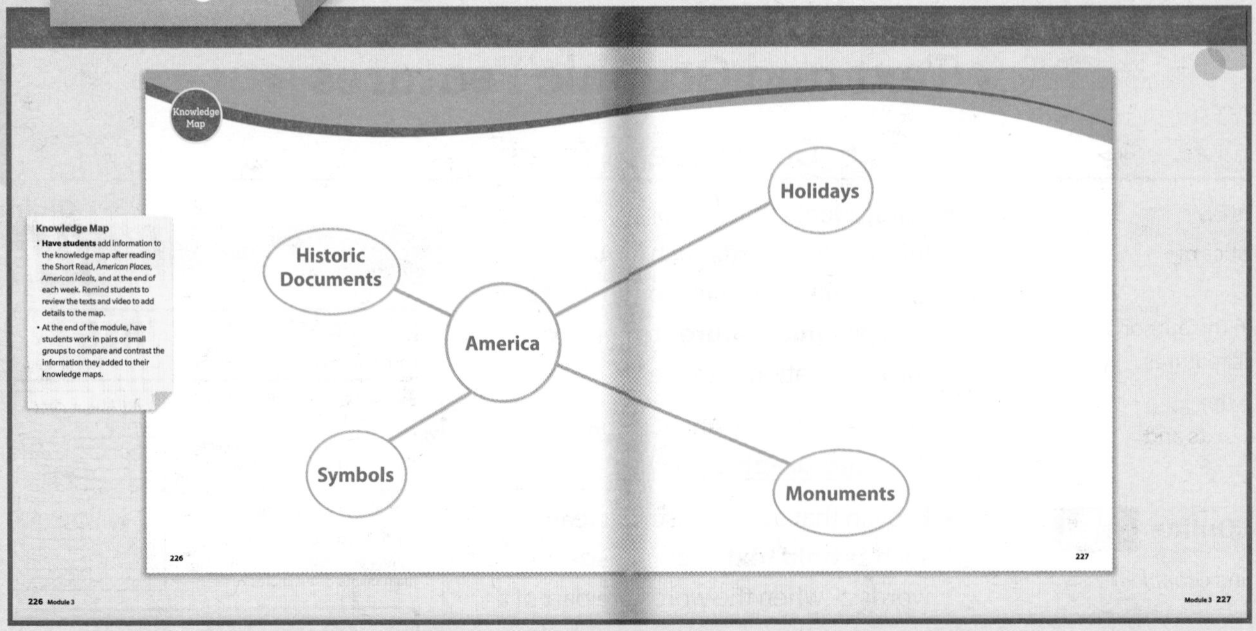

Knowledge Map
Knowledge Map
• **Have students** add information to the knowledge map after reading the Short Read, *American Places, American Ideals*, and at the end of each week. Remind students to review the texts and video to add details to the map.
• At the end of the module, have students work in pairs or small groups to compare and contrast the information they added to their knowledge maps.
Historic Documents
America
Holidays
Symbols
Monuments
226
227
226 Module 3
Module 3 227

Knowledge Focus: Make a Difference

Project Display and Engage: **Knowledge Map 3.1** and have students turn to pages 226–227 in their *my*Book. Tell students they will begin building their knowledge about community leaders and others who make a difference. Explain that they will return to these pages at the end of each week to add new information they learned about the topic.

Genre Focus: Nonfiction

Tell students that in this module they will read several nonfiction selections. Share with students that nonfiction:

- gives only factual information.
- tells about real people, places, and events.
- often includes text features such as headings and captions to help readers find and understand information.

Online Ed

DISPLAY AND ENGAGE: Knowledge Map 3.1

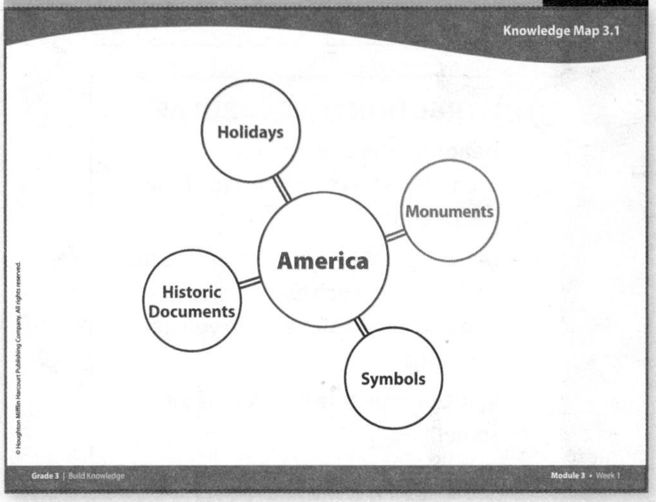

ENGLISH LEARNER SUPPORT: Elicit Participation

SUBSTANTIAL
Ask questions such as: *Is it important for a friend to be loyal?*

MODERATE
Provide this frame: *Someone who is loyal is* ______.

LIGHT
To elicit participation in the topic discussion, ask open-ended questions: *Being loyal means* ______. *It is important to be a loyal citizen because* ______.

Text and Graphic Features

Step 1 Connect and Teach

LEARNING OBJECTIVES

- Recognize characteristics of informational text.
- Recognize and explain the author's use of text and graphic features.
- **Language** Articulate the connections between texts and related visuals.

MATERIALS

Online Ed

Anchor Chart 20 *Text and Graphic Features*

Printable *Anchor Chart 20: Text and Graphic Features*

Teaching Pal *Book 1, pp. 228–229*

myBook *American Places, American Ideals, Book 1, pp. 228–229*

INSTRUCTIONAL VOCABULARY

- **heading** the title for a page or section of a text that helps to organize information
- **map** a graphic picture of an area that shows places such as towns, roads, and bodies of water to help you get somewhere
- **symbol** a picture that stands for something

SPANISH COGNATES

- **text** *texto*
- **map** *mapa*
- **symbol** *símbolo*

- Tell students that authors of informational texts such as *American Places, American Ideals* often use **text and graphic features** to help explain the information in the text.
- Project or display Anchor Chart 20: Text and Graphic Features.
- Explain that authors use text features such as **bold text** to emphasize key words or when the words are part of a name or title.
- Point out that **headings** help readers to notice how a text is organized.
- Review that graphic features such as **photographs, maps,** and **symbols** provide additional details and support for ideas in the text. Explain that the author's purpose for using such features is often to show at a glance something that would take many words to describe.
- Tell students that they will practice using text and graphic features to better understand the important ideas in *American Places, American Ideals*.

Online

ANCHOR CHART 20: Text and Graphic Features

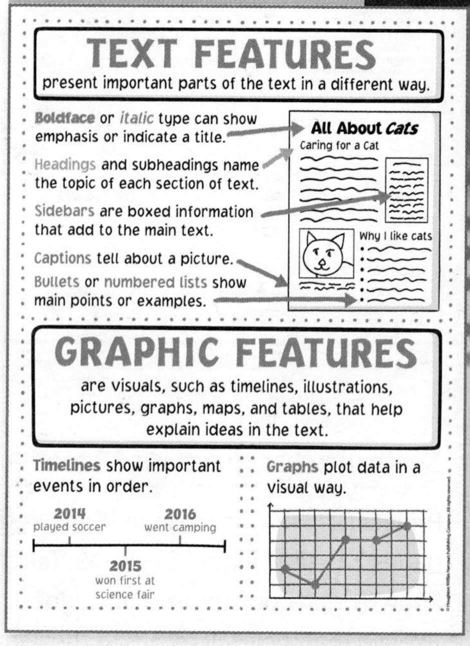

GENRE STUDY: Informational text

Point out to students that *American Places, American Ideals* is an example of informational text. Share this genre information with students.

- In an informational text, the author may explain main ideas and details.
- Informational texts may include visuals, such as the map, symbols, and photographs in this selection.
- Informational text may include text features, such as the bold print and headings in this selection.

Go to Your
Teaching Pal

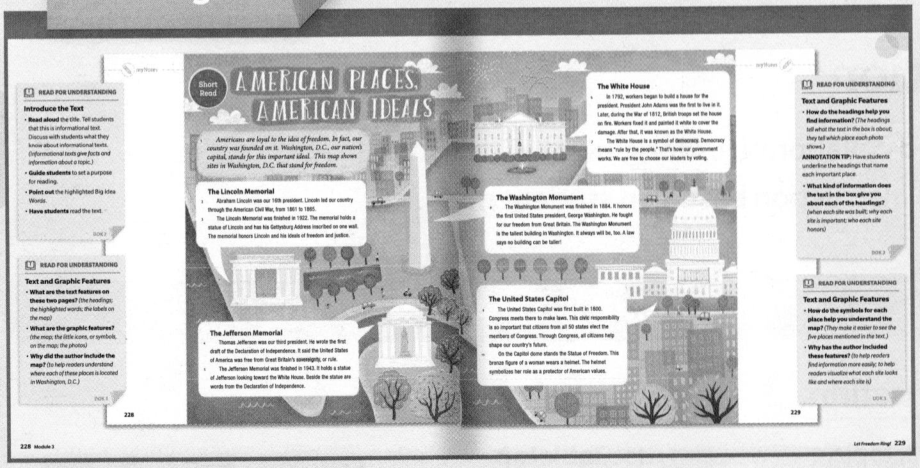

Online Ed

ANNOTATE IT!

Students may use the annotation tools in their eBook.

Step 2 Apply to Text

In your **Teaching Pal**, pages 228–229, use the blue **READ FOR UNDERSTANDING** prompts to guide discussion of *American Places, American Ideals* as students follow along in their *my*Book.

- **Genre Study** Remind students that informational texts give facts and examples about a topic. Ask them what they expect to learn from the reading selection by reviewing the title, headings, and photographs.
- **Set a Purpose** Prompt students to set a purpose for reading based on the title and genre. As needed, use this model: *I will read to find out facts about some important American places.*
- **Read and Comprehend** Use the **READ FOR UNDERSTANDING** routine to have students read the selection. Use the prompts in your **Teaching Pal** to gauge students' understanding and to have them identify and explain the purpose of the text and graphic features the author uses. Refer back to the Anchor Chart as necessary to help students determine the purpose of each text and graphic feature.

Step 3 Engage and Respond

INDEPENDENT PRACTICE: Speaking and Listening

- Remind students of the Essential Question: *How do historic places, documents, and symbols represent our nation?* Then have them read *American Places, American Ideals* to find information that answers the question.
- Have partners use the **COLLABORATIVE DISCUSSION** routine to discuss their ideas and then share with the group. Remind students to listen actively to their partners, to make pertinent comments, and to ask questions, as needed, to clarify information.
- You may want to have students conduct their discussions during daily small-group time.

ENGLISH LEARNER SUPPORT: Support Comprehension

SUBSTANTIAL

Provide this sentence stem to discuss each photograph: *This is the ______. It is important because ______.*

MODERATE

Provide this sentence stem: *This photograph shows the ______. One fact about this place is ______.*

LIGHT

As students share in small groups, encourage them to describe the American places from the article in complete sentences.

LINK TO SMALL-GROUP INSTRUCTION

REINFORCE TEXT AND GRAPHIC FEATURES Review or extend the skill as needed during small-group time to support students' need for differentiation. *See the lesson on p. T33.*

Options for Differentiation

As the class engages in independent and collaborative work, meet with Guided Reading Groups or differentiate instruction based on student need.

GUIDED READING GROUPS

Match Students to Books + Instruction

- Choose just-right books based on level, skill, topic, or genre.

L M N O P Q

Leveled Readers

- Deliver instruction with each book's **Take and Teach Lesson**, choosing appropriate sessions based on need.

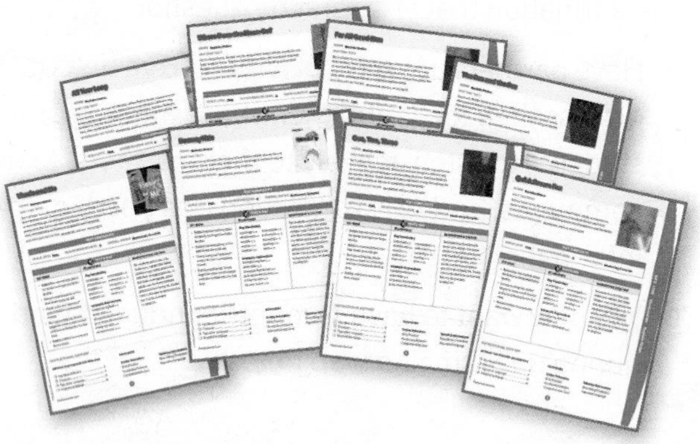

- Check comprehension, reinforce instruction, and extend learning with suggested supporting activities.

Rigby
LEVELED LIBRARY

EL ENGLISH LEARNER SUPPORT

Synthesize

- Use **Tabletop Minilessons: English Language Development 7.1 (Listening)** to introduce and practice the language skill.

Tabletop Minilessons: English Language Development

- Then use the following text-based prompts with *American Places, American Ideals* to guide application of the language skill. Begin with the prompt at the student's identified language proficiency level. As students progress, use lighter supports to encourage increased language proficiency.

SUBSTANTIAL
Read aloud the text that accompanies one of the images. Ask: *What American place is this?* Have students point to the picture of the place the text described and finish the sentence frame: *This American place is* _____.
Repeat with additional places in the text.

MODERATE
Read aloud the text that accompanies an image. Ask students to use what they heard to complete sentence frames: *This American place is* _____. *One fact about it is* _____.

LIGHT
Read aloud the text that accompanies an image. Ask questions such as: *What American place is this? What are three facts you heard about this place?*

REINFORCE TEXT AND GRAPHIC FEATURES

Demonstrate

- Use **Tabletop Minilessons: Reading Card 20** to remind students that authors use **text features** help to organize text and communicate key ideas. For instance, **bold text** or is used to emphasize key words, names, or titles. **Headings** are used to organize ideas in informational text. **Graphic features** are visuals, such as **photographs**, **maps**, and **symbols,** that communicate in a glance what it would take many words to describe.
- Model filling out Printable: Reading Graphic Organizer 16 to make inferences in *American Places, American Ideals.*

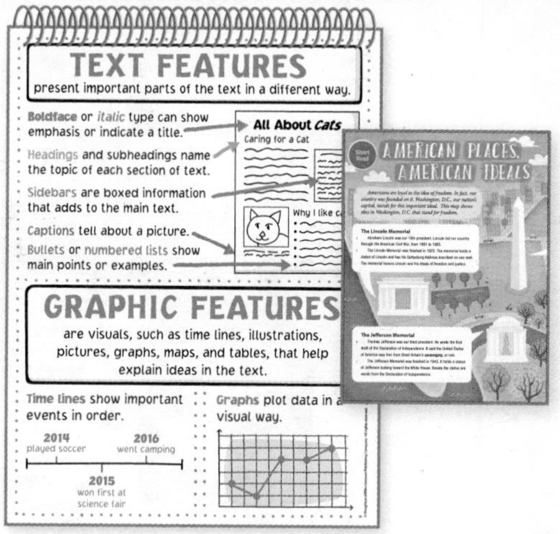

Tabletop Minilessons: Reading

Apply to Independent Reading

- Now have students identify the text and graphic features in an appropriate book or article they are reading independently. Customize these prompts to the texts students choose.
  - » *What text features are in the text?*
  - » *What graphic features are in the text?*
  - » *How do the text and graphic features help to organize the text and communicate key ideas?*
- Have students complete Printable: Reading Graphic Organizer 16 for their independent reading book.

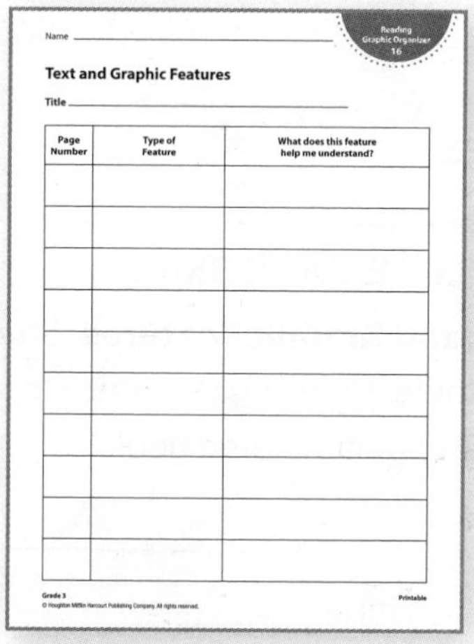

Printable: Reading Graphic Organizer 16

ALMOST THERE

READY FOR MORE

SCAFFOLD AND EXTEND

- Point out text and graphic features. Help students identify how they help readers understand the text.
- Prompt students to identify the text and graphic features and how they communicate information.
- Have students explain how the text and graphic features communicate information in a way that text alone cannot.

ENGLISH LEARNER SUPPORT

SUBSTANTIAL
Have students point to and name each of the text and graphic features. Guide them to find the ideas in the text that are expressed visually.

MODERATE
Have students complete the sentence frames: *This text/graphic feature is ______. It helps me to understand ______.*

LIGHT
Encourage students to explain how text and graphic features helped them understand the text.

Options for Independent and Collaborative Work

While you meet with small groups, have other students engage in literacy activities that reinforce the lesson's learning objectives. Choose from these options.

Independent Reading

Student Choice Library

Rigby
LEVELED LIBRARY

APPLY READING SKILL

Text and Graphic Features Students complete Printable: Reading Graphic Organizer 16 for an independent reading book.

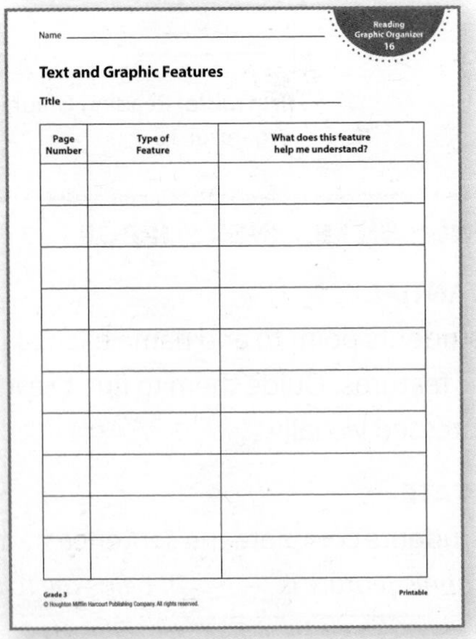

Name

Reading Graphic Organizer 16

Text and Graphic Features

Title

Page Number	Type of Feature	What does this feature help me understand?

Grade 3
© Houghton Mifflin Harcourt Publishing Company. All rights reserved.
Printable

Printable: Reading Graphic Organizer 16

APPLY LANGUAGE SKILL

Synthesize Students complete Printable: Language Graphic Organizer 15 for an independent reading book.

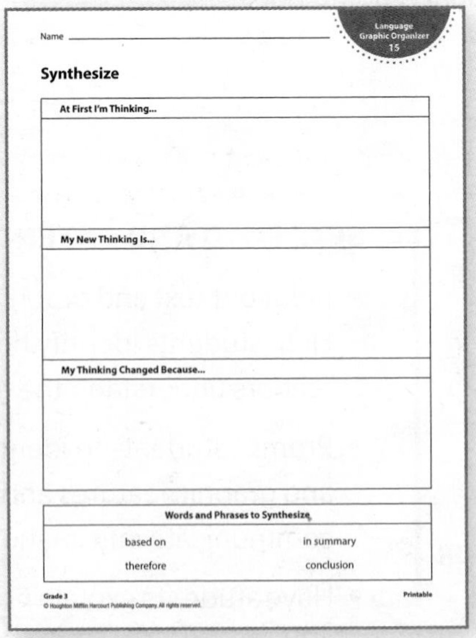

Name

Language Graphic Organizer 15

Synthesize

At First I'm Thinking...

My New Thinking Is...

My Thinking Changed Because...

Words and Phrases to Synthesize

based on, in summary, therefore, conclusion

Grade 3
© Houghton Mifflin Harcourt Publishing Company. All rights reserved.
Printable

Printable: Language Graphic Organizer 15

Literacy Centers

See pp. T24–T25.

- READING CENTER
- VOCABULARY CENTER
- DIGITAL STATION
- WRITING CENTER
- PROJECT CENTER

Speaking and Listening

Partners discuss the Essential Question. *See Engage and Respond, p. T31.*

Additional Skills Practice

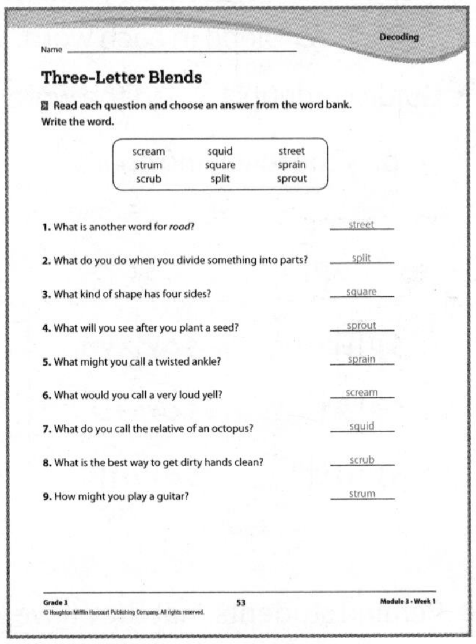

Name ______________________ Decoding

Three-Letter Blends

Read each question and choose an answer from the word bank. Write the word.

scream	squid	street
strum	square	sprain
scrub	split	sprout

1. What is another word for *road*? street
2. What do you do when you divide something into parts? split
3. What kind of shape has four sides? square
4. What will you see after you plant a seed? sprout
5. What might you call a twisted ankle? sprain
6. What would you call a very loud yell? scream
7. What do you call the relative of an octopus? squid
8. What is the best way to get dirty hands clean? scrub
9. How might you play a guitar? strum

Grade 3 53 Module 3 • Week 1

© Houghton Mifflin Harcourt Publishing Company. All rights reserved.

Know It, Show It, p. 53

Wrap-Up

Share Time

At the end of the Reading Workshop, have students reflect on their learning by sharing how they applied **text and graphic features** or another area of focus during independent work time. Choose from these options:

- Use the **SOLO CHAIR** routine. Select a reader each day to come to the front of the class and tell what he or she learned from the reading by using a skill or strategy.
- **THINK-PAIR-SHARE** Students share their thinking with a partner. Select a few pairs each day to share with the whole class.
- **RETURN TO ANCHOR CHART** Have students add sticky notes about their independent reading to the Text and Graphic Features Anchor Chart. Call on a few students to explain what they added and why.

Online Ed

ANCHOR CHART 20: Text and Graphic Features

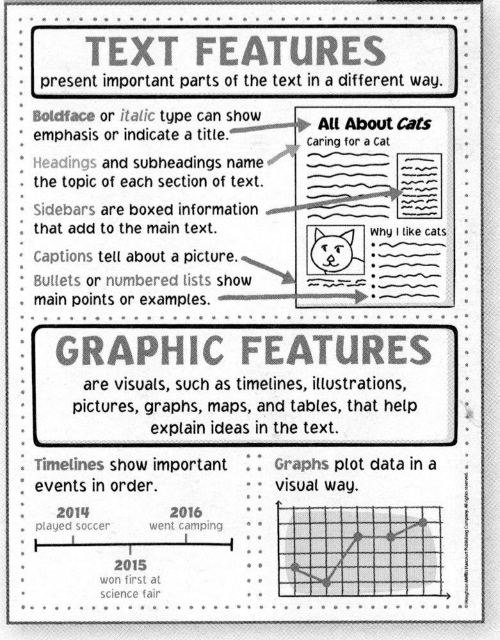

Three-Letter Blends

Step 1 Introduce the Skill

LEARNING OBJECTIVES

- Recognize and decode words with three-letter blends.
- **Language** Read words with three-letter blends and understand their meanings.

MATERIALS Online Ed

Display and Engage *Decoding 3.1*
Know It, Show It *p. 53*

Three-Letter Blends Display and read aloud the word *scratch*.

- Underline the first three letters in the word. Model blending the sounds to read the word. Stretch out the sounds in the word while pointing to each letter.
- Display the words *splash*, *spring*, *stretch*, and *squat* and underline the initial three-letter blend in each word.
- Guide students to read the words aloud.
- Display the following chart.

spl	scr	spr	str	squ
split	scram	sprig	stream	squint
splat	scrub	sprout	strike	squash
splint	scroll	sprung	strand	squawk

- Remind students that they have learned several three-letter blends. Point out the spelling patterns in the top row.
- Then read aloud the example words in each column, emphasizing the initial blend in each while underlining the letters that stand for the sounds.
- Guide students to read the words aloud.

ENGLISH LEARNER SUPPORT: Support Word Meaning

SUBSTANTIAL
Ensure that students understand the meaning of each Blend and Read word by sharing pictures or gestures.

MODERATE
Support students in understanding the meaning of each Blend and Read word by providing oral examples or context sentences. Guide students to think of additional examples or sentences.

LIGHT
Challenge students to create context sentences for some of the Blend and Read words on their own.

Step 2 Guided Practice

- Project Display and Engage: **Decoding 3.1**.
- Have students read the Blend and Read lines aloud. Provide feedback as needed.
- At the end of each of the five lines, prompt a conversation about the words: *How are the sounds and spellings in the words the same? How are they different?*
- Have partners reread the Blend and Read lines and quiz each other on the spellings of three-letter blends.

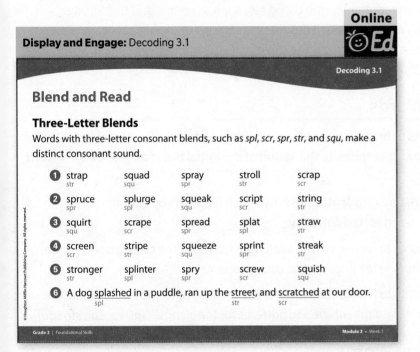

Online Ed

Display and Engage: Decoding 3.1

Decoding 3.1

Blend and Read

Three-Letter Blends

Words with three-letter consonant blends, such as *spl*, *scr*, *spr*, *str*, and *squ*, make a distinct consonant sound.

1	strap (str)	squad (squ)	spray (spr)	stroll (str)	scrap (scr)
2	spruce (spr)	splurge (spl)	squeak (squ)	script (scr)	string (str)
3	squirt (squ)	scrape (scr)	spread (spr)	splat (spl)	straw (str)
4	screen (scr)	stripe (str)	squeeze (squ)	sprint (spr)	streak (str)
5	stronger (str)	splinter (spl)	spry (spr)	screw (scr)	squish (squ)

6 A dog splashed (spl) in a puddle, ran up the street (str), and scratched (scr) at our door.

Grade 3 | Foundational Skills   Module 3 • Week 1

Step 3 Apply

INDEPENDENT PRACTICE

- Have students work in small groups or with partners to complete Know It, Show It page 53.
- Encourage students to share with each other the strategies they use to decode words with three-letter blends.

CORRECT & REDIRECT

If students have trouble decoding words with three-letter blends, use the model below.

- **Correct** the error. *When you see three letters at the beginning of a word, say the sound for each letter.*
- **Model** how to decode the word. */stīk/. That doesn't sound right. I missed one sound at the beginning of the word. The letters str stand for the sounds /str/. So I'll try again: /s/ /t/ /r/ /ī/ /k/,* strike. *That sounds like a word I know.*
- **Guide** students to decode the word *scrub*.
- **Check** students' understanding by displaying the word *sprout*. *What spelling pattern helps you decode this word? (The letters* s, p, r *stand for the sounds /spr/.)*
- **Reinforce** by repeating the process with the word *splint*.

Three-Letter Blends

Introduce the Spelling Words

- Before working with the basic and challenge words, you might want to revisit the review words. These also appear in Printable: Dictation Sentences 3.1. Display one of the Spelling Anchor Chart Printables, as appropriate.
- Cut apart and display the spelling word cards from Printable: Spelling Word Cards 3.1. Read each word aloud and discuss its meaning as needed.
- Tell students you are going to work together to sort the words into categories based on the spelling of the initial blends. Read aloud the words *split*, *scratch*, *sprint*, *strip*, and *squeak* and display those words as column headings.
- Hold up a word containing the blend *spr*, such as *sprain*, and model your thinking: *The word is* sprain. *It has the sounds /spr/ at the beginning. I see the column head* sprint, *which has the same spelling pattern for the blend. So I'll place the word in that column.*

Sort the Words

- Ask students to help you sort the remaining word cards. For two-syllable words such as *straddle*, emphasize the sound of the initial blend as you read the word aloud.
- After sorting, have students read down each list with you to make sure the words have been sorted correctly.
- Guide students to recognize the spelling patterns in the columns. Ask: *What spelling pattern do the words in this column share?*
- Guide students to recognize the different spelling patterns for the initial blends. Ask: *What are the different spelling patterns for the blends?* (spl, scr, spr, str, squ)

Alphabetize Words

- As an extension, show students Anchor Chart 32: Alphabetical Order. Have students sort the word cards into alphabetical order to the first, second, and third letters.

LEARNING OBJECTIVES

- Learn spelling patterns for three-letter blends.
- **Language** Spell words with three-letter blends and understand their meanings.

MATERIALS | Online Ed

Anchor Chart 32 *Alphabetical Order*

Printables *Anchor Chart 32: Alphabetical Order, Dictation Sentences 3.1, Spelling Word Cards 3.1, Proofreading 3.1*

Optional *Use Printable Dictation Sentences 3.1 to administer a pretest.*

SPELLING WORDS

BASIC

1. **splash**
2. **strange**
3. **scratch**
4. **squeeze**
5. **squeak**
6. **squeal**
7. **screen**
8. **split**
9. **splat**
10. **sprain**
11. **sprint**
12. **strip**
13. **strap**
14. **scrap**

REVIEW

15. **easy**
16. **eighteen**
17. **elbow**
18. **program**

CHALLENGE

19. **straddle**
20. **splurge**
21. **scrawl**
22. **squirrel**

ENGLISH LEARNER SUPPORT: Support Word Meaning

ALL LEVELS Make sure students understand the meaning of the spelling words and dictation sentences. If necessary, use visuals or gestures as support. After you've reinforced word meanings, have students practice reading aloud the spelling words.

LINK TO SMALL-GROUP INSTRUCTION

REINFORCE FOUNDATIONAL SKILLS For spelling practice for the remainder of the week: Display this week's spelling words for reference and have students work with Printable: Proofreading 3.1. Remind students to check the spelling words they use in the writing section to confirm they have spelled the words correctly.

Reading Rate

Introduce the Skill

LEARNING OBJECTIVES

- Use appropriate reading rate in order to comprehend text.
- Read aloud grade-level text with fluency and accuracy.
- Apply decoding skills when reading connected text.
- **Language** Comprehend texts using teacher support.

MATERIALS

Online *Ed*

Printable *Fluency 3.1, Word Cards 3.24–3.27*

DECODING ⟶ FLUENCY CONNECTION

The passage on Printable: **Fluency 3.1** includes words that contain this week's decoding element. Use the passage to monitor whether students can accurately and fluently read these grade-level words.

HIGH-FREQUENCY WORDS

- **region**
- **Europe**
- **moon**
- **village**

- Tell students that reading rate is the speed at which you read. Explain that good readers read at a rate that is appropriate to the type of text they are reading, Tell students that they can read at a faster rate when they are reading fiction but that they should read at a slower rate when they are reading nonfiction.
- Distribute Printable: **Fluency 3.1** to students, and project it for whole-group discussion. Model reading the first paragraph at a slow rate that makes the text seem tricky to follow.
- Point out that because the passage is fiction you can speed up your rate in order to enjoy the story. Model reading at an appropriate rate. Discuss with students that reading at an appropriate rate allows readers to gain better understanding and more enjoyment from the reading experience. After you read the entire passage, point out how you decoded the words *sprawled* and *scrimped* by using the three-letter blends at the beginning.

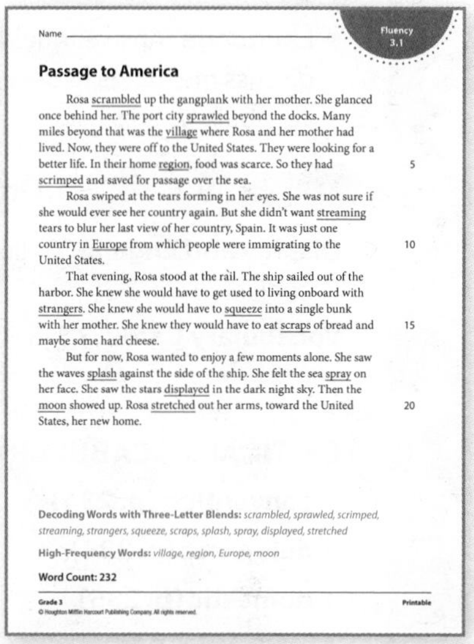

Name ______

Fluency 3.1

Passage to America

Rosa scrambled up the gangplank with her mother. She glanced once behind her. The port city sprawled beyond the docks. Many miles beyond that was the village where Rosa and her mother had lived. Now, they were off to the United States. They were looking for a better life. In their home region, food was scarce. So they had scrimped and saved for passage over the sea.

Rosa swiped at the tears forming in her eyes. She was not sure if she would ever see her country again. But she didn't want streaming tears to blur her last view of her country, Spain. It was just one country in Europe from which people were immigrating to the United States.

That evening, Rosa stood at the rail. The ship sailed out of the harbor. She knew she would have to get used to living onboard with strangers. She knew she would have to squeeze into a single bunk with her mother. She knew they would have to eat scraps of bread and maybe some hard cheese.

But for now, Rosa wanted to enjoy a few moments alone. She saw the waves splash against the side of the ship. She felt the sea spray on her face. She saw the stars displayed in the dark night sky. Then the moon showed up. Rosa stretched out her arms, toward the United States, her new home.

Decoding Words with Three-Letter Blends: *scrambled, sprawled, scrimped, streaming, strangers, squeeze, scraps, splash, spray, displayed, stretched*

High-Frequency Words: *village, region, Europe, moon*

Word Count: 232

Grade 3 Printable

© Houghton Mifflin Harcourt Publishing Company. All rights reserved.

Printable: Fluency 3.1

- After you finish reading the passage, have students read it aloud with you, using the **CHORAL READING** routine.

Apply

- Have students work in pairs or small groups using the **PARTNER READING** routine to read aloud the passage.
- Monitor students for reading rate. Note especially how students handle the more challenging words, such as *gangplank, scarce,* and *immigrating*, and provide support, as needed.

HIGH-FREQUENCY WORDS

Point out the high-frequency words in the passage on **Printable: Fluency 3.1**. Remind students that high-frequency words appear often in texts they read. Students can learn to recognize them, rather than decode them, so that they can read more fluently.

Print and distribute Printables: **Word Cards 3.24–3.27**, which feature this week's high-frequency words, and have students work independently or in pairs to read and complete the activities for each word. For struggling readers, walk through the notes for one or two words before they continue working with a partner.

ENGLISH LEARNER SUPPORT: Support Comprehension

ALL LEVELS As you model reading fluently, have students raise their hand when they hear a word they do not recognize. Work with students to decode the word and practice saying it aloud. Discuss the word's meaning, using gestures or pictures for support if needed. Then have students read the entire sentence chorally. Provide corrective feedback, as needed.

Introduce Critical Vocabulary

Step 1 Introduce the Words

LEARNING OBJECTIVES

- Identify real-life connections between words and their use.
- Use newly acquired vocabulary expressively.
- **Language** Answer questions and discuss meanings to develop vocabulary.

MATERIALS — Online Ed

Display and Engage *Critical Vocabulary 3.2a, 3.2b*

Vocabulary Cards *3.5–3.9*

CRITICAL VOCABULARY

- **convention (p. 234)**
- **delegates (p. 234)**
- **domestic (p. 236)**
- **welfare (p. 236)**
- **posterity (p. 236)**

SPANISH COGNATES

- **convention** *convención*
- **domestic** *doméstico*

Project Display and Engage: Critical Vocabulary 3.2a and Critical Vocabulary 3.2b. Then use the **VOCABULARY** routine to introduce the Critical Vocabulary from *The U.S. Constitution*. You may wish to display the corresponding Vocabulary Card for each word as you discuss it.

DISPLAY AND ENGAGE: Critical Vocabulary 3.2a, 3.2b — Online Ed

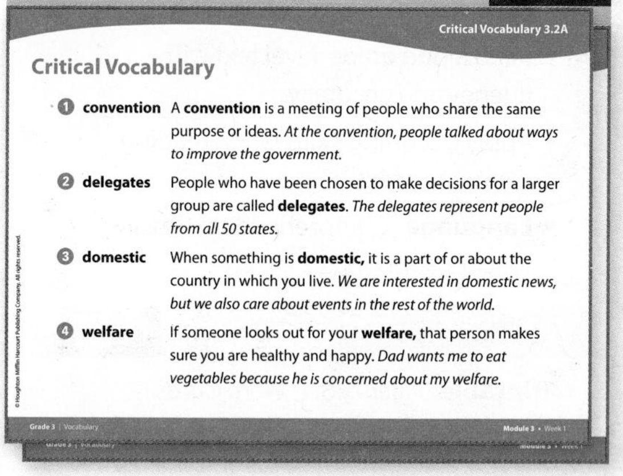
Critical Vocabulary 3.2A
Critical Vocabulary
1 convention A **convention** is a meeting of people who share the same purpose or ideas. *At the convention, people talked about ways to improve the government.*
2 delegates People who have been chosen to make decisions for a larger group are called **delegates**. *The delegates represent people from all 50 states.*
3 domestic When something is **domestic,** it is a part of or about the country in which you live. *We are interested in domestic news, but we also care about events in the rest of the world.*
4 welfare If someone looks out for your **welfare,** that person makes sure you are healthy and happy. *Dad wants me to eat vegetables because he is concerned about my welfare.*

1. Read aloud each word and have students repeat it.
2. Read aloud and discuss each word's student-friendly explanation.
3. Point out the example for the word. Have students suggest other examples.

TEACHER TIP

Encourage students to use Critical Vocabulary words in their writing. You can award students a point each time they use a new vocabulary word correctly in a piece of writing.

ENGLISH LEARNER SUPPORT: Build Vocabulary

SUBSTANTIAL

Show pictures of an elderly person and a baby. Ask students to point to the one who fits the word *posterity*.

MODERATE

Have students complete this sentence frame. *Posterity includes people who* _____ .

LIGHT

Have students share oral context sentences to show the meaning of *posterity*.

Step 2 Guided Practice

Guide students to interact with the words by discussing questions such as these:

- *Are people more likely to agree or disagree at a* ***convention****? Why?*
- *Are there as many* ***delegates*** *in a state as there are people? Explain.*
- *When you read* ***domestic*** *news, are you likely to learn about international events? Why or why not?*
- *If you care about people's* ***welfare,*** *do you care about their political views or their happiness? Explain.*
- *Does* ***posterity*** *include people who lived long ago or people who will be alive in the future? Explain.*

Ask students to name an event that might include a convention and delegates. (Give clues as needed.) Have them give examples of things that are and are not domestic. Ask them why it's important to care about the welfare of posterity.

Step 3 Apply

- Have students work independently to complete steps 3 and 4 on Vocabulary Cards 3.5–3.9.
- Have students use the **TURN AND TALK** routine to discuss with a partner the prompt on each Vocabulary Card.

convention

Vocabulary Cards

LEARNING MINDSET

Grit

Model Reinforce the idea that learning takes effort and progress takes time. *Sometimes I need force myself to keep going when learning something new, especially if I don't get it right the first time. I remind myself that it's OK to not know everything right away. My best learning happens when I have to put forth more time and effort!*

Synthesize

Step 1 Connect and Teach

LEARNING OBJECTIVES

- Synthesize information to create new understanding of text.
- **Language** Articulate the process for synthesizing.

MATERIALS — Online Ed

Anchor Chart 8 *Synthesize*
Printable *Anchor Chart 8: Synthesize*
Teaching Pal *Book 1, pp. 230–243*
myBook *The U. S. Constitution, Book 1, pp. 230–243*
Display and Engage *Meet the Author and Illustrator 3.2*

INSTRUCTIONAL VOCABULARY

- **synthesize** to put together information from different parts of a text to see the author's ideas in new ways

- Tell students that they are going to read an informational text called *The U. S. Constitution*. Explain that when they read informational texts, they **synthesize** new information with what they already know about a topic. As a result, they develop a new understanding of the topic.
- Project or display Anchor Chart 8: Synthesize.
- Explain that good readers make connections when they read by thinking about their own experiences and ideas in other texts. They combine what they know with the information in the text to come to a new understanding.
- Tell students that they can monitor their understanding by asking themselves questions such as, *What did I already know about this topic? After reading, what am I beginning to think? Now what do I understand? What is my new thinking?*
- Tell students that they will practice synthesizing when they read *The U. S. Constitution.*

Online Ed
ANCHOR CHART 8: Synthesize

SYNTHESIZE
When you synthesize, your thinking changes and you form new ideas.
What I know
At first I was thinking . . . because . . .
What I'm learning
When I was reading, I was thinking . . . because . . .
New understanding
By the end, I was thinking . . . because . . .

Notice & Note

3 Big Questions

- The Teaching Pal prompts in this lesson feature the **Notice & Note Signpost: 3 Big Questions.**
- As needed, refer to p. T19 to review the signpost with students.

ASSESSMENT OPTION

Assign the Selection Quiz to check comprehension of *The U. S. Constitution.*

Online

ANNOTATE IT!

Students may use the annotation tools in their eBook.

Step 2 Apply to Text

In your Teaching Pal, pages 230–241, use the blue **READ FOR UNDERSTANDING** prompts and the red **Notice & Note** prompts to read *The U. S. Constitution* as students follow along and annotate their *my*Book.

- **Genre Study** Guide students through the genre information on page 230.
- **Set a Purpose** Read the Set a Purpose section on page 230. Prompt students to set their own purpose for reading *The U. S. Constitution.*
- **Meet the Author and Illustrator** Project Display and Engage: Meet the Author and Illustrator 3.2 and read the information aloud with students. Ask students how it connects to what they already know about American symbols.
- **Read and Comprehend** Use the **READ FOR UNDERSTANDING** routine as you guide students to read the selection. Pause occasionally, using the prompts in your Teaching Pal to gauge students' understanding and to have them synthesize. As students synthesize, have them refer back to the Anchor Chart to determine how they can use new information to change their thinking, and as a result, form new ideas.

Step 3 Engage and Respond

INDEPENDENT PRACTICE: Speaking and Listening

- After reading, use the **COLLABORATIVE CONVERSATION** routine with the Collaborative Discussion questions on Teaching Pal and *my*Book page 247. Have students annotate their *my*Book with details from the text and visuals as evidence to explain their responses.
- Ask volunteers to read aloud the Speaking and Listening tips. Remind students to be prepared to ask follow-up questions when a speaker is not clear, and to respond politely when listeners have questions for them.
- You may want to have students conduct their discussions during daily small-group time.

ENGLISH LEARNER SUPPORT: Facilitate Discussion

SUBSTANTIAL
Provide frames such as the following: *I didn't know that ______. I learned ______. I still want to know ______.*

MODERATE
Guide students to express how they synthesize: *I thought ______, but after reading I understood that ______.*

LIGHT
Invite students to state the process for synthesizing.

LINK TO SMALL-GROUP INSTRUCTION

REINFORCE SYNTHESIZE Review and extend the skill as needed during small-group time to support students' need for differentiation. *See the lesson on p. T45.*

Options for Differentiation

As the class engages in independent and collaborative work, meet with Guided Reading Groups or differentiate instruction based on student need.

GUIDED READING GROUPS

Match Students to Books + Instruction

- Choose just-right books based on level, skill, topic, or genre.

Leveled Readers

- Deliver instruction with each book's **Take and Teach Lesson**, choosing appropriate sessions based on need.

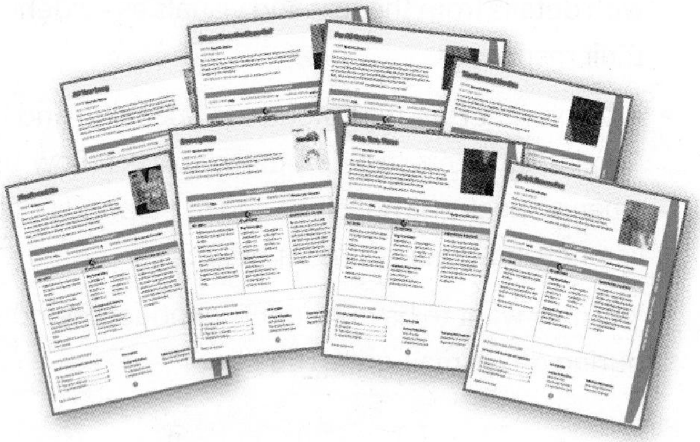

- Check comprehension, reinforce instruction, and extend learning with suggested supporting activities.

ENGLISH LEARNER SUPPORT

Synthesize

- Use **Tabletop Minilessons: English Language Development 7.1 (Speaking)** to reinforce and practice the language skill.

Tabletop Minilessons: English Language Development

- Use the following text-based prompts with *The U.S. Constitution* to guide application of the language skill. Begin with the prompt at the student's identified language proficiency level. As students progress, use lighter supports to encourage increased language proficiency.

SUBSTANTIAL
Have students explain what they learned about the constitution using visuals in the selection. Say: *Point to the executive branch. Who makes up the executive branch?* Allow students to respond in simple words and phrases, or to explain in their first language.

MODERATE
Use the visuals to support students' explanation of the branches of government. Ask: *Why do you think every branch of the U.S. government is equal?* Supply frames like these: *From the text, I learned ______. I think every branch is equal because ______.*

LIGHT
Have students reread the section, "Articles" Ask: *What did you learn about the three branches of government? Why is it important for the branches to be equal?*

REINFORCE SYNTHESIZE

Demonstrate

- Use **Tabletop Minilessons: Reading Card 8** to remind students that when they **synthesize** they put together information from different parts of a text along with what they already know to form new ideas and gain a new understanding.
- Model filling out Printable: Reading Graphic Organizer 8 to synthesize elements of *The U.S. Constitution*.

Apply to Independent Reading

- Now have students synthesize information in an appropriate book or article they are reading independently. Customize these prompts to the texts students choose.
  - » *What did I already know about this topic?*
  - » *What new information did I learn from the text?*
  - » *What is my new thinking about this topic based on what I read?*
- Have students complete Printable: Reading Graphic Organizer 8 for their independent reading book.

Tabletop Minilessons: Reading

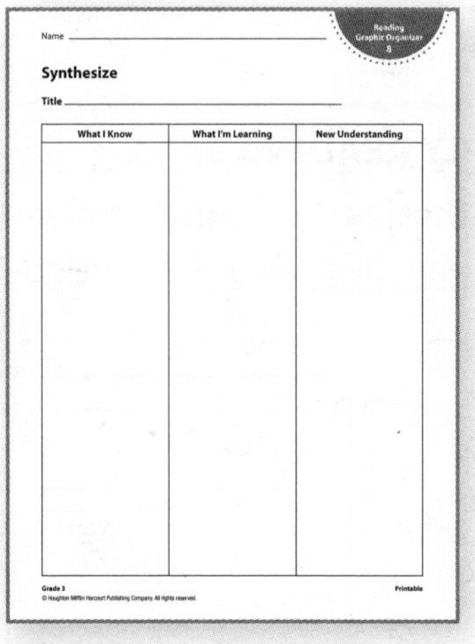

Printable: Reading Graphic Organizer 8

SCAFFOLD AND EXTEND

ALMOST THERE

- Guide students to identify what they already know and what they learned. Then prompt them to synthesize.
- Prompt students to use what they already know and what they learned to synthesize.
- Have students explain how their understanding and synthesis of the text changed from the beginning of their reading to the end.

READY FOR MORE

EL ENGLISH LEARNER SUPPORT

SUBSTANTIAL

Ask yes/no questions to help students synthesize: *Did you already know _____? Is _____ new information? Is _____ a new idea you might have from reading the text?*

MODERATE

Provide sentence frames to help students synthesize: *I already knew _____. I learned _____. I think _____.*

LIGHT

Have students elaborate on their thinking as they answer the questions.

Options for Independent and Collaborative Work

While you meet with small groups, have other students engage in literacy activities that reinforce the lesson's learning objectives. Choose from these options.

Independent Reading

Student Choice Library

Rigby®
LEVELED LIBRARY

APPLY READING SKILL

Synthesize Students complete Printable: Reading Graphic Organizer 8 for an independent reading book.

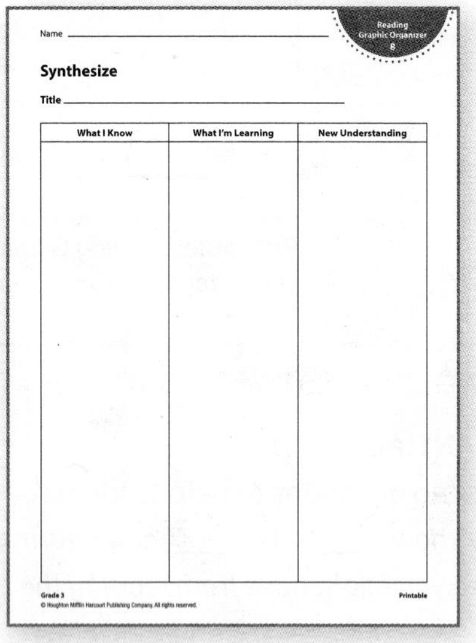

Name

Reading Graphic Organizer 8

Synthesize

Title

What I Know	What I'm Learning	New Understanding

Grade 3 Printable

© Houghton Mifflin Harcourt Publishing Company. All rights reserved.

Printable: Reading Graphic Organizer 8

APPLY LANGUAGE SKILL

Synthesize Students complete Printable: Language Graphic Organizer 15 for an independent reading book.

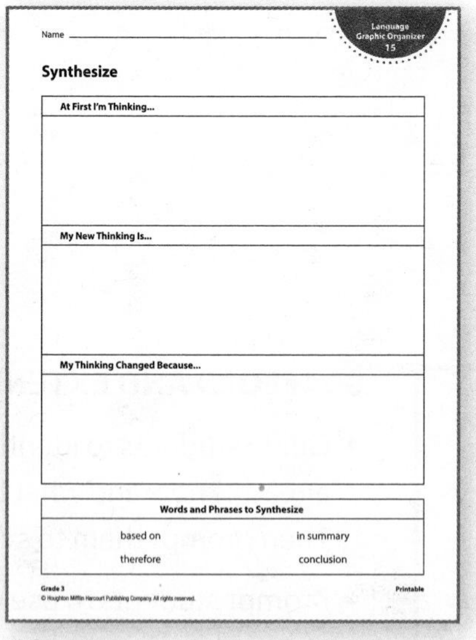

Name

Language Graphic Organizer 15

Synthesize

At First I'm Thinking...

My New Thinking Is...

My Thinking Changed Because...

Words and Phrases to Synthesize	
based on	in summary
therefore	conclusion

Grade 3 Printable

© Houghton Mifflin Harcourt Publishing Company. All rights reserved.

Printable: Language Graphic Organizer 15

Notice & Note

3 Big Questions

When students encounter this signpost, encourage them to ask and answer the Anchor Questions: *What surprised me? What did the author think I already knew? What challenged, changed, or confirmed what I already knew?*

Literacy Centers

See pp. T24–T25.

- READING CENTER
- VOCABULARY CENTER
- DIGITAL STATION
- WRITING CENTER
- PROJECT CENTER

Speaking and Listening

Partners discuss the Collaborative Discussion questions. *See Engage and Respond, p. T43.*

Wrap-Up

Share Time

At the end of the Reading Workshop, have students reflect on their learning by sharing how they applied **synthesize** or another area of focus during independent work time. Choose from these options:

- Use the **SOLO CHAIR** routine. Select a reader each day to come to the front of the class and tell what he or she learned from the reading by using a skill or strategy.
- **THINK-PAIR-SHARE** Students share their thinking with a partner. Select a few pairs each day to share with the whole class.
- **RETURN TO ANCHOR CHART** Have students add sticky notes about their independent reading to the Synthesize Anchor Chart. Call on a few students to explain what they added and why.

Online Ed

ANCHOR CHART 8: Synthesize

SYNTHESIZE
When you synthesize, your thinking changes and you form new ideas.
What I know
At first I was thinking . . . because . . .
What I'm learning
When I was reading, I was thinking . . . because . . .
New understanding
By the end, I was thinking . . . because . . .

Teacher Read-Aloud

Step 1 Introduce the Text

LEARNING OBJECTIVES

- Listen to fluent reading.
- Identify the central idea and supporting facts and details.
- **Language** Summarize to confirm understanding of text read aloud.

MATERIALS

Online Ed

myBook *Book 1, pp. 222–225*

QUICK TEACH WORDS

If students need support for understanding unfamiliar vocabulary they hear, provide the following student-friendly explanations.

- **resonate** When a sound resonates, it fills the room. When an idea resonates, it makes sense.
- **negotiate** To negotiate is to try and work out a deal with the other side: a price, a trade, a compromise.
- **anxious** If you are anxious, you are nervous, worried, tense.
- **inspiration** Inspiration is what put the idea for something in your head.
- **landscape** A landscape is the look of the surrounding land, whether flat or hilly, dirt-brown, or lush green.

SPANISH COGNATE

- **resonate** *resonar*
- **negotiate** *negociar*
- **inspiration** *inspiración*

Tell students that they will be listening to a text you will read aloud about several familiar American patriotic songs. Explain that *patriotic* means having pride in one's country. Work with students to make a list of patriotic tunes, or songs, they know, as well as any facts they know about the songs.

- **Genre Study** Tell students that they will be listening to an informational text. Remind them that informational texts give facts and information about a topic. Tell students that this selection gives the stories and facts about how five patriotic tunes were written and popularized.
- **Set a Purpose** Lead students to set a purpose for listening, such as listening to find out how each song was created and became popular. Encourage students to listen for context clues that will help them determine the meanings of any unfamiliar words they hear.
- **Model Fluency** Tell students to listen to how you read aloud at an appropriate rate. Explain that a rate that is neither too fast nor too slow makes the text easier for listeners to understand and enjoy.
- **Listen and Comprehend** Read the text aloud, pausing occasionally to ask the questions in the margins.

ENGLISH LEARNER SUPPORT: Discuss Language Structures

SUBSTANTIAL

Ask students to draw and label what they just heard.

MODERATE

Ask students to quick write about what they just heard.

LIGHT

Ask: *What is the main or key idea in what you just heard? What details support that idea?*

READ-ALOUD TEXT

Patriotic Tunes

Throughout U.S. history, patriotic songs have rallied Americans' love for their country. Songs celebrated freedom, built pride, and brought Americans together.

Patriotic songs are part of our history and our present. "The songs continue to **resonate** in our culture," says music professor Gerard Floriano at the State University of New York. "They stir in us feelings that are important to our humanness— feelings of family, a shared history, and promise for a better future." Here are the stories behind several timeless American songs. **A**

The Star-Spangled Banner

The War of 1812 gave America "The Star-Spangled Banner." Lawyer Francis Scott Key wrote its lyrics right after the Battle of Fort McHenry in 1814. The day before, Key and diplomat John Skinner had boarded a British ship in the Chesapeake Bay to **negotiate** the release of Dr. William Beanes, who had been captured by the British. The British agreed to release him, but they refused to allow any of the Americans to leave until their planned attack was over.

For 25 hours, the British bombarded Fort McHenry. Key spent an **anxious** night on the British ship. The next morning, he saw that the American flag was still flying. The British attack had failed. A relieved Key started scribbling "Defense of Fort McHenry" on an envelope. **B**

After returning to shore, Key's lyrics were printed and distributed. Thus, the flag became an important American symbol. "The Star- Spangled Banner" became the nation's official anthem in 1931. **C**

Battle Hymn of the Republic

"Battle Hymn of the Republic" was written by Julia Ward Howe. Howe found **inspiration** for her verses after visiting Union troops in northern Virginia in 1861. The Atlantic Monthly paid her five dollars for the poem in 1862. It became a famous Civil War marching tune and today is one of America's most treasured songs.

A **How have patriotic songs been part of American history?** *(The songs have celebrated freedom, pride, love for the country, and brought citizens together.)* DOK 1

What sorts of feelings do people get from patriotic songs? *(The songs stir feelings of family, shared history, and promise for the future.)* DOK 1

B **Why was American lawyer Francis Scott Key watching the Battle of Fort McHenry from on board a British ship?** *(He was there to negotiate a prisoner's release and was not allowed to leave until the battle ended.)* DOK 2

When morning came, how did Key know the British attack had failed? *(The U.S. flag was still there.)* DOK 1

C **When did "The Star-Spangled Banner" become the country's official national anthem?** *(1931)* DOK 1

READ-ALOUD TEXT, *continued*

America the Beautiful

An 1893 hike up Colorado's Pikes Peak inspired Katharine Lee Bates to write her celebratory ode to the nation, "America the Beautiful." The poem was published in 1895, and people loved it.

In 1904, minister Charles Barbour joined Bates' lyrics to a hymn that Samuel Ward wrote in 1882. The song was so popular that many people wanted it to become the national anthem of the United States. "It covers the whole range of what we are and the majesty of the **landscape**," notes music professor Caroline Stoessinger at the City University of New York. (D)

You're a Grand Old Flag

George M. Cohan's first title for a 1906 song from his musical George Washington, Jr., was "You're a Grand Old Rag." His inspiration came from a chance meeting with a Civil War veteran who still carried a tattered flag from the 1863 Battle of Gettysburg.

People thought that the word *rag* was disrespectful, so Cohan changed the words. The song—and his play—were a hit. Later, World War I (1914–1918) cemented the song's place among America's beloved patriotic tunes. (E)

God Bless America

Composer Irving Berlin wrote the first version of "God Bless America" in 1918. However, it sat in a file for two decades. Then, in 1938, singer Kate Smith wanted a special song for the 20th anniversary of the end of World War I. Her manager approached Berlin about "God Bless America." Berlin dug out the song and updated it. Smith sang it on her November 10, 1938, radio show. It gave hope to a nation still suffering through the economic hardships of the Great Depression. Later, the song's message of peace sustained Americans' spirits during World War II (1939–1945).

"God Bless America" brought hope to the country once again after the terrorist attacks on September 11, 2001. (F)

(D) **What inspired Katharine Lee Bates to write "America the Beautiful"?** *(She was inspired by a hike up Colorado's Pikes Peak.)* DOK 1

What tells you how popular the song was? *(The song was so beloved that many people wanted to make it our national anthem.)* DOK 2

(E) **Why was the song originally called "You're a Grand Old Rag," and why did George M. Cohan change it?** *(Cohan based the song on a Civil War veteran who carried a beat-up, old flag. He changed the title because people thought "rag" was disrespectful.)* DOK 1

What does it mean that World War I "cemented" this song's place among patriotic tunes? *(The war made the song important and turned it into one of the classics that people know today.)* DOK 2

(F) **How has "God Bless America" played a role during America's difficult times?** *(The song provided hope amid the Depression. In World War II, its message sustained people's spirits. After September 11, it gave Americans hope in the face of the attacks.)* DOK 1

Step 2 Focus on Fluency

READING RATE

- Remind students that good readers read at an appropriate rate. That means reading neither too fast nor too slow. When reading informational text, readers may read sections with a lot of information more slowly so as to make sure listeners have a chance to hear and comprehend the information.
- Read aloud the introductory paragraph at a very fast rate. Ask students what information they are able to recall. Point out that it can be difficult to hear and recall information from a text that is read too quickly.
- Read aloud the paragraph a second time in a slow and halting manner. Point out that it can be hard for listeners to pay attention and connect ideas in the text when it is read too slowly.
- Read aloud the paragraph a third time, modeling appropriate rate. Guide students to understand that reading at the correct rate is important to help listeners make sense of a text.
- Tell students they will have opportunities to practice appropriate rate as they read other selections in this module.

Step 3 Engage and Respond

COMPARE SELECTIONS

Have students revisit the Essential Question on *my*Book page 223. Then help them recall the Get Curious Video *American Landmarks* and the text *American Places, American Ideals.* Have students discuss the following questions as a class or in small groups. Encourage them to use the Words About Our Nation on page 224 as they do.

1. *What do you now know about how historic places, documents, and symbols represent our nation that you did not know before?* (Responses will vary.)
2. *How is the information in the video about American landmarks and monuments, the informational text about American places, and the selection* Patriotic Tunes *the same and different?* (All are about things that represent our nation. Patriotic Tunes *is about American songs.* Let Freedom Ring, *and* American Places, American Ideals *both include American landmarks and monuments.* Let Freedom Ring *also includes symbols like the Liberty Bell and the Great Seal, as well as the Underground Railroad National Park.*)
3. *What do you hope to learn as you focus on the other selections in this module and search for answers to the Essential Question?* (Responses will vary.)

This discussion is an opportunity to reinforce good speaking and listening behaviors. Remind students to ask relevant questions and to offer comments that connect to the ideas already being discussed.

After the discussion, have students reflect on its effectiveness. Did everyone participate? Did students give everyone who wanted to a chance to speak? Did they listen to one another? Were students' comments and questions relevant to the topic?

ENGLISH LEARNER SUPPORT: Facilitate Discussion

SUBSTANTIAL

Ask students what each of the selections focuses on, using this sentence stem. _____ *is about* _____.

MODERATE

Focus on the content of responses, not grammar or pronunciation.

LIGHT

Ask students to describe what they have learned so far and what they found most interesting about historic places, documents, and symbols that represent our nation.

SOCIAL STUDIES CONNECTION: Extend Learning

National Resources Explain that the U. S. government has many free resources to explore historic places, documents, and symbols:

- Search for and view many historic texts, books, and documents online at The Library of Congress. https://www.loc.gov/families/
- Search for information on national parks in their home state and "from sea to shining sea" through the National Park Service. https://www.nps.gov/findapark/index.htm
- View and learn about American artwork at the National Gallery. https://www.nga.gov/education/kids.html

Review Critical Vocabulary

Step 1 Reinforce Vocabulary

- Project Display and Engage: Critical Vocabulary 3.2 to review and discuss the Critical Vocabulary, student-friendly explanations, and examples of the words. Have students take turns using the words in sentences.

Step 2 Guided Practice

- Display the Critical Vocabulary words. Guide students, as needed, to complete the following sentence stems:

1. *You can't have a convention with just one person because ______.*
2. *The job of delegates is to ______.*
3. *A domestic law probably wouldn't matter to ______.*
4. *When you look out for someone's welfare, you want them to be ______.*
5. *When you think about posterity, you are thinking of people who ______.*

- Invite students to share their own sentences with the class.

Step 3 Apply

INDEPENDENT PRACTICE

- Have students work in small groups or independently. Tell them to complete Know It, Show It page 54. For the last item on the page, tell students to include clues to each word's meaning in their sentences. Have groups share their sentences. Ask listeners to identify the context clue in each sentence.
- You may wish to have students complete the Know It, Show It page during Small Group time.

LEARNING OBJECTIVES

- Review and extend understanding of word meanings.
- Use context to determine the meanings of unfamiliar words.
- **Language** Use newly acquired vocabulary to answer questions.

MATERIALS Online Ed

Display and Engage *Critical Vocabulary 3.2*

Know It, Show It *p. 54*

CRITICAL VOCABULARY

- **convention**
- **delegates**
- **domestic**
- **welfare**
- **posterity**

ENGLISH LEARNER SUPPORT: Support Discussion

SUBSTANTIAL

If you look out for a pet's welfare, what might you do? Draw a picture to show your actions.

MODERATE

If you look out for others' welfare, you ______ about them.

LIGHT

What are ways you might look out for your friends' or family's welfare?

Multiple-Meaning Words

Step 1 Introduce the Strategy

LEARNING OBJECTIVES

- Use context to determine the relevant meanings of multiple-meaning words.
- Use print and digital reference materials to clarify meanings.
- **Language** Identify multiple-meaning words using strategic learning techniques.

MATERIALS Online Ed

Display and Engage *Vocabulary Strategy 3.3a, 3.3b*

INSTRUCTIONAL VOCABULARY

- **multiple-meaning words** words that are spelled the same but have more than one meaning

Online

DISPLAY AND ENGAGE: Vocabulary Strategy 3.3a, 3.3b

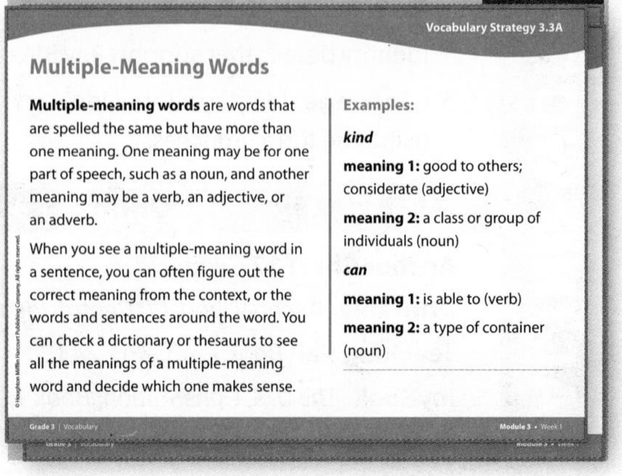
Vocabulary Strategy 3.3A

Multiple-Meaning Words

Multiple-meaning words are words that are spelled the same but have more than one meaning. One meaning may be for only one part of speech, such as a noun, and another meaning may be a verb, an adjective, or an adverb.

When you see a multiple-meaning word in a sentence, you can often figure out the correct meaning from the context, or the words and sentences around the word. You can check a dictionary or thesaurus to see all the meanings of a multiple-meaning word and decide which one makes sense.

Examples:

kind

meaning 1: good to others; considerate (adjective)

meaning 2: a class or group of individuals (noun)

can

meaning 1: is able to (verb)

meaning 2: a type of container (noun)

Grade 3 | Vocabulary — Module 3 • Week 1

- Project Display and Engage: Vocabulary Strategy 3.3a and 3.3b. Read aloud the two paragraphs.
- Tell students that multiple-meaning words are words that have more than one meaning. Explain that identifying these words will help them understand what they read.
- Use the first two examples to show common multiple-meaning words and their meanings. *The multiple-meaning word kind can be an adjective that means "good to others." It can also be a noun that means "a class or group of individuals." The multiple-meaning word can is a verb that means "is able to." It is also a noun that means a type of container.*

Step 2 Guided Practice

- Have students read the other examples of multiple-meaning words and discuss two meanings of each word.
- Challenge students to think of additional meanings for each word.

Step 3 Apply the Strategy

INDEPENDENT PRACTICE

- Point out the word *charge* in *Why We Celebrate the Fourth of July*. Have students work independently to write two or more meanings for the word *charge*. Tell them they can use a dictionary or thesaurus to check meanings.
- Next, challenge students to find other multiple-meaning words in the selection. (Examples include *passed, state,* and *even*.) Have them write down the words and at least two meanings for each. Tell them they can use a dictionary or thesaurus to check meanings.
- Have students exchange the words they identified with a partner and check each other's answers.

ENGLISH LEARNER SUPPORT: Understand Multiple-Meaning Words

SUBSTANTIAL
Offer other simple multiple-meaning words, such as *sink*, to ensure understanding. Then help them find examples in the selection.

MODERATE
Supply sentence stems for multiple-meaning words: Even *is a multiple-meaning word because it can mean "flat," and it can mean* ______.

LIGHT
Ask students to share sentences explaining why the selection words they chose are multiple-meaning words.

Central Idea

Step 1 Connect and Teach

LEARNING OBJECTIVES

- Recognize the central ideas in an informational text.
- Identify details that support key ideas.
- **Language** Identify central ideas using the term *branches*.

MATERIALS Online Ed

Anchor Chart 17 *Central Idea*
Printable *Anchor Chart 17: Central Idea*
Teaching Pal *Book 1, pp. 230–243*
myBook *The U. S. Constitution, Book 1, pp. 230–243*
Know It, Show It *p. 55*

INSTRUCTIONAL VOCABULARY

- **central idea** the big idea, or main idea, that readers should take away from reading a text
- **detail** fact or idea that supports or tells more about the central, or main idea
- **evidence** clues or details in the text that support an answer or idea

SPANISH COGNATES

- **central** *central*
- **idea** *idea*
- **detail** *detalle*
- **evidence** *evidencia*

- Tell students that as they read, they should think about the central, or main, ideas the author wants readers to know. Explain that sometimes an author provides the **central idea** at the beginning or end of a paragraph. At other times, readers have to infer, or figure out, the central idea on their own.
- Project or display Anchor Chart 17: Central Idea. Use the chart to explain the clues that help readers identify a central idea.
- Tell students that informational text is often divided into sections with **headings** that identify key ideas.
- Point out that authors include **evidence** to support main ideas. **Details**, such as facts or examples, provide evidence that tells more about the central idea.
- Tell students that they will practice identifying central ideas and supporting details to gain a deeper understanding of *The U. S. Constitution*.

Online
ANCHOR CHART 17: Central Idea

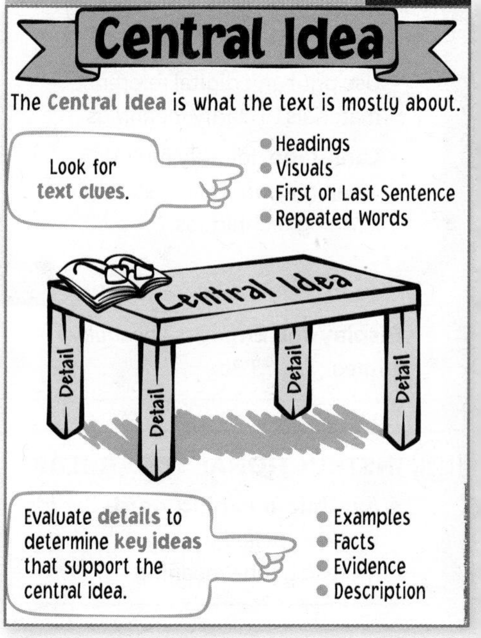
Central Idea
The Central Idea is what the text is mostly about.
Look for text clues.
Headings
Visuals
First or Last Sentence
Repeated Words
Central Idea
Detail
Detail
Detail
Detail
Evaluate details to determine key ideas that support the central idea.
Examples
Facts
Evidence
Description

LEARNING MINDSET

Seeking Challenges

Review Point out that the writers of the U.S Constitution took on an incredible challenge. *They took a risk by trying to find a way to govern their new country in a fair way. We're so lucky that they didn't give up!* Point out that their challenge was part of learning how to do something that had never been tried before: people running their own government.

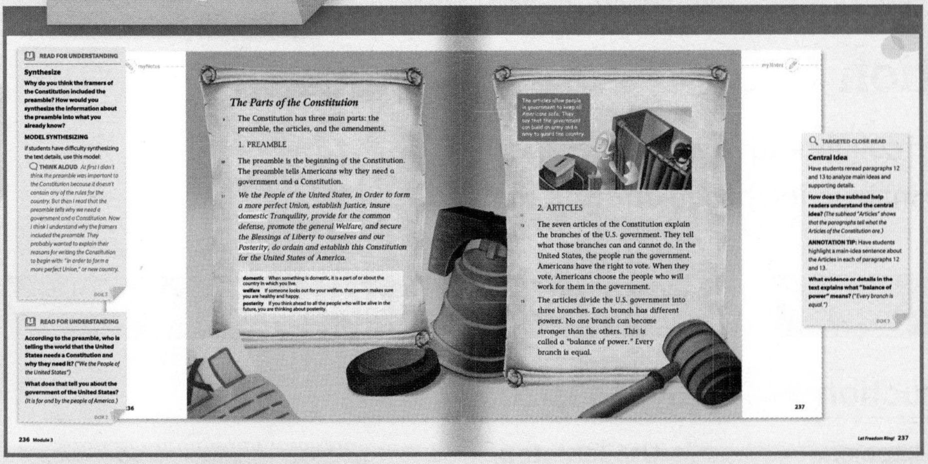

ANNOTATE IT! Online Ed

Students may use the annotation tools in their eBook.

Step 2 Apply to Text

In your **Teaching Pal,** use the purple **TARGETED CLOSE READ** prompts to guide students to apply the Central Idea skill to *The U. S. Constitution* and to cite evidence to support their responses. Use the **CLOSE READING** routine. Students may refer to the questions on Know It, Show It page 55 as you discuss them.

- Read aloud the first question on Teaching Pal page 237 and have students reread paragraphs 12–13 in their *my*Book to determine how the subhead helps readers understand the central idea. *(The subhead "Articles" shows that the paragraphs tell what the Articles of the Constitution are.)*
- Then read the second question on Teaching Pal page 237 and have students respond, using text evidence. *("Every branch is equal.")*
- Refer back to the Anchor Chart as necessary to support the discussion. Have students use sticky notes to add to the Anchor Chart additional examples of central ideas and supporting evidence in *The U. S. Constitution* and in other reading.

Step 3 Engage and Respond

INDEPENDENT PRACTICE: Viewing

Play Close Read **Screencast 3: *The U.S. Constitution.***

- You may want to have students view the Screencast during daily small-group time.

INDEPENDENT PRACTICE: Writing

- **Write An Encyclopedia Entry** Turn to pages 242–243 in your **Teaching Pal**. Have students turn to pages 242–243 in their *my*Book. Use the **WRITING RESPONSE** routine.
- Read the directions with students and use the Teaching Pal prompts to guide them as they plan and complete their encyclopedia entries.
- Provide time for students to share their encyclopedia entries with small groups.
- You may want to have students complete their writing during daily small-group time.
- You may want to have students complete Know It, Show It page 55 during small-group time.

ENGLISH LEARNER SUPPORT: Support Comprehension

SUBSTANTIAL
Use gestures and visuals to help students understand unfamiliar or multiple-meaning terms in the text, such as *branches* and *balance of power.* Ask: *Is one branch more important or are they the same?*

MODERATE
Confirm students' understanding of the text. Expand one-word answers into sentences and have them repeat: *Yes, branches are equal parts.*

LIGHT
Encourage students to use new vocabulary to explain the central idea.

LINK TO SMALL-GROUP INSTRUCTION

REINFORCE CENTRAL IDEA Review and extend the skill as needed during small-group time to support students' need for differentiation. *See the lesson on p. T57.*

Options for Differentiation

As the class engages in independent and collaborative work, meet with Guided Reading Groups or differentiate instruction based on student need.

GUIDED READING GROUPS

Match Students to Books + Instruction

- Choose just-right books based on level, skill, topic, or genre.

L → M → N → O → P → Q

Leveled Readers

- Deliver instruction with each book's **Take and Teach Lesson**, choosing appropriate sessions based on need.

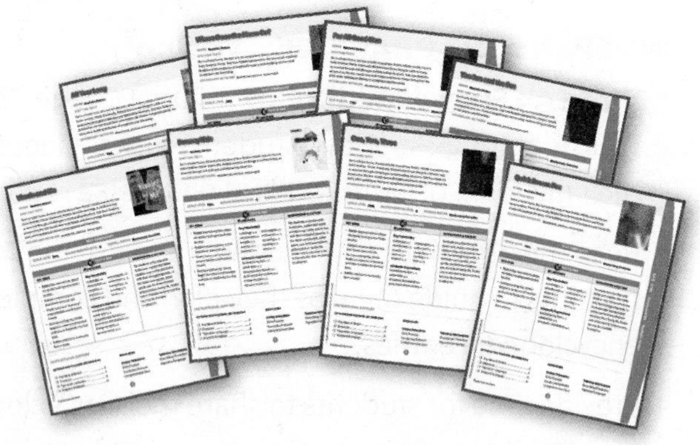

- Check comprehension, reinforce instruction, and extend learning with suggested supporting activities.

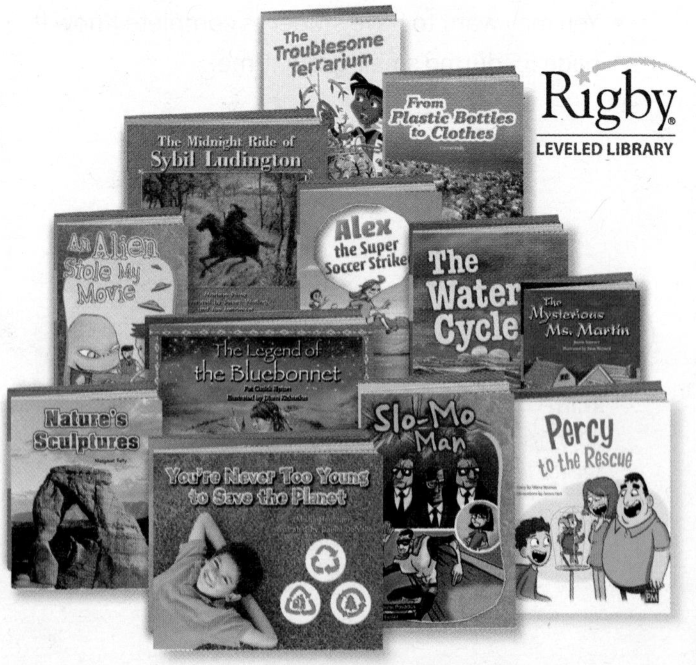

ENGLISH LEARNER SUPPORT

Synthesize

- Use **Tabletop Minilessons: English Language Development 7.2 (Reading)** to reinforce and practice the language skill.

Tabletop Minilessons: English Language Development

- Use the following text-based prompts with *The U.S. Constitution* to guide application of the language skill. Begin with the prompt at the student's identified language proficiency level. As students progress, use lighter supports to encourage increased language proficiency.

SUBSTANTIAL
Choral read with students the final paragraph of the text. Say: *Point to the word that shows how James Madison feels about the Constitution.* (proud) *Do you feel proud of the Constitution, too?*

MODERATE
Ask students to read aloud the last page of the selection. Ask: *How does James Madison feel about the Constitution? Do you agree with him?*

LIGHT
Have partners read the end of the selection together, and then discuss the following questions: *Are your feelings about the Constitution similar to James Madison's? Why or why not?* Have them support their opinions with evidence from the text.

REINFORCE CENTRAL IDEA

Demonstrate

- Use **Tabletop Minilessons: Reading Card 17** to remind students that sometimes an author provides the **central idea** at the beginning or end of a paragraph. At other times, readers have to infer, or figure out, the central idea on their own. Sometimes a **heading** will provide the central idea in a section of text. Authors include **evidence** to support main ideas. **Details**, such as facts or examples, provide evidence that tells more about the central idea.
- Model filling out Printable: Reading Graphic Organizer 17 to identify Central Idea in *The U.S. Constitution.*

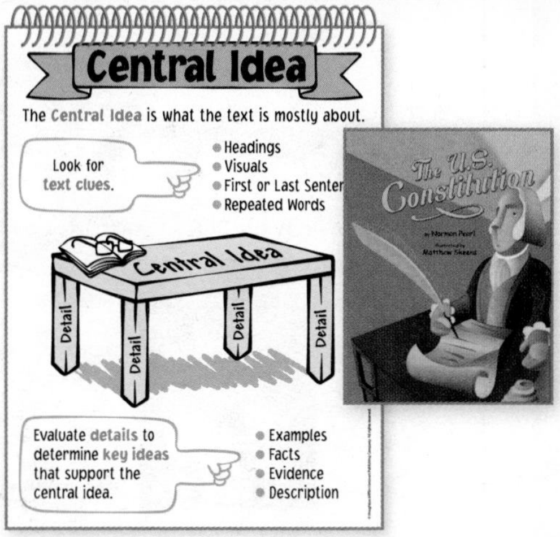

Tabletop Minilessons: Reading

Apply to Independent Reading

- Now have students identify the central idea in an appropriate book or article they are reading independently. Customize these prompts to the texts students choose.
  - » *What is the central idea of this paragraph or section of text?*
  - » *Does the author state the central idea, or did you have to infer it?*
  - » *What evidence and details support the central idea?*
- Have students complete Printable: Reading Graphic Organizer 17 for their independent reading book.

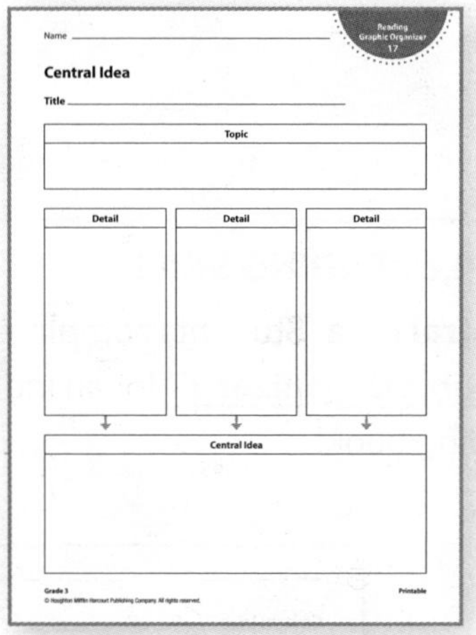

Printable: Reading Graphic Organizer 17

ALMOST THERE

READY FOR MORE

SCAFFOLD AND EXTEND

- Guide students to identify the central idea. Ask them to point out evidence that supports it.
- Prompt students to identify the central idea and the details in the text that support it.
- Have students infer a central idea that is not directly stated, and then explain how they used text evidence to make their inference.

ENGLISH LEARNER SUPPORT

SUBSTANTIAL

Ask *either/or* questions to help students state the central idea: *Is* _____ *or* _____ *the central idea? Is* _____ *or* _____ *a detail that supports the central idea?*

MODERATE

Supply sentence frames such as: *The central idea is* _____. *A detail that supports it is* _____.

LIGHT

Encourage students to explain how they identified the central idea and details that support it.

Options for Independent and Collaborative Work

While you meet with small groups, have other students engage in literacy activities that reinforce the lesson's learning objectives. Choose from these options.

Independent Reading

Student Choice Library

Rigby
LEVELED LIBRARY

APPLY READING SKILL

Central Idea Students complete Printable: Reading Graphic Organizer 17 for an independent reading book.

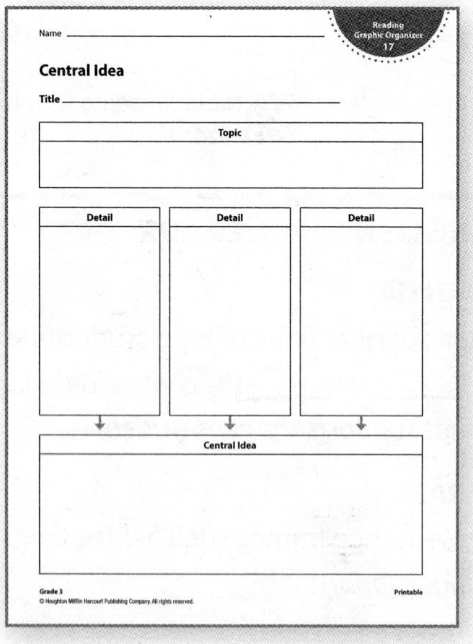
Name
Reading Graphic Organizer 17
Central Idea
Title
Topic
Detail | Detail | Detail
Central Idea
Grade 3
Printable
© Houghton Mifflin Harcourt Publishing Company. All rights reserved.

Printable: Reading Graphic Organizer 17

APPLY LANGUAGE SKILL

Synthesize Students complete Printable: Language Graphic Organizer 15 for an independent reading book.

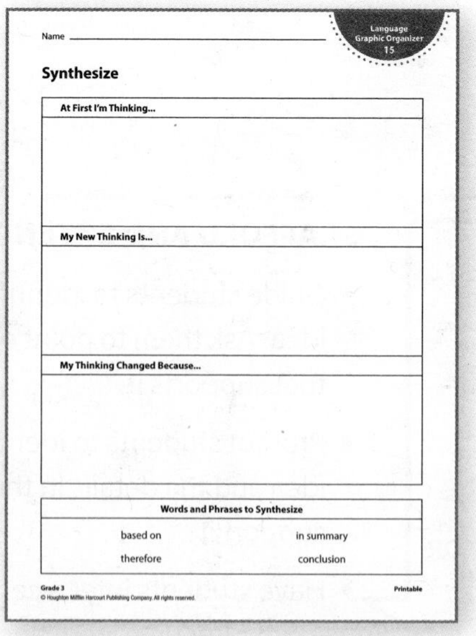
Name
Language Graphic Organizer 15
Synthesize
At First I'm Thinking...
My New Thinking Is...
My Thinking Changed Because...
Words and Phrases to Synthesize

based on	in summary
therefore	conclusion

Grade 3
Printable
© Houghton Mifflin Harcourt Publishing Company. All rights reserved.

Printable: Language Graphic Organizer 15

Literacy Centers

See pp. T24–T25.

- READING CENTER
- VOCABULARY CENTER
- DIGITAL STATION
- WRITING CENTER
- PROJECT CENTER

Writing

Students write an Encyclopedia Entry. *See Engage and Respond, p. T55.*

Close-Read Screencast

Online Ed

Additional Skills Practice

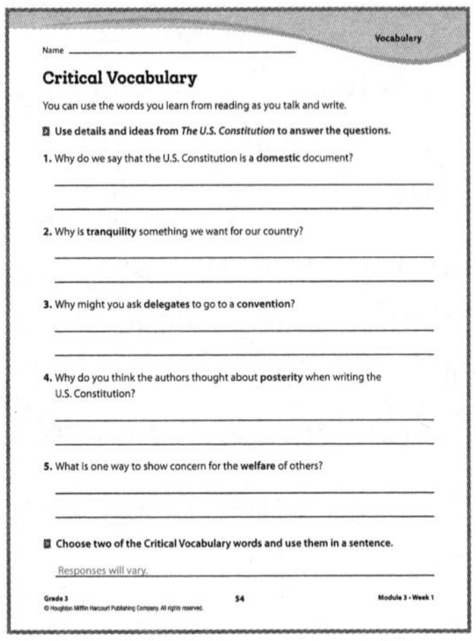

Name ____________ Vocabulary

Critical Vocabulary

You can use the words you learn from reading as you talk and write.

Use details and ideas from *The U.S. Constitution* to answer the questions.

1. Why do we say that the U.S. Constitution is a **domestic** document?
2. Why is **tranquility** something we want for our country?
3. Why might you ask **delegates** to go to a **convention**?
4. Why do you think the authors thought about **posterity** when writing the U.S. Constitution?
5. What is one way to show concern for the **welfare** of others?

Choose two of the Critical Vocabulary words and use them in a sentence.

Responses will vary.

Grade 3 54 Module 3 • Week 1

Know It, Show It, p. 54

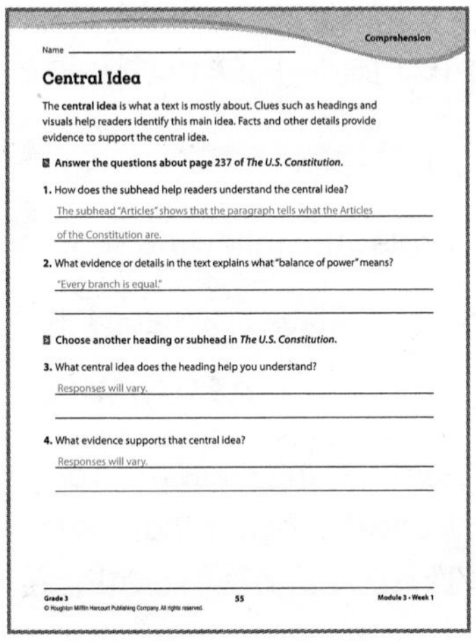

Name ____________ Comprehension

Central Idea

The **central idea** is what a text is mostly about. Clues such as headings and visuals help readers identify this main idea. Facts and other details provide evidence to support the central idea.

Answer the questions about page 237 of *The U.S. Constitution*.

1. How does the subhead help readers understand the central idea?
   The subhead "Articles" shows that the paragraph tells what the Articles of the Constitution are.
2. What evidence or details in the text explains what "balance of power" means?
   "Every branch is equal."

Choose another heading or subhead in *The U.S. Constitution*.

3. What central idea does the heading help you understand?
   Responses will vary.
4. What evidence supports that central idea?
   Responses will vary.

Grade 3 55 Module 3 • Week 1

Know It, Show It, p. 55

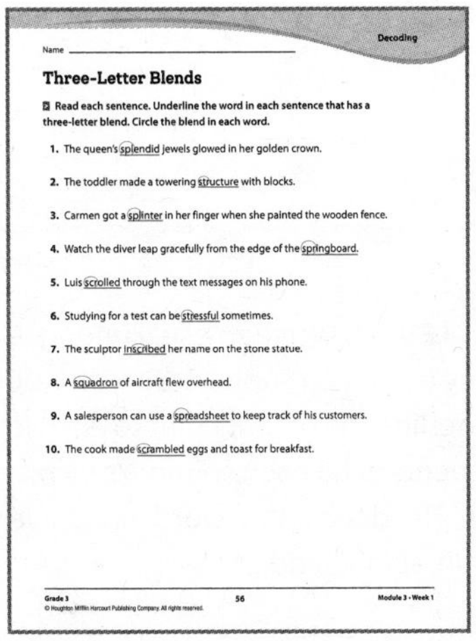

Name ____________ Decoding

Three-Letter Blends

Read each sentence. Underline the word in each sentence that has a three-letter blend. Circle the blend in each word.

1. The queen's splendid jewels glowed in her golden crown.
2. The toddler made a towering structure with blocks.
3. Carmen got a splinter in her finger when she painted the wooden fence.
4. Watch the diver leap gracefully from the edge of the springboard.
5. Luis scrolled through the text messages on his phone.
6. Studying for a test can be stressful sometimes.
7. The sculptor inscribed her name on the stone statue.
8. A squadron of aircraft flew overhead.
9. A salesperson can use a spreadsheet to keep track of his customers.
10. The cook made scrambled eggs and toast for breakfast.

Grade 3 56 Module 3 • Week 1

Know It, Show It, p. 56

Wrap-Up

Share Time

At the end of the Reading Workshop, have students reflect on their learning by sharing how they applied **central idea** or another area of focus during independent work time. Choose from these options:

- Use the **SOLO CHAIR** routine. Select a reader each day to come to the front of the class and tell what he or she learned from the reading by using a skill or strategy.
- **THINK-PAIR-SHARE** Students share their thinking with a partner. Select a few pairs each day to share with the whole class.
- **RETURN TO ANCHOR CHART** Have students add sticky notes about their independent reading to the Central Idea Anchor Chart. Call on a few students to explain what they added and why.

Online Ed

ANCHOR CHART 17: Central Idea

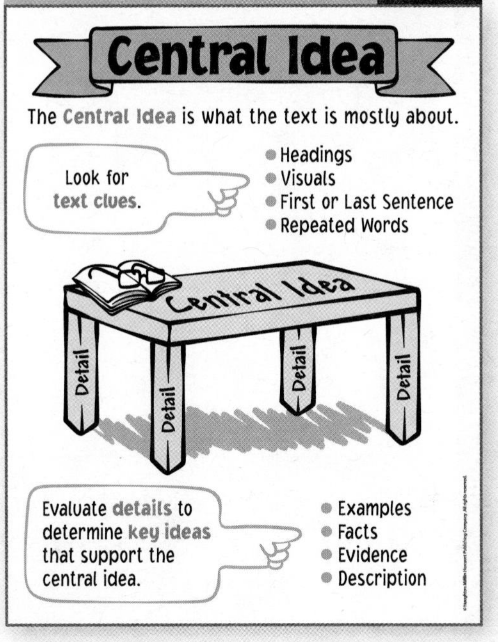
Central Idea
The Central Idea is what the text is mostly about.
Look for text clues.
Headings
Visuals
First or Last Sentence
Repeated Words
Central Idea
Detail
Detail
Detail
Detail
Evaluate details to determine key ideas that support the central idea.
Examples
Facts
Evidence
Description

Three-Letter Blends

Step 1 Reinforce the Skill

LEARNING OBJECTIVES

- Decode and read words with three-letter blends.
- Decode multisyllabic words.
- **Language** Articulate sounds for three-letter blends and read words containing those sounds.

MATERIALS **Online** Ed

Display and Engage *Decoding 3.3*
Know It, Show It *p. 56*

Three-Letter Blends Remind students that they have learned the sounds and spellings of three-letter blends *spl, scr, spr, str,* and *squ*.

- Tell students they can use the strategies they've learned for decoding words with three-letter blends to help them decode longer words.
- Explain that students can divide longer words into syllables to make them easier to read. Draw a line between *n* and *t* to divide *splinter* into syllables. Note that the first syllable ends in a consonant, which means it's a closed syllable. Explain that closed syllables usually have short vowel sounds.
- Repeat with the words *scruffy*, *spreading*, *instrument*, and *squeaky*. Guide students to read aloud the words and to help you identify the three-letter blends in the words: *scr*, *spr*, *str*, *squ*. Point out that in longer words, students may find three-letter blends in the middle of the word, as in *instrument*.
- Display the chart below. Read aloud each word, emphasizing the three-letter blend.

spl	scr	spr	str	squ
splutter	scrutinize	sprinkle	instrument	squiggle

- Display the following sentence and underline the word *scrutinize*.

She needed to scrutinize, or closely review, the assignment before she worked on it.

Say: *If I didn't know the word* scrutinize, *I could look at the blend at the beginning. I know the sounds that the letters* s, c, *and* r *stand for. So I will sound out the word: /skrü/ /tĭ/ /nīz/,* scrutinize. *That sounds right, and it makes sense in the context of the sentence.* Scrutinize *means "to closely review."*

ENGLISH LEARNER SUPPORT: Utilize Language Transfer

ALL LEVELS Vietnamese, Hmong, Cantonese, and Korean do not contain initial *s* blends. They may need support with pronouncing consonant blends. Write the word *spread* and underline the blend. Point to each letter in the blend as you say the sound, and have students echo each sound: /s/, /p/ r/. with you. Then drag out the sounds: /sssssssprrrr/, / spr/. Read the entire word, and have students repeat it. Continue with other words, such as *scrub*, *splash*, and *streak*.

Step 2 Guided Practice

- Project Display and Engage: **Decoding 3.3**.
- Have students read aloud the Blend and Read lines. Provide feedback as needed. At the end of each line, prompt a conversation about the words: *How are the sounds and spellings in the words the same? How are they different?*
- Have partners reread the Blend and Read lines and quiz each other on the spellings of three-letter blends.

Online Ed

DISPLAY AND ENGAGE: Decoding 3.3

Decoding 3.3

Blend and Read

Three-Letter Blends

1	screwdriver (scr)	stretchy (str)	unscramble (scr)	squinting (squ)	sprawling (spr)
2	splatter (spl)	springtime (spr)	squabble (squ)	scrimmage (scr)	display (spl)
3	squeamish (squ)	scrawny (scr)	splashdown (spl)	ostrich (str)	strengthen (str)
4	sprinkler (spr)	strangely (str)	squander (squ)	splotchy (spl)	springboard (spr)
5	straighten (str)	descriptive (scr)	squirmed (squ)	splendor (spl)	bedspread (spr)

6. Jan will recopy her story and scribble (scr) illustrations (str) in her notebook.
7. Dad sprayed (spr) whipped cream straight (str) from the can onto his strawberry (str) shortcake.

Grade 3 | Foundational Skills Module 3 • Week 1

Step 3 Apply

INDEPENDENT PRACTICE

- Have students work in small groups or with partners to complete Know It, Show It page 56.
- Be sure students understand there are two tasks for each sentence: identify the word that contains a three-letter blend, and identify the blend.
- Encourage students to share with each other the strategies they use to decode words with three-letter blends.

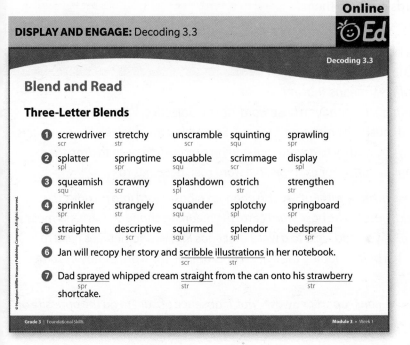

CORRECT & REDIRECT

If students have trouble decoding words with three-letter blends, use the model below.

- **Correct** the error. *When you see three letters at the beginning of a word, say the sound for each letter.*
- **Model** how to decode the word: **/spĭng/.** *That doesn't sound like a word I know. I missed one sound at the beginning of the word. The letters spr stand for the sounds* **/spr/**. *So I'll try reading the word again:* **/sprĭng/**, *spring. That sounds like a word I know.*
- **Guide** students to decode other words: *splatter, scrawny,* and *strengthen.*
- **Check** students' understanding by displaying the word *splotchy. What spelling pattern helps you decode this word? (The letters* s, p, l *stand for the sounds* **/spl/**.*)*
- **Reinforce** by repeating the process with *squinting*.

Suffixes -y, -less; Prefix dis-

Step 1 Introduce the Skill

LEARNING OBJECTIVES

- Determine the meaning of grade-level academic vocabulary with prefixes or suffixes.
- Use a dictionary or glossary to determine the meanings of unknown words.
- **Language** Discuss words with the suffixes *-y* and *-less* and the prefix *dis-* to show understanding of the target suffixes and prefix.

MATERIALS Online Ed

Display and Engage: *Generative Vocabulary 3.4a, 3.4b*

Know It, Show It *p. 57*

INSTRUCTIONAL VOCABULARY

- **suffix** a word part added to the end of a base word that changes the meaning of the word
- **prefix** a word part added to the beginning of a base word that changes the meaning of the word
- **base word** a word in its simplest form, without any word parts added to it

Project Display and Engage: Generative Vocabulary 3.4a and 3.4b. Read aloud the paragraphs.

Online

DISPLAY AND ENGAGE:
Generative Vocabulary 3.4a, 3.4b

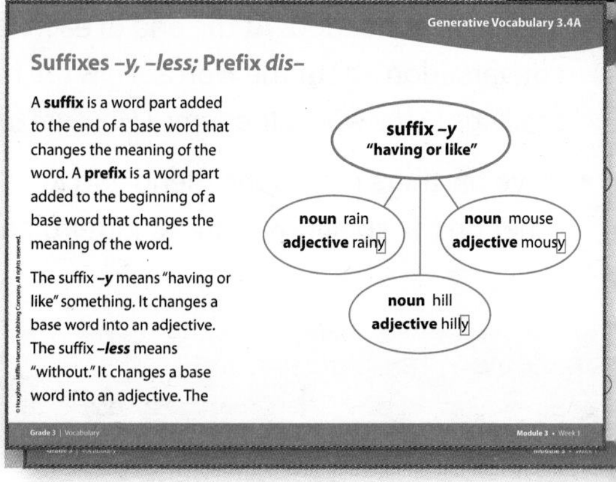
Generative Vocabulary 3.4A
Suffixes -y, -less; Prefix dis-
A suffix is a word part added to the end of a base word that changes the meaning of the word. A prefix is a word part added to the beginning of a base word that changes the meaning of the word.
The suffix -y means "having or like" something. It changes a base word into an adjective.
The suffix -less means "without." It changes a base word into an adjective. The
suffix -y "having or like"
noun rain adjective rainy
noun mouse adjective mousy
noun hill adjective hilly

- Display the words *mushy, careless,* and *disloyal*. Circle the suffixes *-y* and *-less* and the prefix *dis-*. Tell students that knowing the meaning of the suffixes and prefix in these words can help them figure out the words' meanings.
- Then model how to use suffixes to determine the meaning of a word. *The suffix* -y *means "having or like" something. It changes a base word into an adjective. When you add* -y *to the base word* mush, *the meaning changes. Something* mushy *feels like mush or is full of mush. If you add* -y *to a word that ends in* e, *you often need to drop the* e *before adding the suffix. For example, the word* rose *becomes* rosy.

The suffix -less *means "without." It also changes a base word into an adjective. When you add* -less *to the base word* care, *the meaning changes.* Careless *means "without care." If you add* -less *to a word that ends in* y, *you sometimes need to change the* y *to* i *before adding the suffix. For example, the word* penny *becomes* penniless.

The prefix dis- *means "apart or away," "not," "absence of," or "to do the opposite of." When you add* dis- *to the word* loyal, *the meaning changes. If you are* disloyal, *you are not loyal.*

When I see the suffix -y *in a word, I'll know that the word is an adjective that means "having or like" something. When I see the suffix* -less, *I'll know the word is an adjective that means "without" something. When I see the prefix* dis-, *I'll know that the word means "apart or away," "not," "absence of," or "to do the opposite of" something.*

ENGLISH LEARNER SUPPORT: Build Vocabulary

SUBSTANTIAL
Show familiar words with the suffixes *-y* and *-less* and the prefix *dis-*. Discuss each base word's meaning and how the affix changes it.

MODERATE
Ask students to name words with each of the affixes and then identify the base word's meaning and tell how the affix changes it.

LIGHT
Have pairs share sentences with the lesson's *-y, -less, and dis-* words.

Step 2 Guided Practice

- Display the words *flowery, seriously,* and *displace*. Ask students to identify the suffix or prefix in each word and make predictions about the meanings, based on their knowledge of the affixes.
- Then ask students to look up each word in a print or online dictionary to confirm their predictions. Have volunteers provide a definition of each word.

Step 3 Apply the Skill

INDEPENDENT PRACTICE

- Have students work in pairs to complete Know It, Show It p. 57. Tell partners to read the instructions and have them complete the activity together.
- Then have each student write a new sentence for each word. Have partners read their sentences to one another to confirm the meaning of each word. Invite volunteers to read their sentences aloud.
- You may wish to have students complete the Know It, Show It page during Small Group time.

Spiral Review

Suffix *-ly* Remind students that a suffix is a word part added to the end of a word that changes the word's meaning.

- Review that the suffix *–ly* means "in a way that is or like" something. It changes a base word into an adverb that explains how or when something is done. Remind students that the spelling of a base word may change slightly when *–ly* is added. To add *–ly* to a base word ending in *y*, you must replace the final *y* with *i* before adding the suffix.
- Write these words on the board: *fond, crazy, close, wild*. Add the suffix *–ly* to each word. Have volunteers point out the suffix in each word and explain how it changes each word's meaning and part of speech.
- Have students add the suffix *–ly* to the following words: *immediate, merry, month, curious*. Have students explain how the endings change each word's meaning. Invite them to check the words' meanings in a print or online dictionary.

Text Structure

Step 1 Connect and Teach

LEARNING OBJECTIVES

- Recognize a sequence text structure.
- Analyze the author's purpose for using a sequence text structure.
- Recognize transition words that signal a sequence text structure.
- **Language** Identify transition words that signal a sequence text structure.

MATERIALS Online Ed

Anchor Chart 18 *Text Structure*

Printable *Anchor Chart 18: Text Structure*

Teaching Pal *Book 1, pp. 230–243*

myBook *The U. S. Constitution, Book 1, pp. 230–243*

Know It, Show It *p. 58*

INSTRUCTIONAL VOCABULARY

- **organization** the way a text is arranged to help readers understand the information
- **text structure** the way information is organized in a text

SPANISH COGNATES

- **text** *texto*
- **structure** *estructura*
- **sequence** *sequencia*

- Project or display Anchor Chart 18: Text Structure. Explain that **text structure** is the way information is organized in a text. Tell students that authors organize information in different ways, depending on their purpose and the ideas they are presenting. Draw attention to the section of the Anchor Chart that focuses on **sequence** as you explain the following:

Online

ANCHOR CHART 18: Text Structure

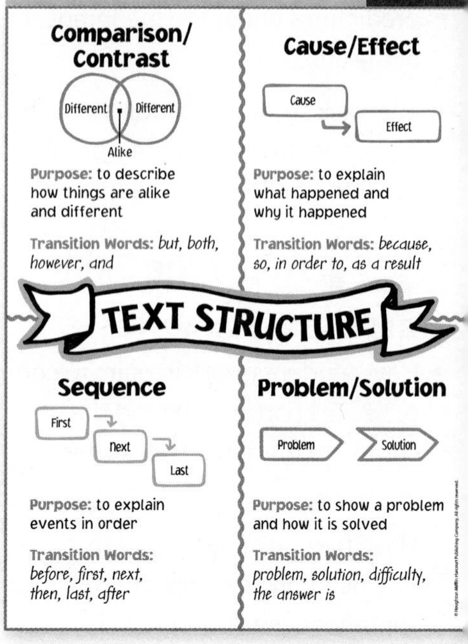

- Recognizing text structures helps readers connect ideas and events. Transition words provide clues to the structure of a text.
- When authors use a sequence text structure their purpose is to show how one event leads to the next. Sequence can indicate time order or steps in a process. Texts that describe historical events often use a sequence text structure to tell about the events in the order they happened.
- Transition words that signal sequence or time order include *before, first, next, then, last,* and *after*. Dates and times also signify sequence.

Discuss with students how identifying a text's structure can help them better understand the information in the text. Tell them that they will practice identifying text structure to gain a deeper understanding of *The U. S. Constitution*.

Go to Your
Teaching Pal

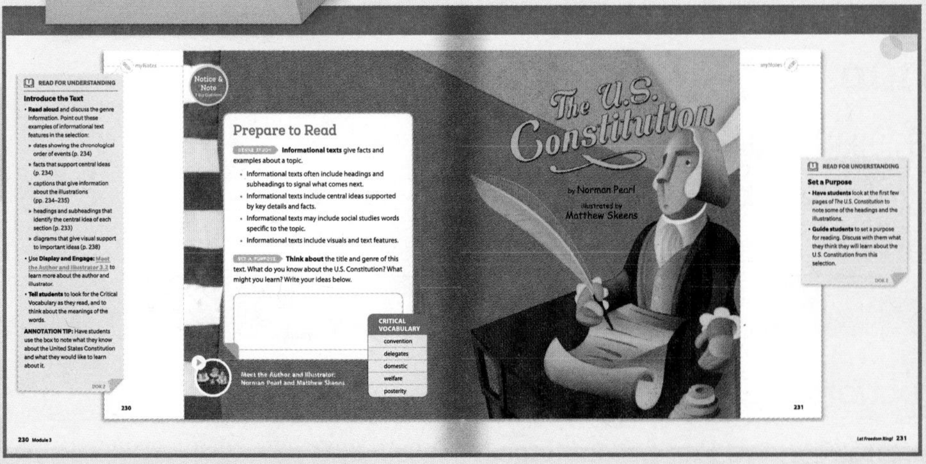
Prepare to Read

Informational texts give facts and examples about a topic.

- Informational texts often include headings and subheadings to signal what comes next.
- Informational texts include central ideas supported by key details and facts.
- Informational texts may include social studies words specific to the topic.
- Informational texts include visuals and text features.

Think about the title and genre of this text. What do you know about the U.S. Constitution? What might you learn? Write your ideas below.

Meet the Author and Illustrator: Norman Pearl and Matthew Skeens

CRITICAL VOCABULARY
convention
delegates
domestic
welfare
posterity

The U.S. Constitution

by Norman Pearl

illustrated by Matthew Skeens

Online Ed

ANNOTATE IT!

Students may use the annotation tools in their eBook.

Step 2 Apply to Text

In your Teaching Pal, use the purple **TARGETED CLOSE READ** prompts on pages 230—243 to guide students to apply the Text Structure skill to *The U. S. Constitution* and to find evidence to support their responses. Use the **CLOSE READING** routine. Students may refer to the questions on Know It, Show It page 58 as you discuss them.

- Read aloud the first question on Teaching Pal page 234. Then have students turn to *my*Book pages 233–234. Tell them to reread paragraphs 3–6 to analyze the text structure. Ask if the author has organized the text by cause-effect, problem-solution, or sequence. *(sequence)*
- Then read the follow-up question on Teaching Pal page 234. Discuss the author's purpose in using this text structure. *(The author wants to explain that the events in planning a new government took place in a particular time order.)*
- Refer back to the Anchor Chart to support the discussion. Students may add sticky notes to the chart to note other examples of a sequence text structure in *The U. S. Constitution*.

Step 3 Engage and Respond

INDEPENDENT PRACTICE: Writing

Explain to students that they are going to write a paragraph explaining how the Constitution was created. Use the **WRITING RESPONSE** routine. Have them review pages 233–235 of *The U. S. Constitution*.

- Suggest that after students reread the text, they make a timeline to show the order of events. They can then refer to the timeline when they write their paragraphs. Remind them to use transition words or phrases to signal the sequence of events.
- Have volunteers read their paragraphs aloud to a partner or small group. Invite other volunteers to identify the transition words used, and to discuss how this text structure helped them better understand the text.
- You may wish to have students complete their writing during daily small-group time.
- You may want to have students complete Know It, Show It page 58 during daily small-group time.

ENGLISH LEARNER SUPPORT: Elicit Participation

SUBSTANTIAL

Point to the words that show when _____. Let's say them together.

MODERATE

Which words show when _____ happened?

LIGHT

What transition words does the author use to show when _____ happened?

LINK TO SMALL-GROUP INSTRUCTION

REINFORCE TEXT STRUCTURE Review and extend the skill as needed during small-group time to support students' need for differentiation. *See the lesson on p. T67.*

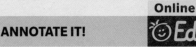

Options for Differentiation

As the class engages in independent and collaborative work, meet with Guided Reading Groups or differentiate instruction based on student need.

GUIDED READING GROUPS

Match Students to Books + Instruction

- Choose just-right books based on level, skill, topic, or genre.

L M N O P Q

Leveled Readers

- Deliver instruction with each book's **Take and Teach Lesson**, choosing appropriate sessions based on need.

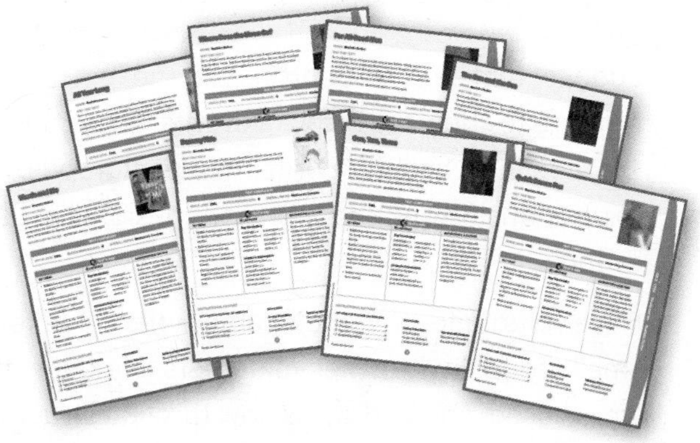

- Check comprehension, reinforce instruction, and extend learning with suggested supporting activities.

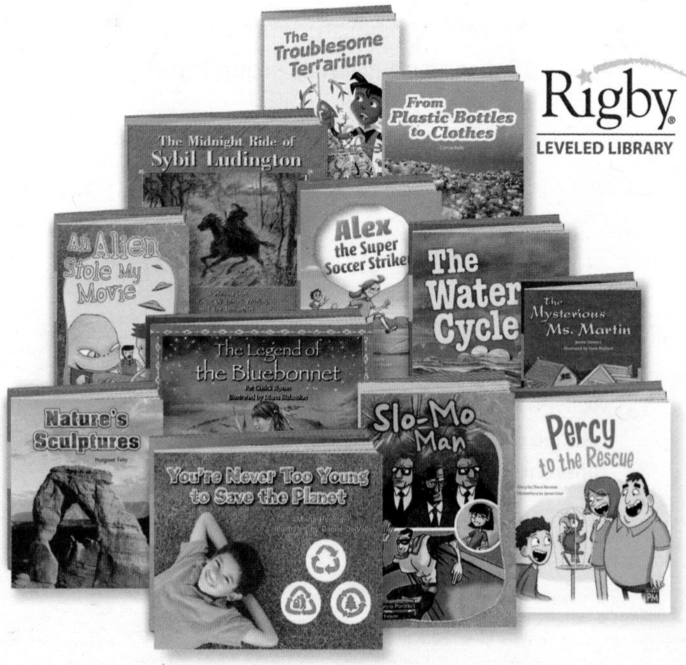

EL ENGLISH LEARNER SUPPORT

Synthesize

- Use **Tabletop Minilessons: English Language Development: 7.2 (Writing)** to reinforce and practice the language skill.

Tabletop Minilessons: English Language Development

- Then use the following text-based prompts with *The U.S. Constitution* to guide application of the language skill. Begin with the prompt at the student's identified language proficiency level. As students progress, use lighter supports to encourage increased language proficiency.

SUBSTANTIAL
Have students draw and label a picture that shows something they learned about the U.S. Constitution.

MODERATE
Have students complete the following written sentence frames: *I learned that the U.S. Constitution is _____ and _____.*

LIGHT
Have students create written responses to the following questions: *What did you know about the U.S. Constitution before you read the selection? What are your thoughts about the U.S. Constitution after having read the selection?*

REINFORCE TEXT STRUCTURE

Demonstrate

- Use **Tabletop Minilessons: Reading Card 18** to remind students that authors use specific kinds of text structure to help them communicate information. Review that one kind of text structure authors use is sequence. Authors use dates, times, and transition words such as *before, after, first, next, then,* and *last* to signal sequence.
- Model filling out Printable: Reading Graphic Organizer 18 to identify text structure in *The U.S. Constitution*.

Apply to Independent Reading

- Now have students identify the text structure in an appropriate book or article they are reading independently. Customize these prompts to the texts students choose.
  - » *What kind of text structure does the author use?*
  - » *What parts of the text help you to identify the text structure?*
  - » *What information does the text structure help to communicate?*
- Have students complete Printable: Reading Graphic Organizer 18 for their independent reading book.

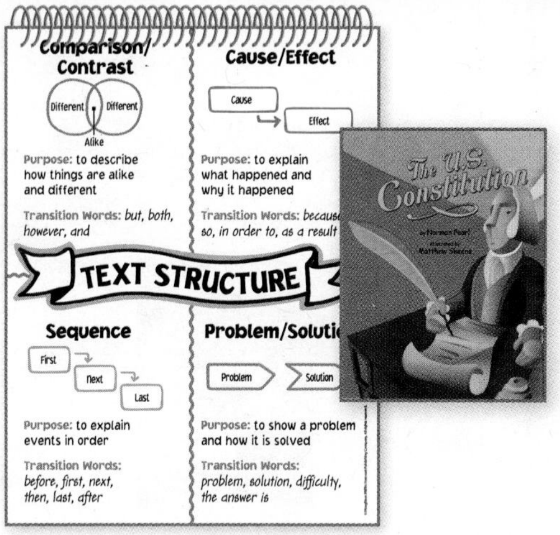

Tabletop Minilessons: Reading

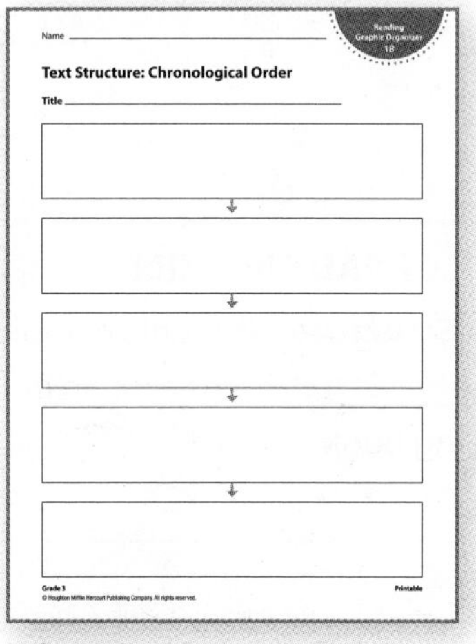

Printable: Reading Graphic Organizer 18

ALMOST THERE

READY FOR MORE

SCAFFOLD AND EXTEND

- Point out details in the text that indicate the text structure. Then help students to identify it.
- Prompt students to identify the text structure, the details in the text that indicate it, and the information it communicates.
- Have students identify the text structure and explain how it helps to communicate the information in the text.

EL ENGLISH LEARNER SUPPORT

SUBSTANTIAL

Have students point to places in the text or illustrations that show the text structure.

MODERATE

Have students complete the sentence frames: *The text structure is _____. An example in the text is _____.*

LIGHT

Encourage students to explain their reasoning as they answer the prompts.

Options for Independent and Collaborative Work

While you meet with small groups, have other students engage in literacy activities that reinforce the lesson's learning objectives. Choose from these options.

Independent Reading

Student Choice Library

Rigby
LEVELED LIBRARY

APPLY READING SKILL

Text Structure Students complete Printable: Reading Graphic Organizer 18 for an independent reading book.

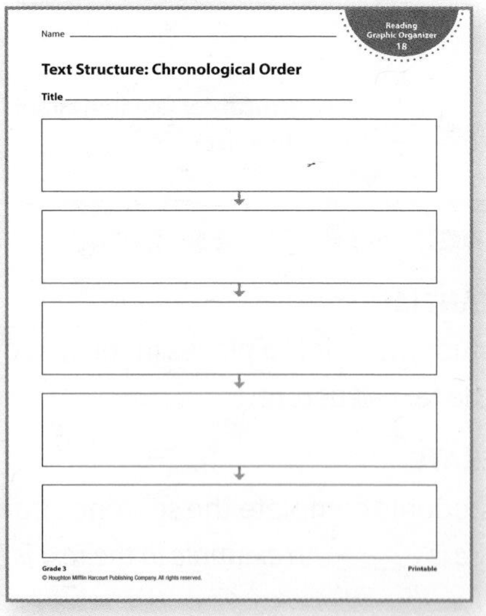

Name

Reading Graphic Organizer 18

Text Structure: Chronological Order

Title

Grade 3

Printable

Printable: Reading Graphic Organizer 18

APPLY LANGUAGE SKILL

Synthesize Students complete Printable: Language Graphic Organizer 15 for an independent reading book.

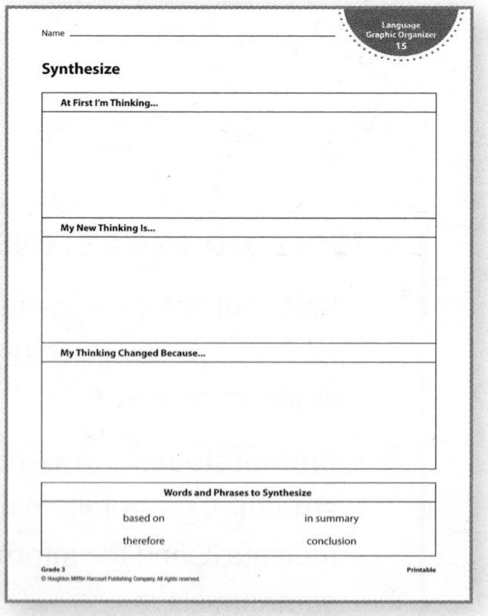

Name

Language Graphic Organizer 15

Synthesize

At First I'm Thinking...

My New Thinking Is...

My Thinking Changed Because...

Words and Phrases to Synthesize

based on	in summary
therefore	conclusion

Grade 3

Printable

Printable: Language Graphic Organizer 15

Literacy Centers

See pp. T24–T25.

- READING CENTER
- VOCABULARY CENTER
- DIGITAL STATION
- WRITING CENTER
- PROJECT CENTER

Writing

Students write a paragraph explaining how the Constitution was created. *See Engage and Respond, p. T65.*

Additional Skills Practice

Generative Vocabulary

Name ________________

Suffixes -y, -less; Prefix dis-

A **suffix** is a word part added to the end of a base word that changes the meaning of the word. A **prefix** is a word part added to the beginning of a base word that changes the meaning of the word.

Add the suffix -y or -less or the prefix dis- to the words below to form words that complete each sentence.

like curve shoe agree grain soap

1. I use lots of ___soapy___ water to wash my dog.
2. Don't give Nick and Trey any pickles because they both ___dislike___ sour foods.
3. Remember to go ___shoeless___ in the house so the floors don't get dirty.
4. This trail is very ___curvy___ and loops around the mountain three times.
5. If you ___disagree___ with me, you're probably wrong.
6. The ___grainy___ beach sand is still stuck between my toes.

Grade 3 57 Module 3 • Week 1

© Houghton Mifflin Harcourt Publishing Company. All rights reserved.

Know It, Show It, p. 57

Comprehension

Name ________________

Text Structure

Text structure is the way information is organized in a text. Authors may use the **sequence** text structure to tell events in the order that they happened. Authors use transition words to provide clues to the structure.

Answer the questions about pages 233–234 of *The U.S. Constitution*.

1. How has the author organized the information, by cause-effect, problem-solution, or sequence?
   sequence
2. Why has the author used the text structure of sequence in this selection?
   The author wants to explain that the events in planning a new government took place in a particular time order.

Choose another section of *The U.S. Constitution*.

3. How has the author organized the information?
   Responses will vary.
4. Why has the author used that text structure in this section?
   Responses will vary.

Grade 3 58 Module 3 • Week 1

© Houghton Mifflin Harcourt Publishing Company. All rights reserved.

Know It, Show It, p. 58

Wrap-Up

Share Time

At the end of the Reading Workshop, have students reflect on their learning by sharing how they applied **text structure** or another area of focus during independent work time. Choose from these options:

- Use the **SOLO CHAIR** routine. Select a reader each day to come to the front of the class and tell what he or she learned from the reading by using a skill or strategy.
- **THINK-PAIR-SHARE** Students share their thinking with a partner. Select a few pairs each day to share with the whole class.
- **RETURN TO ANCHOR CHART** Have students add sticky notes about their independent reading book to the Text Structure Anchor Chart. Call on a few students to explain what they added.

Online Ed

ANCHOR CHART 18: Text Structure

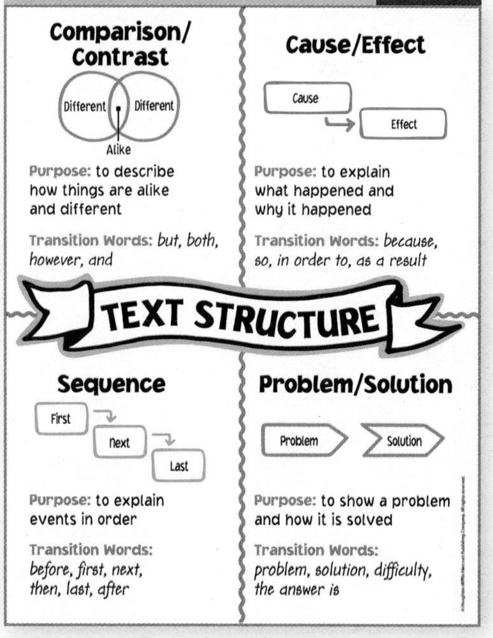

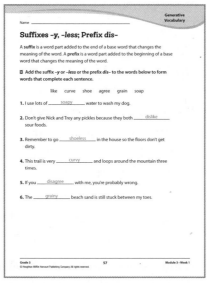

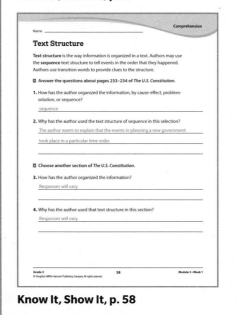

Vocabulary Spiral Review

Step 1 Review Vocabulary

LEARNING OBJECTIVES

- Review vocabulary.
- Identify real-life connections between words and their use.
- Create word webs using vocabulary.
- **Language** Discuss target vocabulary words and expand vocabulary knowledge by creating word webs.

MATERIALS — Online Ed

Display and Engage *2.2a, 2.2b*
Vocabulary Cards *2.1, 2.2, 2.9, 2.13, 2.17, 2.19*
myBook *p. 108*

- Tell students they will review some of the Critical Vocabulary they have learned so far this year and complete an activity based on those words.
- Project Display and Engage: **Critical Vocabulary 2.2a** and **Critical Vocabulary 2.2b** to remind students of the Module 2, Week 2 Critical Vocabulary words and their meanings. Also, use *my*Book page 108 to review the Module 2 Big Idea words.
- After reviewing the meanings, call out words and have volunteers take turns using the words in sentences of their own. If students are having trouble creating sentences, have them give synonyms or antonyms for the word.
- Continue until all students have had a chance to work with one or more of the words.

Online
DISPLAY AND ENGAGE:
Critical Vocabulary 2.2a, 2.2b

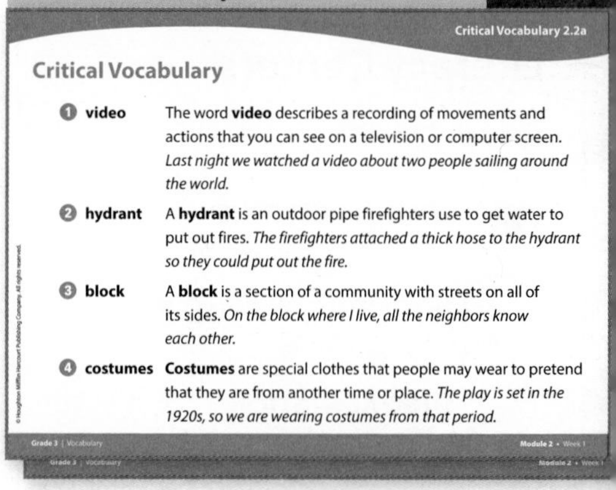
Critical Vocabulary 2.2a

Critical Vocabulary

1 **video** The word **video** describes a recording of movements and actions that you can see on a television or computer screen. *Last night we watched a video about two people sailing around the world.*

2 **hydrant** A **hydrant** is an outdoor pipe firefighters use to get water to put out fires. *The firefighters attached a thick hose to the hydrant so they could put out the fire.*

3 **block** A **block** is a section of a community with streets on all of its sides. *On the block where I live, all the neighbors know each other.*

4 **costumes** **Costumes** are special clothes that people may wear to pretend that they are from another time or place. *The play is set in the 1920s, so we are wearing costumes from that period.*

Grade 3 | Vocabulary   Module 2 • Week 1

Step 2 Guided Practice

- Use Vocabulary Cards 2.1, 2.2, 2.9, 2.13, 2.17, and 2.19 to remind students of the meanings of the words *express, convey, march, speed, assigned,* and *retains*.
- Help students determine that all the words are verbs. If necessary, review with students how verbs are used.
- Write the verb *express* on the board and circle it to form the center of a word web. Elicit from students the word's meaning.

- Add other blank circles radiating out from *express*, and ask students to think of synonyms for the verb. Remind them they can use a dictionary or thesaurus to look for synonyms, being sure to look under the correct part of speech.

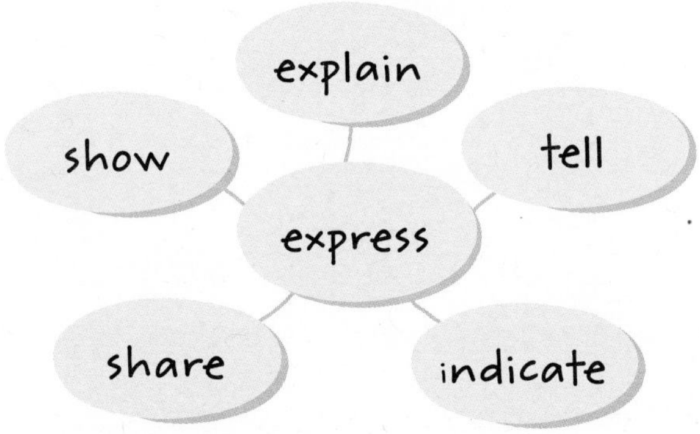

- Display this sentence: *I often _____ my feelings by writing in my journal.* Have students complete the sentence with each of the verbs, noting how the sentence changes.

Step 3 Apply the Skill

- Pair students to create their own word webs using some of the Critical Vocabulary words.
- Have pairs choose three verbs from the Vocabulary Cards and work together to create a word web for each word. Tell students they can use the Vocabulary Cards to remind them of the words' meanings and refer to a dictionary or thesaurus to help them find synonyms.
- Have students create a sentence stem for each web to show the difference in the synonyms' meanings.
- Allow time for students to share their webs and sentences.

ENGLISH LEARNER SUPPORT: Create Word Webs

SUBSTANTIAL
Review word meanings and ask students *yes/no* questions to confirm understanding. Then help guide students to build their webs.

MODERATE
Have students work with more English-fluent partners to discuss the words and to create their word webs.

LIGHT
Facilitate classroom dialogue, including recasting and prompting, as necessary, as partners share ideas and present their webs and sentences.

Text and Graphic Features

Step 1 Connect and Teach

LEARNING OBJECTIVES

- Recognize and explain the author's use of text features.
- **Language** Identify text and graphic features and articulate their purposes.

MATERIALS Online Ed

Anchor Chart 20 *Text and Graphic Features*

Printable *Anchor Chart 20: Text and Graphic Features*

Teaching Pal *Book 1, pp. 230–243*

myBook *The U.S. Constitution, Book 1, pp. 230–243*

Know It, Show It *p. 58*

INSTRUCTIONAL VOCABULARY

- **heading** the title for a page or a section of text that helps to organize
- **label** words that name the parts of a picture
- **sidebar** a feature on a page containing special information about a topic
- **subsection** a smaller part of a section of text
- **text feature** part of a text, such as punctuation, label, or a style of text, that calls out something important

SPANISH COGNATES

- **text** *texto*

- Remind students that authors of informational text often use **text and graphic features** such as headings, subheadings, sidebars, and labels to help explain the ideas in the text.
- Project or display Anchor Chart 20: Text and Graphic Features.
- Explain that authors use **headings** and **subheadings** to let the reader know what each section of text is about. These text features help readers to find information in a text more quickly.
- Tell students that an author might put **labels** on illustrations to help the reader connect the illustrations and the text. They might include **sidebars** to explain or highlight specific information related to the topic.

Online

ANCHOR CHART 20: Text and Graphic Features

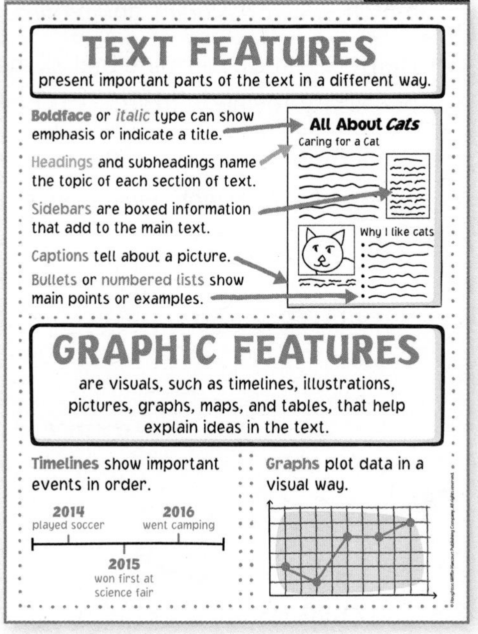

- Tell students that they will practice using these text and graphic features to better understand the important ideas in *The U. S. Constitution.*

LEARNING MINDSET

Grit

Model Remind students that the framers of the U.S. Constitution were determined to make the document better for America. *They knew that they didn't get it right the first time, so they kept trying. I try to be like that when I'm learning something new. Sometimes it's really hard, but I usually get it if I keep trying.*

Go to Your **Teaching Pal**

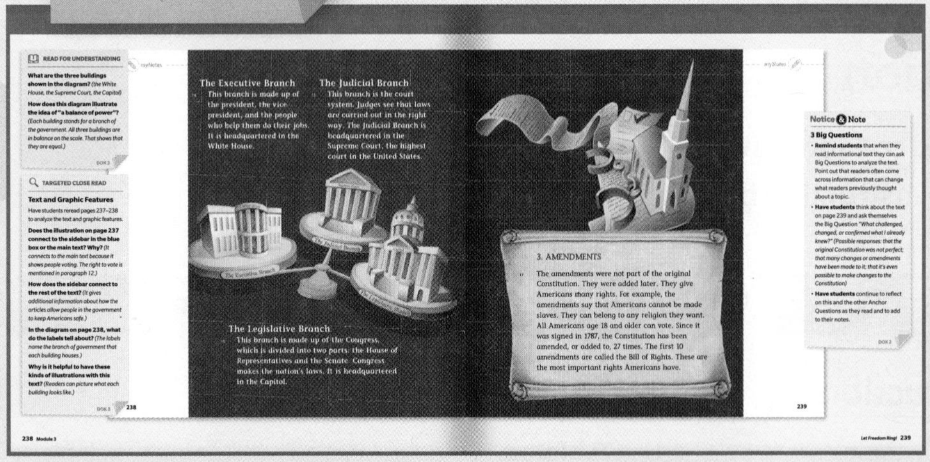

READ FOR UNDERSTANDING

What are the three buildings shown in the diagram? *(the White House, the Supreme Court, the Capitol)*

How does this diagram illustrate the idea of "a balance of power"? *(Each building stands for a branch of the government. All three buildings are in balance on the scale. That shows that they are equal.)*

DOK 3

TARGETED CLOSE READ

Text and Graphic Features

Have students reread pages 237–238 to analyze the text and graphic features.

Does the illustration on page 237 connect to the sidebar in the blue box or the main text? Why? *(It connects to the main text because it shows people voting. The right to vote is mentioned in paragraph 12.)*

How does the sidebar connect to the rest of the text? *(It gives additional information about how the articles allow people in the government to keep Americans safe.)*

In the diagram on page 238, what do the labels tell about? *(The labels name the branch of government that each building houses.)*

Why is it helpful to have these kinds of illustrations with this text? *(Readers can picture what each building looks like.)*

DOK 3

myNotes

The Executive Branch

This branch is made up of the president, the vice president, and the people who help them do their jobs. It is headquartered in the White House.

The Judicial Branch

This branch is the court system. Judges see that laws are carried out in the right way. The Judicial Branch is headquartered in the Supreme Court, the highest court in the United States.

The Legislative Branch

This branch is made up of the Congress, which is divided into two parts: the House of Representatives and the Senate. Congress makes the nation's laws. It is headquartered in the Capitol.

238

3. AMENDMENTS

17 The amendments were not part of the original Constitution. They were added later. They give Americans many rights. For example, the amendments say that Americans cannot be made slaves. They can belong to any religion they want. All Americans age 18 and older can vote. Since it was signed in 1787, the Constitution has been amended, or added to, 27 times. The first 10 amendments are called the Bill of Rights. These are the most important rights Americans have.

myNotes

239

Notice & Note

3 Big Questions

- **Remind students** that when they read informational text they can ask Big Questions to analyze the text. Point out that readers often come across information that can change what readers previously thought about a topic.
- **Have students** think about the text on page 239 and ask themselves the Big Question *"What challenged, changed, or confirmed what I already knew?" (Possible responses: that the original Constitution was not perfect; that many changes or amendments have been made to it; that it's even possible to make changes to the Constitution)*
- **Have students** continue to reflect on this and the other Anchor Questions as they read and to add to their notes.

DOK 2

238 Module 3

Let Freedom Ring! 239

Online Ed

ANNOTATE IT!

Students may use the annotation tools in their eBook.

Step 2 Apply to Text

In your **Teaching Pal**, use the prompt on the purple **TARGETED CLOSE READ** note on page 238 to guide students to apply the Text and Graphic Features skill to *The U. S. Constitution*. Use the **CLOSE READING** routine. Students may refer to the questions on Know It, Show It page 55 as you discuss them.

- Read aloud the first two questions on Teaching Pal page 238. Have students reread pages 237–238 in their *my*Book. Discuss how the illustration and sidebar connect to the text. *(The illustration connects to the main text because it shows people voting. The right to vote is mentioned in paragraph 12. The sidebar gives additional information about how the articles allow people in the government to keep Americans safe.)*
- Then read the last two questions on Teaching Pal page 238. Have students explain the purpose of the graphic features. *(The labels name the branch of government that each building houses. Readers can picture what each building looks like.)*
- Refer to the Anchor Chart to support discussion. Have students use sticky notes to add examples of text and graphic features to the chart as they encounter them.

Step 3 Engage and Respond

INDEPENDENT PRACTICE: Reading

- Have pairs of students look through a science or social studies text to find a section with text and graphic features similar to those in the selection.
- Tell students to use a T-chart to list the text and graphic features they find and explain the purpose of each. Remind them of the text and graphic features they learned about when reading *American Places, American Ideals* and *The U.S. Constitution.*
- Have partners use the **COLLABORATIVE DISCUSSION** routine to discuss text and graphic features. Call on pairs to share their responses.
- You may wish to have students complete the reading activity during daily small-group time.
- You may wish to have students complete Know It, Show It page 55 during daily small-group time.

EL ENGLISH LEARNER SUPPORT: Elicit Participation

SUBSTANTIAL

Point to a _____. Which text feature shows you _____?

MODERATE

Provide this type of sentence frame: *The <label/sidebar/heading> explains _____.*

LIGHT

Invite students to identify and explain the purposes of the text and graphic features.

LINK TO SMALL-GROUP INSTRUCTION

REINFORCE TEXT AND GRAPHIC FEATURES Review or extend the skill as needed during small-group time to support students' need for differentiation. *See p. T75.*

Options for Differentiation

As the class engages in independent and collaborative work, meet with Guided Reading Groups or differentiate instruction based on student need.

GUIDED READING GROUPS

Match Students to Books + Instruction

- Choose just-right books based on level, skill, topic, or genre.

L → M → N → O → P → Q

Leveled Readers

- Deliver instruction with each book's **Take and Teach Lesson**, choosing appropriate sessions based on need.

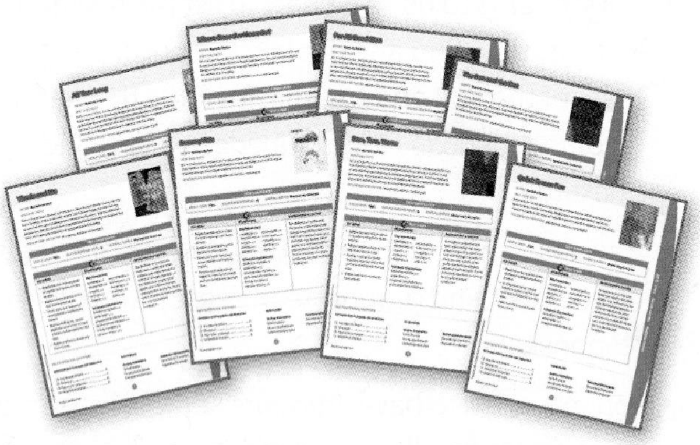

- Check comprehension, reinforce instruction, and extend learning with suggested supporting activities.

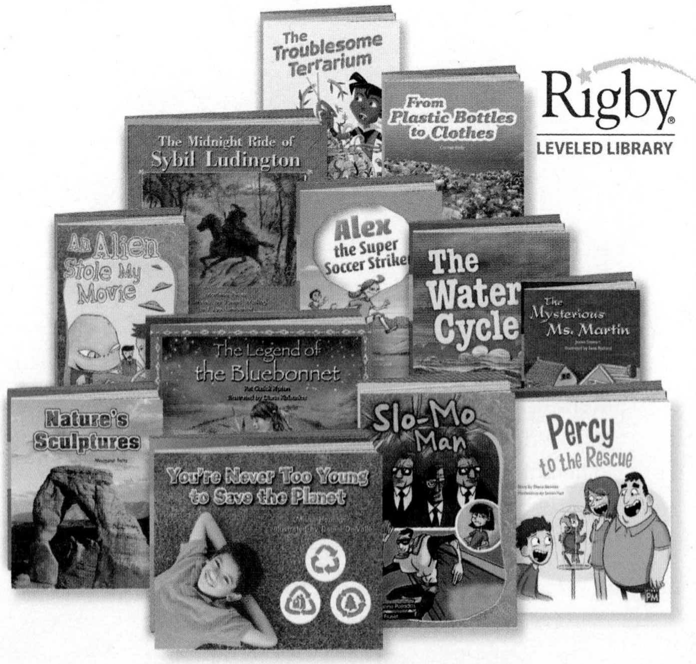

EL ENGLISH LEARNER SUPPORT

Synthesize

- Use **Tabletop Minilessons: English Language Development 7.3 (Collaborative Problem Solving)** to reinforce and practice the language skill.

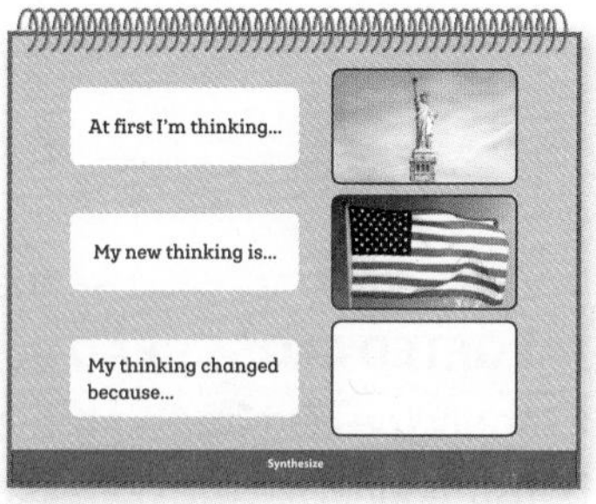

Tabletop Minilessons: English Language Development

- Then use the following text-based prompts with *The U.S. Constitution* to guide application of the language skill. Begin with the prompt at the students' identified language proficiency level. As students progress, use lighter supports to encourage increased language proficiency.

SUBSTANTIAL

Have students work together to draw and label a diagram that shows the three branches of government, and then present it orally.

MODERATE

Guide students to work together to make a poster that answers the question, *So how does the Constitution work for you?* Have them list and illustrate reasons from the text and examples from their own lives.

LIGHT

As a group, have students act out what they imagine the Constitutional Convention was like, using details from the selection.

REINFORCE TEXT AND GRAPHIC FEATURES

Demonstrate

- Use **Tabletop Minilessons: Reading Card 20** to remind students that authors use **text and graphic features** help to organize text and communicate key ideas. For instance, **headings** and **subheadings** let the reader know what sections of text are about. **Labels** help readers connect images to the text. **Sidebars** give information that is not included in the main text, but is related to the topic.
- Model filling out Printable: Reading Graphic Organizer 16 to identify text and graphic features in *American Places, American Ideals*.

Apply to Independent Reading

- Now have students identify the text and graphic features in an appropriate book or article they are reading independently. Customize these prompts to the texts students choose.
  - » *What text and graphic features are in the text?*
  - » *How do the text and graphic features help to organize information?*
  - » *How do the text and graphic features help you to better understand the text?*
- Have students complete Printable: Reading Graphic Organizer 16 for their independent reading book.

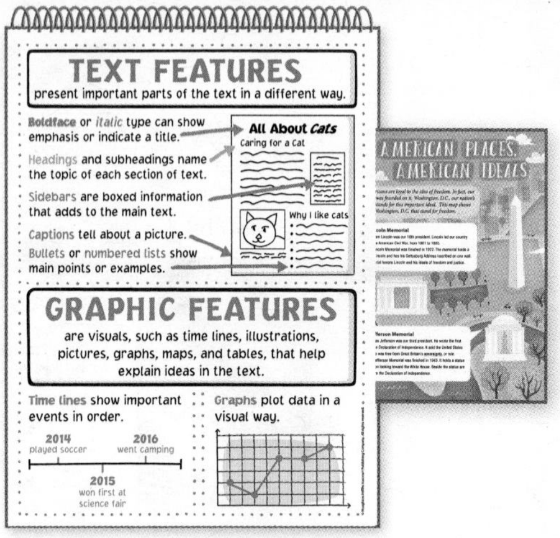

Tabletop Minilessons: Reading

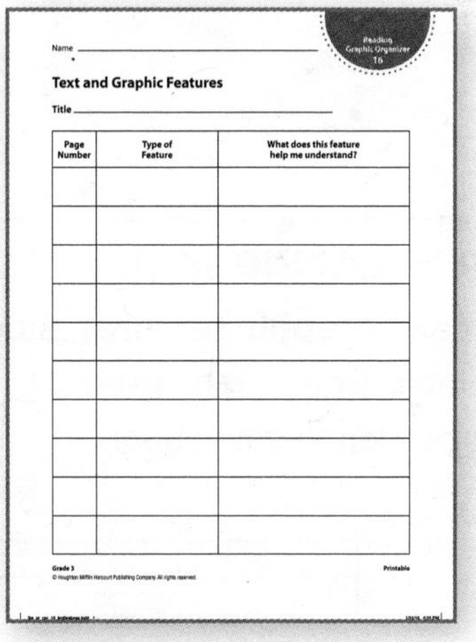

Printable: Reading Graphic Organizer 16

SCAFFOLD AND EXTEND

ALMOST THERE

READY FOR MORE

- Help students identify text and graphic features and how they organize and communicate information.
- Prompt students to identify the text and graphic features and how they communicate information.
- Have students explain how the text and graphic features communicate information in a way that text alone cannot.

EL ENGLISH LEARNER SUPPORT

SUBSTANTIAL
Guide students to point to and name each of the text and graphic features.

MODERATE
Have students complete the sentence frames: *This text/graphic feature is ____. It helps me to understand ____.*

LIGHT
Encourage students to explain how text and graphic features helped them understand the text.

Options for Independent and Collaborative Work

While you meet with small groups, have other students engage in literacy activities that reinforce the lesson's learning objectives. Choose from these options.

Independent Reading

Student Choice Library

Rigby
LEVELED LIBRARY

APPLY READING SKILL

Text and Graphic Features Students complete Printable: Reading Graphic Organizer 16 for an independent reading book.

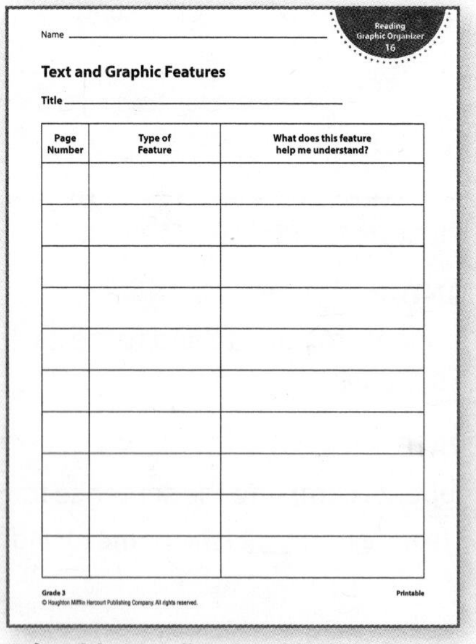

Name ____________

Reading Graphic Organizer 16

Text and Graphic Features

Title ____________

Page Number	Type of Feature	What does this feature help me understand?

Grade 3
© Houghton Mifflin Harcourt Publishing Company. All rights reserved.
Printable

Printable: Reading Graphic Organizer 16

APPLY LANGUAGE SKILL

Synthesize Students complete Printable: Language Graphic Organizer 15 for an independent reading book.

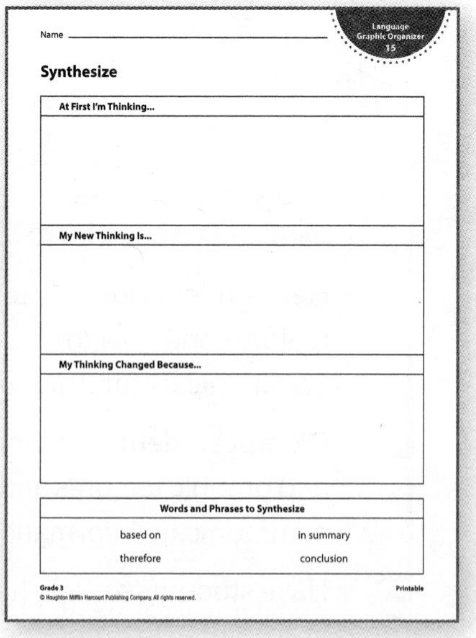

Name ____________

Language Graphic Organizer 15

Synthesize

At First I'm Thinking...

My New Thinking Is...

My Thinking Changed Because...

Words and Phrases to Synthesize	
based on	in summary
therefore	conclusion

Grade 3
© Houghton Mifflin Harcourt Publishing Company. All rights reserved.
Printable

Printable: Language Graphic Organizer 15

Literacy Centers

See pp. T24–T25.

- READING CENTER
- VOCABULARY CENTER
- DIGITAL STATION
- WRITING CENTER
- PROJECT CENTER

Reading

Students read and identify text and graphic features in the text. *See Engage and Respond, p. T73.*

Additional Skills Practice

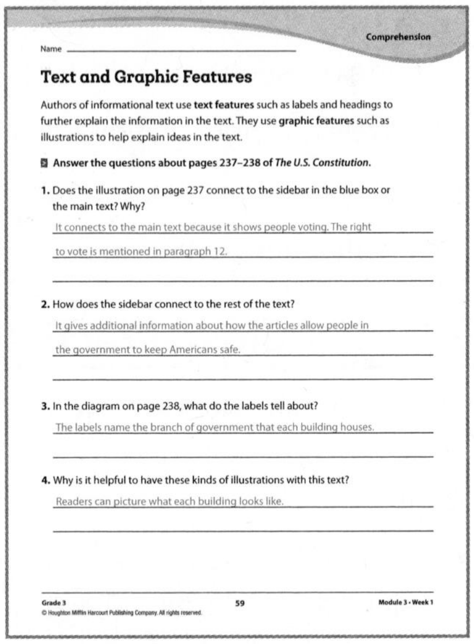
Comprehension

Name ____________

Text and Graphic Features

Authors of informational text use **text features** such as labels and headings to further explain the information in the text. They use **graphic features** such as illustrations to help explain ideas in the text.

Answer the questions about pages 237–238 of *The U.S. Constitution*.

1. Does the illustration on page 237 connect to the sidebar in the blue box or the main text? Why?
   It connects to the main text because it shows people voting. The right to vote is mentioned in paragraph 12.
2. How does the sidebar connect to the rest of the text?
   It gives additional information about how the articles allow people in the government to keep Americans safe.
3. In the diagram on page 238, what do the labels tell about?
   The labels name the branch of government that each building houses.
4. Why is it helpful to have these kinds of illustrations with this text?
   Readers can picture what each building looks like.

Grade 3 59 Module 3 • Week 1
© Houghton Mifflin Harcourt Publishing Company. All rights reserved.

Know It, Show It, p. 59

Wrap-Up

Share Time

At the end of the Reading Workshop, have students reflect on their learning by sharing how they applied **text and graphic geatures** or another area of focus during independent work time. Choose from these options:

- Use the **SOLO CHAIR** routine. Select a reader each day to come to the front of the class and tell what he or she learned from the reading by using a skill or strategy.
- **THINK-PAIR-SHARE** Students share their thinking with a partner. Select a few pairs each day to share with the whole class.
- **RETURN TO ANCHOR CHART** Have students add sticky notes about their independent reading to the Text and Graphic Features Anchor Chart. Call on a few students to explain what they added and why.

ANCHOR CHART 16: Text and Graphic Features

Online Ed

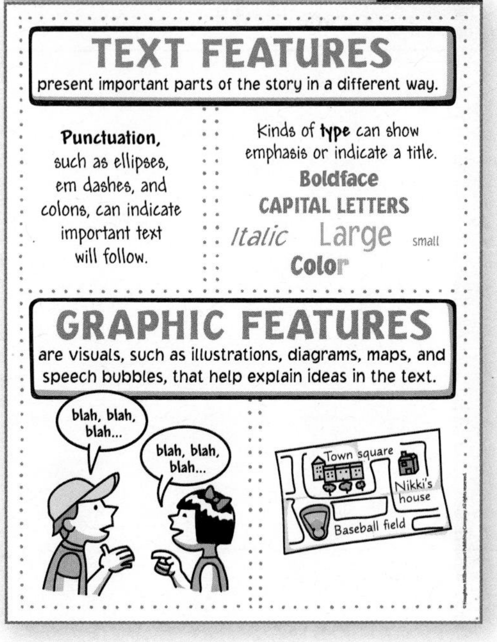

Take Notes

Step 1 Introduce the Skill

Discuss Taking Notes Tell students that taking notes means listing the important facts and details to remember about a topic. They will gather information and take notes to further explore the Essential Question, *How do historic places, documents, and symbols represent our nation?* Discuss note-taking steps.

- Write a question about the topic you are researching.
- Find relevant print or digital sources that can answer the question.
- Write notes in your own words on notecards. Write only one fact per card.
- Write the source's title and author for each note.

Step 2 Guided Practice

Prepare to Take Notes Have students brainstorm a question they want to answer about one historic place, document, or symbol they want to learn more about.

- Guide students to find two relevant print or digital sources that could answer their research question. Tell them they will take notes on these sources.
- Discuss the difference between primary and secondary sources. Say: *You can find the text of the original* U.S. Constitution *online. That's a primary source. The selection we read this week,* The U.S. Constitution, *is about the* Constitution, *but it is not the original document. So it is a secondary source.*
- Model taking notes in your own words, one fact per notecard, with the source title and author listed.

Step 3 Apply the Skill

Take Notes Have students use notecards to take notes on their chosen sources.

- Monitor students to make sure they are following the note-taking rules.
- Have students share their notes with the class, and how they helped to answer their research question.

LEARNING OBJECTIVES

- Gather and sort information to take notes.
- Develop research questions.
- Demonstrate taking notes.
- **Language** Identify and internalize key vocabulary to communicate ideas about a research topic.

MATERIALS

Online Ed

Classroom materials *computer with Internet access, informational books and articles, notecards*

INSTRUCTIONAL VOCABULARY

- **brainstorm:** to think of a lot of ideas quickly before thinking about them more carefully later
- **primary source:** an original document, interview, or information from someone who has witnessed an event
- **research:** to study and find out about a subject
- **secondary source:** books, articles, or reports based on research someone else did

ENGLISH LEARNER SUPPORT: Support Note-Taking

SUBSTANTIAL

Read a portion of the source text aloud. Students may point to words and pictures to explain information they would note. Guide them to write and read their note in English.

MODERATE

Guide students to use key words in the text to help them write their notes. Provide language clarification as needed. Remind them not to copy the text exactly.

LIGHT

Use guiding questions to help students take notes, such as: *Does this information help to answer my research question? How can I say this in my own words?*

Synthesize Topic Knowledge

Genre Focus

- Review with students the characteristics of informational text. Explain that the key feature of informational text is that it gives facts and information about a subject.
- Discuss with students examples of informational text they have encountered this week and why each of them is informational text: *American Places, American Ideals* and *The U.S. Constitution.*
- Ask students to name the topic of the informational text and the key points of information it provides about the topic.

LEARNING OBJECTIVES

- Recognize and describe the features of informational text.
- Synthesize knowledge gained from the week's texts.
- **Language** Articulate what has been learned about the essential question from their reading.

MATERIALS

Online Ed

myBook *Book 1, pp. 226–227, 230–241*

Display and Engage *Knowledge Map 3.5*

Knowledge Focus

- Project Display and Engage: **Knowledge Map 3.5**. Have students turn to *myBook* page 226.
- Tell students to think about what they have learned about how historic places, documents, and symbols represent our nation from reading *American Places, American Ideals.* (Places, such as the Lincoln Memorial, Washington Monument, Jefferson Memorial, White House, and U.S. Capitol are symbols of America and its ideals.)

Online Ed

DISPLAY AND ENGAGE:
Knowledge Map 3.5

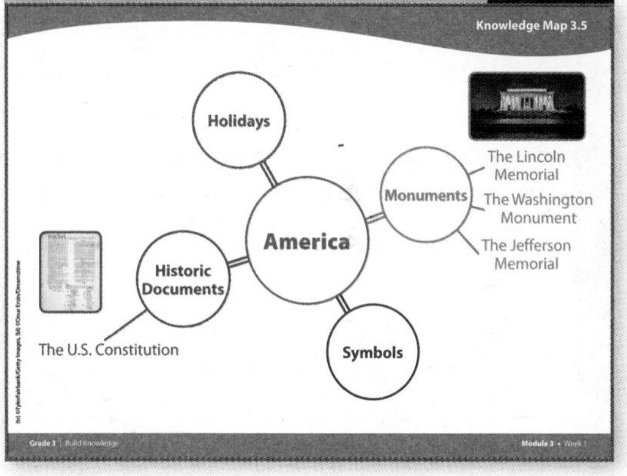

- Then work with students to add information from *The U.S. Constitution* to the "Historical Documents" section of the Knowledge Map.
- Have students discuss their Knowledge Maps and their responses to the Essential Question: *How do historic places, documents, and symbols represent our nation?*
- Tell students that they will return to the Knowledge Map for the Week 2 Make Connections activity.

ENGLISH LEARNER SUPPORT: Facilitate Discussion

SUBSTANTIAL

Help students to connect the reading to the Essential Question: *Some American places that represent our nation are _____. The U.S. Constitution is a _____ that represents our nation.*

MODERATE

Prompt students to connect the reading to the Essential Question. *The U.S. Constitution represents our nation because _____.*

LIGHT

Ask students to connect the reading to the Essential Question. Supply frames such as: ____ *represents our nation by _____.*

Notes

SOCIAL STUDIES CONNECTION:
U.S. History

Let Freedom Ring!

Essential Question How do historic places, documents, and symbols represent our nation?

Essential Skills

VOCABULARY

- Critical Vocabulary: *endowed, declaring, independence, presented, gritty, hoisted, broad*
- Vocabulary Strategy: Multiple Meaning Words
- Generative Vocabulary: Suffix *–er/–est* with spelling change; Spiral Review: Suffixes *–y, –less*; Prefix *dis–*

READING WORKSHOP

- Retell/Summarize
- Media Techniques
- Text Structure
- Content-Area Words

FOUNDATIONAL SKILLS

- Decoding: Words with /j/, /k/, and /kw/
- Spelling: Words with /j/, /k/, and /kw/
- Fluency: Phrasing

COMMUNICATION

- Media Literacy: Interpret/Analyze Media
- Make Connections

WRITING WORKSHOP

- Informational Writing
- Using Commas

LEARNING MINDSET: Grit

THIS WEEK'S SELECTIONS

MEDIA: EDUCATIONAL VIDEO
Why We Celebrate the Fourth of July

NARRATIVE NONFICTION
The Flag Maker

Rigby
LEVELED LIBRARY

WEEK 2

Week at a Glance

Suggested Daily Times

- VOCABULARY 10–15 minutes
- READING WORKSHOP 60–85 minutes
- FOUNDATIONAL SKILLS 15–30 minutes
- COMMUNICATION 15–30 minutes
- WRITING WORKSHOP 30–45 minutes

This Week's Words

BIG IDEA WORDS

loyal *sovereignty* *democracy* *civic*

CRITICAL VOCABULARY WORDS

endowed *declaring* *independence*
presented *gritty* *hoisted*
broad

HIGH-FREQUENCY WORDS

time *months* *century*

INSTRUCTIONAL VOCABULARY

summarize *live action* *media*
media techniques *sound elements* *conflict*
resolution *retell* *sequence*
text structure *content-area words*
context clue

Assessment Options

Online Ed

- **Selection Quiz: *Why We Celebrate the Fourth of July***
- **Selection Quiz: *The Flag Maker***
- **Weekly Assessment**
  - Comprehension: Media Techniques, Text Structure, Content-Area Words
  - Generative Vocabulary: Suffixes *-er/-est* with spelling change
  - Vocabulary Strategy: Multiple Meaning Words
  - Grammar: Using Commas

Intervention

For students needing strategic intervention, choose from daily small-group options for differentiation. Access online Foundational Skills and Word Study Studio for additional support.

LESSON 6

VOCABULARY

Academic Vocabulary, pp. T88–T89

- Introduce Critical Vocabulary: *endowed, declaring, independence, presented*

READING WORKSHOP

Why We Celebrate the Fourth of July

Teaching Pal

GENRE Media: Educational Video

Shared Reading: MINILESSON, pp. T90–T91

- Connect and Teach: Retell/Summarize
- Apply to Text: ***Why We Celebrate the Fourth of July***
- Engage and Respond: Speaking and Listening

SMALL-GROUP INSTRUCTION

Options for Differentiation

- Guided Reading Groups, p. T92
- English Learner Support: Recount Information, p. T92
- Reinforce Retell/Summarize, p. T93

Options for Independent and Collaborative Work, pp. T94–T95

FOUNDATIONAL SKILLS

Decoding, pp. T96–T97

- Words with /j/, /k/, and /kw/

Spelling, p. T98

- Words with /j/, /k/, and /kw/

Fluency, p. T99

- Phrasing

WRITING WORKSHOP

Descriptive Essay, p. W41

- Drafting II: Organizing a Description

Grammar, p. W320

- Commas in a Series of Nouns

LESSON 7

VOCABULARY

Academic Vocabulary, p. T100

- Review Critical Vocabulary: *endowed, declaring, independence, presented*

Vocabulary Strategy, p. T101

- Multiple Meaning Words

READING WORKSHOP

Why We Celebrate the Fourth of July

Teaching Pal

GENRE Media: Educational Video

Shared Reading: MINILESSON, pp. T102–T103

- Connect and Teach: Media Techniques
- Apply to Text: ***Why We Celebrate the Fourth of July***
- Engage and Respond: Write a Summary

SMALL-GROUP INSTRUCTION

Options for Differentiation

- Guided Reading Groups, p. T104
- English Learner Support: Recount Information, p. T104
- Reinforce Media Techniques, p. T105

Options for Independent and Collaborative Work, pp. T106–T107

COMMUNICATION

Project Checkpoint: Write and Create, pp. T17, T85

WRITING WORKSHOP

Descriptive Essay, p. W42

- Drafting III: Moving into the Draft

Grammar, p. W321

- Commas in a Series of Verbs

LESSON 8

VOCABULARY

Academic Vocabulary, pp. T108–T109
- Introduce Critical Vocabulary: *gritty, hoisted, broad*

READING WORKSHOP

The Flag Maker
Teaching Pal
GENRE Narrative Nonfiction
Shared Reading: MINILESSON, pp. T110–T111
- Connect and Teach: Retell/Summarize
- Apply to Text: ***The Flag Maker***
- Engage and Respond: Speaking and Listening

SMALL-GROUP INSTRUCTION

Options for Differentiation
- Guided Reading Groups, p. T112
- English Learner Support: Recount Information, p. T112
- Reinforce Retell/Summarize, p. T113

Options for Independent and Collaborative Work, pp. T114–T115

FOUNDATIONAL SKILLS

Decoding, pp. T116–T117
- Words with /j/, /k/, and /kw/

WRITING WORKSHOP

Descriptive Essay, p. W43
- Drafting IV: Completing the Draft

Grammar, p. W322
- Commas in Addresses

LESSON 9

VOCABULARY

Academic Vocabulary, p. T118
- Review Critical Vocabulary: *gritty, hoisted, broad*

Vocabulary Strategy, p. T119
- Multiple Meaning Words

READING WORKSHOP

The Flag Maker
Teaching Pal
GENRE Narrative Nonfiction
Shared Reading: MINILESSON, pp. T120–T121
- Connect and Teach: Text Structure
- Apply to Text: ***The Flag Maker***
- Engage and Respond: Write an Autobiography

SMALL-GROUP INSTRUCTION

Options for Differentiation
- Guided Reading Groups, p. T122
- English Learner Support: Recount Information, p. T122
- Reinforce Text Structure, p. T123

Options for Independent and Collaborative Work, pp. T124–T125

COMMUNICATION

- **Project Checkpoint: Write and Create,** pp. T17, T85

WRITING WORKSHOP

Descriptive Essay, p. W44
- Revising I: Sentence Variety

Grammar, p. W263
- Review Correct Pronouns

LESSON 10

VOCABULARY

Generative Vocabulary, pp. T126–T127
- Suffixes *–er*/*–est* with spelling change
- Spiral Review: Suffixes *–y*, *–less*; Prefix *dis–*

READING WORKSHOP

The Flag Maker
Teaching Pal
GENRE Narrative Nonfiction
Shared Reading: MINILESSON, pp. T128–T129
- Connect and Teach: Content-Area Words
- Apply to Text: ***The Flag Maker***
- Engage and Respond: Reading

SMALL-GROUP INSTRUCTION

Options for Differentiation
- Guided Reading Groups, p. T130
- English Learner Support: Recount Information, p. T130
- Reinforce Content-Area Words, p. T131

Options for Independent and Collaborative Work, pp. T132–T133

COMMUNICATION

Media Literacy, p. T134
- Interpret/Analyze Media

Make Connections, p. T135
- Synthesize Topic Knowledge

WRITING WORKSHOP

Descriptive Essay, p. W45
- Revising II: Conferencing

Grammar, p. W324
- Connect to Writing: Using Commas

Literacy Centers

- **While you meet with small groups, have students work independently in Literacy Centers. Familiarize students with the week's activities and post a daily rotation schedule.**
- **Have students complete Printable: Exit Ticket for each activity so you can monitor their work.**

READING CENTER

Readers' Theater

- Preview Printable: **Readers' Theater 3**, "Ring the Bell," and assign parts to mixed-ability groups of five students.
- The part of Max is ideal for struggling readers, and the part of Mr. Franklin can be read by a proficient reader.

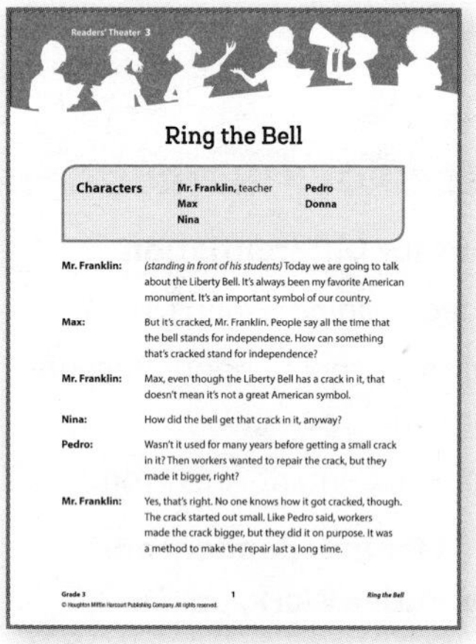
Readers' Theater 3

Ring the Bell

Characters: Mr. Franklin, teacher; Max; Nina; Pedro; Donna

Mr. Franklin: *(standing in front of his students)* Today we are going to talk about the Liberty Bell. It's always been my favorite American monument. It's an important symbol of our country.

Max: But it's cracked, Mr. Franklin. People say all the time that the bell stands for independence. How can something that's cracked stand for independence?

Mr. Franklin: Max, even though the Liberty Bell has a crack in it, that doesn't mean it's not a great American symbol.

Nina: How did the bell get that crack in it, anyway?

Pedro: Wasn't it used for many years before getting a small crack in it? Then workers wanted to repair the crack, but they made it bigger, right?

Mr. Franklin: Yes, that's right. No one knows how it got cracked, though. The crack started out small. Like Pedro said, workers made the crack bigger, but they did it on purpose. It was a method to make the repair last a long time.

Grade 3 1 *Ring the Bell*
© Houghton Mifflin Harcourt Publishing Company. All rights reserved.

Printable: Readers' Theater 3

Independent Reading

- Have students self-select or continue reading an independent reading book.
- Remind students to set a purpose for reading and to record their progress on their Printable: **Reading Log**.
- Have students use Printable: **Independent Reading** for fiction or nonfiction to note key ideas as they read.
- Display and review Anchor Chart 36: **Responding to Texts**.
- You may want to choose from these additional options to have students interact with their books:
  - » **Mixed-Ability Groups** Students discuss their self-selected books, using the questions on the Reading Log.
  - » **Write a Postcard** Students expand on their understanding by writing a postcard to a classmate with a suggestion to help their classmate choose this book.

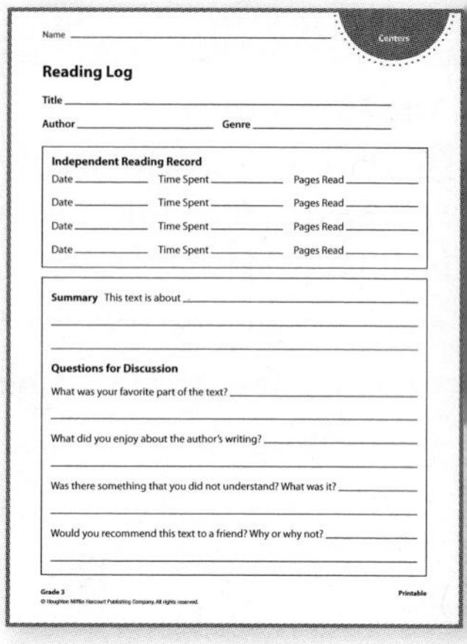
Name ______ Centers

Reading Log

Title ______
Author ______ Genre ______

Independent Reading Record
Date ______ Time Spent ______ Pages Read ______
Date ______ Time Spent ______ Pages Read ______
Date ______ Time Spent ______ Pages Read ______
Date ______ Time Spent ______ Pages Read ______

Summary This text is about ______

Questions for Discussion
What was your favorite part of the text? ______
What did you enjoy about the author's writing? ______
Was there something that you did not understand? What was it? ______
Would you recommend this text to a friend? Why or why not? ______

Grade 3 Printable
© Houghton Mifflin Harcourt Publishing Company. All rights reserved.

Printable: Reading Log

VOCABULARY

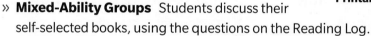

Super Six Words *(Use in Lessons 6–10.)*

- Have students use Printable: **Super Six Words** to list Big Idea Words and this week's Critical Vocabulary words that relate to the module topic.
- Then have students select six words from their lists that they think are most important, interesting, or new to them.
- Tell students to write a sentence for each selected word.
- Explain to students that they will come back to this list at the end of each week in the module.

Name ______ Centers

Super Six Words

1. Take a clean sheet of paper. Write your name at the top. Then write the module title.
2. Create four columns labeled Week 1, Week 2, Week 3, and Super Six.
3. Each week, list words about the topic from the texts you read in that week's column.
4. At the end of each week, choose and circle six words on your weekly list that you think are most important to the topic.
5. Write a sentence for each of those six words. Make sure your sentences show the meanings of the words.
6. At the end of the module, you will have eighteen words and sentences.
7. Now, choose six words from those eighteen words you think are most important to the topic. Write them in the Super Six column.
8. Use your Super Six words to write a summary of what you have learned about the module topic.

Grade 3 Printable
© Houghton Mifflin Harcourt Publishing Company. All rights reserved.

Printable: Super Six Words

DIGITAL STATION

Listener's Choice

Online Ed

- Have students listen to one of this week's selections, *Why We Celebrate the Fourth of July* or *The Flag Maker*, or a Leveled Reader of their choice.
- Tell them to add the title to their Printable: **Listening Log**, as well as list the listening skills they used, a summary of the selection, and questions they have about the selection or book.

Keyboarding

- Have students practice keyboarding using Printable: **Keyboarding 3.2**.

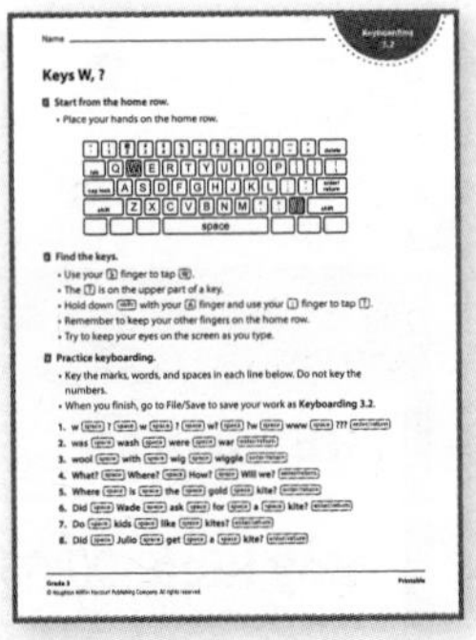

Printable: Keyboarding 3.2

WRITING CENTER

Write a Summary and Write an Autobiography

(Use in Lessons 7, 9, and 10)

- Have students use Printable: **Peer Conferencing Routine** to discuss their writing.
- Tell peers to use the tips on *my*Book pages 249 and 273 as they review the work of others and offer feedback.

Writing Workshop

- Have students work on a piece of writing. They may use the time to prewrite, draft, revise, edit, or publish.
- Students may choose from among tasks such as these:
  - » Revise a draft for correct use of commas.
  - » Conference with a peer about a draft.
- Display Anchor Chart 37: **Cursive Handwriting**.

PROJECT CENTER

Project Checkpoint: Write and Create

- Have students work in groups, using Printable: **Project 3.2** to guide them as they continue the project. Groups should complete the following over the course of the week:

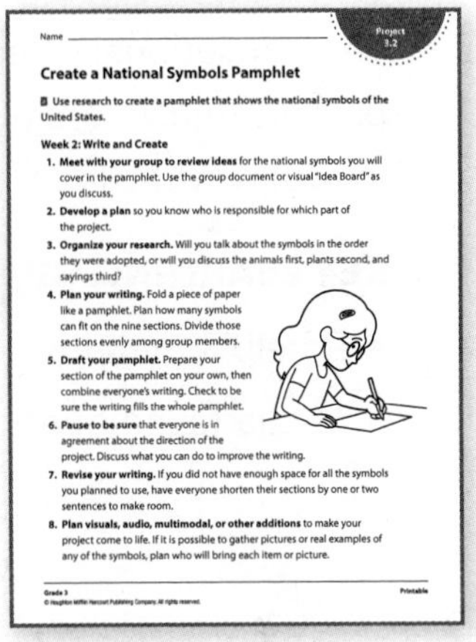

Printable: Project 3.2

- ☑ Draft a list of United States symbols, along with their meanings and history.
- ☑ Come to a consensus about which symbols will appear in the group's pamphlet.
- ☑ Discuss the role each student will play in the project.
- ☑ Create the pamphlet in desktop publishing software.
- ☑ Print copies of the pamphlet for the audience and fold them properly.

Reading Remake

(Use in Lessons 6–10.)

- Have students complete the Make a Documentary activity on Printable: **Reading Remake 6**.
- Ask partners to explain to one another how their documentary shows their understanding of the selection.

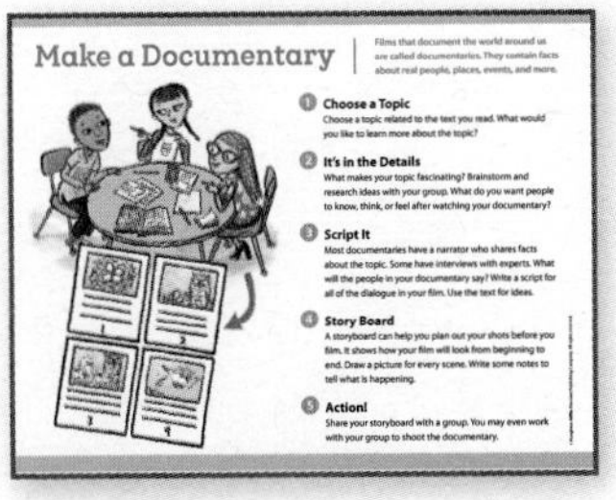

Printable: Reading Remake 6

WEEK 2

Preview Lesson Texts

Build understanding of this week's texts so that you can best support students in making connections, understanding key ideas, and becoming lifelong readers.

Why We Celebrate the Fourth of July by FreeSchool

GENRE Media: Educational Video

myBOO

WHY THIS TEXT?

This educational video provides an opportunity for students to learn and retell how patriotic music and historical scenes and images come together to illustrate the main idea of why the Fourth of July is a patriotic holiday.

KEY LEARNING OBJECTIVES

- Retell/Summarize
- Media Techniques

MAKE CONNECTIONS

BUILD KNOWLEDGE AND LANGUAGE

- **Social Studies Connection:** U.S. History

FOUNDATIONAL SKILLS

- **Words with /j/, /k/, and /kw/:** *charge, changes, Congress, colonies, equal*

WRITING WORKSHOP

- **Informational Text:** Descriptive Essay
- **Using Commas**

TEXT X-RAY

KEY IDEAS

Key Idea *00:05*
The Fourth of July has an important history.

Key Idea *00:28*
In 1787, the thirteen American colonies rebelled against the control of Great Britain and a war began.

Key Idea *00:54*
The colonies wanted to be free and control their own government.

Key Idea *01:40*
The Declaration of Independence was written and ultimately approved.

Key Idea *02:37*
We celebrate on July 4 because that is the day the colonists said they were free.

LANGUAGE

Idiom

sparked a war *00:28* Explain that a spark is a tiny bit of fire that starts a fire and makes it grow bigger. In this selection, "sparked" refers to how the conflict started with smaller rebellions and then escalated to a full-on war.

Content-Area Word

debated *01:31* Students may not understand this term related to government and law-making. Establish a mini-debate in class to demonstrate the concept. Divide students into two groups and choose a topic. Inform each group of their position on the topic and have them give reasons supporting their positions. Give examples before they start.

The Flag Maker by Susan Campbell Bartoletti

GENRE Narrative Nonfiction

WHY THIS TEXT?

Students will summarize the sequence of events in this narrative nonfiction selection about the origin of the American flag. They will identify words (e.g., dates and transitions) that signal a sequence of events and use context to determine the meanings of content-area words.

KEY LEARNING OBJECTIVES

- Retell/Summarize
- Identify Text Structure: Sequence
- Content-Area Words

myBOOK

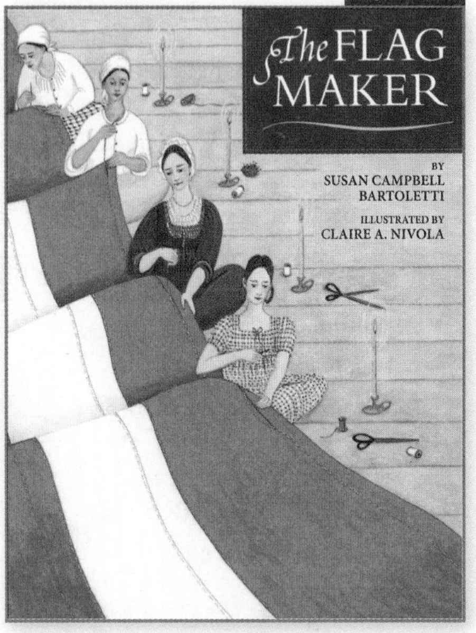

TEXT COMPLEXITY

LEXILE® MEASURE 620L • **GUIDED READING LEVEL** R

OVERALL RATING Complex

This text is comprised of complex social studies concepts and uses general and domain-specific language.

MAKE CONNECTIONS

BUILD KNOWLEDGE AND LANGUAGE

- **Social Studies Connection:** U.S. History

VOCABULARY

- **Suffixes *-er/-est* with spelling change:** *gritty, busier*

FOUNDATIONAL SKILLS

- **High-Frequency Words:** *time, (bed)time*
- **Words with /j/, /k/, and /kw/:** *large, orange, barges, bandages, country, calvary, communicate, cousins*

WRITING WORKSHOP

- **Informational Text:** Descriptive Essay
- **Using Commas**

TEXT X-RAY

KEY IDEAS	LANGUAGE
Key Idea *p. 252* The American flag was originally used to communicate in battle. **Key Idea** *p. 257* A young girl, her mother, and many others were commissioned to make a large flag for Fort McHenry so the British would see it from afar. **Key Idea** *p. 270* Although the Americans had lost many battles, they eventually defeated the British. **Key Idea** *p. 270* The flag was still flying when the last battle was won by the Americans. It served as a symbol of pride, courage, and hope during difficult times.	**Text Structure** ***At midnight...and all was still.*** *Lines 80–83; p. 268* Ask students why they think the writer wrote such short lines here. Explain that writers can use the appearance of the words on the page to make their writing more impactful. In this case, by listing lines one by one, the author communicates the slow passage of time. **Personification** ***tired flag*** *p. 270* Explain to students that writers can give human qualities or characteristics to an animal or object to enrich descriptions. In this case, the flag remained hoisted and flying all night during the last battle the Americans had with the British in Baltimore.

Introduce Critical Vocabulary

Step 1 Introduce the Words

LEARNING OBJECTIVES

- Identify real-life connections between words and their use.
- Use newly acquired vocabulary expressively.
- **Language** Answer questions and discuss meanings to develop vocabulary.

MATERIALS Online Ed

Display and Engage *Critical Vocabulary 3.6*

Vocabulary Cards *3.10–3.13*

CRITICAL VOCABULARY

- **independence**
- **declaring**
- **endowed**
- **presented**

SPANISH COGNATES

independence *independencia*

presented *presentado*

declare *declarar*

Project Display and Engage: Critical Vocabulary 3.6. Then use the **VOCABULARY** routine to introduce the Critical Vocabulary from *Why We Celebrate the Fourth of July*. You may wish to display the corresponding Vocabulary Card for each word as you discuss it.

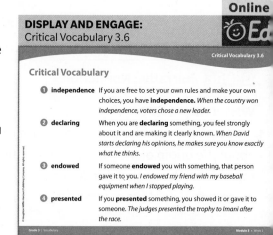

1. Read aloud each word and have students repeat it.
2. Read aloud and discuss each word's student-friendly explanation.
3. Point out the example for the word. Have students suggest other examples.

DISPLAY AND ENGAGE: Online Ed
Critical Vocabulary 3.6

Critical Vocabulary 3.6

Critical Vocabulary

1. **independence** If you are free to set your own rules and make your own choices, you have **independence.** *When the country won independence, voters chose a new leader.*
2. **declaring** When you are **declaring** something, you feel strongly about it and are making it clearly known. *When David starts declaring his opinions, he makes sure you know exactly what he thinks.*
3. **endowed** If someone **endowed** you with something, that person gave it to you. *I endowed my friend with my baseball equipment when I stopped playing.*
4. **presented** If you **presented** something, you showed it or gave it to someone. *The judges presented the trophy to Imani after the race.*

Grade 3 | Vocabulary — Module 3 • Week 2

TEACHER TIP

Encourage authentic **vocabulary usage** in your classroom. Students score a point each time they use a new vocabulary word in conversation.

ENGLISH LEARNER SUPPORT: Build Vocabulary

SUBSTANTIAL

Ask partners to take turns declaring something to each other.

MODERATE

Have students complete this sentence frame. *If I declare something, I ____.*

LIGHT

Have partners write and share sentences in which they declare something.

Step 2 Guided Practice

Guide students to interact with the words by discussing questions such as these:

- *If you gain **independence**, does someone start to take care of you or do you take care of yourself? Explain.*
- *When you are **declaring** something, are you making your ideas clear or asking someone for help? Explain.*
- *If your grandparents **endowed** you with a chair, did they give you the chair or point to it and ask you to sit down? Explain.*
- *If you **presented** something, did you keep it for yourself? Why or why not?*

Ask students to give an example of how they gained independence as they got older. Ask students to share a time they endowed or presented something to a friend or family member. Have students take turns declaring an opinion about the weather or the seasons.

Step 3 Apply

- Have students work independently to complete steps 3 and 4 on Vocabulary Cards **3.10–3.13**.
- Have students use the **TURN AND TALK** routine to discuss the prompt on each Vocabulary Card.

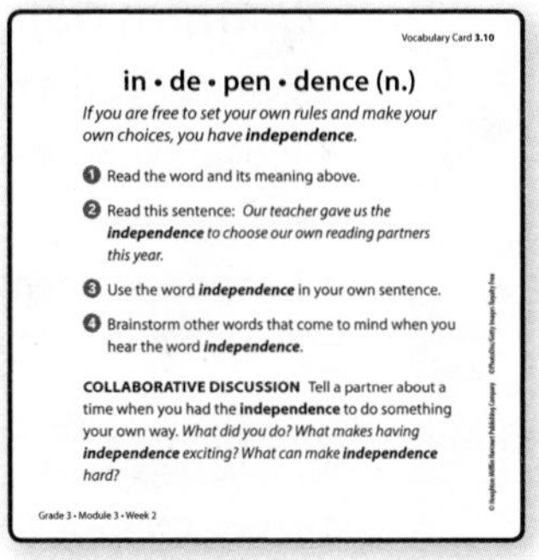
Vocabulary Card **3.10**

in • de • pen • dence (n.)

*If you are free to set your own rules and make your own choices, you have **independence**.*

1. Read the word and its meaning above.
2. Read this sentence: *Our teacher gave us the **independence** to choose our own reading partners this year.*
3. Use the word ***independence*** in your own sentence.
4. Brainstorm other words that come to mind when you hear the word ***independence***.

COLLABORATIVE DISCUSSION Tell a partner about a time when you had the **independence** to do something your own way. *What did you do? What makes having **independence** exciting? What can make **independence** hard?*

Grade 3 • Module 3 • Week 2

Vocabulary Cards

LEARNING MINDSET

Grit

Normalize Explain to students the importance of having grit. *Everyone has days when they feel like they can't complete something or aren't very good at a task. Remember to have the courage to keep going and the determination to do your best. It's not always easy, but if it was too easy you probably won't get as much out of it!*

Summarize

Step 1 Connect and Teach

LEARNING OBJECTIVES
- Summarize the main ideas of a video.
- Provide supporting evidence for main ideas.
- **Language** Identify and articulate key ideas in video content.

MATERIALS Online Ed

Anchor Chart 4 *Summarize*
Printable *Anchor Chart 4: Summarize*
Teaching Pal *pp. 244–249*
myBook *Why We Celebrate the Fourth of July, Book 1, pp. 244–249*
Display and Engage *Build Background 3.6*

INSTRUCTIONAL VOCABULARY
- **summarize** to restate the most important information, or main ideas, in a text in your own words

- Tell students that they are going to view an informational video called *Why We Celebrate the Fourth of July.* Explain that as they watch the video, it is important to pay attention to the key ideas and details presented. This will help them understand and recall what they see. Point out that one way to keep track of main ideas is to **summarize**.
- Explain to students that when they summarize, they restate the most important information, or main ideas, in a text or video.
- Project or display Anchor Chart 4: Summarize. Use it to outline the steps students should follow to summarize.
- Suggest that students turn the title of the video into a question, "Why do we celebrate the Fourth of July?" Have them watch and listen for information that will answer the question.
- Tell students that they will practice summarizing when they view *Why We Celebrate the Fourth of July.*

Online Ed
ANCHOR CHART 4: Summarize

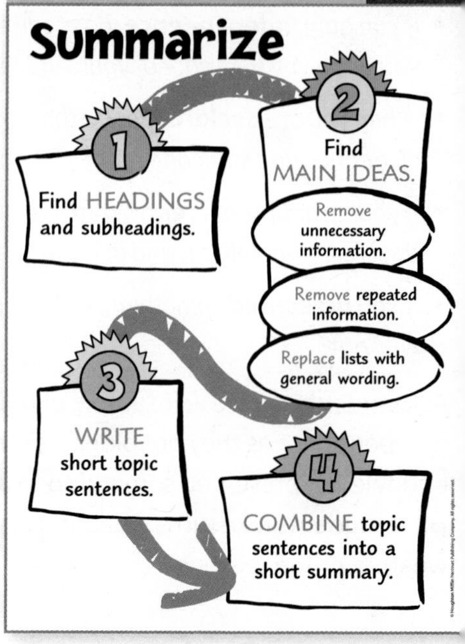
Summarize
1
Find HEADINGS and subheadings.
2
Find MAIN IDEAS.
Remove unnecessary information.
Remove repeated information.
Replace lists with general wording.
3
WRITE short topic sentences.
4
COMBINE topic sentences into a short summary.

ASSESSMENT OPTION

Assign the Selection Quiz to check comprehension of *Why We Celebrate the Fourth of July.*

Go to Your **Teaching Pal**

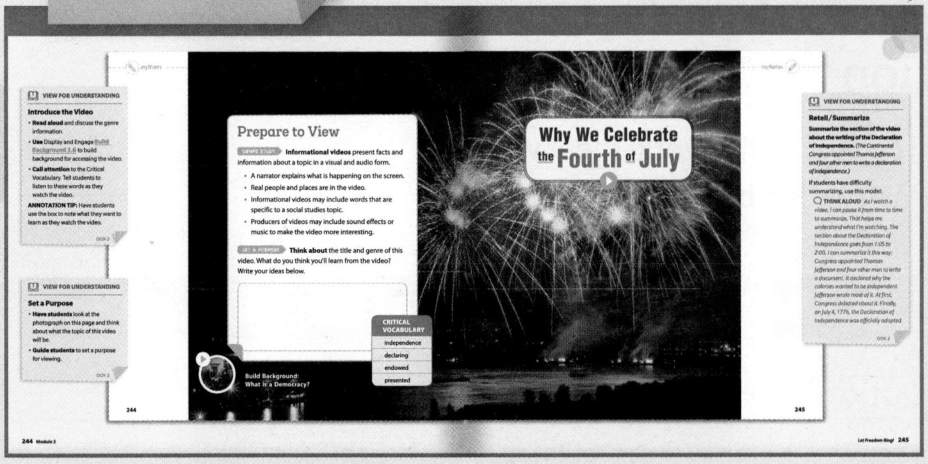

Online

ANNOTATE IT!

Students may use the annotation tools in their eBook.

Step 2 Apply to Text

In your **Teaching Pal**, pages 244–247, use the blue **VIEW FOR UNDERSTANDING** prompts to view *Why We Celebrate the Fourth of July* as students follow along and annotate their *my*Book.

- **Genre Study** Guide students through the genre information on page 244.
- **Build Background** Project Display and Engage 3.6: Build Background and read the information aloud with students. Ask students how the information connects to what they already know about the time when our nation began.
- **Set a Purpose** Read the Set a Purpose section on page 244. Prompt students to set their own purpose for viewing *Why We Celebrate the Fourth of July.*
- **View and Comprehend** Use the **ACTIVE VIEWING** routine as you guide students to view the video. Pause occasionally, using the prompts in your Teaching Pal to gauge students' understanding and to have them summarize. As students summarize, have them refer back to the Anchor Chart to determine how to identify the most important details to include in a summary.

Step 3 Engage and Respond

INDEPENDENT PRACTICE: Speaking and Listening

- After viewing, use the **COLLABORATIVE CONVERSATION** routine with the Collaborative Discussion questions on **Teaching Pal** and *my*Book page 247. Have students annotate their *my*Book with details from the video as evidence to explain their responses.
- Ask volunteers to read aloud the Speaking and Listening tips. Discuss how to make sure their comments and questions help their group focus on the topic.
- You may want to have students conduct their discussions during daily small-group time.

EL ENGLISH LEARNER SUPPORT: Support Comprehension

SUBSTANTIAL
Provide sentence frames to identify main ideas. *The Fourth of July celebrates _____. On the Fourth of July you might see _____.*

MODERATE
Ask: *What is one reason to celebrate the Fourth of July? What is one thing people do to celebrate the Fourth of July?*

LIGHT
Encourage students to rephrase the main ideas of the video in their own words as they summarize.

LINK TO SMALL-GROUP INSTRUCTION

REINFORCE SUMMARIZE Review and extend the skill as needed during small-group time to support students' need for differentiation. *See the lesson on p. T93.*

Options for Differentiation

As the class engages in independent and collaborative work, meet with Guided Reading Groups or differentiate instruction based on student need.

GUIDED READING GROUPS

Match Students to Books + Instruction

- Choose just-right books based on level, skill, topic, or genre.

L M N O P Q

Leveled Readers

- Deliver instruction with each book's **Take and Teach Lesson**, choosing appropriate sessions based on need.

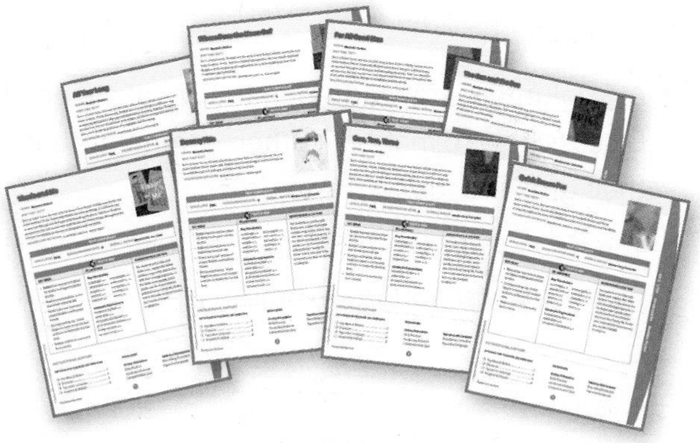

- Check comprehension, reinforce instruction, and extend learning with suggested supporting activities.

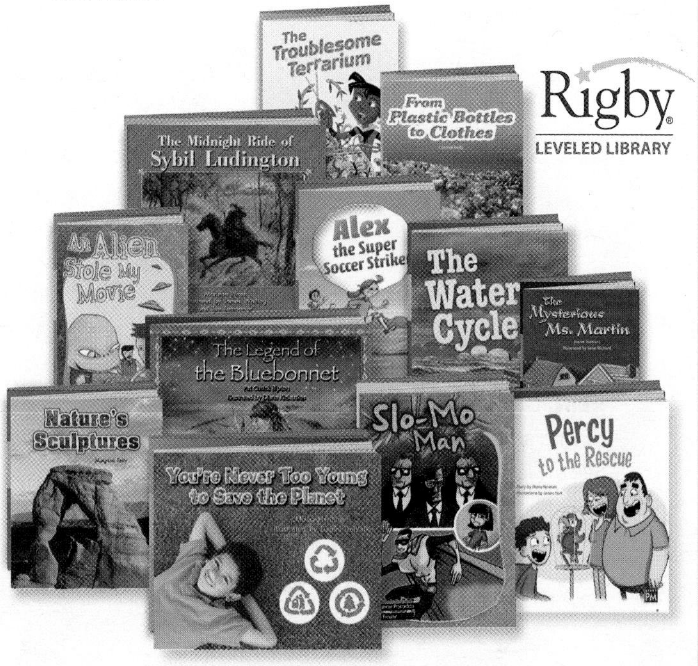

ENGLISH LEARNER SUPPORT

Recount Information

- Use **Tabletop Minilessons: English Language Development 8.1 (Listening)** to introduce and practice the language skill.

Tabletop Minilessons: English Language Development

- Then use the following text-based prompts with *Why We Celebrate the Fourth of July* to guide application of the language skill. Begin with the prompt at the student's identified language proficiency level. As students progress, use lighter supports to encourage increased language proficiency.

SUBSTANTIAL

As students view the video, ask them to raise their hand when they hear the terms "Fourth of July," "Independence Day," and "America's Birthday." Discuss that these are all terms used to discuss the day the United States became a country.

MODERATE

Ask students: *What are two other names for the Fourth of July?* Then have students listen to the video for the answer. Use the sentence frame: *Two other names for the Fourth of July are* _____ *and* _____.

LIGHT

Have students view the video, and then answer the question: *How did the Fourth of July get its name?*

REINFORCE SUMMARIZE

Demonstrate

- Use **Tabletop Minilessons: Reading Card 4** to remind students that when they **summarize**, they restate the most important information, or main ideas, in a text or video. A summary does not need to include all minor details. Summarizing will help students understand and recall what they watch or read.
- Model filling out Printable: Reading Graphic Organizer 4 to summarize *Why We Celebrate the Fourth of July*.

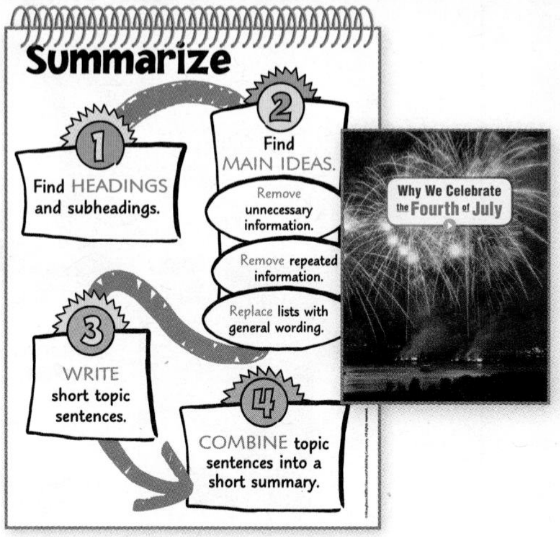
Summarize
1
Find HEADINGS and subheadings.
2
Find MAIN IDEAS.
Remove unnecessary information.
Remove repeated information.
Replace lists with general wording.
3
WRITE short topic sentences.
4
COMBINE topic sentences into a short summary.
Why We Celebrate the Fourth of July

Tabletop Minilessons: Reading

Apply to Independent Reading

- Now have students summarize an appropriate book, article, or video they are reading or viewing independently. Customize these prompts to the texts students choose.
  - » *What main ideas did you include in your summary?*
  - » *What are some minor details that you did not need to include in your summary?*
  - » *How did summarizing help you to understand or remember the text?*
- Have students complete Printable: Reading Graphic Organizer 4 for their independent reading book.

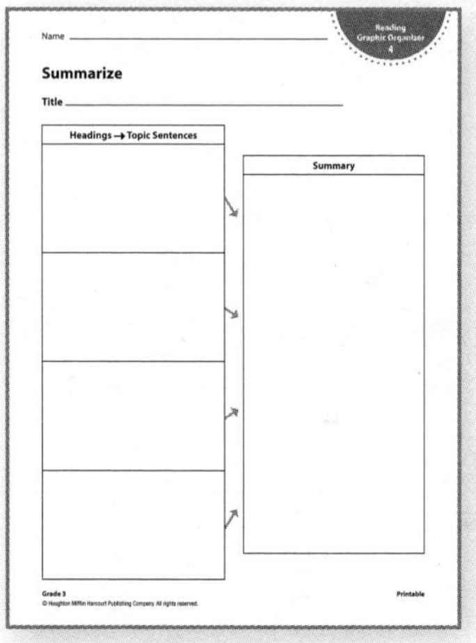
Summarize
Headings → Topic Sentences
Summary

Printable: Reading Graphic Organizer 4

ALMOST THERE

READY FOR MORE

SCAFFOLD AND EXTEND

- Guide students to identify the main ideas and then retell them in a summary.
- Prompt students to identify main ideas and use them to summarize the text.
- Have students explain how they identified which details to include in their summary.

ENGLISH LEARNER SUPPORT

SUBSTANTIAL
Guide students to summarize by pointing to pictures on each page and by using English words to express main ideas.

MODERATE
Supply sentence frames such as: *My summary should include the main ideas _____. I don't need to include _____.*

LIGHT
Have students summarize with a partner and make suggestions to one another as to how to improve their summaries.

INDEPENDENT APPLICATION

Options for Independent and Collaborative Work

While you meet with small groups, have other students engage in literacy activities that reinforce the lesson's learning objectives. Choose from these options.

Independent Reading

Student Choice Library

Rigby
LEVELED LIBRARY

APPLY READING SKILL

Summarize Students complete Printable: Reading Graphic Organizer 4 for an independent reading book.

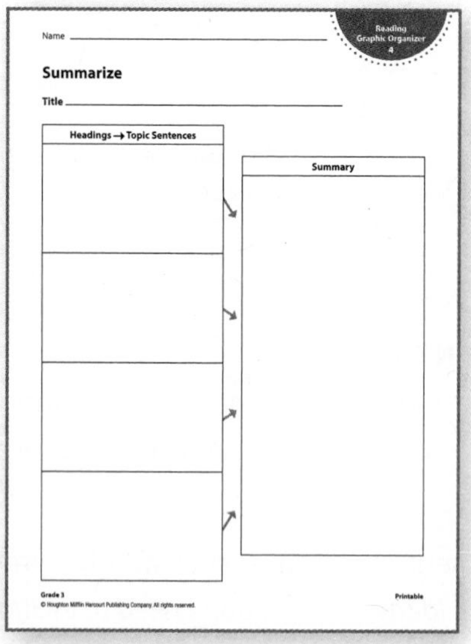

Printable: Reading Graphic Organizer 4

APPLY LANGUAGE SKILL

Recount Information Students complete Printable: Language Graphic Organizer 11 for an independent reading book.

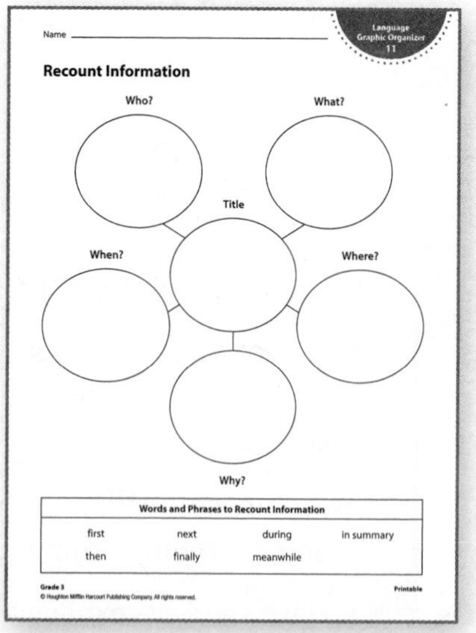

Printable: Language Graphic Organizer 11

Literacy Centers

See pp. T84–T85.

- READING CENTER
- VOCABULARY CENTER
- DIGITAL STATION
- WRITING CENTER
- PROJECT CENTER

Speaking and Listening

Partners discuss the Collaborative Discussion questions. *See Engage and Respond, p. T91.*

Additional Skills Practice

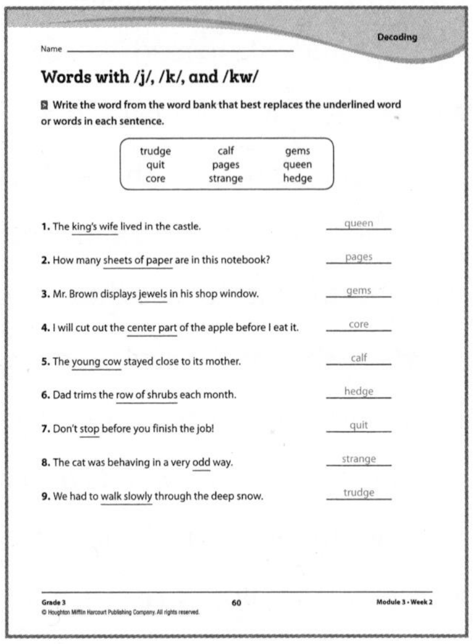
Name ________________________ Decoding

Words with /j/, /k/, and /kw/

Write the word from the word bank that best replaces the underlined word or words in each sentence.

trudge	calf	gems
quit	pages	queen
core	strange	hedge

1. The king's wife lived in the castle. queen
2. How many sheets of paper are in this notebook? pages
3. Mr. Brown displays jewels in his shop window. gems
4. I will cut out the center part of the apple before I eat it. core
5. The young cow stayed close to its mother. calf
6. Dad trims the row of shrubs each month. hedge
7. Don't stop before you finish the job! quit
8. The cat was behaving in a very odd way. strange
9. We had to walk slowly through the deep snow. trudge

Grade 3 60 Module 3 • Week 2

Know It, Show It, p. 60

Wrap-Up

Share Time

At the end of the Reading Workshop, have students reflect on their learning by sharing how they applied **summarize** or another area of focus during independent work time. Choose from these options:

- Use the **SOLO CHAIR** routine. Select a reader each day to come to the front of the class and tell what he or she learned from the reading by using a skill or strategy.
- **THINK-PAIR-SHARE** Students share their thinking with a partner. Select a few pairs each day to share with the whole class.
- **RETURN TO ANCHOR CHART** Have students add sticky notes about their independent reading to the Summarize Anchor Chart. Call on a few students to explain what they added and why.

Online Ed

ANCHOR CHART 4: Summarize

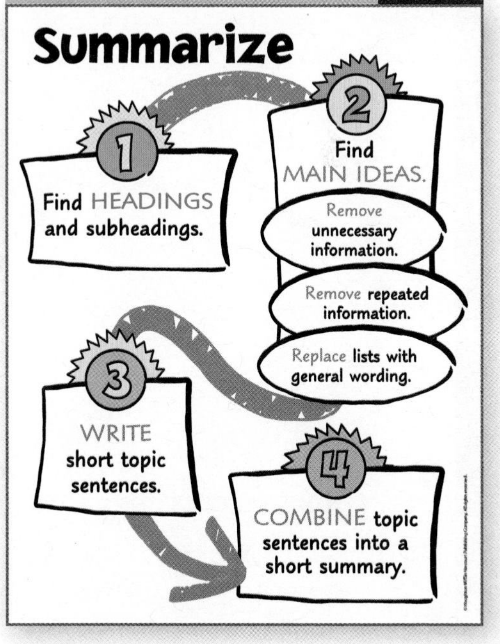
Summarize
1
Find HEADINGS and subheadings.
2
Find MAIN IDEAS.
Remove unnecessary information.
Remove repeated information.
Replace lists with general wording.
3
WRITE short topic sentences.
4
COMBINE topic sentences into a short summary.

Words with /j/, /k/, and /kw/

LEARNING OBJECTIVES

- Decode and read words with /j/, /k/, and /kw/.
- Spell and write words with /j/, /k/, and /kw/.
- **Language** Read words with /j/, /k/, and /kw/ and understand their meanings.

MATERIALS **Online** Ed

Display and Engage *Decoding 3.6*
Know It, Show It *p. 60*

Step 1 Introduce the Skill

Words with /j/ Display and read aloud the words *gem*, *page*, and *edge*.

- Underline *ge* in *gem* and *page* and *dge* in *edge*. Note that the letters *ge* and *dge* stand for the /j/ sound.
- Display the words *huge* and *dodge* and underline *ge* and *dge* in the words.
- Guide students to read aloud the words.

Words with /k/ Display and read aloud the word *cave*.

- Underline *c* and note that in this word the letter *c* stands for the /k/ sound.
- Display the words *cash* and *coat* and underline *c* in the words.
- Guide students to read the words aloud.

Words with /kw/ Display and read aloud the word *queen*.

- Underline *qu* and note that the letters *qu* stand for the /kw/ sound.
- Display the words *quiz* and *quilt* and underline *qu* in the words.
- Guide students to read aloud the words.
- Display the following chart.

ge	dge	c	qu
age	judge	cake	quack
germ	pledge	coach	quote
stage	badge	cool	quench

- Remind students that they have learned multiple ways to spell the sounds /j/, /k/, and /kw/. Point out these spelling patterns in the top row.
- Then read aloud the example words in each column, emphasizing the final sound /j/ and the initial sounds /k/ and /kw/ while underlining the letters that stand for each sound.
- Guide students to read the words aloud.

ENGLISH LEARNER SUPPORT: Support Comprehension

SUBSTANTIAL
Ensure that students understand the meaning of each Blend and Read word by sharing pictures or gestures.

MODERATE
Support students in understanding the meaning of each Blend and Read word by providing oral examples or context sentences. Guide students to think of additional examples or sentences.

LIGHT
Challenge students to create context sentences for some of the Blend and Read words on their own.

Step 2 Guided Practice

- Project Display and Engage: **Decoding 3.6**.
- Have students read aloud the Blend and Read lines. Provide feedback as needed.
- At the end of each line, prompt a conversation about the words: *How are the sounds the same or different? How are the spellings similar or different?*
- Have partners reread the Blend and Read lines and quiz each other on the spellings of /j/, /k/, and /kw/.

Online Ed

Display and Engage: Decoding 3.6

Decoding 3.6

Decoding

Words with /j/, /k/, and /kw/

The letters *ge* and *dge* make the /j/ sound. The letter *c* can make the /k/ sound. The letters *qu* make the /kw/ sound.

1	stage (ge)	ledge (dge)	coast (c)	age (ge)	camel (c)
2	fudge (dge)	wage (ge)	quit (qu)	cast (c)	gentle (ge)
3	quest (qu)	huge (ge)	smudge (dge)	cape (c)	hedge (dge)
4	carton (c)	quill (qu)	bridge (dge)	quaint (qu)	rage (ge)
5	page (ge)	quake (qu)	gene (ge)	coin (c)	trudge (dge)

6 Our hike over the ridge (dge) to the fishing camp (c) lodge (dge) seemed quite (qu) endless.

Grade 3 | Foundational Skills — Module 3 • Week 2

Step 3 Apply

INDEPENDENT PRACTICE

- Have students work in small groups or with partners to complete Know It, Show It page 60.
- Encourage students to share with each other the strategies they use to decode words with the spellings of /j/, /k/, and /kw/.

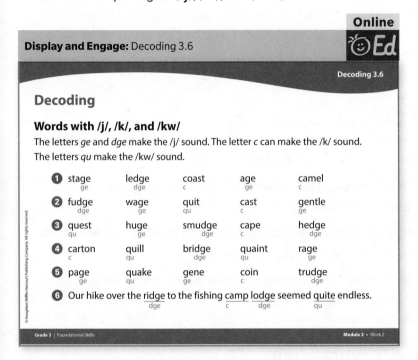

CORRECT & REDIRECT

If students have trouble decoding words with /j/, /k/, and /kw/, use the model below.

- **Correct** the error. *The letters* ge *and* dge *can be pronounced /j/. The letter* c *can be pronounced /k/. The letters* qu *are pronounced /kw/.*
- **Model** how to decode the word. */fŭd/. That doesn't sound like a word I know. We learned that the letters* dge *can stand for the /j/ sound. So I'll try that. /fŭj/.* Fudge *is a word I know.*
- **Guide** students to decode other words: *stage, hedge.*
- **Check** students' understanding by displaying the word *coin. What do you know about the letter* c *that can help you decode this word?* (The letter *c* can be pronounced /k/.)
- **Reinforce** by repeating the process with the word *quest.*

Words with /j/, /k/, and /kw/

LEARNING OBJECTIVES

- Learn spelling patterns for /j/, /k/, and /kw/.
- **Language** Spell words with /j/, /k/, and /kw/ and understand their meanings.

MATERIALS | **Online** Ed

Anchor Chart 37 *Cursive Handwriting*
Printables *Anchor Chart 37: Cursive Handwritng, Dictation Sentences 3.6, Spelling Word Cards 3.6, Proofreading 3.6*
Optional *Use Printable: Dictation Sentences 3.6 to administer a pretest.*

SPELLING WORDS

BASIC

1. **ledge**
2. **nudge**
3. **smudge**
4. **budge**
5. **ridge**
6. **wedge**
7. **quiet**
8. **circus**
9. **second**
10. **quart**
11. **quick**
12. **comma**
13. **stage**
14. **huge**

REVIEW

15. **scratch**
16. **splash**
17. **sprint**
18. **squeal**

CHALLENGE

19. **quiver**
20. **constant**
21. **budget**
22. **enrage**

Introduce the Spelling Words

- Before working with the basic and challenge words, you might want to revisit the review words. These also appear in Printable: Dictation Sentences 3.6. Display the Spelling Anchor Chart Printables, as appropriate.
- Cut out and display the spelling word cards from Printable: Spelling Word Cards 3.6. Read aloud each word and discuss its meaning as needed.
- Tell students you are going to work together to sort the words into categories based on the spelling of the sounds /j/, /k/, and /kw/. Read aloud the words *huge, nudge, comma,* and *quiet*, and display those words as column headings.
- Hold up a word containing *dge*, such as *wedge*, and model your thinking: *The word is* wedge. *It has the /j/ sound at the end. And I see the column head* nudge, *which has the same spelling pattern for the /j/ sound. So I'll place the word in that column.*

Sort the Words

- Ask students to help you sort the remaining word cards. For two-syllable words, emphasize the sound of /j/, /k/, or /kw/.
- After sorting, have students read down each list with you to make sure the words have been sorted correctly.
- Guide students to recognize the spelling patterns in the columns. Ask: *What spelling pattern do the words in this column share?*
- Guide students to recognize the different spelling patterns for the sounds /j/, /k/, and /kw/. Ask: *What are the different spelling patterns for the sounds /j/, /k/, and /kw/? (ge, dge, c, qu)*

Handwriting/Keyboarding

- Display and review Anchor Chart 37: Cursive Handwriting.
- Have students practice handwriting or keyboarding by writing or typing the spelling words. As needed, use the handwriting models from the resources section of this Teacher's Guide.

ENGLISH LEARNER SUPPORT: Build Word Meaning

ALL LEVELS Make sure students understand the meaning of the spelling words and dictation sentences. If necessary, use visuals or gestures as support. For Spanish-speaking students, point out the Spanish cognates *quieto* for *quiet*, *segundo* for *second*, and *constante* for *constant*. After you've reinforced word meanings, have students practice reading the spelling words aloud.

LINK TO SMALL-GROUP INSTRUCTION

REINFORCE FOUNDATIONAL SKILLS For spelling practice for the remainder of the week: Display this week's spelling words for reference and have students work with Printable: Proofreading 3.6. Remind students to check the spelling words they use in the writing section to confirm they have spelled the words correctly.

Phrasing

LEARNING OBJECTIVES

- Read fluently by taking natural pauses at the appropriate places.
- Read aloud grade-level text with fluency and accuracy.
- Apply decoding skills when reading connected text.
- **Language** Comprehend texts using teacher support.

MATERIALS | **Online** Ed

Printable *Fluency 3.6, Word Cards 3.28–3.30*

DECODING ⟶ FLUENCY CONNECTION

The passage on Printable: Fluency 3.6 includes words that contain this week's decoding element. Use the passage to monitor whether students can accurately and fluently read these grade-level words.

HIGH-FREQUENCY WORDS

- **time**
- **months**
- **century**

Introduce the Skill

- Explain that when good readers read aloud, they group words together and pause naturally between phrases. Tell students that readers should use punctuation to help them know where to pause.
- Distribute Printable: Fluency 3.6 to students, and project it for whole-group discussion. Tell students that you will demonstrate how to read the passage with phrasing.
- Read the first paragraph without any natural pauses. Then read the paragraph again and pause at each period, comma, and dash. Ask students which reading was easier to understand. *When you pause, you allow listeners to better understand how the thoughts and phrases are grouped together in the text.* Continue reading to demonstrate taking natural pauses. After you read the entire passage, point out how you decoded the words *qualifies, legends, complete,* and *wedged* by knowing the sounds for *-ge, -dge, c,* and *qu*.

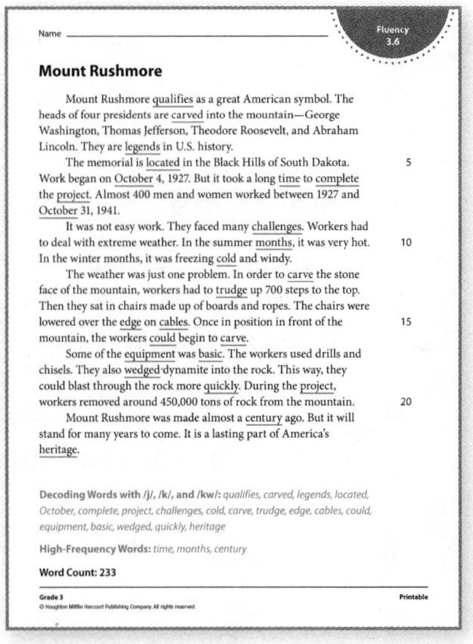

Name ______________________ Fluency 3.6

Mount Rushmore

Mount Rushmore qualifies as a great American symbol. The heads of four presidents are carved into the mountain—George Washington, Thomas Jefferson, Theodore Roosevelt, and Abraham Lincoln. They are legends in U.S. history.

The memorial is located in the Black Hills of South Dakota. Work began on October 4, 1927. But it took a long time to complete the project. Almost 400 men and women worked between 1927 and October 31, 1941.

It was not easy work. They faced many challenges. Workers had to deal with extreme weather. In the summer months, it was very hot. In the winter months, it was freezing cold and windy.

The weather was just one problem. In order to carve the stone face of the mountain, workers had to trudge up 700 steps to the top. Then they sat in chairs made up of boards and ropes. The chairs were lowered over the edge on cables. Once in position in front of the mountain, the workers could begin to carve.

Some of the equipment was basic. The workers used drills and chisels. They also wedged dynamite into the rock. This way, they could blast through the rock more quickly. During the project, workers removed around 450,000 tons of rock from the mountain.

Mount Rushmore was made almost a century ago. But it will stand for many years to come. It is a lasting part of America's heritage.

Decoding Words with /j/, /k/, and /kw/: *qualifies, carved, legends, located, October, complete, project, challenges, cold, carve, trudge, edge, cables, could, equipment, basic, wedged, quickly, heritage*

High-Frequency Words: *time, months, century*

Word Count: 233

Grade 3 | Printable

Printable: Fluency 3.6

- After you finish reading the passage, have students read it aloud with you, using the **CHORAL READING** routine.

Apply

- Have students work in pairs or small groups using the **PARTNER READING** routine to read aloud the passage.
- Monitor students for appropriate phrasing. Note especially how students handle the more challenging words, such as *memorial, extreme,* and *heritage,* and provide support, as needed.

HIGH-FREQUENCY WORDS

Point out the high-frequency words in the passage on Printable: Fluency 3.6. Remind students that high-frequency words appear often in texts they read. Students can learn to recognize them, rather than decode them, so that they can read more fluently.

Print and distribute Printables: Word Cards 3.28–3.30, which feature this week's high-frequency words, and have students work independently or in pairs to read and complete the activities for each word. For struggling readers, walk through the notes for one or two words before they continue working with a partner.

EL ENGLISH LEARNER SUPPORT: Support Comprehension

ALL LEVELS As you model reading with appropriate phrasing, have students raise their hand when they hear a word they do not recognize. Work with students to decode the word and practice saying it aloud. Discuss the word's meaning, using gestures or pictures for support if needed. Then have students read the entire sentence chorally. Provide corrective feedback, as needed.

Review Critical Vocabulary

LEARNING OBJECTIVES

- Review and extend understanding of word meanings.
- Use context to determine the meanings of unfamiliar words.
- **Language** Use newly acquired vocabulary expressively.

MATERIALS **Online** Ed

Display and Engage *Critical Vocabulary 3.6*

Know It, Show It *p. 61*

CRITICAL VOCABULARY

- **independence**
- **declaring**
- **endowed**
- **presented**

Step 1 Reinforce Vocabulary

- Project Display and Engage: Critical Vocabulary 3.6 to review and discuss the Critical Vocabulary, student-friendly explanations, and examples of the words. Have students take turns using the words in sentences.

Step 2 Guided Practice

- Display the Critical Vocabulary words. Have students work in small groups.
- One student in each group gives clues about a Critical Vocabulary word without saying the word. Encourage students to say words that have similar or opposite meanings or examples, or describe times they used or might use the Critical Vocabulary word.
- For example: *If an animal is kept in a cage, it does not have this.* (independence)

Step 3 Apply

INDEPENDENT PRACTICE

- Have students work in small groups or independently. Tell them to complete Know It, Show It page 61. For the last item on the page, tell students to include clues to each word's meaning in their sentences. Have groups share their sentences. Ask listeners to identify the context clue in each sentence.
- You may wish to have students complete the Know It, Show It page during small group time.

ENGLISH LEARNER SUPPORT: Support Discussion

Use tiered supports as needed to help students as they answer questions about the Critical Vocabulary.

SUBSTANTIAL

When you are declaring something, are you talking or moving?

MODERATE

How is declaring something different from asking something?

LIGHT

If you are declaring something, how do you feel about that topic? Explain.

Multiple-Meaning Words

Step 1 Review the Strategy

LEARNING OBJECTIVES

- Use context to determine the relevant meaning of multiple-meaning words.
- Use print and digital reference materials to clarify meanings.
- **Language** Identify the correct meaning of multiple-meaning words using strategic learning techniques.

MATERIALS Online Ed

Display and Engage *Vocabulary Strategy 3.7a, 3.7b, 3.7c*

INSTRUCTIONAL VOCABULARY

- **multiple-meaning words** words that are spelled the same but have more than one meaning

Project Display and Engage: Vocabulary Strategy 3.7 a, 3.7b, and 3.7c. Read aloud the two paragraphs.

Online

DISPLAY AND ENGAGE: Vocabulary Strategy 3.7 a, 3.7b, 3.7c

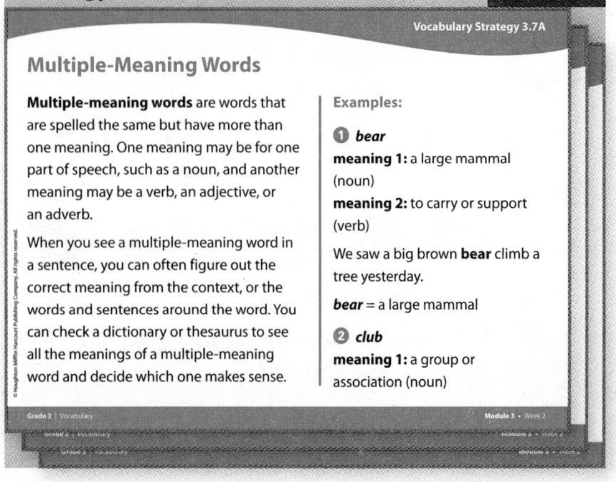
Vocabulary Strategy 3.7A
Multiple-Meaning Words
Multiple-meaning words are words that are spelled the same but have more than one meaning. One meaning may be for one part of speech, such as a noun, and another meaning may be a verb, an adjective, or an adverb.
When you see a multiple-meaning word in a sentence, you can often figure out the correct meaning from the context, or the words and sentences around the word. You can check a dictionary or thesaurus to see all the meanings of a multiple-meaning word and decide which one makes sense.
Examples:
1 bear
meaning 1: a large mammal (noun)
meaning 2: to carry or support (verb)
We saw a big brown bear climb a tree yesterday.
bear = a large mammal
2 club
meaning 1: a group or association (noun)
Grade 3 | Vocabulary
Module 3 • Week 2

- Review with students that multiple-meaning words are words that are spelled the same but have different meanings. Explain that using context clues can help them identify the meaning of these words.
- Use the first two examples to model using context clues to figure out the meaning of the multiple-meaning words *bear* and *club*. *Bear can be a noun that names a kind of mammal, or it can be a verb that means "to carry or support." I can tell from the sentence context that* bear *is a noun. The sentence also says, "climb a tree." Both those clues tell me that in this sentence* bear *means a mammal.* Repeat the process with the second example.

Step 2 Guided Practice

- Have students read the multiple-meaning words *bill* and *box*, their definitions, and the context sentences and determine the correct meaning of each word.
- Ask students how they used context clues to determine the correct word meanings.

Step 3 Apply the Strategy

INDEPENDENT PRACTICE

- Display the following multiple-meaning words from *Why We Celebrate the Fourth of July* and have a volunteer read them aloud: *charge, passed, state, even*. Have students work independently or in pairs to write two or more definitions for each word, using a reference source as needed.
- Next, tell students to locate each word in the selection and write the sentence in which it appears. Have them use context to determine and write the word's meaning.
- Have students exchange responses with a partner and compare their answers, explaining how they chose the correct word meaning.

ENGLISH LEARNER SUPPORT: Understand Multiple-Meaning Words

SUBSTANTIAL
Have students use gestures and oral sentences to show two different meanings of *box*.

MODERATE
Supply sentence frames for the multiple-meaning words: *I can tell* box *has to do with the sport boxing because* _____.

LIGHT
Ask students to explain how they figured out the correct meaning of the words *box* and *bill*.

Media Techniques

Step 1 Connect and Teach

LEARNING OBJECTIVES

- Analyze the use of media techniques to achieve specific purposes.
- Listen actively to analyze and clarify information.
- **Language** Identify and articulate media techniques used in video.

MATERIALS Online Ed

Anchor Chart 29 *Media Techniques*
Printable *Anchor Chart 29: Media Techniques*
Teaching Pal *pp. 244–249*
myBook *Why We Celebrate the Fourth of July, Book 1, pp. 244–249*
Know It, Show It *p. 62*

INSTRUCTIONAL VOCABULARY

- **live action** the scenes of events in media with people, characters, and objects
- **media** the means of communication such as radio, television, newspapers, magazines, and the Internet
- **media techniques** the ways in which an author communicates ideas and information to the viewers, such as animation, live action, sound elements, and visual elements
- **sound elements** the music, sound effects, or narration used in media

- Project or display Anchor Chart 29: Media Techniques. Use the chart to explain the following:
- **Media** refers to different forms of communication, both print and electronic. **Media techniques** are the means authors use to present a topic, idea, or other information.
- **Sound elements** and **expert** speakers provide information and set a mood or tone.
- The use of **live action**, **animation**, and other visuals attract attention. The images may be supported by or combined with sound.
- Encourage students to notice and think about media techniques to gain a deeper understanding of *Why We Celebrate the Fourth of July.*

Online Ed

ANCHOR CHART 29: Media Techniques

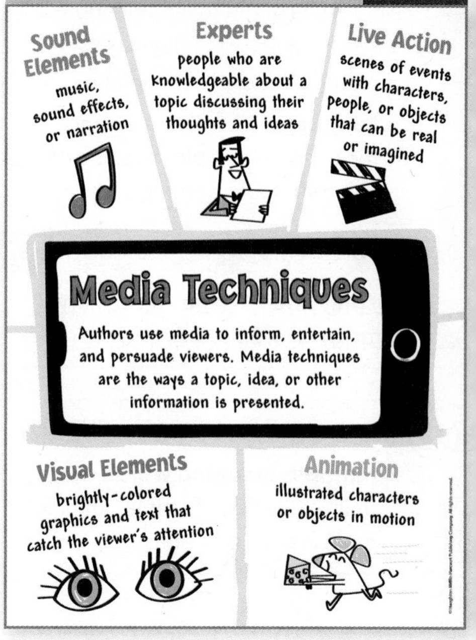

LEARNING MINDSET

Grit

Apply Point out that the writing of the Declaration of Independence didn't happen quickly or easily. *We learned from the video that the committee had to present their writing to Congress, and then go back and make changes to the document. It took effort to get it right.* Discuss ways students can make an effort to evaluate, rework, and improve their written work.

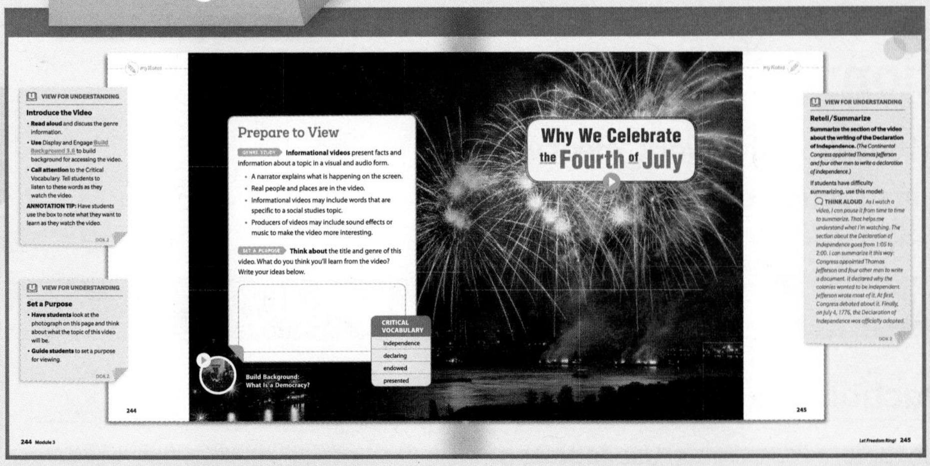

Online *Ed*

ANNOTATE IT!

Students may use the annotation tools in their eBook.

Step 2 Apply to Text

In your **Teaching Pal**, use the purple **TARGETED CLOSE VIEW** prompts on pages 244–247 to guide students to apply the Media Techniques skill to *Why We Celebrate the Fourth of July* and to find evidence to support their responses. Use the **ACTIVE VIEWING** routine. Students may refer to the questions on Know It, Show It page 62 as you discuss them.

- Read aloud the first two questions on Teaching Pal page 246. Then have students view the video to analyze visual and sound elements. *(the flag, images of the first Americans who fought the Revolutionary War; the music is from patriotic songs that are often played on the Fourth of July.)*
- Then read the follow-up questions on page 246. Discuss how the paintings support the information in the video. *(They show the events that the narrator is talking about.)*
- Refer back to the Anchor Chart as necessary to support the discussion. Suggest that students add sticky notes to the chart to note other examples of media techniques they identify in *Why We Celebrate the Fourth of July.*

Step 3 Engage and Respond

INDEPENDENT PRACTICE: Writing

- **Write A Summary** Turn to pages 248–249 in your **Teaching Pal**. Have students turn to pages 248–249 in their *my*Book. Use the **WRITING RESPONSE** routine.
- Read the directions with students and use the Teaching Pal prompts to guide them as they plan and complete their summaries.
- Have students take turns reading their summaries to a partner. Students may compare to see if they have included similar main ideas in their summaries.
- You may wish to have students complete their writing during daily small-group time.
- You may wish to have students complete Know It, Show It page 62 during daily small-group time.

ENGLISH LEARNER SUPPORT: Facilitate Discussion

SUBSTANTIAL
Provide sentence frames: *I can see* ______. *I can hear* ______.

MODERATE
Ask: *What images do you see? What sounds do you hear?*

LIGHT
Encourage students to speak in complete sentences and to use newly acquired vocabulary to describe the media techniques.

LINK TO SMALL-GROUP INSTRUCTION

REINFORCE MEDIA TECHNIQUES Review and extend the skill as needed during small-group time to support students' need for differentiation. *See the lesson on p. T105.*

Options for Differentiation

As the class engages in independent and collaborative work, meet with Guided Reading Groups or differentiate instruction based on student need.

GUIDED READING GROUPS

Match Students to Books + Instruction

- Choose just-right books based on level, skill, topic, or genre.

L → M → N → O → P → Q

Leveled Readers

- Deliver instruction with each book's **Take and Teach Lesson**, choosing appropriate sessions based on need.

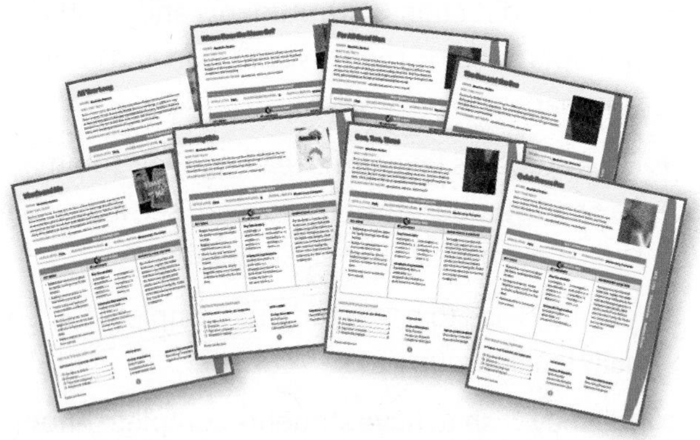

- Check comprehension, reinforce instruction, and extend learning with suggested supporting activities.

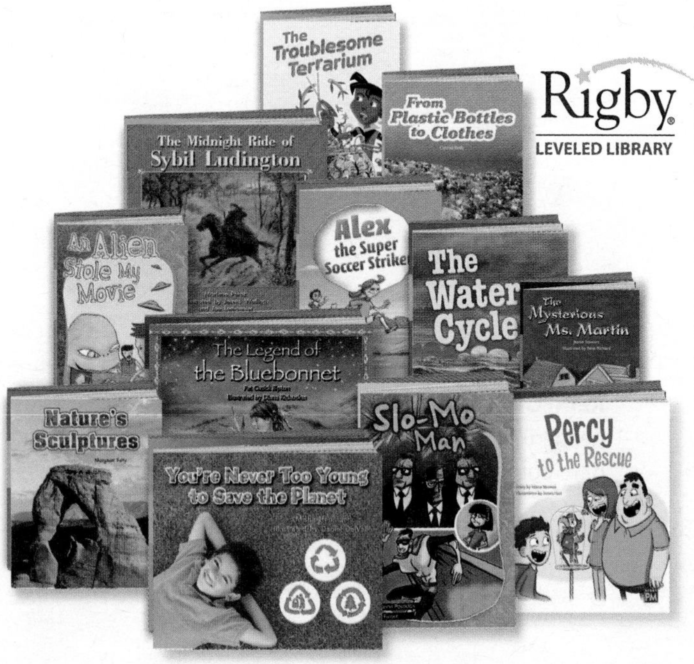

Rigby LEVELED LIBRARY

ENGLISH LEARNER SUPPORT

Recount Information

- Use **Tabletop Minilessons: English Language Development 8.1 (Speaking)** to reinforce and practice the language skill.

Tabletop Minilessons: English Language Development

- Then use the following text-based prompts with *Why We Celebrate the Fourth of July* to guide application of the language skill. Begin with the prompt at the student's identified language proficiency level. As students progress, use lighter supports to encourage increased language proficiency.

SUBSTANTIAL
Ask: *How do we celebrate the Fourth of July?* Allow students to use gestures, English words they know, and their home language to complete oral sentence frames: *The video shows _____. The video says _____.*

MODERATE
Have partners discuss the video using the following: *Why do we celebrate the Fourth of July? The video says we celebrate because _____. How do we celebrate the Fourth of July? The video shows _____.*

LIGHT
Have students discuss the following questions in small groups or pairs: *Why do we celebrate the Fourth of July? What do Americans do on the Fourth of July to celebrate?*

REINFORCE MEDIA TECHNIQUE

Demonstrate

- Use **Tabletop Minilessons: Reading Card 29** to remind students that **media** refers different forms of communication, both print and electronic. **Media techniques** are the means authors use to present a topic, idea, or other information. **Sound elements** and **expert** speakers provide information and set a mood or tone. The use of **live action**, **animation**, and other visuals attract attention.
- Model filling out Printable: Reading Graphic Organizer 29 to identify Media Techniques in *Why We Celebrate the Fourth of July*.

Tabletop Minilessons: Reading

Apply to Independent Reading

- Now have students identify the media techniques in appropriate media they are viewing independently. Customize these prompts to the texts students choose.
  - » *What visuals are used?*
  - » *What sound elements are used?*
  - » *How do the media techniques help you to understand what you are seeing and hearing?*
- Have students complete Printable: Reading Graphic Organizer 29 for their independent media viewing.

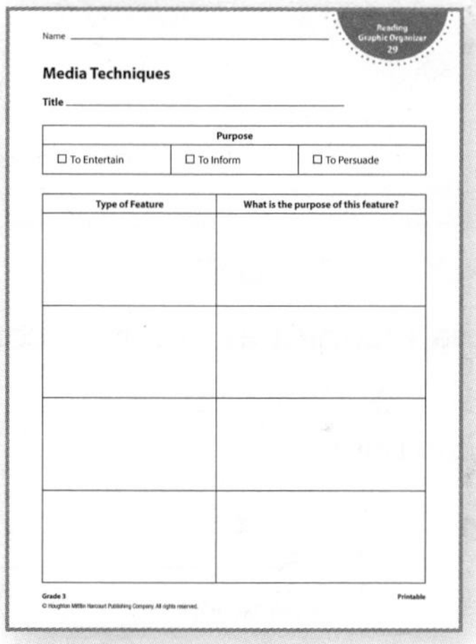

Printable: Reading Graphic Organizer 29

ALMOST THERE

READY FOR MORE

SCAFFOLD AND EXTEND

- Point out details in the text that indicate the Media Technique, and then help students to identify it.
- Prompt students to identify the Media Technique, the details in the text that indicate it, and the information it communicates.
- Have students identify the Media Technique and explain how it helps to communicate the information in the text.

EL ENGLISH LEARNER SUPPORT

SUBSTANTIAL

Provide sentence frames: *I can see* _____. *I can hear* _____.

MODERATE

Ask: *What images do you see? What sounds do you hear?*

LIGHT

Encourage students to explain how they identified the media techniques and used them to improve their understanding.

INDEPENDENT APPLICATION

Options for Independent and Collaborative Work

While you meet with small groups, have other students engage in literacy activities that reinforce the lesson's learning objectives. Choose from these options.

Independent Reading

Student Choice Library

Rigby
LEVELED LIBRARY

APPLY READING SKILL

Media Techniques Students complete Printable: Reading Graphic Organizer 29 for an independent reading book.

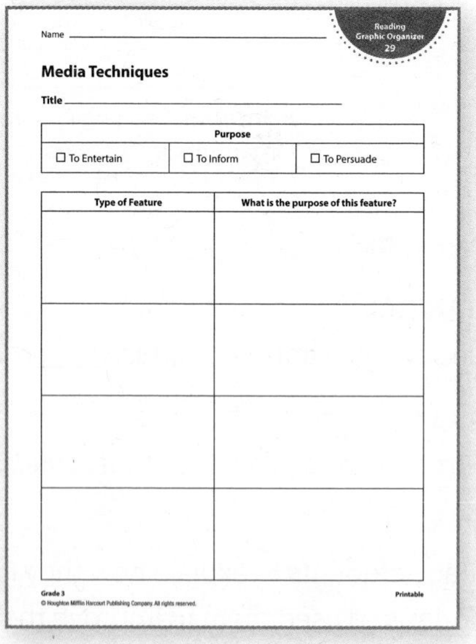
Name

Reading Graphic Organizer 29

Media Techniques

Title

Purpose		
☐ To Entertain	☐ To Inform	☐ To Persuade

Type of Feature	What is the purpose of this feature?

Grade 3 Printable
© Houghton Mifflin Harcourt Publishing Company. All rights reserved.

Printable: Reading Graphic Organizer 29

APPLY LANGUAGE SKILL

Recount Information Students complete Printable: Language Graphic Organize 11 for an independent reading book.

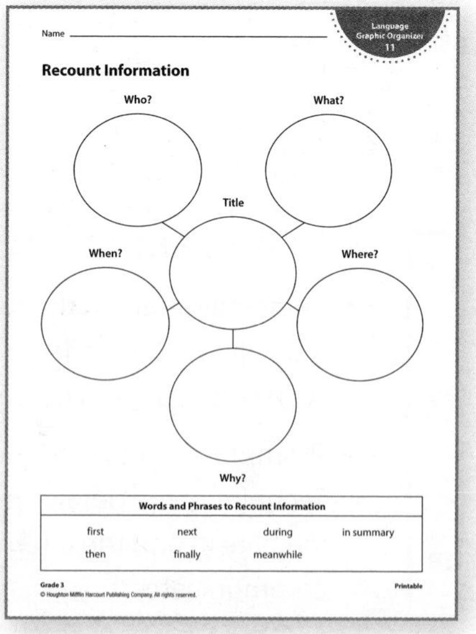

Printable: Language Graphic Organizer 11

Literacy Centers

See pp. T84–T85.

- READING CENTER
- VOCABULARY CENTER
- DIGITAL STATION
- WRITING CENTER
- PROJECT CENTER

Writing

Students write a summary. *See Engage and Respond, p. T103.*

Additional Skills Practice

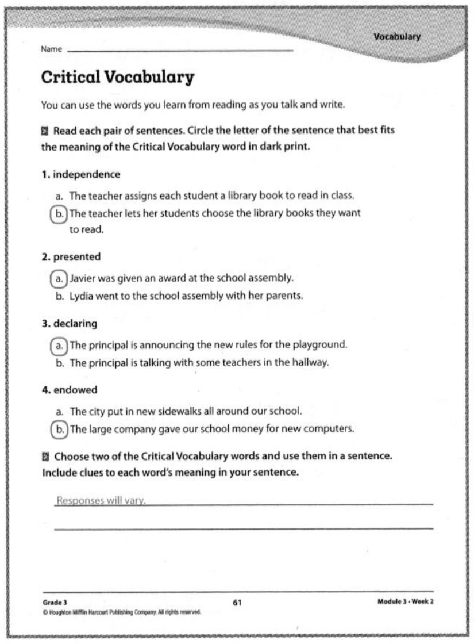

Vocabulary

Name ______________

Critical Vocabulary

You can use the words you learn from reading as you talk and write.

Read each pair of sentences. Circle the letter of the sentence that best fits the meaning of the Critical Vocabulary word in dark print.

1. independence

a. The teacher assigns each student a library book to read in class.
(b.) The teacher lets her students choose the library books they want to read.

2. presented

(a.) Javier was given an award at the school assembly.
b. Lydia went to the school assembly with her parents.

3. declaring

(a.) The principal is announcing the new rules for the playground.
b. The principal is talking with some teachers in the hallway.

4. endowed

a. The city put in new sidewalks all around our school.
(b.) The large company gave our school money for new computers.

Choose two of the Critical Vocabulary words and use them in a sentence. Include clues to each word's meaning in your sentence.

Responses will vary.

Grade 3 | 61 | Module 3 • Week 2

Know It, Show It, p. 61

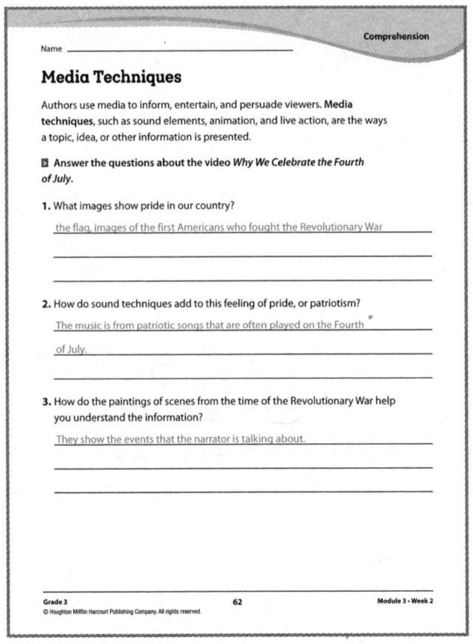

Comprehension

Name ______________

Media Techniques

Authors use media to inform, entertain, and persuade viewers. **Media techniques**, such as sound elements, animation, and live action, are the ways a topic, idea, or other information is presented.

Answer the questions about the video *Why We Celebrate the Fourth of July*.

1. What images show pride in our country?

the flag, images of the first Americans who fought the Revolutionary War

2. How do sound techniques add to this feeling of pride, or patriotism?

The music is from patriotic songs that are often played on the Fourth of July.

3. How do the paintings of scenes from the time of the Revolutionary War help you understand the information?

They show the events that the narrator is talking about.

Grade 3 | 62 | Module 3 • Week 2

Know It, Show It, p. 62

Wrap-Up

Share Time

At the end of the Reading Workshop, have students reflect on their learning by sharing how they applied **media techniques** or another area of focus during independent work time. Choose from these options:

- Use the **SOLO CHAIR** routine. Select a reader each day to come to the front of the class and tell what he or she learned from the reading by using a skill or strategy.
- **THINK-PAIR-SHARE** Students share their thinking with a partner. Select a few pairs each day to share with the whole class.
- **RETURN TO ANCHOR CHART** Have students add sticky notes about their independent reading to the Media Techniques Anchor Chart. Call on a few students to explain what they added and why.

Online Ed

ANCHOR CHART 29: Media Techniques

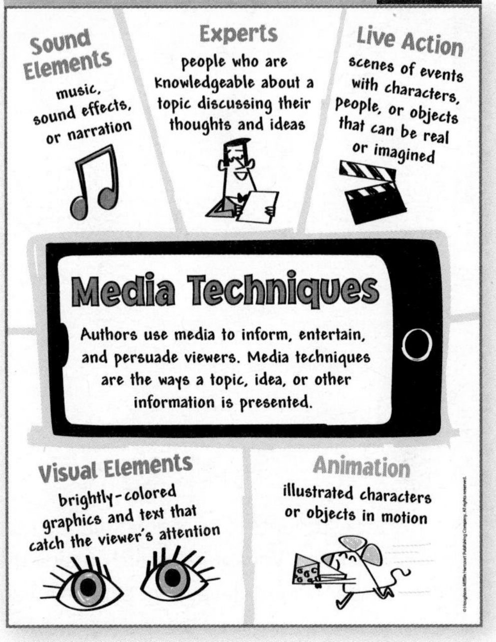

Introduce Critical Vocabulary

Step 1 Introduce the Words

Project Display and Engage: **Critical Vocabulary 3.8**. Then use the **VOCABULARY** routine to introduce the Critical Vocabulary from *The Flag Maker*. You may wish to display the corresponding Vocabulary Card for each word as you discuss it.

Online

DISPLAY AND ENGAGE:
Critical Vocabulary 3.8

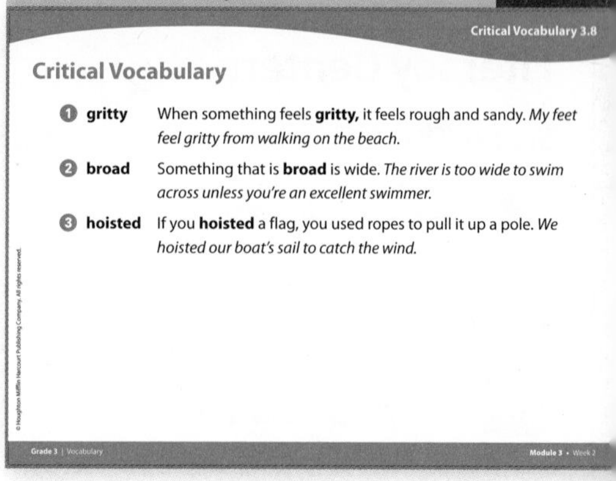
Critical Vocabulary 3.8

Critical Vocabulary

1. **gritty** When something feels **gritty,** it feels rough and sandy. *My feet feel gritty from walking on the beach.*
2. **broad** Something that is **broad** is wide. *The river is too wide to swim across unless you're an excellent swimmer.*
3. **hoisted** If you **hoisted** a flag, you used ropes to pull it up a pole. *We hoisted our boat's sail to catch the wind.*

1. Read aloud each word and have students repeat it.
2. Read aloud and discuss each word's student-friendly explanation.
3. Point out the example for the word. Have students suggest other examples.

LEARNING OBJECTIVES

- Identify real-life connections between words and their use.
- Use newly acquired vocabulary expressively.
- **Language** Answer questions and discuss meanings to develop vocabulary.

MATERIALS

Online Ed

Display and Engage *Critical Vocabulary 3.8*

Vocabulary Cards *3.14–3.16*

CRITICAL VOCABULARY

- **broad (p. 255)**
- **gritty (p. 257)**
- **hoisted (p. 270)**

TEACHER TIP

Ask students to note any time they see a Critical Vocabulary word outside the classroom. Have them explain where they saw or heard the word.

ENGLISH LEARNER SUPPORT: Build Vocabulary

SUBSTANTIAL
Ask students to use gestures to show the meaning of *broad*.

MODERATE
Have students use this sentence frame to explain the meaning of *broad*. *When something is broad, it is* _____.

LIGHT
Have pairs of students write sentences describing things that are broad.

Step 2 Guided Practice

Guide students to interact with the words by discussing questions such as these:

- *When something is **gritty**, is it soft, smooth, or rough? Explain.*
- *If a tunnel is **broad**, is a car likely to get stuck while driving through it? Why or why not?*
- *If you **hoisted** a flag, did you take it down for the night? Explain.*

Ask students to name things in the classroom or outdoors that are broad and things that feel gritty. Have them describe what happens when the school flag is hoisted.

Step 3 Apply

- Have students work independently to complete steps 3 and 4 on Vocabulary Cards 3.14–3.16.
- Have students use the **TURN AND TALK** routine to discuss the prompt on each Vocabulary Card.

Vocabulary Cards

LEARNING MINDSET

Grit

Apply Suggest ways that students can have grit. *You may not understand a new word yet, even after you've read the definition. Do a search for the word in context, or ask a friend how they'd use the word in the sentence. You'll understand and even use the word eventually, with a little time and effort!*

Retell

Step 1 Connect and Teach

LEARNING OBJECTIVES

- Retell the important ideas in a text.
- Evaluate details to determine key ideas.
- **Language** Identify characters, conflict, and resolution to retell the narrative.

MATERIALS — Online Ed

Anchor Chart 3 *Retell*
Printable *Anchor Chart 3: Retell*
Teaching Pal *Book 1, pp. 250–273*
myBook *The Flag Maker, Book 1, pp. 250–273*
Display and Engage *Meet the Author and Illustrator 3.8*

INSTRUCTIONAL VOCABULARY

- **conflict** something in a story that creates a challenge for the characters; also called *problem*
- **resolution** how the conflict in a story is solved
- **retell** to tell a story in your own words

SPANISH COGNATES

- **conflict** *conflicto*
- **resolution** *resolucíon*

- Tell students they are going to read a narrative nonfiction text called *The Flag Maker*. Explain that a good strategy for keeping track of what happens in a narrative is to **retell** key events. Retelling helps readers better understand what they read.
- Project or display Anchor Chart 3: Retell. Use the chart to point out what a good retelling should include: information about important characters, the setting, and the **conflict** or problem that the main character faces. The retelling should also tell about the **resolution**, or how the problem is solved.
- Explain that a good retelling describes the events that happen in the beginning, middle, and end of the story in the order that they happen. Clue words such as *first, next, then, later,* and *finally* signal the sequence of events.
- Tell students that they will practice retelling when they read *The Flag Maker.*

Online — **ANCHOR CHART 3:** Retell

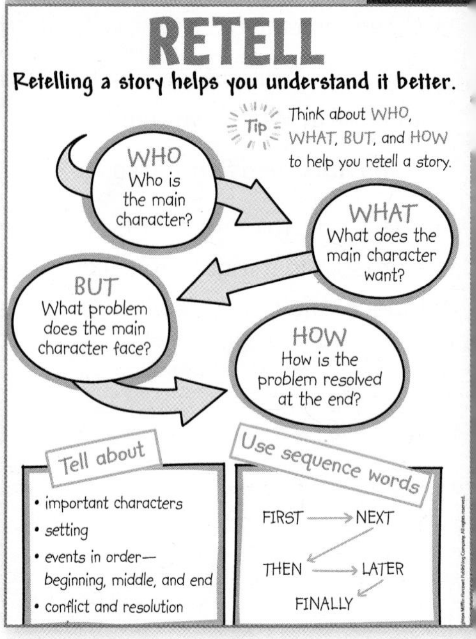
RETELL
Retelling a story helps you understand it better.
Tip
Think about WHO, WHAT, BUT, and HOW to help you retell a story.
WHO Who is the main character?
WHAT What does the main character want?
BUT What problem does the main character face?
HOW How is the problem resolved at the end?
Tell about
• important characters
• setting
• events in order— beginning, middle, and end
• conflict and resolution
Use sequence words
FIRST NEXT
THEN LATER
FINALLY

Notice & Note

Again and Again

- The Teaching Pal prompts in this lesson feature the **Notice & Note Signpost: Again and Again**.
- As needed, refer to p. T18 to review the signpost with students.

ASSESSMENT OPTION

Assign the Selection Quiz to check comprehension of *The Flag Maker.*

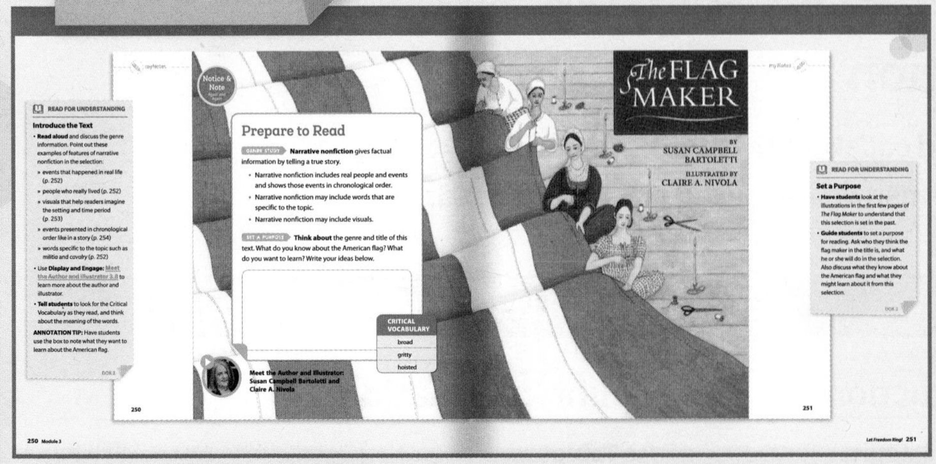

Online

ANNOTATE IT!

Students may use the annotation tools in their eBook.

Step 2 Apply to Text

In your Teaching Pal, pages 250–271, use the blue **READ FOR UNDERSTANDING** prompts and the red **Notice & Note** prompts to read *The Flag Maker* as students follow along and annotate their *my*Book.

- **Genre Study** Guide students through the genre information on page 250.
- **Set a Purpose** Read the Set a Purpose section on page 250. Prompt students to set their own purpose for reading *The Flag Maker*.
- **Meet the Author and Illustrator** Project Display and Engage 3.8: Meet the Author and Illustrator and read the information aloud with students. Ask students how an author and illustrator work together to develop a story.
- **Read and Comprehend** Use the **READ FOR UNDERSTANDING** routine as you guide students to read the selection. Pause occasionally, using the prompts in your Teaching Pal to gauge students' understanding and to have them retell what they have read so far. As students retell the story, have them refer back to the Anchor Chart to try to answer the *Who, What, But What,* and *How* questions.

Step 3 Engage and Respond

INDEPENDENT PRACTICE: Speaking and Listening

- After reading, use the **COLLABORATIVE CONVERSATION** routine with the Collaborative Discussion questions on Teaching Pal and *my*Book page 271. Have students annotate their *my*Book with details from the text and visuals as evidence to explain their responses.
- Ask volunteers to read aloud the Speaking and Listening Tips. Point out that building on others' ideas helps to keep all group members involved in the discussion, and to keep the discussion moving forward.
- You may want to have students conduct their discussions during daily small-group time.

ENGLISH LEARNER SUPPORT: Support Comprehension

SUBSTANTIAL

Prior to reading, do a picture walk to familiarize students with characters and conflict and use the images to support their retellings.

MODERATE

Ask guiding questions: *Who are the main characters? What is their conflict or problem? What is the resolution?*

LIGHT

Have students use complete sentences to identify the main characters, their conflict, and its resolution.

LINK TO SMALL-GROUP INSTRUCTION

REINFORCE RETELL Review and extend the skill as needed during small-group time to support students' need for differentiation. *See the lesson on p. T113.*

Options for Differentiation

As the class engages in independent and collaborative work, meet with Guided Reading Groups or differentiate instruction based on student need.

GUIDED READING GROUPS

Match Students to Books + Instruction

- Choose just-right books based on level, skill, topic, or genre.

L M N O P Q

Leveled Readers

- Deliver instruction with each book's **Take and Teach Lesson**, choosing appropriate sessions based on need.

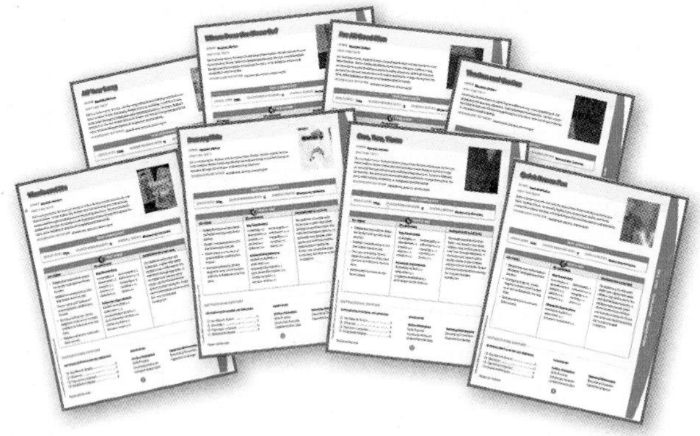

- Check comprehension, reinforce instruction, and extend learning with suggested supporting activities.

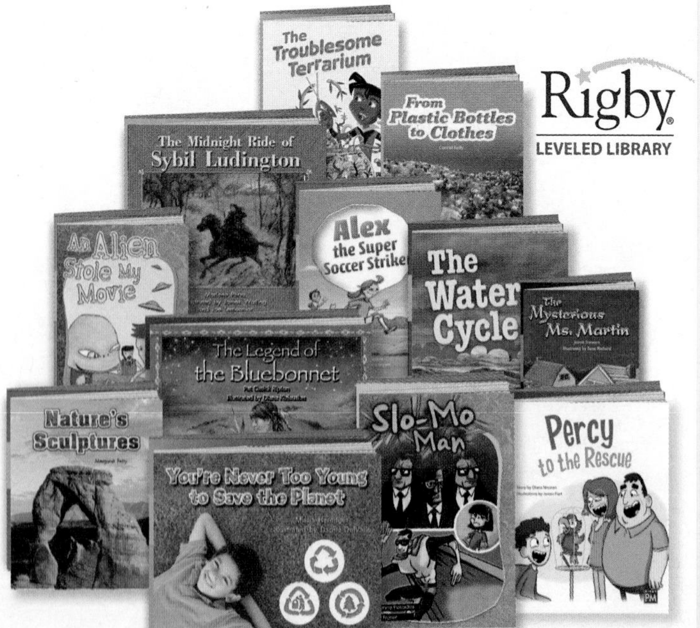

ENGLISH LEARNER SUPPORT

Recount Information

- Use **Tabletop Minilessons: English Language Development 8.2 (Reading)** to reinforce and practice the language skill.

Tabletop Minilessons: English Language Development

- Then use the following text-based prompts with *The Flag Maker* to guide application of the language skill. Begin with the prompt at the student's identified language proficiency level. As students progress, use lighter supports to encourage increased language proficiency.

SUBSTANTIAL
Choral read the first paragraph of the selection. Use the following question-and-answer frames: *When was the United States at war with Britain? The United States was at war with Britain in _____. What did a country at war need? A country at war needed _____.*

MODERATE
Have students take turns reading the first page. After each paragraph, pause to ask a question about the content, and have students answer using information found in the text. For example: *What did Caroline and her mother do? Why did they do it? The text says _____.*

LIGHT
Have students read the first page and then answer the following questions: *What was happening in 1812? Who was Caroline Pickersgill? What did Caroline and her mother do? Why?*

REINFORCE RETELL

Demonstrate

- Use **Tabletop Minilessons: Reading Card 3** to remind students that they can **retell** key events to keep track of what happens in a narrative. A good retelling should include information about the characters and setting as well as the **conflict** and **resolution**. Events should be told in sequence using words, such as *first, next, then,* and *last*.
- Model filling out Printable: Reading Graphic Organizer 3 to retell *The Flag Maker.*

Apply to Independent Reading

- Now have students retell a book or article they are reading independently. Customize these prompts to the texts students choose.
  - » *What is the setting? Who are the characters?*
  - » *What is the conflict and resolution?*
  - » *What is the order of key events?*
- Have students complete Printable: Reading Graphic Organizer 3 for their independent reading book.

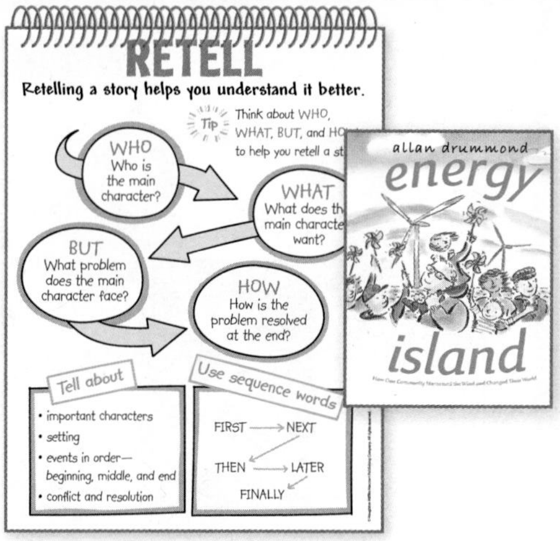
RETELL
Retelling a story helps you understand it better.
Tip
WHO
Who is the main character?
WHAT
BUT
What problem does the main character face?
HOW
How is the problem resolved at the end?
Tell about
• important characters
• setting
• events in order—beginning, middle, and end
• conflict and resolution
Use sequence words
FIRST
NEXT
THEN
LATER
FINALLY
allan drummond
energy
island

Tabletop Minilessons: Reading

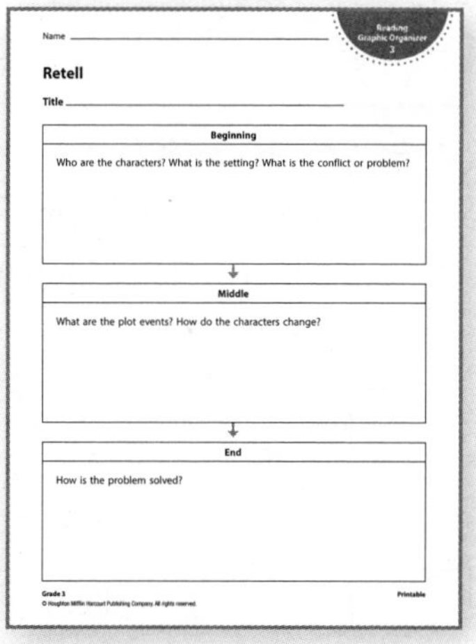
Name
Reading Graphic Organizer 3
Retell
Title
Beginning
Who are the characters? What is the setting? What is the conflict or problem?
Middle
What are the plot events? How do the characters change?
End
How is the problem solved?
Grade 3
Printable

Printable: Reading Graphic Organizer 3

ALMOST THERE

READY FOR MORE

SCAFFOLD AND EXTEND

- Have students name the characters, setting, problem, and solution. Then guide them to retell key events in sequence.
- As students retell, guide them to differentiate between key events and minor events that don't need to be included in the retelling.
- Have students explain why they chose to include particular events and details in their retelling.

ENGLISH LEARNER SUPPORT

SUBSTANTIAL
Supply sentence frames such as: *The characters are* ______. *The setting is* ______. *The problem is* ______. *The solution is* ______.

MODERATE
Supply students with a bank of sequence words and phrases to aid their retelling, such as *first, then, next, after,* and *finally*.

LIGHT
Have students retell to a partner and make suggestions to one another as to how to improve their retellings.

Options for Independent and Collaborative Work

While you meet with small groups, have other students engage in literacy activities that reinforce the lesson's learning objectives. Choose from these options.

Independent Reading

Student Choice Library

Rigby
LEVELED LIBRARY

APPLY READING SKILL

Retell Students complete Printable: Reading Graphic Organizer 3 for an independent reading book.

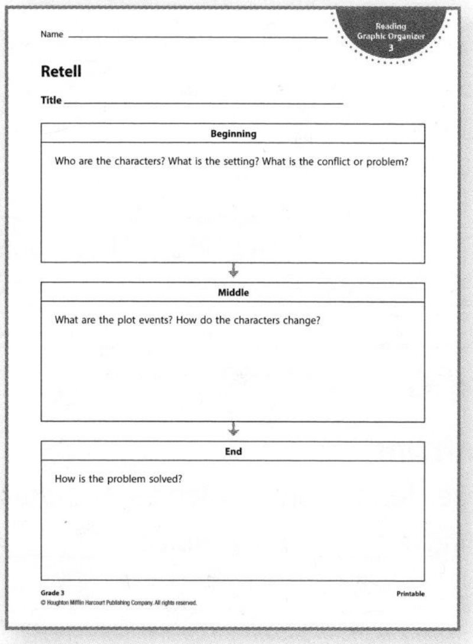

Name

Reading Graphic Organizer 3

Retell

Title

Beginning
Who are the characters? What is the setting? What is the conflict or problem?

Middle
What are the plot events? How do the characters change?

End
How is the problem solved?

Grade 3 Printable

© Houghton Mifflin Harcourt Publishing Company. All rights reserved.

Printable: Reading Graphic Organizer 3

APPLY LANGUAGE SKILL

Recount Information Students complete Printable: Language Graphic Organizer 11 for an independent reading book.

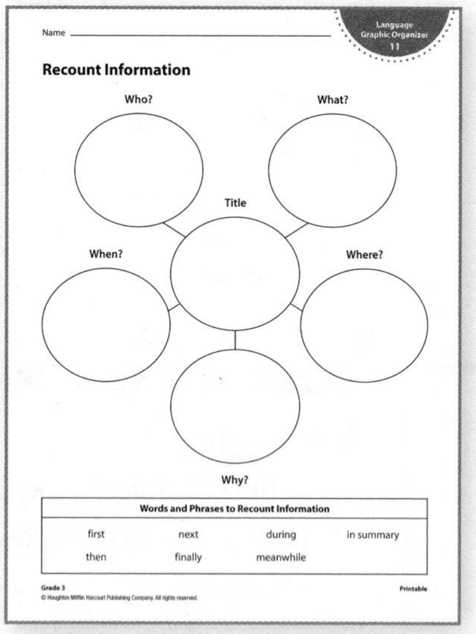

Words and Phrases to Recount Information			
first	next	during	in summary
then	finally	meanwhile	

Grade 3 Printable

© Houghton Mifflin Harcourt Publishing Company. All rights reserved.

Printable: Language Graphic Organizer 11

Notice & Note

Again and Again

When students encounter this signpost in their independent narrative nonfiction reading, encourage them to ask and answer the Anchor Question: *Why might the author bring this up again and again?*

Literacy Centers

See pp. T84–T85.

- READING CENTER
- VOCABULARY CENTER
- DIGITAL STATION
- WRITING CENTER
- PROJECT CENTER

Speaking and Listening

Partners discuss the Collaborative Discussion questions. *See Engage and Respond, p. T111.*

Additional Skills Practice

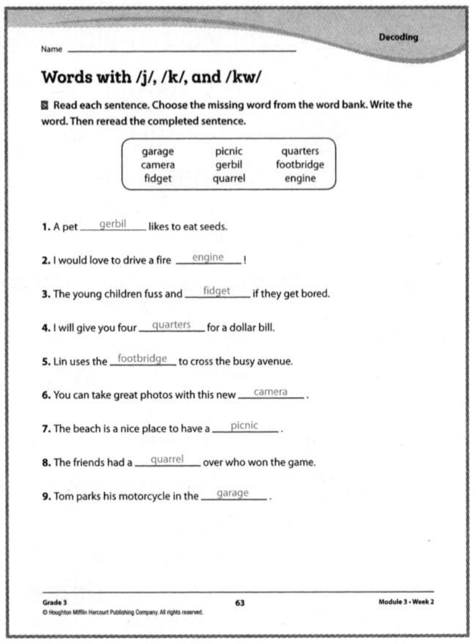
Decoding

Name ____________________

Words with /j/, /k/, and /kw/

Read each sentence. Choose the missing word from the word bank. Write the word. Then reread the completed sentence.

garage	picnic	quarters
camera	gerbil	footbridge
fidget	quarrel	engine

1. A pet gerbil likes to eat seeds.
2. I would love to drive a fire engine !
3. The young children fuss and fidget if they get bored.
4. I will give you four quarters for a dollar bill.
5. Lin uses the footbridge to cross the busy avenue.
6. You can take great photos with this new camera .
7. The beach is a nice place to have a picnic .
8. The friends had a quarrel over who won the game.
9. Tom parks his motorcycle in the garage .

Grade 3 63 Module 3 • Week 2

© Houghton Mifflin Harcourt Publishing Company. All rights reserved.

Know It, Show It, p. 63

Wrap-Up

Share Time

At the end of the Reading Workshop, have students reflect on their learning by sharing how they applied **retell** or another area of focus during independent work time. Choose from these options:

- Use the **SOLO CHAIR** routine. Select a reader each day to come to the front of the class and tell what he or she learned from the reading by using a skill or strategy.
- **THINK-PAIR-SHARE** Students share their thinking with a partner. Select a few pairs each day to share with the whole class.
- **RETURN TO ANCHOR CHART** Have students add sticky notes about their independent reading to the Retell Anchor Chart. Call on a few students to explain what they added and why.

Online Ed

ANCHOR CHART 3: Retell

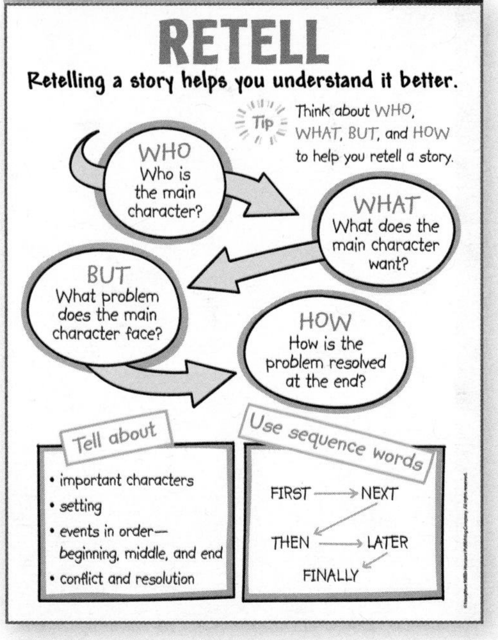

RETELL
Retelling a story helps you understand it better.
Tip
Think about WHO, WHAT, BUT, and HOW to help you retell a story.
WHO
Who is the main character?
WHAT
What does the main character want?
BUT
What problem does the main character face?
HOW
How is the problem resolved at the end?
Tell about
• important characters
• setting
• events in order—beginning, middle, and end
• conflict and resolution
Use sequence words
FIRST
NEXT
THEN
LATER
FINALLY

Words with /j/, /k/, and /kw/

Step 1 Reinforce the Skill

LEARNING OBJECTIVES

- Decode and read multisyllable words with /j/, /k/, and /kw/.
- Recognize spelling patterns for /j/, /k/, and /kw/.
- **Language** Articulate the /j/, /k/, and /kw/ sounds and read words containing those sounds.

MATERIALS Online Ed

Display and Engage *Decoding 3.8*

Know It, Show It *p. 63*

Words with /j/, /k/, and /kw/ Remind students that they have learned the sounds and spellings of /j/, /k/, and /kw/.

- **Transition to Longer Words** Display and read the word *gentle*. Underline the *ge*, pointing out the /j/ sound.
- Tell students they can divide longer words into syllables to make them easier to read. Draw a line between *n* and *t* to divide *gentle* into syllables. Note that the first syllable containing *ge* ends in a consonant, which means it's a closed syllable. Explain that closed syllables usually have short vowel sounds.
- Repeat with the words *passage, gadget, confuse,* and *quickly*. Guide students to read the words aloud and to help you identify the syllables that contain *ge, dge, c,* or *qu*. Point out that in longer words, students may find these letters in the middle of the word, as in *gadget*.
- Display the chart below. Read aloud each word, emphasizing the final sound /j/ and the initial sounds /k/ and /kw/.

ge	dge	c	qu
bandage	knowledge	concert	qualify

- Display the following sentence and underline the word *qualify*.

Rachel ran a fast enough time in the race to qualify for the state meet.

Say: *Let's say I didn't know the word* qualify. *I see the letters* qu *at the beginning and I know that they stand for the /kw/ sound. I divide the word into syllables: /kwŏl/ /ə/ /fī/,* qualify. *That sounds right. It also makes sense in the context of the sentence.* Qualify *means "to have the right skill to do a particular activity."*

ENGLISH LEARNER SUPPORT: Utilize Language Transfer

ALL LEVELS Many English speakers may find difficulty pronouncing the sounds /j/, /k/, and /kw/. Start by making the sound /j/ several times while students focus on your mouth. Have students use mirrors to see how their mouths look as they pronounce /j/. Repeat for /k/ and /kw/.

Step 2 Guided Practice

- Project Display and Engage: **Decoding 3.8**.
- Have students read aloud the Blend and Read lines. Provide feedback as needed. At the end of each line, prompt a conversation about the words: *How are the sounds the same or different? How are the spellings similar or different?*
- Have partners reread the Blend and Read lines and quiz each other on the spellings of /j/, /k/, and /kw/.

Online Ed

Display and Engage: Decoding 3.8

Decoding 3.8

Decoding

Words with /j/, /k/, and /kw/

1	prejudge (dge)	consider (c)	garbage (ge)	question (qu)	picture (c)
2	complete (c)	plastic (c)	equal (qu)	manage (ge)	dislodge (dge)
3	orange (ge)	quickly (qu)	hedgehog (dge)	actor (c)	genius (ge)
4	equipment (qu)	drawbridge (dge)	legend (ge)	request (qu)	oxygen (ge)
5	quality (qu)	general (ge)	cartridge (c, dge)	capital (c)	partridge (dge)

6. It was easy for the three bears to cook (c) porridge (dge) in their cottage (c, ge).
7. The earthquake (qu) caused (c) a lot of damage (ge) to villages (ge) near the equator (qu) and left people helpless.

Grade 3 | Foundational Skills   Module 3 • Week 2

Step 3 Apply

INDEPENDENT PRACTICE

- Have students work in small groups or with partners to complete Know It, Show It page 63.
- Encourage students to share with each other the strategies they use to decode words with the spellings of /j/, /k/, and /kw/.

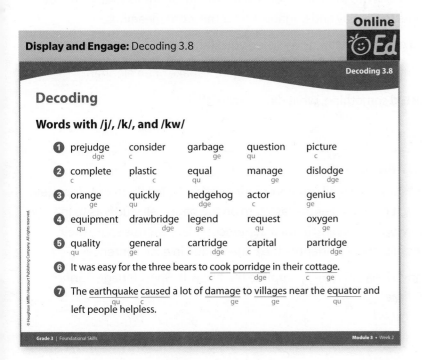

CORRECT & REDIRECT

If students have trouble decoding words with /j/, /k/, and /kw/, use the model below.

- **Correct** the error. *The letters* ge *and* dge *can be pronounced /j/. The letter* c *can be pronounced /k/. The letters* qu *are pronounced /kw/.*
- **Model** how to decode the word. */lĕg/ /ənd/. That doesn't sound right. I'll try reading* ge *with a /j/ sound. /lĕj/ /ənd/. That sounds like a word I know.*
- **Guide** students to decode other words: *genius, dislodge,* and *complete*.
- **Check** students' understanding by displaying the word *equipment*. *What do you know about the letters* qu *that can help you decode this word? (The letters* qu *can be pronounced /kw/.)*
- **Reinforce** by repeating the process with *picture*.

Review Critical Vocabulary

LEARNING OBJECTIVES

- Review and extend understanding of word meanings.
- Use context to determine the meanings of unfamiliar words.
- **Language** Use newly acquired vocabulary expressively.

MATERIALS | Online Ed

Display and Engage *Critical Vocabulary 3.8*

Know It, Show It *p. 64*

CRITICAL VOCABULARY

- **broad**
- **gritty**
- **hoisted**

Step 1 Reinforce Vocabulary

- Project Display and Engage: Critical Vocabulary 3.8 to review and discuss the Critical Vocabulary, student-friendly explanations, and examples of the words. Have students take turns using the words in sentences.

Step 2 Guided Practice

- Have student partners take turns answering questions about the Critical Vocabulary words. Provide questions such as the following for students to ask one another, and invite them to create their own questions as well. As needed, direct students to Display and Engage 3.8 for the word meanings.

1. What kind of surface feels gritty when you stand on it?
2. If something is broad, is it shaped more like a snake or an elephant?
3. If you hoisted something, what did you do with it?

Step 3 Apply

INDEPENDENT PRACTICE

- Have students work in small groups or independently. Tell them to complete Know It, Show It page 64. For the last item on the page, tell students to include clues to each word's meaning in their sentences. Have groups share their sentences. Ask listeners to identify the context clue in each sentence.
- You may wish to have students complete the Know It, Show It page during Small Group time.

ENGLISH LEARNER SUPPORT: Support Discussion

Use tiered supports as needed to help students as they answer questions about the Critical Vocabulary.

SUBSTANTIAL

Show what movements you would make if you hoisted something.

MODERATE

If you hoisted something, which way did you move it?

LIGHT

What do you need to hoist something? What kinds of things might you hoist?

Multiple-Meaning Words

Step 1 Review the Strategy

Project Display and Engage: Vocabulary Strategy 3.9 a, 3.9b, 3.9c, and 3.9d. Read aloud the two paragraphs.

Online Ed

DISPLAY AND ENGAGE: Vocabulary Strategy 3.9a, 3.9b, 3.9c, 3.9d

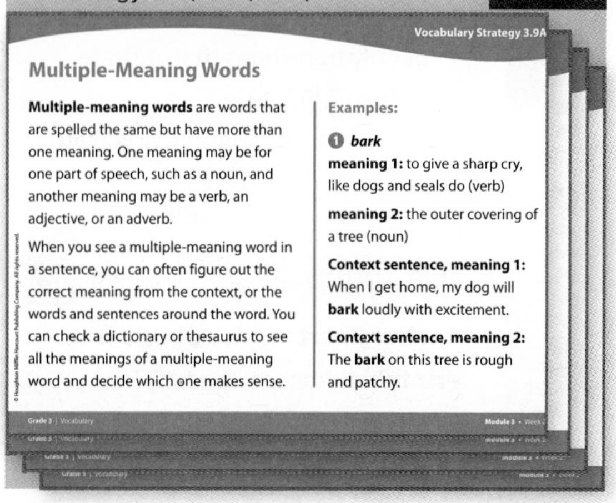
Vocabulary Strategy 3.9A

Multiple-Meaning Words

Multiple-meaning words are words that are spelled the same but have more than one meaning. One meaning may be for one part of speech, such as a noun, and another meaning may be a verb, an adjective, or an adverb.

When you see a multiple-meaning word in a sentence, you can often figure out the correct meaning from the context, or the words and sentences around the word. You can check a dictionary or thesaurus to see all the meanings of a multiple-meaning word and decide which one makes sense.

Examples:

1 ***bark***

meaning 1: to give a sharp cry, like dogs and seals do (verb)

meaning 2: the outer covering of a tree (noun)

Context sentence, meaning 1: When I get home, my dog will **bark** loudly with excitement.

Context sentence, meaning 2: The **bark** on this tree is rough and patchy.

- Review that multiple-meaning words are words that are spelled the same but have different meanings. Remind students that using context clues can help them identify a word's meaning.
- Use the first two examples to model writing context sentences for the multiple-meaning words *bark* and *nail* to show their correct meaning. *Bark can be a verb that means "to give a sharp cry" or a noun that means "the outer coating of a tree." I can write a sentence that gives clues to the word's meaning. The words "my dog" and "loudly" are clues to the first meaning. The words "tree" and "rough and patchy" are clues to the second meaning.* Repeat with *nail*.

Step 2 Guided Practice

- Have students read the definitions for the multiple-meaning words *jam* and *star.* Then ask them to write context sentences for both meanings of the words.
- Ask students to identify their context clues and how they reveal the word meaning.

Step 3 Apply the Strategy

INDEPENDENT PRACTICE

- Have students work independently or in pairs to find these multiple-meaning words in *The Flag Maker*: *ships, felt, room, strike*. Have them use context to determine each word's meaning in the selection. They can use a reference source as needed.
- Next, tell students to write a second meaning for each word, again using a reference source as needed. The have them write a context sentence for this meaning.
- Have students exchange sentences with a partner, identify the meaning of each multiple-meaning word, and identify the context clues.

LEARNING OBJECTIVES

- Use context to determine the relevant meanings of multiple-meaning words and use the words in context sentences.
- Use print and digital reference materials to clarify meanings.
- **Language** Identify and use multiple-meaning words using strategic learning techniques.

MATERIALS Online Ed

Display and Engage *Vocabulary Strategy 3.9a, 3.9b, 3.9c, 3.9d*

INSTRUCTIONAL VOCABULARY

- **multiple-meaning words** words that are spelled the same but have more than one meaning

ENGLISH LEARNER SUPPORT: Use Multiple-Meaning Words

SUBSTANTIAL

Encourage students to use oral context sentences to show two different meanings of *ships*. Offer support as needed.

MODERATE

Supply sentence frames to help students write context sentences: *A word related to ships is _____. I can use that as a context clue.*

LIGHT

Ask students to explain how they decided which context clues to use to show the correct meaning of *ships* in their sentence.

Text Structure

Step 1 Connect and Teach

LEARNING OBJECTIVES

- Analyze the use of text structure to achieve specific purposes.
- Identify transitions that indicate sequence in text.
- **Language** Identify and articulate transition words that indicate a sequence text structure.

MATERIALS

Online Ed

Anchor Chart 18 *Text Structure*

Printable *Anchor Chart 18: Text Structure*

Teaching Pal *Book 1, pp. 250–273*

myBook *The Flag Maker Book 1, pp. 250–273*

Know It, Show It *p. 65*

INSTRUCTIONAL VOCABULARY

- **sequence** an order of events (beginning, middle, and end) in a story
- **text structure** the way information is organized in a text

SPANISH COGNATES

- **text** *texto*
- **structure** *estructura*
- **sequence** *sequencia*

Project or display Anchor Chart 18: Text Structure. Remind students that authors use a specific **text structure** depending on their purpose and the information they are presenting. Draw attention to the sequence section of the chart to discuss the following:

Online

ANCHOR CHART 18: Text Structure Ed

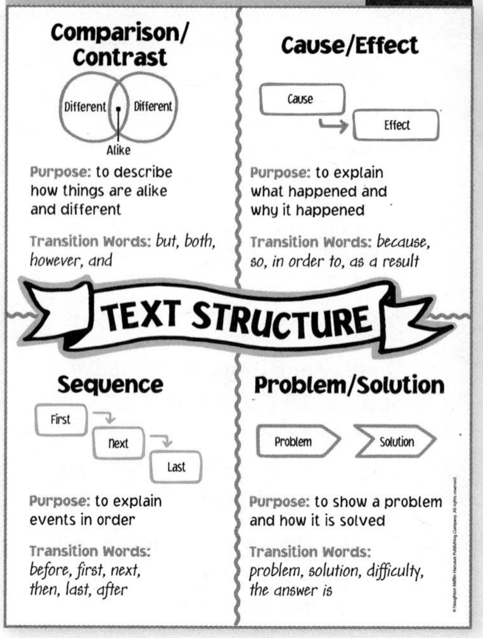

- Authors use a **sequence** text structure when they describe events in the order that they happen. In addition to the transition words shown on the Anchor Chart, an author may use dates and times to signify sequence.
- The author's purpose for telling about events in the order that they happen may be to help readers understand how one event led to another. A sequence text structure also helps to create some suspense for readers as they try to determine what the final outcome will be.
- Discuss with students how identifying a text's structure can help them better understand the information in the text. Tell them that they will practice identifying text structure to gain a deeper understanding of *The Flag Maker*.

LEARNING MINDSET

Grit

Reflect Remind students that people with grit keep trying, even when the task or goal is difficult. *When you have grit, you are strong during hard times. You continue to pursue your goal, just as Caroline and her mother did in* The Flag Maker. Discuss ways students can find the strength to follow their goals and paths and not give up.

Go to Your
Teaching Pal

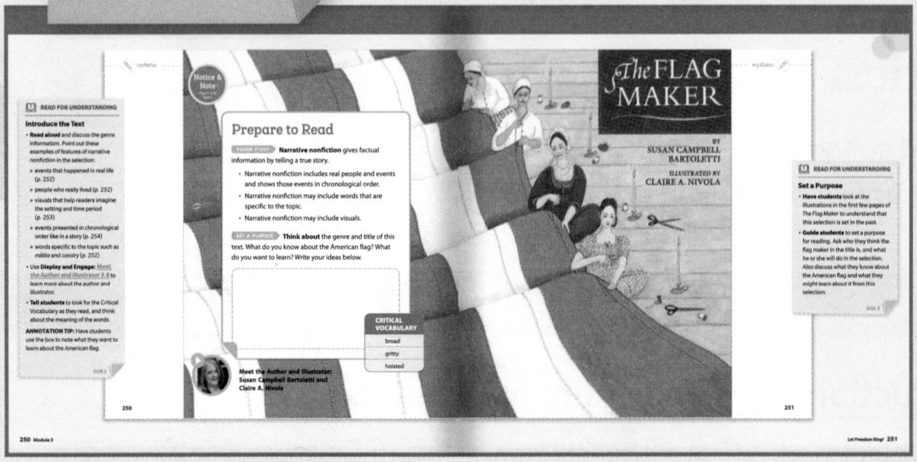

Online

ANNOTATE IT!

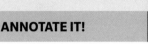

Students may use the annotation tools in their eBook.

Step 2 Apply to Text

In your Teaching Pal, use the purple **TARGETED CLOSE READ** prompts on pages 250–271 to guide students to apply the text structure skill to *The Flag Maker* and to find evidence to support their responses. Use the **CLOSE READING** routine. Students may refer to the questions on Know It, Show It page 65 as you discuss them.

- Read aloud the first question on Teaching Pal page 259. Then have students reread *my*Book paragraphs 21–26. Ask students to identify the text structure of this part of the text and tell how they know. *(sequence; the author shows what happens first, next, and finally.)*
- Read aloud the follow-up question on Teaching Pal page 259. Ask students how knowing the text structure helps them focus on what is happening in the narrative. *(Thinking about the sequence helps you follow the steps in making such an enormous flag.)*
- Refer back to the Anchor Chart to support the discussion. Have students use sticky notes to add to the Anchor Chart more examples of words and phrases that signal sequence in *The Flag Maker*.

Step 3 Engage and Respond

INDEPENDENT PRACTICE: Writing

- **Write an Autobiography** Turn to pages 272–273 in your Teaching Pal. Have students turn to pages 272–273 in their *my*Book. Use the **WRITING RESPONSE** routine.
- Read the directions with students and use the Teaching Pal prompts to guide them as they plan and complete their autobiographies.
- Provide time for students to share their autobiographies with small groups.
- You may want to have students complete their writing during daily small-group time.
- You may want to have students complete Know It, Show It page 65 during small-group time.

ENGLISH LEARNER SUPPORT: Elicit Participation

SUBSTANTIAL

Point to the words that show sequence. Say the words with me.

MODERATE

Which words show the sequence of events? What happened first? Next?

LIGHT

Have students use transition words to describe the sequence of events.

LINK TO SMALL-GROUP INSTRUCTION

REINFORCE TEXT STRUCTURE Review and extend the skill as needed during small-group time to support students' need for differentiation. *See the lesson on p. T123.*

Options for Differentiation

As the class engages in independent and collaborative work, meet with Guided Reading Groups or differentiate instruction based on student need.

GUIDED READING GROUPS

Match Students to Books + Instruction

- Choose just-right books based on level, skill, topic, or genre.

L → M → N → O → P → Q

Leveled Readers

- Deliver instruction with each book's **Take and Teach Lesson**, choosing appropriate sessions based on need.

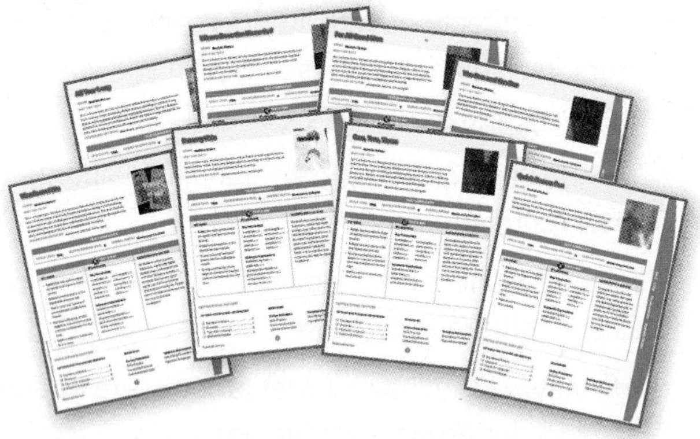

- Check comprehension, reinforce instruction, and extend learning with suggested supporting activities.

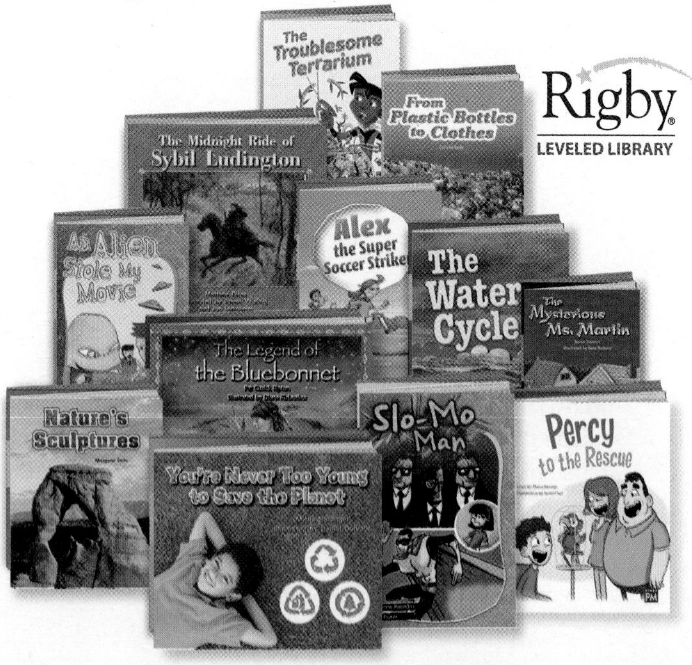

ENGLISH LEARNER SUPPORT

Recount Information

- Use **Tabletop Minilessons: English Language Development 8.2 (Writing)** to reinforce and practice the language skill.

Independence Day is an exciting day in Washington, DC. First, you can watch the parade on Constitution Avenue. Second, you can attend a festival on the National Mall. The festival includes food, music, and dances. Next, you can listen to a music concert at the U.S. Capitol. Finally, you can watch a huge fireworks show!
Recount Information

Tabletop Minilessons: English Language Development

- Then use the following text-based prompts with *The Flag Maker* to guide application of the language skill. Begin with the prompt at the student's identified language proficiency level. As students progress, use lighter supports to encourage increased language proficiency.

SUBSTANTIAL
Have students write sentences that retell three events from the story using sequence words: *First* _____. *Next* _____. *Finally* _____. Guide them to find words and phrases from the text to complete the sentences.

MODERATE
Provide students with a list of sequence words such as *first, second, next,* and *finally*. Have students use the words in a written summary of the important information and events for one page in the story.

LIGHT
Have students write a sequence chart that recounts the key events and information in the story.

REINFORCE TEXT STRUCTURE

Demonstrate

- Use **Tabletop Minilessons: Reading Card 18** to remind students that authors use specific kinds of **text structure** to help them communicate information. Authors use is **sequence** text structure to tell events in the order that they happened. Words such as *first, next, then,* and *last,* help to signal order of events in sequence text structure. Paying attention to sequence text structure can help readers understand how one event leads to another.
- Model filling out Printable: Reading Graphic Organizer 18 to identify text structure in *The Flag Maker*.

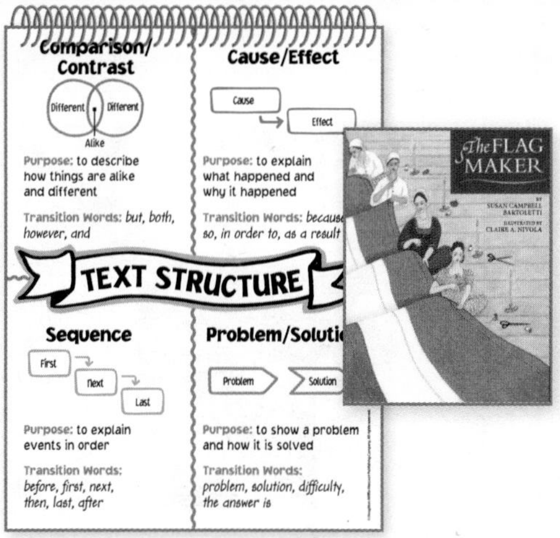

Tabletop Minilessons: Reading

Apply to Independent Reading

- Now have students identify the text structure in an appropriate book or article they are reading independently. Customize these prompts to the texts students choose.
  - » *What kind of text structure does the author use?*
  - » *What words does the author use to signal sequence of events?*
  - » *What is the author's purpose for using this text structure?*
- Have students complete Printable: Reading Graphic Organizer 18 for their independent reading book.

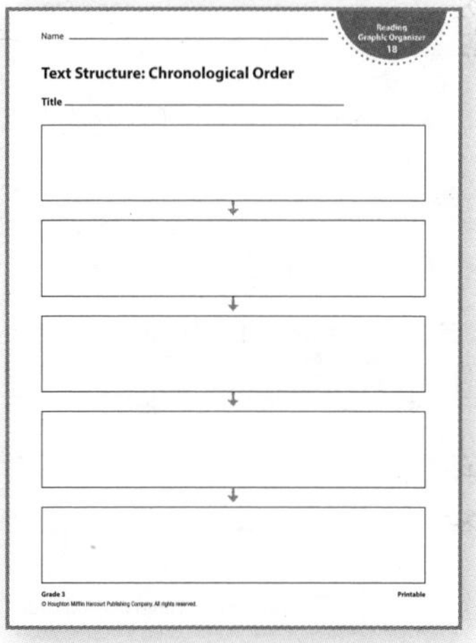

Printable: Reading Graphic Organizer 18

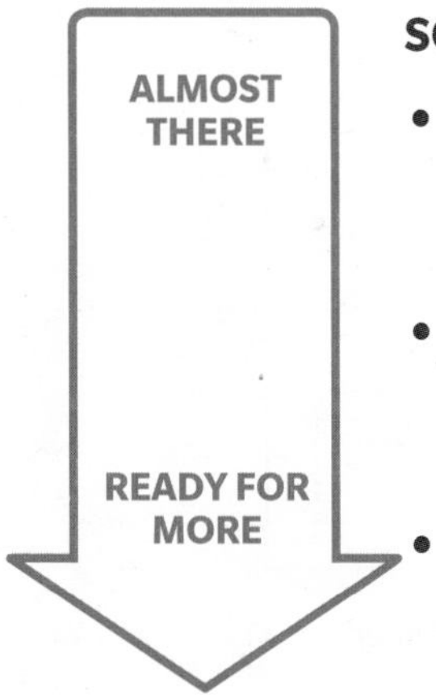

SCAFFOLD AND EXTEND

- Point out details in the text that indicate the text structure. Then help students to identify it.
- Prompt students to identify the text structure and the author's purpose for using it.
- Have students identify the text structure and evaluate whether they think it is the best structure for the text.

ENGLISH LEARNER SUPPORT

SUBSTANTIAL
Have students point to places in the text or illustrations that show the text structure.

MODERATE
Have students complete the sentence frames: *The text structure is ______. The author uses the words ______ to indicate sequence.*

LIGHT
Encourage students to explain their reasoning as they answer the prompts.

Options for Independent and Collaborative Work

While you meet with small groups, have other students engage in literacy activities that reinforce the lesson's learning objectives. Choose from these options.

Independent Reading

Student Choice Library

Rigby
LEVELED LIBRARY

APPLY READING SKILL

Text Structure Students complete Printable: Reading Graphic Organizer 18 for an independent reading book.

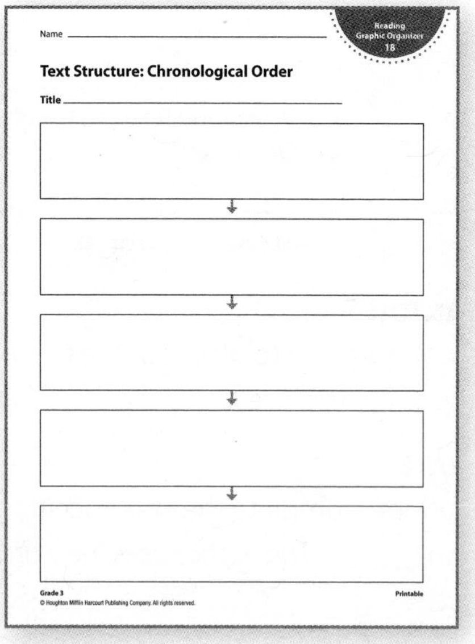

Name ______

Reading Graphic Organizer 18

Text Structure: Chronological Order

Title ______

Grade 3 — Printable
© Houghton Mifflin Harcourt Publishing Company. All rights reserved.

Printable: Reading Graphic Organizer 18

APPLY LANGUAGE SKILL

Recount Information Students complete Printable: Language Graphic Organizer 11 for an independent reading book.

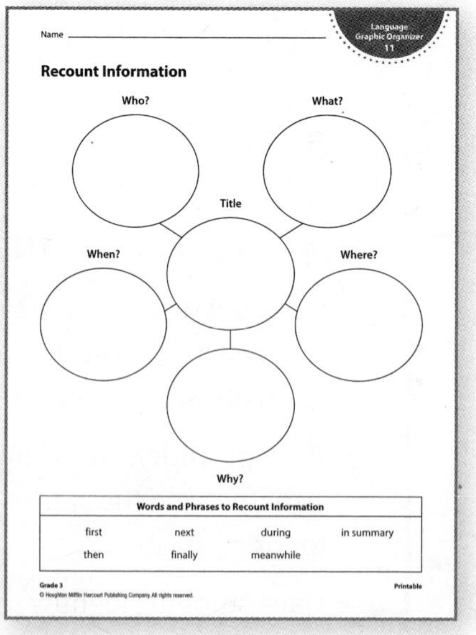

Name ______

Language Graphic Organizer 11

Recount Information

Who? What? Title When? Where? Why?

Words and Phrases to Recount Information			
first	next	during	in summary
then	finally	meanwhile	

Grade 3 — Printable
© Houghton Mifflin Harcourt Publishing Company. All rights reserved.

Printable: Language Graphic Organizer 11

Literacy Centers

See pp. T84–T85.

- READING CENTER
- VOCABULARY CENTER
- DIGITAL STATION
- WRITING CENTER
- PROJECT CENTER

Writing

Students write an autobiography.
See Engage and Respond, p. T121.

Additional Skills Practice

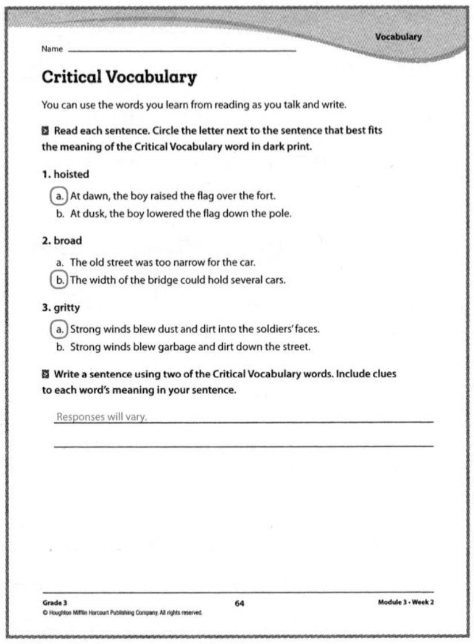
Name ______ Vocabulary

Critical Vocabulary

You can use the words you learn from reading as you talk and write.

Read each sentence. Circle the letter next to the sentence that best fits the meaning of the Critical Vocabulary word in dark print.

1. hoisted
   - (a.) At dawn, the boy raised the flag over the fort.
   - b. At dusk, the boy lowered the flag down the pole.
2. broad
   - a. The old street was too narrow for the car.
   - (b.) The width of the bridge could hold several cars.
3. gritty
   - (a.) Strong winds blew dust and dirt into the soldiers' faces.
   - b. Strong winds blew garbage and dirt down the street.

Write a sentence using two of the Critical Vocabulary words. Include clues to each word's meaning in your sentence.

Responses will vary.

Grade 3 64 Module 3 • Week 2
© Houghton Mifflin Harcourt Publishing Company. All rights reserved.

Know It, Show It, p. 64

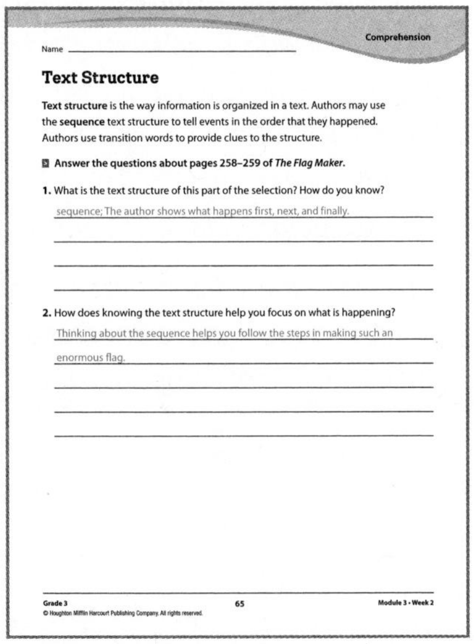
Name ______ Comprehension

Text Structure

Text structure is the way information is organized in a text. Authors may use the **sequence** text structure to tell events in the order that they happened. Authors use transition words to provide clues to the structure.

Answer the questions about pages 258–259 of *The Flag Maker*.

1. What is the text structure of this part of the selection? How do you know?
   sequence; The author shows what happens first, next, and finally.
2. How does knowing the text structure help you focus on what is happening?
   Thinking about the sequence helps you follow the steps in making such an enormous flag.

Grade 3 65 Module 3 • Week 2
© Houghton Mifflin Harcourt Publishing Company. All rights reserved.

Know It, Show It, p. 65

Wrap-Up

Share Time

At the end of the Reading Workshop, have students reflect on their learning by sharing how they applied **text structure** or another area of focus during independent work time. Choose from these options:

- Use the **SOLO CHAIR** routine. Select a reader each day to come to the front of the class and tell what he or she learned from the reading by using a skill or strategy.
- **THINK-PAIR-SHARE** Students share their thinking with a partner. Select a few pairs each day to share with the whole class.
- **RETURN TO ANCHOR CHART** Have students add sticky notes about their independent reading book to the Text Structure Anchor Chart. Call on a few students to explain what they added.

Online Ed

ANCHOR CHART 18: Text Structure

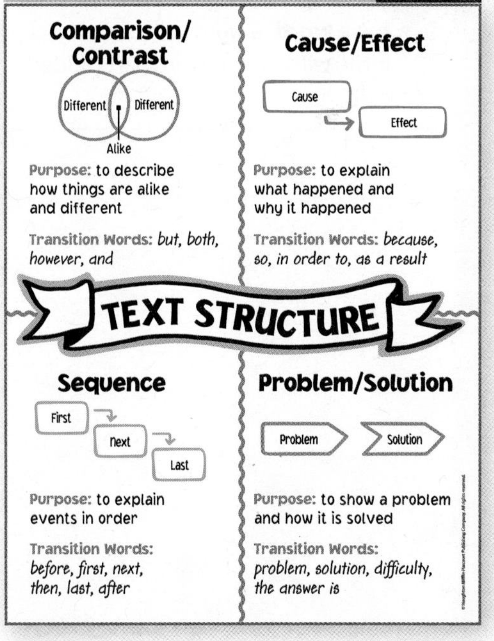

Suffixes -er, -est

Step 1 Introduce the Skill

LEARNING OBJECTIVES

- Determine the meaning of grade-level academic vocabulary with prefixes or suffixes.
- Use a dictionary or glossary to determine the meanings of unknown words.
- **Language** Discuss words with the suffixes *-er* and *-est* to show understanding of the target suffixes and spelling changes to base words when the suffixes are added.

MATERIALS

Online Ed

Display and Engage *Generative Vocabulary 3.10*

Know It, Show It *p. 66*

INSTRUCTIONAL VOCABULARY

- **suffix** a word part added to the end of a base word that changes the meaning of the word
- **prefix** a word part added to the beginning of a base word that changes the meaning of the word
- **base word** a word in its simplest form, without any word parts added to it

Project Display and Engage: Generative Vocabulary 3.10. Read aloud the paragraphs.

DISPLAY AND ENGAGE: Generative Vocabulary 3.10

Online Ed

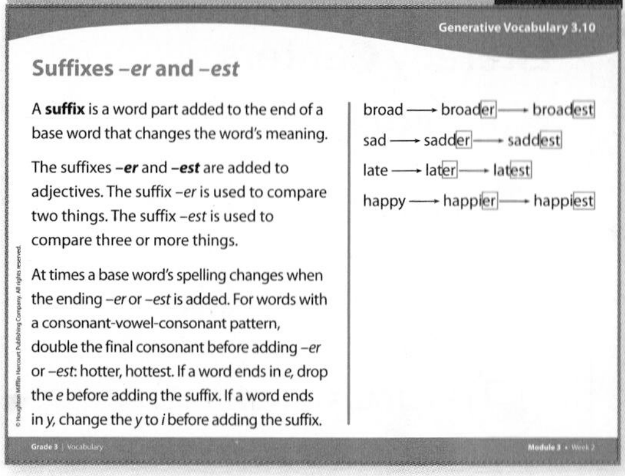
Generative Vocabulary 3.10

Suffixes *–er* and *–est*

A **suffix** is a word part added to the end of a base word that changes the word's meaning.

The suffixes ***–er*** and ***–est*** are added to adjectives. The suffix *–er* is used to compare two things. The suffix *–est* is used to compare three or more things.

At times a base word's spelling changes when the ending *–er* or *–est* is added. For words with a consonant-vowel-consonant pattern, double the final consonant before adding *–er* or *–est*: hotter, hottest. If a word ends in *e*, drop the *e* before adding the suffix. If a word ends in *y*, change the *y* to *i* before adding the suffix.

broad → broader → broadest
sad → sadder → saddest
late → later → latest
happy → happier → happiest

Grade 3 | Vocabulary Module 3 • Week 2

- Write the word *grand*, and ask a volunteer to give the word's meaning. Then write the words *grander* and *grandest*, and underline the suffix in each. Tell students that knowing the meaning of the suffixes *-er* and *-est* plus the meaning of the base word can help them figure out the meaning of each word.
- Then model how to use suffixes to determine the meaning of a word. *The suffixes* –er *and* –est *are added to adjectives. The suffix* –er *is used to compare two things. For example: This castle is grand, but the castle next door to it is grander. The suffix* –est *is used to compare three or more things. For example: This castle is grand, but the castle next door to it is grander. The castle down the street is grandest of all.*

  Sometimes a base word's spelling changes slightly when the ending –er *or* –est *is added. For words such as big or hot, with a consonant-vowel-consonant pattern, I double the final consonant before adding* –er *or* –est*: bigger, biggest; hotter, hottest. For words that end in e, such as fine or pale, I drop the final e before adding the suffix: finer, finest; paler, palest. For words that end in y, such as merry, I change the y to i before adding the suffix: merrier, merriest.*

  When I see the suffix –er *in a word, I will know that the word is an adjective that compares one thing to another. When I see the suffix* –est*, I will know the word is an adjective that compares three or more things.*

ENGLISH LEARNER SUPPORT: Build Vocabulary

SUBSTANTIAL
Share with students familiar words with the suffixes *-er* and *-est*. Discuss each base word's meaning and how the suffix changes it.

MODERATE
Ask students to name words with the suffixes *-er* and *-est* and then identify each base word's meaning and tell how the suffix changes it.

LIGHT
Have pairs write sentences using the lesson's *-er* and *-est* words.

Step 2 Guided Practice

- Display the words *strong*, *stronger*, and *strongest*. Ask a volunteer to give the meaning of *strong*. Then ask students to identify the suffixes in *stronger* and *strongest* and explain how they change the meaning of the base word *strong*. Repeat the exercise with the words *gritty*, *grittier*, and *grittiest*.
- Then ask students to look up each word in a print or online dictionary to confirm their responses. Ask volunteers to use the different forms of each word in context sentences.

Step 3 Apply the Skill

INDEPENDENT PRACTICE

- Have students work in pairs to complete Know It, Show It page 66. Tell partners to read the instructions and then complete the activity together.
- Then have each student write a new sentence for each word with the *-er* or *-est* ending. Have partners read their sentences to one another to confirm the meaning of each word. Invite volunteers to read their sentences aloud.
- You may wish to have students complete the Know It, Show It page during Small Group time.

Spiral Review

Suffixes –*y*, –*less*; Prefix *dis*– Remind students that a suffix is a word part added to the end of a word that changes the word's meaning.

- Review that the suffix –*y* means "having or like" something. It changes a base word into an adjective. The suffix –*less* means "without." It also changes a base word into an adjective. The prefix *dis*– means "apart or away," "not," "absence of," or "to do the opposite of."
- Write these words on the board: *grain, noise*. Add the suffix –*y* to each word, noting that you must drop the final e in noise before adding -*y*. Have volunteers explain how the suffix changes each word's meaning and part of speech. Then write these words: *heart, penny*. Add the suffix –*less* to each word, noting that you must change the final *y* to *i* in penny before adding –*less.* Have volunteers explain how the suffix changes each word's meaning and part of speech. Finally, write these words: *invite, please*. Add the prefix *dis*- to each word, and have volunteers explain how the prefix changes each word's meaning and part of speech.
- Have students add the suffix –*y* to the following words: *wax, scare*. Have them add the suffix –*less* to the following words: *mirror, worry*. Have them add the prefix *dis*– to the following words: *agreement, allow*. Have students explain how the affixes change the words' meanings. Invite them to check the words' meanings in a print or online dictionary.

Content-Area Words

Step 1 Connect and Teach

LEARNING OBJECTIVES

- Use context to determine the meaning of content-area words.
- Use a dictionary or glossary to confirm the meanings of unfamiliar words.
- **Language** Define content-area words using context clues.

MATERIALS Online Ed

Anchor Chart 22 *Content-Area Words*
Printable *Anchor Chart 22: Content-Area Words*
Teaching Pal *Book 1, pp. 250–273*
myBook *The Flag Maker, Book 1, pp. 250–273*
Know It, Show It *p. 67*

INSTRUCTIONAL VOCABULARY

- **content-area words** the words in a text that are specific to a subject such as math, science, or social studies
- **context clue** the words and sentences around an unknown word that can be clues to its meaning

COGNATES

- **content** *contento*
- **area** *area*
- **context** *contexto*

Project or display Anchor Chart 22: Content-Area Words. Use the chart to present the following points:

- Authors may use **content-area words**, or words that are specific to the topic they are writing about. These words might be found in texts related to social studies, science, or math.
- Readers can use **context clues** to help them determine the meaning of content-area words. These clues may appear in the surrounding text, or visuals, such as diagrams or illustrations.
- Readers can confirm their understanding of an unfamiliar content-area word by using a dictionary or glossary.

Online
ANCHOR CHART 22: Content-Area Words

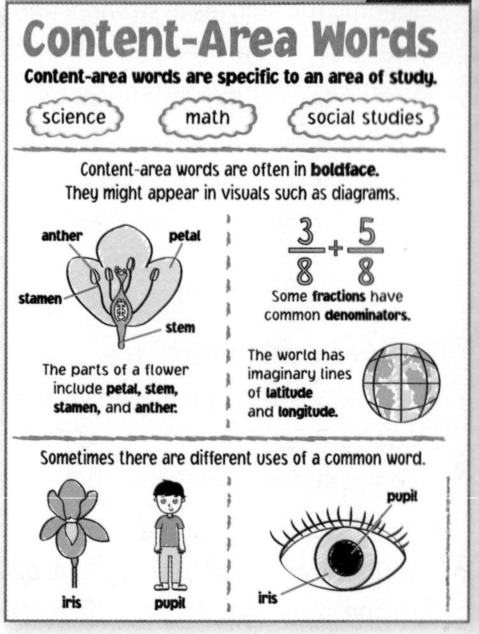

- Tell students that they will practice using context clues to define content-area words to gain a deeper understanding of *The Flag Maker*.

Go to Your
Teaching Pal

READ FOR UNDERSTANDING

How did the video "Why We Celebrate the Fourth of July" use the American flag to create a feeling of pride in the viewer? *(The flag was shown waving in the wind. There were other photographs showing the flag. It created a feeling of patriotism and pride in the country.)*

How is that similar to what Caroline feels? *(Caroline feels proud because she helped to make the flag. But she also seems proud to support the American fight against the British. The Fourth of July celebrates America's victory over the British.)*

DOK 4

TARGETED CLOSE READ

Content-Area Words

Have students reread paragraphs 27–28 to determine the meaning of a content-area word.

What do you think *ramparts* are? *(Ramparts are mounds of earth or walls around a fort that protect it from attack.)*

What clues in the text help you figure out the meaning? *(The text says that the flag is at Fort McHenry and is flying high above the ramparts. That means that ramparts must be part of the fort.)*

How does the illustration also help you with the meaning? *(It shows the fort in the distance, with the flag flying over it. The fort has walls around it, though they are a little hard to see.)*

DOK 2

myNotes

27 The flag was delivered to Fort McHenry, where soldiers raised it high above the ramparts.

28 Each day Caroline looked for her flag as it waved over the fort. It looked tiny in the distance, but she felt proud.

29 Over the next year, the flag shop grew even busier.

30 Caroline and her mother sewed more flags.

31 The Americans fought more battles.

32 Yet they could not defeat the British, once and for all.

33 And so a difficult year passed.

260 Module 3

261

READ FOR UNDERSTANDING

Why do you think the year is described as being a *difficult* one? *(Despite all the battles, the Americans cannot defeat the British.)*

DOK 2

Let Freedom Ring! 261

Online

ANNOTATE IT!

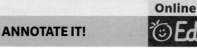

Students may use the annotation tools in their eBook.

Step 2 Apply to Text

In your Teaching Pal, use the purple **TARGETED CLOSE READ** prompt on pages 260 and 263 to guide students to apply the Content-Area Words skill to *The Flag Maker* and to find evidence to support their responses. Use the **CLOSE READING** routine. Students may refer to the questions on Know It, Show It page 67 as you discuss them.

- Read aloud the first two questions on Teaching Pal page 260. Then have students reread *my*Book, paragraphs 27–28, to determine the meaning of *ramparts* using clues in the text. *(*Ramparts *are mounds of earth or walls around a fort that protect it from attack. The text says that the flag is at Fort McHenry and is flying high above the ramparts. That means that ramparts must be part of the fort.)*
- Read aloud the follow-up question on Teaching Pal page 260. Discuss how the illustration supports the meaning. *(It shows the fort in the distance, with the flag flying over it. The fort has walls around it, though they are a little hard to see.)*
- Have students turn to pages 262–263. Use the prompts to have them determine the meanings of content-area words. Refer back to the Anchor Chart to support the discussion. Students may add sticky notes to the chart as they encounter more content-area words in *The Flag Maker*.

Step 3 Engage and Respond

INDEPENDENT PRACTICE: Reading

Assign a section of a social studies lesson that contains content-area words to each pair or small group of students.

- Have students read the section and identify the content-area words and their definitions. Then, have them list the context clues that helped them figure out the meaning of each content-area word.
- Have partners use the **COLLABORATIVE DISCUSSION** routine to discuss the context clues they used. Call on pairs to share their responses.
- You may wish to have students complete Know It, Show It page 67 during daily small-group time.

ENGLISH LEARNER SUPPORT: Support Comprehension

SUBSTANTIAL

Say: *I'm not sure what _____ means. Point to clues in the text or pictures that we can use to figure it out. Let's say the words together.*

MODERATE

Ask: *What details in the text or pictures help you figure out what _____ means?*

LIGHT

Supply this frame: *I can use _____ to figure out the meaning of _____.*

LINK TO SMALL-GROUP INSTRUCTION

REINFORCE CONTENT-AREA WORDS Review and extend the skill as needed during small-group time to support students' need for differentiation. *See the lesson on p. T131.*

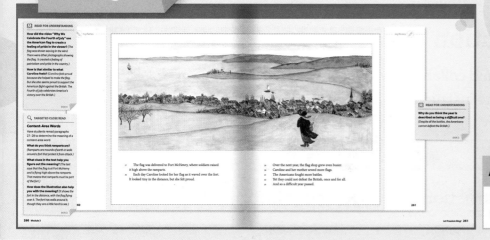

Options for Differentiation

As the class engages in independent and collaborative work, meet with Guided Reading Groups or differentiate instruction based on student need.

GUIDED READING GROUPS

Match Students to Books + Instruction

- Choose just-right books based on level, skill, topic, or genre.

L M N O P Q

Leveled Readers

- Deliver instruction with each book's **Take and Teach Lesson**, choosing appropriate sessions based on need.

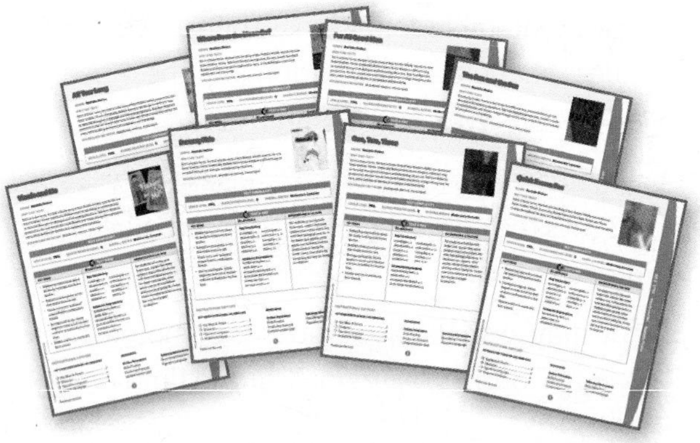

- Check comprehension, reinforce instruction, and extend learning with suggested supporting activities.

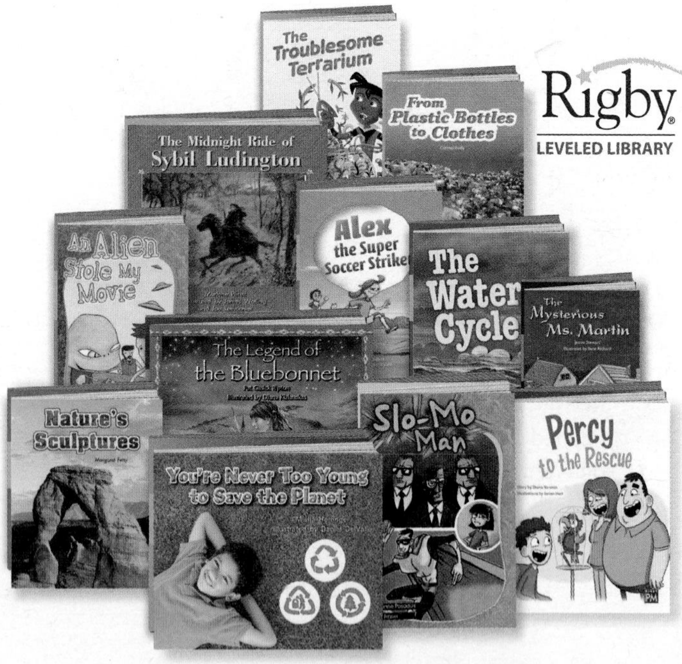

Rigby LEVELED LIBRARY

ENGLISH LEARNER SUPPORT

Recount Information

- Use **Tabletop Minilessons: English Language Development 8.3 (Collaborative Problem Solving)** to reinforce and practice the language skill.

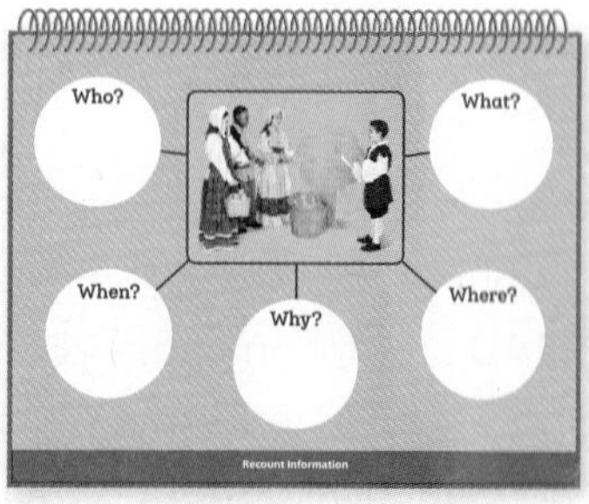

Tabletop Minilessons: English Language Development

- Then use the following text-based prompts with *The Flag Maker* to guide application of the language skill. Begin with the prompt at the student's identified language proficiency level. As students progress, use lighter supports to encourage increased language proficiency.

SUBSTANTIAL
Have students work together to act out a page from the story. Guide them to use words and phrases from the page in their dialogue.

MODERATE
Have students choose a scene from the story and work together to retell it in their own words, making sure to include key information and events.

LIGHT
Have students collaborate to retell what happened to the flag from the time it was made until the end of the story, making sure to include key information and events.

REINFORCE CONTENT-AREA WORDS

Demonstrate

- Use **Tabletop Minilessons: Reading Card 22** to remind students that **content-area words** are words that are specific to the topic an author is writing about. Readers can use **context clues** to help them determine the meaning of content-area words. These clues may appear in the surrounding text, or visuals, such as diagrams or illustrations. Readers can confirm their understanding of an unfamiliar content-area word by using a dictionary or glossary.
- Model filling out Printable: Reading Graphic Organizer 24 to identify content-area words in *The Flag Maker*.

Tabletop Minilessons: Reading

Apply to Independent Reading

- Now have students identify content-area words in an appropriate book or article they are reading independently. Customize these prompts to the texts students choose.
  - » *What is the subject of the text?*
  - » *What content-area words does the author use that are related to the subject?*
  - » *What context clues helped you to figure out the content-area words?*
- Have students complete Printable: Reading Graphic Organizer 24 for their independent reading book.

Printable: Reading Graphic Organizer 24

SCAFFOLD AND EXTEND

ALMOST THERE

READY FOR MORE

- Point out context clues and guide students to determine the meanings of content-area words.
- Prompt students to identify content-area words and explain how they figured out their meanings.
- Have students brainstorm or use a dictionary to help them find additional content-area words related to the subject of their reading text.

EL ENGLISH LEARNER SUPPORT

SUBSTANTIAL
Read aloud content-area words. Use gestures and visuals to clarify meaning for students.

MODERATE
Read aloud content-area words in context with students. Have students use the frame: *The word* _____ *means* _____.

LIGHT
Encourage students to explain how they used context clues or a dictionary or glossary to determine meaning of content area words.

Options for Independent and Collaborative Work

While you meet with small groups, have other students engage in literacy activities that reinforce the lesson's learning objectives. Choose from these options.

Independent Reading

Student Choice Library

Rigby
LEVELED LIBRARY

APPLY READING SKILL

Content-Area Words Students complete Printable: Reading Graphic Organizer 24 for an independent reading book.

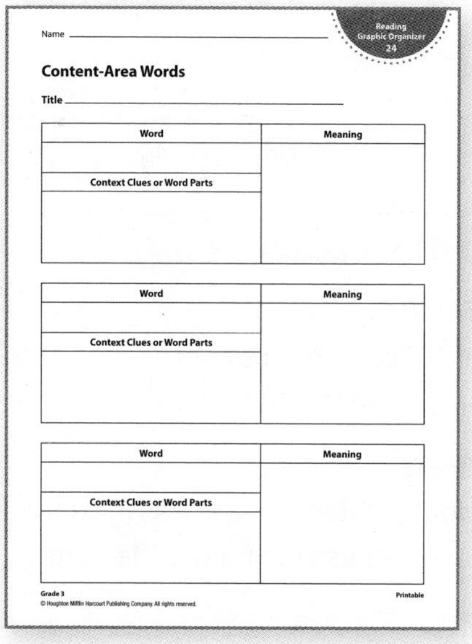
Name

Reading Graphic Organizer 24

Content-Area Words

Title

Word	Meaning
Context Clues or Word Parts	

Word	Meaning
Context Clues or Word Parts	

Word	Meaning
Context Clues or Word Parts	

Grade 3 Printable
© Houghton Mifflin Harcourt Publishing Company. All rights reserved.

Printable: Reading Graphic Organizer 24

APPLY LANGUAGE SKILL

Recount Information Students complete Printable: Language Graphic Organizer 11 for an independent reading book.

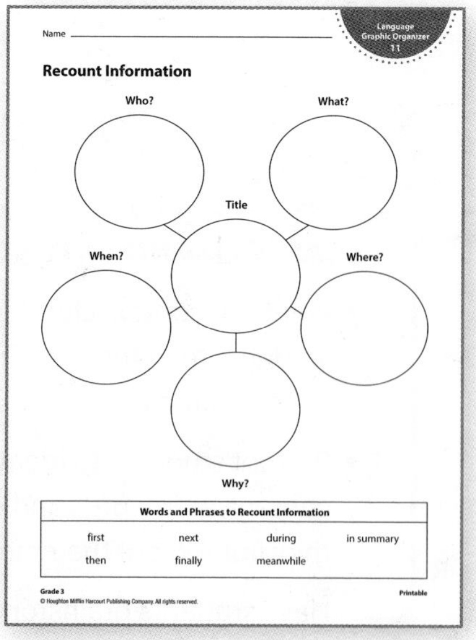

Printable: Language Graphic Organizer 11

Literacy Centers

See pp. T84–T85.

- READING CENTER
- VOCABULARY CENTER
- DIGITAL STATION
- WRITING CENTER
- PROJECT CENTER

Reading

Students read content-area words.
See Engage and Respond, p. T129.

Additional Skills Practice

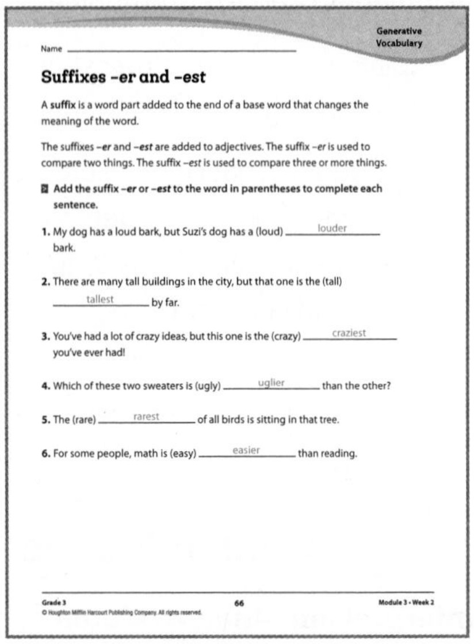
Generative Vocabulary

Name ______

Suffixes -er and -est

A **suffix** is a word part added to the end of a base word that changes the meaning of the word.

The suffixes *-er* and *-est* are added to adjectives. The suffix *-er* is used to compare two things. The suffix *-est* is used to compare three or more things.

Add the suffix *-er* or *-est* to the word in parentheses to complete each sentence.

1. My dog has a loud bark, but Suzi's dog has a (loud) louder bark.
2. There are many tall buildings in the city, but that one is the (tall) tallest by far.
3. You've had a lot of crazy ideas, but this one is the (crazy) craziest you've ever had!
4. Which of these two sweaters is (ugly) uglier than the other?
5. The (rare) rarest of all birds is sitting in that tree.
6. For some people, math is (easy) easier than reading.

Grade 3 66 Module 3 • Week 2

Know It, Show It, p. 66

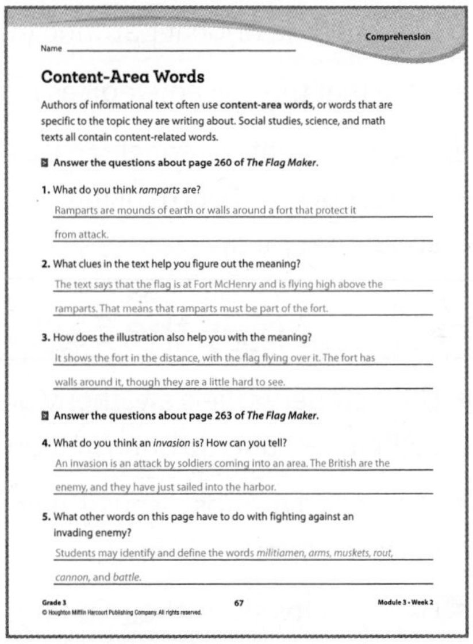
Comprehension

Name ______

Content-Area Words

Authors of informational text often use **content-area words**, or words that are specific to the topic they are writing about. Social studies, science, and math texts all contain content-related words.

Answer the questions about page 260 of *The Flag Maker*.

1. What do you think *ramparts* are?
Ramparts are mounds of earth or walls around a fort that protect it from attack.
2. What clues in the text help you figure out the meaning?
The text says that the flag is at Fort McHenry and is flying high above the ramparts. That means that ramparts must be part of the fort.
3. How does the illustration also help you with the meaning?
It shows the fort in the distance, with the flag flying over it. The fort has walls around it, though they are a little hard to see.

Answer the questions about page 263 of *The Flag Maker*.

4. What do you think an *invasion* is? How can you tell?
An invasion is an attack by soldiers coming into an area. The British are the enemy, and they have just sailed into the harbor.
5. What other words on this page have to do with fighting against an invading enemy?
Students may identify and define the words *militiamen, arms, muskets, rout, cannon,* and *battle*.

Grade 3 67 Module 3 • Week 2

Know It, Show It, p. 67

Wrap-Up

Share Time

At the end of the Reading Workshop, have students reflect on their learning by sharing how they applied **content-area words** or another area of focus during independent work time. Choose from these options:

- Use the **SOLO CHAIR** routine. Select a reader each day to come to the front of the class and tell what he or she learned from the reading by using a skill or strategy.
- **THINK-PAIR-SHARE** Students share their thinking with a partner. Select a few pairs each day to share with the whole class.
- **RETURN TO ANCHOR CHART** Have students add sticky notes about their independent reading to the Content-Area Words Anchor Chart. Call on a few students to explain what they added and why.

Online Ed

ANCHOR CHART 22:
Content-Area Words

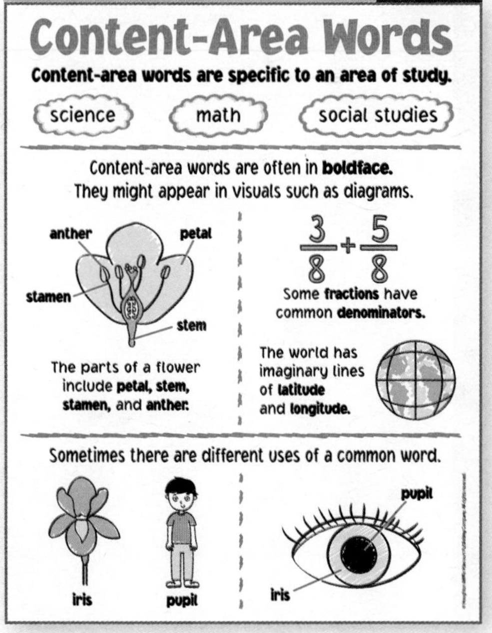

Media Literacy: Interpret/ Analyze Media

LEARNING OBJECTIVES

- Interpret messages in media.
- Analyze media techniques to communicate information.
- **Language** Use content-area words to describe media.

MATERIALS Online Ed

Video *Why We Celebrate the Fourth of July*

INSTRUCTIONAL VOCABULARY

- **analyze** to examine or study something to notice the important details
- **interpret** to understand or explain the meaning of
- **media techniques** the ways in which an author communicates ideas and information to the viewers, such as animation, live action, sound elements, and visual elements

Step 1 Introduce the Skill

Discuss Media Tell students that when they view media, such as a video, they should look for the message the video is communicating, as well as the techniques used to communicate the message.

- Explain that a video's message is connected to its purpose, which may be to entertain, to give information, or to persuade.
- Tell students that both visual (seeing) and audio (hearing) techniques are used to communicate in a video. Visuals may include use of images intended to evoke specific emotions or to give information. Audio may include voiceover, music, and sound effects.
- Say: *When you view media, you should watch and listen attentively. Pay attention to audio and visual techniques to help you determine the video's purpose and message or main ideas.*

Step 2 Guided Practice

Interpret and Analyze Media Model interpreting and analyzing the video *Why We Celebrate the Fourth of July.*

- Point out the upbeat patriotic music and images.
- Note that the voiceover gives information about the Fourth of July holiday.
- Guide students to conclude that the video's purpose is to give information about how the Fourth of July is celebrated, and to make the viewer feel positive about the holiday.

Step 3 Apply the Skill

- Have students view another video, making note of the audio and visual techniques, and the information presented.
- Have small groups discuss their notes and determine the video's purpose and message or main ideas.
- Have groups share their findings with the class.

ENGLISH LEARNER SUPPORT: Support Discussion

SUBSTANTIAL

Point to your eyes or ears and ask: *Did you see _____? Did you hear _____?* Students may answer using sentence frames: *I saw _____. I heard _____.*

MODERATE

Use sentence frames such as: *I saw _____. I heard _____. The video makes me feel _____. I think the video's purpose/message is _____.*

LIGHT

Prompt students to use the words *audio* and *visual* to describe the things they saw and heard in the video. Then have them describe the video's purpose or message.

Synthesize Topic Knowledge

Genre Focus

- Review with students the key features of narrative nonfiction and video. Narrative nonfiction tells about a real event in the form of a story with a beginning, middle, and end. A video uses visual images and sound to communicate information.
- Discuss with students the literature and media they encountered this week. Discuss how *The Flag Maker* and *Why We Celebrate the Fourth of July* communicate information in different ways.
- Ask students to summarize the main points of each selection.

LEARNING OBJECTIVES

- Recognize and describe the features of narrative nonfiction and video.
- Synthesize knowledge gained from the week's texts and video.
- **Language** Compare ideas from two selections using sentence frames for support.

MATERIALS Online Ed

myBook *Book 1, pp. 226–227, 251–271*
Display and Engage *Knowledge Map 3.10*

Knowledge Focus

- Project Display and Engage Knowledge Map 3.10. Have students turn to *myBook* page 251.
- Tell students to think about how the story of *The Flag Maker* shows how the American flag has represented our country. *(The giant American flag flew over Fort McHenry during the War of 1812 as a symbol of America for all to see.)*
- Then work with students to add information about how the holiday Independence Day from the video *Why We Celebrate the Fourth of July.*

Online
DISPLAY AND ENGAGE:
Knowledge Map 3.10

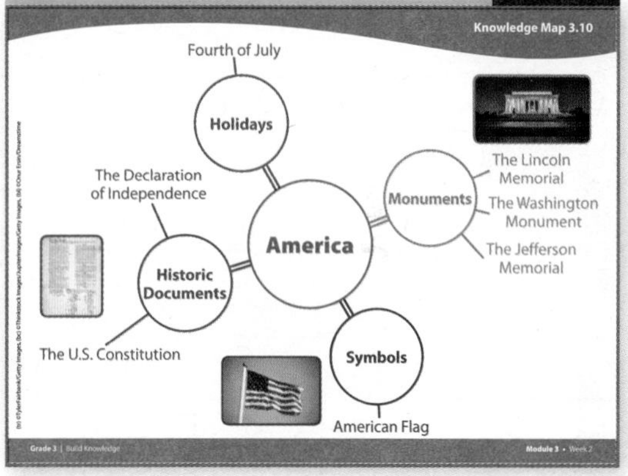

- Have students discuss and compare how the American Flag and the holiday the Fourth of July are different ways to represent America.
- Have students discuss their Knowledge Maps and their responses to the Essential Question: *How do historic places, documents, and symbols represent our nation?*
- Tell students that they will return to the Knowledge Map for the Week 3 Make Connections activity.

ENGLISH LEARNER SUPPORT: Facilitate Discussion

SUBSTANTIAL
Use these frames to help students compare: *The Fourth of July represents America by* _____. *The flag represents America by* _____.

MODERATE
Prompt students to make comparisons: *The flag and the Fourth of July both represent America because* _____.

LIGHT
Ask students to compare and generalize. Supply frames such as *The American flag and the Fourth of July are both* _____.

Notes

SOCIAL STUDIES CONNECTION:
U.S. History

Let Freedom Ring!

Essential Question How do historic places, documents, and symbols represent our nation?

Essential Skills

VOCABULARY

- Critical Vocabulary: *ferry, torch, sculptor, monument, inspired*
- Vocabulary Strategy: Spiral Review: Synonyms/ Antonyms
- Generative Vocabulary: Prefix *im–* (not); Spiral Review: Suffixes *–er, –est* with spelling change

READING WORKSHOP

- Ask and Answer Questions
- Central Idea
- Author's Purpose
- Literary Elements

FOUNDATIONAL SKILLS

- Decoding: Silent letters (*kn, wr, gn, mb, rh*)
- Spelling: Silent Consonants
- Fluency: Expression

COMMUNICATION

- Speaking and Listening: Give a Presentation
- Make Connections

WRITING WORKSHOP

- Informational Writing
- Abstract Nouns

LEARNING MINDSET: Grit

THIS WEEK'S SELECTIONS

NARRATIVE NONFICTION
Why is the Statue of Liberty Green?

Rigby
LEVELED LIBRARY

Week at a Glance

Suggested Daily Times

- VOCABULARY/ SYNTHESIZE AND CONNECT 10–15 minutes
- READING WORKSHOP 60–85 minutes
- FOUNDATIONAL SKILLS 15–30 minutes
- COMMUNICATION 15–30 minutes
- WRITING WORKSHOP 30–45 minutes

This Week's Words

BIG IDEA WORDS

loyal *sovereignty* *democracy* *civic*

CRITICAL VOCABULARY WORDS

ferry *torch* *sculptor*
monument *inspired*

HIGH-FREQUENCY WORDS

raised *held* *picked*

INSTRUCTIONAL VOCABULARY

clarify *prediction* *central idea*
detail *evidence* *author's purpose*
entertain *inform* *persuade*
literary elements *setting*

Assessment Options

Online Ed

- **Selection Quiz: *Why Is the Statue of Liberty Green?***
- **Weekly Assessment**
  - Comprehension: Central Idea, Author's Purpose, Literary Elements
  - Generative Vocabulary: Prefix *im–* (not)
  - Grammar: Abstract Nouns

Intervention

For students needing strategic intervention, choose from daily small-group options for differentiation. Access online Foundational Skills and Word Study Studio for additional support.

LESSON 11

VOCABULARY

Academic Vocabulary, pp. T144–T145

- Introduce Critical Vocabulary: *ferry, torch, sculptor, monument, inspired*

READING WORKSHOP

Why Is the Statue of Liberty Green? Teaching Pal

GENRE Narrative Nonfiction

Shared Reading: MINILESSON, pp. T146–T147

- Connect and Teach: Ask and Answer Questions
- Apply to Text: ***Why Is the Statue of Liberty Green?***
- Engage and Respond: Speaking and Listening

SMALL-GROUP INSTRUCTION

Options for Differentiation

- Guided Reading Groups, p. T148
- English Learner Support: Seek Information, p. T148
- Reinforce Ask and Answer Questions, p. T149

Options for Independent and Collaborative Work, pp. T150–T151

FOUNDATIONAL SKILLS

Decoding, pp. T152–T153

- Silent Letters (*kn, wr, gn, mb, rh*)

Spelling, p. T154

- Silent Consonants

Fluency, p. T155

- Expression

WRITING WORKSHOP

Descriptive Essay, p. W46

- Revising III: Descriptive Words and Phrases

Grammar, p. W240

- Abstract Nouns

LESSON 12

VOCABULARY

Academic Vocabulary, p. T156

- Review Critical Vocabulary: *ferry, torch, sculptor, monument, inspired*

Vocabulary Strategy, p. 157

- Synonyms/Antonyms

READING WORKSHOP

Why Is the Statue of Liberty Green? Teaching Pal

GENRE Narrative Nonfiction

Shared Reading: MINILESSON, pp. T158-T159

- Connect and Teach: Central Idea
- Apply to Text: ***Why Is the Statue of Liberty Green?***
- Engage and Respond: Write an Opinion Letter

SMALL-GROUP INSTRUCTION

Options for Differentiation

- Guided Reading Groups, p. T160
- English Learner Support: Seek Information, p. T160
- Reinforce Central Idea, p. T161

Options for Independent and Collaborative Work, pp. T162–T163

COMMUNICATION

- **Project Checkpoint: Practice and Present,** pp. T17, T141

WRITING WORKSHOP

Descriptive Essay, p. W47

- Editing I: Spelling and Mechanics

Grammar, p. W241

- Identifying Abstract Nouns

LESSON 13

VOCABULARY

Academic Vocabulary, pp. T164–T165
- Prefix *im–* (not)
- Spiral Review: Suffixes *–er*, *–est* with spelling change

READING WORKSHOP

Why Is the Statue of Liberty Green? Teaching Pal
GENRE Narrative Nonfiction
Shared Reading: MINILESSON, pp. T166–T167
- Connect and Teach: Author's Purpose
- Apply to Text: ***Why Is the Statue of Liberty Green?***
- Engage and Respond: Writing

SMALL-GROUP INSTRUCTION

Options for Differentiation
- Guided Reading Groups, p. T168
- English Learner Support: Seek Information, p. T168
- Reinforce Author's Purpose, p. T169

Options for Independent and Collaborative Work, pp. T170–T171

FOUNDATIONAL SKILLS

Decoding, pp. T172–T173
- Silent Letters (*kn, wr, gn, mb, rh*)

WRITING WORKSHOP

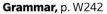

Descriptive Essay, p. W48
- Editing II: Peer Proofreading

Grammar, p. W242
- Using Abstract Nouns

LESSON 14

VOCABULARY

Academic Vocabulary, pp. T174–T175
- Vocabulary Spiral Review

READING WORKSHOP

Why Is the Statue of Liberty Green? Teaching Pal
GENRE Narrative Nonfiction
Shared Reading: MINILESSON, pp. T176–T177
- Connect and Teach: Literary Elements
- Apply to Text: ***Why Is the Statue of Liberty Green?***
- Engage and Respond: Speaking and Listening

SMALL-GROUP INSTRUCTION

Options for Differentiation
- Guided Reading Groups, p. T178
- English Learner Support: Seek Information, p. T178
- Reinforce Literary Elements, p. T179

Options for Independent and Collaborative Work, pp. T180–T181

COMMUNICATION

Speaking and Listening, p. T182
- Give a Presentation

Make Connections, p. T183
- Synthesize Topic Knowledge

WRITING WORKSHOP

Descriptive Essay, p. W49
- Publishing

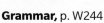

Grammar, p. W278
- Review Verb Tenses

LESSON 15

SYNTHESIZE AND CONNECT

Module Wrap-Up, pp. T184–T185
- Synthesize Knowledge
- Make Connections

READING WORKSHOP

Performance Task, pp. T186–T187 Teaching Pal
- Write an Informative Article

SMALL-GROUP INSTRUCTION

Options for Differentiation
- Guided Reading Groups, p. T188
- English Learner Support: Seek Information, p. T188

Options for Independent and Collaborative Work, p. T189

COMMUNICATION

Project Checkpoint: Project Presentation, pp. T117, T190
- Create a National Symbols Pamphlet

WRITING WORKSHOP

Descriptive Essay, p. W50
- Sharing

Grammar, p. W244
- Connect to Writing: Using Abstract Nouns

Literacy Centers

- **While you meet with small groups, have students work independently in Literacy Centers. Familiarize students with the week's activities and post a daily rotation schedule.**
- **Have students complete Printable: Exit Ticket for each activity so you can monitor their work.**

READING CENTER

Readers' Theater

- Preview Printable: **Readers' Theater 3**, "Ring the Bell," and assign parts to mixed-ability groups of five students.
- The part of Max is ideal for struggling readers, and the part of Mr. Franklin can be read by a proficient reader.

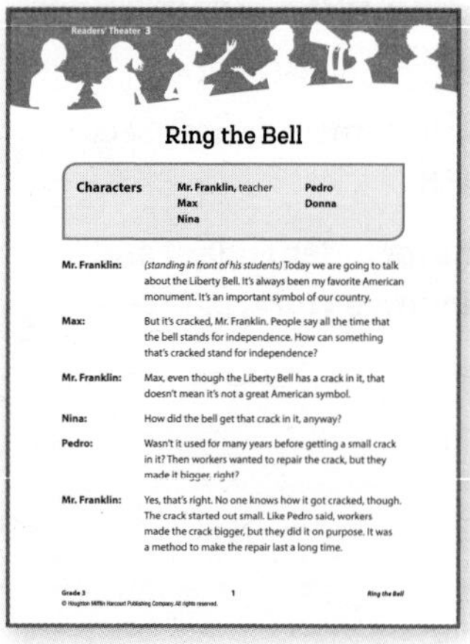
Readers' Theater 3

Ring the Bell

Characters	Mr. Franklin, teacher Max Nina	Pedro Donna

Mr. Franklin:	*(standing in front of his students)* Today we are going to talk about the Liberty Bell. It's always been my favorite American monument. It's an important symbol of our country.
Max:	But it's cracked, Mr. Franklin. People say all the time that the bell stands for independence. How can something that's cracked stand for independence?
Mr. Franklin:	Max, even though the Liberty Bell has a crack in it, that doesn't mean it's not a great American symbol.
Nina:	How did the bell get that crack in it, anyway?
Pedro:	Wasn't it used for many years before getting a small crack in it? Then workers wanted to repair the crack, but they made it bigger, right?
Mr. Franklin:	Yes, that's right. No one knows how it got cracked, though. The crack started out small. Like Pedro said, workers made the crack bigger, but they did it on purpose. It was a method to make the repair last a long time.

Grade 3 1 Ring the Bell
© Houghton Mifflin Harcourt Publishing Company. All rights reserved.

Printable: Readers' Theater 3

Independent Reading

- Have students self-select or continue reading an independent reading book.
- Remind students to set a purpose for reading and to record their progress on their Printable: **Reading Log**.
- Have students use Printable: **Independent Reading** for fiction or nonfiction to note key ideas as they read.
- Display and review Anchor Chart 36: **Respond to Text**.
- You may want to choose from these additional options to have students interact with their books:
  - » **Mixed-Ability Groups** Students discuss their self-selected books using the questions on the Reading Log.
  - » **Write a Blog Entry** Students expand on their correspondence writing by creating an entry in a book review blog to help their classmates choose books.

Name ____ Centers

Reading Log

Title ____

Author ____ Genre ____

Independent Reading Record

Date ____ Time Spent ____ Pages Read ____

Date ____ Time Spent ____ Pages Read ____

Date ____ Time Spent ____ Pages Read ____

Date ____ Time Spent ____ Pages Read ____

Summary This text is about ____

Questions for Discussion

What was your favorite part of the text? ____

What did you enjoy about the author's writing? ____

Was there something that you did not understand? What was it? ____

Would you recommend this text to a friend? Why or why not? ____

Grade 3 Printable
© Houghton Mifflin Harcourt Publishing Company. All rights reserved.

Printable: Reading Log

VOCABULARY

Super Six Words *(Use in Lessons 12–15.)*

- Have students use Printable: **Super Six Words** to list Big Idea Words Critical Vocabulary words that relate to the module topic.
- Then have students select six words from their lists that they think are interesting, or new to them.
- Tell students to write a sentence for each selected word.
- Explain to students that they will come back to this list at the end of module.

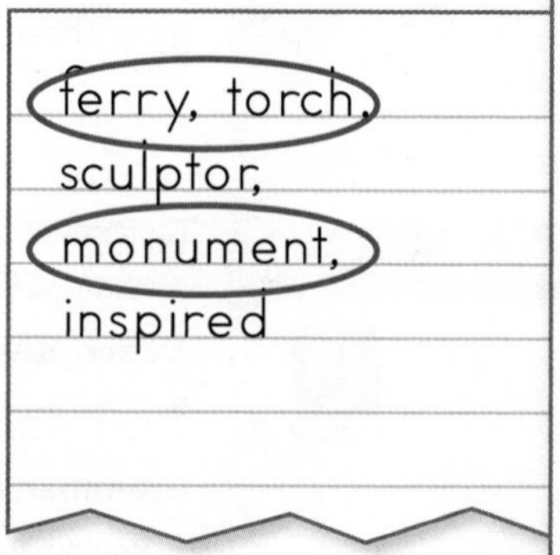

Name ____ Centers

Super Six Words

1. Take a clean sheet of paper. Write your name at the top. Then write the module title.
2. Create four columns labeled Week 1, Week 2, Week 3, and Super Six.
3. Each week, list words about the topic from the texts you read in that week's column.
4. At the end of each week, choose and circle six words on your weekly list that you think are most important to the topic.
5. Write a sentence for each of those six words. Make sure your sentences show the meanings of the words.
6. At the end of the module, you will have eighteen words and sentences.
7. Now, choose six words from those eighteen words you think are most important to the topic. Write them in the Super Six column.
8. Use your Super Six words to write a summary of what you have learned about the module topic.

Grade 3 Printable
© Houghton Mifflin Harcourt Publishing Company. All rights reserved.

Printable: Super Six Words

DIGITAL STATION

Listener's Choice

Online Ed

- Have students listen to this week's selection, *Why Is the Statue of Liberty Green?* or a Leveled Reader of their choice.
- Tell them to add the title to their Printable: **Listening Log**, as well as list the listening skills they used, a summary of the selection, and questions they have about the selection or book.

Keyboarding

- Have students practice keyboarding using Printable: **Keyboarding 3.3**.

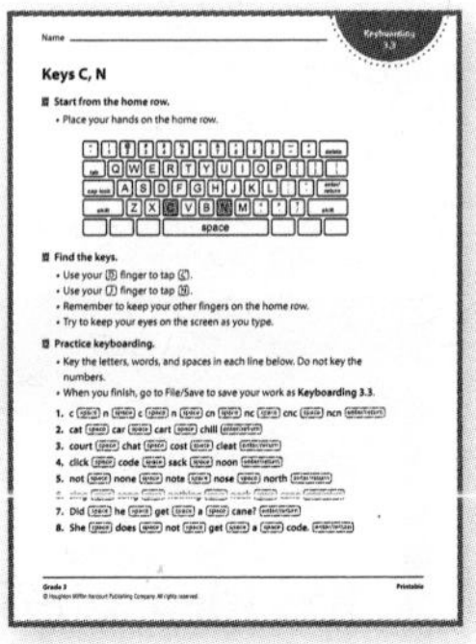
Name ______

Keyboarding 3.3

Keys C, N

Start from the home row.
- Place your hands on the home row.

Find the keys.
- Use your (D) finger to tap (C).
- Use your (J) finger to tap (N).
- Remember to keep your other fingers on the home row.
- Try to keep your eyes on the screen as you type.

Practice keyboarding.
- Key the letters, words, and spaces in each line below. Do not key the numbers.
- When you finish, go to File/Save to save your work as **Keyboarding 3.3**.

1. c (space) n (space) c (space) n (space) cn (space) nc (space) cnc (space) ncn (enter/return)
2. cat (space) car (space) cart (space) chill (enter/return)
3. court (space) chat (space) cost (space) cleat (enter/return)
4. click (space) code (space) sack (space) noon (enter/return)
5. not (space) none (space) note (space) nose (space) north (enter/return)
6. [illegible]
7. Did (space) he (space) get (space) a (space) cane? (enter/return)
8. She (space) does (space) not (space) get (space) a (space) code. (enter/return)

Grade 3 Printable
© Houghton Mifflin Harcourt Publishing Company. All rights reserved.

Printable: Keyboarding 3.3

WRITING CENTER

Write an Opinion Letter *(Use in Lessons 14 and 15.)*

- Have students use Printable: **Peer Conferencing Routine** to discuss their writing.
- Tell peers to use the tips on *my*Book page 291 as they review the work of others and offer feedback.

Writing Workshop

- Have students work on a piece of writing. They may use the time to prewrite, draft, revise, edit, or publish.
- Students may choose from among tasks such as these:
  - » Have peers check punctuation in each other's writing.
  - » Have peers present their writing to each other.
- Display Anchor Chart 37: **Cursive Handwriting**.

PROJECT CENTER

Project Checkpoint:Practice and Present

- Have students work in groups, using Printable: **Project 3.3** to guide them as they conclude the project. Groups should complete the following over the course of the week:
  - ☑ Practice their presentations.
  - ☑ Deliver presentations, and demonstrate good listening skills when not presenting.
  - ☑ Entertain questions from the audience about the symbols they researched.
  - ☑ Discuss what they learned from the presentations.

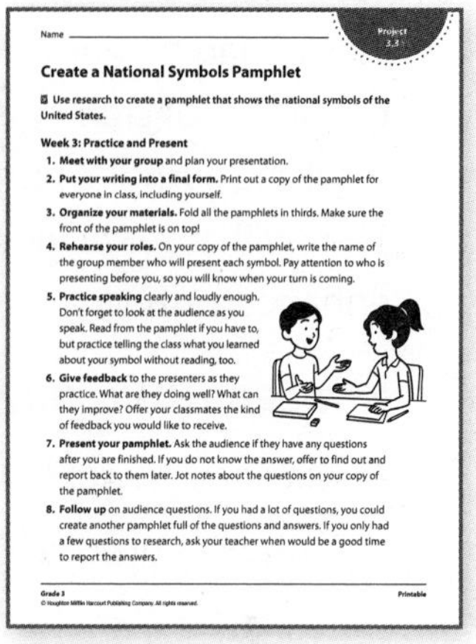
Name ______

Project 3.3

Create a National Symbols Pamphlet

Use research to create a pamphlet that shows the national symbols of the United States.

Week 3: Practice and Present

1. **Meet with your group** and plan your presentation.
2. **Put your writing into a final form.** Print out a copy of the pamphlet for everyone in class, including yourself.
3. **Organize your materials.** Fold all the pamphlets in thirds. Make sure the front of the pamphlet is on top!
4. **Rehearse your roles.** On your copy of the pamphlet, write the name of the group member who will present each symbol. Pay attention to who is presenting before you, so you will know when your turn is coming.
5. **Practice speaking** clearly and loudly enough. Don't forget to look at the audience as you speak. Read from the pamphlet if you have to, but practice telling the class what you learned about your symbol without reading, too.
6. **Give feedback** to the presenters as they practice. What are they doing well? What can they improve? Offer your classmates the kind of feedback you would like to receive.
7. **Present your pamphlet.** Ask the audience if they have any questions after you are finished. If you do not know the answer, offer to find out and report back to them later. Jot notes about the questions on your copy of the pamphlet.
8. **Follow up** on audience questions. If you had a lot of questions, you could create another pamphlet full of the questions and answers. If you only had a few questions to research, ask your teacher when would be a good time to report the answers.

Grade 3 Printable
© Houghton Mifflin Harcourt Publishing Company. All rights reserved.

Printable: Project 3.3

Reading Remake

(Use in Lessons 12–15.)

- Have students complete the Make a Trading Card activity on Printable: **Reading Remake 9**.
- Ask partners to explain to one another how their trading card shows their understanding of the selection.

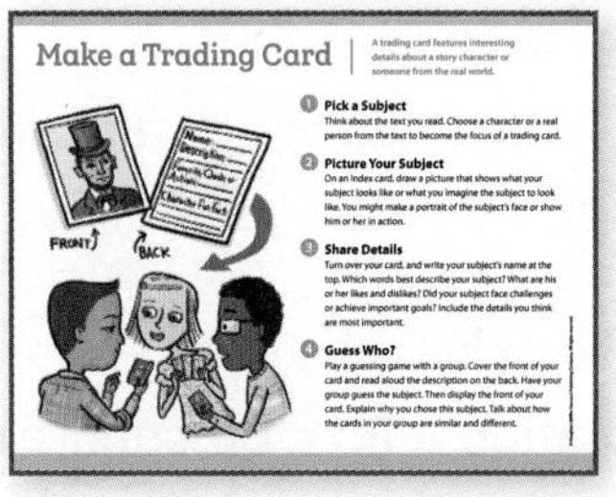
Make a Trading Card

A trading card features interesting details about a story character or someone from the real world.

1. **Pick a Subject** Think about the text you read. Choose a character or a real person from the text to become the focus of a trading card.
2. **Picture Your Subject** On an index card, draw a picture that shows what your subject looks like or what you imagine the subject to look like. You might make a portrait of the subject's face or show him or her in action.
3. **Share Details** Turn over your card, and write your subject's name at the top. Which words best describe your subject? What are his or her likes and dislikes? Did your subject face challenges or achieve important goals? Include the details you think are most important.
4. **Guess Who?** Play a guessing game with a group. Cover the front of your card and read aloud the description on the back. Have your group guess the subject. Then display the front of your card. Explain why you chose this subject. Talk about how the cards in your group are similar and different.

Printable: Reading Remake 9

WEEK 3

Preview Lesson Texts

Build understanding of this week's texts so that you can best support students in making connections, understanding key ideas, and becoming lifelong readers.

Why Is the Statue of Liberty Green? by Martha E.H. Rustad

GENRE Narrative nonfiction

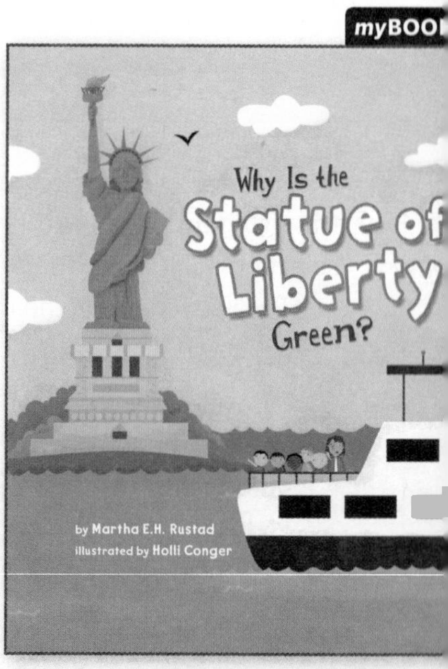

WHY THIS TEXT?

This engaging narrative will prompt students to ask and answer questions about what the Statue of Liberty is and what it represents. They will identify the main/central idea, what the author's purpose is, and be able to provide details to support these features. They will observe more figurative language and discover how literary elements can enhance writing.

KEY LEARNING OBJECTIVES

- Ask and Answer Questions
- Author's Purpose
- Central Idea
- Identify Figurative Language

TEXT COMPLEXITY

LEXILE® MEASURE 560L • **GUIDED READING LEVEL** N

OVERALL RATING Moderately Complex

The genre trait of dialogue in this selection is less common to nonfiction; the text includes some figurative language.

MAKE CONNECTIONS

BUILD KNOWLEDGE AND LANGUAGE

- **Social Studies Connection:** U.S. History

FOUNDATIONAL SKILLS

- **Silent Letters (*kn, wr, gn, mb, rh*):** *wrap, wrote, designed, climb*

WRITING WORKSHOP

- **Informational Text:** Descriptive Essay
- **Abstract Nouns**

TEXT X-RAY

KEY IDEAS

Key Idea *p. 277*
A group of students goes on a field trip to the Statue of Liberty.

Key Idea *p. 278*
The Statue of Liberty was a gift from France and is a symbol of friendship.

Key Idea *pp. 281–283*
The students tour the pedestal area of the statue and learn why the metal surfaces of the monument turned green over time.

Key Idea *p. 287*
The Statue of Liberty represents freedom for all and means different things to different people.

EL LANGUAGE

Personification
The frame is... like Liberty's bones *p. 284* English learners may not understand why bones are being used to describe a metal statue. Explain that, as in the human body, the Statue of Liberty has a skeleton to keep it upright.

Hyperbole
she was as high as the clouds *p. 286* Ask students if they think the Statue of Liberty is tall enough to actually reach the clouds. Explain that authors use exaggerated statements (hyperbole) to more dramatically describe the appearance of something.

Introduce Critical Vocabulary

Step 1 Introduce the Words

Project Display and Engage: Critical Vocabulary 3.11. Then use the **VOCABULARY** routine to introduce the Critical Vocabulary from *Why is the Statue of Liberty Green?* You may wish to display the corresponding Vocabulary Card for each word as you discuss it.

DISPLAY AND ENGAGE: Critical Vocabulary 3.11 — Online Ed

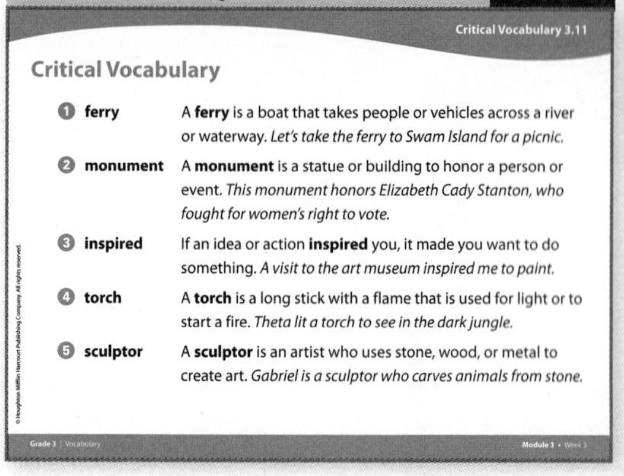

Critical Vocabulary 3.11

Critical Vocabulary

1. **ferry** — A **ferry** is a boat that takes people or vehicles across a river or waterway. *Let's take the ferry to Swam Island for a picnic.*
2. **monument** — A **monument** is a statue or building to honor a person or event. *This monument honors Elizabeth Cady Stanton, who fought for women's right to vote.*
3. **inspired** — If an idea or action **inspired** you, it made you want to do something. *A visit to the art museum inspired me to paint.*
4. **torch** — A **torch** is a long stick with a flame that is used for light or to start a fire. *Theta lit a torch to see in the dark jungle.*
5. **sculptor** — A **sculptor** is an artist who uses stone, wood, or metal to create art. *Gabriel is a sculptor who carves animals from stone.*

1. Read aloud each word and have students repeat it.
2. Read aloud and discuss each word's student-friendly explanation.
3. Point out the example for the word. Have students suggest other examples.

LEARNING OBJECTIVES

- Identify real-life connections between words and their use.
- Use newly acquired vocabulary expressively.
- **Language** Answer questions and discuss meanings to develop vocabulary.

MATERIALS — Online Ed

Display and Engage *Critical Vocabulary 3.11*

Vocabulary Cards *3.17–3.21*

CRITICAL VOCABULARY

- **ferry (p. 278)**
- **monument (p. 278)**
- **inspired (p. 280)**
- **torch (p. 281)**
- **sculptor (p. 284)**

SPANISH COGNATES

monument *monument*

inspired *inspirado*

TEACHER TIP

Continue to use the Vocabulary Cards throughout the year to review words from previous lessons. With repeated exposure, students will find it easier to use the words in everyday conversation and in their writing.

ENGLISH LEARNER SUPPORT: Build Vocabulary

SUBSTANTIAL

Have student pairs pretend to be a sculptor and a monument.

MODERATE

Have students complete these sentence frames. *A sculptor is an ______. He or she might make a monument by using ______.*

LIGHT

Ask partners to write sentences about how a sculptor might make a monument.

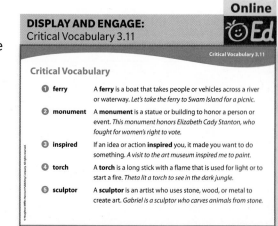

Step 2 Guided Practice

Guide students to interact with the words by discussing questions such as these:

- *Is a **ferry** a good way to get up a mountain? Explain.*
- *What kind of person might get a **monument**?*
- *If you are **inspired**, do you feel sleepy or excited? Explain.*
- *What would you need to make a **torch**?*
- *Where might you find the work of a **sculptor**?*

Ask students to name people or events that have inspired them. Ask them to describe a monument they have seen and to tell whether it may have been made by a sculptor. Have students share whether they have traveled on a ferry or where they would like to go on a ferry. Ask students to explain when it might be useful to have a torch.

Step 2 Apply

- Have students work independently to complete steps 3 and 4 on Vocabulary Cards 3.17–3.21.
- Have students use the **TURN AND TALK** routine with a partner to discuss the prompt on each Vocabulary Card.

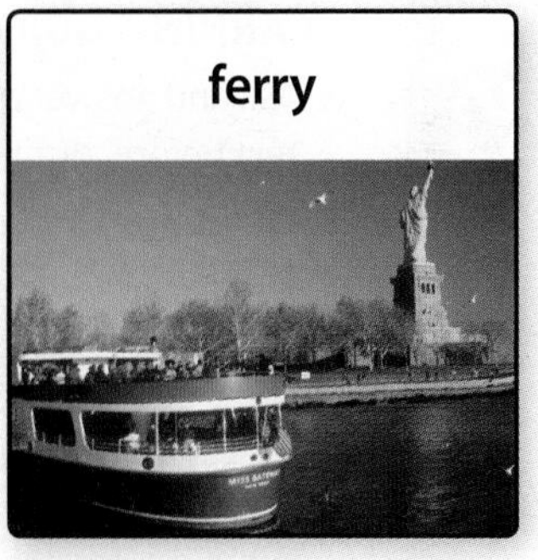

Vocabulary Cards

LEARNING MINDSET

Belonging

Review Remind students that being in a community of learners means that we understand and help each other. *When a friend or classmate is having a hard time or doesn't understand an idea, ask if you can help. Even if you don't have an answer, listening or troubleshooting a problem can make all of the difference!*

Ask and Answer Questions

Step 1 Connect and Teach

LEARNING OBJECTIVES

- Ask and answer questions about a text before, during, and after reading.
- **Language** Articulate questions and answers about the text.

MATERIALS Online Ed

Anchor Chart 1 *Ask and Answer Questions*

Printable *Anchor Chart 1: Ask and Answer Questions*

Teaching Pal *pp. 274–291*

myBook *Why Is the Stature of Liberty Green? Book 1, pp. 274–291*

Display and Engage *Meet the Author and Illustrator 3.11*

INSTRUCTIONAL VOCABULARY

- **clarify** to try to make clear what you don't understand in your reading
- **prediction** a smart guess about what will happen

SPANISH COGNATES

- **question** *cuestión, cuestionar*

- Tell students that they are going to read a narrative nonfiction text called *Why Is the Statue of Liberty Green?* by Martha E.H. Rustad. Explain that asking and answering questions before, during, and after reading will help students better understand the text.
- Project or display Anchor Chart 1: Ask and Answer Questions. Use it to highlight why asking and answering questions will support students' reading and to suggest types of questions students might ask.
- Tell students that they are likely to ask questions about things they are curious about. Then point out that asking and answering questions *before* reading will help students think about what they already know and make **predictions**. Asking and answering questions *during* reading will help students **clarify** anything they don't understand. And asking and answering questions *after* reading, will encourage readers to think more deeply about what they have read.
- Tell students that they will practice asking and answering questions when they read *Why Is the Statue of Liberty Green?*

Online

ANCHOR CHART 1: Ask and Answer Questions

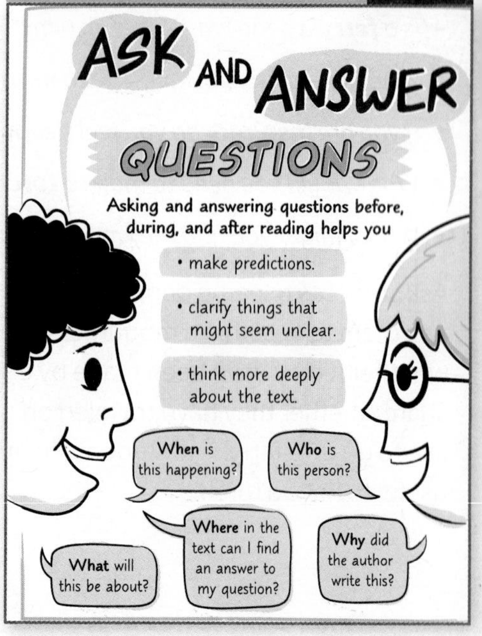
ASK AND ANSWER
QUESTIONS
Asking and answering questions before, during, and after reading helps you
• make predictions.
• clarify things that might seem unclear.
• think more deeply about the text.
When is this happening?
Who is this person?
What will this be about?
Where in the text can I find an answer to my question?
Why did the author write this?

Notice & Note

3 Big Questions

- The Teaching Pal prompts in this lesson feature the **Notice & Note Signpost: 3 Big Questions**
- As needed, refer to p. T19 to review the signpost with students.

ASSESSMENT OPTION

Assign the Selection Quiz to check comprehension of *Why Is the Statue of Liberty Green?*

Go to Your Teaching Pal

Online Ed

ANNOTATE IT!

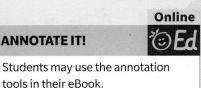

Students may use the annotation tools in their eBook.

Step 2 Apply to Text

In your Teaching Pal, pages 274–291, use the blue **READ FOR UNDERSTANDING** prompts and the red **Notice & Note** prompts to read *Why Is the Statue of Liberty Green?* as students follow along and annotate their *my*Book.

- **Genre Study** Guide students through the genre information on page 274.
- **Meet the Author and Illustrator** Project Display and Engage 3.11: Meet the Author and Illustrator and read the information aloud with students.
- **Set a Purpose** Read the Set a Purpose section on page 274. Prompt students to set their own purpose for reading *Why Is the Statue of Liberty Green?*
- **Read and Comprehend** Use the **READ FOR UNDERSTANDING** routine as you guide students to read the selection. Pause occasionally, using the prompts in your Teaching Pal to gauge students' understanding and to ask and answer questions. As students ask and answer questions, have them refer back to the Anchor Chart to determine if they have asked questions to help them make predictions and clarify information.

Step 3 Engage and Respond

INDEPENDENT PRACTICE: Speaking and Listening

- After reading, use the **COLLABORATIVE CONVERSATION** routine with the Collaborative Discussion questions on Teaching Pal and *my*Book page 289. Have students annotate their *my*Book with details from the text and visuals as evidence to explain their responses.
- Ask volunteers to read aloud the Speaking and Listening Tips. Remind students to follow the agreed-upon rules for discussion, such as listening respectfully and asking questions in a polite way to get more information.
- You may want to have students conduct their discussions during daily small-group time.

ENGLISH LEARNER SUPPORT: Support Comprehension

SUBSTANTIAL

Model asking and answering questions. *Why is the Statue of Liberty green? The Statue of Liberty is green because _____.* Have students repeat.

MODERATE

Provide question frames: *Who _____? What _____? Why _____? When _____?*

LIGHT

Have partners work together to ask and answer questions.

LINK TO SMALL-GROUP INSTRUCTION

REINFORCE ASK AND ANSWER QUESTIONS Review and extend the skill as needed during small-group time to support students' need for differentiation. *See the lesson on p. T149.*

Options for Differentiation

As the class engages in independent and collaborative work, meet with Guided Reading Groups or differentiate instruction based on student need.

GUIDED READING GROUPS

Match Students to Books + Instruction

- Choose just-right books based on level, skill, topic, or genre.

Leveled Readers

- Deliver instruction with each book's **Take and Teach Lesson**, choosing appropriate sessions based on need.

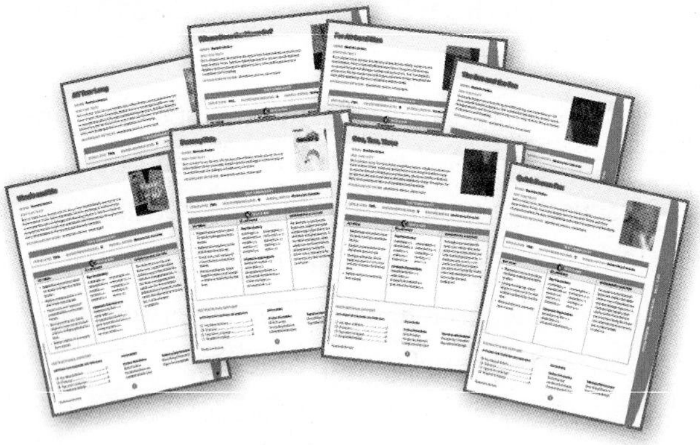

- Check comprehension, reinforce instruction, and extend learning with suggested supporting activities.

ENGLISH LEARNER SUPPORT

Seek Information

- Use **Tabletop Minilessons: English Language Development 9.1 (Listening)** to introduce and practice the language skill.

Tabletop Minilessons: English Language Development

- Then use the following text-based prompts with *Why Is the Statue of Liberty Green?* to guide application of the language skill. Begin with the prompt at the student's identified language proficiency level. As students progress, use lighter supports to encourage increased language proficiency.

SUBSTANTIAL
Have students listen as you read related text to answer the title's question. Guide them to use answer frames: *The Statue of Liberty was _____ when it was new. _____ changed the color to green.*

MODERATE
Ask: *What makes the Statue of Liberty green?* Then have students listen for the answer as you read aloud text to support the question. Have them raise their hand when they hear the answer and use the answer frame: *The Statue of Liberty is green because _____.*

LIGHT
Ask: *Why is the Statue of Liberty green? What is the layer of green called?* Have students listen for answers as you read the related text.

REINFORCE ASK AND ANSWER QUESTIONS

Demonstrate

- Use **Tabletop Minilessons: Reading Card 1** to remind students that they can **ask and answer questions** before, during, and after they read to help them keep track of and understand story events. They can ask and answer questions to **make predictions**, to **clarify** ideas that are unclear, and to think more deeply about the text.
- Model filling out Printable: Reading Graphic Organizer 1 to ask and answer Questions in *Why Is the Statue of Liberty Green?*

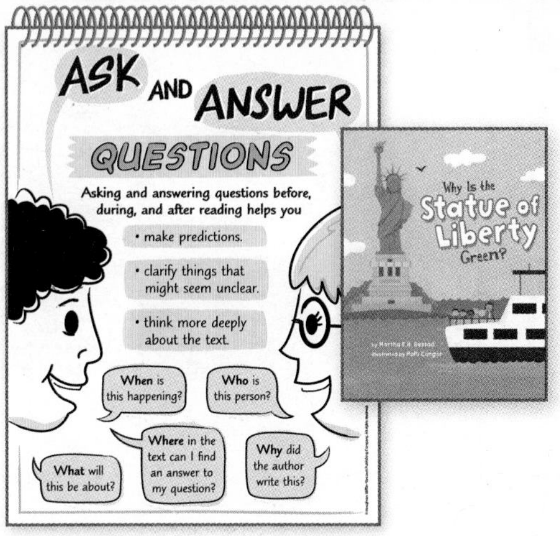

ASK AND ANSWER QUESTIONS
Asking and answering questions before, during, and after reading helps you
• make predictions.
• clarify things that might seem unclear.
• think more deeply about the text.
When is this happening?
Who is this person?
What will this be about?
Where in the text can I find an answer to my question?
Why did the author write this?
Why Is the Statue of Liberty Green?

Tabletop Minilessons: Reading

Apply to Independent Reading

- Now have students ask and answer questions in an appropriate book or article they are reading independently. Customize these prompts to the texts students choose.
  - » *What questions did you ask before you read the text? What answers did you find as you read?*
  - » *What questions did you ask as you were reading the text? How did your questions help you to understand and clarify ideas in the text?*
  - » *What questions did you ask after reading? How did your questions help you to think more deeply about the text?*
- Have students complete Printable: Reading Graphic Organizer 1 for their independent reading book.

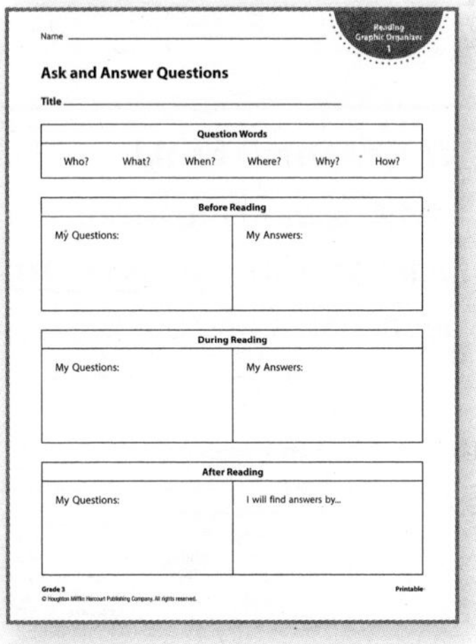
Name
Reading Graphic Organizer 1
Ask and Answer Questions
Title

Question Words					
Who?	What?	When?	Where?	Why?	How?

Before Reading	
My Questions:	My Answers:

During Reading	
My Questions:	My Answers:

After Reading	
My Questions:	I will find answers by...

Grade 1 Printable

Printable: Reading Graphic Organizer 1

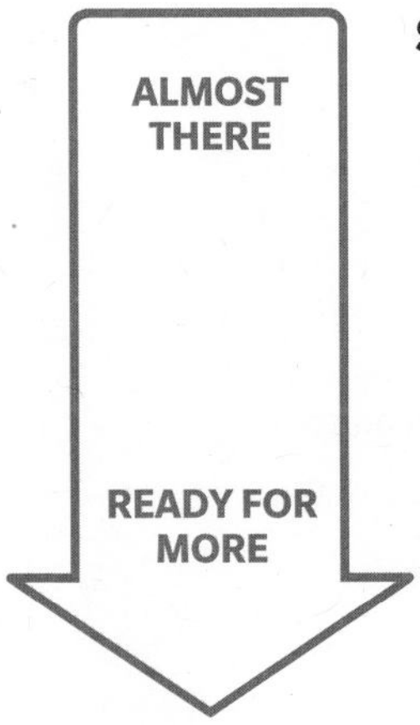

ALMOST THERE
READY FOR MORE

SCAFFOLD AND EXTEND

- Prompt students to ask a question about events in the text. Guide them to read to find answers.
- Prompt students to explain how asking and answering questions helped them clarify ideas and follow events.
- Have students explain what kinds of questions best helped them to clarify ideas and think more deeply about the text.

EL ENGLISH LEARNER SUPPORT

SUBSTANTIAL

Guide students to ask a question using *who, what, when, where, why,* or *how*. Help them read text and use illustrations to answer.

MODERATE

Guide students to form questions using *who, what, when, where why, how*. Have them reuse the question words in their answers. Example: *What happened is* ______.

LIGHT

Have students ask and answer questions with a partner, and then explain how this helped them understand the text.

Options for Independent and Collaborative Work

While you meet with small groups, have other students engage in literacy activities that reinforce the lesson's learning objectives. Choose from these options.

Independent Reading

Student Choice Library

Rigby
LEVELED LIBRARY

APPLY READING SKILL

Ask and Answer Questions Students complete Printable: Reading Graphic Organizer 1 for an independent reading book.

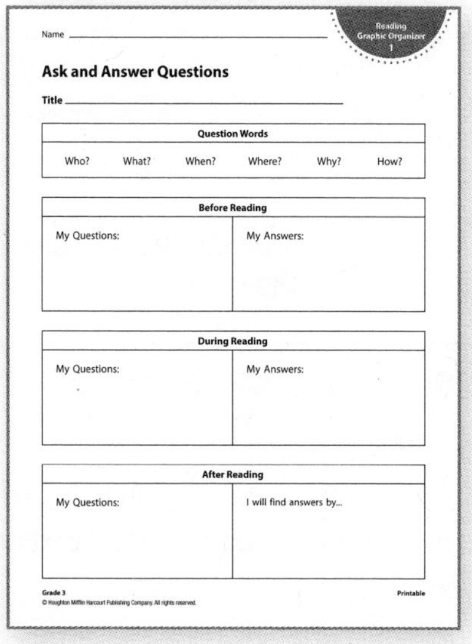
Name
Reading Graphic Organizer 1

Ask and Answer Questions

Title

Question Words					
Who?	What?	When?	Where?	Why?	How?

Before Reading	
My Questions:	My Answers:

During Reading	
My Questions:	My Answers:

After Reading	
My Questions:	I will find answers by...

Grade 3 Printable
© Houghton Mifflin Harcourt Publishing Company. All rights reserved.

Printable: Reading Graphic Organizer 1

APPLY LANGUAGE SKILL

Seek Information Students complete Printable: Language Graphic Organizer 12 for an independent reading book.

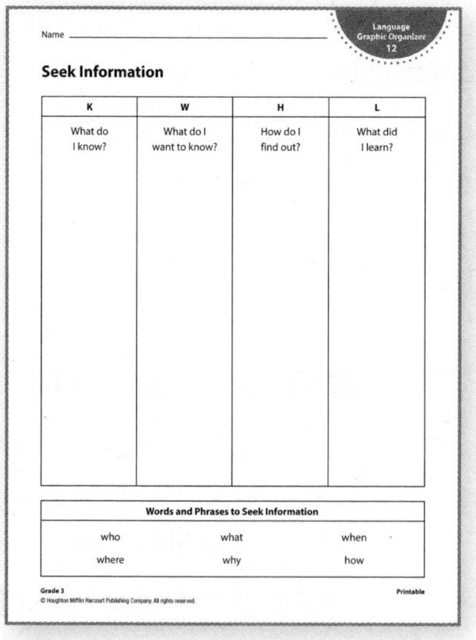
Name
Language Graphic Organizer 12

Seek Information

K	W	H	L
What do I know?	What do I want to know?	How do I find out?	What did I learn?

Words and Phrases to Seek Information		
who	what	when
where	why	how

Grade 3 Printable
© Houghton Mifflin Harcourt Publishing Company. All rights reserved.

Printable: Language Graphic Organizer 12

Notice & Note

3 Big Questions

When students encounter this signpost in their independent historical fiction reading, encourage them to ask and answer the Anchor Questions: *What surprised me? What did the author think I already knew? What challenged, changed or confirmed what I already knew?*

Literacy Centers

See pp. T140–T141.

- READING CENTER
- VOCABULARY CENTER
- DIGITAL STATION
- WRITING CENTER
- PROJECT CENTER

Speaking and Listening

Partners discuss the Collaborative Discussion questions. *See Engage and Respond, p. T147.*

Additional Skills Practice

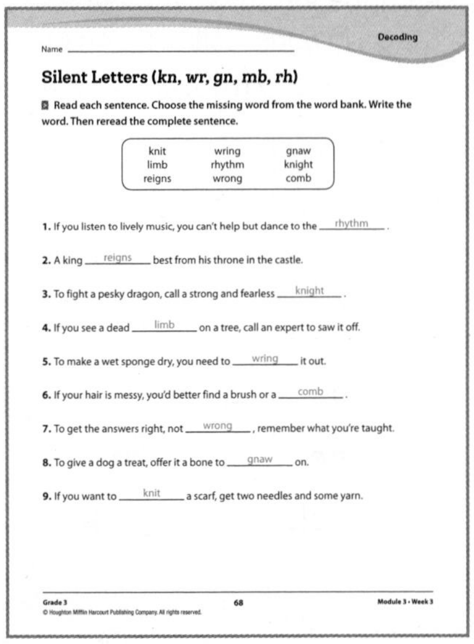

Decoding

Name ______

Silent Letters (*kn, wr, gn, mb, rh*)

Read each sentence. Choose the missing word from the word bank. Write the word. Then reread the complete sentence.

knit	wring	gnaw
limb	rhythm	knight
reigns	wrong	comb

1. If you listen to lively music, you can't help but dance to the rhythm.
2. A king reigns best from his throne in the castle.
3. To fight a pesky dragon, call a strong and fearless knight.
4. If you see a dead limb on a tree, call an expert to saw it off.
5. To make a wet sponge dry, you need to wring it out.
6. If your hair is messy, you'd better find a brush or a comb.
7. To get the answers right, not wrong, remember what you're taught.
8. To give a dog a treat, offer it a bone to gnaw on.
9. If you want to knit a scarf, get two needles and some yarn.

Grade 3 68 Module 3 • Week 3

Know It, Show It, p. 68

Wrap-Up

Share Time

At the end of the Reading Workshop, have students reflect on their learning by sharing how they applied **ask and answer questions** or another area of focus during independent work time. Choose from these options:

- Use the **SOLO CHAIR** routine. Select a reader each day to come to the front of the class and tell what he or she learned from the reading by using a skill or strategy.
- **THINK-PAIR-SHARE** Students share their thinking with a partner. Select a few pairs each day to share with the whole class.
- **RETURN TO ANCHOR CHART** Have students add sticky notes about their independent reading to the Ask and Answer Questions Anchor Chart. Call on a few students to explain what they added and why.

Online Ed

ANCHOR CHART 1: Ask and Answer Questions

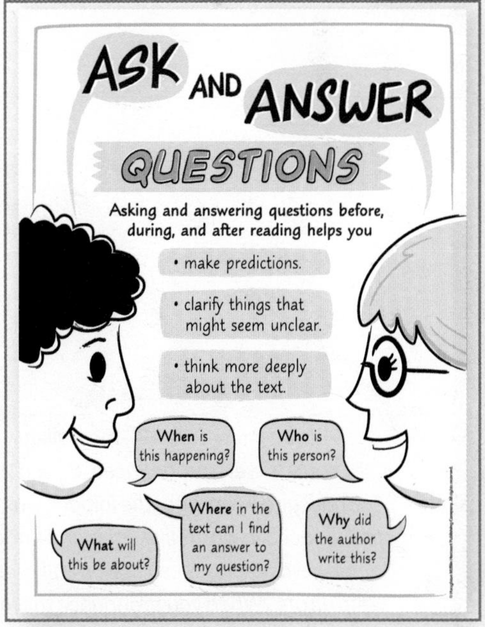
ASK AND ANSWER
QUESTIONS
Asking and answering questions before, during, and after reading helps you
• make predictions.
• clarify things that might seem unclear.
• think more deeply about the text.
When is this happening?
Who is this person?
What will this be about?
Where in the text can I find an answer to my question?
Why did the author write this?

Silent Letters

Step 1 Introduce the Skill

LEARNING OBJECTIVES

- Decode and read words with consonant digraphs with silent letters.
- Spell and write words with consonant digraphs with silent letters.
- **Language** Read words with consonant digraphs with silent letters and understand their meanings.

MATERIALS **Online** Ed

Display and Engage *Decoding 3.11*
Know It, Show It *p. 68*

Silent Letters Display and read aloud the word *know*.

- Underline the *kn*. Point out the silent *k*, emphasizing that *kn* is pronounced /n/.
- Display the words *write*, *gnash*, *lamb*, and *rhino*. Underline the *wr* in *write*, pointing out the silent *w* and explaining that *wr* is pronounced /r/. Repeat for the *gn* in *gnash* (silent *g*, *gn* pronounced /n/), the *mb* in *lamb* (silent *b*, *mb* pronounced /m/), and the *rh* in *rhino* (silent *h*, *rh* pronounced /r/).
- Guide students to read the words aloud.
- Display the following chart.

kn	wr	gn	mb	rh
knot	wrap	gnat	limb	rhyme
knee	wrote	gnome	comb	rhythm
knock	wreck	sign	thumb	rhino

- Remind students that they have learned several consonant digraphs with silent letters. Point out the spelling patterns in the top row.
- Then read aloud the example words in each column, while underlining the consonant digraphs with silent letters.
- Guide students to read aloud the words.

TEACHER TIP

Point out: *Historically, most silent sounds were pronounced. Over a thousand years ago, the initial k was pronounced in words like knee and knock. Initial w was pronounced in words like write and wrote. When you pronounce the first syllable of the word worry, you can get an idea of how wr sounded together.*

ENGLISH LEARNER SUPPORT: Support Comprehension

SUBSTANTIAL
Ensure that students understand the meaning of each Blend and Read word by sharing pictures or gestures.

MODERATE
Support students in understanding the meaning of each Blend and Read word by providing oral examples or context sentences. Guide students to think of additional examples or sentences.

LIGHT
Challenge students to create context sentences for some of the Blend and Read words on their own.

Step 2 Guided Practice

- Project Display and Engage: **Decoding 3.11**.
- Have students read the Blend and Read lines aloud. Provide feedback as needed.
- At the end of each line, prompt a conversation about the words: *What is alike about these words? How are they different?*
- Have partners reread the Blend and Read lines and quiz each other on the spellings of consonant digraphs with silent letters.

Online Ed

DISPLAY AND ENGAGE: Decoding 3.11

Decoding 3.11

Decoding

Silent Letters (*kn, wr, gn, mb, rh*)

1	knob (kn)	crumb (mb)	wrist (wr)	gnaw (gn)	wrong (wr)
2	wren (wr)	knack (kn)	climb (mb)	rhythm (rh)	knife (kn)
3	knit (kn)	gnarl (gn)	numb (mb)	knoll (kn)	wrote (wr)
4	rhino (rh)	knight (kn)	wreath (wr)	gnu (gn)	wrench (wr)
5	comb (mb)	kneel (kn)	gnash (gn)	rhyme (rh)	knew (kn)

6 The player sprained his wrist (wr), bruised his thumb (mb), and reinjured his kneecap (kn).

7 My sister tried to unwrap (wr) the present, but there was a knot (kn) in the ribbon.

Grade 3 | Foundational Skills — Module 3 • Week 3

Step 3 Apply

INDEPENDENT PRACTICE

- Have students work in small groups or with partners to complete Know It, Show It, page 68.
- Encourage students to share with each other the strategies they use to decode the words with consonant digraphs with silent letters.

CORRECT & REDIRECT

If students have trouble decoding words with consonant digraphs with silent letters, use the model below.

- **Correct** the error. *Some consonant digraphs have a silent letter. You don't pronounce both letters.*
- **Model** how to decode the word. */k//n//ŏb/. That doesn't sound right. The word* knob *has the letters* kn *at the beginning. We learned that in this consonant digraph, the letter* k *is silent, and* kn *is pronounced /n/. So I'll try again: /n//ŏb/,* knob. *Now that sounds like a word I know.*
- **Guide** students to decode the words *crumb* and *rhyme*.
- **Check** students' understanding by displaying the word *wrench*. *What spelling pattern helps you decode this word? (The letters* wr *stand for the sound /r/.)*
- **Reinforce** by repeating the process with the word *gnarl*.

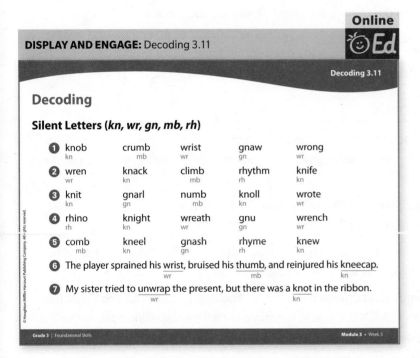

Silent Consonants

Introduce the Spelling Words

- Before working with the basic and challenge words, you might want to revisit the review words. These also appear in Printable: Dictation Sentences 3.11. Display one of the Spelling Anchor Chart Printables, as appropriate.
- Cut apart and display the spelling word cards from Printable: Spelling Word Cards 3.11. Read aloud each word and discuss its meaning as needed.
- Tell students you are going to work together to sort the words into categories based on the spelling of the consonant digraphs with silent letters. Read aloud the words *wreck* and *knee*, and display those words as column headings.
- Hold up a word containing the silent letters *kn*, such as *knock*, and model your thinking: *The word is* knock. *It has the letters* kn *at the beginning. And I see the column head* knee, *which has the same spelling pattern for the consonant digraph with silent letters. So I'll place the word in that column.*

LEARNING OBJECTIVES

- Learn spelling patterns for consonant digraphs with silent letters.
- **Language** Spell words with consonant digraphs with silent letters and understand their meanings.

MATERIALS Online Ed

Anchor Chart 32 *Alphabetical Order*

Printables *Anchor Chart 32: Alphabetical Order, Dictation Sentences 3.11, Spelling Word Cards 3.11, Proofreading 3.11*

Optional *Use Printable: Dictation Sentences 3.11 to administer a pretest.*

SPELLING WORDS

BASIC

1. **wreck**
2. **knee**
3. **wrap**
4. **knot**
5. **knife**
6. **write**
7. **wring**
8. **knew**
9. **knock**
10. **knight**
11. **wrong**
12. **wrench**
13. **wrist**
14. **wrote**

REVIEW

15. **wedge**
16. **second**
17. **quart**
18. **stage**

CHALLENGE

19. **kneel**
20. **knitting**
21. **wreath**
22. **unwrapped**

Sort the Words

- Ask students to help you sort the remaining word cards. For multisyllabic words such as *knitting*, emphasize the consonant digraph sound as you read the word aloud.
- After sorting, have students read down each list with you to make sure the words have been sorted correctly.
- Guide students to recognize the spelling patterns in the columns. Ask: *What spelling pattern do the words in this column share?*
- Guide students to recognize the different spelling patterns for the consonant digraphs with silent letters. Ask: *What are the different spelling patterns for the consonant digraphs with silent letters?* (kn, wr)

Handwriting/Keyboarding

- As an extension, show students Anchor Chart 32: Alphabetical Order. Have students sort the words into alphabetical order to the first, second, and third letters.

ENGLISH LEARNER SUPPORT: Build Vocabulary

SUBSTANTIAL
Use gestures or images to demonstrate the meaning of each spelling word.

MODERATE
Have students complete sentence frames for the spelling words: *I can write ______. I can wrap ______.*

LIGHT
Challenge students to make up sentences for the spelling words.

LINK TO SMALL-GROUP INSTRUCTION

REINFORCE FOUNDATIONAL SKILLS For spelling practice for the remainder of the week: Display this week's spelling words for reference and have students work with Printable: Proofreading 3.11. Remind students to check the spelling words they use in the writing section to confirm they have spelled the words correctly.

Expression

Introduce the Skill

- Explain that when good readers read aloud, they read with expression to make their voices show what the characters say, think, and feel. Point out that the events, descriptions, and dialogue in a story can help readers know which expression is appropriate.
- Distribute Printable: Fluency 3.11 to students, and project it for whole-group discussion. Tell students that you will model how to read the passage with appropriate expression.
- Read the first two sentences with great excitement and then reread them with sadness in your voice. Discuss with students which tone best matches the content of the sentences.
- Model reading the sentences with great excitement again, demonstrating how you use your voice to communicate how the character feels. After you read the entire passage, point out how you decoded the words with consonant digraphs with silent letters.

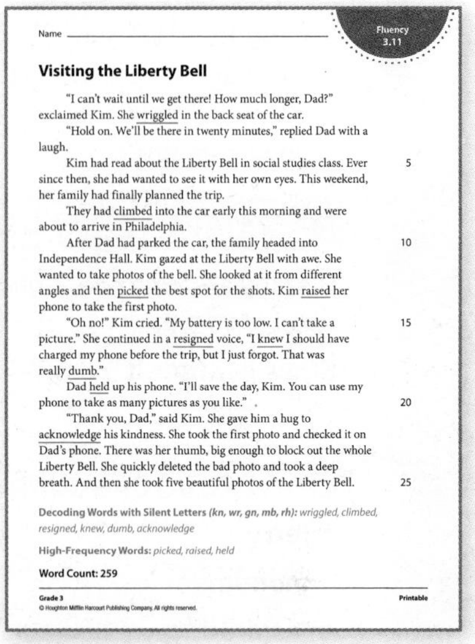

Name ________________

Fluency 3.11

Visiting the Liberty Bell

"I can't wait until we get there! How much longer, Dad?" exclaimed Kim. She wriggled in the back seat of the car.

"Hold on. We'll be there in twenty minutes," replied Dad with a laugh.

Kim had read about the Liberty Bell in social studies class. Ever since then, she had wanted to see it with her own eyes. This weekend, her family had finally planned the trip.

They had climbed into the car early this morning and were about to arrive in Philadelphia.

After Dad had parked the car, the family headed into Independence Hall. Kim gazed at the Liberty Bell with awe. She wanted to take photos of the bell. She looked at it from different angles and then picked the best spot for the shots. Kim raised her phone to take the first photo.

"Oh no!" Kim cried. "My battery is too low. I can't take a picture." She continued in a resigned voice, "I knew I should have charged my phone before the trip, but I just forgot. That was really dumb."

Dad held up his phone. "I'll save the day, Kim. You can use my phone to take as many pictures as you like."

"Thank you, Dad," said Kim. She gave him a hug to acknowledge his kindness. She took the first photo and checked it on Dad's phone. There was her thumb, big enough to block out the whole Liberty Bell. She quickly deleted the bad photo and took a deep breath. And then she took five beautiful photos of the Liberty Bell.

Decoding Words with Silent Letters *(kn, wr, gn, mb, rh)*: *wriggled, climbed, resigned, knew, dumb, acknowledge*

High-Frequency Words: *picked, raised, held*

Word Count: 259

Grade 3 | Printable

Printable: Fluency 3.11

- After you finish reading the passage, use the **CHORAL READING** routine to reread it in sections and have students repeat after you.

Apply

- Have students work in pairs or small groups using the **PARTNER READING** routine to read aloud the passage.
- Monitor students for proper expression. Note especially how students handle the more challenging words, such as *awe, resigned, acknowledge,* and *deleted,* and provide support, as needed.

LEARNING OBJECTIVES

- Read orally with expression.
- Read aloud grade-level text with fluency and accuracy.
- Apply decoding skills when reading connected text.
- **Language** Comprehend texts using teacher support.

MATERIALS

Online Ed

Printable *Fluency 3.11*

Word Cards 3.32–3.34

DECODING ⟶ FLUENCY CONNECTION

The passage on Printable: Fluency 3.11 includes words that contain this week's decoding element. Use the passage to monitor whether students can accurately and fluently read these grade-level words.

HIGH-FREQUENCY WORDS

- **raised**
- **picked**
- **held**

HIGH-FREQUENCY WORDS

Point out the high-frequency words in the passage on Printable: Fluency 3.11. Remind students that high-frequency words appear often in texts they read. Students can learn to recognize them, rather than decode them, so that they can read more fluently.

Print and distribute Printables: Word Cards 3.32–3.34, which feature this week's high-frequency words, and have students work independently or in pairs to read and complete the activities for each word. For struggling readers, walk through the notes for one or two words before they continue working with a partner.

ENGLISH LEARNER SUPPORT: Support Comprehension

ALL LEVELS As you model reading with appropriate expression, have students raise their hand when they hear a word they do not recognize. Work with students to decode the word and practice saying it aloud. Discuss the word's meaning, using gestures or pictures for support if needed. Then have students read the entire sentence chorally. Provide corrective feedback, as needed.

Review Critical Vocabulary

Step 1 Reinforce Vocabulary

- Project Display and Engage: Critical Vocabulary 3.11 to review and discuss the Critical Vocabulary, student-friendly explanations, and examples of the words. Have students take turns using the words in sentences.

Step 2 Guided Practice

- Have students work in pairs to create Four-Square Maps. For each of the Critical Vocabulary words, students should fold a blank sheet of paper into four equal sections. Display the steps below. As needed, direct students to Display and Engage 3.11 for the word meanings, and offer ideas if students get stuck on tricky words. (For example, for the word *inspired* you might suggest drawing someone looking at art, or watching a music or dance performance or sports event.)
  1. In the first section, draw a picture that represents the word.
  2. In the second section, write the meaning of the word.
  3. In the third section, write a sentence using the word.
  4. In the fourth section, write the word.
- Have students use the **THINK-PAIR-SHARE** routine to discuss the sentences they wrote on their Four-Square Maps. Call on pairs to share their sentences. Positively reinforce students' correct word usage.

Step 3 Apply

INDEPENDENT PRACTICE

- Have students work in small groups or independently. Tell them to complete Know It, Show It pages 69–70. For the last item on the page, tell students to include clues to each word's meaning in their sentences. Have groups share their sentences. Ask listeners to identify the context clue in each sentence.
- You may wish to have students complete the Know It, Show It page during Small Group time.

LEARNING OBJECTIVES

- Review and extend understanding of word meanings.
- Use context to determine the meanings of unfamiliar words.
- **Language** Use newly acquired vocabulary expressively to answer questions and demonstrate understanding.

MATERIALS — Online Ed

Display and Engage *Critical Vocabulary 3.11*

Know It, Show It *pp. 69–70*

CRITICAL VOCABULARY

- **ferry**
- **monument**
- **inspired**
- **torch**
- **sculptor**

ENGLISH LEARNER SUPPORT: Support Discussion and Practice

Use tiered supports as needed to help students as they answer questions about the Critical Vocabulary and get ideas for their Four-Square Maps.

SUBSTANTIAL

Show me what you would look like if you were a monument.

MODERATE

A monument can be a building. What else can it be?

LIGHT

Why do people build monuments?

Synonyms/Antonyms

LEARNING OBJECTIVES

- Identify, use, and explain the meaning of synonyms and antonyms in texts.
- Use print and digital reference materials to clarify meanings.
- **Language** Identify and use synonyms and antonyms using strategic learning techniques.

MATERIALS Online Ed

Display and Engage *Vocabulary Strategy 3.12a and 3.12b*

INSTRUCTIONAL VOCABULARY

- **synonym** a word that means the same or almost the same as another word
- **antonym** a word that is opposite in meaning to another word

Step 1 Review the Strategy

Project Display and Engage: Vocabulary Strategy 3.12a and 3.12b. Read aloud the two paragraphs.

Online

DISPLAY AND ENGAGE: Vocabulary Strategy 3.12a, 3.12b

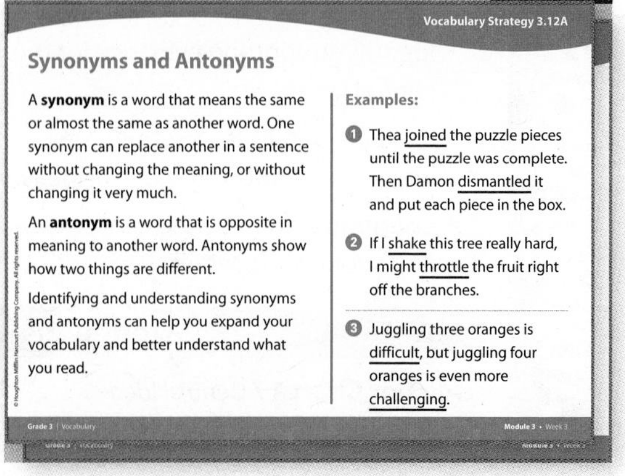
Vocabulary Strategy 3.12A

Synonyms and Antonyms

A **synonym** is a word that means the same or almost the same as another word. One synonym can replace another in a sentence without changing the meaning, or without changing it very much.

An **antonym** is a word that is opposite in meaning to another word. Antonyms show how two things are different.

Identifying and understanding synonyms and antonyms can help you expand your vocabulary and better understand what you read.

Examples:

1. Thea joined the puzzle pieces until the puzzle was complete. Then Damon dismantled it and put each piece in the box.
2. If I shake this tree really hard, I might throttle the fruit right off the branches.
3. Juggling three oranges is difficult, but juggling four oranges is even more challenging.

© Houghton Mifflin Harcourt Publishing Company. All rights reserved.

Grade 3 | Vocabulary — Module 3 • Week 3

- Review that a synonym is a word that means the same or almost the same as another word, and an antonym is a word that is opposite in meaning to another word. Remind students that recognizing and understanding synonyms and antonyms will help them better understand what they read.
- Use the first two examples to show examples of synonyms and antonyms in context. *In the first example, I can tell the word* giving *has a similar meaning to the word* generous. *The sentence context helps me know these words are synonyms. In the second example, I can tell the words* challenging *and* simple *have opposite meanings. The context helps me know these words are antonyms.*

Step 2 Guided Practice

- Have students read sentences 3 and 4 and identify the underlined words as synonyms or antonyms.
- Ask students to explain how they identified the words' relationships and how the words' context helped confirm their ideas.

Step 3 Apply the Strategy

INDEPENDENT PRACTICE

- Display these words from *Why Is the Statue of Liberty Green?: shiny, copy, shouts*. Have students to write a synonym or antonym for each word. Allow students to use a reference source as needed.
- Next, ask students to write a context sentence using each word and its synonym or antonym.
- Have students exchange their work with another pair and compare and discuss their sentences and context clues.

ENGLISH LEARNER SUPPORT: Using Synonyms and Antonyms

SUBSTANTIAL
As needed, guide students to find the antonym *whispers* for *shouts*. Encourage students to use oral sentences for the word pair.

MODERATE
Supply sentence stems for each word. *An antonym for* shouts *is* ______.

LIGHT
Ask students to explain orally what context clues show how their word pairs are related.

Central Idea

LEARNING OBJECTIVES

- Recognize the central, or main, ideas in a text.
- Identify supporting evidence for the central ideas.
- Evaluate details to determine key ideas that support the central ideas.
- **Language** Identify the central idea and supporting details.

MATERIALS Online Ed

Anchor Chart 17 *Central Idea*
Printable *Anchor Chart 17: Central Idea*
Teaching Pal *pp. 274–291*
myBook *Why Is the Statue of Liberty Green? Book 1, pp. 274–291*
Know It, Show It *p. 71*

INSTRUCTIONAL VOCABULARY

- **central idea** the big idea, or main idea, that readers should take away from reading a text
- **detail** fact or idea that supports or tells more about a central, or main idea
- **evidence** clues or details in the text that support an answer or idea

SPANISH COGNATES

- **central** *central*
- **idea** *idea*
- **evidence** *evidencia*
- **detail** *detalle*

Step 1 Connect and Teach

- Recall with students that the **central idea** of a text is what that text is mostly about.
- Project or display Anchor Chart 17: Central Idea.
- Draw attention to the image that shows a central idea supported by details. Point out that authors include different types of **details** or **evidence** to support the central ideas in the text. Supporting evidence may include facts and examples that tell more about the main idea.
- Use the Anchor Chart to review the kinds of text clues that may offer hints about the main, or central, idea of a text.
- Explain that students will practice looking for central ideas and supporting evidence to gain a deeper understanding of *Why Is the Statue of Liberty Green?*

ANCHOR CHART 17: Central Idea — Online Ed

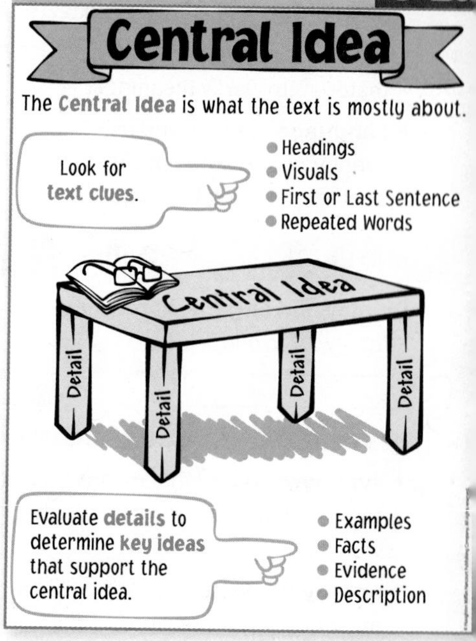

LEARNING MINDSET

Grit

Reflect Point out that people coming to live in the United States faced many challenges and often had to try things again and again to succeed. *We don't always get something right on the first try. Having the desire to try again or using a different strategy can make all the difference in getting it right the next time.*

Go to Your Teaching Pal

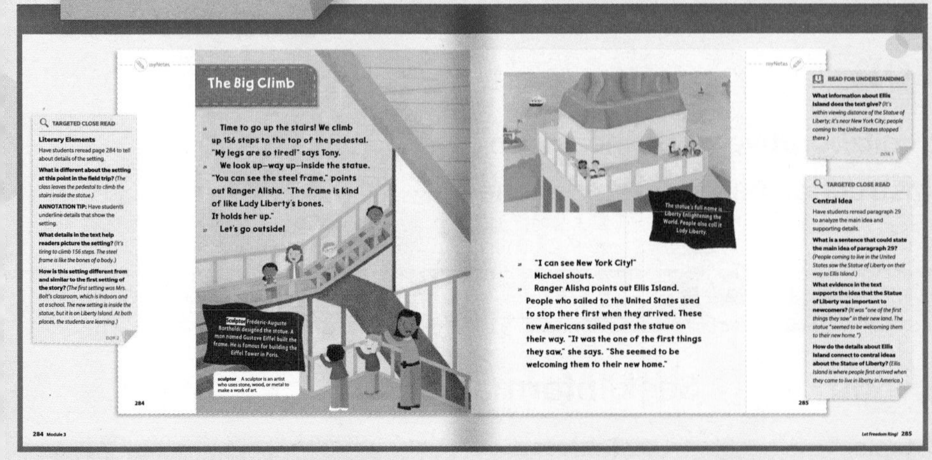

TARGETED CLOSE READ

Literary Elements

Have students reread page 284 to tell about details of the setting.

What is different about the setting at this point in the field trip? *(The class leaves the pedestal to climb the stairs inside the statue.)*

ANNOTATION TIP: Have students underline details that show the setting.

What details in the text help readers picture the setting? *(It's tiring to climb 156 steps. The steel frame is like the bones of a body.)*

How is this setting different from and similar to the first setting of the story? *(The first setting was Mrs. Bolt's classroom, which is indoors and at a school. The new setting is inside the statue, but it is on Liberty Island. At both places, the students are learning.)*

DOK 2

myNotes

The Big Climb

25 Time to go up the stairs! We climb up 156 steps to the top of the pedestal. "My legs are so tired!" says Tony.

26 We look up—way up—inside the statue. "You can see the steel frame," points out Ranger Alisha. "The frame is kind of like Lady Liberty's bones. It holds her up."

27 Let's go outside!

Sculptor Frédéric-Auguste Bartholdi designed the statue. A man named Gustave Eiffel built the frame. He is famous for building the Eiffel Tower in Paris.

sculptor A sculptor is an artist who uses stone, wood, or metal to make a work of art.

284

284 Module 3

The statue's full name is Liberty Enlightening the World. People also call it Lady Liberty.

28 "I can see New York City!" Michael shouts.

29 Ranger Alisha points out Ellis Island. People who sailed to the United States used to stop there first when they arrived. These new Americans sailed past the statue on their way. "It was the one of the first things they saw," she says. "She seemed to be welcoming them to their new home."

285

myNotes

READ FOR UNDERSTANDING

What information about Ellis Island does the text give? *(It's within viewing distance of the Statue of Liberty; it's near New York City; people coming to the United States stopped there.)*

DOK 1

TARGETED CLOSE READ

Central Idea

Have students reread paragraph 29 to analyze the main idea and supporting details.

What is a sentence that could state the main idea of paragraph 29? *(People coming to live in the United States saw the Statue of Liberty on their way to Ellis Island.)*

What evidence in the text supports the idea that the Statue of Liberty was important to newcomers? *(It was "one of the first things they saw" in their new land. The statue "seemed to be welcoming them to their new home.")*

How do the details about Ellis Island connect to central ideas about the Statue of Liberty? *(Ellis Island is where people first arrived when they came to live in liberty in America.)*

Let Freedom Ring! 285

Online Ed

ANNOTATE IT!

Students may use the annotation tools in their eBook.

Step 2 Apply to Text

In your Teaching Pal, use the purple **TARGETED CLOSE READ** prompts on pages 274–289 to guide students to apply the Central Idea skill to *Why Is the Statue of Liberty Green*, and to find evidence to support their responses. Use the **CLOSE READING** routine. Students may refer to the questions on Know It, Show It page 71 as you discuss them.

- Read aloud the first two questions on Teaching Pal page 285. Then have students reread *my*Book paragraph 29. Ask students to identify a sentence that could state the main idea of paragraph 29 and the evidence that supports it. *(People coming to live in the United States saw the Statue of Liberty on their way to Ellis Island. It was "one of the first things they saw" in their new land. The statue "seemed to be welcoming them to their new home.")*
- Read aloud the follow-up question on Teaching Pal page 285. Have students connect Ellis Island to the Statue of Liberty. *(Ellis Island is where people first arrived when they came to live in liberty in America.)*
- Refer back to the Anchor Chart to support the discussion. Students may add sticky notes to the chart to note other central ideas and supporting evidence they identify in *Why Is the Statue of Liberty Green?*

Step 3 Engage and Respond

INDEPENDENT PRACTICE: Writing

- **Write an Opinion Letter** Turn to pages 290–291 in your Teaching Pal. Have students turn to pages 290–291 in their *my*Book. Use the **WRITING RESPONSE** routine.
- Read the directions with students and use the Teaching Pal prompts to guide them as they plan and complete their opinion letters.
- Provide time for students to share their opinion letters with small groups.
- You may want to have students complete their writing during daily small-group time.
- You may want to have students complete Know It, Show It page 71 during small-group time.

ENGLISH LEARNER SUPPORT: Support Comprehension

SUBSTANTIAL

Point to a sentence that states the central idea. Let's read it together.

MODERATE

Which sentence states the central idea? How do you know?

LIGHT

The central idea is ______. ______ is supporting evidence.

LINK TO SMALL-GROUP INSTRUCTION

REINFORCE CENTRAL IDEA Review and extend the skill as needed during small-group time to support students' need for differentiation. *See the lesson on p. T161.*

Options for Differentiation

As the class engages in independent and collaborative work, meet with Guided Reading Groups or differentiate instruction based on student need.

GUIDED READING GROUPS

Match Students to Books + Instruction

- Choose just-right books based on level, skill, topic, or genre.

Leveled Readers

- Deliver instruction with each book's **Take and Teach Lesson**, choosing appropriate sessions based on need.

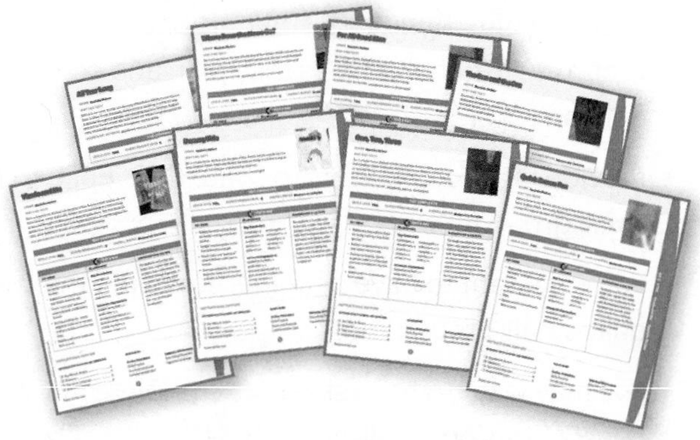

- Check comprehension, reinforce instruction, and extend learning with suggested supporting activities.

ENGLISH LEARNER SUPPORT

Seek Information

- Use **Tabletop Minilessons: English Language Development 9.1 (Speaking)** to reinforce and practice the language skill.

Tabletop Minilessons: English Language Development

- Then use the following text-based prompts with *Why Is the Statue of Liberty Green?* to guide application of the language skill. Begin with the prompt at the student's identified language proficiency level. As students progress, use lighter supports to encourage increased language proficiency.

SUBSTANTIAL

Have students orally complete sentence frames to answer questions such as: *Where did the class go? The class went to visit ______. How tall is the statue? The statue is as tall as ______.* Allow them to complete the frames by pointing to illustrations and using their home language as needed.

MODERATE

Facilitate an oral dialogue using question-and-answer stems such as: *What does ______ mean? ______ means ______. Who was ______? ______ was ______.*

LIGHT

Display question words *who, what, when, where, why,* and *how*. Have students use the words to ask the group questions about the text. Students should answer orally, using text evidence.

REINFORCE CENTRAL IDEA

Demonstrate

- Use **Tabletop Minilessons: Reading Card 17** to remind students that the **central idea** of a text is what the text is mostly about. The central idea is supported by **evidence** such as **details** that give more information about the central idea.
- Model filling out Printable: Reading Graphic Organizer 17 to identify Central Idea in *Why Is the Statue of Liberty Green?*

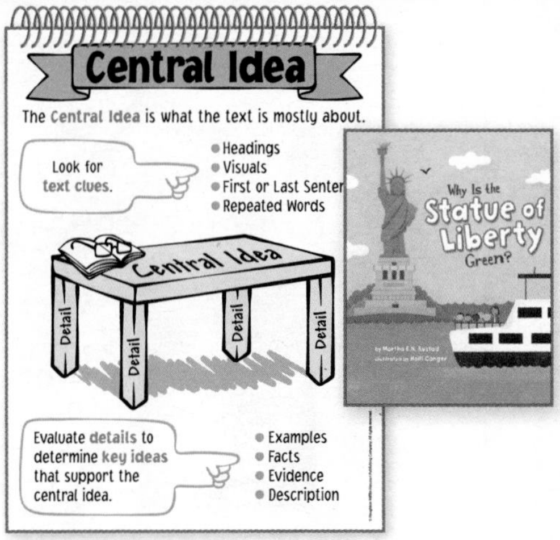

Central Idea
The Central Idea is what the text is mostly about.
Look for text clues.
Headings
Visuals
First or Last Senter
Repeated Words
Central Idea
Detail
Detail
Detail
Detail
Evaluate details to determine key ideas that support the central idea.
Examples
Facts
Evidence
Description
Why Is the Statue of Liberty Green?

Tabletop Minilessons: Reading

Apply to Independent Reading

- Now have students identify the central idea in an appropriate book or article they are reading independently. Customize these prompts to the texts students choose.
  - » *What is the central idea of this text?*
  - » *What details and evidence support the central idea?*
  - » *How does knowing the central idea help you to better understand the text?*
- Have students complete Printable: Reading Graphic Organizer 17 for their independent reading text.

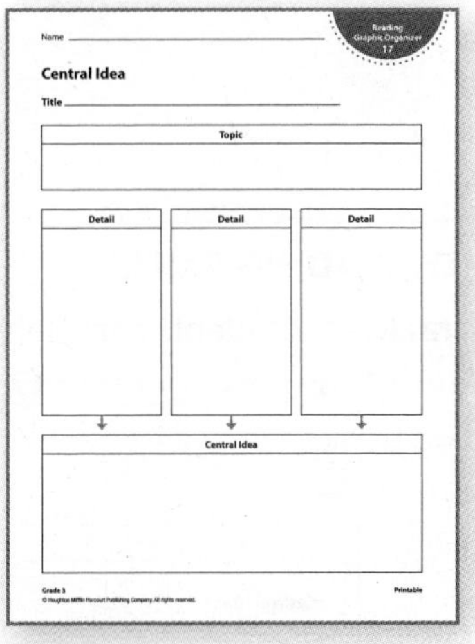

Printable: Reading Graphic Organizer 17

ALMOST THERE

READY FOR MORE

SCAFFOLD AND EXTEND

- Guide students to identify the central idea. Ask them to point out evidence that supports it.
- Prompt students to identify the central idea and the details in the text that support it.
- Have students explain how they used text evidence to identify a central idea not directly stated in the text.

EL ENGLISH LEARNER SUPPORT

SUBSTANTIAL

Help students complete the sentence frame: *The central idea is* ______. Then have them point to words and pictures that support it.

MODERATE

Supply sentence frames such as: *The central idea is* ______. *A detail that supports it is* ______.

LIGHT

Have students tell a partner how they identified the central idea and details that support it.

Options for Independent and Collaborative Work

While you meet with small groups, have other students engage in literacy activities that reinforce the lesson's learning objectives. Choose from these options.

Independent Reading

Student Choice Library

Rigby
LEVELED LIBRARY

APPLY READING SKILL

Central Idea Students complete Printable: Reading Graphic Organizer 17 for an independent reading book.

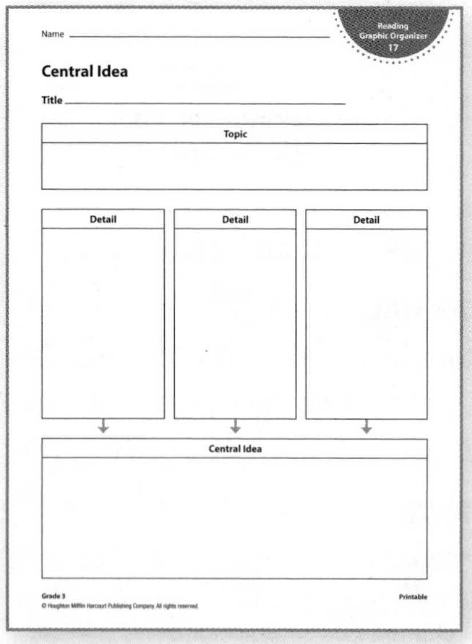
Reading Graphic Organizer 17

Name

Central Idea

Title

Topic

Detail | Detail | Detail

Central Idea

Grade 3
© Houghton Mifflin Harcourt Publishing Company. All rights reserved.
Printable

Printable: Reading Graphic Organizer 17

APPLY LANGUAGE SKILL

Seek Information Students complete Printable: Language Graphic Organizer 12 for an independent reading book.

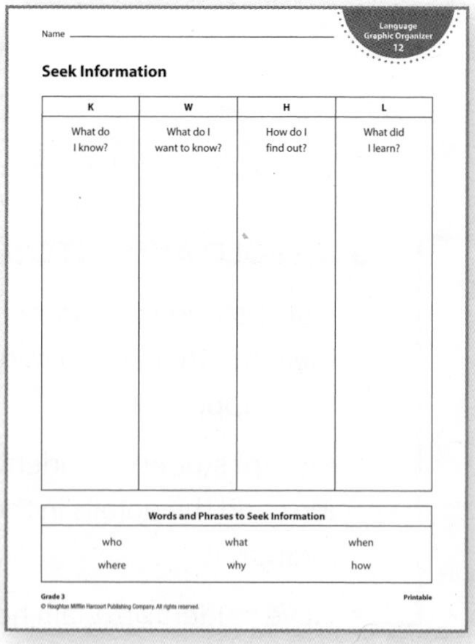
Language Graphic Organizer 12

Name

Seek Information

K	W	H	L
What do I know?	What do I want to know?	How do I find out?	What did I learn?

Words and Phrases to Seek Information

who	what	when
where	why	how

Grade 3
© Houghton Mifflin Harcourt Publishing Company. All rights reserved.
Printable

Printable: Language Graphic Organizer 12

Literacy Centers

See pp. T140–T141.

- READING CENTER
- VOCABULARY CENTER
- DIGITAL STATION
- WRITING CENTER
- PROJECT CENTER

Writing

Students write an opinion letter.
See Engage and Respond, p. T159.

Additional Skills Practice

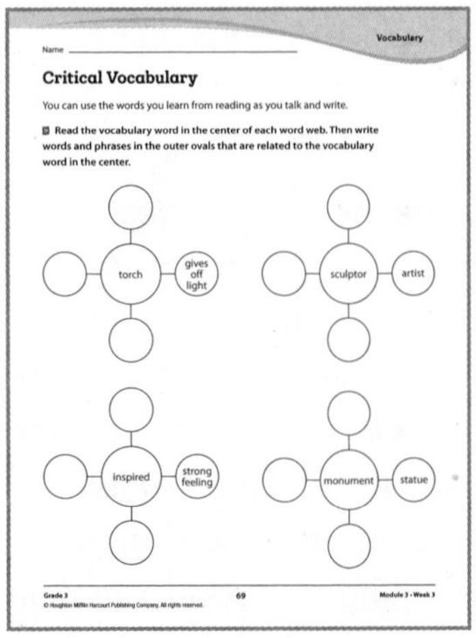
Vocabulary

Name ______

Critical Vocabulary

You can use the words you learn from reading as you talk and write.

Read the vocabulary word in the center of each word web. Then write words and phrases in the outer ovals that are related to the vocabulary word in the center.

torch — gives off light

sculptor — artist

inspired — strong feeling

monument — statue

Grade 3 69 Module 3 • Week 3
© Houghton Mifflin Harcourt Publishing Company. All rights reserved.

Know It, Show It, p. 69

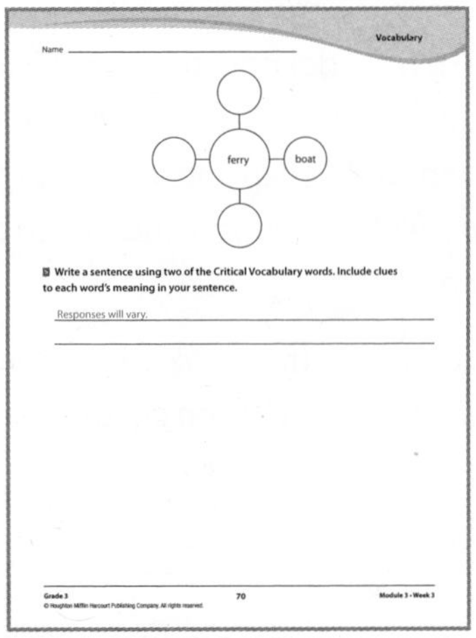
Vocabulary

Name ______

ferry — boat

Write a sentence using two of the Critical Vocabulary words. Include clues to each word's meaning in your sentence.

Responses will vary.

Grade 3 70 Module 3 • Week 3
© Houghton Mifflin Harcourt Publishing Company. All rights reserved.

Know It, Show It, p. 70

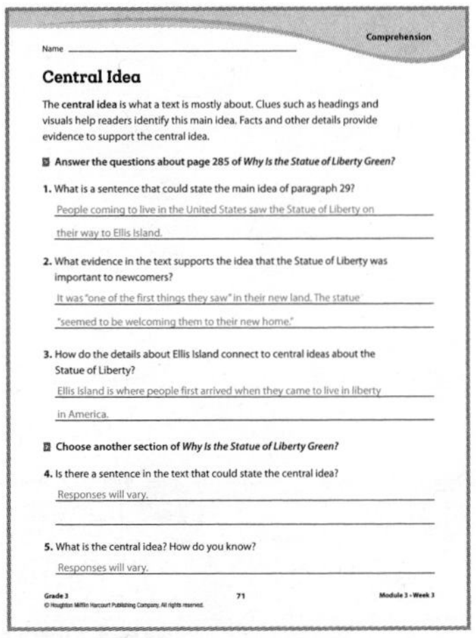
Comprehension

Name ______

Central Idea

The **central idea** is what a text is mostly about. Clues such as headings and visuals help readers identify this main idea. Facts and other details provide evidence to support the central idea.

Answer the questions about page 285 of *Why Is the Statue of Liberty Green?*

1. What is a sentence that could state the main idea of paragraph 29?
People coming to live in the United States saw the Statue of Liberty on their way to Ellis Island.

2. What evidence in the text supports the idea that the Statue of Liberty was important to newcomers?
It was "one of the first things they saw" in their new land. The statue "seemed to be welcoming them to their new home."

3. How do the details about Ellis Island connect to central ideas about the Statue of Liberty?
Ellis Island is where people first arrived when they came to live in liberty in America.

Choose another section of *Why Is the Statue of Liberty Green?*

4. Is there a sentence in the text that could state the central idea?
Responses will vary.

5. What is the central idea? How do you know?
Responses will vary.

Grade 3 71 Module 3 • Week 3
© Houghton Mifflin Harcourt Publishing Company. All rights reserved.

Know It, Show It, p. 71

Wrap-Up

Share Time

At the end of the Reading Workshop, have students reflect on their learning by sharing how they applied **central idea** or another area of focus during independent work time. Choose from these options:

- Use the **SOLO CHAIR** routine. Select a reader each day to come to the front of the class and tell what he or she learned from the reading by using a skill or strategy.
- **THINK-PAIR-SHARE** Students share their thinking with a partner. Select a few pairs each day to share with the whole class.
- **RETURN TO ANCHOR CHART** Have students add sticky notes about their independent reading to the Central Idea Anchor Chart. Call on a few students to explain what they added and why.

Online Ed

ANCHOR CHART 17: Central Idea

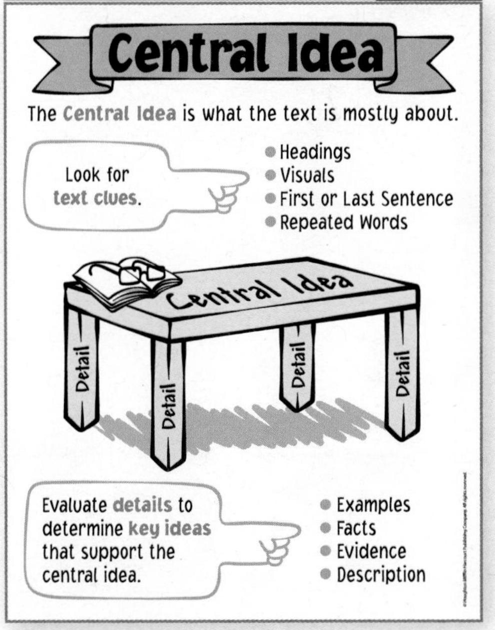

Prefix im- (not)

Step 1 Introduce the Skill

Project Display and Engage: Generative Vocabulary 3.13. Read aloud the paragraphs.

Online

DISPLAY AND ENGAGE:
Generative Vocabulary 3.13

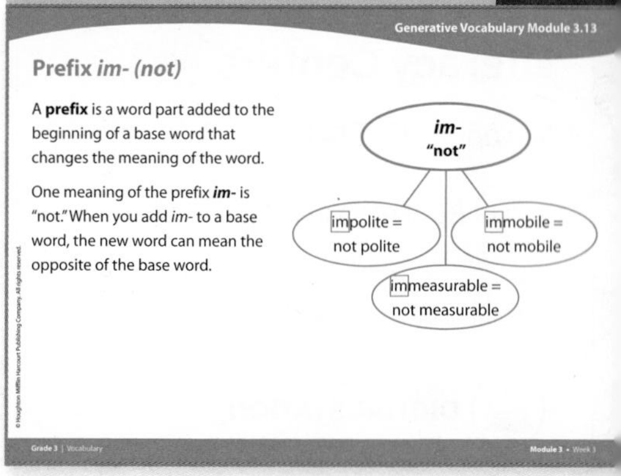
Generative Vocabulary Module 3.13
Prefix *im- (not)*
A **prefix** is a word part added to the beginning of a base word that changes the meaning of the word.
One meaning of the prefix ***im-*** is "not." When you add *im-* to a base word, the new word can mean the opposite of the base word.
im-
"not"
impolite = not polite
immobile = not mobile
immeasurable = not measurable
© Houghton Mifflin Harcourt Publishing Company. All rights reserved.
Grade 3 | Vocabulary
Module 3 • Week 3

- Write the words *perfect* and *possible* on the board. Ask volunteers to share the meaning of each base word. Then add the prefix *im–* to each word to form *imperfect* and *impossible*. Tell students that knowing the meaning of the prefix *im–* can help them figure out the meaning of these words.
- Then model how to use prefixes to determine the meaning of a word. *The prefix* im– *can mean "not." When* im– *means* not, *it changes a base word to mean its opposite. When you add the prefix* im– *to* perfect, *you get* imperfect, *meaning "not perfect." When you add* im– *to* possible, *you get* impossible, *meaning "not possible."*

  When I see the prefix im– *in a word, I will know the word may mean the opposite of the base word. I can check the sentence context to see if this make sense.*

LEARNING OBJECTIVES

- Determine the meaning of grade-level academic vocabulary with prefixes or suffixes.
- Use a dictionary or glossary to determine the meanings of unknown words.
- **Language** Discuss words with the prefix *im-* to show understanding of the target prefix.

MATERIALS Online

Display and Engage *Generative Vocabulary 3.13*
Know It, Show It *p. 72*

INSTRUCTIONAL VOCABULARY

- **prefix** a word part added to the beginning of a base word that changes the meaning of the word
- **suffix** a word part added to the end of a base word that changes the meaning of the word
- **base word** a word in its simplest form, without any word parts added to it.

ENGLISH LEARNER SUPPORT: Build Vocabulary

SUBSTANTIAL
Show familiar words with the prefix *im–*, meaning *not*. Discuss each base word's meaning and how the prefix changes it.

MODERATE
Have students name words with the prefix *im–*, meaning *not*. Ask them to tell the base word's meaning and how the prefix changes it.

LIGHT
Have pairs write sentences with the lesson's *im–* words.

Step 2 Guided Practice

- Display the words *immature and impatient*. Ask volunteers to identify the base word in each and give its meaning. Then ask how the prefix changes the meaning of each base word.
- Ask students to look up each word in a print or online dictionary to confirm their responses. Have volunteers provide a definition of each word.

Step 3 Apply the Skill

INDEPENDENT PRACTICE

- Have students work in pairs to complete Know It, Show It p. 72. Tell partners to read the instructions and then complete the activity together.
- Then have each student write a new sentence for each word with the *im*– prefix. Have partners read their sentences to one another to confirm the meaning of each word. Invite volunteers to read their sentences aloud.

Spiral Review

Suffixes *–er, –est* Remind students that a suffix is a word part added to the end of a base word that changes the meaning of the word.

- Review that the suffixes *–er* and *–est* are added to adjectives to show comparisons. The suffix *–er* compares two things. The suffix *–est* compares three or more things. Review that sometimes a base word's spelling changes slightly when the ending *–er* or *–est* is added. For words with a consonant-vowel-consonant pattern, you double the final consonant before adding *–er* or *–est*. For words that end in *e*, you drop the *e* before adding the suffix. For words that end in *y*, you change the *y* to *i* before adding the suffix.
- Write on the board the following words from *Why Is the Statue of Liberty Green]: green, huge, shiny,* and *tall*. Add the suffixes –er and –est to each word: *greener, greenest; huger, hugest; shinier, shiniest; tall, tallest*. Have volunteers point out the suffix in each word and explain how it changes the base word's meaning.
- Have students add the suffixes *–er* and *–est* to the following words: *wise, fussy, flat, glad, simple*. Have students explain how the affixes change the words' meanings. Invite them to check the words' meanings in a print or online dictionary.

Author's Purpose

Step 1 Connect and Teach

LEARNING OBJECTIVES

- Recognize the author's purpose.
- **Language** Articulate the author's purpose for writing.

MATERIALS Online Ed

Anchor Chart 28 *Author's Purpose*

Printable *Anchor Chart 28: Author's Purpose*

Teaching Pal *pp. 274–291*

myBook *Why Is the Statue of Liberty Green? Book 1, pp. 274–291*

Know It, Show It *p. 73*

INSTRUCTIONAL VOCABULARY

- **author's purpose** the author's reason for writing
- **entertain** to bring joy and fun to the reader through a story
- **inform** to give facts about a topic
- **persuade** to try to convince someone of an idea or to try to get the person to do something

SPANISH COGNATES

- **author** *autor*
- **entertain** *entretener*
- **inform** *informar*
- **persuade** *persuadir*
- **purpose** *proposíto*
- **reason** *razón*

Tell students that authors usually want to share an important lesson or message when they write. Explain that good readers think about the **author's purpose**, or reason, for writing to figure out his or her message.

Project or display **Anchor Chart 28: Author's Purpose.**

Online

ANCHOR CHART 28: Author's Purpose

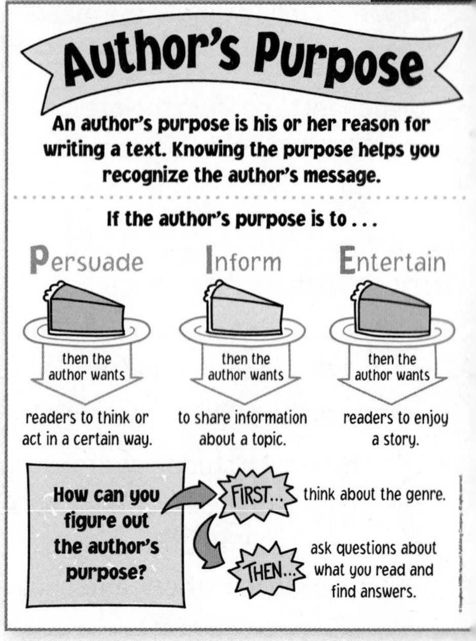

- Draw attention to the graphic to explain the three main purposes an author may have for writing. As you discuss each one, recall familiar texts that **persuade, inform,** and **entertain.**
- Point out that students can ask themselves questions such as the following to help them determine the author's purpose: *Is the author trying to give me facts about a topic? Does the author want to make me laugh? Is the author sharing his or her opinions so that I'll change my opinion?*
- Tell students that they will practice identifying the author's purpose to gain a deeper understanding of *Why Is the Statue of Liberty Green?*

Go to Your
Teaching Pal

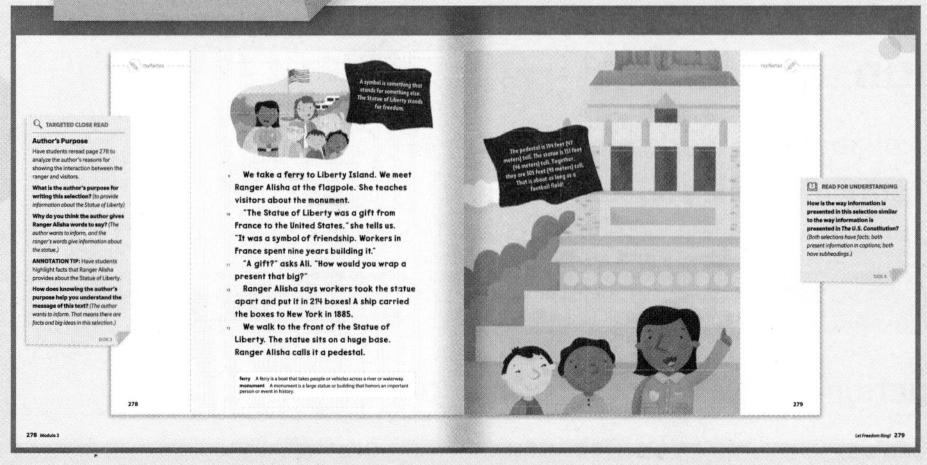

TARGETED CLOSE READ

Author's Purpose

Have students reread page 278 to analyze the author's reasons for showing the interaction between the ranger and visitors.

What is the author's purpose for writing this selection? *(to provide information about the Statue of Liberty)*

Why do you think the author gives Ranger Alisha words to say? *(The author wants to inform, and the ranger's words give information about the statue.)*

ANNOTATION TIP: Have students highlight facts that Ranger Alisha provides about the Statue of Liberty.

How does knowing the author's purpose help you understand the message of this text? *(The author wants to inform. That means there are facts and big ideas in this selection.)*

DOK 3

A symbol is something that stands for something else. The Statue of Liberty stands for freedom.

9 We take a ferry to Liberty Island. We meet Ranger Alisha at the flagpole. She teaches visitors about the monument.

10 "The Statue of Liberty was a gift from France to the United States," she tells us. "It was a symbol of friendship. Workers in France spent nine years building it."

11 "A gift?" asks Ali. "How would you wrap a present that big?"

12 Ranger Alisha says workers took the statue apart and put it in 214 boxes! A ship carried the boxes to New York in 1885.

13 We walk to the front of the Statue of Liberty. The statue sits on a huge base. Ranger Alisha calls it a pedestal.

ferry A ferry is a boat that takes people or vehicles across a river or waterway.
monument A monument is a large statue or building that honors an important person or event in history.

278

The pedestal is 154 feet (47 meters) tall. The statue is 151 feet (46 meters) tall. Together, they are 305 feet (93 meters) tall. That is about as long as a football field!

READ FOR UNDERSTANDING

How is the way information is presented in this selection similar to the way information is presented in *The U.S. Constitution*? *(Both selections have facts; both present information in captions; both have subheadings.)*

DOK 4

279

278 Module 3 Let Freedom Ring! 279

Online

ANNOTATE IT!

Ed

Students may use the annotation tools in their eBook.

Step 2 Apply to Text

In your Teaching Pal, use the purple **TARGETED CLOSE READ** prompts on pages 274–289 to guide students to apply the Author's Purpose skill to *Why Is the Statue of Liberty Green?* and to find evidence to support their responses. Use the **CLOSE READING** routine. Students may refer to the questions on Know It, Show It page 73 as you discuss them.

- Read aloud the first two questions on Teaching Pal page 278. Have students reread *my*Book page 278 and think about the interaction between the ranger and visitors. Discuss the author's purpose for writing and how the ranger's words fit that purpose. *(To provide information about the Statue of Liberty; The author wants to inform, and the ranger's words give information about the statue.)*
- Read aloud the follow-up question on Teaching Pal page 278. Discuss how knowing the author's purpose helps readers understand the message of the text. *(The author wants to inform. That means there are facts and big ideas in this selection.)*
- Refer back to the Anchor Chart to support the discussion. Students may add sticky notes to the chart to note further evidence of the author's purpose in *Why Is the Statue of Liberty Green?*

Step 3 Engage and Respond

INDEPENDENT PRACTICE: Writing

Tell students to think about a place that they find interesting. Have them write a paragraph in which they give information about this place. Use the **WRITING RESPONSE** routine. Remind them to include facts about the place to inform other students about it.

- Have partners exchange paragraphs. Tell each partner to underline the facts they find about their partner's chosen place.
- Then have students discuss how writing to inform affected what they included in their paragraphs.
- You may wish to have students complete their writing during daily small-group time.
- You may want to have students complete Know It, Show It page 73 during daily small-group time.

EL ENGLISH LEARNER SUPPORT: Support Comprehension

SUBSTANTIAL

Does the author want you to laugh or to learn something? Does she inform or entertain?

MODERATE

Provide frames: *The author's purpose is to _____. I know because _____.*

LIGHT

Encourage students to use complete sentences to explain the author's purpose and how they know.

LINK TO SMALL-GROUP INSTRUCTION

REINFORCE AUTHOR'S PURPOSE Review and extend the skill as needed during small-group time to support students' need for differentiation. *See the lesson on p. T169.*

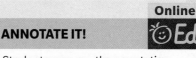

Options for Differentiation

As the class engages in independent and collaborative work, meet with Guided Reading Groups or differentiate instruction based on student need.

GUIDED READING GROUPS

Match Students to Books + Instruction

- Choose just-right books based on level, skill, topic, or genre.

L M N O P Q

Leveled Readers

- Deliver instruction with each book's **Take and Teach Lesson**, choosing appropriate sessions based on need.

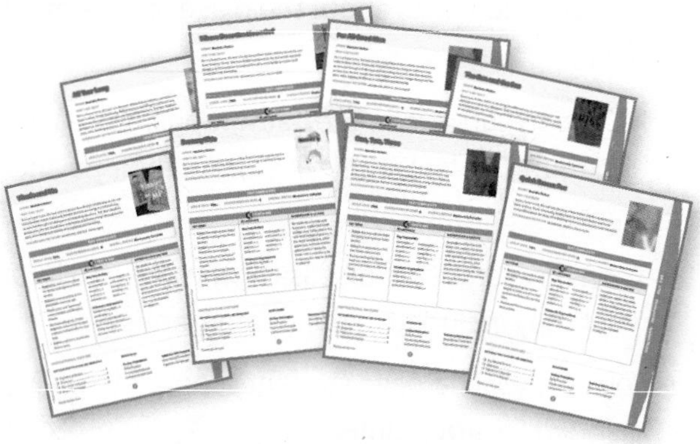

- Check comprehension, reinforce instruction, and extend learning with suggested supporting activities.

ENGLISH LEARNER SUPPORT

Seek Information

- Use **Tabletop Minilessons: English Language Development 9.2 (Reading)** to reinforce and practice the language skill.

Tabletop Minilessons: English Language Development

- Then use the following text-based prompts with *Why Is the Statue of Liberty Green?* to guide application of the language skill. Begin with the prompt at the student's identified language proficiency level. As students progress, use lighter supports to encourage increased language proficiency.

SUBSTANTIAL
Have students find, point to, and read aloud the highlighted words *ferry* and *monument*. Then point to and read together the definitions for those words at the bottom of the page. Clarify the definitions as needed.

MODERATE
Point out the captions and footnotes that contain definitions for content-area words in the section *Why Is the Statue of Liberty Green?* Read them aloud with students. Then have students answer the questions: *What is a ferry? What is a symbol? What is a monument?*

LIGHT
Have students turn to the section *Why Is the Statue of Liberty Green?* Say: *Read the page. Where on the page would you tell someone to look if they wanted to read about what a symbol is? Where would you tell someone to read if they needed to know the meaning of* ferry *or* monument*?*

REINFORCE AUTHOR'S PURPOSE

Demonstrate

- Use **Tabletop Minilessons: Reading Card 28** to remind students that the **author's purpose** is the author's reason for writing a text. Remind students that authors may write to **entertain**, **inform**, or **persuade**. Remind students that they can determine the author's purpose by asking questions such as: *Is the author trying to give me facts about a topic? Does the author want to make me laugh? Is the author sharing his or her opinions so that I'll change my opinion?*
- Model filling out Printable: Reading Graphic Organizer 28 to identify author's purpose in *Why Is the Statue of Liberty Green?*

Apply to Independent Reading

- Now have students identify author's purpose and the author's intended audience in an appropriate book or article they are reading independently. Customize these prompts to the texts students choose.
  - » *Is the author's purpose to entertain, inform, or persuade?*
  - » *What text evidence helps you to determine the author's purpose?*
  - » *How does knowing the author's purpose help you to better understand the text?*
- Have students complete Printable: Reading Graphic Organizer 28 for their independent reading book.

Tabletop Minilessons: Reading

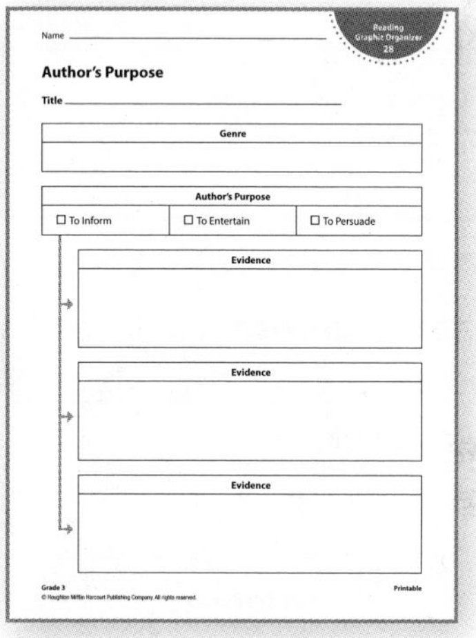

Printable: Reading Graphic Organizer 28

ALMOST THERE

READY FOR MORE

SCAFFOLD AND EXTEND

- Point out details in the text that indicate the author's purpose. Then help students to identify it.
- Prompt students to identify the author's purpose and the details in the text that indicate it.
- Have students explain how the text would be different if the author had the same subject but a different purpose for writing.

EL ENGLISH LEARNER SUPPORT

SUBSTANTIAL

Ask *either/or* questions about the text to help students state the author's purpose. Example: *Does the author try to make you laugh or give you information?*

MODERATE

Supply this sentence frame: *I can tell the author's purpose is ______ because ______.*

LIGHT

Encourage students to explain how they identified the author's purpose.

INDEPENDENT APPLICATION

Options for Independent and Collaborative Work

While you meet with small groups, have other students engage in literacy activities that reinforce the lesson's learning objectives. Choose from these options.

Independent Reading

Student Choice Library

Rigby
LEVELED LIBRARY

APPLY READING SKILL

Author's Purpose Students complete Printable: Reading Graphic Organizer 28 for an independent reading book.

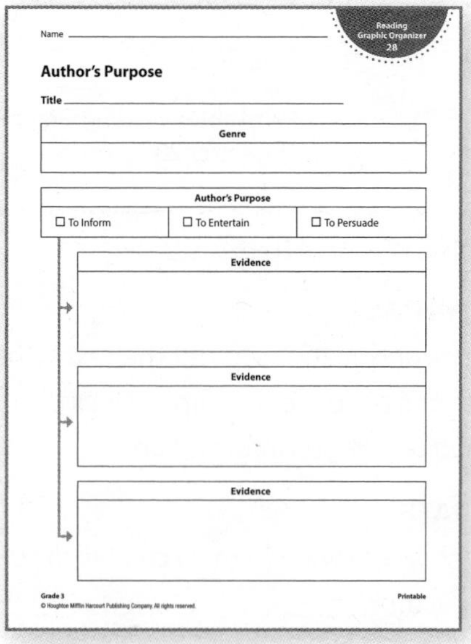

Printable: Reading Graphic Organizer 28

APPLY LANGUAGE SKILL

Seek Information Students complete Printable: Language Graphic Organizer 12 for an independent reading book.

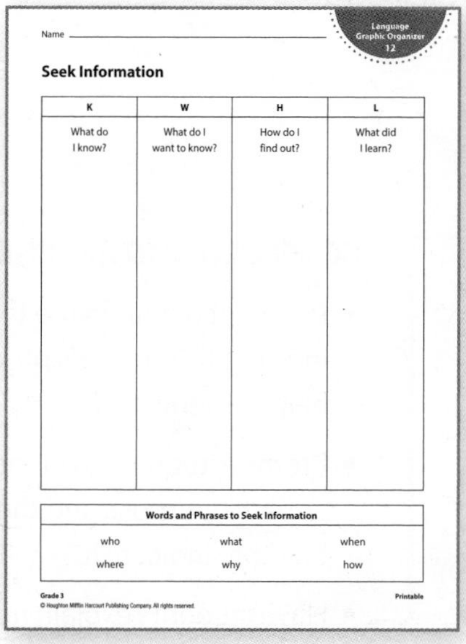

Printable: Language Graphic Organizer 12

Literacy Centers

See pp. T140–T141.

- READING CENTER
- VOCABULARY CENTER
- DIGITAL STATION
- WRITING CENTER
- PROJECT CENTER

Writing

Students write an informational paragraph. *See Engage and Respond, p. T167.*

Additional Skills Practice

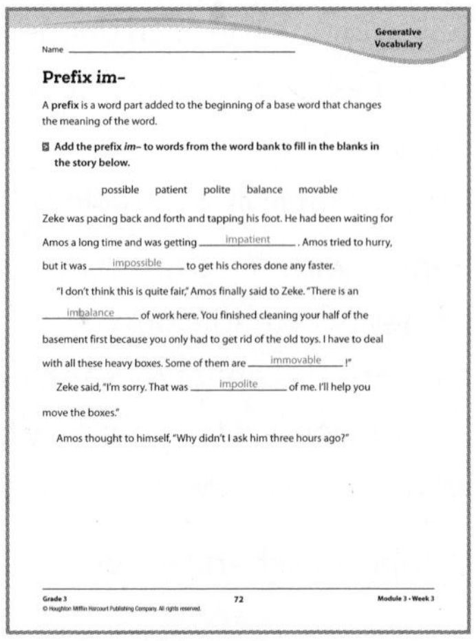

Name ____________ Generative Vocabulary

Prefix im–

A **prefix** is a word part added to the beginning of a base word that changes the meaning of the word.

Add the prefix *im–* to words from the word bank to fill in the blanks in the story below.

possible patient polite balance movable

Zeke was pacing back and forth and tapping his foot. He had been waiting for Amos a long time and was getting impatient. Amos tried to hurry, but it was impossible to get his chores done any faster.

"I don't think this is quite fair," Amos finally said to Zeke. "There is an imbalance of work here. You finished cleaning your half of the basement first because you only had to get rid of the old toys. I have to deal with all these heavy boxes. Some of them are immovable!"

Zeke said, "I'm sorry. That was impolite of me. I'll help you move the boxes."

Amos thought to himself, "Why didn't I ask him three hours ago?"

Grade 3 72 Module 3 • Week 3

Know It, Show It, p. 72

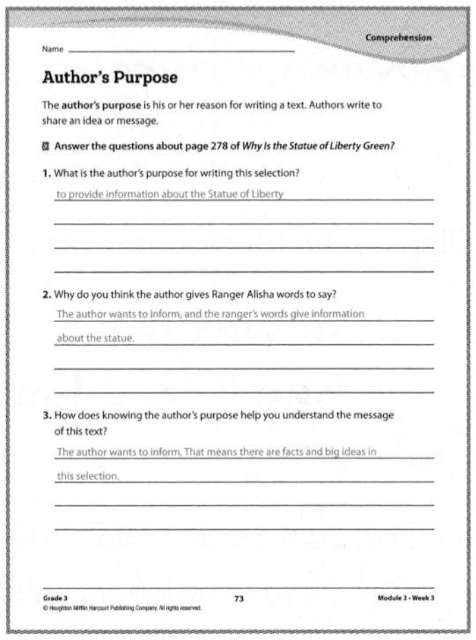

Name ____________ Comprehension

Author's Purpose

The **author's purpose** is his or her reason for writing a text. Authors write to share an idea or message.

Answer the questions about page 278 of *Why Is the Statue of Liberty Green?*

1. What is the author's purpose for writing this selection?
   to provide information about the Statue of Liberty
2. Why do you think the author gives Ranger Alisha words to say?
   The author wants to inform, and the ranger's words give information about the statue.
3. How does knowing the author's purpose help you understand the message of this text?
   The author wants to inform. That means there are facts and big ideas in this selection.

Grade 3 73 Module 3 • Week 3

Know It, Show It, p. 73

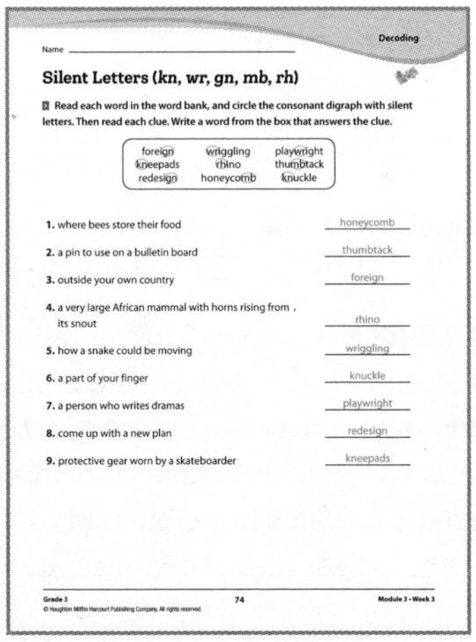

Name ____________ Decoding

Silent Letters (kn, wr, gn, mb, rh)

Read each word in the word bank, and circle the consonant digraph with silent letters. Then read each clue. Write a word from the box that answers the clue.

foreign	wriggling	playwright
kneepads	rhino	thumbtack
redesign	honeycomb	knuckle

1. where bees store their food — honeycomb
2. a pin to use on a bulletin board — thumbtack
3. outside your own country — foreign
4. a very large African mammal with horns rising from its snout — rhino
5. how a snake could be moving — wriggling
6. a part of your finger — knuckle
7. a person who writes dramas — playwright
8. come up with a new plan — redesign
9. protective gear worn by a skateboarder — kneepads

Grade 3 74 Module 3 • Week 3

Know It, Show It, p. 74

Wrap-Up

Share Time

At the end of the Reading Workshop, have students reflect on their learning by sharing how they applied **author's purpose** or another area of focus during independent work time. Choose from these options:

- Use the **SOLO CHAIR** routine. Select a reader each day to come to the front of the class and tell what he or she learned from the reading by using a skill or strategy.
- **THINK-PAIR-SHARE** Students share their thinking with a partner. Select a few pairs each day to share with the whole class.
- **RETURN TO ANCHOR CHART** Have students add sticky notes about their independent reading to the Author's Purpose Anchor Chart. Call on a few students to explain what they added and why.

ANCHOR CHART 28: Text and Graphic Features

Online Ed

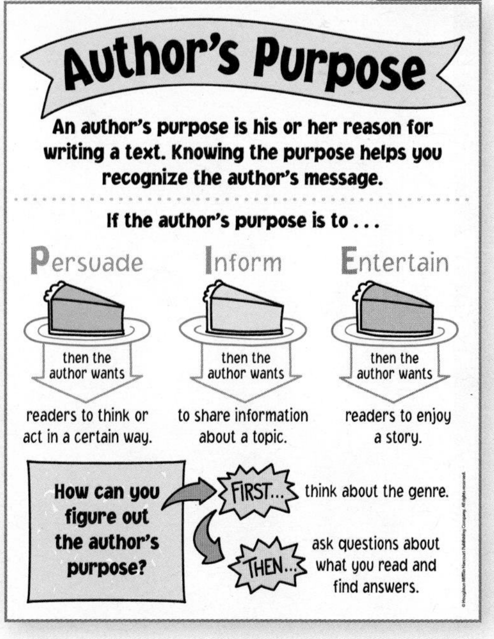

Author's Purpose
An author's purpose is his or her reason for writing a text. Knowing the purpose helps you recognize the author's message.
If the author's purpose is to . . .
Persuade
then the author wants
readers to think or act in a certain way.
Inform
then the author wants
to share information about a topic.
Entertain
then the author wants
readers to enjoy a story.
How can you figure out the author's purpose?
FIRST...
think about the genre.
THEN...
ask questions about what you read and find answers.

LEARNING OBJECTIVES

- Decode and read words with consonant digraphs with silent letters.
- Recognize spelling patterns for consonant digraphs with silent letters.
- **Language** Articulate the /r/ sound and read words containing that sound.

MATERIALS **Online** Ed

Display and Engage *Decoding 3.13*
Know It, Show It *p. 74*

Silent Letters

Step 1 Reinforce the Skill

Silent Letters Remind students that they have learned the sounds and spellings of consonant digraphs with silent letters: *kn*, *wr*, *gn*, *mb*, and *rh*.

- **Transition to Longer Words** Display and read the word *knothole*. Underline the *kn*, pointing out the /n/ sound.
- Tell students they can divide longer words into syllables to make them easier to read. Draw a line between *t* and *h* to divide *knothole* into syllables. Note that the first syllable ends in a consonant, which means it's a closed syllable. Explain that closed syllables usually have short vowel sounds.
- Repeat with the words *typewriter*, *assignment*, *climber*, and *rhyming*. Guide students to read aloud the words and to help you identify the syllables that contain consonant digraphs with silent letters: *wr, gn, mb, rh*. Point out that in longer words, students may find these consonant digraphs in the middle of words, as in *typewriter, assignment,* and *climber*.
- Display the chart below. Read each word aloud.

kn	wr	gn	mb	rh
knowingly	wrangler	signpost	breadcrumb	rhubarb

- Display the following sentence and underline the word *wrangler*.

Dina was the best wrangler on the ranch, because she had herded and cared for cattle for more than ten years.

Say: *Let's say I didn't know the word* wrangler. *I look for a spelling pattern that can help me. I know the letters* wr *stand for the /r/ sound. So I will sound out the word: /răng/ /glər/,* wrangler. *That sounds right. It also makes sense. From context clues in the sentence, I can figure out that a wrangler is a person who takes care of cattle on a ranch.*

ENGLISH LEARNER SUPPORT: Utilize Language Transfer

ALL LEVELS Pronouncing the /r/ sound may present difficulty to some English learners. The sound may not exist in the primary language, may exist but be pronounced somewhat differently, or may be confused with another sound. Support speakers of Spanish, Hmong, Cantonese, Haitian Creole, and Korean by making the sound /r/ several times. Direct students to watch how you hold your mouth. Have students use mirrors to see how their mouths look as they pronounce /r/.

Step 2 Guided Practice

- Project Display and Engage: **Decoding 3.13**.
- Have students read aloud the Blend and Read lines. Provide feedback as needed. At the end of each line, prompt a conversation about the words: *What is alike about these words? How are they different?*
- Have partners reread the Blend and Read lines and quiz each other on the spellings of consonant digraphs with silent letters.

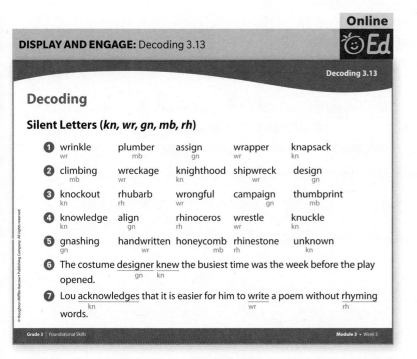

Online Ed

DISPLAY AND ENGAGE: Decoding 3.13

Decoding 3.13

Decoding

Silent Letters (*kn, wr, gn, mb, rh*)

1	wrinkle (wr)	plumber (mb)	assign (gn)	wrapper (wr)	knapsack (kn)
2	climbing (mb)	wreckage (wr)	knighthood (kn)	shipwreck (wr)	design (gn)
3	knockout (kn)	rhubarb (rh)	wrongful (wr)	campaign (gn)	thumbprint (mb)
4	knowledge (kn)	align (gn)	rhinoceros (rh)	wrestle (wr)	knuckle (kn)
5	gnashing (gn)	handwritten (wr)	honeycomb (mb)	rhinestone (rh)	unknown (kn)

6 The costume designer (gn) knew (kn) the busiest time was the week before the play opened.

7 Lou acknowledges (kn) that it is easier for him to write (wr) a poem without rhyming (rh) words.

Grade 3 | Foundational Skills   Module 3 • Week 3

Step 3 Apply

INDEPENDENT PRACTICE

- Have students work in small groups or with partners to complete Know It, Show It page 74.
- Be sure students understand there are two tasks for each sentence. First read each word in the box and circle the consonant digraph with the silent letter. Then write a word that answers the clue.
- Encourage students to share with each other the strategies they use to decode the words with consonant digraphs with silent letters.

CORRECT & REDIRECT

If students have trouble decoding words with consonant digraphs with silent letters, use the model below.

- **Correct** the error. *Some consonant digraphs have a silent letter. You don't pronounce both letters.*
- **Model** how to decode the word. */ə/ /līgn/. That doesn't sound like a word I know. The word* align *has the letters* gn *at the end. I know that in this consonant digraph, the letter* g *is silent, and* gn *is pronounced /n/. So I'll try it again: /ə/ /līn/,* align. *That sounds right.*
- **Guide** students to decode the words *knuckle* and *wrestle*.
- **Check** students' understanding by displaying the word *thumbprint*. *What spelling pattern helps you decode this word?* (The letters mb stand *for the sound /m/.*)
- **Reinforce** by repeating the process with *rhinestone*.

Vocabulary Spiral Review

Step 1 Review Vocabulary

LEARNING OBJECTIVES

- Review vocabulary.
- Identify real-life connections between words and their uses.
- Practice vocabulary by playing charades.
- **Language** Discuss target vocabulary words and expand vocabulary knowledge.

MATERIALS

Online Ed

Display and Engage *2.6, 2.8, 2.11*

Vocabulary Cards *2.5, 2.6, 2.8, 2.10, 2.11, 2.15, 2.16, 2.18, 2.21*

- Tell students they will review some of the Critical Vocabulary they have learned so far this year and complete an activity based on those words.
- Project Display and Engage: Critical Vocabulary 2.6, Critical Vocabulary 2.8, and Critical Vocabulary 2.11 to remind students of the Module 2, Week 2 and Week 3 Critical Vocabulary words and their meanings.

Online Ed

DISPLAY AND ENGAGE: Critical Vocabulary 2.6,2.8, and 2.11

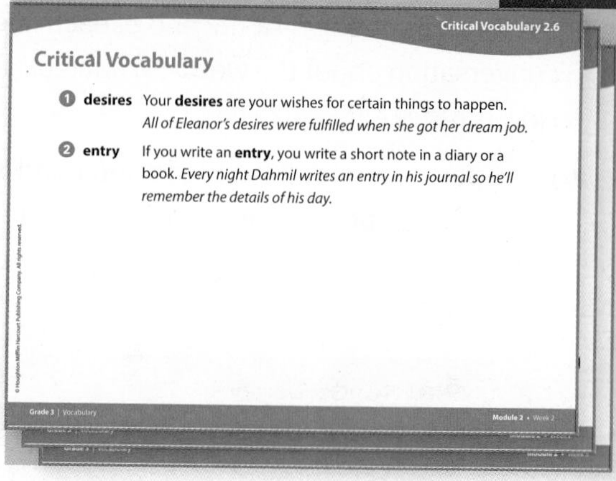

- After reviewing the meanings, call out words and have volunteers take turns using the words in sentences of their own. If students are having trouble creating sentences, have them give synonyms or antonyms for the word.
- Continue until all students have had a chance to work with one or more of the words.

Step 2 Guided Practice

- Use Vocabulary Cards 2.5, 2.6, 2.8, 2.10, 2.11, 2.15, 2.16, 2.18, and 2.21 to remind students of the meanings of the words *video, hydrant, costumes, desires, entry, conductor, projects, mosaics,* and *demolition*.
- Ask students how all the words are alike. If necessary, point out that all the words are nouns, and review how nouns are used.
- Tell students they will use these words to play a game of charades.
- Explain the rules. Students will play in groups. One member will silently act out a word from the Vocabulary Cards. No mouthing words, either! Team members will try to guess the word. The student who guesses correctly scores a point. You may choose to use a timer to limit each round to one minute.
- Model the activity by acting out one of the vocabulary words and asking students to make guesses.

Step 3 Apply the Skill

- Divide students into groups of four or more to play the game on their own.
- Display the vocabulary words where students can easily see them.
- Have a volunteer from each group take the first turn choosing and acting out a word, as team members call out guesses. The first student to correctly guess the word gets a point.
- For the next round, a different student will choose and act out a word.
- Have students keep playing until everyone on a team has acted out at least one word.

ENGLISH LEARNER SUPPORT: Play Charades with Vocabulary

SUBSTANTIAL

Make sure students understand the charade rules. Have pairs practice acting out words as you give suggestions as needed.

MODERATE

Have students work with an English-fluent partner to act out the charade words.

LIGHT

Challenge students to offer a context sentence for each charade word they guess correctly, offering an extra game point for doing so.

TEACHER TIP

Encourage students to suggest additional rules for the charades game to make it (a little bit!) easier or harder, and allow them to incorporate the rules as they begin a new round.

Literary Elements

Step 1 Connect and Teach

LEARNING OBJECTIVES

- Identify the setting in a narrative nonfiction text.
- Recognize changes in setting and their influence on the plot.
- **Language** Identify and articulate the settings in a narrative nonfiction text.

MATERIALS Online Ed

Anchor Chart 12 *Literary Elements*
Printable *Anchor Chart 12: Literary Elements*
Teaching Pal *pp. 274–291*
***my*Book** *Why Is the Statue of Liberty Green? Book 1, pp. 274–291*
Know It, Show It *p. 75*

INSTRUCTIONAL VOCABULARY

- **literary elements** the pieces that make up a story, such as characters, setting, plot, and events
- **setting** where and when a story takes place

SPANISH COGNATES

- **literary** *literario*

- Project or display Anchor Chart 12: Literary Elements. Recall with students that **literary elements** are the pieces that make up a story. Draw attention to the corresponding area of the Anchor Chart as you review **characters**, **setting**, **plot**, and **events**.
- Point out that clues in the text and in the illustrations can reveal a story's setting. For example, skyscrapers suggest a city setting, while crops and animals may indicate a farm or other rural environment. Similarly, characters' clothing and other details in the illustrations can show if the story is set in the past, present, or future.
- Explain that a story's setting may influence its plot. Characters in a city may face different problems than those in a desert or mountainous setting. Those characters would have to choose different ways to solve their problems.
- Tell students that they will practice identifying literary elements to gain a deeper understanding of *Why Is the Statue of Liberty Green?*

ANCHOR CHART 12: Literary Elements — Online Ed

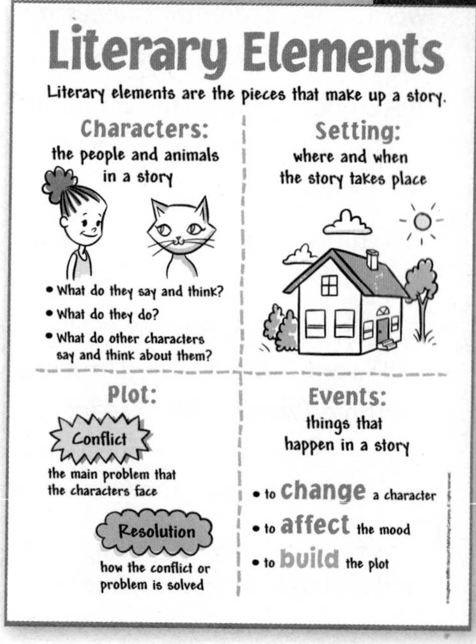
Literary Elements
Literary elements are the pieces that make up a story.
Characters:
the people and animals in a story
• What do they say and think?
• What do they do?
• What do other characters say and think about them?
Setting:
where and when the story takes place
Plot:
Conflict
the main problem that the characters face
Resolution
how the conflict or problem is solved
Events:
things that happen in a story
• to change a character
• to affect the mood
• to build the plot

LEARNING MINDSET

Grit

Normalize Explain that it's normal to feel overwhelmed when taking on a new challenge. *Sometimes it seems like you'll never be able to complete a big task or learn a new idea. That happens to everyone! It takes some grit to just get started. That first step is a big one!*

Go to Your
Teaching Pal

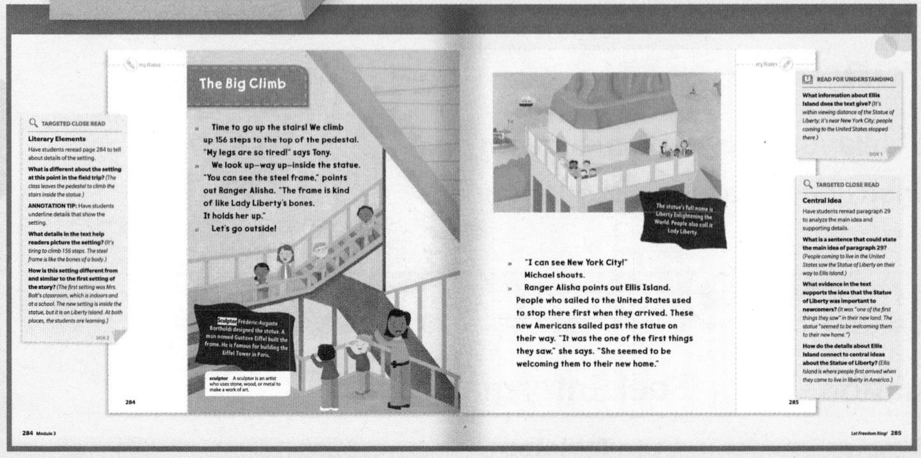

TARGETED CLOSE READ

Literary Elements

Have students reread page 284 to tell about details of the setting.

What is different about the setting at this point in the field trip? *(The class leaves the pedestal to climb the stairs inside the statue.)*

ANNOTATION TIP: Have students underline details that show the setting.

What details in the text help readers picture the setting? *(It's tiring to climb 156 steps. The steel frame is like the bones of a body.)*

How is this setting different from and similar to the first setting of the story? *(The first setting was Mrs. Bolt's classroom, which is indoors and at a school. The new setting is inside the statue, but it is on Liberty Island. At both places, the students are learning.)*

DOK 2

The Big Climb

Time to go up the stairs! We climb up 156 steps to the top of the pedestal. "My legs are so tired!" says Tony.

We look up—way up—inside the statue. "You can see the steel frame," points out Ranger Alisha. "The frame is kind of like Lady Liberty's bones. It holds her up."

Let's go outside!

Sculptor Frédéric-Auguste Bartholdi designed the statue. A man named Gustave Eiffel built the frame. He is famous for building the Eiffel Tower in Paris.

sculptor A sculptor is an artist who uses stone, wood, or metal to make a work of art.

284

284 Module 3

The statue's full name is Liberty Enlightening the World. People also call it Lady Liberty.

"I can see New York City!" Michael shouts.

Ranger Alisha points out Ellis Island. People who sailed to the United States used to stop there first when they arrived. These new Americans sailed past the statue on their way. "It was the one of the first things they saw," she says. "She seemed to be welcoming them to their new home."

285

READ FOR UNDERSTANDING

What information about Ellis Island does the text give? *(It's within viewing distance of the Statue of Liberty; it's near New York City; people coming to the United States stopped there.)*

DOK 1

TARGETED CLOSE READ

Central Idea

Have students reread paragraph 29 to analyze the main idea and supporting details.

What is a sentence that could state the main idea of paragraph 29? *(People coming to live in the United States saw the Statue of Liberty on their way to Ellis Island.)*

What evidence in the text supports the idea that the Statue of Liberty was important to newcomers? *(It was "one of the first things they saw" in their new land. The statue "seemed to be welcoming them to their new home.")*

How do the details about Ellis Island connect to central ideas about the Statue of Liberty? *(Ellis Island is where people first arrived when they came to live in liberty in America.)*

Let Freedom Ring! 285

Online

ANNOTATE IT! Ed

Students may use the annotation tools in their eBook.

Step 2 Apply to Text

In your Teaching Pal, use the purple **TARGETED CLOSE READ** prompts on page 274-291 to guide students to apply the Literary Elements skill to *Why Is the Statue of Liberty Green?* and to find evidence to support their responses. Use the **CLOSE READING** routine. Students may refer to the questions on Know It, Show It page 75 as you discuss them.

- Read aloud the first two questions on Teaching Pal page 284. Then have students reread *my*Book page 284 to tell about details that help readers picture the change in setting at this point in the field trip. *(The class leaves the pedestal to climb the stairs inside the statue. It's tiring to climb 156 steps. The steel frame is like the bones of a body.)*
- Read aloud the follow-up question on Teaching Pal page 284 and discuss how the setting differs from the beginning of the story. *(The first setting was Mrs. Bolt's classroom, which is indoors and at a school. The new setting is inside the statue, on Liberty Island. At both places, the students are learning.)*
- Refer back to the Anchor Chart to support the discussion. Students may add sticky notes to the chart to note literary elements they identify in *Why Is the Statue of Liberty Green?*

Step 3 Engage and Respond

INDEPENDENT PRACTICE: Speaking and Listening

Remind students that the setting is where and when a story takes place. Point out that the setting may influence what happens in a story, and it is important for the reader to notice when this happens.

- Have partners use the **COLLABORATIVE DISCUSSION** routine to discuss the various setting changes in *Why Is the Statue of Liberty Green?* Encourage them to note the setting at the beginning, middle, and end of the story. To help them identify each setting, suggest that students ask themselves, *Where are the characters now? How does the setting affect what happens?*
- You may want to have students conduct their discussions during daily small-group time.
- You may want to have students complete Know It, Show It page 75 during daily small-group time.

ENGLISH LEARNER SUPPORT: Elicit Participation

SUBSTANTIAL

Guide students to identify setting changes: *Now the class is ______. I know because ______.*

MODERATE

Supply this sentence stem: *I know the setting is ______ because ______.*

LIGHT

Have partners identify the setting and its impact in complete sentences.

LINK TO SMALL-GROUP INSTRUCTION

REINFORCE LITERARY ELEMENTS Review and extend the skill as needed during small-group time to support students' need for differentiation. *See the lesson on p. T179.*

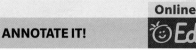

Options for Differentiation

As the class engages in independent and collaborative work, meet with Guided Reading Groups or differentiate instruction based on student need.

GUIDED READING GROUPS

Match Students to Books + Instruction

- Choose just-right books based on level, skill, topic, or genre.

L M N O P Q

Leveled Readers

- Deliver instruction with each book's **Take and Teach Lesson**, choosing appropriate sessions based on need.

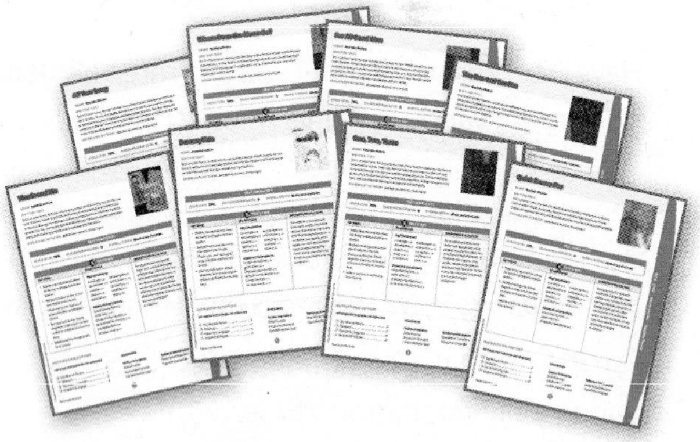

- Check comprehension, reinforce instruction, and extend learning with suggested supporting activities.

ENGLISH LEARNER SUPPORT

Seek Information

- Use **Tabletop Minilessons: English Language Development 9.2 (Writing)** to reinforce and practice the language skill.

Tabletop Minilessons: English Language Development

- Then use the following text-based prompts with *Why Is the Statue of Liberty Green?* to guide application of the language skill. Begin with the prompt at the student's identified language proficiency level. As students progress, use lighter supports to encourage increased language proficiency.

SUBSTANTIAL

Have students draw a picture of the Statue of Liberty and label the pedestal, the torch, and the flame.

MODERATE

Have students write a fact caption for the Statue of Liberty using a frame such as: *The Statue of Liberty is a symbol of _____. It was given to the United States by _____ in _____. It is built out of _____. It is _____ tall.*

LIGHT

Have students write a fact sheet for the Statue of Liberty that includes facts from the text such as how tall it is, what it is made out of, who built it, when it was built, and how it was built.

REINFORCE LITERARY ELEMENTS

Demonstrate

- Use **Tabletop Minilessons: Reading Card 12** to remind students that all stories have certain **literary elements** that are the same: main **characters** and minor characters; the **setting**, or where and when a story takes place; and the **plot**, or story **events**. Review that characters and setting can have an effect on the events.
- Model filling out Printable: Reading Graphic Organizer 12 to identify literary elements in *Why Is the Statue of Liberty Green?*

Apply to Independent Reading

- Now have students identify literary elements in an appropriate book or article they are reading independently. Customize these prompts to the texts students choose.
  - » *Who are the characters?*
  - » *What is the setting?*
  - » *What are the main story events, and how are they affected by characters and setting?*
- Have students complete Printable: Reading Graphic Organizer 12 for their independent reading book.

Literary Elements
Literary elements are the pieces that make up a story.
Characters:
the people and animals in a story
• What do they say and think?
• What do they do?
• What do other characters say and think about them?
Setting:
where and when the story takes place
Plot:
Conflict
the main problem that the characters face
Resolution
how the conflict or problem is solved
Events:
things that happen in a story
• to change a character
• to affect the mood
• to build the plot
Why Is the Statue of Liberty Green?

Tabletop Minilessons: Reading

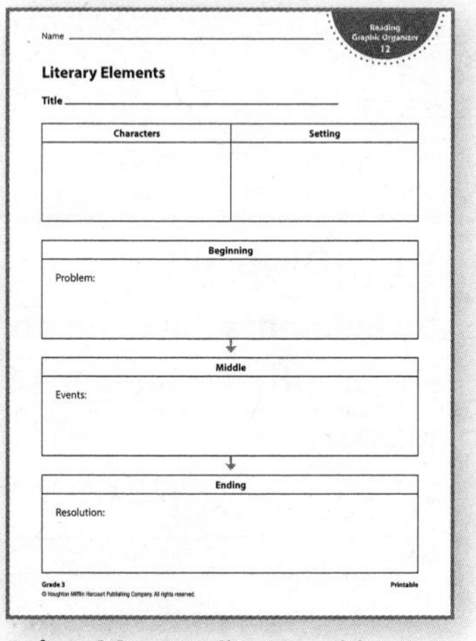
Name
Literary Elements
Title
Characters	Setting

Beginning
Problem:

Middle
Events:

Ending
Resolution:

Grade 3 Printable

Printable: Reading Graphic Organizer 12

ALMOST THERE

READY FOR MORE

SCAFFOLD AND EXTEND

- Guide students to identify the characters and setting. Help them find examples of how the characters and setting affect story events.
- Prompt students to identify the characters and setting, and how they affect story events.
- Have students explain how story events might be different if the characters or setting in the story were changed.

EL ENGLISH LEARNER SUPPORT

SUBSTANTIAL
Have students point to pictures and words in the selection that indicate characters, setting, and events.

MODERATE
Have students complete sentence frames: *The characters are ______. The setting is ______. The main story events are ______.*

LIGHT
Encourage students to explain how they think the characters and setting affect the events of the story.

Options for Independent and Collaborative Work

While you meet with small groups, have other students engage in literacy activities that reinforce the lesson's learning objectives. Choose from these options.

Independent Reading

Student Choice Library

Rigby
LEVELED LIBRARY

APPLY READING SKILL

Literary Elements Students complete Printable: Reading Graphic Organizer 12 for an independent reading book.

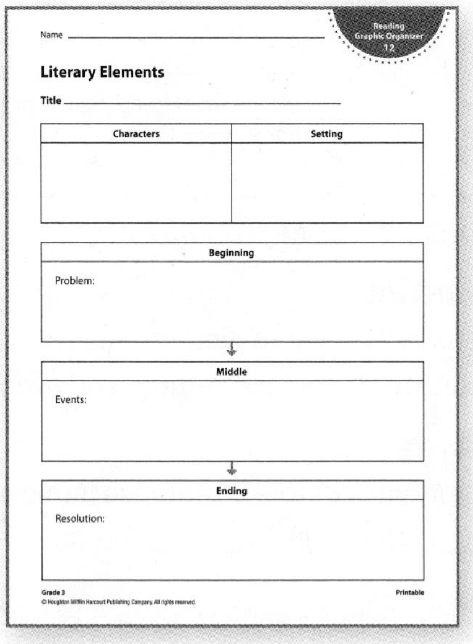

Name

Reading Graphic Organizer 12

Literary Elements

Title

Characters	Setting

Beginning
Problem:

Middle
Events:

Ending
Resolution:

Grade 3 Printable

© Houghton Mifflin Harcourt Publishing Company. All rights reserved.

Printable: Reading Graphic Organizer 12

APPLY LANGUAGE SKILL

Seek Information Students complete Printable: Language Graphic Organizer 12 for an independent reading book.

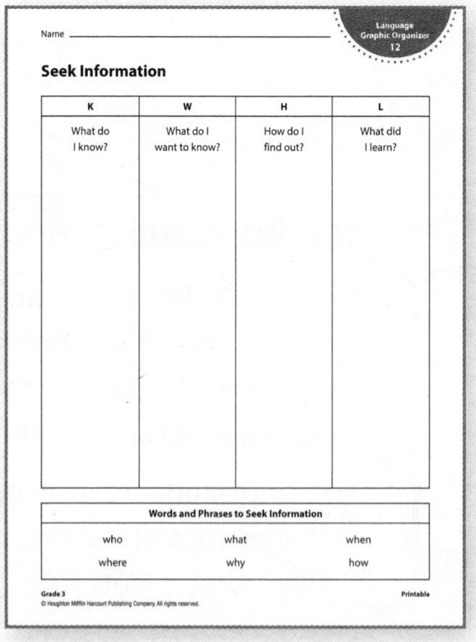

Name

Language Graphic Organizer 12

Seek Information

K	W	H	L
What do I know?	What do I want to know?	How do I find out?	What did I learn?

Words and Phrases to Seek Information		
who	what	when
where	why	how

Grade 3 Printable

© Houghton Mifflin Harcourt Publishing Company. All rights reserved.

Printable: Language Graphic Organizer 12

Literacy Centers

See pp. T140–T141.

- READING CENTER
- VOCABULARY CENTER
- DIGITAL STATION
- WRITING CENTER
- PROJECT CENTER

Speaking and Listening

Partners discuss literary elements.
See Engage and Respond, p. T177.

Additional Skills Practice

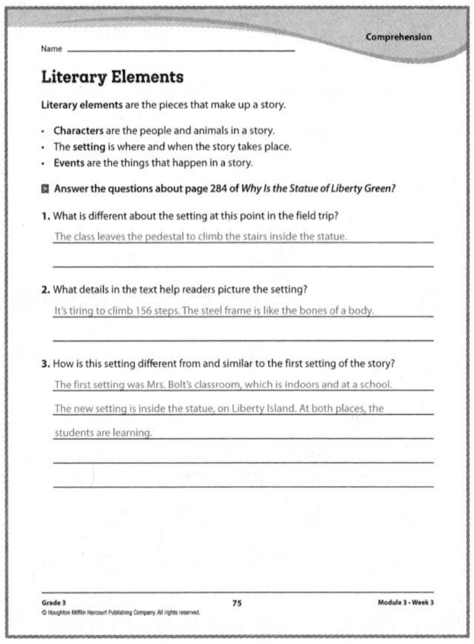

Name ______

Comprehension

Literary Elements

Literary elements are the pieces that make up a story.

- **Characters** are the people and animals in a story.
- The **setting** is where and when the story takes place.
- **Events** are the things that happen in a story.

Answer the questions about page 284 of *Why Is the Statue of Liberty Green?*

1. What is different about the setting at this point in the field trip?
   The class leaves the pedestal to climb the stairs inside the statue.
2. What details in the text help readers picture the setting?
   It's tiring to climb 156 steps. The steel frame is like the bones of a body.
3. How is this setting different from and similar to the first setting of the story?
   The first setting was Mrs. Bolt's classroom, which is indoors and at a school. The new setting is inside the statue, on Liberty Island. At both places, the students are learning.

Grade 3 75 Module 3 • Week 3

© Houghton Mifflin Harcourt Publishing Company. All rights reserved.

Know It, Show It, p. 75

Wrap-Up

Share Time

At the end of the Reading Workshop, have students reflect on their learning by sharing how they applied **literary elements** or another area of focus during independent work time. Choose from these options:

- Use the **SOLO CHAIR** routine. Select a reader each day to come to the front of the class and tell what he or she learned from the reading by using a skill or strategy.
- **THINK-PAIR-SHARE** Students share their thinking with a partner. Select a few pairs each day to share with the whole class.
- **RETURN TO ANCHOR CHART** Have students add sticky notes about their independent reading book to the Literary Elements Anchor Chart. Call on a few students to explain what they added.

Online Ed

ANCHOR CHART 12: Literary Elements

Literary Elements
Literary elements are the pieces that make up a story.
Characters:
the people and animals in a story
• What do they say and think?
• What do they do?
• What do other characters say and think about them?
Setting:
where and when the story takes place
Plot:
Conflict
the main problem that the characters face
Resolution
how the conflict or problem is solved
Events:
things that happen in a story
• to change a character
• to affect the mood
• to build the plot

Give a Presentation

LEARNING OBJECTIVES

- Plan and give a short presentation about a personal experience.
- Demonstrate active listening skills.
- **Language** Use acquired language skills to give a presentation.

MATERIALS

Online Ed

notecards

INSTRUCTIONAL VOCABULARY

- **bullet points** a list of important ideas about a concept
- **formal language** a style for speaking or writing, following the rules of English
- **pacing** the rate at which a person speaks
- **presentation** a formal talk about a subject

Step 1 Introduce the Skill

Discuss an Effective Presentation Tell students that they will give a short presentation about a personal experience they have had with a historic place, event, or symbol of our nation. Discuss these guidelines for a presentation.

- Follow an organized plan. A presentation should open with a topic sentence, provide supporting details, and end with a concluding statement.
- Write key talking points as a bulleted list or on notecards. Do not simply read your notes. Use them as a guide. Speak clearly at an understandable pace, and use formal language.
- If necessary, use visuals to support the information.
- Offer details and elaborate on responses to questions.
- Always take time to practice before presenting to the class.

Step 2 Guided Practice

Choose a Topic Guide students to choose a topic related to a personal experience with an American symbol, place, or event.

Provide Strong Introductions Discuss ways students can begin a presentation, such as asking a question, using a quotation, or stating an interesting fact.

Organize Ideas Model how to list key words or phrases on notecards, rather than complete sentences. Organize and number them in sequence.

Practice Have students practice with a partner and provide feedback based on the guidelines above.

Step 3 Apply the Skill

Present Have students give their presentations. Emphasize that they should speak at an understandable pace. Provide time for students to ask questions about the information from the speaker. Remind speakers to offer elaboration and detail in their responses.

Listen Actively Remind students that when they listen to a presentation they should listen actively. As they listen, they should think of relevant questions they can ask the speaker when he or she is finished presenting.

ENGLISH LEARNER SUPPORT: Support Presenting

SUBSTANTIAL
Provide time-order sentence stems to help students organize their presentations: *First,* ______. *Next,* ______. *Then* ______. *Finally,* ______.

MODERATE
Provide students with a list of time-order words to help them organize their presentations. Guide them to use formal English and to speak in complete sentences.

LIGHT
Have students practice with a partner. Give them a checklist for: a strong introduction, proper sequence, conclusion, even pacing, and formal language.

Synthesize Topic Knowledge

LEARNING OBJECTIVES

- Recognize and describe the features of narrative nonfiction.
- Synthesize knowledge gained from the week's texts.
- **Language** Discuss the connection between their reading and the essential question.

MATERIALS Online Ed

myBook *Book 1, pp. 226–227, 275–289*

Display and Engage
Knowledge *Map 3.14*

Genre Focus

- Review with students the key features of narrative nonfiction. Narrative nonfiction gives facts on a topic, and has the elements of a story with a beginning, middle, and end.
- Discuss with students the literature they encountered this week. Discuss what makes *Why Is the Statue of Liberty Green?* a narrative nonfiction selection.
- Ask students to identify the key ideas and information, as well as the story elements in the text.

Knowledge Focus

- Project Display and Engage: **Knowledge Map 3.14**. Have students turn to *myBook* page 226.
- Tell students to think about what they have learned about how the Statue of Liberty represents our nation in *Why Is the Statue of Liberty Green? (It is an American monument; it welcomes immigrants to our country; it stands for freedom.)*
- Work with students to add this information to the "Monuments" section of the Knowledge Map.

Online Ed

DISPLAY AND ENGAGE:
Knowledge Map 3.14

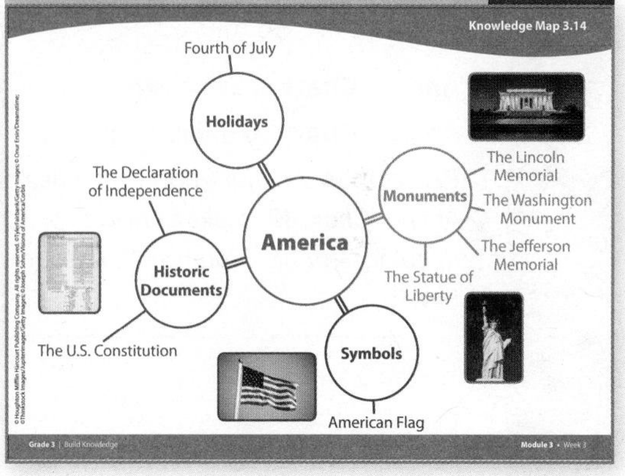

- Have students discuss their completed Knowledge Maps and synthesize what they learned by connecting it to the Essential Question: *How do historic places, documents, and symbols represent our nation?*

ENGLISH LEARNER SUPPORT: Support Discussion

SUBSTANTIAL
Support discussion with sentence frames: *A place I read about is* _____. *A document I read about is* _____. *A symbol I read about is* _____.

MODERATE
Have students complete sentence frames for each American place, symbol, or document they read about: *This week I learned about* _____. *It represents America because* _____.

LIGHT
Ask students to explain how the week's reading helped them to answer the Essential Question.

Synthesize Knowledge

Revisit Vocabulary Network and Knowledge Map

- Project or display Anchor Chart 8: Synthesize. Read it with students.
- Tell students that they will synthesize what they learned in *Let Freedom Ring!* Have students page through the selections in *my*Book Module 3.
- Next, have students revisit the vocabulary network they completed on *my*Book pages 224–225. Draw the web on the board or on chart paper, and invite volunteers to write words they added. Discuss how the words relate to freedom. Ask volunteers to use the words in oral sentences.
- Then have students turn to *my*Book pages 226–227 to review the knowledge map they built throughout the module. Project Display and Engage: Knowledge Map 3.14. Discuss with students the ideas and concepts in the knowledge map, and invite students to add ideas of their own.

Online

ANCHOR CHART 8: Synthesize

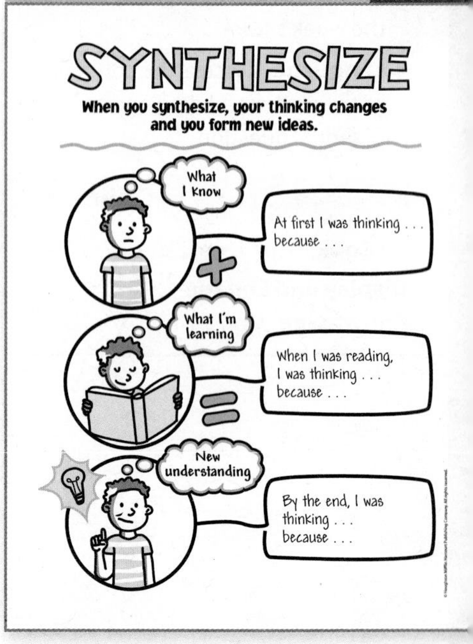
SYNTHESIZE
When you synthesize, your thinking changes and you form new ideas.
What I know
At first I was thinking . . . because . . .
What I'm learning
When I was reading, I was thinking . . . because . . .
New understanding
By the end, I was thinking . . . because . . .

Apply Module Knowledge

- Ask students to use Printable: Reading Graphic Organizer 8 to note evidence from the selections and information from the knowledge map as they discuss and respond to the questions below. Encourage students to use the vocabulary network entries in their responses.
  - » *What did you learn about American places, documents, and symbols in this module?*
  - » *What new idea or information did you learn that was unexpected?*
  - » *How did the selections in this module give you a new understanding about our country?*

LEARNING OBJECTIVES

- Synthesize information from multiple selections.
- Discuss vocabulary about a topic.
- Evaluate and reflect on module selections.
- Make connections between and to module selections.
- **Language** Articulate ideas and opinions about module selections.

MATERIALS

Online

myBook *Book 1, pp. 222–295*

Display and Engage *Knowledge Map 3.14*

Anchor Chart 8 *Synthesize*

Anchor Chart 30 *Make Connections*

Printables *Anchor Chart 8: Synthesize; Anchor Chart 30: Make Connections; Reading Graphic Organizer 8; Selection Review*

ENGLISH LEARNER SUPPORT: Facilitate Discussion

SUBSTANTIAL

Use sentence frames such as *I learned that America* _____.

MODERATE

Use sentence frames such as *I learned that* _____ *stands for America.* _____ *changed the way I think about* _____.

LIGHT

Use sentence frames such as *I thought that* _____, *but I learned that* _____.

Make Connections

Reflect on Module Selections

- Project or display Anchor Chart 30: **Make Connections** or begin one of your own. Tell students that good readers find ways to make connections to the texts they read.

Online

ANCHOR CHART 30: Make Connections

Make Connections
When you read, find ways that the text is like things in your own life and other texts you have read.
Text to Self
Connect the text to your life. This reminds me of when I . . .
Text to Text
Connect the text to a text you've read. This is like another book I read . . .
Text to World
Connect the text to the world around you. This is like something that happened in my community . . .

- As you point to the corresponding parts of the Anchor Chart, explain to students that they can connect what they read to their personal experiences, to ideas in other texts, and to society, or the world around them.
- Then have students turn to *my*Book pages 222–223. Read the module title, quote, and essential question aloud. Have students discuss the module as a whole, explaining how the selections they read connect to the module topic, quote, and essential question.

Evaluate Module Selections

- Have students turn to the Table of Contents on *my*Book page 7. Ask students to rate each selection in Module 3, based on how much they enjoyed it, learned from it, or would recommend it to others.
- Have students mark each selection in the Table of Contents with 1–4 stars, based on these ratings: four stars = loved it, three stars = liked it, two stars = it was OK, and one star = did not like it.
- Have students turn to a partner and share their selection ratings.
- **Write a Review** Have students work independently to complete Printable: **Selection Review** to write a review of their favorite selection in this module.

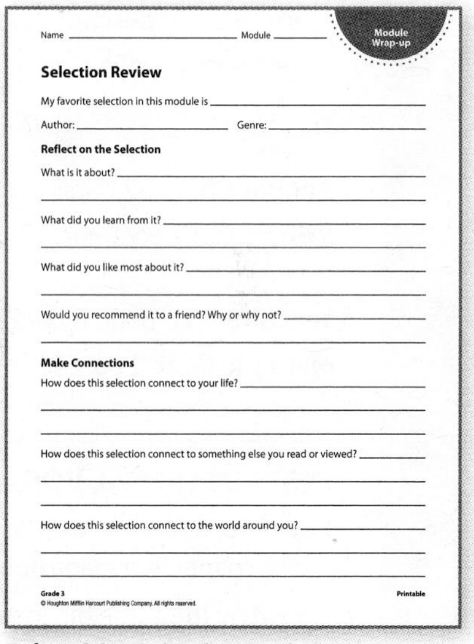
Name ____ Module ____ Module Wrap-up

Selection Review

My favorite selection in this module is ____

Author: ____ Genre: ____

Reflect on the Selection

What is it about? ____

What did you learn from it? ____

What did you like most about it? ____

Would you recommend it to a friend? Why or why not? ____

Make Connections

How does this selection connect to your life? ____

How does this selection connect to something else you read or viewed? ____

How does this selection connect to the world around you? ____

Grade 3 Printable

Printable: Selection Review

- Point out and explain the section of the review where students will make connections to their favorite selection.
- **Discuss Reviews** Pair students who reviewed the same selection and students who reviewed different selections to discuss their reviews. What did they both like? Why is that selection their favorite? Can their partner be persuaded to like the other selection? Encourage students to state their opinions and offer reasons and support. Then gather the class to discuss overall results. Encourage volunteers to share their reviews with the class.

LEARNING MINDSET

Grit

Reflect As students review the module selections discuss what each one showed about the value of continued effort and grit. *Very few things are perfect the first time we try. Just like what happened in the selections we read, we have to keep at it until we get it right. Continuing to try shows determination and grit.*

ENGLISH LEARNER SUPPORT: Elicit Participation

SUBSTANTIAL
Ask students to rate their favorite selection using these frames: *I give this selection ____ stars. I like that ____.*

MODERATE
Prompt students to use sentence frames to evaluate the selection. *I gave ____ the most stars because ____.*

LIGHT
Ask students to share what they learned from their favorite selection. *____ is my favorite selection because I learned that ____.*

Performance Task

Step 1 Discuss Writing to a Prompt

- Point out the Prompt label on *my*Book page 292. Tell students that many writing tasks they will encounter begin with a prompt that explains the task.
- Tell students that the prompt tells exactly what they have to do and that it is important to understand all the parts of the prompt before beginning to write.
- Share with students the steps below. Tell them to follow these steps when responding to writing task prompts.
  1. Read the prompt carefully.
  2. Ask yourself, "What is the prompt asking me to do? What am I supposed to write?" Make sure you understand whether you are being asked to write a story, an opinion essay, an informational essay, or some other kind of writing.
  3. Restate the prompt in your own words to make sure you understand it.
  4. Decide which selection(s) you may need to look back at to use in your writing.
  5. Complete the parts of the writing process: plan, draft, revise and edit, and publish.
- Display and read aloud the prompt on *my*Book page 292. Use the Think Aloud below to model how to break apart the prompt and note key words in it.

THINK ALOUD *The first sentence of the prompt reminds me that the selections in this module were about our nation.*

The next sentence presents my reason for writing: to help create a display that will inform others about the United States. The next sentence identifies the topic and kind of writing: an article about something that stands for our country. That means I need to present facts and evidence, not use my imagination. The last sentence reminds me to use evidence from the selections and the video in my article.

LEARNING OBJECTIVES

- Learn and apply strategies for writing to a prompt.
- Write an informative article that presents a central idea and uses text evidence as support.
- Gather information from sources to use in writing.
- Follow the steps of the writing process: plan, draft, revise and edit, and publish.
- **Language** Compose an informative article using descriptive language from a word bank.

MATERIALS

Online Ed

Anchor Chart 37 *Cursive Handwriting*
Printable *Anchor Chart 37: Cursive Handwriting*
Teaching Pal *Book 1, pp. 292–295*
***my*Book** *Book 1, pp. 292–295*

INSTRUCTIONAL VOCABULARY

- **article** a piece of writing in a newspaper or a magazine
- **central idea** the big idea, or main idea, that readers should take away from reading a text
- **conclusion** a statement you make or an idea you have about a text based on thinking about the information in the text
- **detail** fact or idea that supports or tells more about a central, or main idea
- **topic** the person or thing a text is about

ENGLISH LEARNER SUPPORT: Support Comprehension

SUBSTANTIAL
Ask questions. *Will you write an article or a story? Will you write facts or made-up details?*

MODERATE
Which words tell you what kind of writing you should do? Where should you find facts and details for your article?

LIGHT
I will write an _____ about _____. I will use evidence from _____ to support my topic.

Go to Your
Teaching Pal

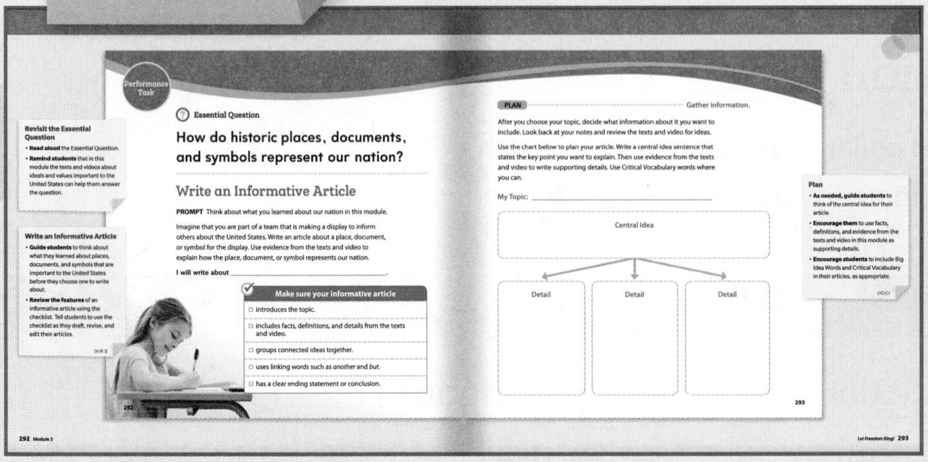

Performance Task

Revisit the Essential Question
- **Read aloud** the Essential Question.
- **Remind students** that in this module the texts and videos about ideals and values important to the United States can help them answer the question.

Write an Informative Article
- **Guide students** to think about what they learned about places, documents, and symbols that are important to the United States before they choose one to write about.
- **Review the features** of an informative article using the checklist. Tell students to use the checklist as they draft, revise, and edit their articles.

DOK 2

Essential Question

How do historic places, documents, and symbols represent our nation?

Write an Informative Article

PROMPT Think about what you learned about our nation in this module.

Imagine that you are part of a team that is making a display to inform others about the United States. Write an article about a place, document, or symbol for the display. Use evidence from the texts and video to explain how the place, document, or symbol represents our nation.

I will write about ______________________.

Make sure your informative article
- ☐ introduces the topic.
- ☐ includes facts, definitions, and details from the texts and video.
- ☐ groups connected ideas together.
- ☐ uses linking words such as *another* and *but*.
- ☐ has a clear ending statement or conclusion.

292

292 Module 3

PLAN ········· Gather information.

After you choose your topic, decide what information about it you want to include. Look back at your notes and review the texts and video for ideas.

Use the chart below to plan your article. Write a central idea sentence that states the key point you want to explain. Then use evidence from the texts and video to write supporting details. Use Critical Vocabulary words where you can.

My Topic: ______________________

Central Idea

Detail | Detail | Detail

Plan
- **As needed, guide students** to think of the central idea for their article.
- **Encourage them** to use facts, definitions, and evidence from the texts and video in this module as supporting details.
- **Encourage students** to include Big Idea Words and Critical Vocabulary in their articles, as appropriate.

DOK 2

293

Let Freedom Ring! 293

Online
ANNOTATE IT!
Ed

Students may use the annotation tools in their eBook.

Step 2 Apply

WRITING PROCESS

Teaching Pal

In your **Teaching Pal**, use the yellow prompts to guide students as they complete the steps of the writing process.

- Read through the checklist on page 292 with students. Tell them that as they write, they should return to this checklist to make sure their informative articles reflect everything in it.
- Before filling in their graphic organizer for the Plan step, tell students to think about the central idea, or main point, that they want to share with readers. What do they most want readers to understand about why the place, document, or symbol stands for the United States? Explain that the answer to that question will be the central idea of the informative article. Remind students that the details they write in the graphic organizer should support or tell more about the central idea.
- As students draft the introduction to the informative article, suggest that they use a question or a surprising fact to grab readers' attention. Remind them to state a clear central idea and to organize supporting details, facts, and examples in an order that makes sense, such as order of importance or by grouping related details.
- Remind students to use transition, or linking, words to clearly show how ideas are connected.
- Explain that the end of the article should review the central idea and supporting details.
- Review the rubric on page 295 with students. As partners confer to revise and edit, remind them to look for what the writer has done well before making suggestions for improvement. Have students use the rubric to self-evaluate their work.

Step 3 Publish

- After students have created a final copy, discuss each method of sharing the informative article. Ask students which one they would prefer and why. Then offer these additional options.
- Share the article in small groups with others who have written about the same place, document, or symbol. Discuss how the articles are alike and different.
- Create an audio recording of the informative article. Make it available to others along with images of the place, document, or symbol.
- Display and Review Anchor Chart 37: Cursive Handwriting.

EL

ENGLISH LEARNER SUPPORT: Scaffold Writing

SUBSTANTIAL
Provide a word bank related to the places, documents, or symbols and guide students to complete sentence frames.

MODERATE
Supply paragraph frames to help students begin their informative articles. As needed, refer students to a topic-related word bank.

LIGHT
Guide students to use descriptive language from a topic-related word bank as they develop their drafts.

Options for Differentiation

As the class engages in independent and collaborative work, meet with Guided Reading Groups or differentiate instruction based on student need.

GUIDED READING GROUPS

Match Students to Books + Instruction

- Choose just-right books based on level, skill, topic, or genre.

L → M → N → O → P → Q

Leveled Readers

- Deliver instruction with each book's **Take and Teach Lesson**, choosing appropriate sessions based on need.

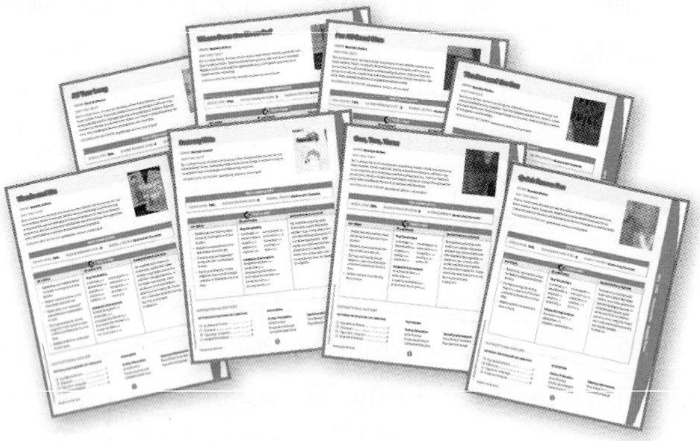

- Check comprehension, reinforce instruction, and extend learning with suggested supporting activities.

Rigby® LEVELED LIBRARY

ENGLISH LEARNER SUPPORT

Seek Information

- Use **Tabletop Minilessons: English Language Development 9.3 (Collaborative Problem Solving)** to reinforce and practice the language skill.

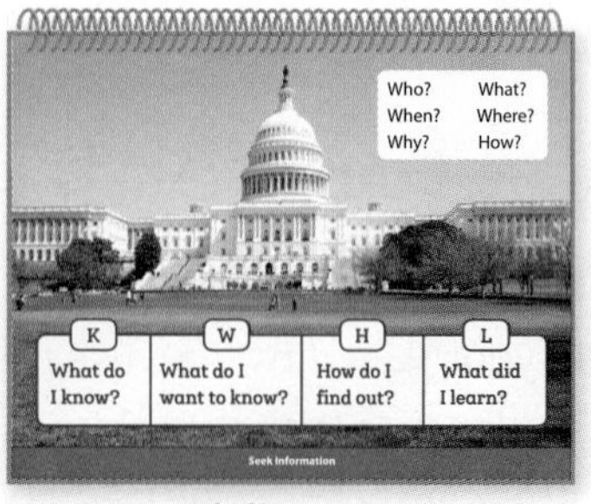

Tabletop Minilessons: English Language Development

- Then use the following prompts to guide application of the language skill to students' understanding of the module topic. Begin with the prompt at the student's identified language proficiency level. As students progress, use lighter supports to encourage increased language proficiency.

SUBSTANTIAL

Have students share with the group something they hope to learn more about, using the sentence frame: *I wonder _____.*

MODERATE

Have students share with the group something they hope to learn more about. Guide them to use sentence frames such as: *How does _____ work? What is/are _____? I wonder why _____? When will/does _____? Who is/are _____?*

LIGHT

Have students share with a partner or the group something they hope to learn more about. Ask them to form questions using the words *who, what, when, where, why,* and *how*.

Options for Independent and Collaborative Work

While you meet with small groups, have other students engage in literacy activities that reinforce the lesson's learning objectives. Choose from these options.

Independent Reading

Student Choice Library

Rigby
LEVELED LIBRARY

APPLY READING SKILL

Synthesize Students complete Printable: Reading Graphic Organizer 8 for an independent reading book.

APPLY LANGUAGE SKILL

Seek Information Students complete Printable: Language Graphic Organizer 12 for an independent reading book.

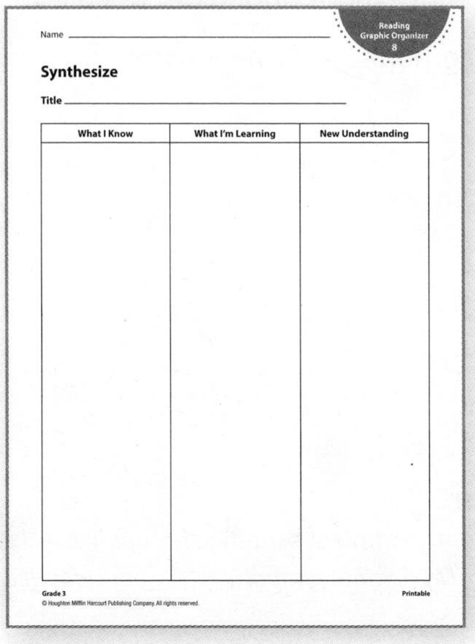

Reading Graphic Organizer 8

Name ______

Synthesize

Title ______

What I Know	What I'm Learning	New Understanding

Grade 3
© Houghton Mifflin Harcourt Publishing Company. All rights reserved.
Printable

Printable: Reading Graphic Organizer 8

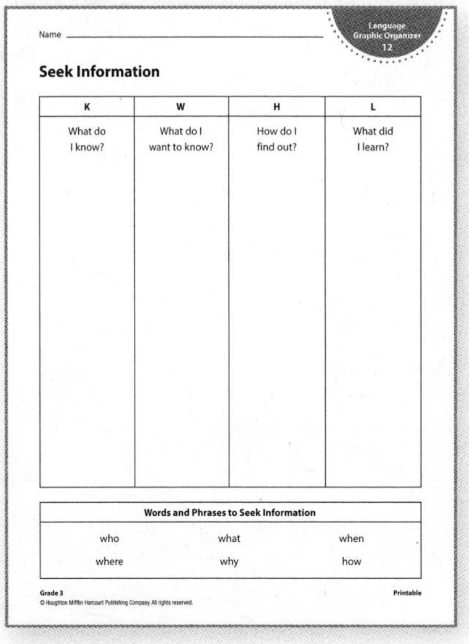

Language Graphic Organizer 12

Name ______

Seek Information

K	W	H	L
What do I know?	What do I want to know?	How do I find out?	What did I learn?

Words and Phrases to Seek Information		
who	what	when
where	why	how

Grade 3
© Houghton Mifflin Harcourt Publishing Company. All rights reserved.
Printable

Printable: Language Graphic Organizer 12

Create a National Symbols Pamphlet

LEARNING OBJECTIVES

- Present a project.
- Listen actively and provide feedback during discussion.
- Self-assess project work using a rubric.
- **Language** Have students react to presentations.

MATERIALS | **Online** Ed

Printable *Project 3.3 Project Rubric*

Classroom materials

handwritten notes

copies of group pamphlet

SUGGESTED PACING

Students worked on their projects in groups during Small Group or during a designated time for project work, using the pacing below as a general guide.

WEEK 1 Introduce and Research

WEEK 2 Write and Create

WEEK 3 Practice and Present/Assess

Practice and Present

Prepare and Rehearse Allow students time to organize their presentation materials and rehearse their roles with their groups.

Deliver Presentations Give each group a designated timeframe in which to present their projects. You may want to invite family members and other students.

- Remind audience members to listen attentively and be polite to the presenters. Encourage listeners to take notes and to ask questions at the end.
- Briefly discuss each presentation. Provide feedback questions such as these: *What did this group do well? What part of the presentation did you enjoy most? What do you like about the pamphlet?*

Reflect and Celebrate Establish a time for students to reflect on the project and on what they've learned, and to celebrate their achievements.

- After groups have presented, have students discuss as a whole class what they learned about United States symbols.
- Ask the class what other objects might make good national symbols for the United States.

Assess

☑ **Speaking and Listening** Do students speak clearly and use presentation techniques such as eye contact? Do students demonstrate active listening skills? Do students work collaboratively?

☑ **Writing** Are students' pamphlets clear and well organized? Do they appeal to an appropriate audience?

☑ **Collaboration** Do students take turns speaking while working on their project? Do they ask and answer questions during discussion?

☑ **Presentation** Do students incorporate information from their research in their presentation?

ENGLISH LEARNER SUPPORT: Elicit Participation

SUBSTANTIAL
Have students complete sentence frames like, *I liked the part when ____, My favorite symbol is _____, or I wonder _____.*

MODERATE
Have students ask questions about one of the symbols after each presentation.

LIGHT
Encourage students to explain which national symbol is their favorite and why.

Stories on Stage

MODULE 4

Essential Question
Why might some stories be better told as plays?

LANGUAGE ARTS CONNECTION:
Drama

In this module, students will listen to, read, and view a variety of texts and media that give them information about the features of drama.

A genre focus on drama provides students with opportunities to identify elements of drama and literary elements in order to better understand unfamiliar texts. Students will also encounter fables and video to build knowledge across genres.

As students build their vocabulary and synthesize topic knowledge, they will learn more about the value of drama and the key differences between stories and plays.

Building Knowledge Networks

As students read, view, and interact with the texts and media in this module, they build deep topic knowledge about the features and value of drama and how this information connects to their lives.

Online Ed

DISPLAY AND ENGAGE: Knowledge Map 4.14

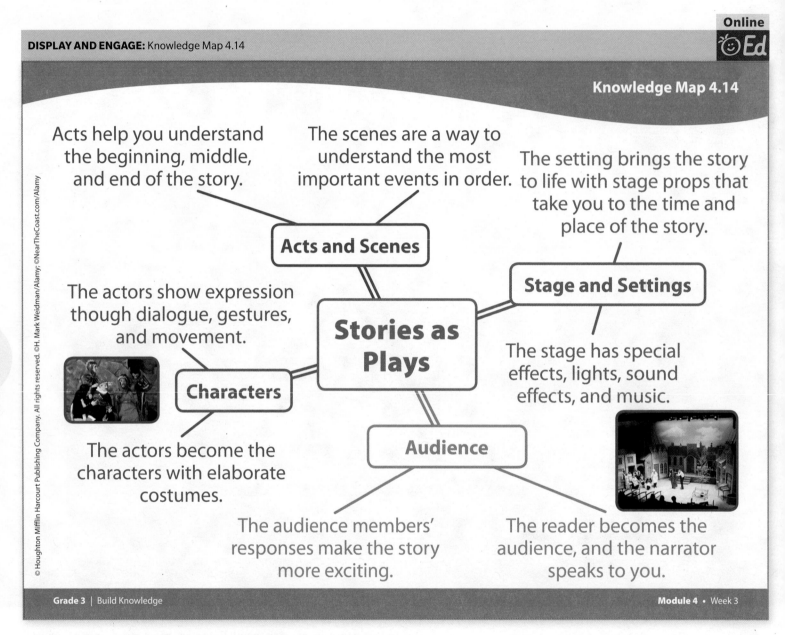

Knowledge Map 4.14

Stories as Plays

Acts and Scenes
- Acts help you understand the beginning, middle, and end of the story.
- The scenes are a way to understand the most important events in order.

Stage and Settings
- The setting brings the story to life with stage props that take you to the time and place of the story.
- The stage has special effects, lights, sound effects, and music.

Characters
- The actors show expression though dialogue, gestures, and movement.
- The actors become the characters with elaborate costumes.

Audience
- The audience members' responses make the story more exciting.
- The reader becomes the audience, and the narrator speaks to you.

Grade 3 | Build Knowledge — Module 4 • Week 3

Synthesizing Knowledge

1. At the beginning of the module, introduce the module topic. Point students to *my*Book, Book 1, page 300, and use Display and Engage: Knowledge Map 4.1 to give students the first step in building their Knowledge Maps throughout the module.
2. After reading each text, have students add to the Knowledge Map in their *my*Book. At the end of each week, use Display and Engage: Knowledge Map 4.5, 4.10, or 4.14 and discuss the added information.
3. At the end of the module, students will synthesize what they have learned about the topic and make connections to self, society, and other texts.

Fostering a Learning Mindset

Throughout this module, look for the Learning Mindset feature to introduce the Learning Mindset focus—**self-reflection**—and use the suggestions to weave it throughout students' literacy instruction as they encounter new texts and practice new skills.

Key Messages

- Looking back and self-reflecting allows us to catch mistakes and learn new things.
- Self-reflection means reflecting on your work and asking yourself how to make your work better.
- Mistakes are a sign of progress, they give us opportunities to self-reflect and think about how to improve.
- Display Anchor Chart 31: My Learning Mindset throughout the year. Refer to it to introduce self-reflection and to reinforce the skills you introduced in previous modules.
- Recognize when students consistently exhibit a Learning Mindset focus.

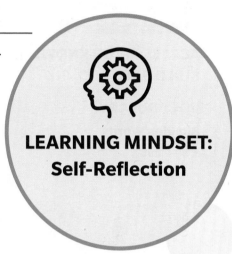

LEARNING MINDSET: Self-Reflection

Online Ed

ANCHOR CHART 31: My Learning Mindset

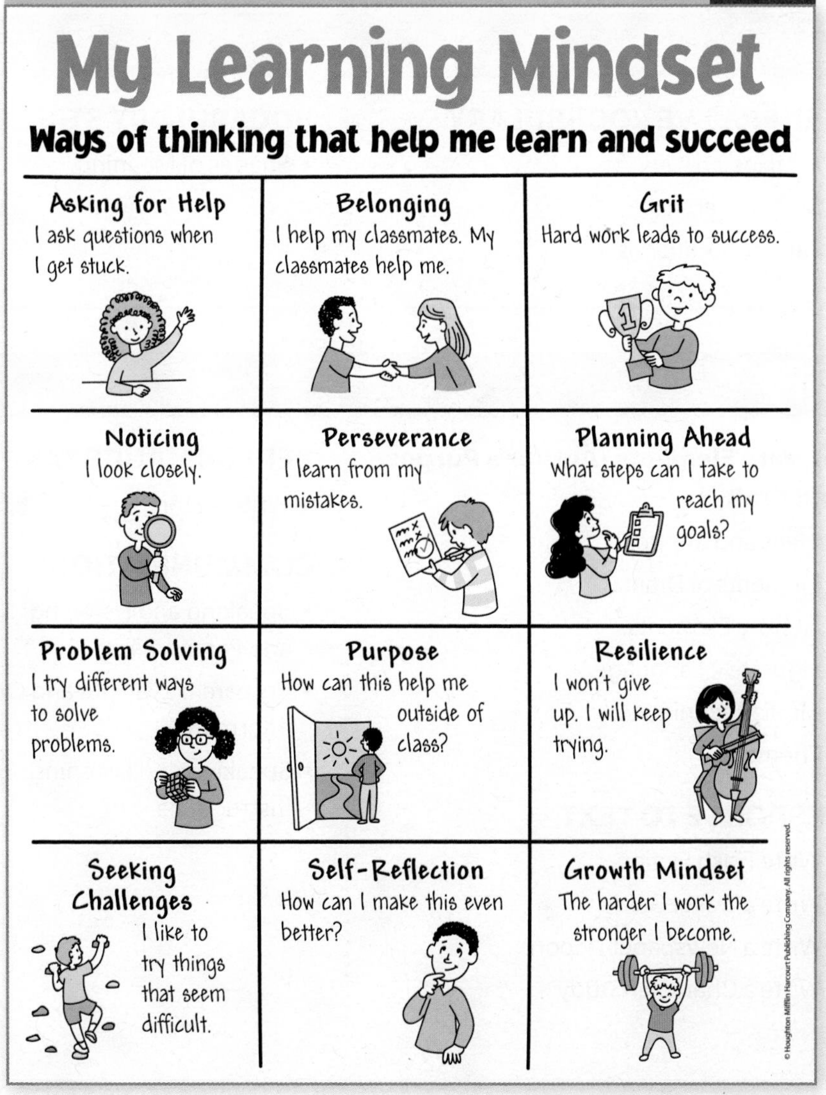

Developing Knowledge and Skills

Students build topic knowledge and develop academic vocabulary, reading, communication, and writing skills through daily whole- and small-group instruction.

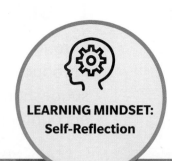

LEARNING MINDSET: Self-Reflection

Build Knowledge and Language

ACCESS PRIOR KNOWLEDGE/ BUILD BACKGROUND

VOCABULARY

Big Idea Words

- *audition*
- *rehearse*
- *ability*
- *actor*

MULTIMEDIA

Active Listening and Viewing

- Get Curious Video: Auditions

Online

GET CURIOUS VIDEO

Vocabulary

ACADEMIC VOCABULARY

- Critical Vocabulary
- Instructional Vocabulary

GENERATIVE VOCABULARY

- Prefixes *im–, in–*
- Suffixes *–er, –or*
- Latin roots *aud, vis*

VOCABULARY STRATEGY

- Shades of Meaning

Reading Workshop & Vocabulary

MULTIPLE GENRES

Genre Focus: Drama

- Drama
- Educational Video
- Classic Tale

COMPREHENSION

Use Metacognitive Skills

- Visualize
- Retell/Summarize
- Monitor and Clarify

Literary Elements/Author's Purpose and Craft

- Ideas and Support
- Elements of Drama
- Literary Elements
- Figurative Language
- Media Techniques
- Theme

RESPONSE TO TEXT

- Write Flash Fiction
- Write a Travel Guide
- Write a Newspaper Report
- Write a Character Study

PERFORMANCE TASK

- Write a Story

COMMUNICATION

- Speaking and Listening: Summarizing and Paraphrasing
- Research: Evaluate and Organize Information
- Speaking and Listening: Oral Instructions

Essential Question

Why might some stories be better told as plays?

Foundational Skills

DECODING

- Consonant Digraphs *ch, tch, sh, wh, th, ph, ng*
- Vowel Diphthongs *ow, ou*
- Vowel Sounds *au, aw, al, o*

SPELLING

- Spelling the /ch/ Sound
- Vowel Sound in *town*
- Vowel Sound in *talk*

FLUENCY

- Expression
- Intonation
- Reading Rate

Writing Workshop

WRITING PROCESS

Narrative

- Plan and Generate Ideas
- Organize
- Draft
- Revise and Edit
- Publish and Present

WRITING FORM

Story

GRAMMAR

Conventions

- Pronouns and Antecedents
- More Plural Nouns
- Writing Quotations

Demonstrate Knowledge

INQUIRY & RESEARCH PROJECT

- Write a Play

ASSESS LEARNING

Formative Assessments

- Selection Quizzes
- Weekly Assessments
- Module Assessments

Performance-Based Assessments

- Informative Writing
- Inquiry and Research Project

Teaching with Text Sets

Carefully selected, content-rich text sets help students build topic knowledge and reading skills.

WEEK 1

Online

Auditions

Students view and respond to the video *Auditions* to learn more about the features of drama.

READ ALOUD

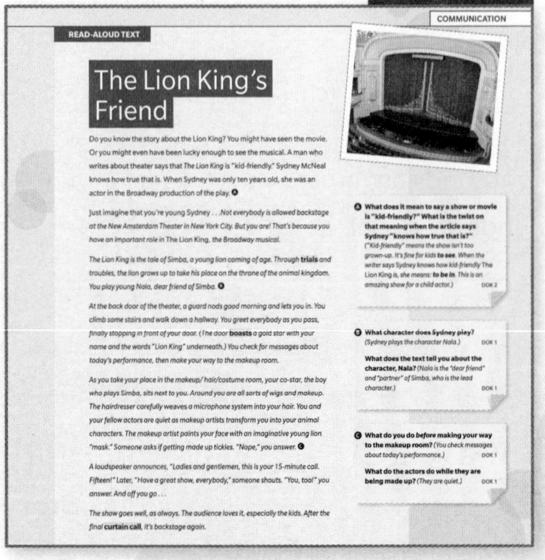
COMMUNICATION

READ-ALOUD TEXT

The Lion King's Friend

Do you know the story about the Lion King? You might have seen the movie. Or you might even have been lucky enough to see the musical. A man who writes about theater says that *The Lion King* is "kid-friendly." Sydney McNeal knows how true that is. When Sydney was only ten years old, she was an actor in the Broadway production of the play. A

Just imagine that you're young Sydney . . . *Not everybody is allowed backstage at the New Amsterdam Theater in New York City. But you are! That's because you have an important role in* The Lion King, *the Broadway musical.*

The Lion King is the tale of Simba, a young lion coming of age. Through **trials** *and troubles, the lion grows up to take his place on the throne of the animal kingdom. You play young Nala, dear friend of Simba.* B

At the back door of the theater, a guard nods good morning and lets you in. You climb some stairs and walk down a hallway. You greet everybody as you pass, finally stopping in front of your door. (The door **boasts** *a gold star with your name and the words "Lion King" underneath.) You check for messages about today's performance, then make your way to the makeup room.*

As you take your place in the makeup/ hair/costume room, your co-star, the boy who plays Simba, sits next to you. Around you are all sorts of wigs and makeup. The hairdresser carefully weaves a microphone system into your hair. You and your fellow actors are quiet as makeup artists transform you into your animal characters. The makeup artist paints your face with an imaginative young lion "mask." Someone asks if getting made up tickles. "Nope," you answer. C

A loudspeaker announces, "Ladies and gentlemen, this is your 15-minute call. Fifteen!" Later, "Have a great show, everybody," someone shouts. "You, too!" you answer. And off you go . . .

The show goes well, as always. The audience loves it, especially the kids. After the final **curtain call**, *it's backstage again.*

A **What does it mean to say a show or movie is "kid-friendly?" What is the twist on that meaning when the article says Sydney "knows how true that is?"** *("Kid-friendly" means the show isn't too grown-up. It's fine for kids* **to see**. *When the writer says Sydney knows how kid-friendly The Lion King is, she means:* **to be in**. *This is an amazing show for a child actor.)* DOK 2

B **What character does Sydney play?** *(Sydney plays the character Nala.)* DOK 1

What does the text tell you about the character, Nala? *(Nala is the "dear friend" and "partner" of Simba, who is the lead character.)* DOK 1

C **What do you do *before* making your way to the makeup room?** *(You check messages about today's performance.)* DOK 1

What do the actors do while they are being made up? *(They are quiet.)* DOK 1

Genre: Informational Text

my BOOK

Short Read

THAT'S ENTERTAINMENT!

1 Anyone who has seen a great play will agree: theater is one of the most exciting forms of entertainment. Nothing beats watching skilled actors bringing a story to life on the stage.

2 At the audition, each actor must work hard to win a part as one of the characters. Then it's time to rehearse. The actors take weeks to learn their roles. They read the script and practice their dialogue, or the words they speak on stage. They follow stage directions, which tell actors how to behave and move.

3 Meanwhile, the crew builds sets for the stage to show the play's different settings. The sets include props such as furniture or painted scenery. Each act or scene is like a chapter in a story and may require a different set. Costume designers decide what the actors should wear. The director oversees everything.

4 The play *Peter Pan* is theater at its best. A great script, exciting roles, and colorful stage sets—this play has it all! Written by J. M. Barrie, the play was first performed in 1904. Today, it's as popular as ever. Barrie mixes fantasy and reality to tell an irresistible story. The main character is a boy who never

Genre: Opinion Text
Lexile® Measure: 730L

my BOOK

Genre: Drama/Tall Tale

? Essential Question
Why might some stories be better told as plays?

WEEK 2

my BOOK

Genre: Educational Video

my BOOK

Genre: Drama/Classic Tale

WEEK 3

my BOOK

Genre: Drama/Myth

WRITING FOCAL TEXT

Genre: Historical Fiction
Lexile® Measure: AD640L
Guided Reading Level: T

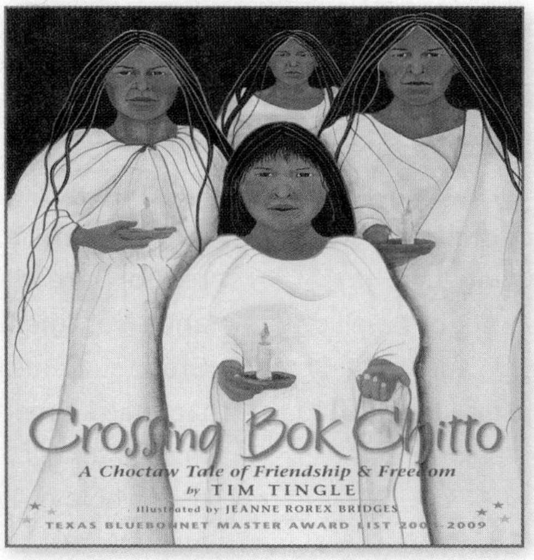

Reading Workshop

During Reading Workshop, students will engage daily in a variety of whole-group, small-group, and independent literacy activities. Multiple options for differentiated instruction allow teachers to tailor instruction based on student need.

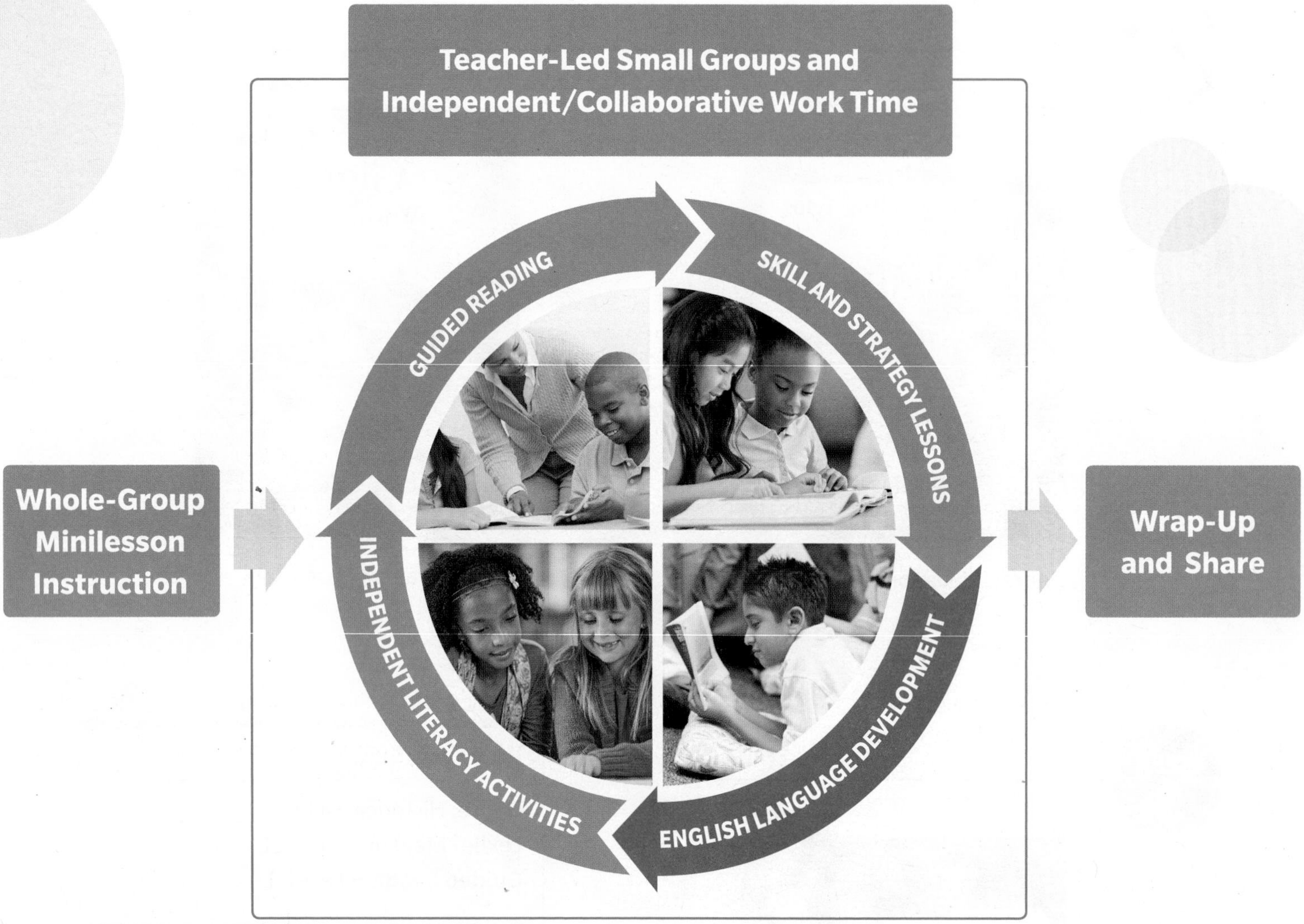

GUIDED READING

Teacher works with students at their instructional guided reading level.
Using the Rigby Leveled Library, pull just-right books to facilitate guided reading lessons.

SKILL AND STRATEGY LESSONS

Teacher works with small groups to reinforce reading skills and strategies.
Group students for targeted support. Lessons may be connected to the daily whole-group minilesson or based on student need.

ENGLISH LANGUAGE DEVELOPMENT

Teacher works with small groups to support English language acquisition.
Lessons provide students with opportunities to engage in language skills across all the literacy domains in a safe small-group environment.

INDEPENDENT LITERACY ACTIVITIES

While teacher works with small groups, other students work independently.
Students engage in literacy activities that reinforce the lesson's learning objectives.

Forming Small Groups

Guided Reading Groups

- Assess students periodically, using running records or other diagnostic assessments to determine each student's guided reading level.
- Choose books from the Rigby Leveled Library based on reading level or choose strategies that you plan to teach or practice with each group.
- Use assessment data and information from conferences to frequently regroup students based on reading level.
- Refer to Take & Teach lessons to guide reading instruction, check comprehension, and extend learning.
- Access online Printables, comprehension quizzes, and additional resources that promote revisiting the Leveled Readers for multiple purposes.

Skill and Strategy Groups

- Observe students during whole-group minilessons to determine who may benefit from targeted support or extension of the day's reading skill. Use assessment data and information to group students according to need.
- Use Tabletop Minilessons: Reading to scaffold students' understanding of the skill through an Anchor Chart and supporting lesson.
- Access online Printables for students to apply their understanding of the skill to an independent reading book.

English Language Development

- Use Tabletop Minilessons: English Language Development to teach and practice language skills. Guide students to apply them to each lesson's text at their identified language proficiency level.
- Access online Printables for students to apply the skill to an independent reading book.

SETTING READING GOALS AND CONFERRING

- Talk to students about their strengths and areas for growth during conferences.
- Work with students to set realistic reading goals that will support them in reaching the next guided reading level.
- Teach strategies that will help students achieve their goals and remind them to use the strategies when they read. Review strategies frequently with different books.

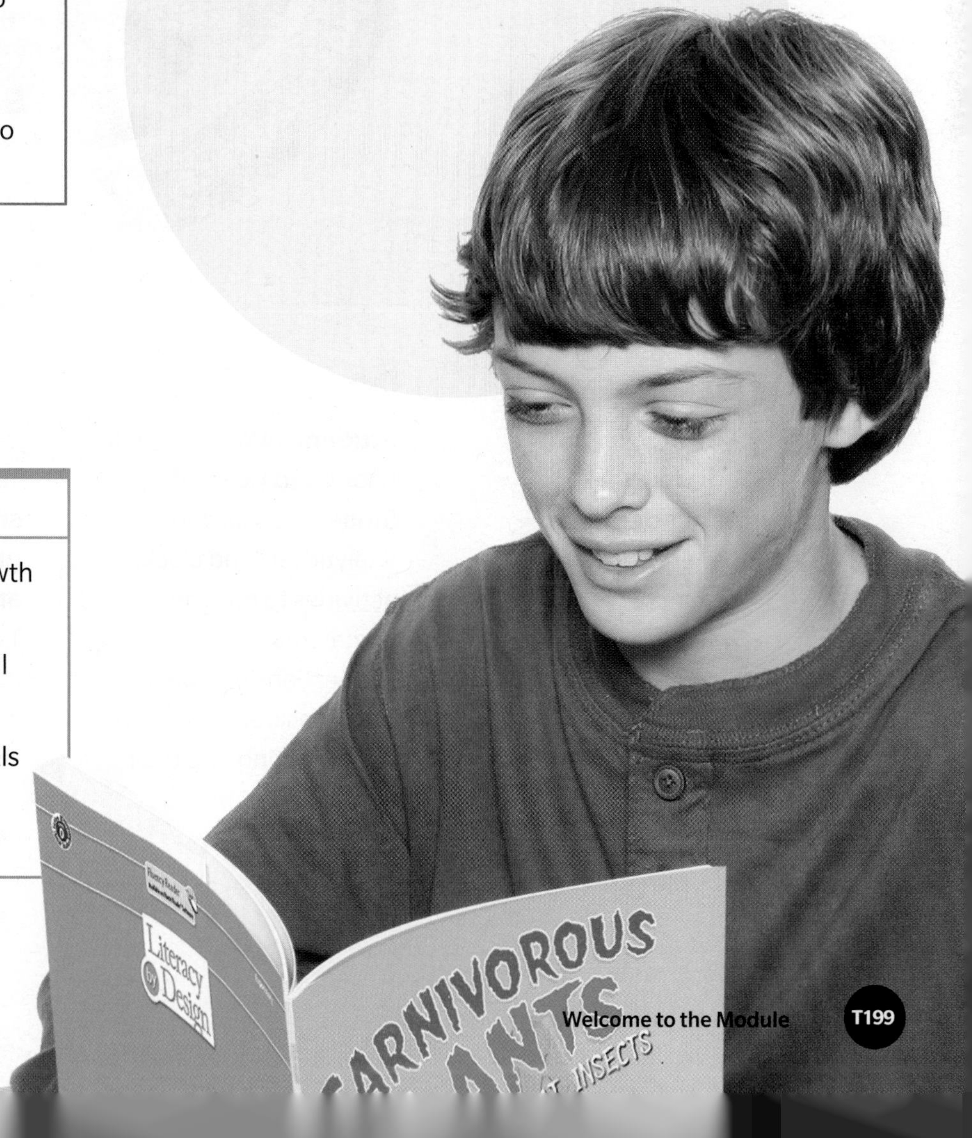

Writing Workshop

Students will engage in the full writing process to produce a story during this three-week module. The Writing Workshop Teacher's Guide provides explicit instruction and ample opportunity for students to write daily.

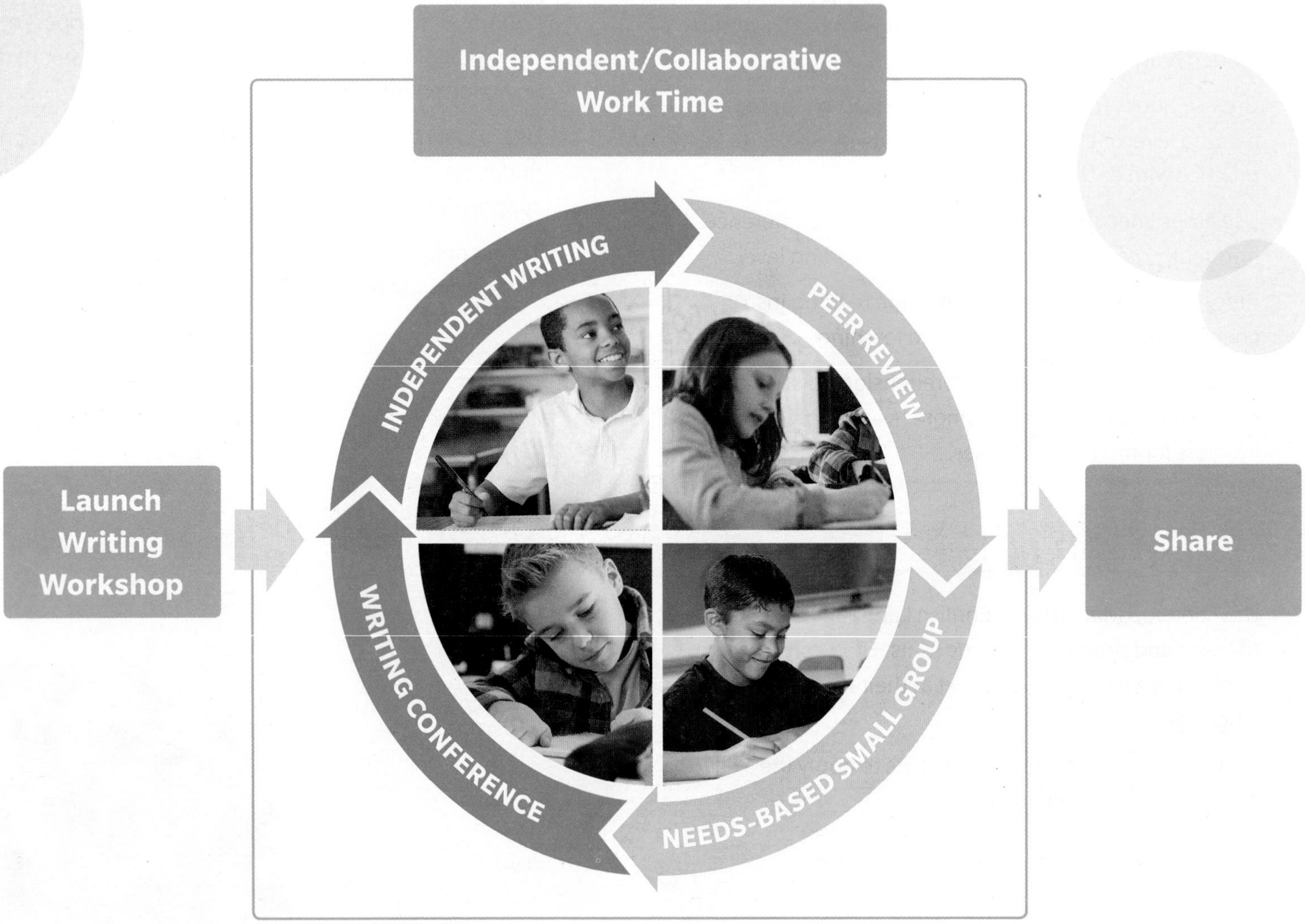

INDEPENDENT WRITING

Students work independently to:

- generate ideas/ research
- prewrite
- draft
- write
- revise and edit
- publish

PEER REVIEW

Students work in small groups to peer edit. Students engage in analytic talk and clocking activities to provide comments and suggestions that peers may consider incorporating into their writing.

NEEDS-BASED SMALL GROUP

Teacher works with small needs-based groups on grammar and writing skills. Targeted minilessons support development of writing and grammar skills in areas of need.

WRITING CONFERENCE

One-on-One Conferring
Teachers meet with students one-on-one to set writing goals and to provide feedback throughout the writing process.

Story Writing Module Overview

Writing Workshop Teacher's Guide, pp. W51–W66

WEEK 1

- Priming the Students
- Priming the Text
- The Read
- Vocabulary
- Prewriting II: Preparing to Write

WEEK 2

- Drafting I: Beginning the Draft
- Drafting II: Writing the Middle
- Drafting III: Completing the Draft
- Revising I: Integrating Narrative Elements
- Revising II: Conferencing

WEEK 3

- Revising III: Adding Dialogue
- Editing I: Grammar and Mechanics
- Editing II: Peer Proofreading
- Publishing
- Sharing

FOCAL TEXT

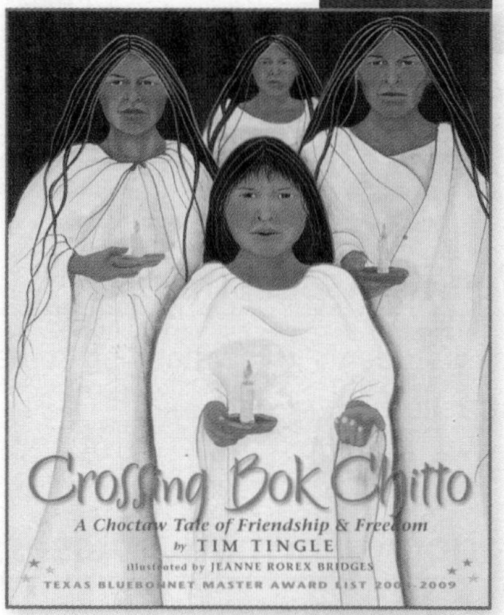

Crossing Bok Chitto
A Choctaw Tale of Friendship & Freedom
by TIM TINGLE
illustrated by JEANNE ROREX BRIDGES
TEXAS BLUEBONNET MASTER AWARD LIST 2008–2009

Crossing Bok Chitto by Tim Tingle

WRITING MODE Narrative

WRITING FORM Story

FOCAL STATEMENT How a person helps someone can make an interesting story to tell.

Writing Prompt

- **READ** this sentence: How a person helps someone can make an interesting story to tell.
- **THINK** about someone you know whose help made a difference in another person's life.
- **WRITE** a story about this person's life and what they did to help someone else.

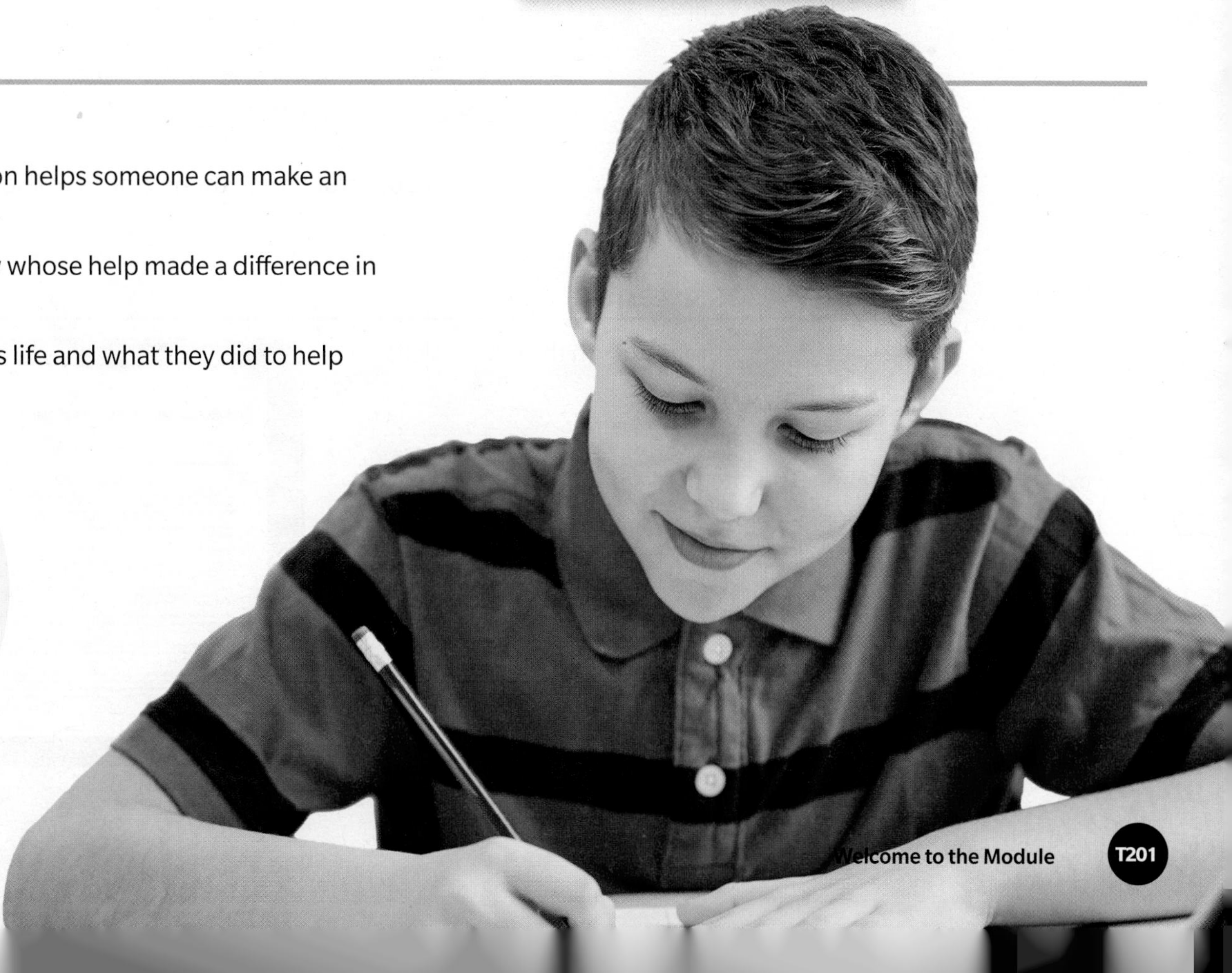

Assessment and Progress Monitoring

Ongoing formative assessment guides daily instruction, while performance-based assessments demonstrate student progress toward mastery of module skills and standards.

FORMATIVE ASSESSMENT

Selection Quizzes

Assess comprehension of the *my*Book text selections:

Weekly Assessments

Assess students' understanding of the key Reading and Writing skills, covered during each week of instruction.

Ongoing Formative Assessment Tools

- Leveled Readers Cards
- Selection Quizzes
- Running Records
- 1:1 Observation Records
- Daily Lesson Checks and Correct & Redirect opportunities in the Teacher's Guide

Module Assessment

Measure student's proficiency in the critical skills covered in this module:

- Generative Vocabulary
- Vocabulary Strategies
- Comprehension
- Grammar
- Writing

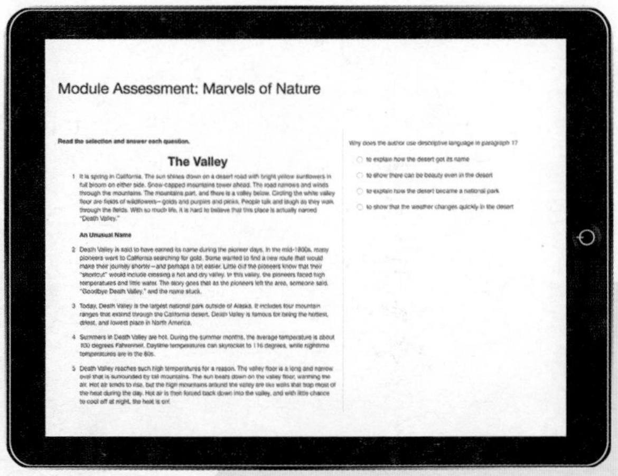

PERFORMANCE-BASED ASSESSMENTS

Performance Task

Students synthesize what they have learned from the module's text set and demonstrate their genre and topic knowledge by completing a Performance Task in response to the Essential Question.

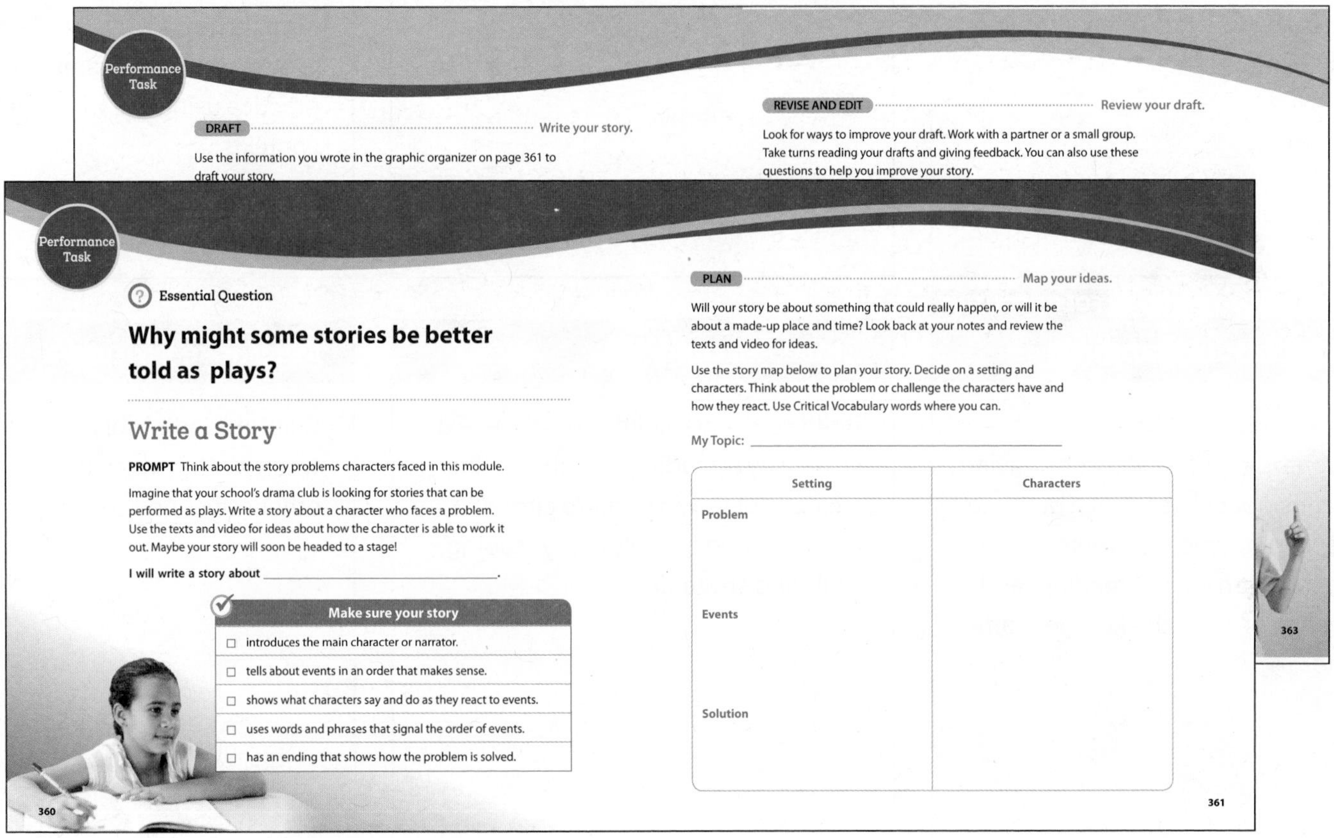
Performance Task

DRAFT .... Write your story.

Use the information you wrote in the graphic organizer on page 361 to draft your story.

REVISE AND EDIT .... Review your draft.

Look for ways to improve your draft. Work with a partner or a small group. Take turns reading your drafts and giving feedback. You can also use these questions to help you improve your story.

363

Performance Task

Essential Question

Why might some stories be better told as plays?

Write a Story

PROMPT Think about the story problems characters faced in this module.

Imagine that your school's drama club is looking for stories that can be performed as plays. Write a story about a character who faces a problem. Use the texts and video for ideas about how the character is able to work it out. Maybe your story will soon be headed to a stage!

I will write a story about ______________.

Make sure your story

- ☐ introduces the main character or narrator.
- ☐ tells about events in an order that makes sense.
- ☐ shows what characters say and do as they react to events.
- ☐ uses words and phrases that signal the order of events.
- ☐ has an ending that shows how the problem is solved.

360

PLAN .... Map your ideas.

Will your story be about something that could really happen, or will it be about a made-up place and time? Look back at your notes and review the texts and video for ideas.

Use the story map below to plan your story. Decide on a setting and characters. Think about the problem or challenge the characters have and how they react. Use Critical Vocabulary words where you can.

My Topic: ______________

Setting	Characters
Problem	
Events	
Solution	

361

Tailor Instruction to Meet Student Needs

Throughout the course of the module, in Writing Workshop, students work through the stages of the writing process. Student writing can be evaluated according to the rubric provided for the module's writing form, located in the Teacher Resource Book.

Teaching with Instructional Routines

Use recursive, research-informed instructional routines to support lesson planning and maximize students' learning.

Active Viewing

Build and extend students' knowledge about a topic by having them actively view and respond to both the Get Curious Videos at the beginning of each module and the videos that appear as selections within the modules.

Active Listening

Increase students' familiarity with fluent reading and develop their listening comprehension by having them actively listen and respond to a text on the module topic read aloud.

Vocabulary

Explicitly teach the meaning of topic-related and academic vocabulary words from the texts, provide relevant examples, and practice using the words in familiar contexts.

FOCUS ROUTINE

Read for Understanding

Develop students' reading comprehension of a full text by having them consider genre to set a purpose before reading, monitor their comprehension during reading, and summarize or retell the key ideas after reading.

Close Reading

Build students' ability to analyze text closely by rereading and annotating sections of text in order to cite evidence and actively apply reading skills and strategies.

Response Writing

Build students' ability to cite evidence when writing in response to texts and other selections.

Additional Routines

ENGAGEMENT ROUTINES

- Choral Reading
- Partner Reading
- Echo Reading
- Turn and Talk
- Think-Pair-Share
- Solo Chair
- Collaborative Discussion

Refer to the **GPS guide** for support with using the routines embedded throughout the lessons.

FOCUS ROUTINE

Read for Understanding

Use the **READ FOR UNDERSTANDING** routine to

- practice reading comprehension of a full text.
- consider genre to set a purpose before reading.
- monitor comprehension during reading.
- summarize or retell key ideas after readings.

READ FOR UNDERSTANDING ROUTINE MATERIALS

Use the ***my*****Book selections** and corresponding **Teaching Pal** pages to engage students in reading and responding to texts.

- Ensure that all students have access to their own *my*Book or to one shared with a partner.
- Encourage students to take notes in the margins of their *my*Book to capture questions, predictions, and notable ideas.

READ FOR UNDERSTANDING ROUTINE IN ACTION

ROUTINE STEP	MODEL LANGUAGE
1 **Set a purpose for reading.** Encourage students to consider the genre as they set a purpose.	*Think about the genre of this selection. Then look at the first few pages of the selection to find elements that are clues to that genre. As you set your purpose for reading, ask yourself what you think you will learn from this selection.*
2 **Read the text.** Guide students to read through the text. Ask them the questions that appear on the blue flags in the Teaching Pal. Use the Annotation Tips to guide students in marking their responses. Make sure that students' responses indicate that they understand the gist of the selection.	*As you read, make sure you understand what you're reading. Take time to look at the visuals and think about how they support the text. What additional information do the visuals provide? Underline or highlight ideas in the selection that you want to remember. Write in the margins notes and questions you have about the text.*
3 **Respond to the text.** Use **TURN AND TALK** to have partners discuss their notes and questions about the key ideas of the selection.	*Revisit the purpose you set before reading. What did you learn from the text? Look back at the notes you took and the questions you wrote. Summarize or retell what you learned. Be sure to cite text evidence to support your responses.*

Inquiry and Research Project

WRITE A PLAY Over the next three weeks, students will collaborate to generate ideas, research, complete, and present an inquiry-based project.

WEEK 1 Launch the Project: Brainstorm and Research

LEARNING OBJECTIVES

- Participate in shared research projects.
- Gather information and evidence from sources.
- Work collaboratively with others to develop a plan of shared responsibilities.

MATERIALS

- **Printable** *Project 4.1*
- pens, pencils, notepaper
- informational books, magazines, and approved websites
- student anthologies

WEEKLY FOCUS Set a Goal and Gather Information

Clarify Project Goals Tell students that over the next few weeks, they will work in groups to research a traditional story, then rewrite and perform it as a play. First, students will use research to make a list of famous folktales, fairy tales, or legends. Then they will narrow the list to two or three they think might make good plays. After reading the narrative versions, students will discuss the options and choose one to rewrite as a play.

Build Background Preview the reading selections in this module with students. Ask how these texts are different from the texts in previous modules.

- Point out that almost any story can be written as a traditional narrative or a play. Create a Venn diagram to list similarities and differences between traditional stories and plays. Discuss why a writer might choose one format over the other.
- Make a list of the features of a play, such as the list of characters, stage directions, setting, dialogue, acts, and scenes. Define each concept aloud and ask students to point out examples of each in their anthologies.

Begin Group Work and Research Organize students into groups of three or four.

- Guide groups to create an Idea Board or group document for brainstorming, recording and discussing ideas, and sharing quotations and other information from their research.
- Remind students that there are numerous sources of research they can use beyond their *my*Book selections, such as anthologies of folktales and fairy tales, existing plays, and websites for or about playwrights.
- Assign each group member one or more story types to research, such as folktales, fairy tales, fables, legends, and myths. Have them gather information about the characteristics of each type of traditional story, as well as two to three examples of each type.

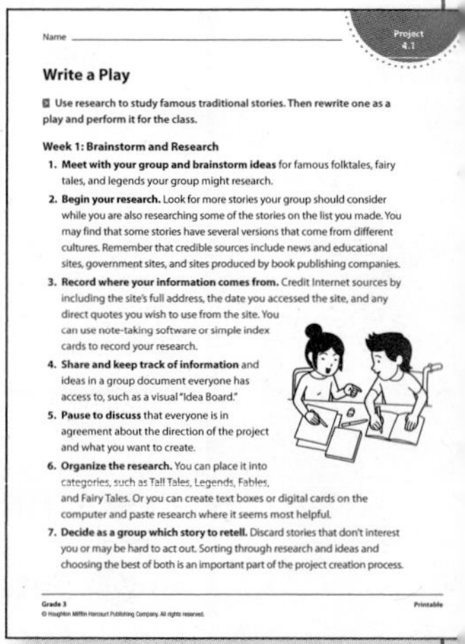
Name ______

Project 4.1

Write a Play

Use research to study famous traditional stories. Then rewrite one as a play and perform it for the class.

Week 1: Brainstorm and Research

1. **Meet with your group and brainstorm ideas** for famous folktales, fairy tales, and legends your group might research.
2. **Begin your research.** Look for more stories your group should consider while you are also researching some of the stories on the list you made. You may find that some stories have several versions that come from different cultures. Remember that credible sources include news and educational sites, government sites, and sites produced by book publishing companies.
3. **Record where your information comes from.** Credit Internet sources by including the site's full address, the date you accessed the site, and any direct quotes you wish to use from the site. You can use note-taking software or simple index cards to record your research.
4. **Share and keep track of information** and ideas in a group document everyone has access to, such as a visual "Idea Board."
5. **Pause to discuss** that everyone is in agreement about the direction of the project and what you want to create.
6. **Organize the research.** You can place it into categories, such as Tall Tales, Legends, Fables, and Fairy Tales. Or you can create text boxes or digital cards on the computer and paste research where it seems most helpful.
7. **Decide as a group which story to retell.** Discard stories that don't interest you or may be hard to act out. Sorting through research and ideas and choosing the best of both is an important part of the project creation process.

Grade 3 Printable

- Tell students that as they research famous stories, they will discover that many cultures have their own version of the same story (such as Cinderella). Point out that the plots are not always the same and sometimes the endings are different, so they may want to read more than one version of the story they select before they write their plays.
- Have the group meet to share their research with each other. After hearing or reading all the examples, ask the group to come to a consensus about which story they will rewrite as a play.

EL ENGLISH LEARNER SUPPORT: Generate Ideas

Display a sentence frame and ideas to support discussion of which story to choose: *I like ______ more than ______ because ______.*

WEEK 2 Write and Create

LEARNING OBJECTIVE

- Record notes and use them to choose a traditional story and rewrite it as a play.

MATERIALS

- **Printable** *Project 4.2*
- pens, pencils, notepaper
- desktop publishing software
- student anthologies

WEEKLY FOCUS Develop Ideas

Plan and Draft Have students reread the story they chose as a group. Then have the group make a list of the most important characters and plot points.

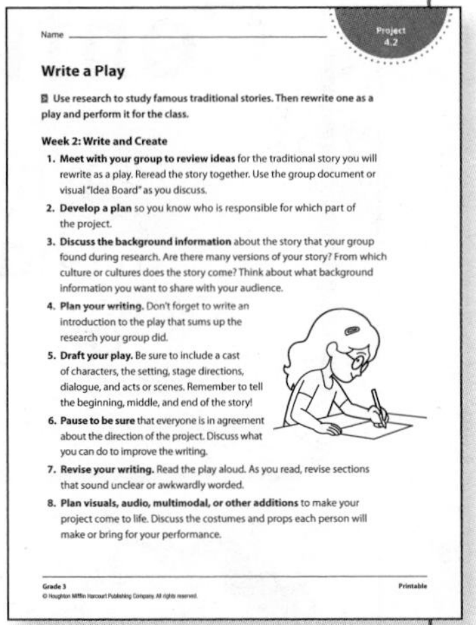

Name ______

Project 4.2

Write a Play

Use research to study famous traditional stories. Then rewrite one as a play and perform it for the class.

Week 2: Write and Create

1. **Meet with your group to review ideas** for the traditional story you will rewrite as a play. Reread the story together. Use the group document or visual "Idea Board" as you discuss.
2. **Develop a plan** so you know who is responsible for which part of the project.
3. **Discuss the background information** about the story that your group found during research. Are there many versions of your story? From which culture or cultures does the story come? Think about what background information you want to share with your audience.
4. **Plan your writing.** Don't forget to write an introduction to the play that sums up the research your group did.
5. **Draft your play.** Be sure to include a cast of characters, the setting, stage directions, dialogue, and acts or scenes. Remember to tell the beginning, middle, and end of the story!
6. **Pause to be sure** that everyone is in agreement about the direction of the project. Discuss what you can do to improve the writing.
7. **Revise your writing.** Read the play aloud. As you read, revise sections that sound unclear or awkwardly worded.
8. **Plan visuals, audio, multimodal, or other additions** to make your project come to life. Discuss the costumes and props each person will make or bring for your performance.

Grade 3 Printable
© Houghton Mifflin Harcourt Publishing Company. All rights reserved.

- When versions differ in important ways, help the group reach a consensus on which version to retell.
- Remind students that a story has a beginning, a middle, and an ending, whether it is a narrative or a play.

Revise and Format Encourage students to compare the formatting of their rough drafts to those of the plays in the Module 4 anthology. Tell them to format their plays in the same way. Remind them to double check to ensure they did not forget any elements of a play.

Create and Integrate Visuals Give students a little time to plan costumes and props.

EL ENGLISH LEARNER SUPPORT: Generate Ideas

Have students complete these sentence frames when the group is summarizing ideas: *The first thing that happened was* ______. *Then,* ______. *After that,* ______. *Next,* ______. *Finally* ______.

WEEK 3 Present and Reflect

LEARNING OBJECTIVE

- Participate in the presentation of a play.

MATERIALS

- **Printable:** *Project 4.3*
- play scripts
- paper and pencil

WEEKLY FOCUS Present and Reflect

Practice and Present Have students practice presenting with a small group. See Lesson 15, p. T380.

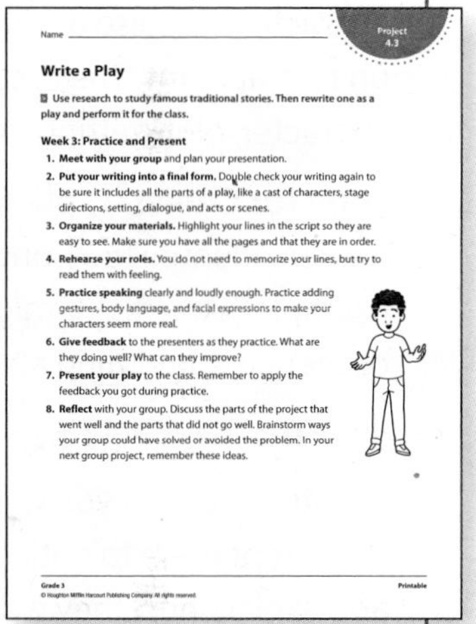

Name ______

Project 4.3

Write a Play

Use research to study famous traditional stories. Then rewrite one as a play and perform it for the class.

Week 3: Practice and Present

1. **Meet with your group** and plan your presentation.
2. **Put your writing into a final form.** Double check your writing again to be sure it includes all the parts of a play, like a cast of characters, stage directions, setting, dialogue, and acts or scenes.
3. **Organize your materials.** Highlight your lines in the script so they are easy to see. Make sure you have all the pages and that they are in order.
4. **Rehearse your roles.** You do not need to memorize your lines, but try to read them with feeling.
5. **Practice speaking** clearly and loudly enough. Practice adding gestures, body language, and facial expressions to make your characters seem more real.
6. **Give feedback** to the presenters as they practice. What are they doing well? What can they improve?
7. **Present your play** to the class. Remember to apply the feedback you got during practice.
8. **Reflect** with your group. Discuss the parts of the project that went well and the parts that did not go well. Brainstorm ways your group could have solved or avoided the problem. In your next group project, remember these ideas.

Grade 3 Printable
© Houghton Mifflin Harcourt Publishing Company. All rights reserved.

- As students present, remind them to speak clearly and at a comfortable pace, to use gestures, and to show the character's emotions through body language and facial expressions.
- Allow students to read from scripts if they so choose.
- Remind listeners to be attentive and polite, and to take notes if they wish.

ASSESS LEARNING

Online Ed

See the Inquiry and Research Project Rubric in the Resources section of the Teacher's Guide.

EL ENGLISH LEARNER SUPPORT: Read Aloud

Work with students to rehearse their presentations. Coach them to mark their copies of the play with pronunciations for words that are hard to remember.

MODULE 4

Welcome to the Module

Notice & Note

Introduce this module's Signposts, using these lessons. Revisit the Anchor Charts, as needed, as you encounter the Signposts during Shared Reading.

FICTION Contrasts and Contradictions

INTRODUCE THE SIGNPOST

- Remind students that they have already encountered the Contrasts and Contradictions Signpost. If students successfully applied the Signpost, focus on the Look for Clues! and Anchor Question sections.
- Tell students that sometimes the way a character acts contrasts, or is different from, the way the reader would expect someone to act. The character may also act in the opposite way he or she has been acting up to that point. These contrasts tell something important about the character, plot, setting, or theme.
- **Look for Clues!** Explain that there are often story clues that help readers identify the Contrasts and Contradictions Signpost. For example, a character might suddenly act or think in a different way, or there is something about the setting that seems strange.

NOTICE & NOTE IN ACTION!

- Tell students that you will pause as you read certain myBook stories to prompt them to notice the Contrasts and Contradictions Signpost and explain how they would apply it to the text. You will also ask students to note things in the text or visuals that will help them remember the Signpost and why it is important to the story.

ANCHOR QUESTION

Display Anchor Chart 43: Contrasts and Contradictions and discuss the Anchor Question. Tell students that they will ask themselves this question after noticing the Contrasts and Contradictions Signpost .

Online Ed

ANCHOR CHART 43: Contrasts and Contradictions

Contrasts and Contradictions
Why would the character feel or act this way?

This module's Signposts are featured with the texts below, which contain strong examples of the Signposts as well as complementary comprehension skills. Encourage students to use their growing bank of known Signposts as they read different texts.

LESSON	TEXT	GENRE	COMPREHENSION SKILL	SIGNPOST
2	The Saga of Pecos Bill	drama	Visualize	Contrasts and Contradictions
8	Gigi and the Wishing Ring	drama	Retell/Summarize	Words of the Wiser
11	Two Bear Cubs	drama/myth	Monitor and Clarify	Contrasts and Contradictions

Professional Learning

RESEARCH FOUNDATIONS

"Stories may be imaginative, made-up, unreal, but they teach us real lessons about our lives."

—Beers & Probst (2017)

See the **GPS guide** to learn more.

FICTION Words of the Wiser

INTRODUCE THE SIGNPOST

- Tell students that stories often have wise characters that give advice or insight about life to the main characters. These smarter characters are usually older.
- **Look for Clues!** Explain that there are usually clues in the story that help readers identify the Words of the Wiser Signpost. One of these clues is when the characters go off somewhere and have a quiet, serious moment by themselves. The wiser character then shares advice that helps the main character solve a problem or make an important decision.

NOTICE & NOTE IN ACTION!

- Tell students that as they read with you certain *my*Book stories in this module, you will prompt them to notice the Words of the Wiser Signpost and explain how they would apply it to that page or pages. You will also ask students to note in their books things in the text or visuals that will help them remember the Signpost and why it is important to the story.

ANCHOR QUESTION

- Display Anchor Chart 38: Words of the Wiser, and discuss the Anchor Question. Tell students that they will ask themselves this question after noticing the Words of the Wiser Signpost. Answering this question will help them think about and explain the story's theme, or its big idea, moral, or lesson.

Online Ed

ANCHOR CHART 38: Words of the Wiser

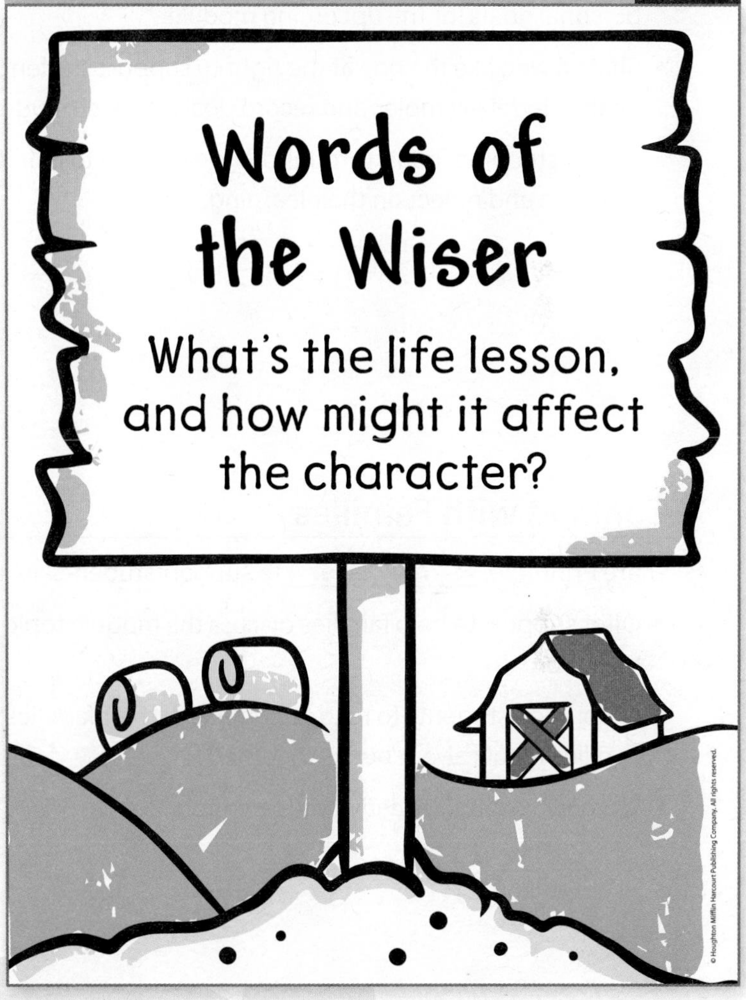

Kicking Off the Module!

Get started with Module 4 by setting goals with students and connecting with families.

Set Goals with Students

Tell students that over the next few weeks, they will build and strengthen their reading, writing, listening, speaking, and thinking skills as they explore drama:

- Encourage students to reflect on their prior learning and to set personal goals for the upcoming module.
- Share a web like the one at the right to support students in setting goals. Model examples and record goals for each student.
- Revisit students' goals throughout the module to help them track progress and reflect on their learning.

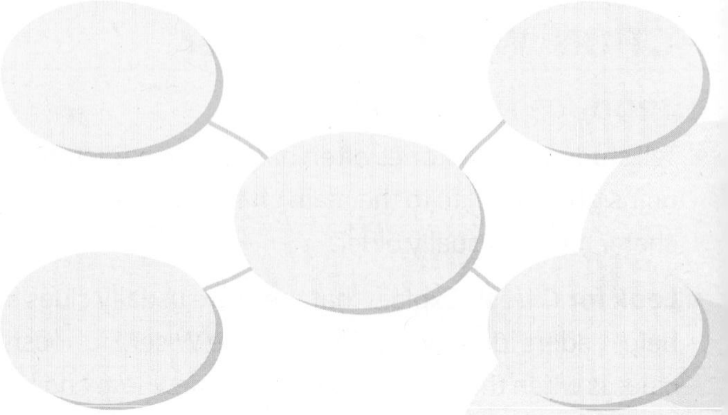

Connect with Families

Share Printable: Family Letter 4 to support students' learning at home:

- Offer support to help families discuss the module topic and the module's Big Idea Words.
- Encourage students to read at home with their families, and provide ideas for families to talk about books together.
- Suggest vocabulary activities to support literacy.

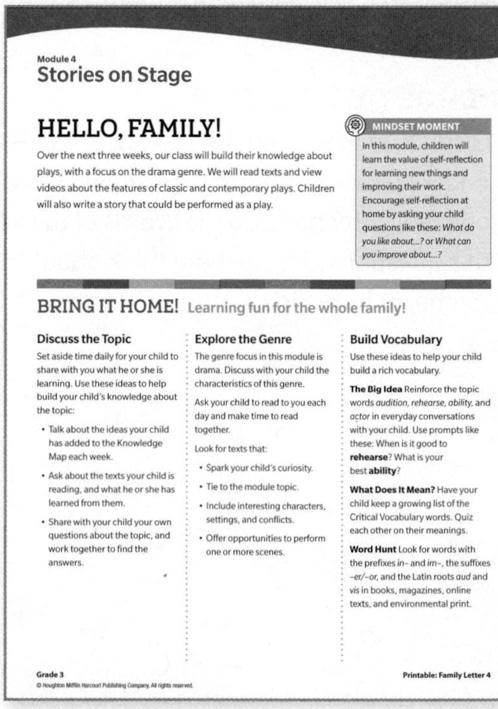

Module 4
Stories on Stage

HELLO, FAMILY!

Over the next three weeks, our class will build their knowledge about plays, with a focus on the drama genre. We will read texts and view videos about the features of classic and contemporary plays. Children will also write a story that could be performed as a play.

MINDSET MOMENT
In this module, children will learn the value of self-reflection for learning new things and improving their work. Encourage self-reflection at home by asking your child questions like these: *What do you like about...?* or *What can you improve about...?*

BRING IT HOME! Learning fun for the whole family!

Discuss the Topic
Set aside time daily for your child to share with you what he or she is learning. Use these ideas to help build your child's knowledge about the topic:
- Talk about the ideas your child has added to the Knowledge Map each week.
- Ask about the texts your child is reading, and what he or she has learned from them.
- Share with your child your own questions about the topic, and work together to find the answers.

Explore the Genre
The genre focus in this module is drama. Discuss with your child the characteristics of this genre.

Ask your child to read to you each day and make time to read together.

Look for texts that:
- Spark your child's curiosity.
- Tie to the module topic.
- Include interesting characters, settings, and conflicts.
- Offer opportunities to perform one or more scenes.

Build Vocabulary
Use these ideas to help your child build a rich vocabulary.

The Big Idea Reinforce the topic words *audition, rehearse, ability,* and *actor* in everyday conversations with your child. Use prompts like these: When is it good to **rehearse**? What is your best **ability**?

What Does It Mean? Have your child keep a growing list of the Critical Vocabulary words. Quiz each other on their meanings.

Word Hunt Look for words with the prefixes *in–* and *im–*, the suffixes *–er/–or,* and the Latin roots *aud* and *vis* in books, magazines, online texts, and environmental print.

Grade 3

Printable: Family Letter 4

Printable: Family Letter 4

LANGUAGE ARTS CONNECTION: Drama

Stories on Stage

Essential Question Why might some stories be better told as plays?

Essential Skills

VOCABULARY

- Critical Vocabulary: *audition, rehearse, ability, actor, saga, genuine, coiled, whirled, tame*
- Vocabulary Strategy: Shades of Meaning
- Generative Vocabulary: Prefixes *in– (not), im– (into)*; Spiral Review: Prefix *im– (not)*

READING WORKSHOP

- Ideas and Support
- Visualize
- Elements of Drama
- Literary Elements
- Figurative Language

FOUNDATIONAL SKILLS

- Decoding: Consonant digraphs (*ch, tch, sh, wh, th, ph, ng*)
- Spelling: Spelling the /ch/ sound
- Fluency: Expression

COMMUNICATION

- Listening Comprehension
- Speaking and Listening: Summarizing/ Paraphrasing
- Make Connections

WRITING WORKSHOP

- Narrative Writing: Story
- Pronouns and Antecedents

LEARNING MINDSET: Self-Reflection

THIS WEEK'S SELECTIONS

INFORMATIONAL TEXT
The Lion King's Friend

ARGUMENT / OPINION ESSAY
That's Entertainment!

DRAMA / TALL TALE
The Saga of Pecos Bill

Rigby LEVELED LIBRARY

WEEK 1

Week at a Glance

Suggested Daily Times

• BUILD KNOWLEDGE & LANGUAGE/ VOCABULARY	10–15 minutes
• READING WORKSHOP	60–85 minutes
• FOUNDATIONAL SKILLS	15–30 minutes
• COMMUNICATION	15–30 minutes
• WRITING WORKSHOP	30–45 minutes

This Week's Words

BIG IDEA WORDS

audition *rehearse* *ability* *actor*

CRITICAL VOCABULARY WORDS

saga	*genuine*	*coiled*
whirled	*tame*	

HIGH-FREQUENCY WORDS

dance *speak* *paint*

INSTRUCTIONAL VOCABULARY

audience	*claim*	*fact*
opinion	*visualize*	*act*
cast of characters	*dialogue*	*drama*
scene	*script*	*stage direction*
conflict	*event*	*literary elements*
plot	*resolution*	*figurative language*
hyperbole	*imagery*	

Assessment Options

Online Ed

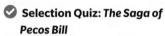

- **Selection Quiz: *The Saga of Pecos Bill***
- **Weekly Assessment**
  - Comprehension: Elements of Drama, Literary Elements, Figurative Language
  - Generative Vocabulary: Prefixes *in–* (not), *im–* (into)
  - Vocabulary Strategy: Shades of Meaning
  - Grammar: Pronouns and Antecedents

Intervention

For students needing strategic intervention, choose from daily small-group options for differentiation. Access online Foundational Skills and Word Study Studio for additonal support.

LESSON 1

BUILD KNOWLEDGE & LANGUAGE

Teaching Pal

Module Launch, pp. T218–T219
- **Introduce the Topic:** Stories on Stage
- Big Idea Words: *audition, rehearse, ability, actor*

READING WORKSHOP

Teaching Pal

That's Entertainment!
GENRE Argument/Opinion Essay
Shared Reading: MINILESSON, pp. T220–T221
- Connect and Teach: Ideas and Support
- Apply to Text: ***That's Entertainment***!
- Engage and Respond: Speaking and Listening

SMALL-GROUP INSTRUCTION

Options for Differentiation
- Guided Reading Groups, p. T222
- English Learner Support: Infer, p. T222
- Reinforce Ideas and Support, p. T223

Options for Independent and Collaborative Work, pp. T224–T225

FOUNDATIONAL SKILLS

Decoding, pp. T226–T227
- Consonant digraphs (*ch, tch, sh, wh, th, ph, ng*)

Spelling, p. T228
- Spelling the /ch/ sound

Fluency, p. T229
- Expression

WRITING WORKSHOP

Narrative Writing: Story, p. W52
- Priming the Students

Grammar, p. W255
- Subject Pronouns

LESSON 2

VOCABULARY

Academic Vocabulary, pp. T230–T231
- Introduce Critical Vocabulary: *saga, genuine, coiled, whirled, tame*

READING WORKSHOP

Teaching Pal

The Saga of Pecos Bill
GENRE Drama/Tall Tale
Shared Reading: MINILESSON, pp. T232–T233
- Connect and Teach: Visualize
- Apply to Text: ***The Saga of Pecos Bill***
- Engage and Respond: Speaking and Listening

SMALL-GROUP INSTRUCTION

Options for Differentiation
- Guided Reading Groups, p. T234
- English Learner Support: Infer, p. T234
- Reinforce Visualize, p. T235

Options for Independent and Collaborative Work, pp. T236–T237

COMMUNICATION

Listening Comprehension, pp. T238–T241
- Teacher Read-Aloud: *The Lion King's Friend*
- Focus on Fluency: Reading Rate
- Engage and Respond: Speaking and Listening

WRITING WORKSHOP

Narrative Writing: Story, p. W53
- Priming the Text

Grammar, p. W256
- Object Pronouns

LESSON 3

VOCABULARY

Academic Vocabulary, p. T242
- Review Critical Vocabulary: *saga, genuine, coiled, whirled, tame*

Vocabulary Strategy, T243
- Shades of Meaning

READING WORKSHOP

The Saga of Pecos Bill
Teaching Pal
GENRE Drama/Tall Tale
Shared Reading: MINILESSON, pp. T244–T245
- Connect and Teach: Elements of Drama
- Apply to Text: ***The Saga of Pecos Bill***
- Engage and Respond: Close Read Screencast
- Engage and Respond: Write Flash Fiction

SMALL-GROUP INSTRUCTION

Options for Differentiation
- Guided Reading Groups, p. T246
- English Learner Support: Infer, p. T246
- Reinforce Elements of Drama, p. T247

Options for Independent and Collaborative Work, pp. T248–T249

FOUNDATIONAL SKILLS

Decoding, pp. T250–T251
- Consonant digraphs (*ch, tch, sh, wh, th, ph, ng*)

WRITING WORKSHOP

Narrative Writing: Story, p. W54
- The Read

Grammar, p. W257
- Pronoun-Antecedent Agreement

LESSON 4

VOCABULARY

Generative Vocabulary, pp. T252–T253
- Prefixes *in–* *(not), im–* *(into)*
- Spiral Review: Prefix *im–* *(not)*

READING WORKSHOP

The Saga of Pecos Bill
Teaching Pal
GENRE Drama/Tall Tale
Shared Reading: MINILESSON, pp. T254–T255
- Connect and Teach: Literary Elements
- Apply to Text: ***The Saga of Pecos Bill***
- Engage and Respond: Writing

SMALL-GROUP INSTRUCTION

Options for Differentiation
- Guided Reading Groups, p. T256
- English Learner Support: Infer, p. T256
- Reinforce Literary Elements, p. T257

Options for Independent and Collaborative Work, pp. T258–T259

COMMUNICATION

Project Checkpoint: Brainstorm and Research, pp. T206, T215

WRITING WORKSHOP

Narrative Writing: Story, p. W55
- Vocabulary

Grammar, p. W238
- Review Plural Nouns with *–s* and *–es*

LESSON 5

VOCABULARY

Academic Vocabulary, pp. T260–T261
- Vocabulary Spiral Review

READING WORKSHOP

The Saga of Pecos Bill
Teaching Pal
GENRE Drama/Tall Tale
Shared Reading: MINILESSON, pp. T262–T263
- Connect and Teach: Figurative Language
- Apply to Text: ***The Saga of Pecos Bill***
- Engage and Respond: Writing

SMALL-GROUP INSTRUCTION

Options for Differentiation
- Guided Reading Groups, p. T264
- English Learner Support: Infer, p. T264
- Reinforce Figurative Language, p. T265

Options for Independent and Collaborative Work, pp. T266–T267

COMMUNICATION

Speaking and Listening, p. T268
- Summarizing and Paraphrasing

Make Connections, p. T269
- Synthesize Topic Knowledge

WRITING WORKSHOP

Narrative Writing: Story, p. W56
- Prewriting: Preparing to Write

Grammar, p. W259
- Connect to Writing: Using Pronouns and Antecedents

Literacy Centers

- **While you meet with small groups, have students work independently in Literacy Centers. Familiarize students with the week's activities and post a daily rotation schedule.**
- **Have students complete Printable: Exit Ticket for each activity so you can monitor their work.**

READING CENTER

Readers' Theater

- Preview Printable: **Readers' Theater 4**, "A Tale with a Twist," and assign parts to mixed-ability groups of five students.
- The part of Carlos is ideal for struggling readers, and the part of Carrie can be read by a proficient reader.

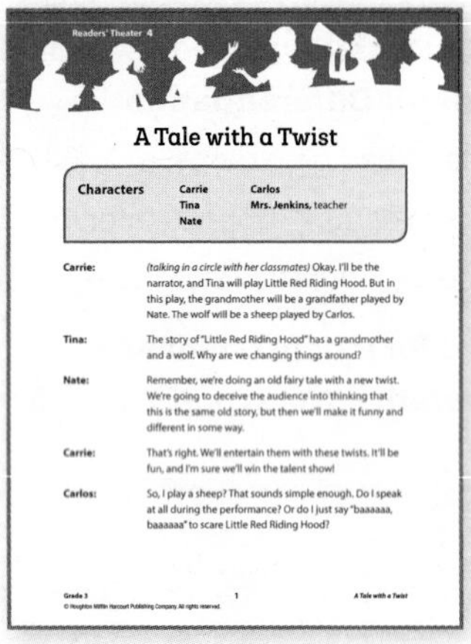
Readers' Theater 4

A Tale with a Twist

Characters	Carrie	Carlos
	Tina	Mrs. Jenkins, teacher
	Nate	

Carrie: *(talking in a circle with her classmates)* Okay. I'll be the narrator, and Tina will play Little Red Riding Hood. But in this play, the grandmother will be a grandfather played by Nate. The wolf will be a sheep played by Carlos.

Tina: The story of "Little Red Riding Hood" has a grandmother and a wolf. Why are we changing things around?

Nate: Remember, we're doing an old fairy tale with a new twist. We're going to deceive the audience into thinking that this is the same old story, but then we'll make it funny and different in some way.

Carrie: That's right. We'll entertain them with these twists. It'll be fun, and I'm sure we'll win the talent show!

Carlos: So, I play a sheep? That sounds simple enough. Do I speak at all during the performance? Or do I just say "baaaaaa, baaaaaa" to scare Little Red Riding Hood?

Grade 3 1 A Tale with a Twist

Printable: Readers' Theater 4

Independent Reading

- Display and review Anchor Chart 35: **Choosing a Book**.
- Have students self-select or continue reading an independent reading book.
- Remind students to set a purpose for reading and to record their progress on their Printable: **Reading Log**.
- Have students use Printable: **Independent Reading** for fiction or nonfiction to note key ideas as they read.
- You may want to choose from these additional options to have students interact with their books:
- **Mixed-Ability Groups** Students discuss their self-selected books, using the questions on the Reading Log.
- **Book Review** Students expand on their opinions by writing a short book review to help their classmates choose books.

Name ______ Centers

Reading Log

Title ______

Author ______ Genre ______

Independent Reading Record

Date ______ Time Spent ______ Pages Read ______

Date ______ Time Spent ______ Pages Read ______

Date ______ Time Spent ______ Pages Read ______

Date ______ Time Spent ______ Pages Read ______

Summary This text is about ______

Questions for Discussion

What was your favorite part of the text? ______

What did you enjoy about the author's writing? ______

Was there something that you did not understand? What was it? ______

Would you recommend this text to a friend? Why or why not? ______

Grade 3 Printable

Printable: Reading Log

VOCABULARY CENTER

Super Six Words *(Use in Lessons 2–5.)*

- Have students use Printable: **Super Six Words** to list Big Idea Words and this week's Critical Vocabulary words that relate to the module topic.
- Then have students select six words from their lists that they think are most important, interesting, or new to them.
- Tell students to write a sentence for each selected word.
- Explain to students that they will come back to this list at the end of each week in the module.

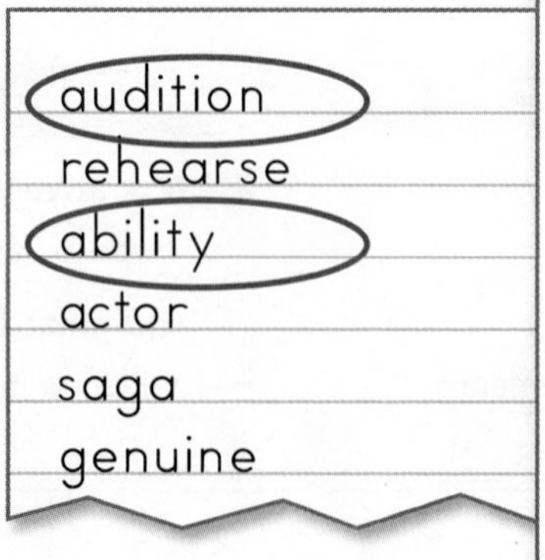

Name ______ Centers

Super Six Words

1. Take a clean sheet of paper. Write your name at the top. Then write the module title.
2. Create four columns labeled Week 1, Week 2, Week 3, and Super Six.
3. Each week, list words about the topic from the texts you read in that week's column.
4. At the end of each week, choose and circle six words on your weekly list that you think are most important to the topic.
5. Write a sentence for each of those six words. Make sure your sentences show the meanings of the words.
6. At the end of the module, you will have eighteen words and sentences.
7. Now, choose six words from those eighteen words you think are most important to the topic. Write them in the Super Six column.
8. Use your Super Six words to write a summary of what you have learned about the module topic.

Grade 3 Printable

Printable: Super Six Words

DIGITAL STATION

Listener's Choice

- Have students listen to this week's selection, *The Saga of Pecos Bill*, or a Leveled Reader of their choice.
- Tell them to add the title to their Printable: Listening Log, as well as listing the listening skills they used, a summary of the selection, and questions they have about the selection or book.

Keyboarding

- Have students practice keyboarding using Printable: Keyboarding 4.1.

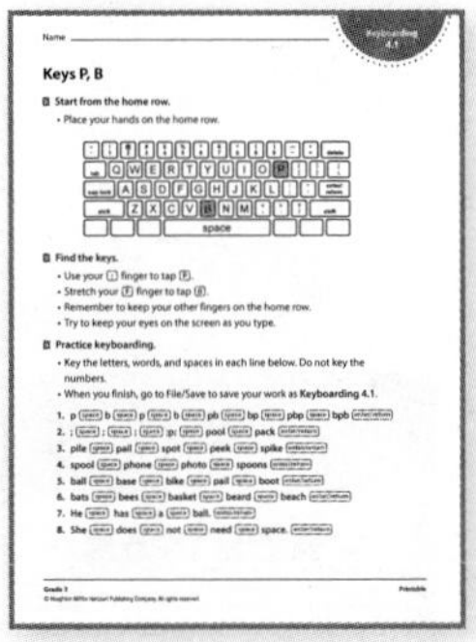

Printable: Keyboarding 4.1

WRITING CENTER

Write Flash Fiction *(Use in Lessons 3–5.)*

- Have students use Printable: Peer Conferencing Routine to discuss their writing.
- Tell peers to use the tips on *my*Book page 317 as they review the work of others and offer feedback.

Writing Workshop

- Have students work on a piece of writing. They may use the time to prewrite, draft, revise, edit, or publish.
- Students may choose from among tasks such as these:
  - » Brainstorm words associated with a selected topic.
  - » Free-write on your topic. Have a partner check the subject pronouns, object pronouns, and antecedents.
- Display Anchor Chart 37: Cursive Handwriting.

PROJECT CENTER

Project Checkpoint: Brainstorm and Research

- Have students work in groups, using Printable: Project 4.1 to guide them as they begin the project. Groups should complete the following over the course of the week:

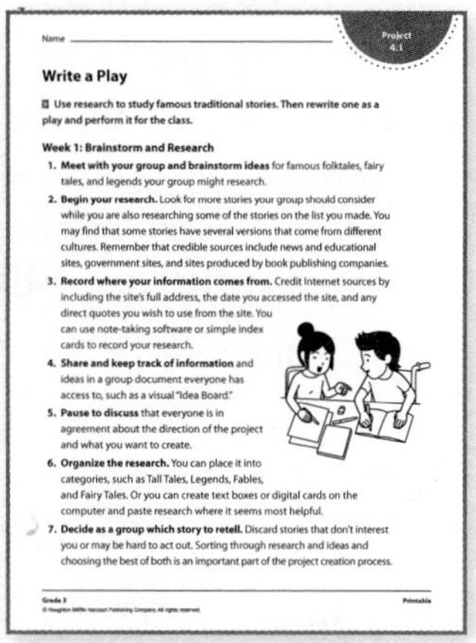
Name
Project 4.1

Write a Play

Use research to study famous traditional stories. Then rewrite one as a play and perform it for the class.

Week 1: Brainstorm and Research

1. **Meet with your group and brainstorm ideas** for famous folktales, fairy tales, and legends your group might research.
2. **Begin your research.** Look for more stories your group should consider while you are also researching some of the stories on the list you made. You may find that some stories have several versions that come from different cultures. Remember that credible sources include news and educational sites, government sites, and sites produced by book publishing companies.
3. **Record where your information comes from.** Credit Internet sources by including the site's full address, the date you accessed the site, and any direct quotes you wish to use from the site. You can use note-taking software or simple index cards to record your research.
4. **Share and keep track of information** and ideas in a group document everyone has access to, such as a visual "Idea Board."
5. **Pause to discuss** that everyone is in agreement about the direction of the project and what you want to create.
6. **Organize the research.** You can place it into categories, such as Tall Tales, Legends, Fables, and Fairy Tales. Or you can create text boxes or digital cards on the computer and paste research where it seems most helpful.
7. **Decide as a group which story to retell.** Discard stories that don't interest you or may be hard to act out. Sorting through research and ideas and choosing the best of both is an important part of the project creation process.

Grade 3
Printable

Printable: Project 4.1

- ☑ Brainstorm ideas and conduct research on traditional stories and folktales.
- ☑ Discuss the plot of the stories on their list, or read the stories for the first time if possible.
- ☑ Determine how they will share and keep track of their information and ideas.
- ☑ Think about how their research fits into the project plan.
- ☑ Pause during research to confirm that everyone is in agreement about the direction of the project.

Reading Remake

(Use in Lessons 2–5.)

- Have students complete the Make a Flipbook activity on Printable: Reading Remake 5.
- Ask partners to explain to one another how their flipbook shows their understanding of the selection.

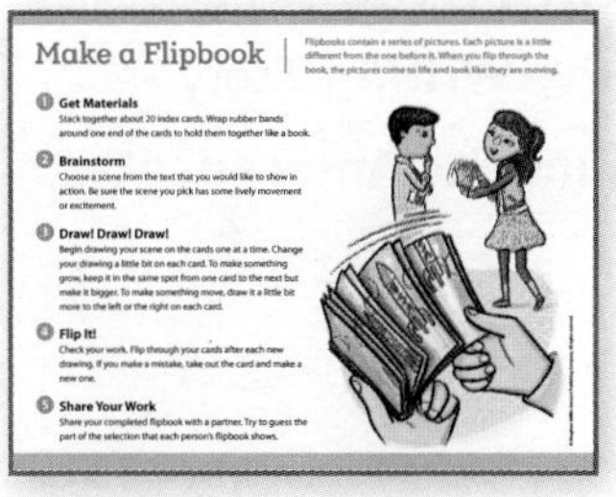

Printable: Reading Remake 5

WEEK 1 Preview Lesson Texts

Build understanding of this week's texts so that you can best support students in making connections, understanding key ideas, and becoming lifelong readers.

That's Entertainment!

GENRE Opinion/Argument

WHY THIS TEXT?

After reading this opinion/argument text about theater productions, students should be able to identify the author's claim, provide supporting details, and distinguish fact from opinion.

KEY LEARNING OBJECTIVES

- Explain the author's ideas and support them with details

myBOO

Short Read

THAT'S ENTERTAINMENT!

1 Anyone who has seen a great play will agree: theater is one of the most exciting forms of entertainment. Nothing beats watching skilled actors bringing a story to life on the stage.

2 At the audition, each actor must work hard to win a part as one of the characters. Then it's time to rehearse. The actors take weeks to learn their roles. They read the script and practice their dialogue, or the words they speak on stage. They follow stage directions, which tell actors how to behave and move.

3 Meanwhile, the crew builds sets for the stage to show the play's different settings. The sets include props such as furniture or painted scenery. Each act or scene is like a chapter in a story and may require a different set. Costume designers decide what the actors should wear. The director oversees everything.

4 The play *Peter Pan* is theater at its best. A great script, exciting roles, and colorful stage sets—this play has it all! Written by J. M. Barrie, the play was first performed in 1904. Today, it's as popular as ever. Barrie mixes fantasy and reality to tell an irresistible story. The main character is a boy who never

TEXT COMPLEXITY

OVERALL RATING 730L Slightly Complex

This text has a clearly stated and sequential organization of main idea and details.

MAKE CONNECTIONS

BUILD KNOWLEDGE AND LANGUAGE

- **Language Arts Connection:** Drama

FOUNDATIONAL SKILLS

- **High-Frequency Words:** *speak, paint*
- **Consonant Digraphs *ch, tch, sh, wh, th, ph, ng*:** *each, coach, watching, with, nothing, range*

WRITING WORKSHOP

- **Narrative Writing:** Story
- **Pronouns and Antecedents**

TEXT X-RAY

KEY IDEAS

Key Idea *pp. 302–303*
Live theater performances are one of the most exciting forms of entertainment.

Key Idea *pp. 302–303*
A theater production requires preparation by actors, crew, and costume designers.

Key Idea *pp. 302–303*
The play *Peter Pan* is an excellent example of theater at its best: amazing scenery, costumes, and effects.

Key Idea *pp. 302–303*
The participants in theater productions need to be creative and talented to have the encourage them to perform their best.

LANGUAGE

Alliteration
audience is in awe *pp. 302–303* Explain that *awe* means "a strong feeling of wonder/amazement." Alliteration is the repetition of the same beginning sounds in words near each other (*au-*, *awe*) to further dramatize what is being said. In this case, it emphasizes how exciting the show is.

Idiom
make them sparkle *pp. 302–303* English learners may understand that *sparkle* means "small flashes of light." If possible, demonstrate using something in the classroom. Explain that when a person makes someone "sparkle," it means they guide them to have an impact (e.g., acting, designing, coaching).

The Saga of Pecos Bill by Anthony D. Fredericks

GENRE Drama/Tall Tale

Online

CLOSE-READ SCREENCAST Ed

The Saga of Pecos Bill Have students tap the Closer Look icons to access a screencast in which readers discuss and annotate the key passage. As a class, view and discuss the video.

myBOOK

WHY THIS TEXT?

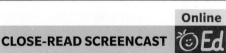

In this "tall tale" drama, students should be able to visualize the narrators and characters playing parts, as well as the setting in which the tale is being told. Additionally, students will identify elements of drama, such as dialogue and acts/scenes, and explore how they, along with figurative language, can influence the plot and the author's purpose.

KEY LEARNING OBJECTIVES

- Visualize
- Elements of Drama
- Literary Elements
- Figurative Language

TEXT COMPLEXITY

OVERALL RATING Slightly Complex

This selection has a less familiar concept and uses some unfamiliar informal language.

MAKE CONNECTIONS

BUILD KNOWLEDGE AND LANGUAGE

- **Language Arts Connection:** Drama

FOUNDATIONAL SKILLS

- **Consonant Digraphs *ch, tch, sh, wh, th, ph, ng*:** *ranch, such, reach, teach, match, slung, swung, hangin'*

WRITING WORKSHOP

- **Narrative Writing:** Story
- **Pronouns and Antecedents**

TEXT X-RAY

KEY IDEAS

Key Idea *pp. 306–308*
A group of narrators give the background on Pecos Bill's childhood explaining how he was separated from his family and raised by coyotes.

Key Idea *p. 311*
Pecos Bill's ability to tame animals was noticed by other cowboys and he offered to help them with whatever they needed.

Key Idea *pp. 312–314*
Pecos Bill wrestles a tornado to protect the people of Texas. Modern-day land characteristics are attributed to this tall tale.

LANGUAGE

Informal Language
like you was a regular coyote *p. 308* Students may not recognize informal language, such as the improper use of verb tenses and words like "ain't." Explain that the characters are from a certain time period and different level of education, which can affect speech and language.

Simile
like it was full of about a hundred wildcats *p. 312* Explain that similes compare two things. This enhances the images that students visualize when reading the story. The author gives an extensive, lively description of the tornado that Pecos Bill battles, comparing it to the wild behavior of large group of animals.

Introduce the Topic: Stories on Stage

LEARNING OBJECTIVES

- Share information and ideas about a topic under discussion.
- Ask relevant questions to clarify information.
- Recognize characteristics of informational texts.
- **Language** Answer questions related to the theme using module vocabulary.

MATERIALS — Online Ed

Display and Engage *Knowledge Map 4.1*
Teaching Pal *Book 1, pp. 296–301*
***my*Book** *Book 1, pp. 296–301*
Get Curious Video *Auditions*
Vocabulary Cards *4.1–4.4*

Access Prior Knowledge

- Tell students that in this module they will read texts and view media related to the drama genre, including both classic and modern plays.
- Have students turn to *my*Book pages 296–297. Read aloud the title *Stories on Stage* and begin a discussion about what it means.
- Have students share what they know about plays, including the names of any plays they have seen or taken part in.

Build Background

In your Teaching Pal, pages 296–299, use the prompts to guide students through an introduction to the module as they follow along in their *my*Book.

- **Discuss the Quotation** Lead a discussion about the quotation by Stella Adler.
- **Essential Question** Introduce the Essential Question. Then use the **ACTIVE VIEWING** routine with the Get Curious Video: Auditions. Tell students that the video is informational, so they should expect to see and hear facts about the topic.
- **Big Idea Words** Use the **VOCABULARY** routine and Vocabulary Cards 4.1–4.4 to introduce the topic vocabulary: *audition, rehearse, ability,* and *actor*. Then have students begin the vocabulary network on page 299. Encourage them to add to it throughout the module.

Vocabulary Cards

LEARNING MINDSET

Self-Reflection

Introduce Explain the meaning of self-reflection. Point out examples of self-reflection or ways to practice self-reflection throughout this module. *Looking back on what we do and say allows us to see how we may do things even better the next time. Mistakes are often a part of self-reflection. Once we make a mistake, we have the opportunity to improve because we know what to do differently in the future.*

Go to
Teaching Pal

MODULE 4

Introduce the Topic

- **Read aloud** the module title, *Stories on Stage.*
- **Tell students** that in this module they will be reading dramas that are also called plays and viewing a video about a theater where plays are performed.
- **Have students** explain what a play is and how actors act out written words on a page. Discuss how acting out a play is different from reading a story aloud.
- **Ask** students to discuss what a stage is and what happens when actors perform a drama on stage. *(Possible responses: A stage is a place where actors perform. In a drama, or play, actors act out a story on a stage.)*

Discuss the Quotation

- **Read aloud** the quotation by Stella Adler.
- **Lead a discussion** in which students discuss what it means when someone says that a play is not just about the words. Explain the meaning of the quote, as needed: *The words of a play are written on a page, but the actors turn these words into actions in a performance.*
- **Ask students** to give examples of plays they have seen or performed in. *(Accept reasonable responses.)*

MODULE 4

Stories on Stage

"The play is not in the words. It's behind the words."
—Stella Adler

Essential Question

Why might some stories be better told as plays?

Get Curious Video

296 297

Introduce the Essential Question

- **Read aloud** the Essential Question.
- **Tell** students that throughout this module, they will read dramas and watch a video that will help them answer the Essential Question.
- **Make sure** students understand that stories can be told in different ways. Discuss how reading a story is different from hearing a storyteller tell a story or from watching actors perform a story as a play.

View and Respond to a Video

- Use the ACTIVE VIEWING routine with the Get Curious Video: *Auditions.*

296 Module 4

Module 4 297

Teaching Pal, pp.296–297

Knowledge Focus: Make a Difference

Project Display and Engage: Knowledge Map 4.1 and have students turn to pages 300–301 in their *my*Book. Tell students they will begin building their knowledge about stories that are told as plays and performed on a stage. Explain that they will return to these pages at the end of each week to add new information they learned about the topic.

Online Ed

DISPLAY AND ENGAGE: Knowledge Map 4.1

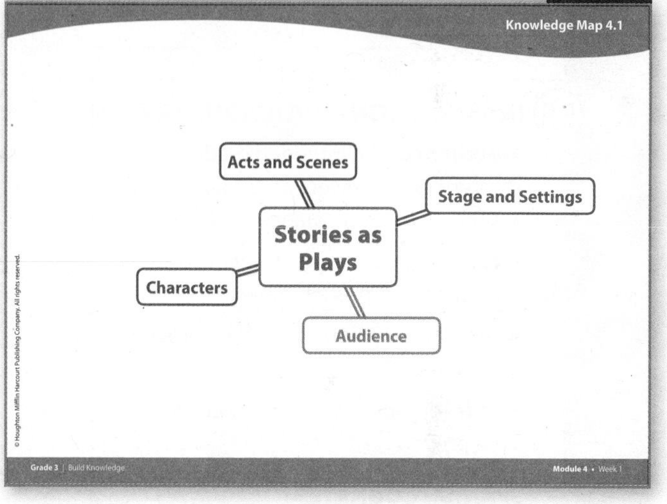

Genre Focus: Drama/Plays

Tell students that in this module they will read several plays. Share with students that plays:

- are written to be performed on a stage, by actors, in front of an audience.
- consist of dialogue, or the words spoken by characters.
- can include made-up events and characters or events and characters from real life.
- are written in acts (larger sections) and scenes (smaller sections set in a particular place).

ENGLISH LEARNER SUPPORT: Elicit Participation

SUBSTANTIAL
Ask questions such as: *Can you put on a play without an actor?*

MODERATE
Provide frames such as this: *You can't put on a play without an actor because* ______.

LIGHT
To elicit participation in the topic discussion, ask open-ended questions: *A play is different from a story because* ______. *To act in a play, an actor* ______.

Ideas and Support

Step 1 Connect and Teach

LEARNING OBJECTIVES

- Recognize characteristics of an argumentative text.
- Identify the author's claim, supporting facts, and intended audience.
- Distinguish facts and opinions.
- **Language** Identify and state the author's claim and supporting facts.

MATERIALS — Online Ed

Anchor Chart 21 *Ideas and Support*

Printable *Anchor Chart 21: Ideas and Support*

Teaching Pal *Book 1, pp. 302–303*

myBook *Book 1, That's Entertainment!, pp. 302–303*

INSTRUCTIONAL VOCABULARY

- **audience** the intended readers, listeners, or viewers of a story, speech, or performance
- **claim** the main argument in an opinion or argumentative text
- **fact** information that can be proved to be true
- **opinion** ideas or beliefs that cannot be proved

SPANISH COGNATES

- **opinion** *opinión*

- Tell students that as they read, it is important to think about the **ideas** in the text and how the author **supports** them.
- Project or display Anchor Chart 21: **Ideas and Support**.
- Explain that in an argumentative text, the author makes a **claim** and supports it with reasons and details. The author has a specific audience in mind and chooses reasons and details that will appeal to those readers.
- Point out that an author's claim is often an **opinion**. Explain that authors support their opinions with **facts**.
- Tell students that it is important to know if the author is stating a fact or an opinion. Review the information on the Anchor Chart as you explain how to identify facts and opinions. Tell students to look for these details as they read.
- Tell students that they will practice identifying ideas and support as they read the argumentative text *That's Entertainment!*

Online Ed

ANCHOR CHART 21: Ideas and Support

GENRE STUDY: Argumentative Text

Point out to students that *That's Entertainment!* is an argumentative text. Share this genre information with students.

- An argumentative text gives the author's opinion about a topic.
- In an argumentative text, the author tries to convince readers to believe that opinion.
- Argumentative texts include evidence such as facts and examples to support the author's viewpoint.

Go to Your **Teaching Pal**

Online

ANNOTATE IT!

Students may use the annotation tools in their eBook.

Step 2 Apply to Text

In your **Teaching Pal**, pages 302–303, use the blue **READ FOR UNDERSTANDING** prompts to guide discussion of *That's Entertainment!* as students follow along in their *my*Book.

- **Genre Study** Remind students that in an argumentative text, the author makes a claim or states his or her opinion. The author supports that opinion with details such as facts. Ask students what they expect to learn from reading the selection by previewing the title and photographs.
- **Set a Purpose** Prompt students to set a purpose for reading based on the title and genre. As needed, use this model: *I will read to find the author's claim and how it is supported.*
- **Read and Comprehend** Use the **READ FOR UNDERSTANDING** routine to have students read the selection. Use the prompts in your Teaching Pal to gauge students' understanding and to have them identify the author's claim, as well as facts and opinions in the text. Discuss the author's intended audience for the selection. Refer back to the Anchor Chart as necessary to help students understand the differences between facts and opinions.

Step 3 Engage and Respond

INDEPENDENT PRACTICE: Speaking and Listening

- Remind students of the Essential Question: *Why might some stories be better told as plays?* Then have them read *That's Entertainment!* to find information that answers the question.
- Have partners use the **THINK-PAIR-SHARE** routine to discuss their ideas and then share with the group. Remind students to listen actively to their partners, speak coherently, and ask questions to clarify information.
- You may want to have students conduct their discussions during daily small-group time.

ENGLISH LEARNER SUPPORT: Facilitate Discussion

SUBSTANTIAL

Provide frames such as *The author thinks* Peter Pan _____. *One fact is* _____.

MODERATE

Have partners ask and answer: *What is the author's opinion? What facts does the author give?*

LIGHT

Have students use complete sentences to state the author's opinion and identify the supporting facts and details.

LINK TO SMALL-GROUP INSTRUCTION

REINFORCE IDEAS AND SUPPORT Review or extend the skill as needed during small-group time to support students' need for differentiation. *See the lesson on p. T223.*

Options for Differentiation

As the class engages in independent and collaborative work, meet with Guided Reading Groups or differentiate instruction based on student need.

GUIDED READING GROUPS

Match Students to Books + Instruction

- Choose just-right books based on level, skill, topic, or genre.

L — M — N — O — P — Q

Leveled Readers

- Deliver instruction with each book's **Take and Teach Lesson**, choosing appropriate sessions based on need.

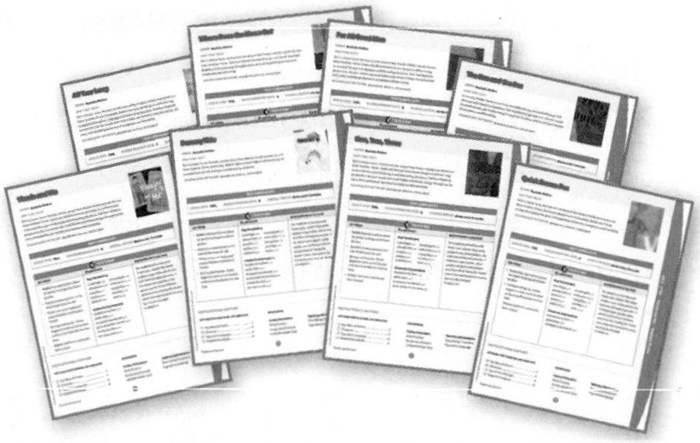

- Check comprehension, reinforce instruction, and extend learning with suggested supporting activities.

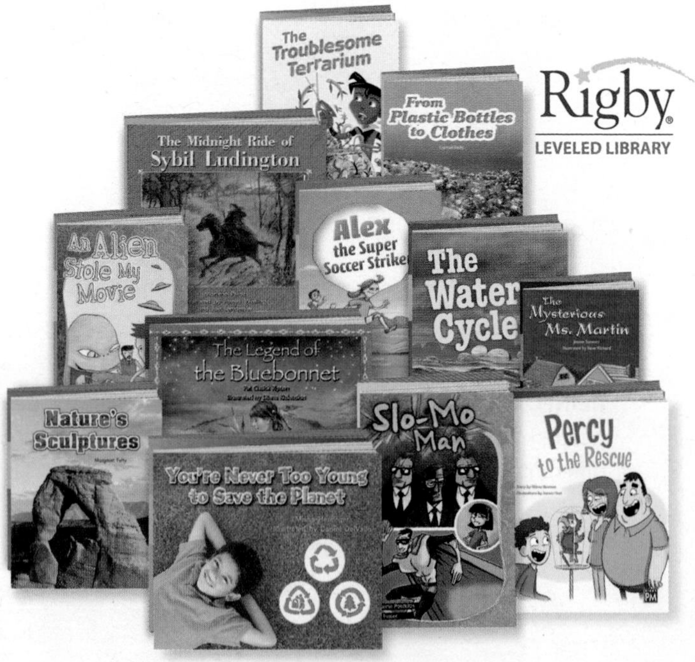

ENGLISH LEARNER SUPPORT

Infer

- Use **Tabletop Minilessons: English Language Development 10.1 (Listening)** to introduce and practice the language skill.

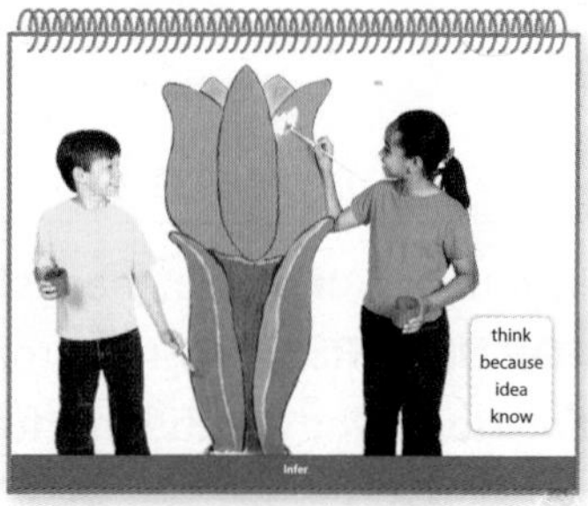

Tabletop Minilessons: English Language Development

- Then use the following text-based prompts with *That's Entertainment!* to guide application of the language skill. Begin with the prompt at the student's identified language proficiency level. As students progress, use lighter supports to encourage increased language proficiency.

SUBSTANTIAL
Read aloud paragraph 2. Ask: *Do you think it is easy or hard to rehearse for a play?* Then read the paragraph again. Ask students to raise their hand when they hear text evidence that supports their inference.

MODERATE
Read aloud paragraphs 1–3. Ask students who they think has the hardest job in a play: an actor, set designer, costume designer, or director. Have them complete sentence frames: *I think the* ______ *has the hardest job because the text says* ______.

LIGHT
Read aloud paragraph 4. Say: *Make an inference about why Peter Pan is still a popular play today. What text evidence supports your inference?*

REINFORCE IDEAS AND SUPPORT

Demonstrate

- Use **Tabletop Minilessons: Reading Card 21** to remind students that as they read, it is important to think about the **ideas** in the text and how the author **supports** them. In an argumentative text, the author makes a **claim**, which is often an **opinion**, and supports it with **facts** and details that will appeal to the specific audience the author has in mind. Readers will be better able to understand and evaluate persuasive text when they know whether the writer is stating a fact or opinion.
- Model filling out Printable: Reading Graphic Organizer 23 to identify ideas and support in *That's Entertainment!*

Tabletop Minilessons: Reading

Apply to Independent Reading

- Now have students identify the ideas and support in an appropriate book or article they are reading independently. Customize these prompts to the texts students choose.
  - » *What is the author's claim? Is it a fact or opinion?*
  - » *What details support the author's ideas?*
  - » *Who is the author's intended audience?*
- Have students complete Printable: Reading Graphic Organizer 23 for their independent reading book.

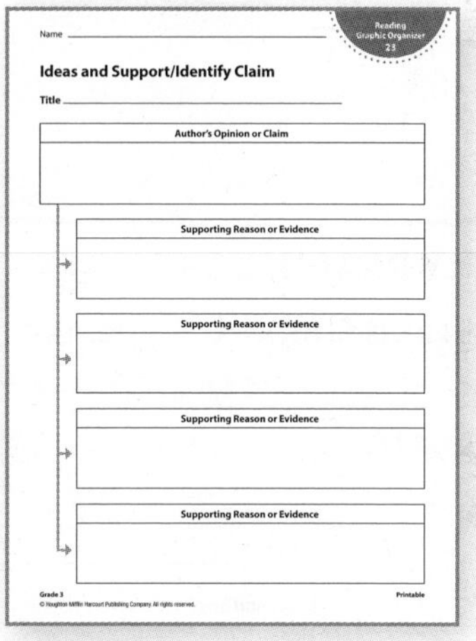

Printable: Reading Graphic Organizer 23

ALMOST THERE

READY FOR MORE

SCAFFOLD AND EXTEND

- Guide students to identify the author's claim. Point out a supporting detail. Have students find more supporting details.
- Prompt students to identify the author's claim, supporting details, audience, and whether the author states facts or opinions.
- Have students suggest how the author's support for the claim could be made stronger for his or her audience.

EL ENGLISH LEARNER SUPPORT

SUBSTANTIAL
Ask *yes/no* questions such as: *Is this the author's claim? Does this detail support the claim? Is this a fact? Is it an opinion?*

MODERATE
Have students complete the sentence frames: *The author's claim is ______. A detail that supports it is ______.*

LIGHT
Encourage students to explain their reasoning as they answer the prompts.

Options for Independent and Collaborative Work

While you meet with small groups, have other students engage in literacy activities that reinforce the lesson's learning objectives. Choose from these options.

Independent Reading

Student Choice Library

Rigby
LEVELED LIBRARY

APPLY READING SKILL

Ideas and Support Students complete Printable: Reading Graphic Organizer 23 for an independent reading book.

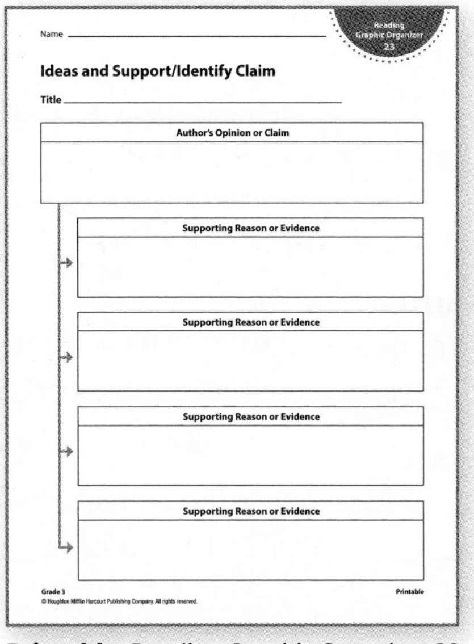

Name ______

Reading Graphic Organizer 23

Ideas and Support/Identify Claim

Title ______

Author's Opinion or Claim

Supporting Reason or Evidence

Supporting Reason or Evidence

Supporting Reason or Evidence

Supporting Reason or Evidence

Grade 3
© Houghton Mifflin Harcourt Publishing Company. All rights reserved.
Printable

Printable: Reading Graphic Organizer 23

APPLY LANGUAGE SKILL

Infer Students complete Printable: Language Graphic Organizer 7 for an independent reading book.

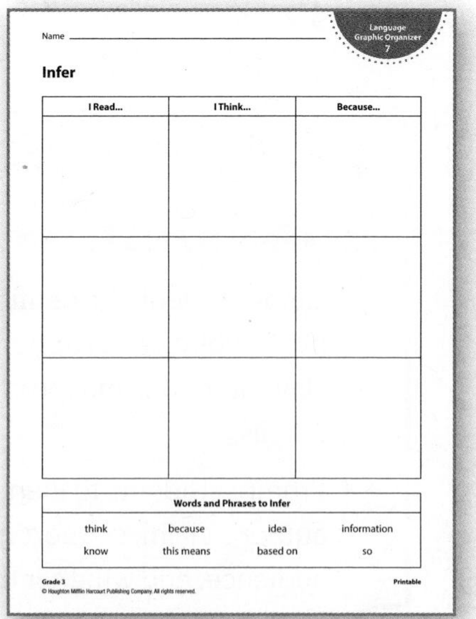

Name ______

Language Graphic Organizer 7

Infer

I Read...	I Think...	Because...

Words and Phrases to Infer			
think	because	idea	information
know	this means	based on	so

Grade 3
© Houghton Mifflin Harcourt Publishing Company. All rights reserved.
Printable

Printable: Language Graphic Organizer 7

Literacy Centers

See pp. T214–T215.

- READING CENTER
- VOCABULARY CENTER
- DIGITAL STATION
- WRITING CENTER
- PROJECT CENTER

Speaking and Listening

Partners discuss the Essential Question. *See Engage and Respond, p. T221.*

Additional Skills Practice

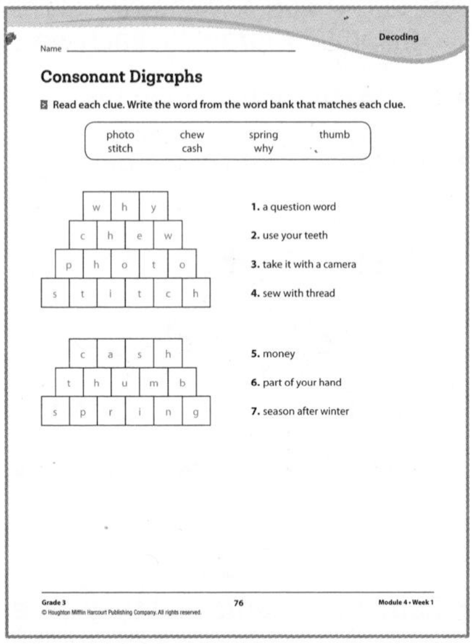
Name ______________ Decoding

Consonant Digraphs

Read each clue. Write the word from the word bank that matches each clue.

photo	chew	spring	thumb
stitch	cash	why	

1. a question word — w h y
2. use your teeth — c h e w
3. take it with a camera — p h o t o
4. sew with thread — s t i t c h
5. money — c a s h
6. part of your hand — t h u m b
7. season after winter — s p r i n g

Grade 3 76 Module 4 • Week 1

© Houghton Mifflin Harcourt Publishing Company. All rights reserved.

Know It, Show It, p. 76

Wrap-Up

Share Time

At the end of the Reading Workshop, have students reflect on their learning by sharing how they applied **ideas and support** or another area of focus during independent work time. Choose from these options:

- Use the **SOLO CHAIR** routine. Select a reader each day to come to the front of the class and tell what he or she learned from the reading by using a skill or strategy.
- **THINK-PAIR-SHARE** Students share their thinking with a partner. Select a few pairs each day to share with the whole class.
- **RETURN TO ANCHOR CHART** Have students add sticky notes about their independent reading to the Ideas and Support Anchor Chart. Call on a few students to explain what they added and why.

ANCHOR CHART 21: Ideas and Support

Online Ed

Consonant Digraphs

Step 1 Introduce the Skill

Consonant Digraphs Display and read aloud the word *chop*, emphasizing the initial sound /ch/.

- Underline *ch*. Note that the letters *ch* stand for the /ch/ sound.
- Display the words *catch, shape, wheel, think, phase,* and *king* and underline the consonant digraph in each word.
- Guide students to read the words aloud.
- Display the following chart.

ch	tch	sh	wh	th	ph	ng
chase	sketch	shine	whine	thin	photo	thing
chill	pitch	short	what	thump	phone	bang
such	ditch	brush	whiz	math	graph	long

- Remind students that they have learned to spell several consonant digraphs. Point out the spelling patterns in the top row of the chart.
- Then read aloud the example words in each column, emphasizing the consonant digraph in each while underlining the letters that stand for the sound.
- Guide students to read the words aloud.

LEARNING OBJECTIVES

- Recognize and decode words with consonant digraphs *ch, tch, sh, wh, th, ph,* and *ng*.
- Spell and write words with consonant digraphs .
- **Language** Read words with consonant digraphs and understand their meanings.

MATERIALS Online Ed

Display and Engage *Decoding 4.1*
Know It, Show It *p. 76*

EL ENGLISH LEARNER SUPPORT: Support Word Meaning

SUBSTANTIAL
Ensure that students understand the meaning of each Blend and Read word by sharing pictures or gestures.

MODERATE
Support students in understanding the meaning of each Blend and Read word by providing oral examples or context sentences. Guide students to think of additional examples or sentences.

LIGHT
Challenge students to create context sentences for some of the Blend and Read words on their own.

Step 2 Guided Practice

- Project Display and Engage: **Decoding 4.1**.
- Have students read the Blend and Read lines aloud. Provide feedback as needed.
- At the end of each line, prompt a conversation about the words: *How are the sounds and spellings in the words the same? How are they different?*
- Have partners reread the Blend and Read lines and quiz each other on the spellings of the consonant digraphs.

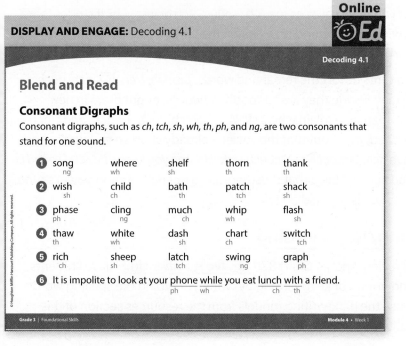

Online Ed

DISPLAY AND ENGAGE: Decoding 4.1

Decoding 4.1

Blend and Read

Consonant Digraphs

Consonant digraphs, such as *ch, tch, sh, wh, th, ph,* and *ng*, are two consonants that stand for one sound.

1	song (ng)	where (wh)	shelf (sh)	thorn (th)	thank (th)
2	wish (sh)	child (ch)	bath (th)	patch (tch)	shack (sh)
3	phase (ph)	cling (ng)	much (ch)	whip (wh)	flash (sh)
4	thaw (th)	white (wh)	dash (sh)	chart (ch)	switch (tch)
5	rich (ch)	sheep (sh)	latch (tch)	swing (ng)	graph (ph)

6 It is impolite to look at your phone (ph) while (wh) you eat lunch (ch) with (th) a friend.

Grade 3 | Foundational Skills Module 4 • Week 1

Step 3 Apply

INDEPENDENT PRACTICE

- Have students work in small groups or with partners to complete Know It, Show It page 76.
- Encourage students to share with each other the strategies they use to decode words with consonant digraphs.

CORRECT & REDIRECT

If students have trouble decoding words with consonant digraphs, use the model below.

- **Correct** the error. *The letters* ph *can stand for the /f/ sound.*
- **Model** how to decode the word *graph*. */grăp/. That does not sound right. I will try another sound for the letters* ph*: /grăf/,* graph*. That sounds like a word I know.*
- **Guide** students to decode other words: *chart, shelf, white*, and *cling*.
- **Check** students' understanding by displaying the word *switch*. *What spelling pattern helps you decode this word?*
- **Reinforce** by repeating the process with the word *thorn*.

Spelling the /ch/ Sound

LEARNING OBJECTIVES

- Learn spelling patterns for consonant digraphs *ch* and *tch*.
- **Language** Spell words with consonant digraphs *ch* and *tch* and understand their meanings.

MATERIALS **Online** Ed

Anchor Chart 37 *Cursive Handwriting*

Printables *Anchor Chart 37: Cursive Handwriting, Dictation Sentences 4.1, Spelling Word Cards 4.1, Proofreading 4.1*

Optional *Use Printable Dictation Sentences 4.1 to administer a pretest.*

SPELLING WORDS

BASIC	REVIEW
1. fetch	**15. wreck**
2. stretch	**16. knock**
3. roach	**17. wrist**
4. each	**18. wrong**
5. peach	**CHALLENGE**
6. screech	**19. stretcher**
7. snatch	**20. switching**
8. hatch	**21. launch**
9. branch	**22. slouch**
10. clutch	
11. trench	
12. cinch	
13. ouch	
14. couch	

Introduce the Spelling Words

- Before working with the basic and challenge words, you might want to revisit the review words. These also appear in Printable: **Dictation Sentences 4.1**. Display one of the Spelling Anchor Chart Printables, as appropriate.
- Cut apart and display the spelling word cards from Printable: **Spelling Word Cards 4.1**. Read each word aloud and discuss its meaning as needed.

Sort the Words

- Sort the words *fetch, stretch, roach, each, peach, screech, snatch, hatch,* and *clutch* into two columns, *–ch* and *–tch.* Ask: *What do you notice? Are there any clues that tell you when you spell the /ch/ sound –tch or just –ch?* If students are unsure, ask what vowel sound they hear in the *-ch* column (long) and the *–tch* column (short). *What generalization tells us when to use –ch or –tch?*
- Next, ask students to sort the remaining words: *branch, trench, cinch, ouch, couch.* They may decide they are all "oddball" words, or put them in new columns. Ask them to explain why. Ask: *Why don't* branch, trench, *and* cinch *end in* tch? As needed, point out that the vowel is already short so you don't need *tch*—you have *nch*. For *ouch* and *couch*, ask: *How do you know the /ch/ sound is spelled* ch *and not* tch? Elicit that these words do not have a short vowel sound, so the /ch/ sound is not spelled *tch*.

Handwriting/Keyboarding

- Display and review Anchor Chart 37: **Cursive Handwriting**. Have students practice handwriting or keyboarding by writing or typing the spelling words. As needed, use the handwriting models from the resources section of this Teacher's Guide.

Teacher Tip

- Point out: *There are many ways to spell the same sound in English. The spelling of sounds often depends on where they occur, their position, in words. Remembering this will help narrow down possible spellings for a sound. Although the* **/ch/** sound is spelled two ways at the end of words or syllables, it is spelled only one way, ch, at the beginning of a word.

ENGLISH LEARNER SUPPORT: Support Word Meaning

ALL LEVELS Make sure students understand the meaning of the spelling words and dictation sentences. If necessary, use visuals or gestures as support. After you've reinforced word meanings, have students practice reading the spelling words aloud.

LINK TO SMALL-GROUP INSTRUCTION

REINFORCE FOUNDATIONAL SKILLS For spelling practice for the remainder of the week: Display this week's spelling words for reference and have students work with Printable: **Proofreading 4.1**. Remind students to check the spelling words they use in the writing section to confirm they have spelled the words correctly.

Expression

Introduce the Skill

LEARNING OBJECTIVES

- Read orally with expression.
- Read aloud grade-level text with fluency and accuracy.
- Apply decoding skills when reading connected text.
- **Language** Comprehend texts using teacher support.

MATERIALS **Online** Ed

Printable *Fluency 4.1*
Word Cards *3.34–3.36*

DECODING ⟶ FLUENCY CONNECTION

The passage on Printable: Fluency 4.1 includes words that contain this week's decoding element. Use the passage to monitor whether students can accurately and fluently read these grade-level words.

HIGH-FREQUENCY WORDS

- **dance**
- **speak**
- **paint**

- Explain that when good readers read aloud, they match the expression in their voices to the words in the selection.
- Distribute Printable: **Fluency 4.1** to students, and project it for whole-group discussion. Tell students that you will demonstrate how to read the passage with appropriate expression.
- Read aloud the first paragraph with no expression as students follow along. Then reread it with appropriate expression. Ask students which was an example of good reading. Point out words, phrases, and punctuation that helped you decide what kind of expression to use. Then read the entire passage. Point out how you decoded the words *athlete, challenge, trophies,* and *theme* by using the consonant digraphs.
- After you finish reading the passage, have students read it aloud with you, using the **CHORAL READING** routine.

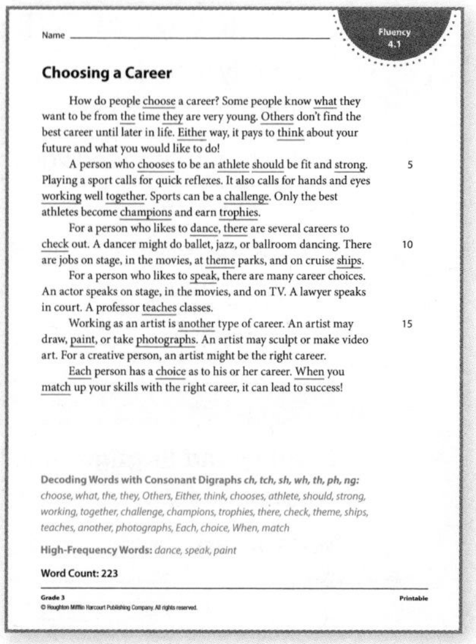
Name ______

Fluency 4.1

Choosing a Career

How do people choose a career? Some people know what they want to be from the time they are very young. Others don't find the best career until later in life. Either way, it pays to think about your future and what you would like to do!

A person who chooses to be an athlete should be fit and strong. Playing a sport calls for quick reflexes. It also calls for hands and eyes working well together. Sports can be a challenge. Only the best athletes become champions and earn trophies.

For a person who likes to dance, there are several careers to check out. A dancer might do ballet, jazz, or ballroom dancing. There are jobs on stage, in the movies, at theme parks, and on cruise ships.

For a person who likes to speak, there are many career choices. An actor speaks on stage, in the movies, and on TV. A lawyer speaks in court. A professor teaches classes.

Working as an artist is another type of career. An artist may draw, paint, or take photographs. An artist may sculpt or make video art. For a creative person, an artist might be the right career.

Each person has a choice as to his or her career. When you match up your skills with the right career, it can lead to success!

Decoding Words with Consonant Digraphs ***ch, tch, sh, wh, th, ph, ng:*** *choose, what, the, they, Others, Either, think, chooses, athlete, should, strong, working, together, challenge, champions, trophies, there, check, theme, ships, teaches, another, photographs, Each, choice, When, match*

High-Frequency Words: *dance, speak, paint*

Word Count: 223

Grade 3 Printable

Printable: Fluency 4.1

Apply

- Have students work in pairs or small groups using the **PARTNER READING** routine to read aloud the passage.
- Monitor students' reading for expression. Note especially how students handle the more challenging words, such as *reflexes, ballet, creative,* and *success,* and provide support, as needed.

HIGH-FREQUENCY WORDS

Point out the high-frequency words in the passage on Printable: **Fluency 4.1**. Remind students that high-frequency words appear often in texts they read. Students can learn to recognize them, rather than decode them, so that they can read more fluently.

Print and distribute **Word Cards 3.34–3.36**, which feature this week's high-frequency words, and have students work independently or in pairs to read and complete the activities for each word. For struggling readers, walk through the notes for one or two words before they continue working with a partner.

EL **ENGLISH LEARNER SUPPORT: Support Comprehension**

ALL LEVELS As you model reading fluently, have students raise their hand when they hear a word they do not recognize. Work with students to decode the word and practice saying it aloud. Discuss the word's meaning, using gestures or pictures for support if needed. Then have students read the entire sentence chorally. Provide corrective feedback, as needed.

Introduce Critical Vocabulary

Step 1 Introduce the Words

LEARNING OBJECTIVES

- Identify real-life connections between words and their use.
- Use newly acquired vocabulary expressively.
- **Language** Answer questions and discuss meanings to develop vocabulary.

MATERIALS

Online Ed

Display and Engage *Critical Vocabulary 4.2*

Vocabulary Cards *4.5–4.9*

CRITICAL VOCABULARY

- **genuine (p. 306)**
- **saga (p. 307)**
- **coiled (p. 310)**
- **whirled (p. 312)**
- **tame (p. 312)**

SPANISH COGNATES

genuine *genuino*

Project Display and Engage: Critical Vocabulary 4.2. Then use the **VOCABULARY** routine to introduce the Critical Vocabulary from *The Saga of Pecos Bill*. You may wish to display the corresponding Vocabulary Card for each word as you discuss it.

1. Read aloud each word and have students repeat it.
2. Read aloud and discuss each word's student-friendly explanation.
3. Point out the example for the word. Have students suggest other examples.

Online Ed

DISPLAY AND ENGAGE:
Critical Vocabulary 4.2

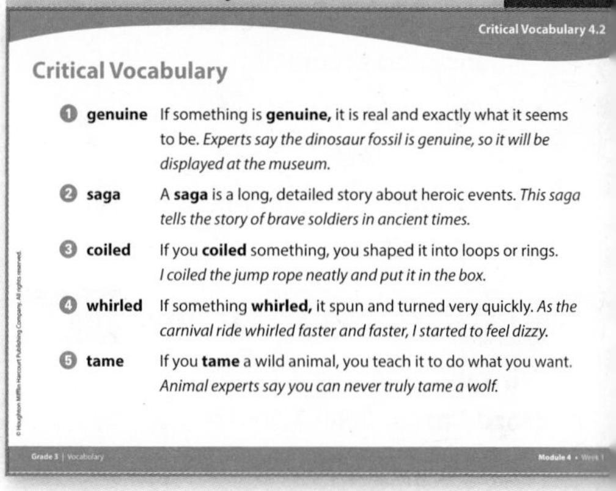
Critical Vocabulary 4.2

Critical Vocabulary

1. **genuine** If something is **genuine,** it is real and exactly what it seems to be. *Experts say the dinosaur fossil is genuine, so it will be displayed at the museum.*
2. **saga** A **saga** is a long, detailed story about heroic events. *This saga tells the story of brave soldiers in ancient times.*
3. **coiled** If you **coiled** something, you shaped it into loops or rings. *I coiled the jump rope neatly and put it in the box.*
4. **whirled** If something **whirled,** it spun and turned very quickly. *As the carnival ride whirled faster and faster, I started to feel dizzy.*
5. **tame** If you **tame** a wild animal, you teach it to do what you want. *Animal experts say you can never truly tame a wolf.*

TEACHER TIP

Encourage authentic **vocabulary usage** in your classroom. Students score a point each time they use a new vocabulary word in conversation.

ENGLISH LEARNER SUPPORT: Build Vocabulary

SUBSTANTIAL

Ask partners to demonstrate the word *whirled* using classroom objects (or themselves).

MODERATE

Have students use this sentence frame to explain the word *whirled*: *If something whirled, it* _____.

LIGHT

Have pairs make up context sentences describing something that whirled.

Step 2 Guided Practice

Guide students to interact with the words by discussing questions such as these:

- *If something is **genuine,** should you be suspicious that it is fake? Why or why not?*
- *Might a **saga** be about what happened today at lunch? Why or why not?*
- *If you **coiled** something, would it end up long and straight? Explain.*
- *When you come across an animal in the forest, is it likely to be **tame?** Why or why not?*
- *If you **whirled,** would you jump up and down, move from side to side, or go around in circles?*

Ask students to point to something in the room that can be coiled, and have them demonstrate with gestures how something would look if it whirled. Ask students how they can tell when something is genuine or fake. Have students tell what makes a story a saga. Ask them to name animals that might be hard to tame.

Step 3 Apply

- Have students work independently to complete steps 3 and 4 on Vocabulary Cards 4.5–4.9.
- Have students use the **TURN AND TALK** routine to discuss with a partner the prompt on each Vocabulary Card.

Vocabulary Cards

LEARNING MINDSET

Self-Reflection

Model Explain to students one way that you have benefited from self-reflection. *Sometimes, I have to look closely at how I learn to help me apply the new knowledge. For example, when I see or hear a new word, I have to look up the meaning and use it in a sentence. I know that if I don't, I could forget the word's meaning.*

Visualize

Step 1 Connect and Teach

LEARNING OBJECTIVES

- Create mental images while reading.
- **Language** Articulate visualizations using details from the text.

MATERIALS Online Ed

Anchor Chart 6 *Visualize*
Printable *Anchor Chart 6: Visualize*
Teaching Pal *Book 1, pp. 304–317*
***my*Book** *Book 1, The Saga of Pecos Bill, pp. 304–317*
Display and Engage *Build Background 4.2*

INSTRUCTIONAL VOCABULARY

- **visualize** when a reader creates or pictures images in his or her mind in order to understand a text.

- Tell students that they are going to read a drama called *The Saga of Pecos Bill* by Anthony D. Fredericks. Tell students that as they read dramas, or plays, they should use their senses (sight, smell, hearing, taste, and touch) to **visualize,** or create pictures in their mind.
- Project or display Anchor Chart 6: Visualize. Use the chart to explain that authors include details that connect to readers' senses. Point out that these details make a story come to life by helping readers see, smell, hear, taste, and feel what's happening.
- Point out that as they read, it is a good strategy to ask themselves questions about the text. Review the questions for each sense on the Anchor Chart.
- Tell students that they will practice visualizing when they read *The Saga of Pecos Bill.*

Online
ANCHOR CHART 6: Visualize

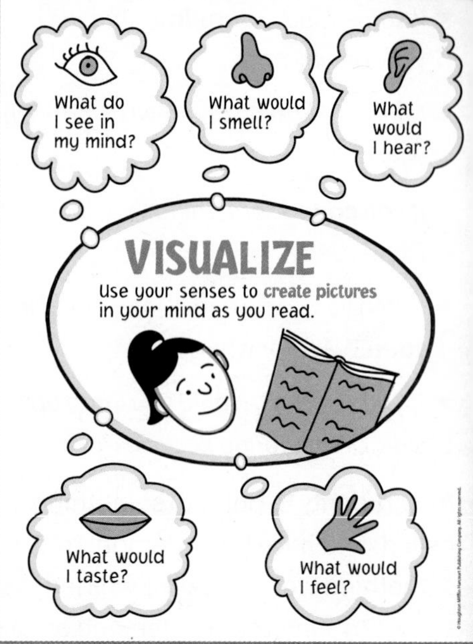

What do I see in my mind?
What would I smell?
What would I hear?
VISUALIZE
Use your senses to create pictures in your mind as you read.
What would I taste?
What would I feel?

Notice & Note

Contrasts and Contradictions

- The Teaching Pal prompts in this lesson feature the **Notice & Note Signpost: Contrasts and Contradictions.**
- As needed, refer to p. T208 to review the signpost with students.

ASSESSMENT OPTION

Assign the Selection Quiz to check comprehension of *The Saga of Pecos Bill.*

Go to Your Teaching Pal

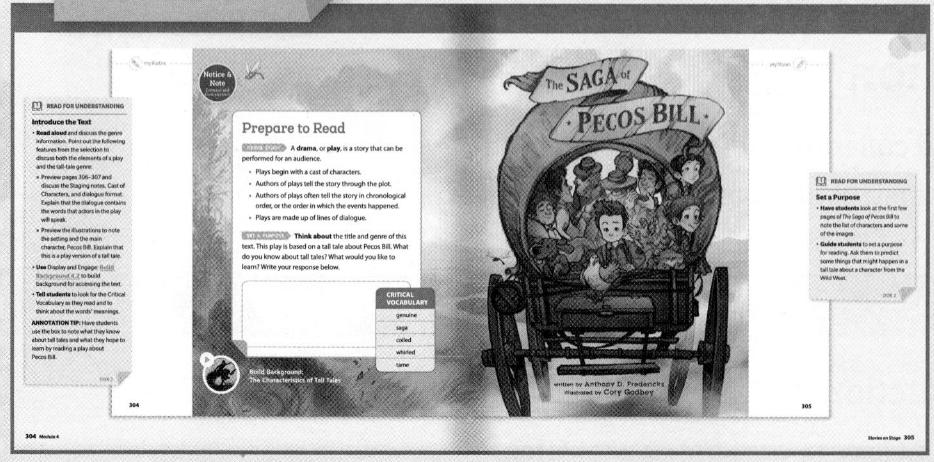

READ FOR UNDERSTANDING

Introduce the Text

- **Read aloud** and discuss the genre information. Point out the following features from the selection to discuss both the elements of a play and the tall-tale genre:
  - Preview pages 306–307 and discuss the Staging notes, Cast of Characters, and dialogue format. Explain that the dialogue contains the words that actors in the play will speak.
  - Preview the illustrations to note the setting and the main character, Pecos Bill. Explain that this is a play version of a tall tale.
- **Use** Display and Engage: Build Background 4.2 to build background for accessing the text.
- **Tell students** to look for the Critical Vocabulary as they read and to think about the words' meanings.

ANNOTATION TIP: Have students use the box to note what they know about tall tales and what they hope to learn by reading a play about Pecos Bill.

DOK 2

myNotes

Notice & Note

Prepare to Read

GENRE STUDY A **drama**, or **play**, is a story that can be performed for an audience.

- Plays begin with a cast of characters.
- Authors of plays tell the story through the plot.
- Authors of plays often tell the story in chronological order, or the order in which the events happened.
- Plays are made up of lines of dialogue.

SET A PURPOSE **Think about** the title and genre of this text. This play is based on a tall tale about Pecos Bill. What do you know about tall tales? What would you like to learn? Write your response below.

CRITICAL VOCABULARY: genuine, saga, coiled, whirled, tame

Build Background: The Characteristics of Tall Tales

304

The SAGA of PECOS BILL

written by Anthony D. Fredericks
illustrated by Cory Godbey

305

myNotes

READ FOR UNDERSTANDING

Set a Purpose

- **Have students** look at the first few pages of *The Saga of Pecos Bill* to note the list of characters and some of the images.
- **Guide students** to set a purpose for reading. Ask them to predict some things that might happen in a tall tale about a character from the Wild West.

DOK 2

304 Module 4

Stories on Stage 305

Online Ed

ANNOTATE IT!

Students may use the annotation tools in their eBook.

Step 2 Apply to Text

In your Teaching Pal, pages 304–317, use the blue **READ FOR UNDERSTANDING** prompts and the red **Notice & Note** prompts to read *The Saga of Pecos Bill* as students follow along and annotate their *my*Book.

- **Genre Study** Guide students through the genre information on page 304.
- **Set a Purpose** Read the Set a Purpose section on page 304. Prompt students to set their own purpose for reading *The Saga of Pecos Bill*.
- **Build Background** Project Display and Engage: Build Background 4.2. and read the information aloud with students. Ask students what might be challenging about presenting a tall tale as a play on stage.
- **Read and Comprehend** Use the **READ FOR UNDERSTANDING** routine as you guide students to read the selection. Pause occasionally, using the prompts in your Teaching Pal to gauge students' understanding and to have them visualize what is happening. As students visualize, have them refer back to the Anchor Chart to determine which senses they are using.

Step 3 Engage and Respond

INDEPENDENT PRACTICE: Speaking and Listening

- After reading, use the **COLLABORATIVE CONVERSATION** routine with the Collaborative Discussion questions on Teaching Pal and *my*Book page 315. Have students annotate their *my*Book with details from the text and visuals as evidence to explain their responses.
- Ask volunteers to read aloud the Speaking and Listening tips. Remind students to speak clearly so that they are understood by everyone. Tell group members to do their part to keep the discussion focused on the selection and the questions.
- You may want to have students conduct their discussions during daily small-group time.

EL ENGLISH LEARNER SUPPORT: Facilitate Discussion

SUBSTANTIAL

Supply sentence frames: *The words _____ make me see/smell/hear/taste/feel _____.*

MODERATE

Provide frames such as the following: *When I read _____, I visualize _____.*

LIGHT

Encourage students to add more detail as they describe what they visualize from the text.

LINK TO SMALL-GROUP INSTRUCTION

REINFORCE VISUALIZE Review and extend the skill as needed during small-group time to support students' need for differentiation. *See the lesson on p. T235.*

Options for Differentiation

As the class engages in independent and collaborative work, meet with Guided Reading Groups or differentiate instruction based on student need.

GUIDED READING GROUPS

Match Students to Books + Instruction

- Choose just-right books based on level, skill, topic, or genre.

L → M → N → O → P → Q

Leveled Readers

- Deliver instruction with each book's **Take and Teach Lesson**, choosing appropriate sessions based on need.

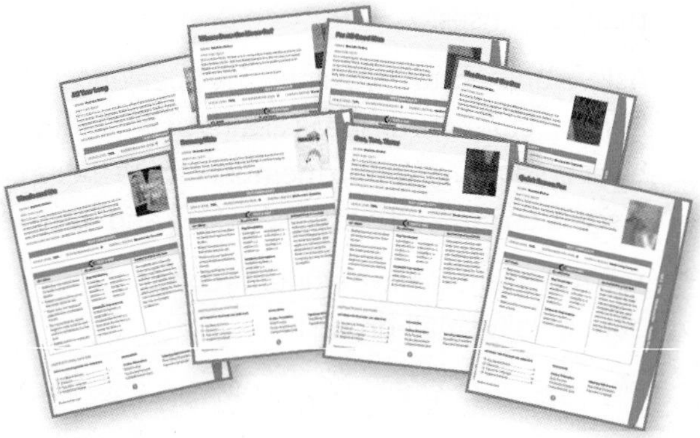

- Check comprehension, reinforce instruction, and extend learning with suggested supporting activities.

Rigby LEVELED LIBRARY

EL ENGLISH LEARNER SUPPORT

Infer

- Use **Tabletop Minilessons: English Language Development 10.1 (Speaking)** to reinforce and practice the language skill.

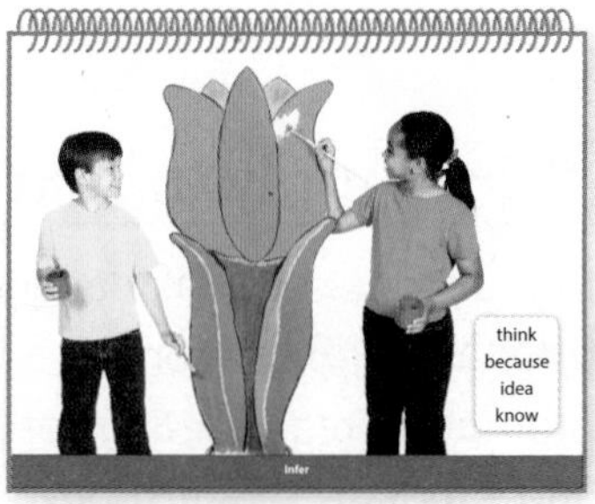

Tabletop Minilessons: English Language Development

- Then use the following text-based prompts with *The Saga of Pecos Bill* to guide application of the language skill. Begin with the prompt at the student's identified language proficiency level. As students progress, use lighter supports to encourage increased language proficiency.

SUBSTANTIAL
Read aloud paragraph 3. Clarify meaning as needed. Then ask: *Can a real baby take home a bear from the woods? Is this story realistic? Is the author using exaggeration.*

MODERATE
Read paragraph 3 with students. Ask: *Is this play realistic or fantasy?* Have students answer using text evidence and the sentence frame: *I can infer that this text is _____ because it says _____.*

LIGHT
After students have read the text, ask: *Is this play supposed to be realistic or fantasy? How can you tell?* Have students answer orally.

REINFORCE VISUALIZE

Demonstrate

- Use **Tabletop Minilessons: Reading Card 6** to remind students that when they **visualize,** they create pictures in their mind based on details in the text. To help them visualize, they should pay attention to details that describe the five senses of sight, smell, hearing, touch, and taste.
- Model filling out Printable: Reading Graphic Organizer 6 to visualize elements of *The Saga of Pecos Bill.*

Tabletop Minilessons: Reading

Apply to Independent Reading

- Now have students visualize information in an appropriate book or article they are reading independently. Customize these prompts to the texts students choose.
  » *What details describe sight, smell, hearing, touch, or taste?*
  » *What did the details in the text help you to visualize?*
  » *How did visualizing help you better understand what you read?*
- Have students complete Printable: Reading Graphic Organizer 6 for their independent reading book.

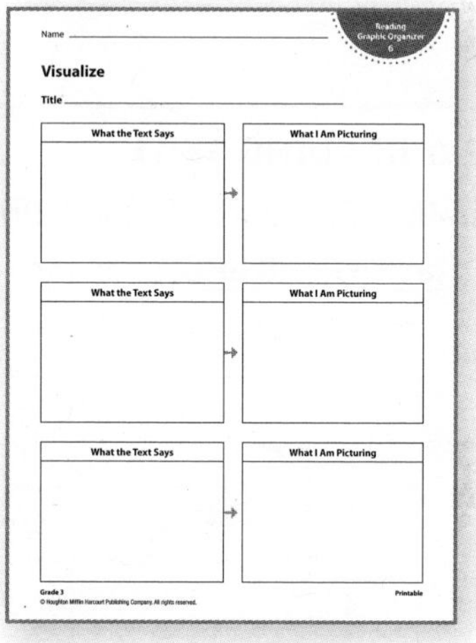
Name
Reading Graphic Organizer 6
Visualize
Title

What the Text Says	What I Am Picturing

Grade 3 Printable

Printable: Reading Graphic Organizer 6

ALMOST THERE

READY FOR MORE

SCAFFOLD AND EXTEND

- Point out a detail in the text. Prompt students to say what it helps them visualize.
- Prompt students to visualize using details in the text and tell how it helped them in their reading.
- Have students elaborate on how visualizing helped them better understand the text.

EL ENGLISH LEARNER SUPPORT

SUBSTANTIAL
Use gestures to ask about the five senses in the text. Example: *What word describes something you hear? The word* ______.

MODERATE
Provide sentence frames to help students visualize: *I read the details* ______. *They helped me visualize* ______.

LIGHT
Have students explain their thinking as they answer the questions.

Options for Independent and Collaborative Work

While you meet with small groups, have other students engage in literacy activities that reinforce the lesson's learning objectives. Choose from these options.

Independent Reading

Student Choice Library

Rigby
LEVELED LIBRARY

APPLY READING SKILL

Visualize Students complete Printable: Reading Graphic Organizer 6 for an independent reading book.

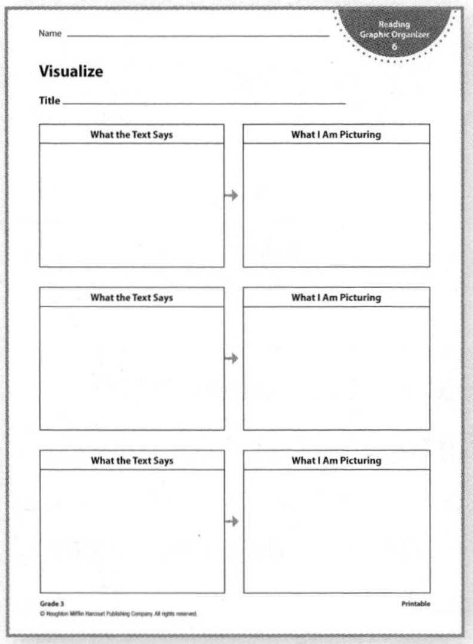

Name

Reading Graphic Organizer 6

Visualize

Title

What the Text Says	What I Am Picturing

What the Text Says	What I Am Picturing

What the Text Says	What I Am Picturing

Grade 3 Printable
© Houghton Mifflin Harcourt Publishing Company. All rights reserved.

Printable: Reading Graphic Organizer 6

APPLY LANGUAGE SKILL

Infer Students complete Printable: Language Graphic Organizer 7 for an independent reading book.

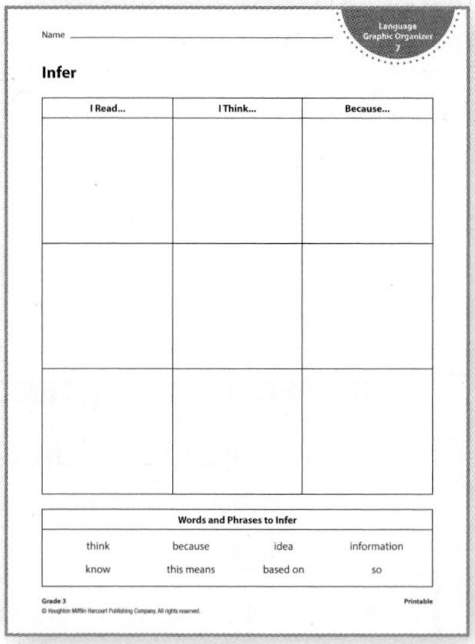

Name

Language Graphic Organizer 7

Infer

I Read...	I Think...	Because...

Words and Phrases to Infer			
think	because	idea	information
know	this means	based on	so

Grade 3 Printable
© Houghton Mifflin Harcourt Publishing Company. All rights reserved.

Printable: Language Graphic Organizer 7

Notice & Note

Contrasts and Contradictions

When students encounter this signpost in their independent biography reading, encourage them to ask and answer the Anchor Question: *Why would the character feel/act this way?*

Literacy Centers

See pp. T214–T215.

- READING CENTER
- VOCABULARY CENTER
- DIGITAL STATION
- WRITING CENTER
- PROJECT CENTER

Speaking and Listening

Partners discuss the Collaborative Discussion questions. *See Engage and Respond, p. T233.*

Wrap-Up

Share Time

At the end of the Reading Workshop, have students reflect on their learning by sharing how they applied **visualize** or another area of focus during independent work time. Choose from these options:

- Use the **SOLO CHAIR** routine. Select a reader each day to come to the front of the class and tell what he or she learned from the reading by using a skill or strategy.
- **THINK-PAIR-SHARE** Students share their thinking with a partner. Select a few pairs each day to share with the whole class.
- **RETURN TO ANCHOR CHART** Have students add sticky notes about their independent reading to the Visualize Anchor Chart. Call on a few students to explain what they added and why.

Online Ed

ANCHOR CHART 6: Visualize

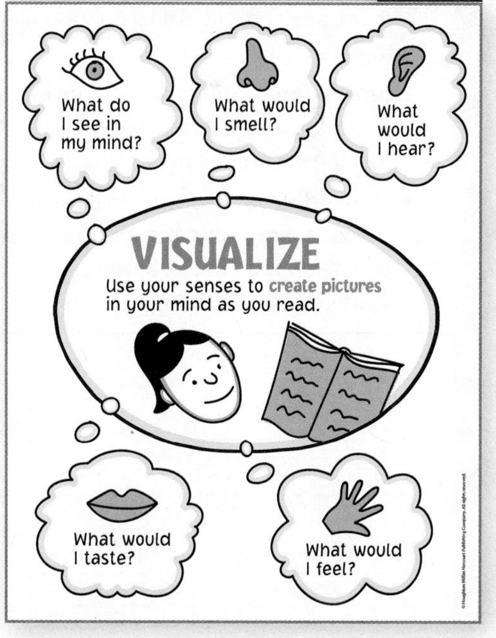

Teacher Read-Aloud

Step 1 Introduce the Text

LEARNING OBJECTIVES

- Listen to fluent reading.
- Use details to connect to meaning.
- **Language** Comprehend details to connect to meaning.

MATERIALS

Online Ed

myBook *Book 1, pp. 296–299*

QUICK TEACH WORDS

If students need support for understanding unfamiliar vocabulary they hear, provide the following student friendly explanations.

- **trials** Trials are difficult challenges that test a person's strength or courage. They are sometimes tough to overcome.
- **boasts** This is talking or bragging too much about oneself.
- **curtain call** You know the show is over when the performers come out for their curtain call. They step forward while the audience claps for them, and end with a final bow all together.
- **professional** Someone working in an occupation that requires special training is a professional.
- **focused** To be focused is to have all of your energy, your attention, directed toward the task. You aren't scattered or distracted.

Tell students that they will be listening to a text you will read aloud about a kid who is an actor in a well-known musical play called *The Lion King*. Ask students if they are familiar with the particular play or if they have ever seen a play. Have them share what they know in general about how plays are performed. Explain the roles of actors, acts and scenes, the stage, and the audience. Then discuss what things an actor might need to do to prepare for a role on stage.

- **Genre Study** Tell students that they will be listening to an informational text. Remind them that informational texts give facts and information about a topic. Explain that this selection describes what it is like to act in a play, based on the experience of Sydney McNeal, a real child actor in the play. It includes words specific to preparing for and performing in a play.
- **Set a Purpose** Lead students to set a purpose for listening, such as listening to find out what it is like to be an actor. Encourage students to listen for context clues that will help them determine the meanings of any unfamiliar words they hear.
- **Model Fluency** Tell students to listen to how you read aloud accurately with intonation and expression and at an appropriate rate.
- **Listen and Comprehend** Read the text aloud, pausing occasionally to ask the questions in the margins.

ENGLISH LEARNER SUPPORT: Connect to Meaning

SUBSTANTIAL/MODERATE

Ask students to draw and label what they just heard about.

LIGHT

To help students connect to meaning, call out specific details about Sydney McNeal's experience while reading. Then ask: *What does this tell you about what it's like to be an actor?*

READ-ALOUD TEXT

The Lion King's Friend

Do you know the story about the Lion King? You might have seen the movie. Or you might even have been lucky enough to see the musical. A man who writes about theater says that *The Lion King* is "kid-friendly." Sydney McNeal knows how true that is. When Sydney was only ten years old, she was an actor in the Broadway production of the play. **A**

Just imagine that you're young Sydney . . .*Not everybody is allowed backstage at the New Amsterdam Theater in New York City. But you are! That's because you have an important role in* The Lion King, *the Broadway musical.*

The Lion King is the tale of Simba, a young lion coming of age. Through **trials** *and troubles, the lion grows up to take his place on the throne of the animal kingdom. You play young Nala, dear friend of Simba.* **B**

At the back door of the theater, a guard nods good morning and lets you in. You climb some stairs and walk down a hallway. You greet everybody as you pass, finally stopping in front of your door. (The door **boasts** *a gold star with your name and the words "Lion King" underneath.) You check for messages about today's performance, then make your way to the makeup room.*

As you take your place in the makeup/ hair/costume room, your co-star, the boy who plays Simba, sits next to you. Around you are all sorts of wigs and makeup. The hairdresser carefully weaves a microphone system into your hair. You and your fellow actors are quiet as makeup artists transform you into your animal characters. The makeup artist paints your face with an imaginative young lion "mask." Someone asks if getting made up tickles. "Nope," you answer. **C**

A loudspeaker announces, "Ladies and gentlemen, this is your 15-minute call. Fifteen!" Later, "Have a great show, everybody," someone shouts. "You, too!" you answer. And off you go . . .

The show goes well, as always. The audience loves it, especially the kids. After the final **curtain call**, *it's backstage again.*

A What does it mean to say a show or movie is "kid-friendly?" What is the twist on that meaning when the article says Sydney "knows how true that is?" *("Kid-friendly" means the show isn't too grown-up. It's fine for kids* ***to see****. When the writer says Sydney knows how kid-friendly* The Lion King *is, she means:* ***to be in****. This is an amazing show for a child actor.)* DOK 2

B What character does Sydney play? *(Sydney plays the character Nala.)* DOK 1

What does the text tell you about the character, Nala? *(Nala is the "dear friend" and "partner" of Simba, who is the lead character.)* DOK 1

C What do you do *before* making your way to the makeup room? *(You check messages about today's performance.)* DOK 1

What do the actors do while they are being made up? *(They are quiet.)* DOK 1

READ-ALOUD TEXT, *continued*

D **What is balance? What does it mean to "balance" school and acting?** *(Balance is when two things are even. To balance school and acting means not letting one take up all your time and energy.)* DOK 2

At the time, young Sydney and her family lived in Montclair, New Jersey. She had taken dance and voice lessons but had little **professional** experience on stage before the role of young Nala came along. It wasn't easy to balance school and acting, but Sydney loved being onstage. **D**

"Imagine living your dream at age 10!" she exclaims. "Seriously, you have to be really **focused** to do this. Your family has to be supportive. If mine wasn't, I'd have had 500 nervous breakdowns." Teachers at Sydney's school have been understanding, too, she says. And "my best friends don't treat me differently." **E**

E **How does Sydney feel about landing a major role in a hit Broadway show?** *(It's her dream.)* DOK 1

Why does her family need to be supportive? *(If her family wasn't supportive, she says she would have had "500 nervous breakdowns.")* **What does that tell you this experience is like, besides being a "dream"?** *(It means the experience can be hugely stressful.)* DOK 2

How do Sydney's friends and teachers treat her? *(They are understanding and don't treat her differently.)* DOK 1

Sydney has some advice for anyone who *has been bitten by the acting bug*: "Never give up. Even if someone says you're not good enough. Just keep going." **F**

F **What do you think it means to be "bitten by the acting bug"?** *(You've been "infected" with a passion for acting.)* DOK 2

An advertisement for the play says, "*The Lion King*. See it now. Remember it forever." Sydney certainly will.

Step 2 Focus on Fluency

EXPRESSION

- Remind students that good readers use appropriate expression when they read aloud. That means showing with your voice the emotion and feelings the words express.
- Model reading aloud paragraph 10, which begins: *"Imagine living your dream at age 10!"* Read with a flat, emotionless expression.
- Read aloud the paragraph a second time with appropriate expression. Point out that the text is more interesting and easier to understand when you read with appropriate expression.
- Tell students they will have opportunities to practice reading with expression as they read other selections in this module.

Step 3 Engage and Respond

COMPARE SELECTIONS

Have students revisit the Essential Question on *my*Book page 297. Then help them recall the Get Curious Video *Auditions* and the text *That's Entertainment!* Have students discuss the following questions as a class or in small groups. Encourage them to use the Words About Plays on page 298 as they do.

1. *What do you now know about plays and how they are performed that you did not know before? (Responses will vary.)*
2. *How is the information in the video about auditions, the informational text* That's Entertainment!*, and the selection* The Lion King's Friend *the same and different? (All tell about how plays are performed. The video shows what auditions are and how they take place.* That's Entertainment *shows all the backstage workings of how a play is put on, and gives examples from the play* Peter Pan. The Lion King's Friend *tells what it is like to be an actor from the point of view of a real child actor.)*
3. *What do you hope to learn as you focus on the other selections in this module and search for answers to the Essential Question? (Responses will vary.)*

This discussion is an opportunity to reinforce good speaking and listening behaviors. Remind students to ask relevant questions and to offer comments that connect to the ideas already being discussed.

After the discussion, have students reflect on its effectiveness. Did everyone participate? Did students give everyone who wanted to a chance to speak? Did they listen to one another? Were students' comments and questions relevant to the topic?

EL ENGLISH LEARNER SUPPORT: Compare and Discuss

SUBSTANTIAL
Ask students what each of the selections focuses on using this sentence stem. ______ *is about* ______.

MODERATE
Focus on the content of student responses, not grammar or pronunciation.

LIGHT
Ask students to describe what they have learned so far about plays, and to describe what they found most interesting.

Review Critical Vocabulary

Step 1 Reinforce Vocabulary

- Project Display and Engage: Critical Vocabulary 4.2 to review and discuss the Critical Vocabulary, student-friendly explanations, and examples of the words. Have students take turns using the words in sentences.

Step 2 Guided Practice

- Have students work in pairs to create Four-Square Maps. For each of the Critical Vocabulary words, students should fold a blank sheet of paper into four equal sections. Display the steps below. As needed, direct students to Display and Engage 4.2 for the word meanings, and offer ideas if students get stuck on tricky words. (For example, for the word *genuine* you might suggest drawing a friendly, smiling person.)

1. In the first section, draw a picture that represents the word.
2. In the second section, write the meaning of the word.
3. In the third section, write a sentence using the word.
4. In the fourth section, write the word.

- Have students use the **COLLABORATIVE DISCUSSION** routine to discuss the sentences they wrote on their Four-Square Maps. Call on pairs to share their sentences. Positively reinforce students' correct word usage.

Step 3 Apply

INDEPENDENT PRACTICE

- Have students work in small groups or independently. Tell them to complete Know It, Show It page 77. For the last item on the page, tell students to include clues to each word's meaning in their sentences. Have groups share their sentences. Ask listeners to identify the context clue in each sentence.
- You may wish to have students complete the Know It, Show It page during Small Group time.

LEARNING OBJECTIVES

- Review and extend understanding of word meanings.
- Use context to determine the meanings of unfamiliar words.
- **Language** Use newly acquired vocabulary to answer questions and demonstrate understanding.

MATERIALS Online Ed

Display and Engage *Critical Vocabulary 4.2*

Know It, Show It *p. 77*

CRITICAL VOCABULARY

- **genuine**
- **saga**
- **coiled**
- **whirled**
- **tame**

ENGLISH LEARNER SUPPORT: Support Discussion and Practice

Use tiered supports as needed to help students as they answer questions about the Critical Vocabulary and generate ideas for their Four-Square Maps.

SUBSTANTIAL

Can a rope be coiled? Can a ladder be coiled?

MODERATE

If something is coiled, does it look bigger or smaller? Why?

LIGHT

What are some things that are often coiled?

Shades of Meaning

LEARNING OBJECTIVES

- Understand that synonyms are differentiated by shades of meaning and identify shades of meaning between synonyms.
- Use print and digital reference materials to clarify meanings.
- **Language** Identify shades of meaning using strategic learning techniques.

MATERIALS **Online** Ed

Display and Engage *Vocabulary Strategy 4.3*

INSTRUCTIONAL VOCABULARY

- **shades of meaning** small differences between words that mean almost the same thing

Step 1 Introduce the Strategy

Project Display and Engage: **Vocabulary Strategy 4.3**. Read aloud the two paragraphs.

Online Ed

DISPLAY AND ENGAGE:
Vocabulary Strategy 4.3

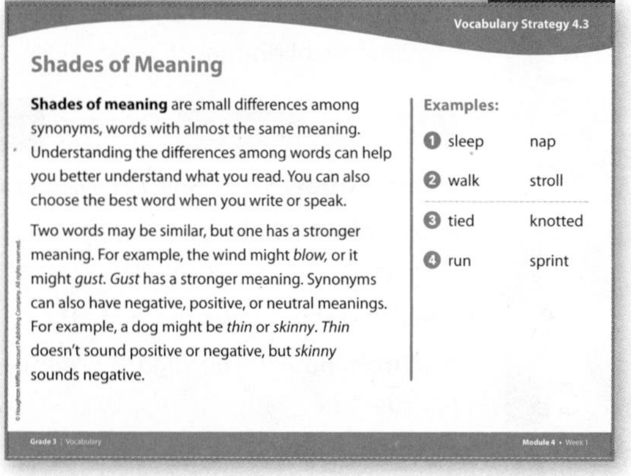
Vocabulary Strategy 4.3

Shades of Meaning

Shades of meaning are small differences among synonyms, words with almost the same meaning. Understanding the differences among words can help you better understand what you read. You can also choose the best word when you write or speak.

Two words may be similar, but one has a stronger meaning. For example, the wind might *blow*, or it might *gust*. *Gust* has a stronger meaning. Synonyms can also have negative, positive, or neutral meanings. For example, a dog might be *thin* or *skinny*. *Thin* doesn't sound positive or negative, but *skinny* sounds negative.

Examples:

1. sleep nap
2. walk stroll
3. tied knotted
4. run sprint

Grade 3 | Vocabulary Module 4 • Week 1

- Tell students that synonyms, or words with similar meanings, usually don't mean exactly the same thing. There are small differences between them, and these are called shades of meaning. Explain that identifying shades of meaning will help them better understand what they read.
- Use the first two examples to model shades of meaning. *The words* tall *and* towering *are synonyms. They have similar meanings.* Towering *means "tall", but it has a different shade of meaning. If something is* towering, *it is extremely tall, especially in comparison with the things around it. The words* walk *and* stroll *are also synonyms. When you* stroll, *you are walking. However,* stroll *has a different shade of meaning. To* stroll *means to "walk in a relaxed way for a short distance."*

Step 2 Guided Practice

- Have students read the next two pairs of words and identify their shades of meaning. Invite them to use a reference source as needed to check the definitions.
- Ask students to explain the differences between the words in each pair.

Step 3 Apply the Strategy

INDEPENDENT PRACTICE

- Point out the words *saga* and *survive* in *The Saga of Pecos Bill.* Have students work independently to find a synonym for each word, using reference sources as needed.
- For each word and its synonym, ask students to write a sentence or two explaining how the words are similar and how they differ in shades of meaning.
- Have students exchange their word pairs and sentences with partners and discuss one another's responses.

ENGLISH LEARNER SUPPORT: Understand Shades of Meaning

SUBSTANTIAL

Offer additional simple synonyms with shades of meaning and invite students to use oral sentences or gestures to explain their differences.

MODERATE

Supply sentence stems for each pair of synonyms: _____ *is a synonym for* _____*, but it's different because* _____.

LIGHT

Ask students to explain what makes each pair of words alike and what makes them different.

Elements of Drama

Step 1 Connect and Teach

- Tell students that a **drama,** or play, is a story performed by actors on a stage.
- Project or display the Anchor Chart 14: **Elements of Drama.**
- Explain that dramas, like stories, also have characters, dialogue, and settings. Point out that reading a drama is really reading a **script,** or the text of a play.
- Tell students that the script for a drama has features that a story does not often have. Use the Anchor Chart to define and describe narrator, **cast of characters, dialogue,** and **stage directions.**
- Tell students that just as a book is divided into chapters, a drama is also divided into parts. Review the information about **acts** and **scenes.** Explain that each scene builds on a previous scene to move the story forward.
- Tell students they will identify the elements of a drama to gain a deeper understanding of *The Saga of Pecos Bill.*

Online

ANCHOR CHART 14: Elements of Drama

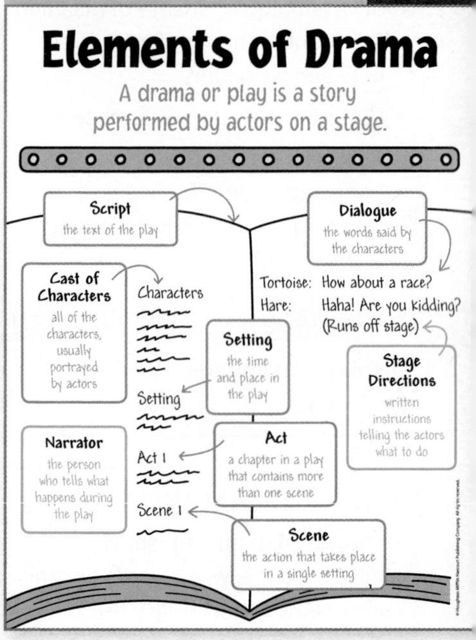
Elements of Drama
A drama or play is a story performed by actors on a stage.
Script
the text of the play
Dialogue
the words said by the characters
Cast of Characters
all of the characters, usually portrayed by actors
Characters
Tortoise: How about a race?
Hare: Haha! Are you kidding? (Runs off stage)
Setting
the time and place in the play
Stage Directions
written instructions telling the actors what to do
Setting
Narrator
the person who tells what happens during the play
Act
a chapter in a play that contains more than one scene
Act 1
Scene 1
Scene
the action that takes place in a single setting

LEARNING OBJECTIVES

- Identify elements of a drama.
- **Language** Identify and articulate the elements of drama.

MATERIALS | Online

Anchor Chart 14 *Elements of Drama*

Printable *Anchor Chart 14: Elements of Drama*

Teaching Pal *Book 1, pp. 304–317*

myBook *Book 1, The Saga of Pecos Bill, pp. 304–317*

Know It, Show It *p. 78*

INSTRUCTIONAL VOCABULARY

- **act** a chapter in a play that contains more than one scene
- **cast of characters** the characters in a drama or play
- **dialogue** the words that characters in a story or drama say aloud to each other
- **drama** a play or story that is acted out by people in a performance
- **scene** the action in a play that takes place in a single setting
- **script** the text of the play that includes the dialogue and the stage directions
- **stage direction** information in a drama that tells actors where to move, how to look or speak, or information about the set

Go to Your
Teaching Pal

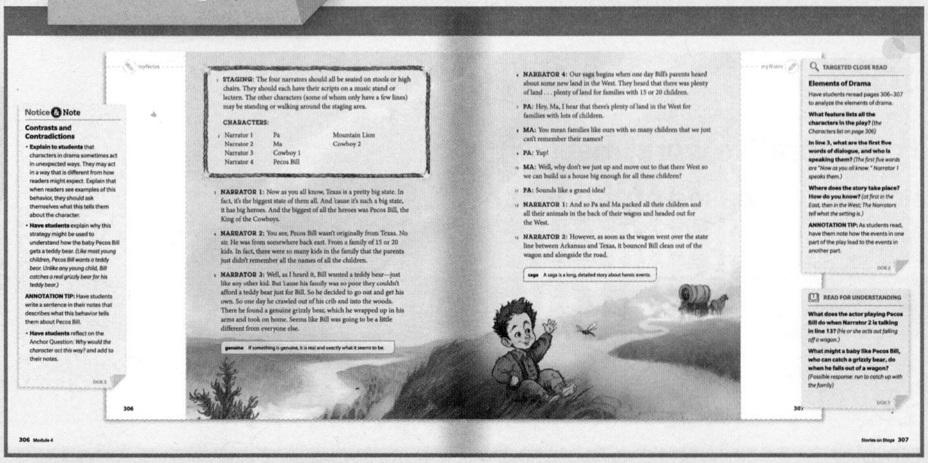

Notice & Note

Contrasts and Contradictions

- **Explain to students** that characters in drama sometimes act in unexpected ways. They may act in a way that is different from how readers might expect. Explain that when readers see examples of this behavior, they should ask themselves what this tells them about the character.
- **Have students** explain why this strategy might be used to understand how the baby Pecos Bill gets a teddy bear. *(Like most young children, Pecos Bill wants a teddy bear. Unlike any young child, Bill catches a real grizzly bear for his teddy bear.)*

ANNOTATION TIP: Have students write a sentence in their notes that describes what this behavior tells them about Pecos Bill.

- **Have students** reflect on the Anchor Question: *Why would the character act this way?* and add to their notes.

DOK 3

myNotes

1 **STAGING:** The four narrators should all be seated on stools or high chairs. They should each have their scripts on a music stand or lectern. The other characters (some of whom only have a few lines) may be standing or walking around the staging area.

CHARACTERS:

2 Narrator 1, Narrator 2, Narrator 3, Narrator 4, Pa, Ma, Cowboy 1, Pecos Bill, Mountain Lion, Cowboy 2

3 **NARRATOR 1:** Now as you all know, Texas is a pretty big state. In fact, it's the biggest state of them all. And 'cause it's such a big state, it has big heroes. And the biggest of all the heroes was Pecos Bill, the King of the Cowboys.

4 **NARRATOR 2:** You see, Pecos Bill wasn't originally from Texas. No sir. He was from somewhere back east. From a family of 15 or 20 kids. In fact, there were so many kids in the family that the parents just didn't remember all the names of all the children.

5 **NARRATOR 3:** Well, as I heard it, Bill wanted a teddy bear—just like any other kid. But 'cause his family was so poor they couldn't afford a teddy bear just for Bill. So he decided to go out and get his own. So one day he crawled out of his crib and into the woods. There he found a genuine grizzly bear, which he wrapped up in his arms and took on home. Seems like Bill was going to be a little different from everyone else.

genuine If something is genuine, it is real and exactly what it seems to be.

306

306 Module 4

6 **NARRATOR 4:** Our saga begins when one day Bill's parents heard about some new land in the West. They heard that there was plenty of land . . . plenty of land for families with 15 or 20 children.

7 **PA:** Hey, Ma, I hear that there's plenty of land in the West for families with lots of children.

8 **MA:** You mean families like ours with so many children that we just can't remember their names?

9 **PA:** Yup!

10 **MA:** Well, why don't we just up and move out to that there West so we can build us a house big enough for all these children?

11 **PA:** Sounds like a grand idea!

12 **NARRATOR 1:** And so Pa and Ma packed all their children and all their animals in the back of their wagon and headed out for the West.

13 **NARRATOR 2:** However, as soon as the wagon went over the state line between Arkansas and Texas, it bounced Bill clean out of the wagon and alongside the road.

saga A saga is a long, detailed story about heroic events.

307

myNotes

TARGETED CLOSE READ

Elements of Drama

Have students reread pages 306–307 to analyze the elements of drama.

What feature lists all the characters in the play? *(the Characters list on page 306)*

In line 3, what are the first five words of dialogue, and who is speaking them? *(The first five words are "Now as you all know." Narrator 1 speaks them.)*

Where does the story take place? How do you know? *(at first in the East, then in the West; The Narrators tell what the setting is.)*

ANNOTATION TIP: As students read, have them note how the events in one part of the play lead to the events in another part.

DOK 2

READ FOR UNDERSTANDING

What does the actor playing Pecos Bill do when Narrator 2 is talking in line 13? *(He or she acts out falling off a wagon.)*

What might a baby like Pecos Bill, who can catch a grizzly bear, do when he falls out of a wagon? *(Possible response: run to catch up with the family)*

DOK 3

Stories on Stage 307

Online **Ed**

ANNOTATE IT!

Students may use the annotation tools in their eBook.

Step 2 Apply to Text

In your Teaching Pal, use the purple **TARGETED CLOSE READ** prompts to guide students to apply the Elements of Drama skill to *The Saga of Pecos Bill* and to cite evidence to support their responses. Use the **CLOSE READING** routine. Students may refer to the questions on Know It, Show It page 78 as you discuss them.

- Read aloud the first two questions on Teaching Pal page 307 and have students reread pages 306–307 in their *my*Book to identify the cast of characters and dialogue. *(the Characters list on page 306; The first five words are "Now as you all know." Narrator 1 speaks them.)*
- Then read the last question on Teaching Pal page 307 and have students describe the drama's setting and how they know. *(at first in the East, then in the West; The Narrators tell what the setting is.)*
- Refer back to the Anchor Chart as necessary to support the discussion. Have students use sticky notes to add to the Anchor Chart additional examples of elements of drama in *The Saga of Pecos Bill* and in other reading.

Step 3 Engage and Respond

INDEPENDENT PRACTICE: Viewing

- **Close-Read Screencast** Play Close-Read Screencast 2: The Saga of Pecos Bill.
- You may want to have students view the Screencast during daily small-group time.

INDEPENDENT PRACTICE: Viewing

- **Write Flash Fiction** Turn to pages 316–317 in your Teaching Pal. Have students turn to pages 316–317 in their *my*Book. Use the **WRITING RESPONSE** routine.
- Read the directions with students and use the Teaching Pal prompts to guide them as they plan and complete their flash fiction summaries.
- Provide time for students to share their flash fiction summaries with small groups.
- You may want to have students complete their writing during daily small-group time.
- You may want to have students complete Know It, Show It page 78 during daily small-group time.

ENGLISH LEARNER SUPPORT: Support Comprehension

SUBSTANTIAL

Point to the cast of characters. Point to the stage directions. Say those words with me.

MODERATE

Have students identify the elements of drama: *How many characters are there? Where are the stage directions?*

LIGHT

Have partners ask and answer questions. *What do you learn from the cast of characters? From the stage directions?*

LINK TO SMALL-GROUP INSTRUCTION

REINFORCE ELEMENTS OF DRAMA Review and extend the skill as needed during small-group time to support students' need for differentiation. *See the lesson on p. T247.*

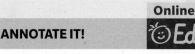

Options for Differentiation

As the class engages in independent and collaborative work, meet with Guided Reading Groups or differentiate instruction based on student need.

GUIDED READING GROUPS

Match Students to Books + Instruction

- Choose just-right books based on level, skill, topic, or genre.

L → M → N → O → P → Q

Leveled Readers

- Deliver instruction with each book's **Take and Teach Lesson**, choosing appropriate sessions based on need.

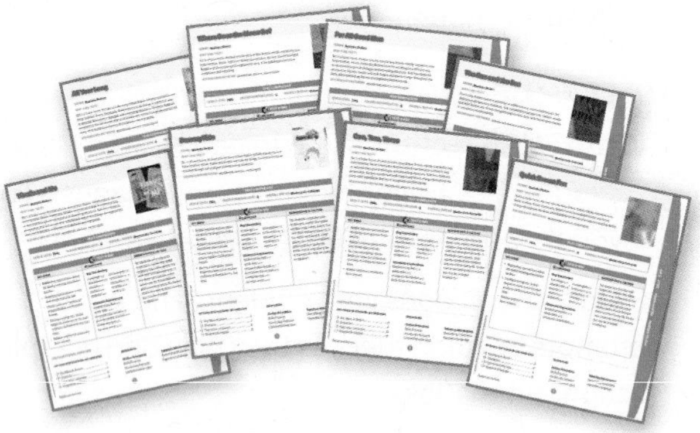

- Check comprehension, reinforce instruction, and extend learning with suggested supporting activities.

ENGLISH LEARNER SUPPORT

Infer

- Use **Tabletop Minilessons: English Language Development 10.2 (Reading)** to reinforce and practice the language skill.

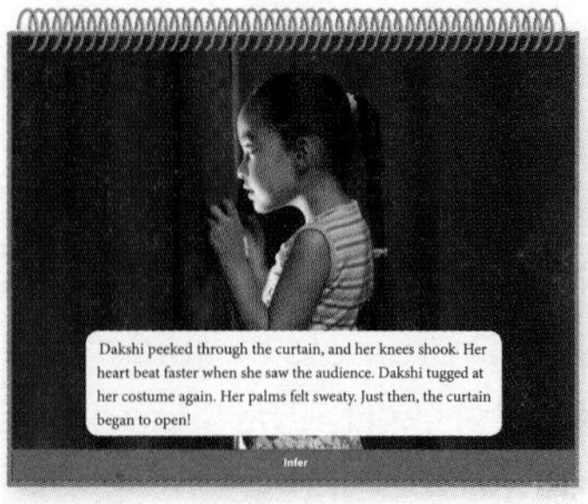

Tabletop Minilessons: English Language Development

- Then use the following text-based prompts with *The Saga of Pecos Bill* to guide application of the language skill. Begin with the prompt at the student's identified language proficiency level. As students progress, use lighter supports to encourage increased language proficiency.

SUBSTANTIAL
Read the third page of the drama and explain to students the meaning of the word *coyote*. Ask: *What does the last sentence in the paragraph say Bill is?* (*a regular coyote*) *Is Bill really a coyote?* (*no*)

MODERATE
Ask students to read aloud the parts of Pecos Bill and Cowboy 1 on the third page. Then have them use text evidence to complete sentence frames: *Bill thinks he is a ______. I can tell Bill isn't really a coyote because ______.*

LIGHT
Define the word *exaggeration*. Then have partners find and reread parts of the drama that clarify the meaning of the word. Ask: *Where does the author use exaggeration? How can you tell?* Have them support their inferences with evidence from the text.

REINFORCE ELEMENTS OF DRAMA

Demonstrate

- Use **Tabletop Minilessons: Reading Card 14** to remind students that a **drama**, or play, is a story performed by actors on a stage. The *script* is the text of the drama, which may be divided into **acts**, like chapters, and *scenes*, which are smaller parts of acts. The **cast of characters** tells who is in the play. **Dialogue** is the words the characters speak. **Stage directions** tell what the characters do onstage.
- Model filling out Printable: Reading Graphic Organizer 14 to identify elements of drama in *The Saga of Pecos Bill.*

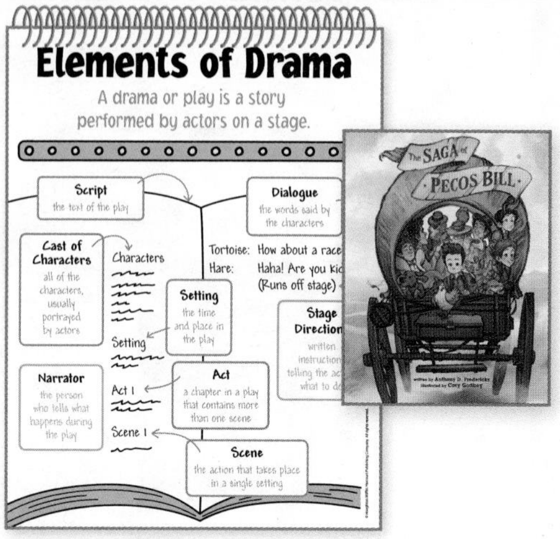

Elements of Drama
A drama or play is a story performed by actors on a stage.
Script
the text of the play
Dialogue
the words said by the characters
Cast of Characters
all of the characters, usually portrayed by actors
Characters
Tortoise: How about a race
Hare: Haha! Are you kid
(Runs off stage)
Setting
the time and place in the play
Setting
Stage Direction
Narrator
the person who tells what happens during the play
Act 1
Act
a chapter in a play that contains more than one scene
Scene 1
Scene
the action that takes place in a single setting
The SAGA of PECOS BILL

Tabletop Minilessons: Reading

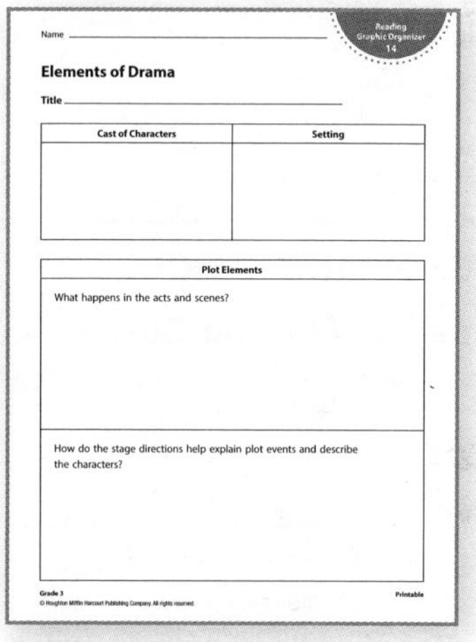
Name
Reading Graphic Organizer 14
Elements of Drama
Title

Cast of Characters	Setting

Plot Elements
What happens in the acts and scenes?
How do the stage directions help explain plot events and describe the characters?

Grade 3 Printable

Printable: Reading Graphic Organizer 14

Apply to Independent Reading

- Now have students identify the elements of drama in an appropriate play that they are reading independently. Customize these prompts to the texts students choose.
  - » *Who are the characters in the drama?*
  - » *How is the drama divided into acts or scenes?*
  - » *How can you identify dialogue and stage directions?*
- Have students complete Printable: Reading Graphic Organizer 14 for their independent reading book.

ALMOST THERE

READY FOR MORE

SCAFFOLD AND EXTEND

- Guide students to identify any acts, scenes, characters, dialogue, and stage directions in the drama.
- Prompt students to identify which elements of drama their independent reading includes.
- Have students explain how the elements of drama help them to picture what the drama would look like on stage.

EL ENGLISH LEARNER SUPPORT

SUBSTANTIAL
Have students point to and name the cast of characters, lines of dialogue, stage directions, and acts or scenes in the text.

MODERATE
Supply sentence frames such as: *The characters are* ______. *An example of dialogue is* ______. *An example of stage directions are* ______.

LIGHT
Encourage students to explain how they identified the elements of drama and how they help them picture the play onstage.

Options for Independent and Collaborative Work

While you meet with small groups, have other students engage in literacy activities that reinforce the lesson's learning objectives. Choose from these options.

Independent Reading

Student Choice Library

Rigby
LEVELED LIBRARY

APPLY READING SKILL

Elements of Drama Students complete Printable: Reading Graphic Organizer 14 for an independent reading book.

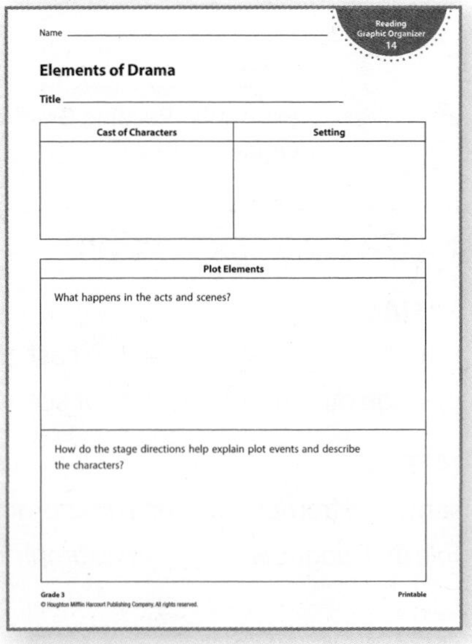

Name ______ Reading Graphic Organizer 14

Elements of Drama

Title ______

Cast of Characters	Setting

Plot Elements
What happens in the acts and scenes?
How do the stage directions help explain plot events and describe the characters?

Grade 3 Printable
© Houghton Mifflin Harcourt Publishing Company. All rights reserved.

Printable: Reading Graphic Organizer 14

APPLY LANGUAGE SKILL

Infer Students complete Printable: Language Graphic Organizer 7 for an independent reading book.

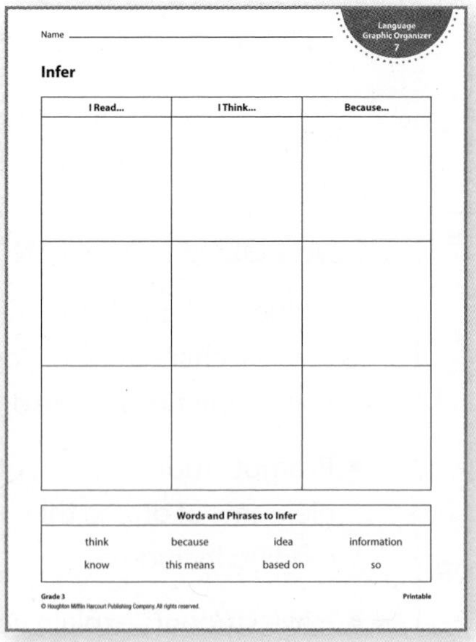

Name ______ Language Graphic Organizer 7

Infer

I Read...	I Think...	Because...

Words and Phrases to Infer			
think	because	idea	information
know	this means	based on	so

Grade 3 Printable
© Houghton Mifflin Harcourt Publishing Company. All rights reserved.

Printable: Language Graphic Organizer 7

Literacy Centers

See pp. T214–T215.

- READING CENTER
- VOCABULARY CENTER
- DIGITAL STATION
- WRITING CENTER
- PROJECT CENTER

Viewing

Students view the Close-Read Screencast. *See Engage and Respond, p. T245.*

Close-Read Screencast

Online Ed

Additional Skills Practice

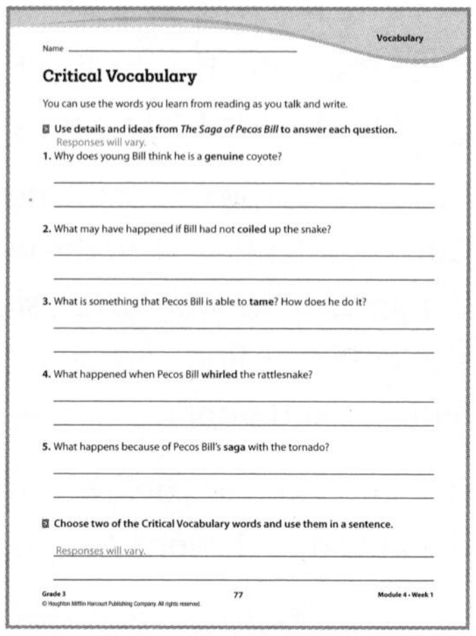
Vocabulary

Name

Critical Vocabulary

You can use the words you learn from reading as you talk and write.

Use details and ideas from *The Saga of Pecos Bill* to answer each question.
Responses will vary.

1. Why does young Bill think he is a **genuine** coyote?
2. What may have happened if Bill had not **coiled** up the snake?
3. What is something that Pecos Bill is able to **tame**? How does he do it?
4. What happened when Pecos Bill **whirled** the rattlesnake?
5. What happens because of Pecos Bill's **saga** with the tornado?

Choose two of the Critical Vocabulary words and use them in a sentence.

Responses will vary.

Grade 3 77 Module 4 • Week 1
© Houghton Mifflin Harcourt Publishing Company. All rights reserved.

Know It, Show It, p. 77

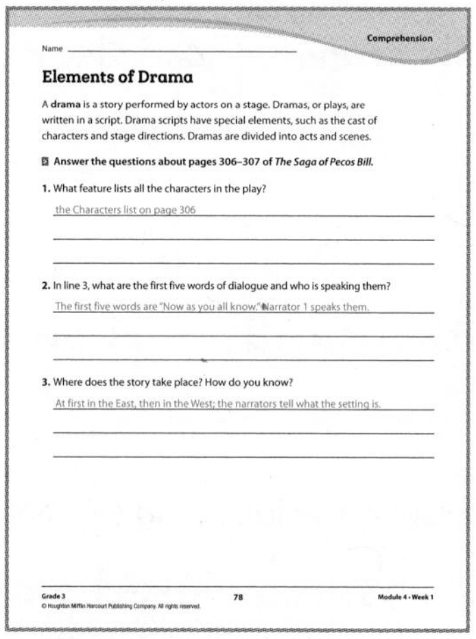
Comprehension

Name

Elements of Drama

A **drama** is a story performed by actors on a stage. Dramas, or plays, are written in a script. Drama scripts have special elements, such as the cast of characters and stage directions. Dramas are divided into acts and scenes.

Answer the questions about pages 306–307 of *The Saga of Pecos Bill.*

1. What feature lists all the characters in the play?
   the Characters list on page 306
2. In line 3, what are the first five words of dialogue and who is speaking them?
   The first five words are "Now as you all know." Narrator 1 speaks them.
3. Where does the story take place? How do you know?
   At first in the East, then in the West; the narrators tell what the setting is.

Grade 3 78 Module 4 • Week 1
© Houghton Mifflin Harcourt Publishing Company. All rights reserved.

Know It, Show It, p. 78

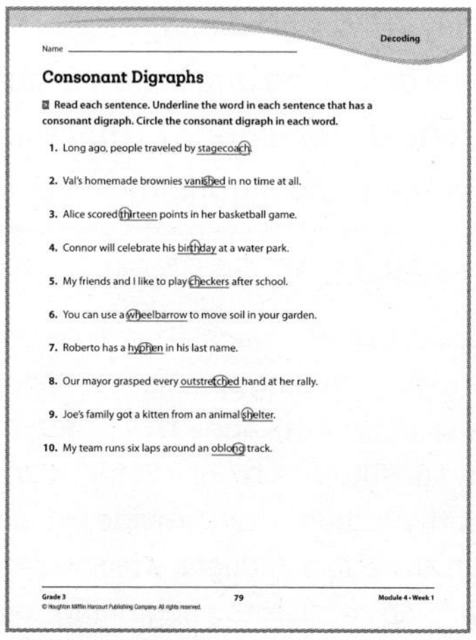
Decoding

Name

Consonant Digraphs

Read each sentence. Underline the word in each sentence that has a consonant digraph. Circle the consonant digraph in each word.

1. Long ago, people traveled by stagecoach.
2. Val's homemade brownies vanished in no time at all.
3. Alice scored thirteen points in her basketball game.
4. Connor will celebrate his birthday at a water park.
5. My friends and I like to play checkers after school.
6. You can use a wheelbarrow to move soil in your garden.
7. Roberto has a hyphen in his last name.
8. Our mayor grasped every outstretched hand at her rally.
9. Joe's family got a kitten from an animal shelter.
10. My team runs six laps around an oblong track.

Grade 3 79 Module 4 • Week 1
© Houghton Mifflin Harcourt Publishing Company. All rights reserved.

Know It, Show It, p. 79

Wrap-Up

Share Time

At the end of the Reading Workshop, have students reflect on their learning by sharing how they applied **elements of drama** or another area of focus during independent work time. Choose from these options:

- Use the **SOLO CHAIR** routine. Select a reader each day to come to the front of the class and tell what he or she learned from the reading by using a skill or strategy.
- **THINK-PAIR-SHARE** Students share their thinking with a partner. Select a few pairs each day to share with the whole class.
- **RETURN TO ANCHOR CHART** Have students add sticky notes about their independent reading to the Elements of Drama Anchor Chart. Call on a few students to explain what they added and why.

Online Ed

ANCHOR CHART 14: Elements of Drama

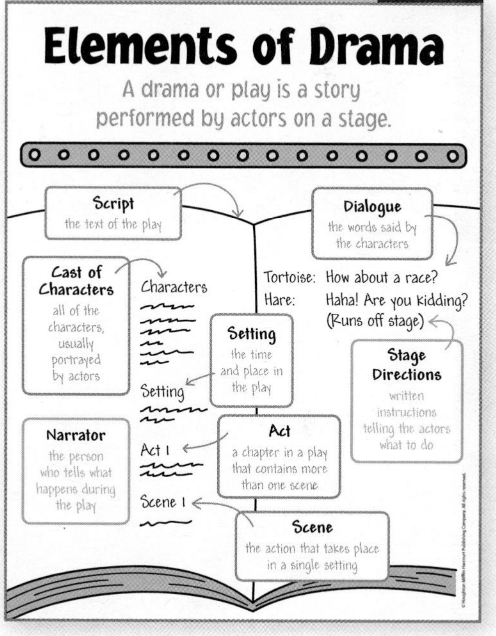
Elements of Drama
A drama or play is a story performed by actors on a stage.
Script
the text of the play
Dialogue
the words said by the characters
Cast of Characters
all of the characters, usually portrayed by actors
Characters
Tortoise: How about a race?
Hare: Haha! Are you kidding? (Runs off stage)
Setting
the time and place in the play
Setting
Stage Directions
written instructions telling the actors what to do
Narrator
the person who tells what happens during the play
Act I
Act
a chapter in a play that contains more than one scene
Scene I
Scene
the action that takes place in a single setting

LEARNING OBJECTIVES

- Decode and read with consonant digraphs *ch, tch, sh, wh, th, ph,* and *ng*.
- Recognize spelling patterns for consonant digraphs.
- **Language** Articulate sounds for consonant digraphs and read words containing those sounds.

MATERIALS Online Ed

Display and Engage *Decoding 4.3*
Know It, Show It *p. 79*

Consonant Digraphs

Step 1 Reinforce the Skill

Consonant Digraphs Remind students that they have learned the sounds and spellings of consonant digraphs *ch, tch, sh, wh, th, ph,* and *ng*.

- **Transition to Longer Words** Display and read the word *chosen*, emphasizing the /ch/ sound. Explain that students can divide longer words into syllables to make them easier to read. Draw a line between *o* and *s* to divide *chosen* into syllables. Note that the first syllable ends in a vowel, which means it's an open syllable. Explain that open syllables usually have long vowel sounds.
- Repeat with the words *pitcher*, *shovel*, *whitecap*, *bathtub*, *trophy*, and *along*. Guide students to read the words aloud and to help you identify the consonant digraphs in the words: *tch, sh, wh, th, ph,* and *ng*. Point out that in longer words, students may find consonant digraphs in the middle of the word, as in *pitcher*, *bathtub*, and *trophy*.
- Display the charts below. Read each word aloud, emphasizing the consonant digraph in each word and underlining it.

ch	tch	sh	wh
chicken	catcher	sharpen	whisker

th	ph	ng
thousand	phonics	lengthen

- Display the following sentences and underline the word *shoddy*.

Susan ordered a cheap toy in the mail. Unfortunately, the shoddy toy was broken when it arrived.

Say: *Let's say I didn't recognize the word* shoddy. *I see the consonant digraph* sh *at the beginning and I know it stands for the /sh/ sound. So I will sound out the word: /shŏd/ /ē/,* shoddy. *That sounds right. Also, the context clues* cheap *and* broken *help me understand the meaning, "something poorly made."*

ENGLISH LEARNER SUPPORT: Utilize Language Transfer

ALL LEVELS Preteach /th/, /sh/, /wh/, and /ch/ for language transfer. Some English learners (including speakers of Spanish and several Asian languages) may have trouble with the sounds /wh/ and /th/. In addition, speakers of Spanish, Vietnamese, and Cantonese may substitute /ch/ or /s/ for /sh/. Say each sound several times as students study your mouth position. Then provide extra modeling and practice with words, such as *ship, shell, shop, thick, thin, thought, whip, whale, when*. Have students chorally repeat each word after you, then vocalize the beginning sound, before saying the whole word again. Use each word in a sentence to reinforce meaning.

Step 2 Guided Practice

- Project Display and Engage: **Decoding 4.3**.
- Have students read the Blend and Read lines aloud. Provide feedback as needed. At the end of each line, prompt a conversation about the words: *How are the sounds and spellings in the words the same? How are they different?*
- Have partners reread the Blend and Read lines and quiz each other on the spellings of the consonant digraphs. Challenge students to find words that contain two consonant digraphs.

Online Ed

DISPLAY AND ENGAGE: Decoding 4.3

Decoding 4.3

Blend and Read

Consonant Digraphs

1	belong (ng)	shadow (sh)	dolphin (ph)	pitchfork (tch)	channel (ch)
2	whirlpool (wh)	sandwich (ch)	seventh (th)	unsung (ng)	ketchup (tch)
3	bleachers (ch)	typhoon (ph)	finish (sh)	wheelchair (wh, ch)	thoughtful (th)
4	shower (sh)	photoflash (ph, sh)	champion (ch)	kingdom (ng)	publish (sh)
5	kitchen (tch)	underneath (th)	sunshine (sh)	whisper (wh)	thunder (th)

6. This imperfect graphic does not match the text in the chapter. (Th, ph, tch, ch)
7. My young nephew becomes impatient when he is thirsty. (ph, wh, th)

Grade 3 | Foundational Skills — Module 4 • Week 1

Step 3 Apply

INDEPENDENT PRACTICE

- Have students work in small groups or with partners to complete Know It, Show It page 79.
- Be sure students understand there are two tasks for each sentence: identify the word that contains a consonant digraph, and identify the consonant digraph.
- Encourage students to share with each other the strategies they use to decode words with consonant digraphs.

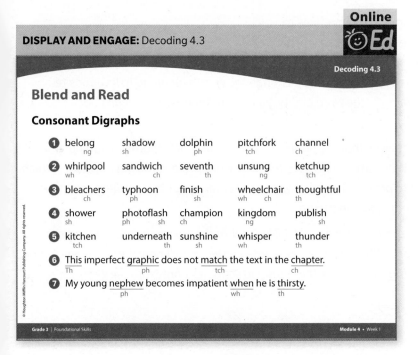

CORRECT & REDIRECT

If students have trouble decoding words with consonant digraphs, use the model below.

- **Correct** the error. *The letters* sh *stand for the /sh/ sound.*
- **Model** how to decode the word *publish*. */pŭb/ /lĭs/. That doesn't sound like a word I know. I see the letters* sh *at the end, so I'll try the /sh/ sound. I'll try reading the word again: /pŭb/ /lĭsh/,* publish. *That sounds like a word I know.*
- **Guide** students to decode other words: *channel, ketchup, underneath,* and *typhoon*.
- **Check** students' understanding by displaying the word *whisper*. *What spelling pattern helps you decode this word?*
- **Reinforce** by repeating the process with *kingdom*.

Prefixes *in–* (not), *im–* (into)

Step 1 Introduce the Skill

LEARNING OBJECTIVES

- Determine the meaning of the grade-level academic vocabulary with prefixes or suffixes.
- Use a dictionary or glossary to determine the meanings of unknown words.
- **Language** Discuss words with the prefixes *in–* and *im–* to show understanding of the target prefixes.

MATERIALS Online Ed

Display and Engage *Generative Vocabulary 4.4*

Know It, Show It, *p. 80*

INSTRUCTIONAL VOCABULARY

- **prefix** a word part added to the beginning of a base word that changes the meaning
- **base word** a word in its simplest form, without any word parts added to it

Project Display and Engage: Generative Vocabulary 4.4. Read aloud the paragraphs.

Online

DISPLAY AND ENGAGE:
Generative Vocabulary 4.4

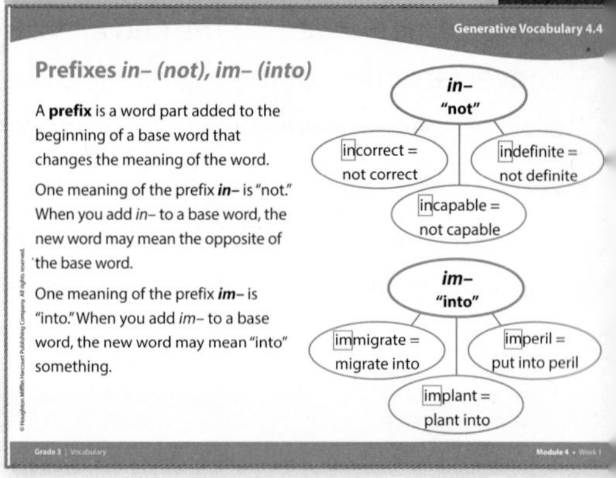
Generative Vocabulary 4.4
Prefixes in– (not), im– (into)
A prefix is a word part added to the beginning of a base word that changes the meaning of the word.
One meaning of the prefix in– is "not." When you add in– to a base word, the new word may mean the opposite of the base word.
One meaning of the prefix im– is "into." When you add im– to a base word, the new word may mean "into" something.
in– "not"
incorrect = not correct
indefinite = not definite
incapable = not capable
im– "into"
immigrate = migrate into
imperil = put into peril
implant = plant into

- Display the words *inability* and *imprison*. Circle the prefixes *in–* and *im–*. Tell students that knowing the meaning of the prefixes in these words can help them figure out the words' meaning.
- Then model how to use prefixes to determine the meaning of a word.

The prefix in– *can mean "not." When* in– *is added to a base word, it can change the word's meaning to its opposite. When you add* in– *to the word* ability, *you get* inability, *which means "lack of ability."*

We learned last week that the prefix im– *can mean "not." Another meaning for* im– *is "into." When* im– *is added to the base word* prison, *you get* imprison, *which means "put into prison." The base word and sentence context will help you know the correct meaning of* im– *in a word.*

When I see the prefix in– *in a word, I'll know that the word may mean the opposite of the base word. When I see the prefix* im– *in a word, I'll know the word may mean "into" something. I can check the word and sentence context to see if this makes sense.*

ENGLISH LEARNER SUPPORT: Build Vocabulary

SUBSTANTIAL
Show familiar words with the prefixes *in– (not)* and *im– (into)*. Discuss each base word's meaning and how the prefix changes it.

MODERATE
Ask students to name words with *in– (not)* and *im– (into)* and then identify the base word's meaning and tell how the prefix changes it.

LIGHT
Have pairs share sentences with the lesson's *in– and im–* words.

Step 2 Guided Practice

- Display the words *insincere* and *implant*. Ask volunteers to identify the base word in each and give its meaning. Then ask how the prefix changes the meaning of each base word.
- Then ask students to look up each word in a print or online dictionary to confirm their predictions. Have volunteers provide a definition of each word.

Step 3 Apply the Skill

INDEPENDENT PRACTICE

- Have students work in pairs to complete Know It, Show It p. 80. Tell partners to read the instructions and have them complete the activity together.
- Then have each student write a new sentence for each *in-* and *im–* word. Have partners read their sentences to one another to confirm the meaning of each word. Invite volunteers to read their sentences aloud.
- You may wish to have students complete the Know It, Show It page during Small Group time.

Spiral Review

Prefix *im– (not)* Remind students that a prefix is a word part added to the beginning of a base word that changes the meaning of the word.

- Review that the prefix *im–* can mean "not". When *im–*, meaning "not", is added to a base word, the new word means the opposite of the base word.
- Write on the board the following words for review: *imperfect, impossible, immature, immoral*. Guide students to identify the base word and prefix in each word and explain how the prefix changes the base word's meaning.
- Have students add the prefix *im–* to the following words for review: *movable, probable, balance, polite, measurable.* Have students explain how the prefix change the words' meaning. Invite them to check the words' meanings in a print or online dictionary.

Literary Elements

LEARNING OBJECTIVES

- Analyze plot elements.
- Analyze how plot elements reveal the author's purpose.
- **Language** Identify and articulate the conflict and resolution in a drama.

MATERIALS Online Ed

Anchor Chart 12 *Literary Elements*

Printable *Anchor Chart 12: Literary Elements*

Teaching Pal *Book 1, pp. 304–317*

***my*Book** *Book 1, The Saga of Pecos Bill, pp. 304–317*

Know It, Show It *p. 81*

INSTRUCTIONAL VOCABULARY

- **conflict** challenge in a story
- **event** occurrence in a story
- **literary elements** parts of a story, characters, setting, plot, and events
- **plot** conflict, events, and resolution that make up a story's structure
- **resolution** how the conflict in a story is solved

SPANISH COGNATES

- **conflict** *conflicto*
- **element** *elemento*
- **event** *evento*
- **literary** *literario*
- **resolution** *resolución*

Step 1 Connect and Teach

- Project or display Anchor Chart 12: Literary Elements. Remind students that both stories and dramas include characters, settings, plot, and events. These pieces of a story are called **literary elements.**
- Explain that the **plot** of a story or drama has different elements. The plot includes a sequence of **events** that happen in the story. The events are what move the story or drama along.
- Explain that authors include events for specific purposes, or reasons. Review the information about events on the Anchor Chart. Point out how each event in the drama *The Saga of Pecos Bill* builds toward creating Bill's character and entertaining readers.

Online Ed

ANCHOR CHART 12: Literary Elements

Literary Elements
Literary elements are the pieces that make up a story.
Characters:
the people and animals in a story
• What do they say and think?
• What do they do?
• What do other characters say and think about them?
Setting:
where and when the story takes place
• affects the plot because certain events happen in certain settings
• affects the plot by creating its mood
Plot:
Conflict
the main problem that the characters face
Resolution
how the conflict or problem is solved
Events:
things that happen in a story
• to change a character
• to affect the mood
• to build the plot

- Use the Anchor Chart to review that a plot also includes a problem, or **conflict,** that must be solved. The solution to the problem is the **resolution.**
- Tell students they will practice analyzing literary elements, including plot, to gain a deeper understanding of *The Saga of Pecos Bill.*

Go to Your
Teaching Pal

Online Ed

ANNOTATE IT!

Students may use the annotation tools in their eBook.

Step 2 Apply to Text

In your Teaching Pal, use the purple **TARGETED CLOSE READ** prompts on page 313 to guide students to apply the Literary Elements skill to *The Saga of Pecos Bill* and to find evidence to support their responses. Use the **CLOSE READING** routine. Students may refer to the questions on Know It, Show It page 81 as you discuss them.

- Read aloud the first question on Teaching Pal page 313. Then have students reread *my*Book pages 311–313. Tell students to look for clues in the text that tell about the conflict. *(He has to tame the tornado.)*
- Then read and discuss the last two questions on Teaching Pal page 313. Discuss how story events are connected and lead to a resolution. *(The tornado gives up, leaves Texas, and creates California's Death Valley. This fits with the author's purpose to show how amazing Pecos Bill was, and to show a tall tale explanation for Death Valley.)*
- Refer back to the Anchor Chart to support the discussion. Students may add sticky notes to the chart to note the settings, conflicts, resolutions, and events they identify in *The Saga of Pecos Bill.*
- Reinforce Literary Elements by having students retell the tale in their own words. Extend the the discussion by asking them to identify the theme.

Step 3 Engage and Respond

INDEPENDENT PRACTICE: Writing

Provide students with a storyboard template. (You may want to show students a completed storyboard for reference.)

- Have students reread pages 307–309. Ask students to identify the events, the conflict, and the resolution in this part of the play. Use the **WRITING RESPONSE** routine.
- Have students illustrate the main events for that section of text and write what's happening below each illustration. Remind students to choose key events that move the plot forward. Encourage students to add speech bubbles with dialogue for the characters.
- Have small groups share their storyboards and discuss what they have learned about plot.
- You may wish to have students complete their writing during daily small-group time.
- You may want to have students complete Know It, Show It page 81 during daily small-group time.

ENGLISH LEARNER SUPPORT: Elicit Participation

SUBSTANTIAL

Does Bill help end the drought? Was Bill afraid of the tornado?

MODERATE

Why is the drought a problem? What does Bill do solve it? How does Bill help with the tornado?

LIGHT

Have partners ask and answer questions. *What problems does Bill have? What does he do to solve them?*

LINK TO SMALL-GROUP INSTRUCTION

REINFORCE LITERARY ELEMENTS Review and extend the skill as needed during small-group time to support students' need for differentiation. *See the lesson on p. T257.*

Options for Differentiation

As the class engages in independent and collaborative work, meet with Guided Reading Groups or differentiate instruction based on student need.

GUIDED READING GROUPS

Match Students to Books + Instruction

- Choose just-right books based on level, skill, topic, or genre.

L M N O P Q

Leveled Readers

- Deliver instruction with each book's **Take and Teach Lesson**, choosing appropriate sessions based on need.

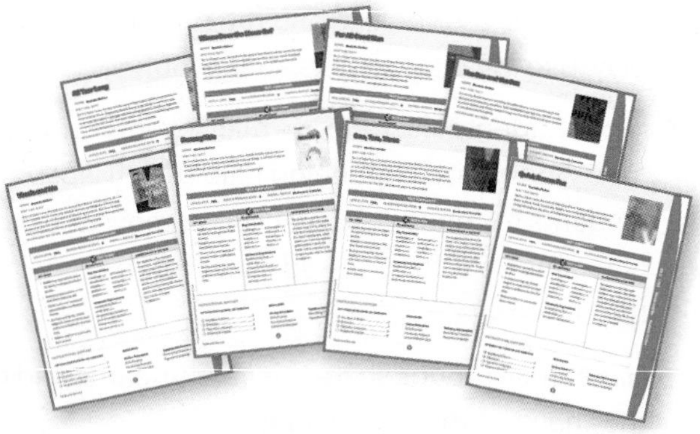

- Check comprehension, reinforce instruction, and extend learning with suggested supporting activities.

ENGLISH LEARNER SUPPORT

Infer

- Use **Tabletop Minilessons: English Support: 10.2 (Writing)** to reinforce and practice the language skill.

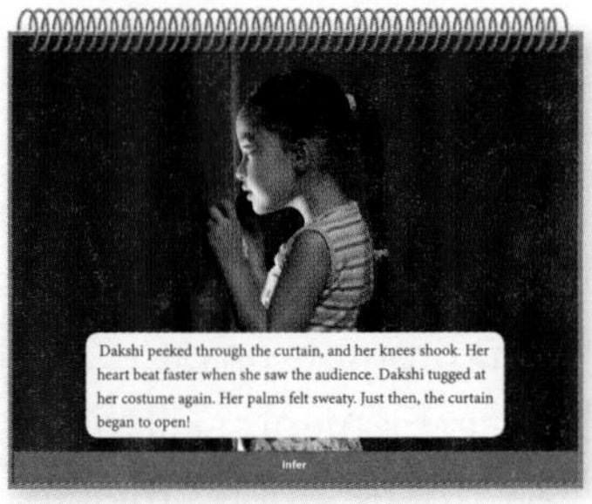

Tabletop Minilessons: English Language Development

- Then use the following text-based prompts with *The Saga of Pecos Bill* to guide application of the language skill. Begin with the prompt at the student's identified language proficiency level. As students progress, use lighter supports to encourage increased language proficiency.

SUBSTANTIAL
Read aloud a section of dialogue between Pecos Bill and the Mountain Lion. Have students write to complete the following: *In this story, the mountain lion [talks/does not talk]. I know that mountain lions [do/do not] talk. This story [is/is not] realistic.*

MODERATE
Have students complete the following written sentence frame to make an inference: *An inference I can make is _____ because the text says _____.*

LIGHT
After students have read the text, have them write responses to the following questions: *What is an inference you made about the text? What did you already know that helped you make the inference? What in the text helped you to make the inference?*

REINFORCE LITERARY ELEMENTS

Demonstrate

- Use **Tabletop Minilessons: Reading Card 12** to remind students that all stories and dramas have certain **literary elements** that are the same: characters, setting, plot, and events. Review that plot includes the sequence of events that make up a story or drama. The plot often includes a problem, or **conflict,** that must be solved. The solution to the problem is the **resolution**.
- Model filling out Printable: Reading Graphic Organizer 12 to identify literary elements in *The Saga of Pecos Bill.*

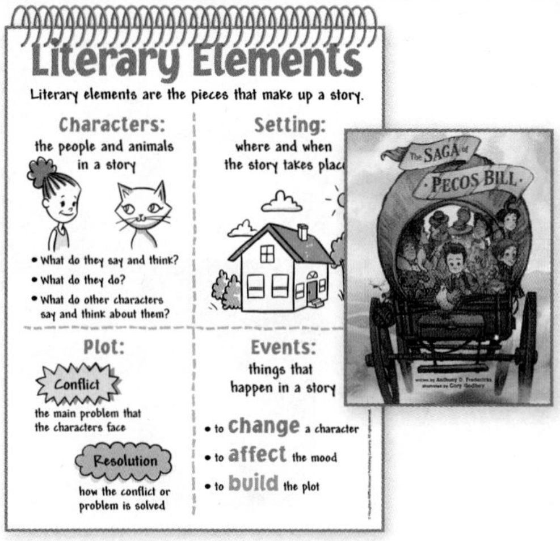

Literary Elements
Literary elements are the pieces that make up a story.
Characters:
the people and animals in a story
• What do they say and think?
• What do they do?
• What do other characters say and think about them?
Setting:
where and when the story takes plac
Plot:
Conflict
the main problem that the characters face
Resolution
how the conflict or problem is solved
Events:
things that happen in a story
• to change a character
• to affect the mood
• to build the plot
The SAGA of PECOS BILL

Tabletop Minilessons: Reading

Apply to Independent Reading

- Now have students identify literary elements in an appropriate book or article they are reading independently. Customize these prompts to the texts students choose.
  - » *What is the problem or conflict?*
  - » *What plot events happen as a result of the conflict?*
  - » *How is the conflict resolved?*
- Have students complete Printable: Reading Graphic Organizer 12 for their independent reading book.

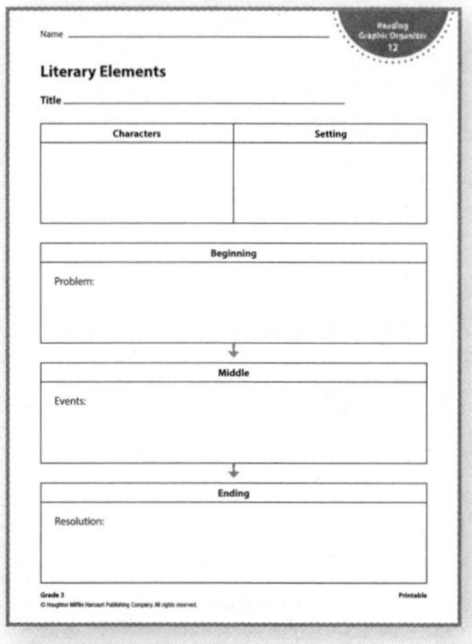
Name
Literary Elements
Title
Characters | Setting
Beginning
Problem:
Middle
Events:
Ending
Resolution:
Grade 3
Printable

Printable: Reading Graphic Organizer 12

SCAFFOLD AND EXTEND

ALMOST THERE

READY FOR MORE

- Guide students to identify the problem, main events, and resolution.
- Prompt students to identify the problem, sequence of events, and resolution.
- Have students elaborate on how the sequence of events leads to the resolution of the problem.

ENGLISH LEARNER SUPPORT

SUBSTANTIAL

Have students point to the text and use English words they know to complete sentence frames: *The problem is* ______. *The resolution is* ______.

MODERATE

Have students complete sentence frames: *The problem is* ______. *The main events are* ______. *The resolution is* ______.

LIGHT

Have students name and then explain how they identified the problem, main events, and resolution.

INDEPENDENT APPLICATION

Options for Independent and Collaborative Work

While you meet with small groups, have other students engage in literacy activities that reinforce the lesson's learning objectives. Choose from these options.

Independent Reading

Student Choice Library

Rigby
LEVELED LIBRARY

APPLY READING SKILL

Literary Elements Students complete Printable: Reading Graphic Organizer 12 for an independent reading book.

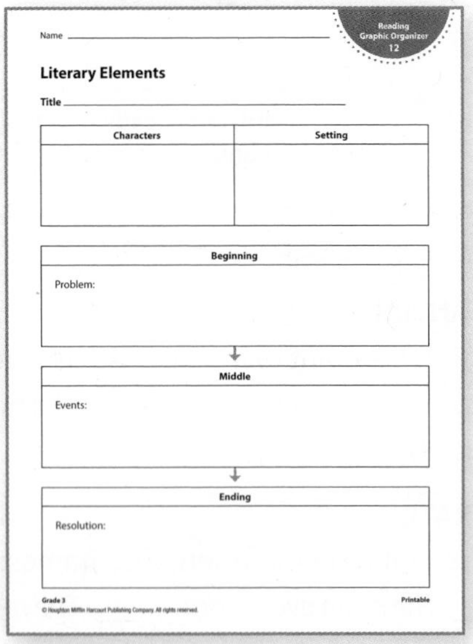

Name

Reading Graphic Organizer 12

Literary Elements

Title

Characters	Setting

Beginning
Problem:

Middle
Events:

Ending
Resolution:

Grade 3 · © Houghton Mifflin Harcourt Publishing Company. All rights reserved. · Printable

Printable: Reading Graphic Organizer 12

APPLY LANGUAGE SKILL

Infer Students complete Printable: Language Graphic Organizer 7 for an independent reading book.

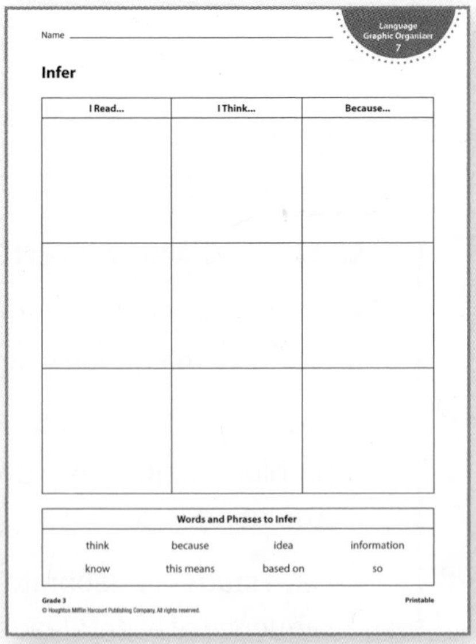

Name

Language Graphic Organizer 7

Infer

I Read...	I Think...	Because...

Words and Phrases to Infer

think	because	idea	information
know	this means	based on	so

Grade 3 · © Houghton Mifflin Harcourt Publishing Company. All rights reserved. · Printable

Printable: Language Graphic Organizer 7

Literacy Centers

See pp. T214–T215.

- READING CENTER
- VOCABULARY CENTER
- DIGITAL STATION
- WRITING CENTER
- PROJECT CENTER

Writing

Students write a storyboard. *See Engage and Respond, p. T255.*

Additional Skills Practice

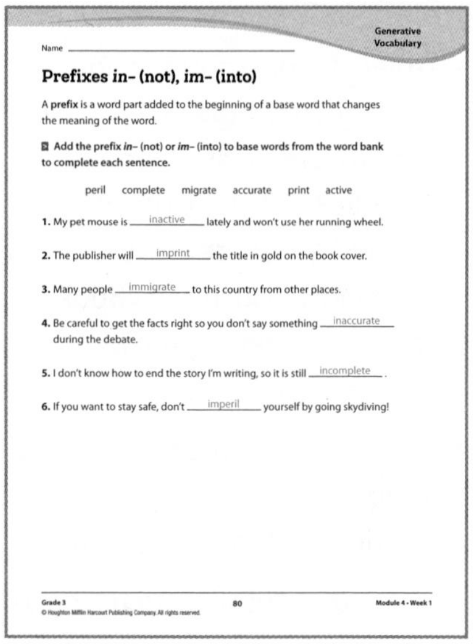
Name

Generative Vocabulary

Prefixes in– (not), im– (into)

A **prefix** is a word part added to the beginning of a base word that changes the meaning of the word.

Add the prefix *in*– (not) or *im*– (into) to base words from the word bank to complete each sentence.

peril complete migrate accurate print active

1. My pet mouse is inactive lately and won't use her running wheel.
2. The publisher will imprint the title in gold on the book cover.
3. Many people immigrate to this country from other places.
4. Be careful to get the facts right so you don't say something inaccurate during the debate.
5. I don't know how to end the story I'm writing, so it is still incomplete .
6. If you want to stay safe, don't imperil yourself by going skydiving!

Grade 3 80 Module 4 • Week 1

© Houghton Mifflin Harcourt Publishing Company. All rights reserved.

Know It, Show It, p. 80

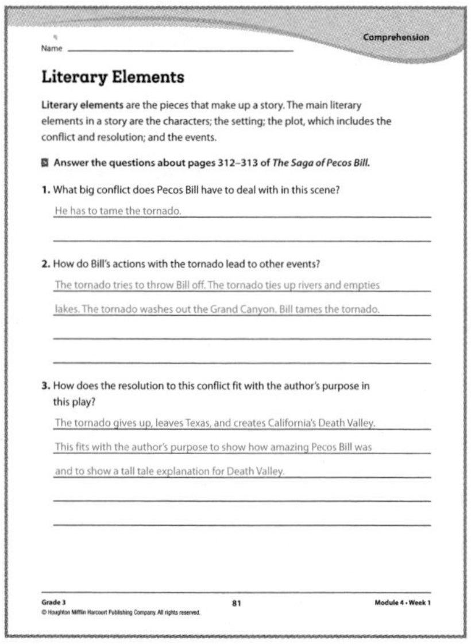
Name

Comprehension

Literary Elements

Literary elements are the pieces that make up a story. The main literary elements in a story are the characters; the setting; the plot, which includes the conflict and resolution; and the events.

Answer the questions about pages 312–313 of *The Saga of Pecos Bill.*

1. What big conflict does Pecos Bill have to deal with in this scene?
He has to tame the tornado.
2. How do Bill's actions with the tornado lead to other events?
The tornado tries to throw Bill off. The tornado ties up rivers and empties lakes. The tornado washes out the Grand Canyon. Bill tames the tornado.
3. How does the resolution to this conflict fit with the author's purpose in this play?
The tornado gives up, leaves Texas, and creates California's Death Valley. This fits with the author's purpose to show how amazing Pecos Bill was and to show a tall tale explanation for Death Valley.

Grade 3 81 Module 4 • Week 1

© Houghton Mifflin Harcourt Publishing Company. All rights reserved.

Know It, Show It, p. 81

Wrap-Up

Share Time

At the end of the Reading Workshop, have students reflect on their learning by sharing how they applied **Literary Elements** or another area of focus during independent work time. Choose from these options:

- Use the **SOLO CHAIR** routine. Select a reader each day to come to the front of the class and tell what he or she learned from the reading by using a skill or strategy.
- **THINK-PAIR-SHARE** Students share their thinking with a partner. Select a few pairs each day to share with the whole class.
- **RETURN TO ANCHOR CHART** Have students add sticky notes about their independent reading book to the Literary Elements Anchor Chart. Call on a few students to explain what they added.

Online Ed

ANCHOR CHART 12: Literary Elements

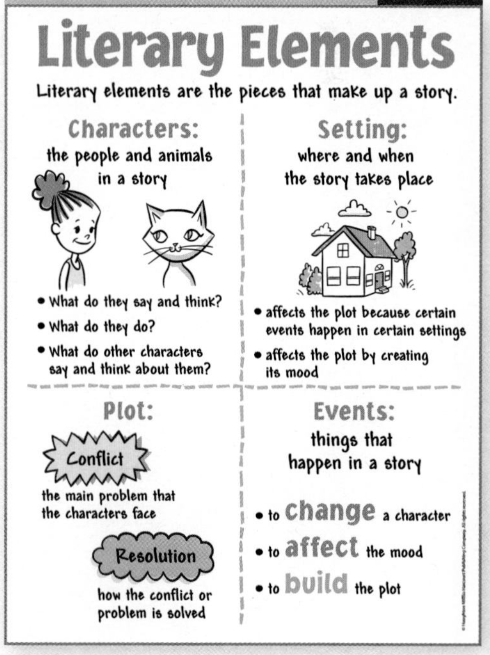
Literary Elements
Literary elements are the pieces that make up a story.
Characters:
the people and animals in a story
• What do they say and think?
• What do they do?
• What do other characters say and think about them?
Setting:
where and when the story takes place
• affects the plot because certain events happen in certain settings
• affects the plot by creating its mood
Plot:
Conflict
the main problem that the characters face
Resolution
how the conflict or problem is solved
Events:
things that happen in a story
• to change a character
• to affect the mood
• to build the plot

Vocabulary Spiral Review

Step 1 Review Vocabulary

LEARNING OBJECTIVES

- Review vocabulary.
- Identify real-life connections between words and their use.
- Play a word-guessing game using vocabulary.
- **Language** Discuss target vocabulary words and expand vocabulary knowledge by playing a word game.

MATERIALS Online Ed

- **Display and Engage** *Critical Vocabulary 3.2a, 3.2b*
- **Vocabulary Cards** *3.1, 3.2, 3.3, 3.4, 3.5, 3.6, 3.7, 3.8, 3.9*
- ***myBook*** *Book 1, p. 224*

- Tell students they will review some of the Critical Vocabulary they have learned so far this year and complete an activity based on those words.
- Project Display and Engage: **Critical Vocabulary 3.2a** and **3.2b** to remind students of the Module 3, Week 1 Critical Vocabulary words and their meanings. Also, use *my*Book page 224 to review the Module 3 Big Idea words.

Online Ed

DISPLAY AND ENGAGE:
Critical Vocabulary 3.2a and 3.2b

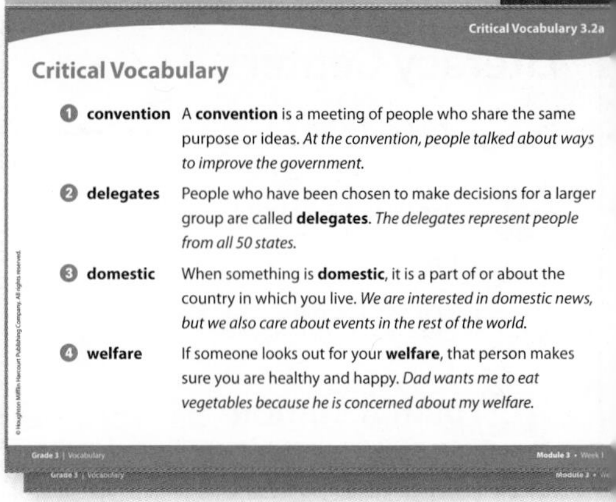
Critical Vocabulary 3.2a

Critical Vocabulary

1. **convention** A **convention** is a meeting of people who share the same purpose or ideas. *At the convention, people talked about ways to improve the government.*
2. **delegates** People who have been chosen to make decisions for a larger group are called **delegates**. *The delegates represent people from all 50 states.*
3. **domestic** When something is **domestic**, it is a part of or about the country in which you live. *We are interested in domestic news, but we also care about events in the rest of the world.*
4. **welfare** If someone looks out for your **welfare**, that person makes sure you are healthy and happy. *Dad wants me to eat vegetables because he is concerned about my welfare.*

Grade 3 | Vocabulary Module 3 • Week 1

- After reviewing the meanings, call out words and have volunteers take turns using the words in sentences of their own. If students are having trouble creating sentences, have them give synonyms or antonyms for the word.
- Continue until all students have had a chance to work with one or more of the words.

Step 2 Guided Practice

- Use Vocabulary Cards 3.1, 3.2, 3.3, 3.4, 3.5, 3.6, 3.7, 3.8, and 3.9 to remind students of the meanings of the words *loyal, sovereignty, democracy, civic, convention, delegates, domestic, welfare,* and *posterity.*
- Tell students they will play a game of What's My Word? with these vocabulary words. One player will give clues about a word, and the other players in the group will guess the word based on the clues.
- Write the rules where students can easily see them, and go over them with the class.
- One student in each group will choose a vocabulary card at random. (You can make sets of index cards containing the words, or ask students to make them.)
- The student will give clues about the word using only words and gestures. The clues must be about the word's meaning, not what it sounds like or what letters are in it. Clue givers can't repeat the definitions on the Vocabulary Cards; they must use their own words.
- Model the game by choosing a word and giving clues about it. For example, *domestic: This doesn't have to do with things that happen in other parts of the world. This has to do with things nearby that affect us.*
- Invite students to guess as you give clues. The first person to guess correctly scores a point.

Step 3 Apply the Skill

- Divide students into small groups of 4 or 5 students to play What's My Word? Give each group a set of index cards. You may also wish to provide a timer to limit each round to a minute or two.
- Ask a volunteer from each group to choose the first word and start giving clues. The other students should make guesses until someone gets the right answer. That person scores a point.
- Have students in each group take turns being the clue-giver until they have used all the words.

ENGLISH LEARNER SUPPORT: Guess Vocabulary Words

SUBSTANTIAL
Review the Vocabulary Cards with students before the game. Allow them to work in pairs and encourage them to use drawings as clues.

MODERATE
Pair students with English-fluent partners to give clues in the game, Allow them to review the Vocabulary Cards to remember definitions.

LIGHT
Let partners discuss ideas for word clues before the game begins, consulting the Vocabulary Cards as needed.

TEACHER TIP

Use the Vocabulary Cards throughout the year to review words from previous modules. With repeated exposure, students will find it easier to use the words in everyday conversations and in their writing.

Figurative Language

Step 1 Connect and Teach

LEARNING OBJECTIVES

- Explain the author's use of figurative language achieves a purpose.
- Write sentences using imagery.
- **Language** Articulate the author's purpose for using hyperbole.

MATERIALS | Online Ed

Anchor Charts 25 & 26 *Figurative Language*
Printable *Anchor Charts 25 & 26: Figurative Language*
Teaching Pal *Book 1, pp. 304–317*
myBook *Book 1, The Saga of Pecos Bill, pp. 304–317*
Know It, Show It *p. 82*

INSTRUCTIONAL VOCABULARY

- **figurative language** words or expressions that mean something different from their dictionary definitions
- **hyperbole** an exaggerated statement
- **imagery** words that create images in the readers' mind

- Help students recall that authors often use **figurative language** to make their stories and dramas more interesting. Review that figurative language is words or phrases that do not have their normal dictionary meaning.
- Project or display Anchor Charts 25 & 26: Figurative Language.
- Use Anchor Chart 25 to point out that one type of figurative language is **hyperbole**. Discuss how the example sentence shows exaggeration. Help students understand that hyperbole is often used to create a humorous effect.
- Review the information about **imagery** on Anchor Chart 26. Discuss with students how the example sentence appeals to their senses of taste and touch. Explain that authors use imagery to appeal to the readers' five senses, helping them create mental images.
- Explain that figurative language (such as the example sentence for hyperbole) is often informal. Contrast an example of informal figurative language with more formal language.
- Tell students they will analyze figurative language to gain a deeper understanding of *The Saga of Pecos Bill.*

Online Ed
ANCHOR CHARTS 25 & 26:
Figurative Language

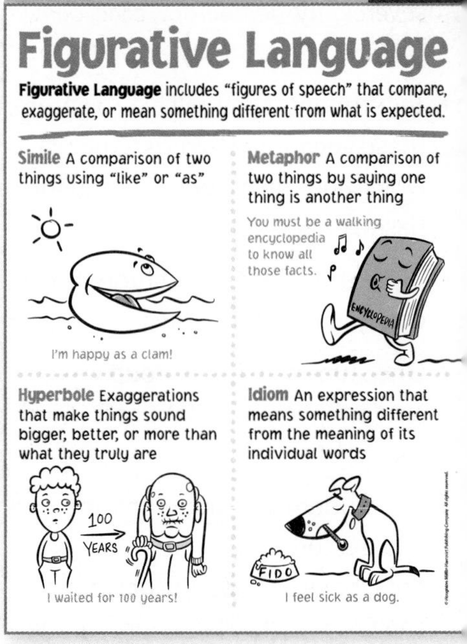

Figurative Language
Figurative Language includes "figures of speech" that compare, exaggerate, or mean something different from what is expected.
Simile A comparison of two things using "like" or "as"
I'm happy as a clam!
Metaphor A comparison of two things by saying one thing is another thing
You must be a walking encyclopedia to know all those facts.
Hyperbole Exaggerations that make things sound bigger, better, or more than what they truly are
100 YEARS
I waited for 100 years!
Idiom An expression that means something different from the meaning of its individual words
FIDO
I feel sick as a dog.

LEARNING MINDSET

Self-Reflection

Normalize Explain to students that when you look back at your work and see mistakes, you may feel frustrated. This is normal. *Everyone makes mistakes! Making mistakes helps us become better learners. When we find mistakes in our work, it is a chance to self-reflect and think about how we can improve.*

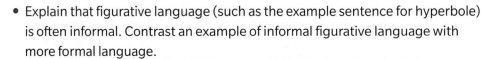

Go to Your
Teaching Pal

myNotes

TARGETED CLOSE READ

Figurative Language

Have students reread the description of Pecos Bill and the snake in lines 33–35 to analyze the figurative language.

How do repeated words in line 33 help create the image of a twirling rope? *(They describe how the snake changes by spinning it round and round.)*

What details make this scene a good example of hyperbole, or exaggeration? *(A real person couldn't twirl a snake into a 30-foot rope.)*

How is the language of Narrator 3 in line 33 different from the language in the Staging note on page 306? *(The Narrator uses informal language. It is fun and like people talk in cowboy stories. The Staging note is formal. It just provides information.)*

DOK 3

NARRATOR 2: They hadn't gone but 10 miles when a 10-foot rattlesnake swung out of a cactus plant and down on top of them.

NARRATOR 3: Bill jumped off the mountain lion's back and grabbed the end of that snake. He swung that snake around and around his head. As the snake was spinning round and round, it grew thinner and thinner. It also got longer and longer. By the time Bill was done, that 10-foot rattlesnake was 30 feet long.

NARRATOR 4: Bill coiled up that 30-foot snake just like it was a rope and slung it over his shoulder. From then on cowboys always carried a rope with them just like Pecos Bill carried a 30-foot snake with him wherever he went.

coiled If you coiled something, you shaped it into loops or rings.

310

310 Module 4

NARRATOR 1: After that, Bill and the cowboy rode on until they got to the ranch alongside the Pecos River. The other cowboys didn't know what to make of Bill, riding his mountain lion and carrying a snake wrapped across his shoulders. But I guess they could see that he was a good man, so they figured he'd be a good cowboy, too.

PECOS BILL: Howdy, folks, I'm new in these here parts. I just want to learn how to be a cowboy and help you fellas out.

COWBOY 2: Well, friend, you're welcome to stay as long as you want. We're always looking for new help, seeing as we have the whole state of Texas to take care of and lots of cattle to keep an eye on.

PECOS BILL: I appreciate that. By the way, what would you like to have me do now?

COWBOY 2: Well, I don't think it's anything you can help us with. See, we're just in the biggest drought that Texas ever had. We ain't had no water for months and months now.

myNotes

READ FOR UNDERSTANDING

Visualize

How can you visualize what happens when Bill uses the snake like a rope? *(Students should use their senses to visualize the action in the scene.)*

If students have difficulty visualizing, use this model:

THINK ALOUD *I see the actor playing Bill spinning a fake snake around and around. I can hear snake-hissing sound effects. It makes a whirring sound in the air as Bill spins it. Bill is probably hollering, too. Yee-ha!!*

DOK 3

READ FOR UNDERSTANDING

What do the cowboys think of Bill? How do you know? *(They didn't know what to make of him. They think he is a good man.)*

ANNOTATION TIP: Have students underline the text that shows how the cowboys react to Bill.

DOK 2

311

Stories on Stage 311

Online

ANNOTATE IT!

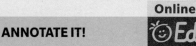

Students may use the annotation tools in their eBook.

Step 2 Apply to Text

In your Teaching Pal, use the prompt on the purple **TARGETED CLOSE READ** note on page 310 to guide students to apply the Figurative Language skill to *The Saga of Pecos Bill* and to find evidence to support their responses. Use the **CLOSE READING** routine. Students may refer to the questions on Know It, Show It page 82 as you discuss them.

- Read aloud the first question on Teaching Pal page 310. Have students reread paragraphs 34–36 on *my*Book page 310. Discuss the author's use of imagery. *(They describe how the snake changes by spinning it round and round.)*
- Read aloud the last two questions on Teaching Pal page 310. Discuss the effect of the author's use of hyperbole, as well as formal and informal language. *(A real person couldn't ride a mountain lion like a horse or twirl a snake into a 30-foot rope. The Narrator uses informal language. It is fun and like people talk in cowboy stories. The Staging note is formal. It just provides information about the play.)*
- Refer to the Anchor Chart to support discussion. Have students use sticky notes to add other examples of figurative language to the chart as they encounter them.

Step 3 Engage and Respond

INDEPENDENT PRACTICE: Writing

- Remind students that authors use imagery to make their writing more interesting and to appeal to readers' senses. Ask students to work in pairs. Have pairs write five very simple sentences about *The Saga of Pecos Bill*. For example: *Bill saw a mountain lion*. Use the **WRITING RESPONSE** routine.
- Have partners trade papers with another pair. Have partners read the sentences they receive and add words and phrases that appeal to the senses. For example: *Bill saw an angry mountain lion with long sharp teeth.*
- Have partners use the **COLLABORATIVE DISCUSSION** routine to discuss how they used imagery to improve the sentences. Students should discuss what specific words or phrases help them see, smell, hear, taste, or feel. Call on pairs to share their responses.
- You may wish to have students complete their writing during daily small-group time.
- You may wish to have students complete Know It, Show It page 82 during daily small-group time.

ENGLISH LEARNER SUPPORT: Support Comprehension

SUBSTANTIAL

Show me something Bill does that a real person could not do. Say it with me: Bill rides a mountain lion.

MODERATE

What does Bill do that a real person could not do? What does the author want readers to think about Bill?

LIGHT

Why does the author use hyperbole to describe what Bill does?

LINK TO SMALL-GROUP INSTRUCTION

REINFORCE FIGURATIVE LANGUAGE Review or extend the skill as needed during small-group time to support students' need for differentiation. *See the lesson on p. T265.*

Options for Differentiation

As the class engages in independent and collaborative work, meet with Guided Reading Groups or differentiate instruction based on student need.

GUIDED READING GROUPS

Match Students to Books + Instruction

- Choose just-right books based on level, skill, topic, or genre.

L M N O P Q

Leveled Readers

- Deliver instruction with each book's **Take and Teach Lesson**, choosing appropriate sessions based on need.

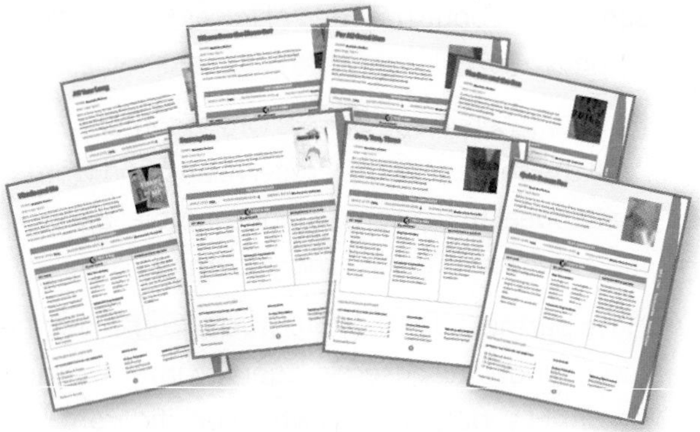

- Check comprehension, reinforce instruction, and extend learning with suggested supporting activities.

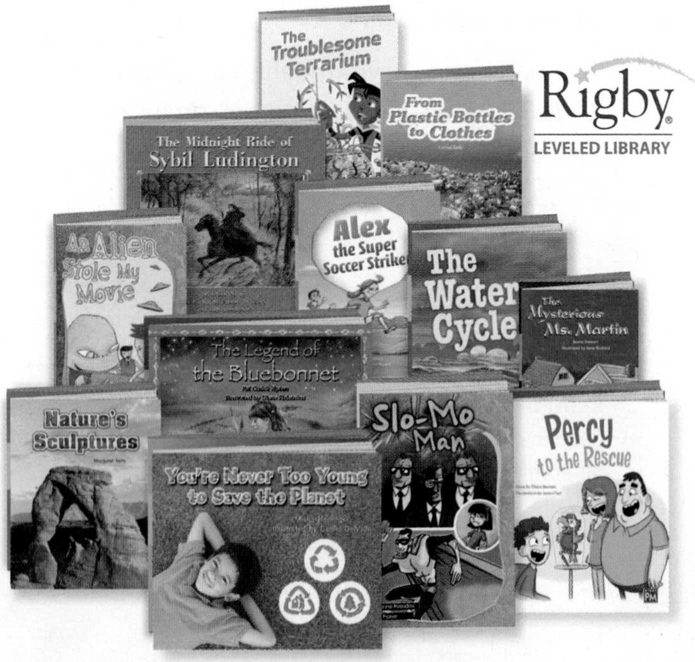

ENGLISH LEARNER SUPPORT

Infer

- Use **Tabletop Minilessons: English Language Development 10.3 (Collaborative Problem Solving)** to reinforce and practice the language skill.

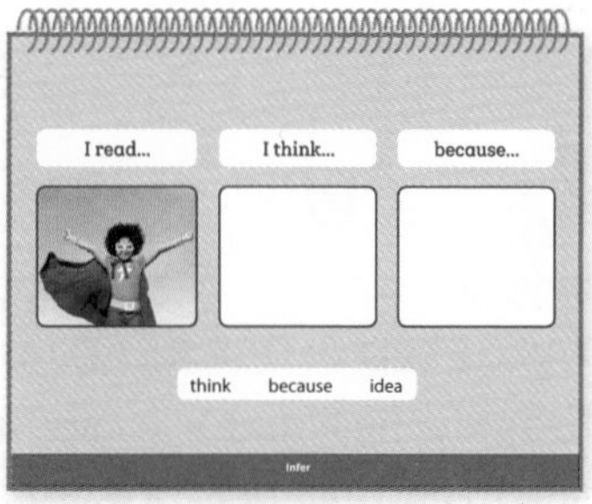

Tabletop Minilessons: English Language Development

- Then use the following text-based prompts with *The Saga of Pecos Bill* to guide application of the language skill. Begin with the prompt at the student's identified language proficiency level. As students progress, use lighter supports to encourage increased language proficiency.

SUBSTANTIAL
Have students work together to draw and label a poster that shows three examples of hyperbole in the text.

MODERATE
Have students take turns acting out scenes from the play and being audience members. Ask audience members to identify examples of hyperbole in the scenes and explain: *I know _____ is hyperbole because _____.*

LIGHT
Have partners rewrite a scene from *The Saga of Pecos Bill* to include a new example of hyperbole. Have them read their scene to other students, who should identify the hyperbole and explain how they identified it.

REINFORCE FIGURATIVE LANGUAGE

Demonstrate

- Use **Tabletop Minilessons: Reading Cards 25 & 26** to remind students that **figurative language** is words or phrases that mean something different from their dictionary definitions. Authors use figurative language to make stories or dramas more interesting. **Hyperbole** is exaggeration used to add humor. **Imagery** appeals to the five senses of taste, hearing, sight, smell, and touch.
- Model filling out Printable: Reading Graphic Organizers 25 & 26 to identify figurative language in *The Saga of Pecos Bill.*

Apply to Independent Reading

- Now have students identify the figurative language in an appropriate book or article they are reading independently. Customize these prompts to the texts students choose.
  - » *What imagery in the selection appeals to the sense of taste, hearing, sight, smell, or touch?*
  - » *What examples of hyperbole or exaggeration does the author include?*
  - » *How does the figurative language make the text more interesting?*
- Have students complete Printable: Reading Graphic Organizer 25 & 26 for their independent reading book.

Tabletop Minilessons: Reading

Printable: Reading Graphic Organizers 25 & 26

ALMOST THERE

READY FOR MORE

SCAFFOLD AND EXTEND

- Help students to identify imagery. Prompt them to tell what it describes.
- Prompt students to identify examples of imagery and tell what it helps them to picture or feel.
- Have students explain how the imagery adds to their understanding or interest in the text.

EL ENGLISH LEARNER SUPPORT

SUBSTANTIAL

Use motions to indicate the five senses as you ask: *Does the figurative language describe something you see? hear? touch? taste? smell?*

MODERATE

Have students use sentence: *An example of imagery is ______. An example of hyperbole is ______. It makes the text more ______.*

LIGHT

Prompt students to identify imagery and hyperbole, and describe how the figurative language affects the text.

Options for Independent and Collaborative Work

While you meet with small groups, have other students engage in literacy activities that reinforce the lesson's learning objectives. Choose from these options.

Independent Reading

Student Choice Library

Rigby
LEVELED LIBRARY

APPLY READING SKILL

Figurative language Students complete Printable: Reading Graphic Organizers 25 & 26 for an independent reading book.

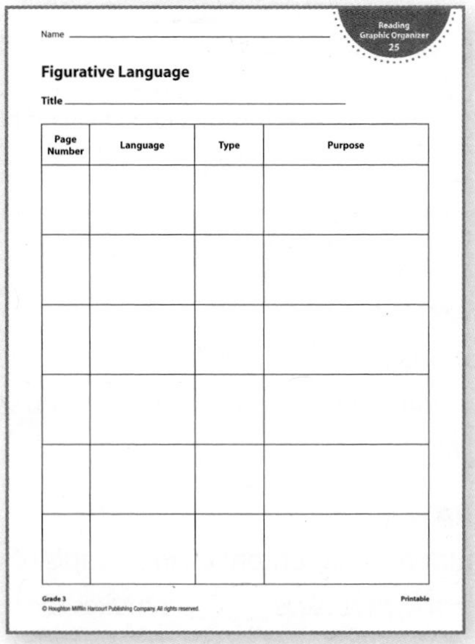

Name ______ Reading Graphic Organizer 25

Figurative Language

Title ______

Page Number	Language	Type	Purpose

Grade 3 Printable
© Houghton Mifflin Harcourt Publishing Company. All rights reserved.

Printable: Reading Graphic Organizers 25 & 26

APPLY LANGUAGE SKILL

Infer Students complete Printable: Language Graphic Organizer 7 for an independent reading book.

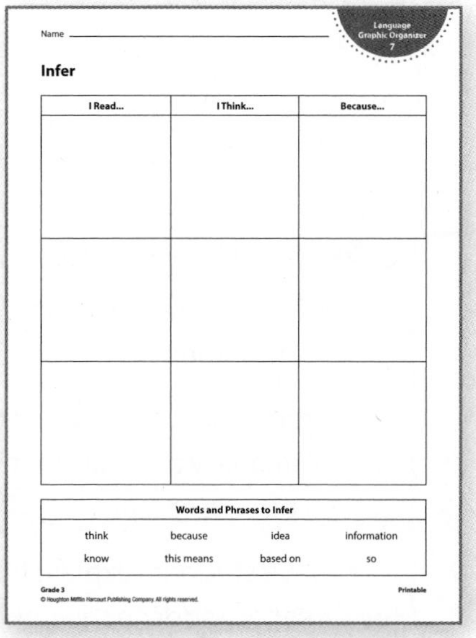

Name ______ Language Graphic Organizer 7

Infer

I Read...	I Think...	Because...

Words and Phrases to Infer			
think	because	idea	information
know	this means	based on	so

Grade 3 Printable
© Houghton Mifflin Harcourt Publishing Company. All rights reserved.

Printable: Language Graphic Organizer 7

Literacy Centers

See pp. T214–T215.

- READING CENTER
- VOCABULARY CENTER
- DIGITAL STATION
- WRITING CENTER
- PROJECT CENTER

Writing

Students write using figurative language. *See Engage and Respond, p. T263.*

Additional Skills Practice

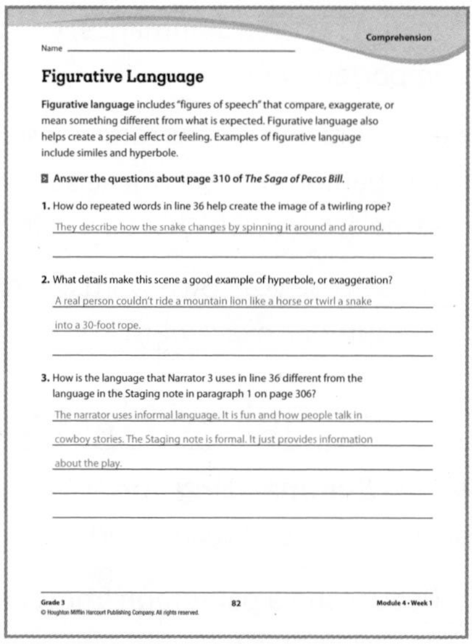

Name ______________________ Comprehension

Figurative Language

Figurative language includes "figures of speech" that compare, exaggerate, or mean something different from what is expected. Figurative language also helps create a special effect or feeling. Examples of figurative language include similes and hyperbole.

Answer the questions about page 310 of *The Saga of Pecos Bill*.

1. How do repeated words in line 36 help create the image of a twirling rope?

They describe how the snake changes by spinning it around and around.

2. What details make this scene a good example of hyperbole, or exaggeration?

A real person couldn't ride a mountain lion like a horse or twirl a snake into a 30-foot rope.

3. How is the language that Narrator 3 uses in line 36 different from the language in the Staging note in paragraph 1 on page 306?

The narrator uses informal language. It is fun and how people talk in cowboy stories. The Staging note is formal. It just provides information about the play.

Grade 3 82 Module 4 • Week 1

© Houghton Mifflin Harcourt Publishing Company. All rights reserved.

Know It, Show It, p. 82

Wrap-Up

Share Time

At the end of the Reading Workshop, have students reflect on their learning by sharing how they applied **figurative language** or another area of focus during independent work time. Choose from these options:

- Use the **SOLO CHAIR** routine. Select a reader each day to come to the front of the class and tell what he or she learned from the reading by using a skill or strategy.
- **THINK-PAIR-SHARE** Students share their thinking with a partner. Select a few pairs each day to share with the whole class.
- **RETURN TO ANCHOR CHART** Have students add sticky notes about their independent reading to the Figurative Language Anchor Charts. Call on a few students to explain what they added and why.

Online Ed

ANCHOR CHARTS 25 & 26: Figurative Language

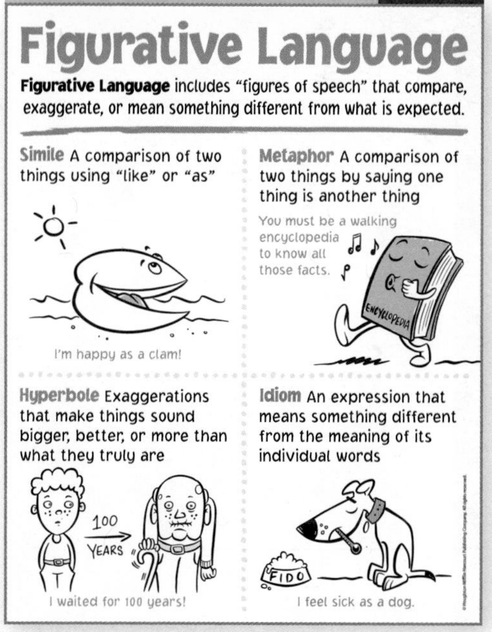

Figurative Language
Figurative Language includes "figures of speech" that compare, exaggerate, or mean something different from what is expected.
Simile A comparison of two things using "like" or "as"
I'm happy as a clam!
Metaphor A comparison of two things by saying one thing is another thing
You must be a walking encyclopedia to know all those facts.
ENCYCLOPEDIA
Hyperbole Exaggerations that make things sound bigger, better, or more than what they truly are
100 YEARS
I waited for 100 years!
Idiom An expression that means something different from the meaning of its individual words
FIDO
I feel sick as a dog.

Summarizing/Paraphrasing

LEARNING OBJECTIVES
- Paraphrase information read aloud.
- Summarize information read aloud.
- **Language** Use acquired language to summarize and paraphrase information.

MATERIALS Online Ed

Classroom materials Read Aloud *Becoming an Actor*, pp. T239–T240

INSTRUCTIONAL VOCABULARY
- **paraphrase** to put someone else's ideas in your own words
- **summarize** to restate the most important information, or main ideas in a text, in your own words

Step 1 Introduce the Skill

Discuss Summarizing and Paraphrasing Explain to students that summarizing and paraphrasing are both ways to recount information in a text in your own words.

- Summarizing means restating the key information and important details in a text. When you summarize, you don't need to retell every minor detail, just the important ones.
- Paraphrasing means retelling someone else's ideas in your own words. When you paraphrase, you make sure to include all the important information in the same order in which it occurs in the text.
- Always use your own words when summarizing and paraphrasing. Never use the author's exact words.

Step 2 Guided Practice

Model Summarizing and Paraphrasing Model how to summarize and paraphrase a text read aloud.

- Read aloud a paragraph from a text, such as Read Aloud *Becoming an Actor* on pages T239–T240.
- Model paraphrasing the paragraph. Point out how to change the author's words into your own words. Guide students to paraphrase the same paragraph in their own words.
- Then summarize the main ideas in the paragraph. Point out that you don't include all the minor details in a summary. Guide students to create their own summary.

Step 3 Apply the Skill

Summarize/Paraphrase Information Read Aloud Have students paraphrase and summarize another paragraph from *Becoming an Actor* or another text.

- Read aloud a paragraph and give students some time to paraphrase or tell a summary of what they heard to a partner.
- Have students share their summaries and discuss what makes a good summary.

ENGLISH LEARNER SUPPORT: Support Paraphrasing and Summarizing

SUBSTANTIAL
Read aloud a single sentence. Allow students to restate it using whatever language is accessible. Then help them clarify and correct language as needed.

MODERATE
Use sentence frames: *The key idea is* ______. *The important details are* ______.

LIGHT
Use guiding questions such as these to help students paraphrase and summarize: *What is the key idea and important details? How would you say that in your own words?*

Synthesize Topic Knowledge

LEARNING OBJECTIVES

- Recognize and describe the features of a drama.
- Synthesize knowledge gained from the week's texts.
- **Language** Articulate what has been learned about the essential question from their reading.

MATERIALS Online Ed

myBook *Book 1, pp. 300–301, 304–315*

Display and Engage *Knowledge Map 4.5*

Genre Focus

- Review with students the characteristics of a drama. Explain that a drama is written to be performed on stage. Key features include a cast of characters, dialogue, and stage directions. Like a story, a drama has characters, setting, and a plot with a beginning, middle, and end. A drama may be divided into acts and scenes, which are like chapters in a book.
- Discuss with students that the selection of the week, *The Saga of Pecos Bill,* is an example of a drama.
- Ask students to name the features of a drama that appear in the selection, and how these features help them to understand the story and help them to picture it being performed on a stage.

Knowledge Focus

- Project Display and Engage: Knowledge Map 4.5. Have students turn to *my*Book page 300.
- Tell students to think about what makes *The Saga of Pecos Bill* a good story to tell as a play. *(It has settings that can be shown on a stage, exciting action, interesting characters, and dialogue that can be easily performed.)*
- Then work with students to add information from *The Saga of Pecos Bill* to the Knowledge Map.

Online

DISPLAY AND ENGAGE:
Knowledge Map 4.5

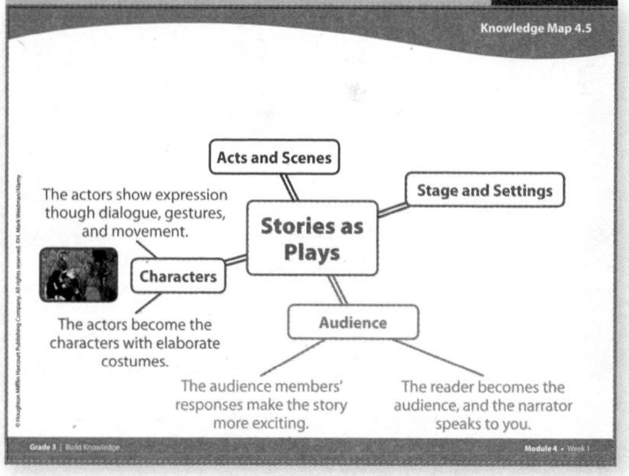

- Have students discuss their Knowledge Maps and their responses to the Essential Question: *Why might some stories be better told as plays?*
- Tell students that they will return to the Knowledge Map for the Week 2 Make Connections activity.

ENGLISH LEARNER SUPPORT: Facilitate Discussion

SUBSTANTIAL

Use these frames to help students connect the reading the Essential Question: *A play has _____.* The Saga of Pecos Bill *also has _____.*

MODERATE

Prompt students to connect the reading to the Essential Question. The Saga of Pecos Bill *is better performed as a play because _____.*

LIGHT

Ask students to connect the reading to the Essential Question. Ask: *What makes* The Saga of Pecos Bill *a good story for a play?*

Notes

LANGUAGE ARTS CONNECTION: Drama

Stories on Stage

Essential Question Why might some stories be better told as plays?

Essential Skills

VOCABULARY

- Critical Vocabulary: *baroque, pulleys, backdrop, performance, eminent, peasant, stately, deceive, superior, merciful*
- Vocabulary Strategy: Shades of Meaning
- Generative Vocabulary: Suffixes *–er/–or* "one who"; Spiral Review: Prefixes *in– (not), im– (into)*

READING WORKSHOP

- Retell/Summarize
- Media Techniques
- Elements of Drama
- Theme

FOUNDATIONAL SKILLS

- Vowel Diphthongs *ow, ou*
- Spelling: Vowel Sound in *town*
- Fluency: Intonation

COMMUNICATION

- Research: Evaluate and Organize Information
- Make Connections

WRITING WORKSHOP

- Narrative Writing: Story
- More Plural Nouns

LEARNING MINDSET: Self-Reflection

THIS WEEK'S SELECTIONS

myBOOK

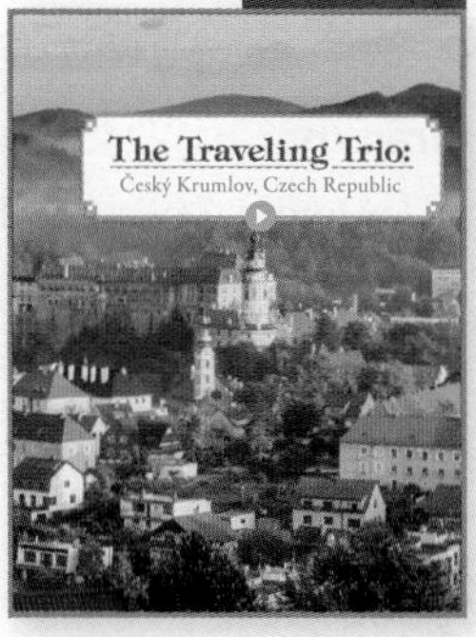

MEDIA: EDUCATIONAL VIDEO
The Traveling Trio: Český Krumlov, Czech Republic

myBOOK

DRAMA/CLASSIC TALE
Gigi and the Wishing Ring

Rigby®
LEVELED LIBRARY

WEEK 2

Week at a Glance

Suggested Daily Times

- VOCABULARY 10–15 minutes
- READING WORKSHOP 60–85 minutes
- FOUNDATIONAL SKILLS 15–30 minutes
- COMMUNICATION 15–30 minutes
- WRITING WORKSHOP 30–45 minutes

This Week's Words

BIG IDEA WORDS

audition *rehearse* *ability* *actor*

CRITICAL VOCABULARY WORDS

baroque	*pulleys*	*backdrop*
performance	*eminent*	*peasant*
stately	*deceive*	*superior*
merciful		

HIGH-FREQUENCY WORDS

clothes	*instruments*	*direction*
center		

INSTRUCTIONAL VOCABULARY

main idea	*summarize*	*animation*
live action	*media*	*sound elements*
visual elements	*retell*	*act*
dialogue	*scene*	*stage direction*
moral	*theme*	*topic*

Assessment Options

Online Ed

- **Selection Quiz: *The Traveling Trio: Český Krumlov, Czech Republic***
- **Selection Quiz: *Gigi and the Wishing Ring***
- **Weekly Assessment**
  - Comprehension: Media Techniques, Elements of Drama, Theme
  - Generative Vocabulary: Suffixes *-er/-or* "one who..."; Spiral Review: Prefixes *in-* (not), *im-* (into)
  - Vocabulary Strategy: Shades of Meaning
  - Grammar: More Plural Nouns

Intervention

For students needing strategic intervention, choose from daily small-group options for differentiation. Access online Foundational Skills and Word Study Studio for additional support.

LESSON 6

VOCABULARY

Academic Vocabulary, pp. T278–T279

- Introduce Critical Vocabulary: *baroque, pulleys, backdrop, performance*

READING WORKSHOP

Teaching Pal

The Traveling Trio: Český Krumlov, Czech Republic

GENRE Media: Educational Video

Shared Reading: MINILESSON, pp. T280–T281

- Connect and Teach: Retell/Summarize
- Apply to Video: ***The Traveling Trio: Český Krumlov, Czech Republic***
- Engage and Respond: Speaking and Listening

SMALL-GROUP INSTRUCTION

Options for Differentiation

- Guided Reading Groups, p. T282
- English Learner Support: Recount Information, p. T282
- Reinforce Retell/Summarize, p. T283

Options for Independent and Collaborative Work, pp. T284–T285

FOUNDATIONAL SKILLS

Decoding, pp. T286–T287

- Vowel Diphthongs *ow, ou*

Spelling, p. T288

- Vowel Sound in *town*

Fluency, p. T289

- Intonation

WRITING WORKSHOP

Narrative Writing: Story, p. W57

- Drafting I: Beginning the Draft

Grammar, p. W245

- Change *y* to *i*

LESSON 7

VOCABULARY

Academic Vocabulary, p. T290

- Review Critical Vocabulary: *baroque, pulleys, backdrop, performance*

Vocabulary Strategy, p. T291

- Shades of Meaning

READING WORKSHOP

Teaching Pal

The Traveling Trio: Český Krumlov, Czech Republic

GENRE Media: Educational Video

Shared Reading: MINILESSON, pp. T292–T293

- Connect and Teach: Media Techniques
- Apply to Video: ***The Traveling Trio: Český Krumlov, Czech Republic***
- Engage and Respond: Write a Travel Guide

SMALL-GROUP INSTRUCTION

Options for Differentiation

- Guided Reading Groups, p. T294
- English Learner Support: Recount Information, p. T294
- Reinforce Media Techniques, p. T295

Options for Independent and Collaborative Work, pp. T296–T297

COMMUNICATION

Project Checkpoint: Write and Create, pp. T207, T275

WRITING WORKSHOP

Narrative Writing: Story, p. W58

- Drafting II: Writing the Middle

Grammar, p. W246

- Adding *-s* or *-es* to Nouns

LESSON 8

VOCABULARY

Academic Vocabulary, pp. T298–T299

- Introduce Critical Vocabulary: *eminent, peasant, stately, deceive, superior, merciful*

READING WORKSHOP

Gigi and the Wishing Ring

Teaching Pal

GENRE Drama/Classic Tale

Shared Reading: MINILESSON, pp. T300–T301

- Connect and Teach: Retell/Summarize
- Apply to Text: ***Gigi and the Wishing Ring***
- Engage and Respond: Speaking and Listening

SMALL-GROUP INSTRUCTION

Options for Differentiation

- Guided Reading Groups, p. T302
- English Learner Support: Recount Information, p. T302
- Reinforce Retell/Summarize, p. T303

Options for Independent and Collaborative Work, pp. T304–T305

FOUNDATIONAL SKILLS

Decoding, pp. T306–T307

- Vowel Diphthongs *ow, ou*

WRITING WORKSHOP

Narrative Writing: Story, p. W59

- Drafting III: Completing the Draft

Grammar, p. W247

- Forming Irregular Plural Nouns

LESSON 9

VOCABULARY

Academic Vocabulary, p. T308

- Review Critical Vocabulary: *eminent, peasant, stately, deceive, superior, merciful*

Vocabulary Strategy, p. T309

- Shades of Meaning

READING WORKSHOP

Gigi and the Wishing Ring

Teaching Pal

GENRE Drama/Classic Tale

Shared Reading: MINILESSON, pp. T310–T311

- Connect and Teach: Elements of Drama
- Apply to Text: ***Gigi and the Wishing Ring***
- Engage and Respond: Write a Newspaper Report

SMALL-GROUP INSTRUCTION

Options for Differentiation

- Guided Reading Groups, p. T312
- English Learner Support: Recount Information, p. T312
- Reinforce Elements of Drama, p. T313

Options for Independent and Collaborative Work, pp. T314–T315

COMMUNICATION

Project Checkpoint: Write and Create, pp. T207, T275

WRITING WORKSHOP

Narrative Writing: Story, p. W60

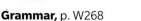

- Revising I: Integrating Narrative Elements

Grammar, p. W268

- Reviewing Action and Being Verbs

LESSON 10

VOCABULARY

Generative Vocabulary, pp. T316–T317

- Suffixes *–er/–or* "one who..."
- Spiral Review: Prefixes *in– (not), im– (into)*

READING WORKSHOP

Gigi and the Wishing Ring

Teaching Pal

GENRE Drama/Classic Tale

Shared Reading: MINILESSON, pp. T318–T319

- Connect and Teach: Theme
- Apply to Text: ***Gigi and the Wishing Ring***
- Engage and Respond: Reading

SMALL-GROUP INSTRUCTION

Options for Differentiation

- Guided Reading Groups, p. T320
- English Learner Support: Recount Information, p. T320
- Reinforce Theme, p. T131

Options for Independent and Collaborative Work, pp. T322–T323

COMMUNICATION

Research, p. T324

- Evaluate and Organize Information

Make Connections, p. T325

- Synthesize Topic Knowledge

WRITING WORKSHOP

Narrative Writing: Story, p. W61

- Revising II: Conferencing

Grammar, p. W249

- Connect to Writing: Using Plural Nouns

Literacy Centers

- **While you meet with small groups, have students work independently in Literacy Centers. Familiarize students with the week's activities and post a daily rotation schedule.**
- **Have students complete Printable: Exit Ticket for each activity so you can monitor their work.**

READING CENTER

Readers' Theater

- Preview Printable: **Readers' Theater 4**, "A Tale with a Twist," and assign parts to mixed-ability groups of five students.
- The part of Carlos is ideal for struggling readers, and the part of Carrie can be read by a proficient reader.

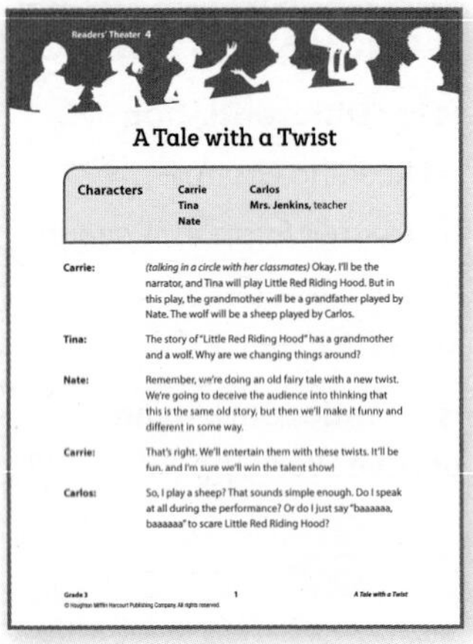
Readers' Theater 4

A Tale with a Twist

Characters: Carrie, Tina, Nate, Carlos, Mrs. Jenkins, teacher

Carrie: (talking in a circle with her classmates) Okay. I'll be the narrator, and Tina will play Little Red Riding Hood. But in this play, the grandmother will be a grandfather played by Nate. The wolf will be a sheep played by Carlos.

Tina: The story of "Little Red Riding Hood" has a grandmother and a wolf. Why are we changing things around?

Nate: Remember, we're doing an old fairy tale with a new twist. We're going to deceive the audience into thinking that this is the same old story, but then we'll make it funny and different in some way.

Carrie: That's right. We'll entertain them with these twists. It'll be fun, and I'm sure we'll win the talent show!

Carlos: So, I play a sheep? That sounds simple enough. Do I speak at all during the performance? Or do I just say "baaaaaa, baaaaaa" to scare Little Red Riding Hood?

Printable: Readers' Theater 4

Independent Reading

- Have students self-select or continue reading an independent reading book.
- Remind students to set a purpose for reading and to record their progress on their Printable: **Reading Log**.
- Have students use Printable: **Independent Reading** for fiction or nonfiction to note key ideas as they read.
- Display and review Anchor Chart 36: **Respond to Text**.
- You may want to choose from these additional options to have students interact with their books:
- **Mixed-Ability Groups** Students discuss their self-selected books, using the questions on the Reading Log.
- **Write a Postcard** Students expand on their understanding by writing a postcard to a classmate with a suggestion to help their classmate choose this book.

Name ______ Centers

Reading Log

Title ______

Author ______ Genre ______

Independent Reading Record

Date ______ Time Spent ______ Pages Read ______

Date ______ Time Spent ______ Pages Read ______

Date ______ Time Spent ______ Pages Read ______

Date ______ Time Spent ______ Pages Read ______

Summary This text is about ______

Questions for Discussion

What was your favorite part of the text? ______

What did you enjoy about the author's writing? ______

Was there something that you did not understand? What was it? ______

Would you recommend this text to a friend? Why or why not? ______

Printable: Reading Log

VOCABULARY CENTER

Super Six Words *(Use in Lessons 6–10.)*

- Have students use Printable: **Super Six Words** to list Big Idea Words and this week's Critical Vocabulary words that relate to the module topic.
- Then have students select six words from their lists that they think are most important, interesting, or new to them.
- Tell students to write a sentence for each selected word.
- Explain to students that they will come back to this list at the end of each week in the module.

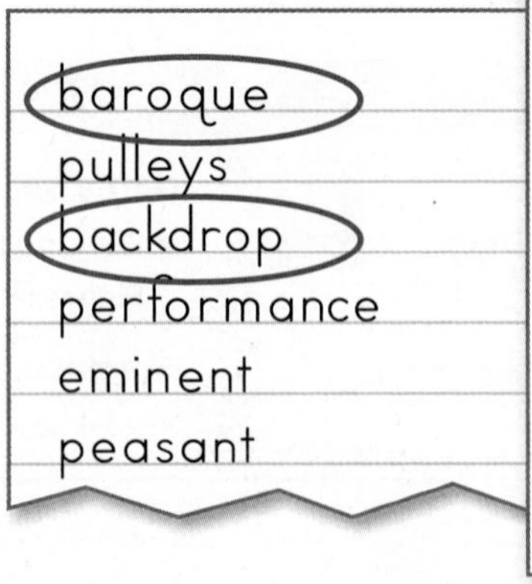

Name ______ Centers

Super Six Words

1. Take a clean sheet of paper. Write your name at the top. Then write the module title.
2. Create four columns labeled Week 1, Week 2, Week 3, and Super Six.
3. Each week, list words about the topic from the texts you read in that week's column.
4. At the end of each week, choose and circle six words on your weekly list that you think are most important to the topic.
5. Write a sentence for each of those six words. Make sure your sentences show the meanings of the words.
6. At the end of the module, you will have eighteen words and sentences.
7. Now, choose six words from those eighteen words you think are most important to the topic. Write them in the Super Six column.
8. Use your Super Six words to write a summary of what you have learned about the module topic.

Printable: Super Six Words

DIGITAL STATION

Listener's Choice

Online Ed

- Have students listen to one of this week's selections, *The Traveling Trio*, or *Gigi and the Wishing Ring*, or a Leveled Reader of their choice.
- Tell them to add the title to their Printable: **Listening Log**, as well as listing the listening skills they used, a summary of the selection, and questions they have about the selection or book.

Keyboarding

- Have students practice keyboarding using Printable: **Keyboarding 4.2**.

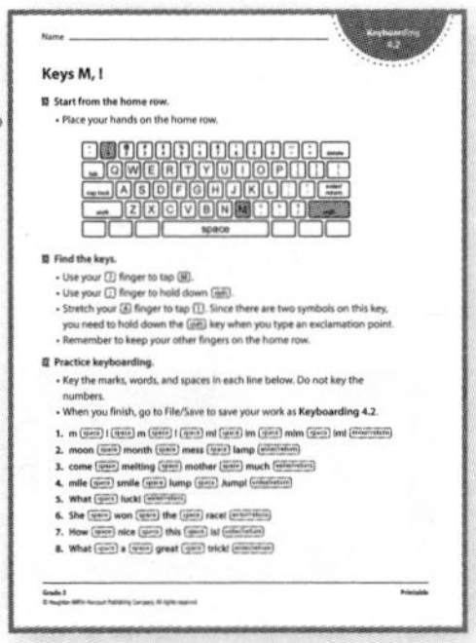
Name

Keyboarding 4.2

Keys M, !

Start from the home row.
- Place your hands on the home row.

Find the keys.
- Use your finger to tap M.
- Use your finger to hold down shift.
- Stretch your finger to tap !. Since there are two symbols on this key, you need to hold down the shift key when you type an exclamation point.
- Remember to keep your other fingers on the home row.

Practice keyboarding.
- Key the marks, words, and spaces in each line below. Do not key the numbers.
- When you finish, go to File/Save to save your work as **Keyboarding 4.2**.

1. m space ! space m space ! space m! space !m space m!m space !m!
2. moon space month space mess space lamp
3. come space melting space mother space much
4. mile space smile space lump space Jump!
5. What space luck!
6. She space won space the space race!
7. How space nice space this space is!
8. What space a space great space trick!

Grade 3 Printable

Printable: Keyboarding 4.2

WRITING CENTER

Write a Travel Guide and Write a Newspaper Report *(Use in Lessons 7, 9, and 10)*

- Have students use Printable: **Peer Conferencing Routine** to discuss their writing.
- Tell peers to use the tips on *my*Book pages 317 and 341 as they review the work of others and offer feedback.

Writing Workshop

- Have students work on a piece of writing. Depending on where students are in their writing, they may use the time to prewrite, draft, revise, edit, or publish.
- Students may choose from among tasks such as these:
  - » Revise a draft for proper use of parts of speech, subject-verb agreement, or punctuation in dialogue.
- Display Anchor Chart 37: **Cursive Handwriting**.

PROJECT CENTER

Project Checkpoint: Write and Create

- Have students work in groups, using Printable: **Project 4.2** to guide them as they continue the project. Groups should complete the following over the course of the week:

☑ Come to a consensus about which story the group will rewrite as a play.

☑ Discuss the role each student will play in the project.

☑ Draft the play script.

☑ Prepare costumes and props if desired.

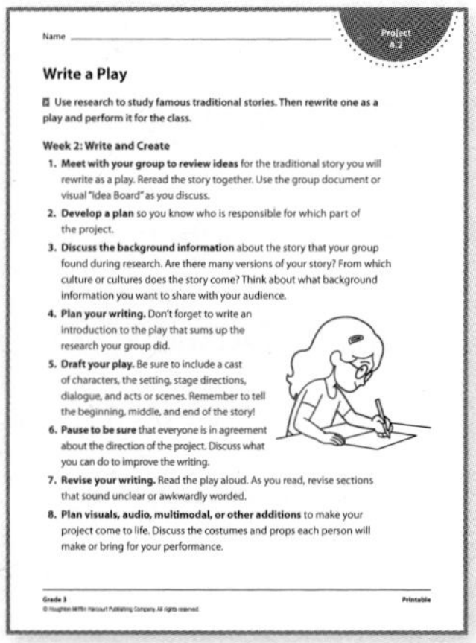
Name

Project 4.2

Write a Play

Use research to study famous traditional stories. Then rewrite one as a play and perform it for the class.

Week 2: Write and Create

1. **Meet with your group to review ideas** for the traditional story you will rewrite as a play. Reread the story together. Use the group document or visual "Idea Board" as you discuss.
2. **Develop a plan** so you know who is responsible for which part of the project.
3. **Discuss the background information** about the story that your group found during research. Are there many versions of your story? From which culture or cultures does the story come? Think about what background information you want to share with your audience.
4. **Plan your writing.** Don't forget to write an introduction to the play that sums up the research your group did.
5. **Draft your play.** Be sure to include a cast of characters, the setting, stage directions, dialogue, and acts or scenes. Remember to tell the beginning, middle, and end of the story!
6. **Pause to be sure** that everyone is in agreement about the direction of the project. Discuss what you can do to improve the writing.
7. **Revise your writing.** Read the play aloud. As you read, revise sections that sound unclear or awkwardly worded.
8. **Plan visuals, audio, multimodal, or other additions** to make your project come to life. Discuss the costumes and props each person will make or bring for your performance.

Grade 3 Printable

Printable: Project 4.2

Reading Remake

(Use in Lessons 6–10.)

- Have students complete the Make a Flipbook activity on Printable: **Reading Remake 7**.
- Ask partners to explain to one another how their mural shows their understanding of the selection.

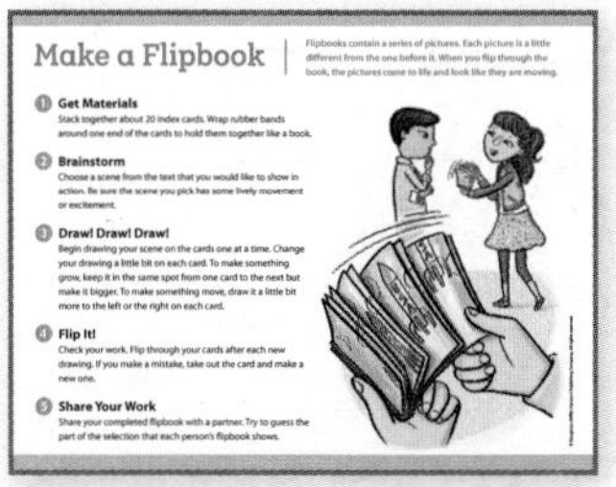
Make a Flipbook

Flipbooks contain a series of pictures. Each picture is a little different from the one before it. When you flip through the book, the pictures come to life and look like they are moving.

1. **Get Materials**
Stack together about 20 index cards. Wrap rubber bands around one end of the cards to hold them together like a book.
2. **Brainstorm**
Choose a scene from the text that you would like to show in action. Be sure the scene you pick has some lively movement or excitement.
3. **Draw! Draw! Draw!**
Begin drawing your scene on the cards one at a time. Change your drawing a little bit on each card. To make something grow, keep it in the same spot from one card to the next but make it bigger. To make something move, draw it a little bit more to the left or the right on each card.
4. **Flip It!**
Check your work. Flip through your cards after each new drawing. If you make a mistake, take out the card and make a new one.
5. **Share Your Work**
Share your completed flipbook with a partner. Try to guess the part of the selection that each person's flipbook shows.

Printable: Reading Remake 7

WEEK 2 Preview Lesson Texts

Build understanding of this week's texts so that you can best support students in making connections, understanding key ideas, and becoming lifelong readers.

The Traveling Trio: Český Krumlov, Czech Republic

GENRE Media: Educational Video

WHY THIS VIDEO?

This educational video provides an opportunity for students to see and retell historical and present-day details about a treasured Baroque theater in the Czech Republic. Students will get a tour of the building and explore areas that the audience doesn't get to see, such as backstage and under the stage.

KEY LEARNING OBJECTIVES

- Retell/Summarize
- Media Techniques

myBOO

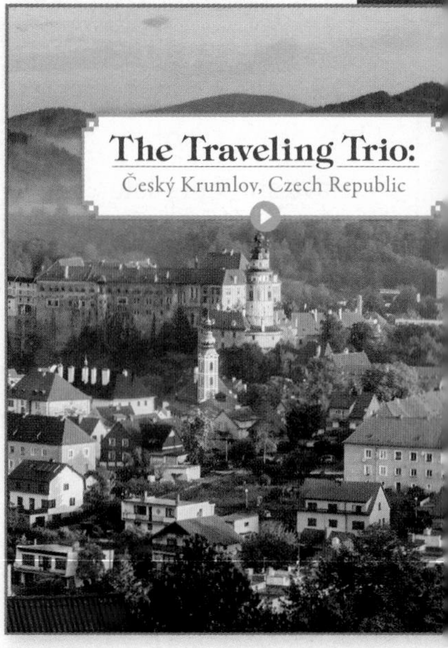

MAKE CONNECTIONS

BUILD KNOWLEDGE AND LANGUAGE

- **Language Arts Connection:** Drama

VOCABULARY

- **Suffixes *-er/-or* "one who...":** *actors*

FOUNDATIONAL SKILLS

- **Vowel Diphthongs *ow, ou*:** *town, towering, allowed, down, downstairs, nowadays*

WRITING WORKSHOP

- **Narrative Writing: Story**
- **More Plural Nouns**

TEXT X-RAY

KEY IDEAS

Key Idea *06:57*
Stage plays have been a big part of European culture for hundreds of years.

Key Idea *07:03*
The Český Krumlov theater was originally built for the royal family 250 years ago.

Key Idea *07:18*
Unfortunately, many theaters like this burned down due to the use of candles to light the stage (pre-electricity days).

Key Idea *08:43*
Due to its uniqueness, this theater is being preserved by limiting its use to three times per year.

LANGUAGE

Content-Area Word
culture *06:57* Students have most likely heard the term "culture". Encourage them to define it via a word association game and write down their responses on a white board. Explain that while "culture" is a somewhat complex concept, it is important to understand its meaning to better learn about the wide variety of cultures in the world. Key word ideas: *beliefs, customs, arts, society, group, place, time.*

Content-Area Word
nowadays *08:43* English learners may not recognize this term. Explain that it is another way of saying "at the present time." Give an example: "Nowadays, [smart phones] are very popular."

Gigi and the Wishing Ring Adapted from an Italian Fairy Tale

GENRE Drama/Classic Tale

myBOOK

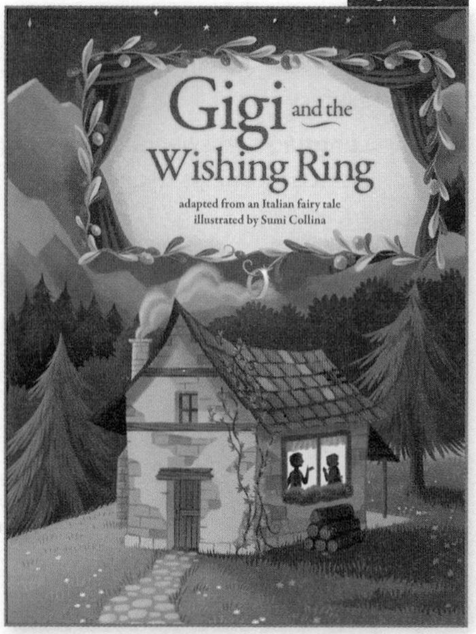

WHY THIS TEXT?

This stage adaption of a classic Italian fairy tale will provide an opportunity for students to retell/summarize the events in the story. They will learn to identify characters, dialogue, setting, and acts/scenes in a drama. In addition, students will identify the theme and understand how it is different from a topic.

KEY LEARNING OBJECTIVES

- Retell/Summarize
- Elements of Drama
- Theme

TEXT COMPLEXITY

OVERALL RATING Slightly Complex

This selection has a conventional structure with a simple theme and conversational language.

MAKE CONNECTIONS

BUILD KNOWLEDGE AND LANGUAGE

- **Language Arts Connection:** Drama

VOCABULARY

- **Suffixes–er/–or "one who":** *narrator, waiter*

FOUNDATIONAL SKILLS

- **High-Frequency Words:** *clothes, center*
- **Vowel Diphthongs ow, ou:** *down, bows, wow, meow, how, howl(ing)*

WRITING WORKSHOP

- **Narrative Writing:** Story
- **More Plural Nouns**

TEXT X-RAY

KEY IDEAS

Key Idea *p. 327*
Gigi wants to leave home and explore the world. His mother advises him that "you only *get* from people what you *give* to people."

Key Idea *pp. 328–329*
He meets an old woman who gives him her cat, dog, and a wishing ring to thank him for helping her carry a heavy load.

Key Idea *p. 331*
Gigi meets beautiful Maliarda and gives away the secret of the ring.

Key Idea *p. 338*
Maliarda then uses it against Gigi. He recovers it and gives her a taste of her own medicine.

LANGUAGE

Content-Area Word

backdrop *Line 82; p. 331*
Theatre productions can use a set background tool called a "backdrop" to enhance the scenery. They are usually created on large pieces of fabric or strong paper that are hung behind the actors. It adds detail without requiring a lot of props.

Idiom

to give him/her a taste of their own medicine *p. 338*
Explain to English Learners that there is no real medicine involved here. This idiom, which is a phrase that means something different from what the individual words say, means to treat someone as poorly as they treated you. In other words, to seek revenge using the same method.

Introduce Critical Vocabulary

Step 1 Introduce the Words

LEARNING OBJECTIVES

- Identify real-life connections between words and their use.
- Use newly acquired vocabulary expressively.
- **Language** Answer questions and discuss meanings to develop vocabulary.

MATERIALS Online Ed

Display and Engage *Critical Vocabulary 4.6*

Vocabulary Cards *4.10–4.13*

CRITICAL VOCABULARY

- **Baroque**
- **pulleys**
- **backdrop**
- **performance**

SPANISH COGNATES

- **Baroque** *barroco*

Project Display and Engage: Critical Vocabulary 4.6. Then use the **VOCABULARY** routine to introduce the Critical Vocabulary from *The Traveling Trio: Česky Krumlov, Czech Republic*. You may wish to display the corresponding Vocabulary Card for each word as you discuss it.

DISPLAY AND ENGAGE: Critical Vocabulary 4.6 — Online Ed

Critical Vocabulary 4.6

Critical Vocabulary

1 **Baroque**	The **Baroque** Period was many years ago. The buildings of that time were very fancy and decorated. *You can tell this church is from the Baroque Period because of its high domes and twisted columns.*
2 **pulleys**	**Pulleys** are wheels wrapped with rope that people can use to lift heavy objects. *We use pulleys to lift the heavy velvet stage curtain when it's time for the play to start.*
3 **backdrop**	On a stage, a **backdrop** is a painted curtain or wall that shows the setting of the scene. *Students painted trees and grass on the backdrop to show the scene was set in the park.*
4 **performance**	If you sing, dance, or speak in front of a group, you give a **performance.** *After the band's performance, the audience clapped and yelled for more.*

Grade 3 | Vocabulary — Module 4 • Week 2

1. Read aloud each word and have students repeat it.
2. Read aloud and discuss each word's student-friendly explanation.
3. Point out the example for the word. Have students suggest other examples.

TEACHER TIP

Encourage authentic **vocabulary usage** in your classroom. Students score a point each time they use a new vocabulary word in conversation.

ENGLISH LEARNER SUPPORT: Build Vocabulary

SUBSTANTIAL

Ask pairs to act out giving a performance.

MODERATE

Have students use this sentence frame to describe a performance. *During a performance, a person might* _____ *or* _____.

LIGHT

Ask partners to discuss different kinds of performances they have seen or would like to see.

Step 2 Guided Practice

Guide students to interact with the words by discussing questions such as these:

- *If something is **Baroque**, is it new and modern? Explain.*
- *Do **pulleys** help move things forward, backward, or up and down? Explain.*
- *Does a **backdrop** always show sky, trees, and other parts of nature? Why or why not?*
- *If you sing to yourself in your room, is that a **performance?** Why or why not?*

Ask students to describe how the school is different from a Baroque building. Have them explain what pulleys might be used for. Ask students what might be included in a backdrop for a play set in a big city, and ask where they might see a performance.

Step 3 Apply

- Have students work independently to complete steps 3 and 4 on Vocabulary Cards 4.10–4.13.
- Have students use the **TURN AND TALK** routine to discuss with a partner the prompt on each Vocabulary Card.

Vocabulary Cards

LEARNING MINDSET

Self-Reflection

Normalize Explain to students that it is normal to feel uncomfortable when using self-reflection. *It can be hard to look back at your work when you wanted a different outcome, but that's when you learn more strategies. Add these tools to your toolkit! Then you can pick the right tool for the next task!*

Summarize

LEARNING OBJECTIVES

- Summarize the main ideas of an informational video.
- **Language** Ask and answer questions about the content of an informational video.

MATERIALS **Online** Ed

Anchor Chart 4 *Summarize*
Printable *Anchor Chart 4: Summarize*
Teaching Pal *Book 1, pp. 318–323*
myBook *Book 1, The Traveling Trio, pp. 318–323*
Display and Engage *Build Background 4.6*

INSTRUCTIONAL VOCABULARY

- **main idea** the central idea of a text or what the text is mostly about
- **summarize** to restate the most important information, or main ideas, in a text in your own words

Step 1 Connect and Teach

- Tell students that they are going to watch a video called *The Traveling Trio: Český Krumlov, Czech Republic*. Tell students that when they view the video, it is important to keep track of key ideas and details.
- Project or display Anchor Chart 4: Summarize. Explain to students that when they **summarize,** they restate the most important information, or **main ideas,** in a text or video.
- Review step 1 on the Anchor Chart. Tell students that as they view, they should look for headings, or text on screen that gives important information and tells what each section is about.
- Review steps 2, 3, and 4 on the Anchor Chart. Remind students that they should use their own words when they summarize.
- Tell students that they will practice summarizing when they view *The Traveling Trio.*

Online Ed

ANCHOR CHART 4: Summarize

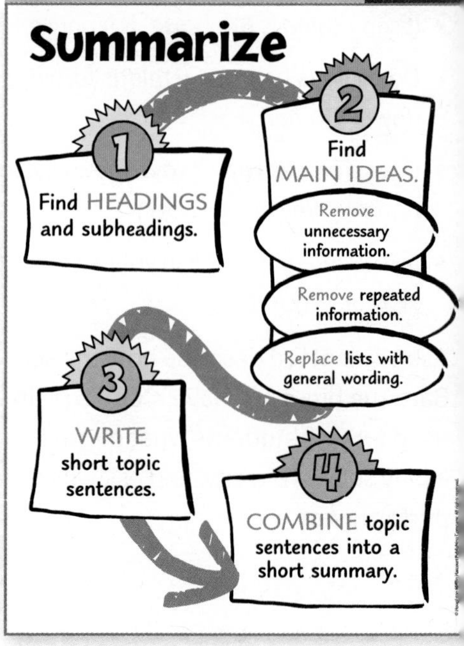
Summarize
1
Find HEADINGS and subheadings.
2
Find MAIN IDEAS.
Remove unnecessary information.
Remove repeated information.
Replace lists with general wording.
3
WRITE short topic sentences.
4
COMBINE topic sentences into a short summary.

ASSESSMENT OPTION

Assign the Selection Quiz to check comprehension of *The Traveling Trio.*

Go to Your
Teaching Pal

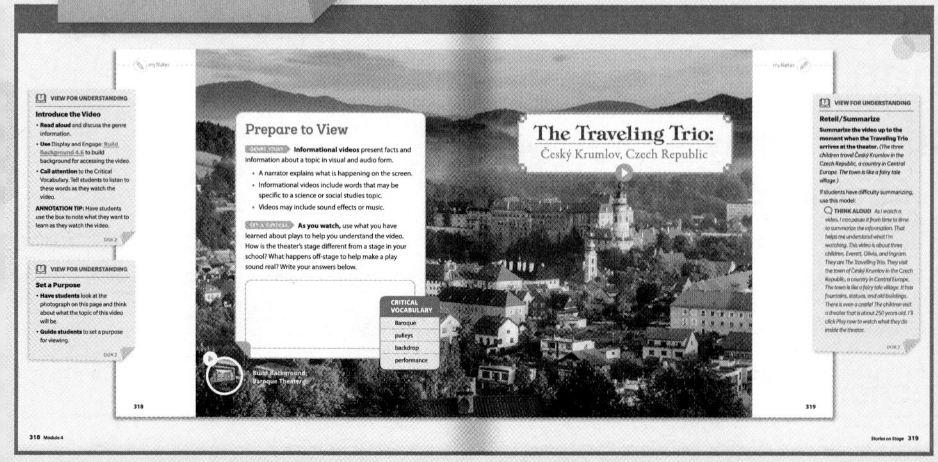

Online Ed

ANNOTATE IT!

Students may use the annotation tools in their eBook.

Step 2 Apply to Text

In your Teaching Pal, pages 318–321, use the blue **VIEW FOR UNDERSTANDING** prompts to view *The Traveling Trio* as students follow along and annotate their *my*Book.

- **Genre Study** Guide students through the genre information on page 318.
- **Build Background** Project Display and Engage 4.6: Build Background and read the information aloud with students. Ask students how the information connects to what they have already learned about plays.
- **Set a Purpose** Read the Set a Purpose section on page 318. Prompt students to set their own purpose for viewing *The Traveling Trio.*
- **View and Comprehend** Use the **ACTIVE VIEWING** routine as you guide students to view the video. Pause occasionally, using the prompts in your Teaching Pal to gauge students' understanding and to have them summarize. As students summarize, have them refer back to the Anchor Chart to determine what information to include in their summaries.

Step 3 Engage and Respond

INDEPENDENT PRACTICE: Speaking and Listening

- After viewing, use the **COLLABORATIVE CONVERSATION** routine with the Collaborative Discussion questions on Teaching Pal and *my*Book page 321. Have students annotate their *my*Book with details from the videos and visuals as evidence to explain their responses.
- Ask volunteers to read aloud the Speaking and Listening tips. Remind students that as they speak, they should pay attention to others' reactions to check that everyone understands what is being said.
- You may want to have students conduct their discussions during daily small-group time.

ENGLISH LEARNER SUPPORT: Elicit Participation

SUBSTANTIAL

Supply frames to support summarizing: *The children go to _____. They learn about_____.*

MODERATE

Where do the children go? What makes their visit special?

LIGHT

Encourage students to use complete sentences as they summarize key points in the video.

LINK TO SMALL-GROUP INSTRUCTION

REINFORCE SUMMARIZE Review and extend the skill as needed during small-group time to support students' need for differentiation. *See the lesson on p. T283.*

Options for Differentiation

As the class engages in independent and collaborative work, meet with Guided Reading Groups or differentiate instruction based on student need.

GUIDED READING GROUPS

Match Students to Books + Instruction

- Choose just-right books based on level, skill, topic, or genre.

L M N O P Q

Leveled Readers

- Deliver instruction with each book's **Take and Teach Lesson**, choosing appropriate sessions based on need.

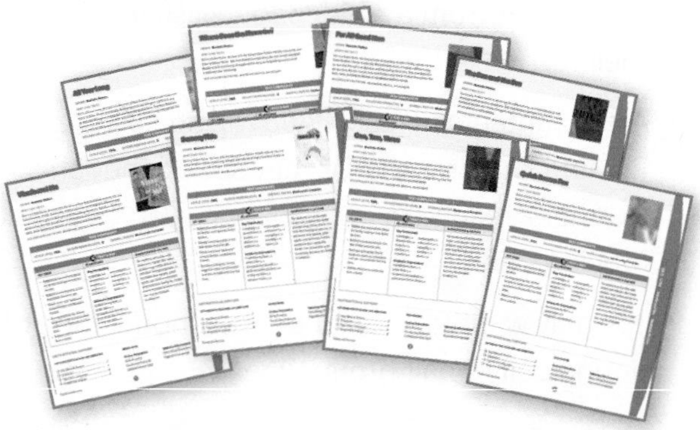

- Check comprehension, reinforce instruction, and extend learning with suggested supporting activities.

ENGLISH LEARNER SUPPORT

Recount Information

- Use **Tabletop Minilessons: English Language Development 11.1 (Listening)** to introduce and practice the language skill.

Tabletop Minilessons: English Language Development

- Then use the following text-based prompts with *The Traveling Trio* to guide application of the language skill. Begin with the prompt at the student's identified language proficiency level. As students progress, use lighter supports to encourage increased language proficiency.

SUBSTANTIAL

As students view the video, ask them to raise their hand when they hear the words that complete the sentence frames: *The Czech Republic is located in central _____. The Český Krumlov Baroque Theater was built about _____ years ago.*

MODERATE

Have students view the video, and then use the sentence frames to recount information: *The Český Krumlov is a _____. It was built _____. It is located in the country of _____.*

LIGHT

Have students view the video, and then answer the questions: *What is the Český Krumlov? Where is it located? When was it built?*

REINFORCE SUMMARIZE

Demonstrate

- Use **Tabletop Minilessons: Reading Card 4** to remind students that when they **summarize,** they restate the most important information, or **main ideas,** in a text or video. A summary does not need to include all minor details. Recall that summarizing will help students understand and recall what they watch or read.
- Model filling out Printable: Reading Graphic Organizer 4 to summarize *The Traveling Trio.*

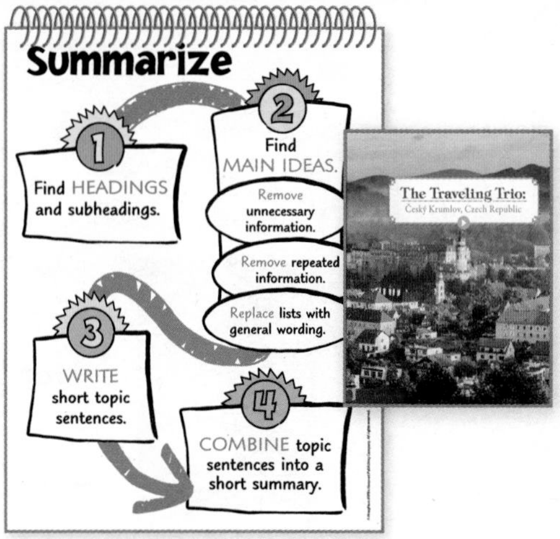
Summarize
1
Find HEADINGS and subheadings.
2
Find MAIN IDEAS.
Remove unnecessary information.
Remove repeated information.
Replace lists with general wording.
3
WRITE short topic sentences.
4
COMBINE topic sentences into a short summary.
The Traveling Trio:
Český Krumlov, Czech Republic

Tabletop Minilessons: Reading

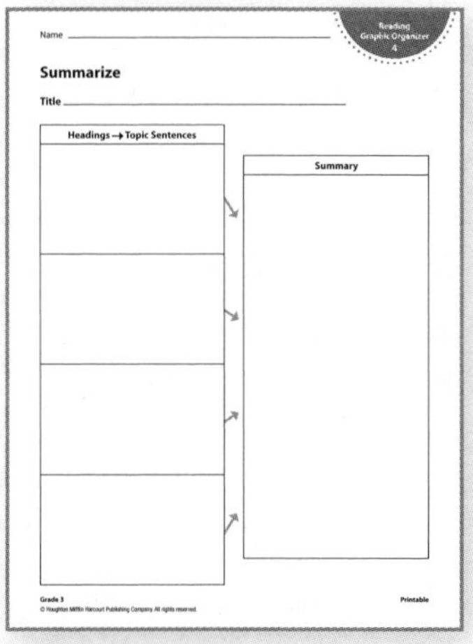
Name
Summarize
Title
Headings → Topic Sentences
Summary
Printable

Printable: Reading Graphic Organizer 4

Apply to Independent Reading

- Now have students summarize an appropriate book, article, or video they are reading or viewing independently. Customize these prompts to the texts students choose.
  - » *What main ideas did you include in your summary?*
  - » *What are some minor details that you did not need to include in your summary?*
  - » *How did summarizing help you to understand or remember the text?*
- Have students complete Printable: Reading Graphic Organizer 4 for their independent reading book.

ALMOST THERE
READY FOR MORE

SCAFFOLD AND EXTEND

- Guide students to identify the main ideas and then retell them in a summary.
- Prompt students to identify main ideas and use them to summarize the text.
- Have students explain how they identified which details to include in their summary.

EL ENGLISH LEARNER SUPPORT

SUBSTANTIAL
Guide students to summarize by pointing to pictures in the text and using English words to express main ideas.

MODERATE
Supply students with sentence frames such as: *My summary should include the main ideas _____. I don't need to include _____.*

LIGHT
Have partners listen to each other's summaries of the text. Then ask them to discuss the main ideas and offer suggestions to one another on how to improve the summary.

Options for Independent and Collaborative Work

While you meet with small groups, have other students engage in literacy activities that reinforce the lesson's learning objectives. Choose from these options.

Independent Reading

Student Choice Library

Rigby
LEVELED LIBRARY

APPLY READING SKILL

Summarize Students complete Printable: Reading Graphic Organizer 4 for an independent reading book.

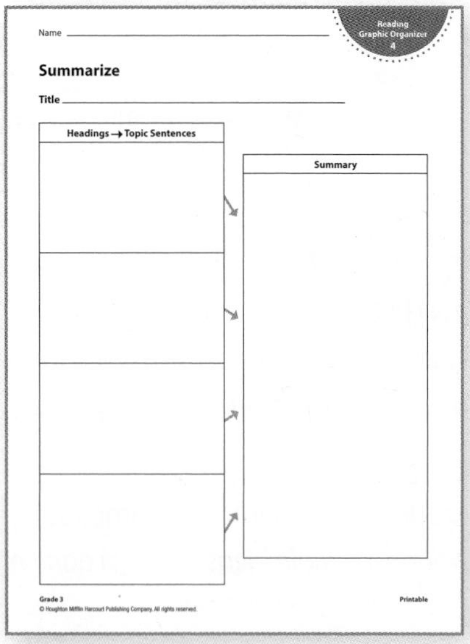
Reading Graphic Organizer 4
Name
Summarize
Title
Headings → Topic Sentences
Summary
Grade 3
Printable

Printable: Reading Graphic Organizer 4

APPLY LANGUAGE SKILL

Recount Information Students complete Printable: Language Graphic Organizer 11 for an independent reading book.

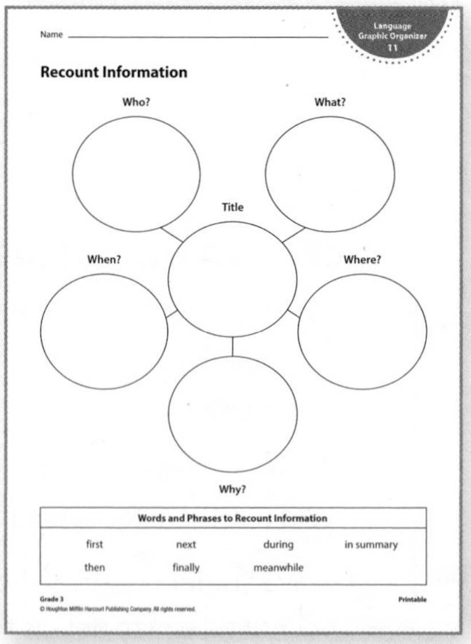
Language Graphic Organizer 11
Name
Recount Information
Who? What? Title When? Where? Why?

Words and Phrases to Recount Information			
first	next	during	in summary
then	finally	meanwhile	

Grade 3
Printable

Printable: Language Graphic Organizer 11

Literacy Centers

See pp. T274–T275.

- READING CENTER
- VOCABULARY CENTER
- DIGITAL STATION
- WRITING CENTER
- PROJECT CENTER

Speaking and Listening

Partners discuss the Collaborative Discussion questions. *See Engage and Respond, p. T281.*

Additional Skills Practice

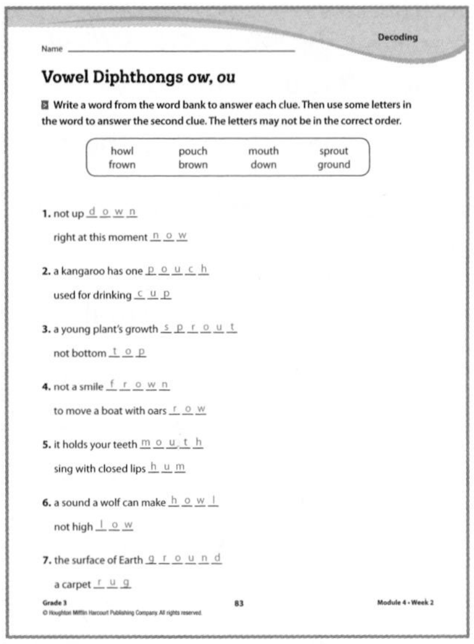
Decoding

Name ____________________

Vowel Diphthongs ow, ou

Write a word from the word bank to answer each clue. Then use some letters in the word to answer the second clue. The letters may not be in the correct order.

howl	pouch	mouth	sprout
frown	brown	down	ground

1. not up d o w n
   right at this moment n o w
2. a kangaroo has one p o u c h
   used for drinking c u p
3. a young plant's growth s p r o u t
   not bottom t o p
4. not a smile f r o w n
   to move a boat with oars r o w
5. it holds your teeth m o u t h
   sing with closed lips h u m
6. a sound a wolf can make h o w l
   not high l o w
7. the surface of Earth g r o u n d
   a carpet r u g

Grade 3 83 Module 4 • Week 2

Know It, Show It, p. 83

Wrap-Up

Share Time

At the end of the Reading Workshop, have students reflect on their learning by sharing how they applied **summarize** or another area of focus during independent work time. Choose from these options:

- Use the **SOLO CHAIR** routine. Select a reader each day to come to the front of the class and tell what he or she learned from the reading by using a skill or strategy.
- **THINK-PAIR-SHARE** Students share their thinking with a partner. Select a few pairs each day to share with the whole class.
- **RETURN TO ANCHOR CHART** Have students add sticky notes about their independent reading to the Summarize Anchor Chart. Call on a few students to explain what they added and why.

Online Ed

ANCHOR CHART 4: Summarize

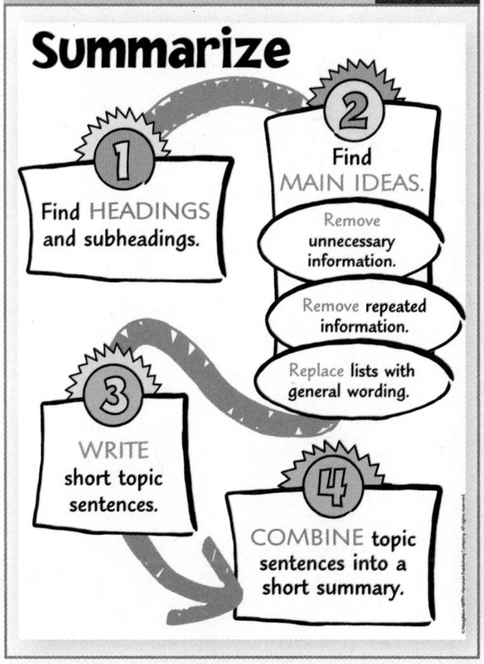
Summarize
1
Find HEADINGS and subheadings.
2
Find MAIN IDEAS.
Remove unnecessary information.
Remove repeated information.
Replace lists with general wording.
3
WRITE short topic sentences.
4
COMBINE topic sentences into a short summary.

LEARNING OBJECTIVES

- Recognize and decode words with vowel diphthongs *ow* and *ou*.
- **Language** Read words with vowel diphthongs *ow* and *ou* and understand their meanings.

MATERIALS **Online** *Ed*

Display and Engage *Decoding 4.6*
Know It, Show It *p. 83*

Vowel Diphthongs *ow, ou*

Step 1 Introduce the Skill

Vowel Diphthong *ow* Display and read aloud the word *down*, emphasizing the vowel sound /ou/.

- Underline *ow* and note that in this word the letters *ow* stand for the /ou/ sound.
- Display the words *cow, owl,* and *growl*. Underline the *ow* in each word. Note that the letters *ow* stand for the /ou/ sound in all of these words.
- Guide students to read the words aloud.

Vowel Diphthong *ou* Display and read aloud the word *loud*, emphasizing the vowel sound /ou/.

- Underline *ou* and note that in this word the letters *ou* stand for the /ou/ sound.
- Display the words *hound, shout,* and *ground*. Underline the *ou* in each word. Note that the letters *ou* stand for the /ou/ sound in all of these words.
- Guide students to read the words aloud.
- Display the following chart.

ow	ou
crowd	proud
howl	crouch
plow	mouth

- Remind students that they have learned two spellings for the /ou/ sound. Point out the spelling patterns in the top row.
- Then read aloud the example words in each column, emphasizing the vowel diphthong in each while underlining the letters that stand for the sound.
- Guide students to read the words aloud.

ENGLISH LEARNER SUPPORT: Support Word Meaning

SUBSTANTIAL
Ensure that students understand the meaning of each Blend and Read word by sharing pictures or gestures.

MODERATE
Guide students to understand the meanings of the Blend and Read words that are homophones: *flower/flour, foul/fowl.*

LIGHT
Challenge partners to use each of the Blend and Read homophones (*flower/flour, foul/fowl*) in a sentence to demonstrate their understanding of its meaning.

Step 2 Guided Practice

- Project Display and Engage: **Decoding 4.6**.
- Have students read the Blend and Read lines aloud. Provide feedback as needed.
- At the end of each line, prompt a conversation about the words: *How are the vowel sounds the same? How are the spellings the same or different?*
- Have partners reread the Blend and Read lines and quiz each other on the spellings of the vowel diphthongs.

Online Ed

DISPLAY AND ENGAGE: Decoding 4.6

Decoding 4.6

Blend and Read

Vowel Diphthongs *ow, ou*

The diphthongs *ow* and *ou* make the /ou/ sound, as in *cow*.

1	count ou	brown ow	couch ou	house ou	ounce ou
2	flower ow	flour ou	scout ou	vowel ow	slouching ou
3	mouse ou	thousand ou	gown ow	chow ow	sprout ou
4	mound ou	now ow	stout ou	clown ow	pouted ou
5	snout ou	wow ow	pouch ou	shower ow	thousand ou

6 The boy frowned (ow) when he found (ou) out (ou) how (ow) many he had to do.

7 The visitors were bound (ou) for a town (ow) in the south (ou) of the country.

Grade 3 | Foundational Skills   Module 4 • Week 2

Step 3 Apply

INDEPENDENT PRACTICE

- Have students work in small groups or with partners to complete Know It, Show It page 83.
- Be sure students understand that the answer to the second clue contains fewer letters than the answer to the first clue.
- Encourage students to share with each other the strategies they use to decode words with vowel diphthongs.

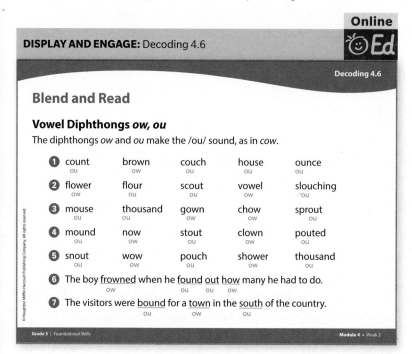

CORRECT & REDIRECT

If students have trouble decoding words with vowel diphthongs, use the model below.

- **Correct** the error. *The letters ow and ou can be pronounced /ou/.*
- **Model** how to decode the word *brown*. */brōn/. That does not sound right. Since I know the letters ow can stand for /ou/, I'll try that sound: /broun/, brown. That sounds like a word I know.*
- **Guide** students to decode the words *chow* and *mound*.
- **Check** students' understanding by displaying the word *stout*. *What spelling pattern helps you decode this word?*
- **Reinforce** by repeating the process with the word *vow*.

Spelling the /ou/ Sound

Introduce the Spelling Words

- Before working with the basic and challenge words, you might want to revisit the review words. These also appear in Printable: Dictation Sentences 4.6. Display one of the Spelling Anchor Printables, as appropriate.
- Cut out and display the spelling word cards from Printable: Spelling Word Cards 4.6. Read each word aloud and discuss its meaning as needed.
- Tell students that you are going to work together to sort the words into categories based on the spelling of the /ou/ sound. Read aloud the words *clown* and *sound*, and display those cards as column headings.
- Hold up a word containing the /ou/ sound spelled *ou*, such as *count*, and model your thinking: *The word is* count. *The /ou/ sound is spelled* ou. *I see the column head sound, which has the same /ou/ sound and spelling pattern. So I'll place the word in that column.*

Sort the Words

- Ask students to help you sort the remaining word cards. For multisyllabic words such as *thousand*, emphasize the /ou/ sound as you read the word aloud.
- After sorting, have students read down each list with you to make sure the words have been sorted correctly based on the spellings *ow* and *ou*.
- Guide students to recognize the spelling patterns in the columns. Ask: *What vowel sound do the words in this column share? What spelling pattern do they share?*
- Guide students to recognize the different spelling patterns for the /ou/ sound. Ask: *What are the different spelling patterns for the /ou/ sound?* (ow, ou)

Alphabetize the Words

- As an extension, show students **Anchor Chart 32:** Alphabetical Order. Have students sort the word cards into alphabetical order to the first, second, and third letters.

LEARNING OBJECTIVES

- Learn spelling patterns for vowel diphthongs *ow* and *ou*.
- **Language** Spell words with vowel diphthongs *ow* and *ou* and understand their meanings.

MATERIALS Online Ed

Anchor Chart 32 *Alphabetical Order*

Printables *Anchor Chart 32: Alphabetical Order, Dictation Sentences 4.6, Spelling Word Cards 4.6, Proofreading 4.6*

Optional *Use Printable: Dictation Sentences 4.6 to administer a pretest.*

SPELLING WORDS

BASIC

1. **clown**
2. **round**
3. **bow**
4. **cloud**
5. **power**
6. **crown**
7. **thousand**
8. **crowd**
9. **sound**
10. **count**
11. **powder**
12. **blouse**
13. **frown**
14. **pound**

REVIEW

15. **couch**
16. **peach**
17. **stretch**
18. **trench**

CHALLENGE

19. **mountain**
20. **announce**
21. **vowel**
22. **coward**

ENGLISH LEARNER SUPPORT: Support Word Meaning

ALL LEVELS Make sure students understand the meaning of the spelling words and dictation sentences. If necessary, use visuals or gestures as support. For Spanish-speaking students, point out the Spanish cognates *redondo* for *round*, *poder* for *power*, *corona* for *crown*, *sonido* for *sound*, *conde* for *count*, *blusa* for *blouse*, *montaña* for *mountain*, *anunciar* for *announce*, and *cobarde* for *coward*. After you've reinforced word meanings, have students practice reading the spelling words aloud.

LINK TO SMALL-GROUP INSTRUCTION

REINFORCE FOUNDATIONAL SKILLS For spelling practice for the remainder of the week: Display this week's spelling words for reference and have students work with Printable: Proofreading 4.6. Remind students to check the spelling words they use in the writing section to confirm they have spelled the words correctly. Have students use the Spelling Anchor Chart Printables to reinforce spelling knowledge.

Intonation

Introduce the Skill

- Explain that when good readers read aloud, they use intonation. That means they make their voice rise and fall.
- Distribute Printable: Fluency 4.6 to students, and project it for whole-group discussion. Tell students that you will demonstrate how to read the passage using rising and falling intonation.
- Read aloud the first two paragraphs in a flat tone. Then, reread the paragraphs with intonation. Ask: *In which reading did I use intonation?* Point out that end punctuation marks and commas help you know how and when to use rising or falling intonation. Model your thinking: *As I read, I paid close attention to the punctuation marks. When I saw a comma or a period, I lowered my voice. When I saw an exclamation point or a question mark, I raised my voice.* Then read the entire passage. Point out how you decoded the words *tryouts* and *frowned* by using the vowel diphthongs.
- After you finish reading the passage, have students read it aloud with you, using the **CHORAL READING** routine.

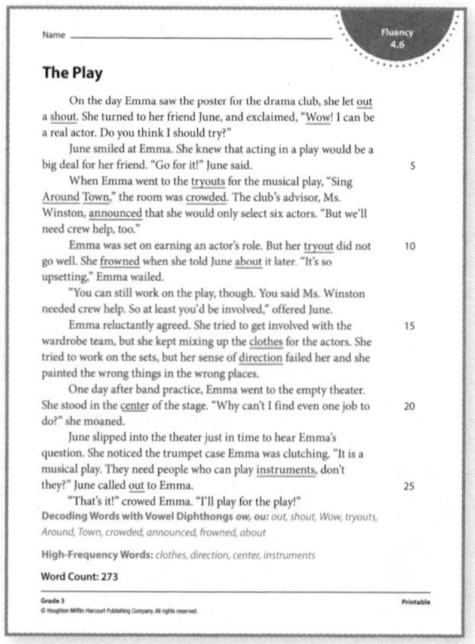
Name ______________________ Fluency 4.6

The Play

On the day Emma saw the poster for the drama club, she let out a shout. She turned to her friend June, and exclaimed, "Wow! I can be a real actor. Do you think I should try?"

June smiled at Emma. She knew that acting in a play would be a big deal for her friend. "Go for it!" June said.

When Emma went to the tryouts for the musical play, "Sing Around Town," the room was crowded. The club's advisor, Ms. Winston, announced that she would only select six actors. "But we'll need crew help, too."

Emma was set on earning an actor's role. But her tryout did not go well. She frowned when she told June about it later. "It's so upsetting," Emma wailed.

"You can still work on the play, though. You said Ms. Winston needed crew help. So at least you'd be involved," offered June.

Emma reluctantly agreed. She tried to get involved with the wardrobe team, but she kept mixing up the clothes for the actors. She tried to work on the sets, but her sense of direction failed her and she painted the wrong things in the wrong places.

One day after band practice, Emma went to the empty theater. She stood in the center of the stage. "Why can't I find even one job to do?" she moaned.

June slipped into the theater just in time to hear Emma's question. She noticed the trumpet case Emma was clutching. "It is a musical play. They need people who can play instruments, don't they?" June called out to Emma.

"That's it!" crowed Emma. "I'll play for the play!"

Decoding Words with Vowel Diphthongs ow, ou: *out, shout, Wow, tryouts, Around, Town, crowded, announced, frowned, about*

High-Frequency Words: *clothes, direction, center, instruments*

Word Count: 273

Grade 3 Printable

© Houghton Mifflin Harcourt Publishing Company. All rights reserved.

Printable: Fluency 4.6

Apply

- Have students work in pairs or small groups using the **PARTNER READING** routine to read aloud the passage.
- Monitor students for intonation. Note especially how students handle the more challenging words, such as *musical, announced, involved*, and *reluctantly,* and provide support, as needed.

LEARNING OBJECTIVES

- Read orally with intonation.
- Read aloud grade-level text with fluency and accuracy.
- Apply decoding skills when reading connected text.
- **Language** Comprehend texts using teacher support.

MATERIALS — Online Ed

Printable *Fluency 4.6*
Word Cards *3.37–3.40*

DECODING → FLUENCY CONNECTION

The passage on Printable: Fluency 4.6 includes words that contain this week's decoding element. Use the passage to monitor whether students can accurately and fluently read these grade-level words.

HIGH-FREQUENCY WORDS

- **clothes**
- **direction**
- **instruments**
- **center**

HIGH-FREQUENCY WORDS

Point out the high-frequency words in the passage on Printable: Fluency 4.6. Remind students that high-frequency words appear often in texts they read. Students can learn to recognize them, rather than decode them, so that they can read more fluently.

Print and distribute Word Cards 3.37–3.40, which feature this week's high-frequency words, and have students work independently or in pairs to read and complete the activities for each word. For struggling readers, walk through the notes for one or two words before they continue working with a partner.

EL ENGLISH LEARNER SUPPORT: Support Comprehension

ALL LEVELS As you model reading fluently, have students raise their hand when they hear a word they do not recognize. Work with students to decode the word and practice saying it aloud. Discuss the word's meaning, using gestures or pictures for support if needed. Then have students read the entire sentence chorally. Provide corrective feedback, as needed.

VOCABULARY

Review Critical Vocabulary

Step 1 Reinforce Vocabulary

- Project Display and Engage: **Critical Vocabulary 4.6** to review and discuss the Critical Vocabulary, student-friendly explanations, and examples of the words. Have students take turns using the words in sentences.

Step 2 Guided Practice

- Display the Critical Vocabulary words. Guide students, as needed, to complete the following sentence stems:

1. *If a building is from the Baroque Period, it will be _____ and _____.*
2. *Pulleys made from _____ and are used to _____ .*
3. *A backdrop is a _____ that you might see _____.*
4. *When you look out for someone's welfare, you want them to be _____.*
5. *During a performance, someone might _____ or _____.*

- Invite students to share their own sentences with the class.

Step 3 Apply

INDEPENDENT PRACTICE

- Have students work in small groups or independently. Tell them to complete Know It, Show It page 84. For the last item on the page, tell students to include clues to each word's meaning in their sentences. Have groups share their sentences. Ask listeners to identify the context clue in each sentence.
- You may wish to have students complete the Know It, Show It page during Small Group time.

LEARNING OBJECTIVES

- Review and extend understanding of word meanings.
- Use context to determine the meanings of unfamiliar words.
- **Language** Use newly acquired vocabulary expressively.

MATERIALS

Online Ed

Display and Engage *Critical Vocabulary 4.6*

Know It, Show It *p. 84*

CRITICAL VOCABULARY

- **Baroque**
- **pulleys**
- **backdrop**
- **performance**

ENGLISH LEARNER SUPPORT: Support Discussion

Use tiered supports as needed to help students as they answer questions about the Critical Vocabulary.

SUBSTANTIAL

Draw what might be on a backdrop for a play set in the city.

MODERATE

If a play had no backdrop, the audience might not know _____.

LIGHT

Why is a backdrop important? What would happen if it were missing?

Shades of Meaning

LEARNING OBJECTIVES

- Identify shades of meaning in synonyms.
- Use print and digital reference materials to clarify meanings.
- **Language** Identify shades of meaning using strategic learning techniques.

MATERIALS Online Ed

Display and Engage *Vocabulary Strategy 4.7*

INSTRUCTIONAL VOCABULARY

- **shades of meaning** small differences between words that mean almost the same thing

Step 1 Review the Strategy

Project Display and Engage: **Vocabulary Strategy 4.7**. Read aloud the two paragraphs.

Online

DISPLAY AND ENGAGE: Strategy 4.7

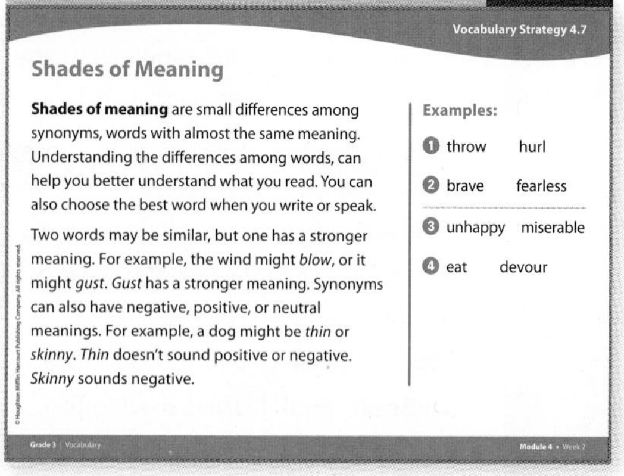
Vocabulary Strategy 4.7

Shades of Meaning

Shades of meaning are small differences among synonyms, words with almost the same meaning. Understanding the differences among words, can help you better understand what you read. You can also choose the best word when you write or speak.

Two words may be similar, but one has a stronger meaning. For example, the wind might *blow*, or it might *gust*. *Gust* has a stronger meaning. Synonyms can also have negative, positive, or neutral meanings. For example, a dog might be *thin* or *skinny*. *Thin* doesn't sound positive or negative. *Skinny* sounds negative.

Examples:

1. throw hurl
2. brave fearless
3. unhappy miserable
4. eat devour

© Houghton Mifflin Harcourt Publishing Company. All rights reserved.

Grade 3 | Vocabulary Module 4 • Week 2

- Discuss how synonyms won't always have exactly the same meanings. One synonym can have a stronger meaning or feeling. These slight differences are called shades of meaning. Explain the differences in degrees of certainty or states of mind.
- Use the first word pair to model and discuss shades of meaning. *The words* throw *and* hurl *are synonyms. They have similar meanings.* Hurl *means "throw", but it has a stronger meaning. If you hurl something, you throw it very hard. The words* brave *and* fearless *are also synonyms. When you're* fearless, *you are* brave. *However,* fearless *has a stronger meaning because it means you're never afraid of* anything.

Step 2 Guided Practice

- Have students read the next two pairs of words and identify which word has a more stronger meaning. Invite them to use a reference source as needed to check the definitions.
- Ask students to explain why one word in each pair has a stronger meaning.

Step 3 Apply the Strategy

INDEPENDENT PRACTICE

- Point out the synonyms *tasty* and *delicious* and the synonyms *house* and *mansion* in *Gigi and the Wishing Ring*. Have students work independently to write a definition for each word, using reference sources as needed.
- Ask students to write a sentence or two explaining how the words are similar and which word has a stronger meaning.

ENGLISH LEARNER SUPPORT: Identifying Shades of Meaning

SUBSTANTIAL

Use simple language or images to explain the difference between *eat* and *devour*. Then ask students to act out each word to show the difference.

MODERATE

Supply sentence frames for each pair of synonyms: _____ *is a stronger word than* _____.

LIGHT

Ask students to explain why *devour* is a stronger word than *eat*.

Media Techniques

Step 1 Connect and Teach

LEARNING OBJECTIVES

- Identify media techniques and analyze their effects.
- **Language** Identify and articulate media techniques used in video.

MATERIALS Online Ed

Anchor Chart 29 *Media Techniques*

Printable *Anchor Chart 29: Media Techniques*

Teaching Pal *Book 1, pp. 318–323*

myBook *Book 1, The Traveling Trio, pp. 318–323*

Know It, Show It *p. 85*

INSTRUCTIONAL VOCABULARY

- **animation** the movement of illustrations of characters, objects, and events used in media
- **live action** the scenes of events in media with people, characters, and objects
- **media** the means of communication such as radio, television, newspapers, magazines, and the Internet
- **sound elements** the music, sound effects, or narration used in media
- **visual elements** brightly colored graphics and text in media that catch the viewer's attention

SPANISH COGNATES

- **animation** *animación*

Project or display Anchor Chart 29: Media Techniques.

Online

ANCHOR CHART 29: Media Techniques

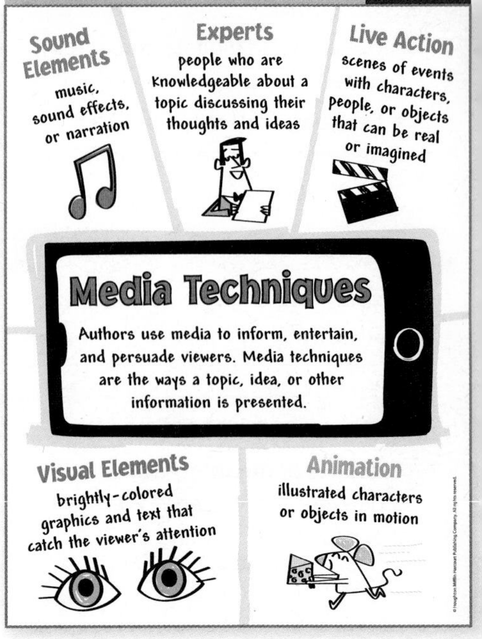

Review the introductory information about **media techniques** at the center. Explain that these techniques offer a variety of ways to present information in a video. Use the relevant sections of the Anchor Chart as you make the following points:

- **Sound elements** may include background sounds, music, voiceovers, and sound effects. These elements may create a humorous or somber mood, or even a feeling of suspense.
- A video may also include **live action** that creates a realistic feeling or **animation** that suggests something more imaginative.
- Tell students they will practice identifying media techniques to gain a deeper understanding of *The Traveling Trio: Český Krumlov, Czech Republic.*

Go to Your Teaching Pal

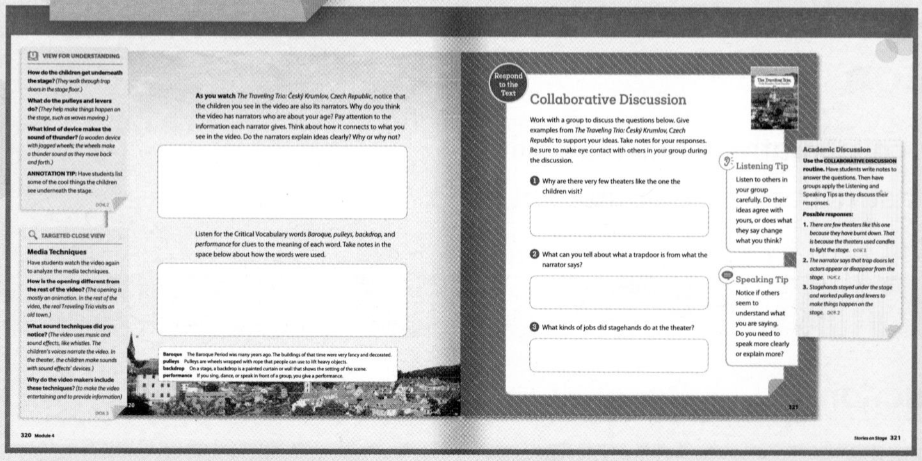

VIEW FOR UNDERSTANDING

How do the children get underneath the stage? *(They walk through trap doors in the stage floor.)*

What do the pulleys and levers do? *(They help make things happen on the stage, such as waves moving.)*

What kind of device makes the sound of thunder? *(a wooden device with jagged wheels; the wheels make a thunder sound as they move back and forth.)*

ANNOTATION TIP: Have students list some of the cool things the children see underneath the stage.

DOK 2

TARGETED CLOSE VIEW

Media Techniques

Have students watch the video again to analyze the media techniques.

How is the opening different from the rest of the video? *(The opening is mostly an animation. In the rest of the video, the real Traveling Trio visits an old town.)*

What sound techniques did you notice? *(The video uses music and sound effects, like whistles. The children's voices narrate the video. In the theater, the children make sounds with sound effects' devices.)*

Why do the video makers include these techniques? *(to make the video entertaining and to provide information)*

DOK 3

As you watch *The Traveling Trio: Český Krumlov, Czech Republic*, notice that the children you see in the video are also its narrators. Why do you think the video has narrators who are about your age? Pay attention to the information each narrator gives. Think about how it connects to what you see in the video. Do the narrators explain ideas clearly? Why or why not?

Listen for the Critical Vocabulary words *Baroque, pulleys, backdrop,* and *performance* for clues to the meaning of each word. Take notes in the space below about how the words were used.

Baroque The Baroque Period was many years ago. The buildings of that time were very fancy and decorated.
pulleys Pulleys are wheels wrapped with rope that people can use to lift heavy objects.
backdrop On a stage, a backdrop is a painted curtain or wall that shows the setting of the scene.
performance If you sing, dance, or speak in front of a group, you give a performance.

320 Module 4

Respond to the Text

Collaborative Discussion

Work with a group to discuss the questions below. Give examples from *The Traveling Trio: Český Krumlov, Czech Republic* to support your ideas. Take notes for your responses. Be sure to make eye contact with others in your group during the discussion.

1. Why are there very few theaters like the one the children visit?
2. What can you tell about what a trapdoor is from what the narrator says?
3. What kinds of jobs did stagehands do at the theater?

Listening Tip
Listen to others in your group carefully. Do their ideas agree with yours, or does what they say change what you think?

Speaking Tip
Notice if others seem to understand what you are saying. Do you need to speak more clearly or explain more?

Academic Discussion

Use the COLLABORATIVE DISCUSSION routine. Have students write notes to answer the questions. Then have groups apply the Listening and Speaking Tips as they discuss their responses.

Possible responses:

1. *There are few theaters like this one because they have burnt down. That is because the theaters used candles to light the stage.* DOK 1
2. *The narrator says that trap doors let actors appear or disappear from the stage.* DOK 2
3. *Stagehands stayed under the stage and worked pulleys and levers to make things happen on the stage.* DOK 2

321

Stories on Stage 321

Online

ANNOTATE IT!

Students may use the annotation tools in their eBook.

Step 2 Apply to Text

In your Teaching Pal, use the purple **TARGETED CLOSE READ** prompts on page 320 to guide students to apply the Media Techniques skill to *The Traveling Trio* and to find evidence to support their responses. Use the **ACTIVE VIEWING** routine. Students may refer to the questions on Know It, Show It page 85 as you discuss them.

- Read aloud the first question on Teaching Pal page 320. Then have students watch the video again to identify how the opening differs from the rest of the video. *(The opening is mostly an animation. In the rest of the video, the real Traveling Trio visits an old town.)*
- Then read the last two questions on Teaching Pal page 320. Discuss the purpose and effect of the media techniques. *(The video uses music and sound effects like whistles. The children's voices narrate the video. In the theater, the children make sounds with sound effects devices; to make the video entertaining and to provide information.)*
- Refer back to the Anchor Chart to support the discussion. Students may add sticky notes to the chart to note media techniques they identify in *The Traveling Trio.*

Step 3 Engage and Respond

INDEPENDENT PRACTICE: Writing

- **Write a Travel Guide** Turn to pages 322–323 in your Teaching Pal. Have students turn to pages 322–323 in their *my*Book. Use the **WRITING RESPONSE** routine.
- Read the directions with students and use the Teaching Pal prompts to guide them as they plan and complete their travel guides.
- Provide time for students to share their travel guides with small groups.
- You may want to have students complete their writing during daily small-group time.
- You may want to have students complete Know It, Show It page 85 during daily small-group time.

ENGLISH LEARNER SUPPORT: Facilitate Discussion

SUBSTANTIAL

Provide sentence frames: *The opening has _____. I can hear_____.*

MODERATE

Ask: *When did you see animation? Live action? What sounds do you hear?*

LIGHT

Encourage students to speak in complete sentences and use newly acquired vocabulary to describe the media techniques.

LINK TO SMALL-GROUP INSTRUCTION

REINFORCE MEDIA TECHNIQUES Review and extend the skill as needed during small-group time to support students' need for differentiation. *See the lesson on p. T295.*

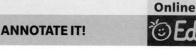

Options for Differentiation

As the class engages in independent and collaborative work, meet with Guided Reading Groups or differentiate instruction based on student need.

GUIDED READING GROUPS

Match Students to Books + Instruction

- Choose just-right books based on level, skill, topic, or genre.

L M N O P Q

Leveled Readers

- Deliver instruction with each book's **Take and Teach Lesson**, choosing appropriate sessions based on need.

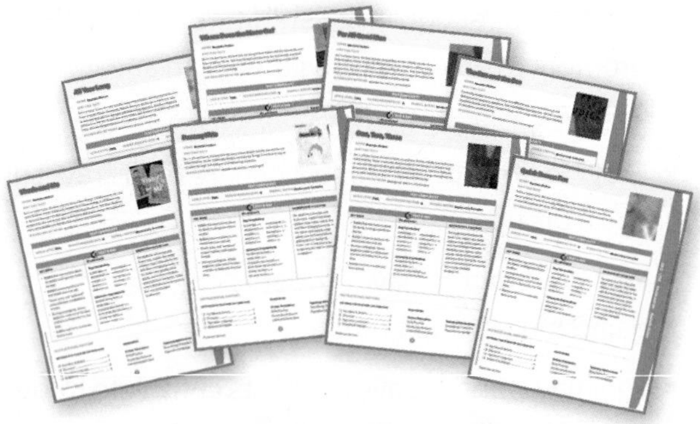

- Check comprehension, reinforce instruction, and extend learning with suggested supporting activities.

Rigby LEVELED LIBRARY

EL ENGLISH LEARNER SUPPORT

Recount Information

- Use **Tabletop Minilessons: English Language Development 11.1 (Speaking)** to reinforce and practice the language skill.

Tabletop Minilessons: English Language Development

- Then use the following text-based prompts with *The Traveling Trio* to guide application of the language skill. Begin with the prompt at the student's identified language proficiency level. As students progress, use lighter supports to encourage increased language proficiency.

SUBSTANTIAL

Ask: *What sound effects can be made at the Český Krumlov theater?* Allow students to use gestures, English words, and their home language to complete the following oral sentence frame: *The theater can make the sound effects for _____, _____, and _____.*

MODERATE

Have partners take turns using the following question and answer frames: *How is the sound effect _____ made? The sound effect _____ is made by _____.*

LIGHT

Have students discuss the following questions in small groups or pairs: *What were some of the things stage hands would do at the theater? What sound effects could the stage hands make? Why is the theater only used three times a year today?* Monitor discussions as needed.

REINFORCE MEDIA TECHNIQUES

Demonstrate

- Use **Tabletop Minilessons: Reading Card 29** to remind students that **media techniques** offer a variety of ways to present information in a video. **Sound elements** may include background sounds, music, voice-overs, and sound effects. A video may also include **live action** that creates a realistic feeling or **animation**, which is more like a cartoon.
- Model filling out Printable: Reading Graphic Organizer 29 to identify Media Techniques in *The Traveling Trio.*

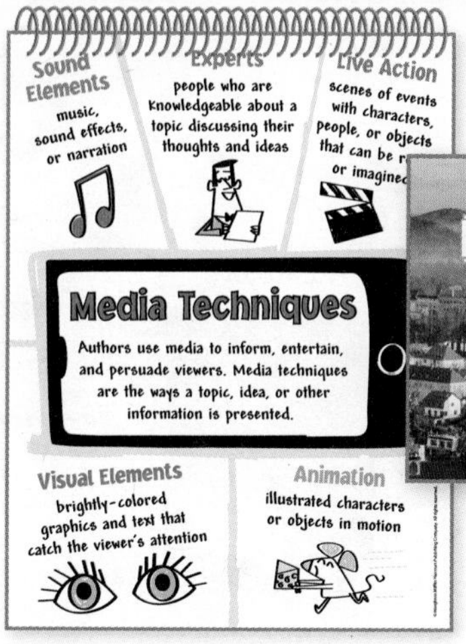

Tabletop Minilessons: Reading

Apply to Independent Reading

- Now have students identify the media techniques in appropriate media they are viewing independently. Customize these prompts to the texts students choose.
  - » *Is the video live action or animation? How can you tell?*
  - » *What sound elements are used?*
  - » *How do the media techniques affect how you understand and feel about the video?*
- Have students complete Printable: Reading Graphic Organizer 29 for their independent media viewing.

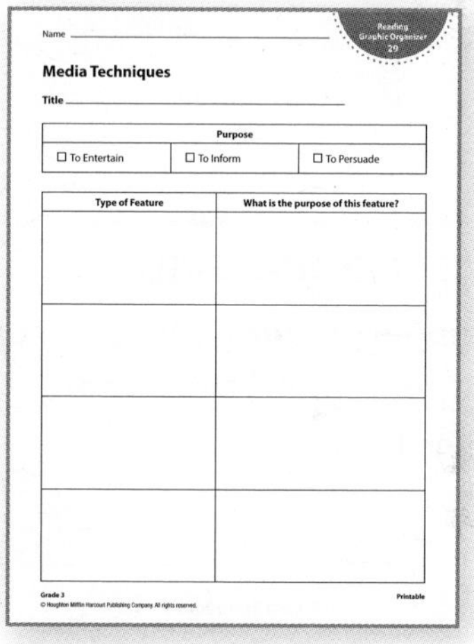

Printable: Reading Graphic Organizer 29

ALMOST THERE

READY FOR MORE

SCAFFOLD AND EXTEND

- Prompt students to identify the media techniques. Guide them to understand how they affect the viewing of the video.
- Prompt students to identify the media techniques and how they understand and feel about the video.
- Have students explain how changing one of the media techniques would change their experience of the video.

EL ENGLISH LEARNER SUPPORT

SUBSTANTIAL

Ask *yes/no* questions: *Is the video live action? Is the video animation? Does it have music/voice-over/sound effects?*

MODERATE

Ask questions such as: *Is the video live action or animation? What sound elements do you hear?*

LIGHT

Have students identify the media techniques and explain how they affected their viewing of the video.

Options for Independent and Collaborative Work

While you meet with small groups, have other students engage in literacy activities that reinforce the lesson's learning objectives. Choose from these options.

Independent Reading

Student Choice Library

Rigby
LEVELED LIBRARY

APPLY READING SKILL

Media Techniques Students complete Printable: Reading Graphic Organizer 29 for an independent reading book.

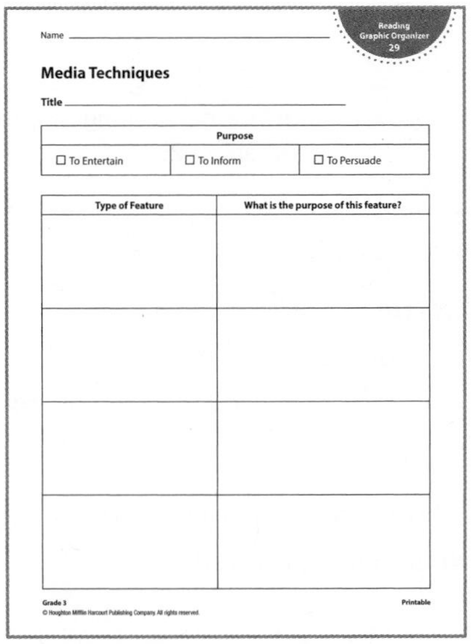

Name
Reading Graphic Organizer 29

Media Techniques

Title

Purpose		
☐ To Entertain	☐ To Inform	☐ To Persuade

Type of Feature	What is the purpose of this feature?

Grade 3
© Houghton Mifflin Harcourt Publishing Company. All rights reserved.
Printable

Printable: Reading Graphic Organizer 29

APPLY LANGUAGE SKILL

Recount Information Students complete Printable: Language Graphic Organizer 11 for an independent reading book.

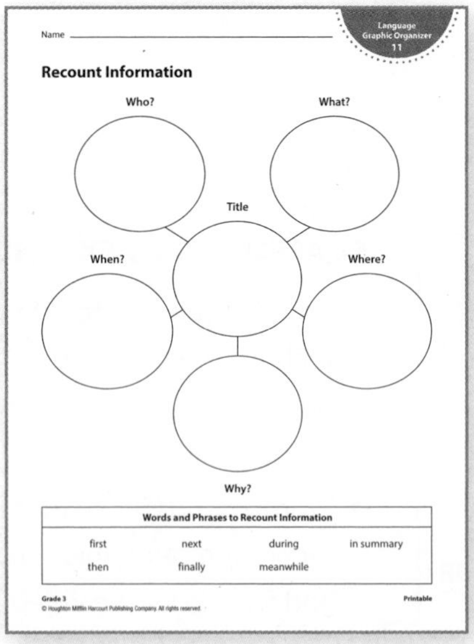

Name
Language Graphic Organizer 11

Recount Information

Words and Phrases to Recount Information			
first	next	during	in summary
then	finally	meanwhile	

Grade 3
© Houghton Mifflin Harcourt Publishing Company. All rights reserved.
Printable

Printable: Language Graphic Organizer 11

Literacy Centers

See pp. T274–T275.

- READING CENTER
- VOCABULARY CENTER
- DIGITAL STATION
- WRITING CENTER
- PROJECT CENTER

Writing

Students write a travel guide. *See Engage and Respond, p. T293.*

Additional Skills Practice

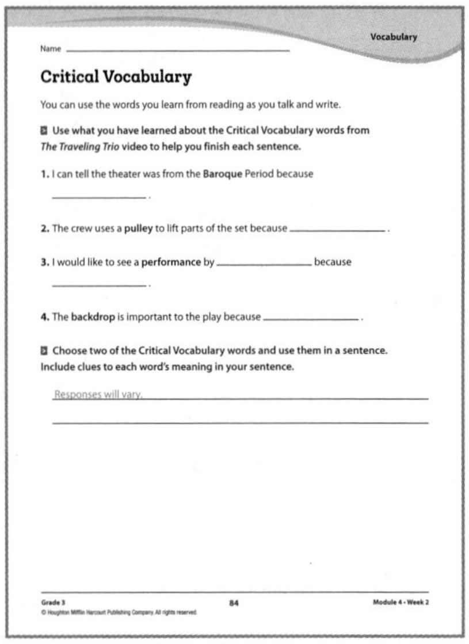
Vocabulary

Name ______________

Critical Vocabulary

You can use the words you learn from reading as you talk and write.

Use what you have learned about the Critical Vocabulary words from *The Traveling Trio* video to help you finish each sentence.

1. I can tell the theater was from the **Baroque** Period because ____________.
2. The crew uses a **pulley** to lift parts of the set because ____________.
3. I would like to see a **performance** by ____________ because ____________.
4. The **backdrop** is important to the play because ____________.

Choose two of the Critical Vocabulary words and use them in a sentence. Include clues to each word's meaning in your sentence.

Responses will vary.

Grade 3 — 84 — Module 4 • Week 2
© Houghton Mifflin Harcourt Publishing Company. All rights reserved.

Know It, Show It, p. 84

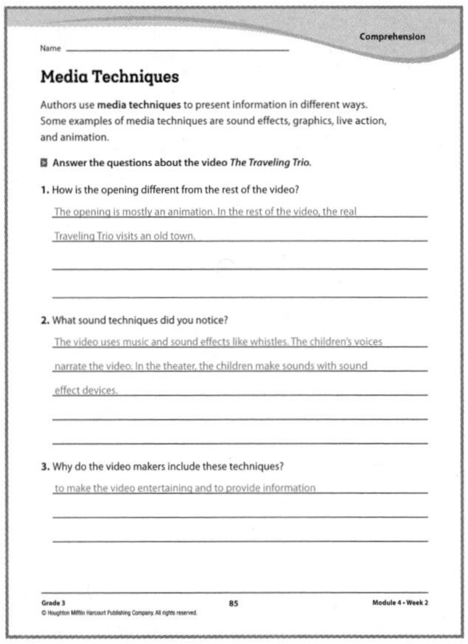
Comprehension

Name ______________

Media Techniques

Authors use **media techniques** to present information in different ways. Some examples of media techniques are sound effects, graphics, live action, and animation.

Answer the questions about the video *The Traveling Trio.*

1. How is the opening different from the rest of the video?
   The opening is mostly an animation. In the rest of the video, the real Traveling Trio visits an old town.
2. What sound techniques did you notice?
   The video uses music and sound effects like whistles. The children's voices narrate the video. In the theater, the children make sounds with sound effect devices.
3. Why do the video makers include these techniques?
   to make the video entertaining and to provide information

Grade 3 — 85 — Module 4 • Week 2
© Houghton Mifflin Harcourt Publishing Company. All rights reserved.

Know It, Show It, p. 85

Wrap-Up

Share Time

At the end of the Reading Workshop, have students reflect on their learning by sharing how they applied **media techniques** or another area of focus during independent work time. Choose from these options:

- Use the **SOLO CHAIR** routine. Select a reader each day to come to the front of the class and tell what he or she learned from the reading by using a skill or strategy.
- **THINK-PAIR-SHARE** Students share their thinking with a partner. Select a few pairs each day to share with the whole class.
- **RETURN TO ANCHOR CHART** Have students add sticky notes about their independent reading to the Media Techniques Anchor Chart. Call on a few students to explain what they added and why.

Online Ed

ANCHOR CHART 29:
Media Techniques

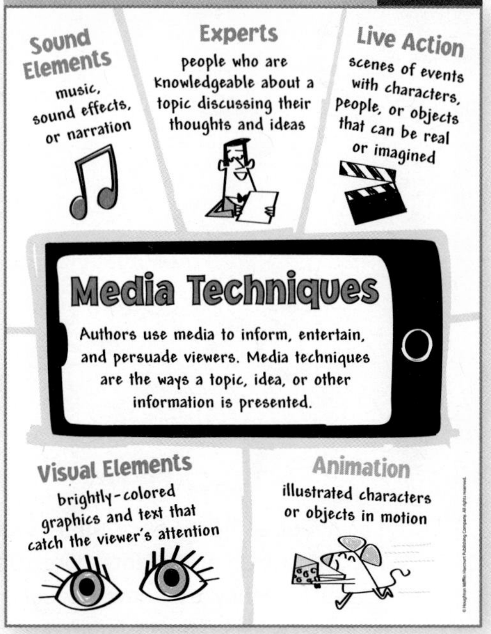

LEARNING OBJECTIVES

- Identify real-life connections between words and their use.
- Use newly acquired vocabulary expressively.
- **Language** Answer questions and discuss meanings to develop vocabulary.

MATERIALS **Online** Ed

Display and Engage *Critical Vocabulary 4.8a and 4.8b*

Vocabulary Cards *4.14–4.19*

CRITICAL VOCABULARY

- **eminent (p. 330)**
- **peasant (p. 331)**
- **stately (p. 331)**
- **deceive (p. 332)**
- **superior (p. 332)**
- **merciful (p. 338)**

SPANISH COGNATE

- **superior** *superior*

Introduce Critical Vocabulary

Step 1 Introduce the Words

Project Display and Engage: **Critical Vocabulary 4.8a** and **4.8b**. Then use the **VOCABULARY** routine to introduce the Critical Vocabulary from *Gigi and the Wishing Ring*. You may wish to display the corresponding Vocabulary Card for each word as you discuss it.

Online Ed

DISPLAY AND ENGAGE:
Critical Vocabulary 4.8a and 4.8b

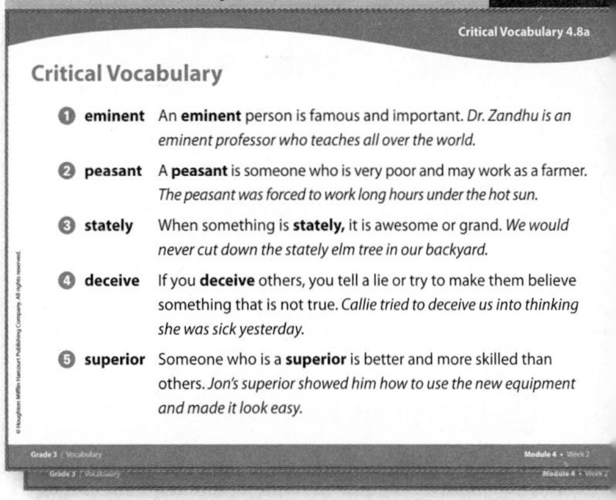
Critical Vocabulary 4.8a

Critical Vocabulary

1. **eminent** An **eminent** person is famous and important. *Dr. Zandhu is an eminent professor who teaches all over the world.*
2. **peasant** A **peasant** is someone who is very poor and may work as a farmer. *The peasant was forced to work long hours under the hot sun.*
3. **stately** When something is **stately,** it is awesome or grand. *We would never cut down the stately elm tree in our backyard.*
4. **deceive** If you **deceive** others, you tell a lie or try to make them believe something that is not true. *Callie tried to deceive us into thinking she was sick yesterday.*
5. **superior** Someone who is a **superior** is better and more skilled than others. *Jon's superior showed him how to use the new equipment and made it look easy.*

1. Read aloud each word and have students repeat it.
2. Read aloud and discuss each word's student-friendly explanation.
3. Point out the example for the word. Have students suggest other examples.

TEACHER TIP

Encourage authentic **vocabulary usage** in your classroom. Students score a point each time they use a new vocabulary word in conversation.

ENGLISH LEARNER SUPPORT: Build Vocabulary

SUBSTANTIAL

Ask pairs to point to someone who is eminent or something that is stately in a classroom book or other resource.

MODERATE

Have students complete this sentence frame. *A building might be stately if it is ______.*

LIGHT

Ask partners to write sentences describing items that are stately.

Step 2 Guided Practice

Guide students to interact with the words by discussing questions such as these:

- *If you are **eminent**, are you working hard to become successful? Explain.*
- *Is it more likely for a **peasant** to work outdoors or in an office? Explain.*
- *Is a flea usually thought of as a **stately** creature? Why or why not?*
- *When you **deceive** people, do you help them understand the truth about something? Explain.*
- *If someone is your **superior**, is he or she likely to ask you how to do something? Why or why not?*
- *Would a **merciful** person make a good friend? Why or why not?*

Ask students to name someone eminent and describe the traits of a peasant, a superior, someone who is merciful, and something stately. Have students explain whether it is good or bad to deceive, and why.

Step 3 Apply

- Have students work independently to complete steps 3 and 4 on Vocabulary Cards 4.14–4.19.
- Have students use the **TURN AND TALK** routine to discuss with a partner the prompt on each Vocabulary Card.

eminent

Vocabulary Cards

LEARNING MINDSET

Self-Reflection

Reflect Remind students of the importance of self-reflection. *Think about the words you use outside the classroom. Do you use many of the same words over and over again? Might you be able to add some new words your vocabulary?* Ask students how they can use one or more of this week's vocabulary words when they talk or write. Invite them to give examples.

Retell

Step 1 Connect and Teach

LEARNING OBJECTIVES

- Evaluate details to determine key ideas.
- Retell a drama in ways that maintain meaning and order.
- **Language** Retell key events in a drama using sequence words.

MATERIALS Online Ed

Anchor Chart 3 *Retell*
Printable *Anchor Chart 3: Retell*
Teaching Pal *Book 1, pp. 324–341*
myBook *Book 1, Gigi and the Wishing Ring, pp. 324–341*
Display and Engage *Build Background 4.8*

INSTRUCTIONAL VOCABULARY

- **retell** to tell a story in your own words

- Tell students they are going to read a drama called *Gigi and the Wishing Ring*. Explain that a good way to keep track of events in a drama is to **retell** the story.
- Project or display Anchor Chart 3: Retell. Review the Tip and questions on the Anchor Chart. Explain that answering these questions ensures that students evaluate and include key details when they retell the story.
- Explain that using sequence words helps the listener understand the order of events and follow what you are saying.
- Remind students that when they retell a story, they use their own words.
- Tell students that they will practice retelling when they read the tale/fable *Gigi and the Wishing Ring*.

Online Ed

ANCHOR CHART 3: Retell

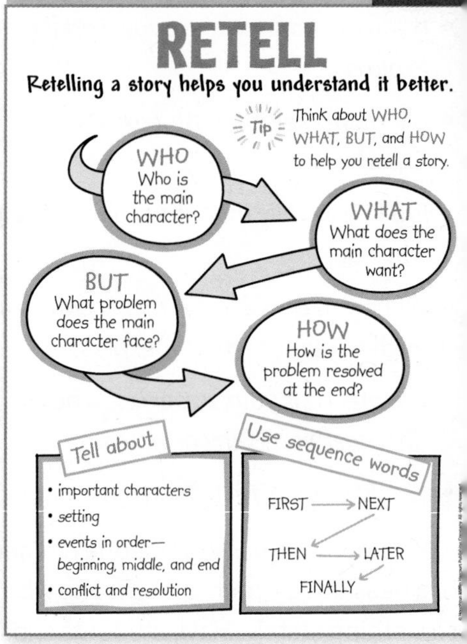
RETELL
Retelling a story helps you understand it better.
Tip
Think about WHO, WHAT, BUT, and HOW to help you retell a story.
WHO Who is the main character?
WHAT What does the main character want?
BUT What problem does the main character face?
HOW How is the problem resolved at the end?
Tell about
• important characters
• setting
• events in order— beginning, middle, and end
• conflict and resolution
Use sequence words
FIRST → NEXT
THEN → LATER
FINALLY

Notice & Note

Words of the Wiser

- The Teaching Pal prompts in this lesson feature the **Notice & Note Signpost: Words of the Wiser.**
- As needed, refer to p. T209 to review the signpost with students.

ASSESSMENT OPTION

Assign the Selection Quiz to check comprehension of *Gigi and the Wishing Ring*.

Go to Your **Teaching Pal**

Online Ed

ANNOTATE IT!

Students may use the annotation tools in their eBook.

Step 2 Apply to Text

In your **Teaching Pal,** pages 324–339, use the blue **READ FOR UNDERSTANDING** prompts and the red **Notice & Note** prompts to read *Gigi and the Wishing Ring* as students follow along and annotate their *my*Book.

- **Genre Study** Guide students through the genre information on page 324. Remind students that this drama is an adaption of classic tale or fable.
- **Set a Purpose** Read the Set a Purpose section on page 324. Prompt students to set their own purpose for reading *Gigi and the Wishing Ring.*
- **Build Background** Project Display and Engage 4.8: Build Background and read the information aloud with students. Ask students how the information might connect to a story with a title that includes the words *wishing ring*.
- **Read and Comprehend** Use the **READ FOR UNDERSTANDING** routine as you guide students to read the selection. Pause occasionally, using the prompts in your Teaching Pal to gauge students' understanding and to have them retell parts of the drama. As students retell, have them refer back to the Anchor Chart to make sure their retellings have answered the questions on the chart.

Step 3 Engage and Respond

INDEPENDENT PRACTICE: Speaking and Listening

- After reading, use the **COLLABORATIVE CONVERSATION** routine with the Collaborative Discussion questions on **Teaching Pal** and *my*Book page 339. Have students annotate their *my*Book with details from the text and visuals as evidence to explain their responses.
- Ask volunteers to read aloud the Speaking and Listening tips. Remind students to ask questions to check their understanding of what the speaker has said. Point out that they should be as specific as possible when asking for clarification.
- You may want to have students conduct their discussions during daily small-group time.

EL ENGLISH LEARNER SUPPORT: Elicit Participation

SUBSTANTIAL
Have partners use the illustrations to retell the story using the words *first, next,* and *then.*

MODERATE
Have students retell the story with words *first, next, then, later,* and *finally*.

LIGHT
Have students retell the story using details and time-order words.

LINK TO SMALL-GROUP INSTRUCTION

REINFORCE RETELL Review and extend the skill as needed during small-group time to support students' need for differentiation. *See the lesson on p. T303.*

Options for Differentiation

As the class engages in independent and collaborative work, meet with Guided Reading Groups or differentiate instruction based on student need.

GUIDED READING GROUPS

Match Students to Books + Instruction

- Choose just-right books based on level, skill, topic, or genre.

L → M → N → O → P → Q

Leveled Readers

- Deliver instruction with each book's **Take and Teach Lesson**, choosing appropriate sessions based on need.

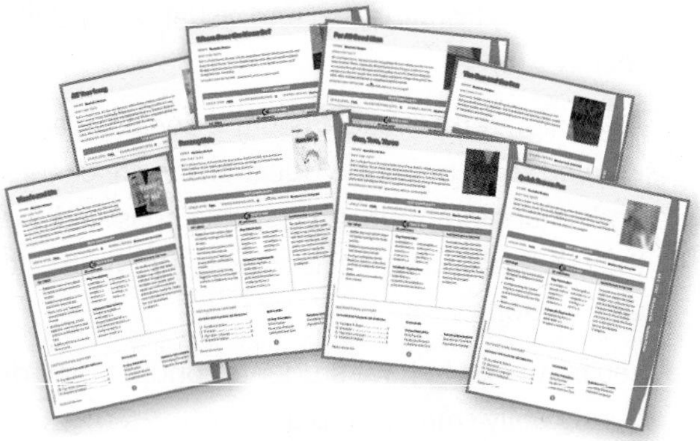

- Check comprehension, reinforce instruction, and extend learning with suggested supporting activities.

ENGLISH LEARNER SUPPORT

Recount Information

- Use **Tabletop Minilessons: English Language Development 11.2 (Reading)** to reinforce and practice the language skill.

Tabletop Minilessons: English Language Development

- Then use the following text-based prompts with *Gigi and the Wishing Ring* to guide application of the language skill. Begin with the prompt at the student's identified language proficiency level. As students progress, use lighter supports to encourage increased language proficiency.

SUBSTANTIAL
Have students choral read the names under the Cast of Characters. Then ask students to reread each individual name and point to a picture of the character in the text.

MODERATE
Have students take turns reading aloud the roles of Gigi and his mother in Act I, Scene 1. Then have them recount details to complete the sentence frames: *Gigi wants to ______. Gigi's mother tells him ______.*

LIGHT
Have students read Act I, and then answer the following questions: *Where is Gigi going? What advice does Gigi's mother give him?*

REINFORCE RETELL

Demonstrate

- Use **Tabletop Minilessons: Reading Card 3** to remind students that they can **retell** key events to keep track of what happens in a drama. A good retelling includes characters, setting, and major events of the drama told using sequence words such as *first, next, then,* and *last*.
- Model filling out Printable: Reading Graphic Organizer 3 to retell *Gigi and the Wishing Ring.*

Apply to Independent Reading

- Now have students retell a book or drama they are reading independently. Customize these prompts to the texts students choose.
  - » *What is the setting?*
  - » *Who are the characters?*
  - » *What is the order of key events?*
- Have students complete Printable: Reading Graphic Organizer 3 for their independent reading book.

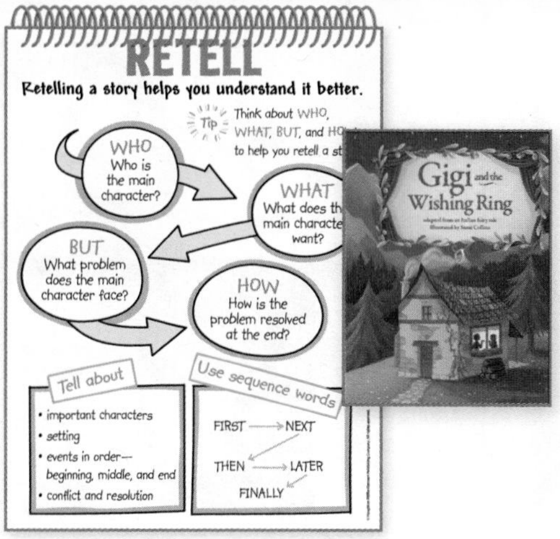
RETELL
Retelling a story helps you understand it better.
Tip
Think about WHO, WHAT, BUT, and HO
to help you retell a st
WHO
Who is the main character?
WHAT
What does th main characte want?
BUT
What problem does the main character face?
HOW
How is the problem resolved at the end?
Tell about
• important characters
• setting
• events in order— beginning, middle, and end
• conflict and resolution
Use sequence words
FIRST
NEXT
THEN
LATER
FINALLY
Gigi and the Wishing Ring

Tabletop Minilessons: Reading

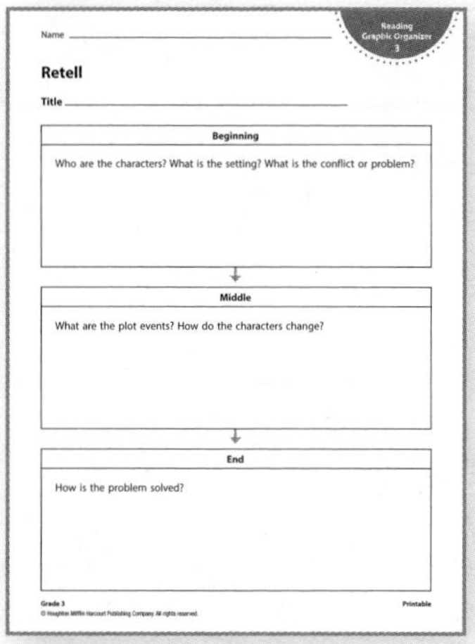

Name

Reading Graphic Organizer 3

Retell

Title

Beginning

Who are the characters? What is the setting? What is the conflict or problem?

Middle

What are the plot events? How do the characters change?

End

How is the problem solved?

Grade 3 Printable

Printable: Reading Graphic Organizer 3

SCAFFOLD AND EXTEND

ALMOST THERE

READY FOR MORE

- Have students name characters and setting for each act or scene. Guide them to retell key events in sequence.
- As students retell, guide them to differentiate between key events and minor events.
- Have students explain why they chose to include particular events and details in their retelling.

EL ENGLISH LEARNER SUPPORT

SUBSTANTIAL

Supply sentence frames such as: *The characters are* ______. *The setting is* ______. *The first/next/last event is* ______.

MODERATE

Supply students with a bank of sequence words and phrases to aid their retelling, such as *first, then, next, after, finally.*

LIGHT

Have students retell to a partner and make suggestions to one another as to how to improve their retellings.

Options for Independent and Collaborative Work

While you meet with small groups, have other students engage in literacy activities that reinforce the lesson's learning objectives. Choose from these options.

Independent Reading

Student Choice Library

Rigby
LEVELED LIBRARY

APPLY READING SKILL

Retell Students complete Printable: Reading Graphic Organizer 3 for an independent reading book.

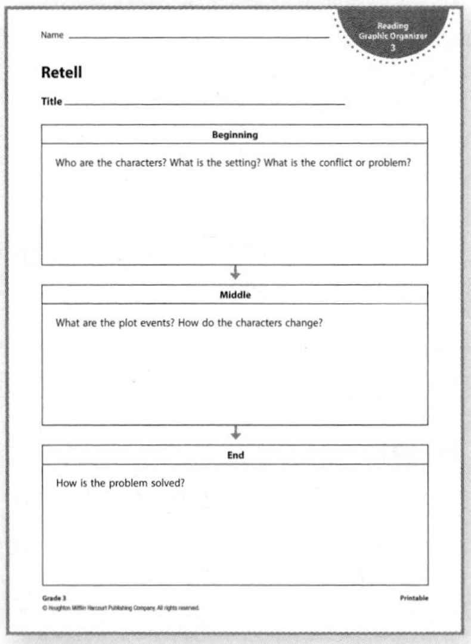

Name ______ Reading Graphic Organizer 3

Retell

Title ______

Beginning
Who are the characters? What is the setting? What is the conflict or problem?

Middle
What are the plot events? How do the characters change?

End
How is the problem solved?

Grade 3 Printable

Printable: Reading Graphic Organizer 3

APPLY LANGUAGE SKILL

Recount Information Students complete Printable: Language Graphic Organizer 11 for an independent reading book.

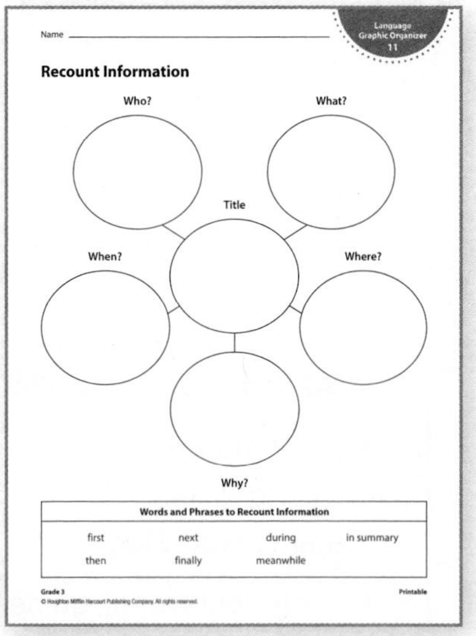

Name ______ Language Graphic Organizer 11

Recount Information

Who? What? Title When? Where? Why?

Words and Phrases to Recount Information			
first	next	during	in summary
then	finally	meanwhile	

Grade 3 Printable

Printable: Language Graphic Organizer 11

Notice & Note

Words of the Wiser

When students encounter this signpost in their independent reading, encourage them to ask and answer the Anchor Question: *What's the life lesson and how might it affect the character?*

Literacy Centers

See pp. T274–T275.

READING CENTER

VOCABULARY CENTER

DIGITAL STATION

WRITING CENTER

PROJECT CENTER

Speaking and Listening

Partners discuss the Collaborative Discussion questions. *See Engage and Respond, p. T301.*

Additional Skills Practice

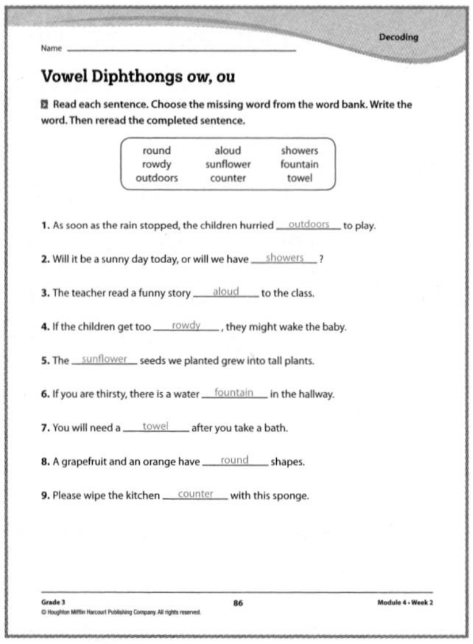
Decoding

Name ____________

Vowel Diphthongs ow, ou

Read each sentence. Choose the missing word from the word bank. Write the word. Then reread the completed sentence.

round	aloud	showers
rowdy	sunflower	fountain
outdoors	counter	towel

1. As soon as the rain stopped, the children hurried __outdoors__ to play.
2. Will it be a sunny day today, or will we have __showers__ ?
3. The teacher read a funny story __aloud__ to the class.
4. If the children get too __rowdy__, they might wake the baby.
5. The __sunflower__ seeds we planted grew into tall plants.
6. If you are thirsty, there is a water __fountain__ in the hallway.
7. You will need a __towel__ after you take a bath.
8. A grapefruit and an orange have __round__ shapes.
9. Please wipe the kitchen __counter__ with this sponge.

Grade 3 | 86 | Module 4 • Week 2

Know It, Show It, p. 86

Wrap-Up

Share Time

At the end of the Reading Workshop, have students reflect on their learning by sharing how they applied **retell** or another area of focus during independent work time. Choose from these options:

- Use the **SOLO CHAIR** routine. Select a reader each day to come to the front of the class and tell what he or she learned from the reading by using a skill or strategy.
- **THINK-PAIR-SHARE** Students share their thinking with a partner. Select a few pairs each day to share with the whole class.
- **RETURN TO ANCHOR CHART** Have students add sticky notes about their independent reading to the Retell Anchor Chart. Call on a few students to explain what they added and why.

Online Ed

ANCHOR CHART 3: Retell

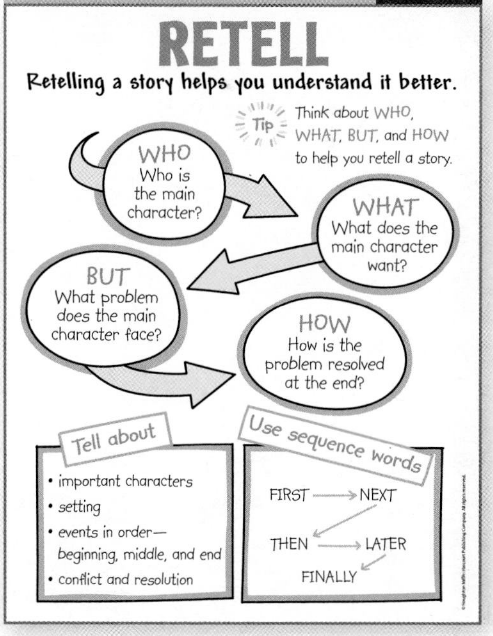
RETELL
Retelling a story helps you understand it better.
Tip
Think about WHO, WHAT, BUT, and HOW to help you retell a story.
WHO Who is the main character?
WHAT What does the main character want?
BUT What problem does the main character face?
HOW How is the problem resolved at the end?
Tell about
• important characters
• setting
• events in order—beginning, middle, and end
• conflict and resolution
Use sequence words
FIRST NEXT
THEN LATER
FINALLY

Vowel Diphthongs *ow, ou*

Step 1 Reinforce the Skill

LEARNING OBJECTIVES

- Decode and read with vowel diphthongs *ow* and *ou*.
- Recognize spelling patterns for vowel diphthongs *ow* and *ou*.
- **Language** Articulate sounds for vowel diphthongs *ow* and *ou* and read words containing those sounds.

MATERIALS Online Ed

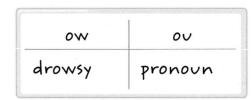

Display and Engage *Decoding 4.8*
Know It, Show It *p. 86*

Vowel Diphthongs *ow, ou* Remind students that they have learned the sounds and spellings of the vowel diphthongs *ow* and *ou*.

- **Transition to Longer Words** Display the word *powder*. Explain that students can divide longer words into syllables to make them easier to decode and read.
- Draw a line between *w* and *d* in *powder*. Say each syllable: /pow/ /dər/. Underline the *ow* in the first syllable. Point out that the /ou/ sound is in the first syllable.
- Repeat with the words *allow, background,* and *trousers*. Guide students to read the words and identify the /ou/ sound spelled *ow* and *ou*.
- Display the chart below. Read each word aloud, emphasizing the /ou/ sound and underlining the vowel diphthong in each word.

ow	ou
drowsy	pronoun

- Display the following sentences and underline the word *drowsy*.

Playing soccer all afternoon made Eric feel so drowsy that he went inside and took a nap.

Say: *Let's say I didn't recognize the word* drowsy. *I see the vowel diphthong* ow *in the first syllable, which I know can stand for the /ou/ sound. That can help me sound out the word: /drou/ /zē/,* drowsy. *It sounds like a word I've heard, but I need to check the meaning. I can tell from the context clues in the sentence that* drowsy *means "sleepy."*

ENGLISH LEARNER SUPPORT: Utilize Language Transfer

ALL LEVELS In Spanish, vowel sounds tend to be spelled consistently. Point out that in English, the vowel diphthongs *ow* and *ou* can both stand for the same sound, /ou/. Write *found, loud, power,* and *tower*. Say each word, emphasize the /ou/ sound, and have students repeat. Ask volunteers to underline the letters in each word that stand for the /ou/ sound.

Step 2 Guided Practice

- Project Display and Engage: **Decoding 4.8**.
- Have students read the Blend and Read lines aloud. Provide feedback as needed. At the end of each line, prompt a conversation about the words: *How are the vowel sounds the same? How are the spellings the same or different?*
- Have partners reread the Blend and Read lines and quiz each other on the spellings of the vowel diphthongs. Challenge students to find words that contain two vowel diphthongs.

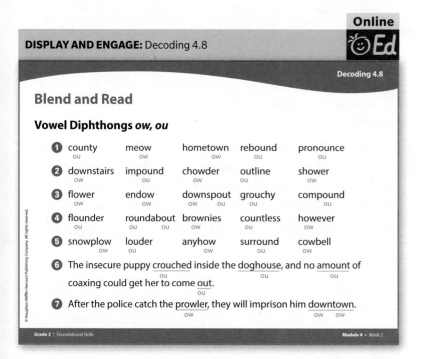

Online Ed

DISPLAY AND ENGAGE: Decoding 4.8

Decoding 4.8

Blend and Read

Vowel Diphthongs *ow, ou*

1	county (ou)	meow (ow)	hometown (ow)	rebound (ou)	pronounce (ou)
2	downstairs (ow)	impound (ou)	chowder (ow)	outline (ou)	shower (ow)
3	flower (ow)	endow (ow)	downspout (ow, ou)	grouchy (ou)	compound (ou)
4	flounder (ou)	roundabout (ou, ou)	brownies (ow)	countless (ou)	however (ow)
5	snowplow (ow)	louder (ou)	anyhow (ow)	surround (ou)	cowbell (ow)

6 The insecure puppy crouched (ou) inside the doghouse (ou), and no amount (ou) of coaxing could get her to come out (ou).

7 After the police catch the prowler (ow), they will imprison him downtown (ow, ow).

Grade 3 | Foundational Skills Module 4 • Week 2

Step 3 Apply

INDEPENDENT PRACTICE

- Have students work in small groups or with partners to complete Know It, Show It page 86.
- Encourage students to share with each other the strategies they use to decode words with vowel diphthongs.

CORRECT & REDIRECT

If students have trouble decoding words with vowel diphthongs, use the model below.

- **Correct** the error. *The letters ow and ou can be pronounced /ou/.*
- **Model** how to decode the word *compound*. */cŏm/ /pŏnd/. That doesn't sound right. In the second syllable, I see the letters ou. I know that ou can stand for the /ou/ sound. I'll try that: /cŏm/ /pound/,* compound. Compound *is a word I know.*
- **Guide** students to decode the words *flounder* and *chowder*.
- **Check** students' understanding by displaying the word *endow*. *What spelling pattern helps you decode this word?*
- **Reinforce** by repeating the process with *impound*.

Review Critical Vocabulary

LEARNING OBJECTIVES

- Review and extend understanding of word meanings.
- Use context to determine the meanings of unfamiliar words.
- **Language** Use newly acquired vocabulary expressively.

MATERIALS | Online Ed

Display and Engage *Critical Vocabulary 4.8*

Know It, Show It *p. 87*

CRITICAL VOCABULARY

- **eminent**
- **peasant**
- **stately**
- **deceive**
- **superior**
- **merciful**

Step 1 Reinforce Vocabulary

- Project Display and Engage: **Critical Vocabulary 4.8** to review and discuss the Critical Vocabulary, student-friendly explanations, and examples of the words. Have students take turns using the words in sentences.

Step 2 Guided Practice

- Display the Critical Vocabulary words. Have students work in small groups.
- One student in each group gives clues about a Critical Vocabulary word without saying the word. Encourage students to say words that have similar or opposite meanings or examples, or describe times they used or might use the Critical Vocabulary word.
- For example: *This word is the opposite of unimportant.* (eminent)

Step 3 Apply

INDEPENDENT PRACTICE

- Have students work in small groups or independently. Tell them to complete Know It, Show It page 87. For the last item on the page, tell students to include clues to each word's meaning in their sentences. Have groups share their sentences. Ask listeners to identify the context clue in each sentence.
- You may wish to have students complete the Know It, Show It page during small-group time.

ENGLISH LEARNER SUPPORT: Support Discussion

Use tiered supports as needed to help students as they answer questions about the Critical Vocabulary.

SUBSTANTIAL

Draw or describe something that is stately.

MODERATE

Something that is stately is _____.

LIGHT

What qualities make someone or something stately? Give examples.

Shades of Meaning

Step 1 Introduce the Strategy

LEARNING OBJECTIVES

- Identify shades of meaning in synonyms.
- Use print and digital reference materials to clarify meanings.
- **Language** Identify shades of meaning using strategic learning techniques.

MATERIALS Online Ed

Display and Engage *Vocabulary Strategy 4.9*

INSTRUCTIONAL VOCABULARY

- **shades of meaning** small differences between words that mean almost the same thing

Project Display and Engage: **Vocabulary Strategy 4.9**. Read aloud the two paragraphs.

Online

DISPLAY AND ENGAGE: Strategy 4.9

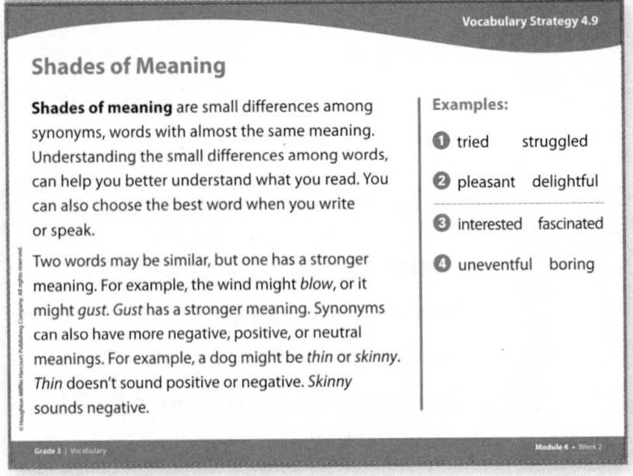
Vocabulary Strategy 4.9

Shades of Meaning

Shades of meaning are small differences among synonyms, words with almost the same meaning. Understanding the small differences among words, can help you better understand what you read. You can also choose the best word when you write or speak.

Two words may be similar, but one has a stronger meaning. For example, the wind might *blow*, or it might *gust*. *Gust* has a stronger meaning. Synonyms can also have more negative, positive, or neutral meanings. For example, a dog might be *thin* or *skinny*. *Thin* doesn't sound positive or negative. *Skinny* sounds negative.

Examples:

1. tried struggled
2. pleasant delightful
3. interested fascinated
4. uneventful boring

Grade 3 | Vocabulary   Module 4 • Week 2

- Remind students that synonyms won't always have exactly the same meanings. There are slight differences called shades of meaning. Sometimes one synonym has a more positive or negative feeling or implication. Explain the differences in degrees of certainty or states of mind.
- Use the first two word pairs to model shades of meaning. Tried *and* struggled *are synonyms.* Struggled *means "tried", but it has a more negative meaning. If you* struggled *to do something, you had a hard time doing it.* Pleasant *and* delightful *are also synonyms. However,* delightful *has a more positive meaning. When something is* delightful, *it is much more than just* pleasant!

Step 2 Guided Practice

- Have students read the next two pairs of words and identify which word has a more positive or negative meaning. Invite them to use a reference source as needed.
- Ask students to explain why the words have a more positive or negative meaning.

Step 3 Apply the Strategy

INDEPENDENT PRACTICE

- Have students find the words *live, ask,* and *silly* in *Gigi and the Wishing Ring*. For each word, ask students to write a synonym with a more negative or positive connotation. (For example: *thrive, survive; demand; foolish*) Allow them to use reference sources.
- Have students write a sentence or two explaining why each word they chose has a more negative or positive meaning than its synonym.
- Have students exchange their sentences with partners and discuss one another's responses.

ENGLISH LEARNER SUPPORT: Identify Shades of Meaning

SUBSTANTIAL
Help students identify positive or negative synonyms. Have them use gestures and oral sentences to share meanings.

MODERATE
Supply sentence frames for synonyms: _____ *has a more positive meaning than* _____.

LIGHT
Ask students to explain orally why one synonym has a more negative or positive meaning than another.

READING WORKSHOP

Elements of Drama

Step 1 Connect and Teach

LEARNING OBJECTIVES

- Identify and discuss elements of drama.
- **Language** Identify elements of drama using the terms *stage direction* and *setting*.

MATERIALS Online Ed

Anchor Chart 14 *Elements of Drama*
Printable *Anchor Chart 14: Elements of Drama*
Teaching Pal *Book 1, pp. 324–341*
myBook *Book 1, Gigi and the Wishing Ring, pp. 324–341*
Know It, Show It *p. 88*

INSTRUCTIONAL VOCABULARY

- **act** a chapter in a play that contains more than one scene
- **dialogue** the words that characters in a story or drama say aloud to each other
- **scene** the action in a play that takes place in a single setting
- **stage direction** information in a drama that tells actors where to move, how to look or speak, or information about the set

SPANISH COGNATES

- **dialogue** *diálogo*

- Remind students that a **drama,** or play, is a story performed by actors on a stage.
- Project or display Anchor Chart 14: Elements of Drama.
- Review that dramas have characters, dialogue, and settings, just like stories.
- Use the Anchor Chart to discuss the elements of drama that differ from stories: script, narrator, cast of characters, **dialogue,** and **stage directions.**
- Point out the corresponding sections of the Anchor Chart as you remind students that dramas are divided into **acts** and **scenes**. Discuss how the events in a scene build on what happened in the previous scenes.
- Tell students they will identify the elements of drama to gain a deeper understanding of *Gigi and the Wishing Ring*.

Online
ANCHOR CHART 14: Elements of Drama

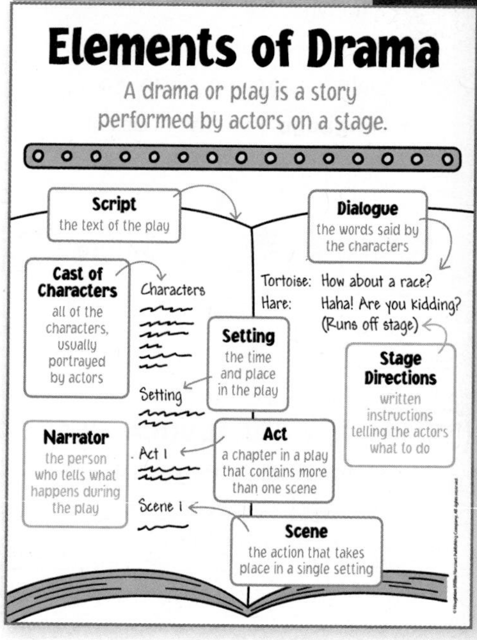

Elements of Drama
A drama or play is a story performed by actors on a stage.
Script
the text of the play
Dialogue
the words said by the characters
Cast of Characters
all of the characters, usually portrayed by actors
Characters
Tortoise: How about a race?
Hare: Haha! Are you kidding? (Runs off stage)
Setting
the time and place in the play
Stage Directions
written instructions telling the actors what to do
Setting
Narrator
the person who tells what happens during the play
Act 1
Act
a chapter in a play that contains more than one scene
Scene 1
Scene
the action that takes place in a single setting

LEARNING MINDSET

Self-Reflection

Apply Have students look back at their news reports from page T311 to reflect on their writing. *As you look back at your work, note things that you did well. Also, what mistakes do you notice? What details can you improve? How would you fix these things the next time you write? Write down your answers.*

Go to Your **Teaching Pal**

Online Ed

ANNOTATE IT!

Students may use the annotation tools in their eBook.

Step 2 Apply to Text

In your Teaching Pal, use the purple **TARGETED CLOSE READ** prompts on pages 334 and 337 to guide students to apply the Elements of Drama skill to *Gigi and the Wishing Ring* and to cite evidence to support their responses. Use the **CLOSE READING** routine. Students may refer to the questions on Know It, Show It page 88 as you discuss them.

- Read aloud the first two questions on Teaching Pal page 334 and have students reread pages 329–334 in their *my*Book to identify and discuss the parts of the play. *(Narrator; The stage directions on page 331 tell how the setting magically changes to a mansion.)*
- Then read the last question on Teaching Pal page 334 and discuss how events build on previous scenes. *(In Scene 2, Old Woman gives Gigi the ring and warns him never to tell anyone about the ring. In Scene 3, he does not follow the warning. Maliarda uses the ring to send him and his friends to the mountaintop.)*
- Have students turn to page 337. Use the prompts to have them analyze elements of drama. Refer back to the Anchor Chart as necessary to support the discussion. Students may add sticky notes to the chart to note other elements of drama in *Gigi and the Wishing Ring* and in other readings.

Step 3 Engage and Respond

INDEPENDENT PRACTICE: Writing

- **Write a Newspaper Report** Turn to pages 340–341 in your Teaching Pal. Have students turn to pages 340–341 in their *my*Book. Use the **WRITING RESPONSE** routine.
- Read the directions with students and use the Teaching Pal prompts to guide them as they plan and complete their newspaper reports.
- Provide time for students to share their newspaper reports with small groups.
- You may want to have students complete their writing during daily small-group time.
- You may want to have students complete Know It, Show It page 88 during daily small-group time.

ENGLISH LEARNER SUPPORT: Build Vocabulary

SUBSTANTIAL

Point to the stage directions. Which words tell about the setting?

MODERATE

What do the stage directions tell about the setting? How do you know?

LIGHT

Have partners use academic vocabulary such as *stage directions* and *setting* to explain and analyze elements of drama.

LINK TO SMALL-GROUP INSTRUCTION

REINFORCE ELEMENTS OF DRAMA Review and extend the skill as needed during small-group time to support students' need for differentiation. *See the lesson on p. T313.*

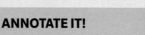

Options for Differentiation

As the class engages in independent and collaborative work, meet with Guided Reading Groups or differentiate instruction based on student need.

GUIDED READING GROUPS

Match Students to Books + Instruction

- Choose just-right books based on level, skill, topic, or genre.

L M N O P Q

Leveled Readers

- Deliver instruction with each book's **Take and Teach Lesson**, choosing appropriate sessions based on need.

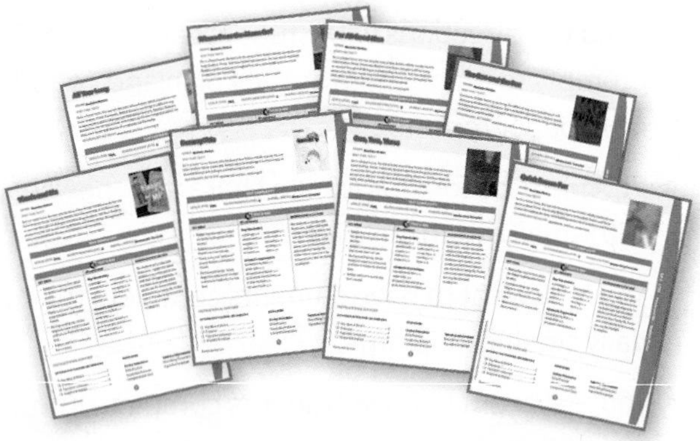

- Check comprehension, reinforce instruction, and extend learning with suggested supporting activities.

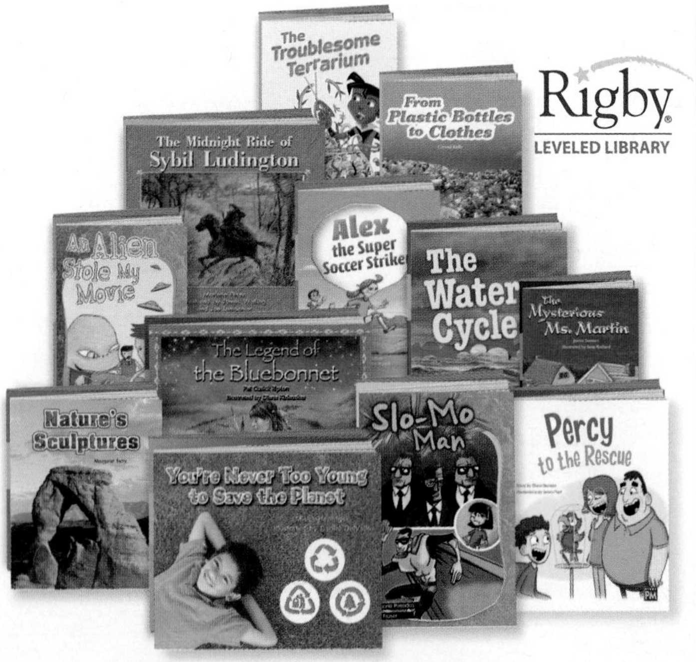

Rigby
LEVELED LIBRARY

ENGLISH LEARNER SUPPORT

Recount Information

- Use **Tabletop Minilessons: English Language Development 11.2 (Writing)** to reinforce and practice the language skill.

Tabletop Minilessons: English Language Development

- Then use the following text-based prompts with *Gigi and the Wishing Ring* to guide application of the language skill. Begin with the prompt at the student's identified language proficiency level. As students progress, use lighter supports to encourage increased language proficiency.

SUBSTANTIAL
Guide students to find words and phrases from the text to complete the sentence frames with sequential events from one scene in the drama: *First* _____. *Next* _____. *Finally* _____.

MODERATE
Provide students with a list of sequence words, such as *first, second, next, finally.* Have students use the words in a written summary of the important information and events for one scene in the drama.

LIGHT
Have students write a sequence chart that recounts the key events and information in the drama.

REINFORCE ELEMENTS OF DRAMA

Demonstrate

- Use **Tabletop Minilessons: Reading Card 14** to remind students that a **drama**, or play, is a story performed by actors on a stage. The script of a drama may be divided into **acts**, like chapters, and **scenes**, which are smaller parts of acts. A **cast of characters** tells who the characters are in the play. **Dialogue** is the words the characters speak. **Stage directions** tell what the characters do onstage.
- Model filling out Printable: Reading Graphic Organizer 14 to identify elements of drama in *Gigi and the Wishing Ring.*

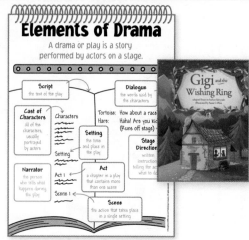

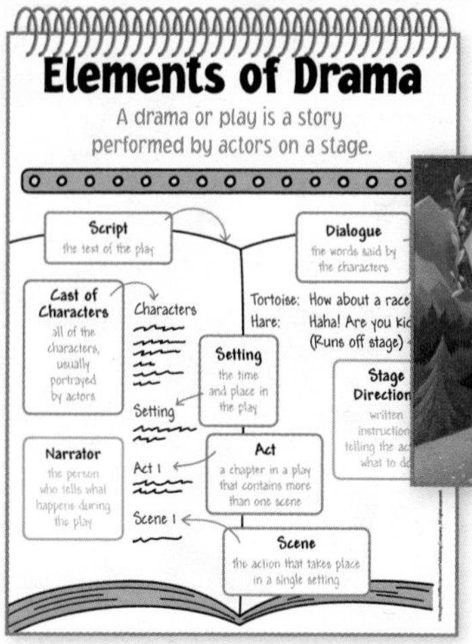

Tabletop Minilessons: Reading

Apply to Independent Reading

- Now have students identify the elements of drama in an appropriate play that they are reading independently. Customize these prompts to the texts students choose.
  - » *Who is in the cast of characters?*
  - » *What is the setting in each act or scene?*
  - » *How do the dialogue and stage directions help you to understand the characters and events?*
- Have students complete Printable: Reading Graphic Organizer 14 for their independent reading book.

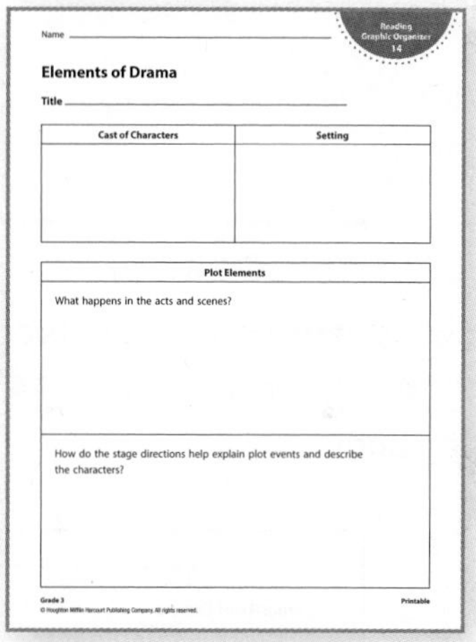

Printable: Reading Graphic Organizer 14

ALMOST THERE

READY FOR MORE

SCAFFOLD AND EXTEND

- Guide students to locate each element of drama in their reading. Then prompt them to recall major events.
- Prompt students to identify the characters, setting, dialogue, and stage directions for each act or scene.
- Have students explain how events in each act or scene are communicated through setting, stage directions, and the characters' dialogue.

EL ENGLISH LEARNER SUPPORT

SUBSTANTIAL

Say: *Point to the cast of characters. Point to a line of dialogue/stage directions. Show me where a new act starts.*

MODERATE

Supply sentence frames such as: *The setting of this act/scene is _____. The characters are _____. The main events are _____.*

LIGHT

Encourage students to explain how they identified the elements of drama and how they help them understand the play.

Options for Independent and Collaborative Work

While you meet with small groups, have other students engage in literacy activities that reinforce the lesson's learning objectives. Choose from these options.

Independent Reading

Student Choice Library

Rigby
LEVELED LIBRARY

APPLY READING SKILL

Elements of drama Students complete Printable: Reading Graphic Organizer 14 for an independent reading book.

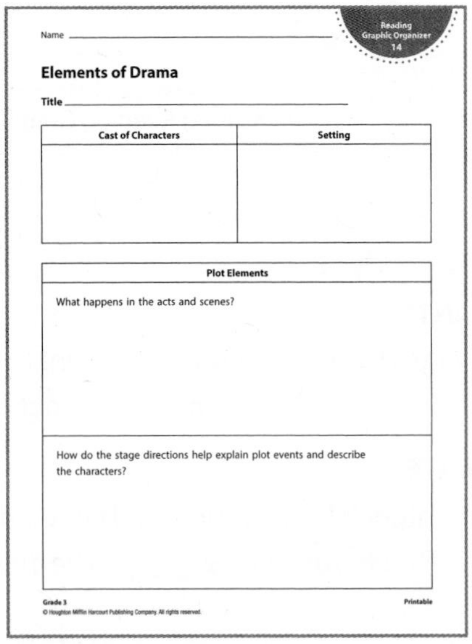
Name ____
Reading Graphic Organizer 14

Elements of Drama

Title ____

Cast of Characters	Setting

Plot Elements

What happens in the acts and scenes?

How do the stage directions help explain plot events and describe the characters?

Grade 3 Printable
© Houghton Mifflin Harcourt Publishing Company. All rights reserved.

Printable: Reading Graphic Organizer 14

APPLY LANGUAGE SKILL

Recount Information Students complete Printable: Language Graphic Organizer 11 for an independent reading book.

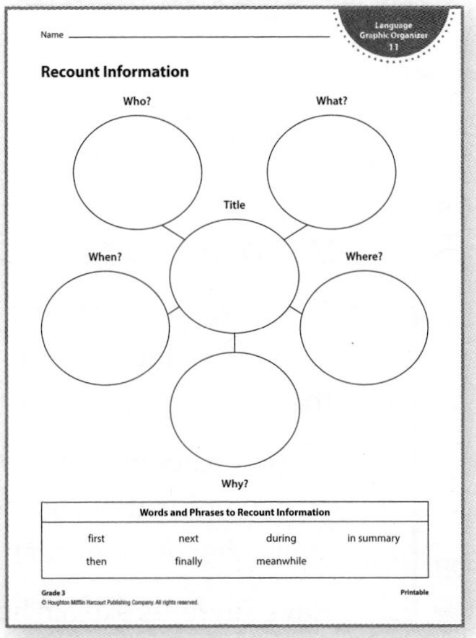
Name ____
Language Graphic Organizer 11

Recount Information

Who? What? Title When? Where? Why?

Words and Phrases to Recount Information			
first	next	during	in summary
then	finally	meanwhile	

Grade 3 Printable
© Houghton Mifflin Harcourt Publishing Company. All rights reserved.

Printable: Language Graphic Organizer 11

Literacy Centers

See pp. T274–T275.

- READING CENTER
- VOCABULARY CENTER
- DIGITAL STATION
- WRITING CENTER
- PROJECT CENTER

Writing

Students write a newspaper report.
See Engage and Respond, p. T311.

Additional Skills Practice

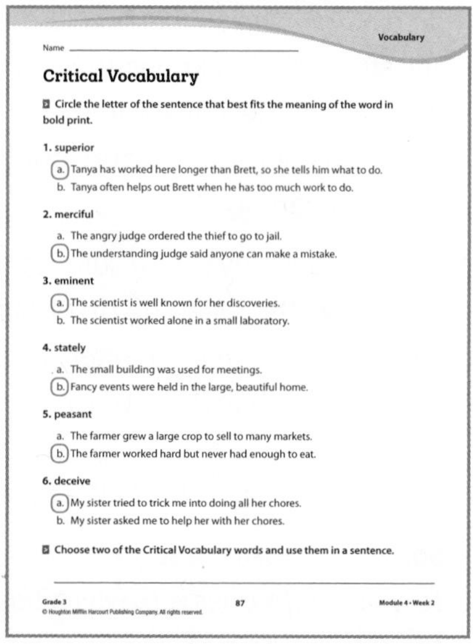

Name ______ Vocabulary

Critical Vocabulary

Circle the letter of the sentence that best fits the meaning of the word in bold print.

1. **superior**
   a. Tanya has worked here longer than Brett, so she tells him what to do.
   b. Tanya often helps out Brett when he has too much work to do.
2. **merciful**
   a. The angry judge ordered the thief to go to jail.
   b. The understanding judge said anyone can make a mistake.
3. **eminent**
   a. The scientist is well known for her discoveries.
   b. The scientist worked alone in a small laboratory.
4. **stately**
   a. The small building was used for meetings.
   b. Fancy events were held in the large, beautiful home.
5. **peasant**
   a. The farmer grew a large crop to sell to many markets.
   b. The farmer worked hard but never had enough to eat.
6. **deceive**
   a. My sister tried to trick me into doing all her chores.
   b. My sister asked me to help her with her chores.

Choose two of the Critical Vocabulary words and use them in a sentence.

Grade 3 87 Module 4 • Week 2

Know It, Show It, p. 87

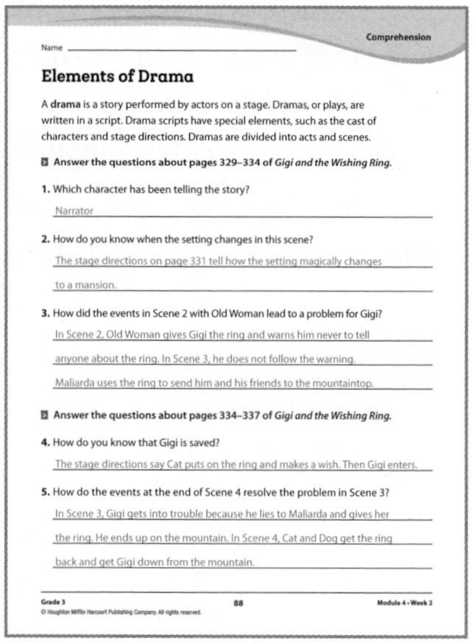

Name ______ Comprehension

Elements of Drama

A **drama** is a story performed by actors on a stage. Dramas, or plays, are written in a script. Drama scripts have special elements, such as the cast of characters and stage directions. Dramas are divided into acts and scenes.

Answer the questions about pages 329–334 of *Gigi and the Wishing Ring.*

1. Which character has been telling the story?
   Narrator
2. How do you know when the setting changes in this scene?
   The stage directions on page 331 tell how the setting magically changes to a mansion.
3. How did the events in Scene 2 with Old Woman lead to a problem for Gigi?
   In Scene 2, Old Woman gives Gigi the ring and warns him never to tell anyone about the ring. In Scene 3, he does not follow the warning. Maliarda uses the ring to send him and his friends to the mountaintop.

Answer the questions about pages 334–337 of *Gigi and the Wishing Ring.*

4. How do you know that Gigi is saved?
   The stage directions say Cat puts on the ring and makes a wish. Then Gigi enters.
5. How do the events at the end of Scene 4 resolve the problem in Scene 3?
   In Scene 3, Gigi gets into trouble because he lies to Maliarda and gives her the ring. He ends up on the mountain. In Scene 4, Cat and Dog get the ring back and get Gigi down from the mountain.

Grade 3 88 Module 4 • Week 2

Know It, Show It, p. 88

Wrap-Up

Share Time

At the end of the Reading Workshop, have students reflect on their learning by sharing how they applied **elements of drama** or another area of focus during independent work time. Choose from these options:

- Use the **SOLO CHAIR** routine. Select a reader each day to come to the front of the class and tell what he or she learned from the reading by using a skill or strategy.
- **THINK-PAIR-SHARE** Students share their thinking with a partner. Select a few pairs each day to share with the whole class.
- **RETURN TO ANCHOR CHART** Have students add sticky notes about their independent reading book to the Elements of Drama Anchor Chart. Call on a few students to explain what they added.

Online Ed

ANCHOR CHART 14: Elements of Drama

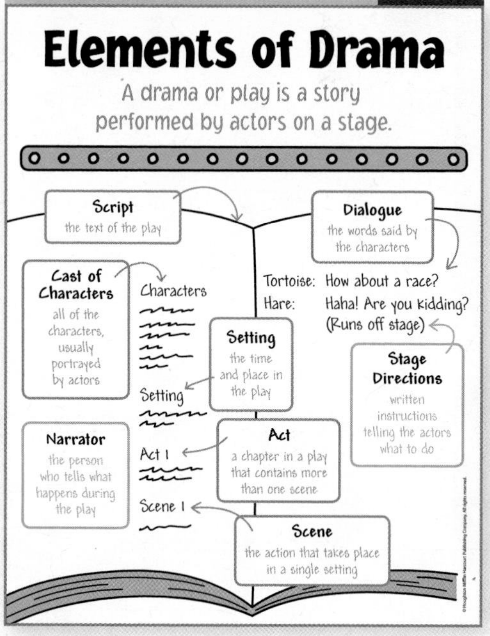

Elements of Drama
A drama or play is a story performed by actors on a stage.
Script
the text of the play
Dialogue
the words said by the characters
Cast of Characters
all of the characters, usually portrayed by actors
Characters
Tortoise: How about a race?
Hare: Haha! Are you kidding? (Runs off stage)
Setting
the time and place in the play
Setting
Stage Directions
written instructions telling the actors what to do
Narrator
the person who tells what happens during the play
Act 1
Act
a chapter in a play that contains more than one scene
Scene 1
Scene
the action that takes place in a single setting

VOCABULARY

Suffixes -er, -or (one who)

Step 1 Introduce the Skill

Project Display and Engage: Generative Vocabulary 4.10a and 4.10b. Read aloud the paragraphs.

Online

DISPLAY AND ENGAGE:
Generative Vocabulary 4.10a and 4.10b

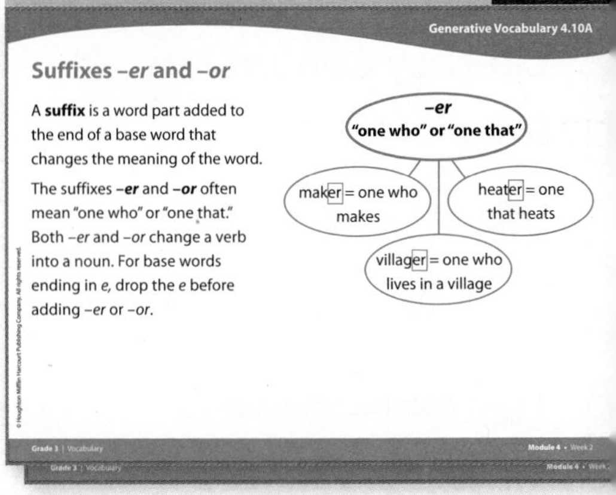

Generative Vocabulary 4.10A
Suffixes –er and –or
A suffix is a word part added to the end of a base word that changes the meaning of the word.
The suffixes –er and –or often mean "one who" or "one that." Both –er and –or change a verb into a noun. For base words ending in e, drop the e before adding –er or –or.
–er
"one who" or "one that"
maker = one who makes
heater = one that heats
villager = one who lives in a village

- Display the words *teacher* and *actor.* Circle the suffixes *–er* and *–or.* Tell students that knowing the meaning of the suffixes in these words can help them figure out the words' meaning.
- Then model how to use suffixes to determine the meaning of a word.

*The suffixes –*er *and –*or *often mean "one who" or "one that." When either suffix is added to a verb, the verb becomes a noun.* Teach *is a verb. When you add –*er *to* teach, *it becomes* teacher: *one who teaches.* Act *is a verb too. When you add -*or *to* act, *it becomes* actor: *one who acts.*

*Some verbs take the suffix –*er, *and others take the suffix –*or. *There is no easy guide to which suffix goes with which base word. The best plan is to check a dictionary or thesaurus to be sure.*

*Sometimes a word's spelling changes slightly when you add the suffix –*er *or –*or. *For most verbs that end in* e, *you drop the* e *before adding the suffix:* race *becomes* racer. *For verbs that end in a vowel followed by a consonant, you double the consonant when adding the suffix:* run *becomes* runner.

*When I see the suffix –*er *or –*or, *I'll know that the word is a noun that may mean "one who" or "one that" does something.*

LEARNING OBJECTIVES

- Determine the meaning of grade-level academic vocabulary with prefixes or suffixes.
- Use a dictionary or glossary to determine the meanings of unknown words.
- **Language** Discuss words with the suffixes *–er* and *–or* to show understanding of the target suffixes.

MATERIALS Online Ed

Display and Engage *Generative Vocabulary 4.10a, 4.10b*

Know It, Show It *p. 89*

INSTRUCTIONAL VOCABULARY

- **suffix** a word part added to the end of a base word that changes the meaning of the word
- **prefix** a word part added to the beginning of a base word that changes the meaning of the word
- **base word** a word in its simplest form, without any word parts added to it

ENGLISH LEARNER SUPPORT: Build Vocabulary

SUBSTANTIAL
Show familiar words with the suffixes *–er* and *–or (one who/that).* Discuss each base word's meaning and how the suffix changes it.

MODERATE
Have students name words with the suffix *–er* or *–or (one who/that)* and explain the base word's meaning and how the suffix changes it.

LIGHT
Have partners write sentences with the lesson's *–er and –or* words.

Step 2 Guided Practice

- Display the words *sculptor* and *presenter*. Ask volunteers to identify the base word in each and give its meaning. Then ask how the suffixes change the meaning of each base word.
- Then ask students to look up each word in a print or online dictionary to confirm their predictions. Have volunteers provide a definition of each word.

Step 3 Apply the Skill

INDEPENDENT PRACTICE

- Have students work in pairs to complete Know It, Show It page 89. Tell partners to read the instructions and have them complete the activity together.
- Then have each student write a new sentence for each *–er* and *–or* word. Have partners read their sentences to one another to confirm the meaning of each word. Invite volunteers to read their sentences aloud.
- You may wish to have students complete the Know It, Show It page during small-group time.

Spiral Review

Prefixes *in–* (not), *im–* (into) Remind students that a prefix is a word part added to the beginning of a base word that changes the meaning of the word.

- Review that the prefix *in–* can mean "not." When *in–*, meaning "not," is added to a base word, the new word means the opposite of the base word. Review also that the prefix *im–* can mean "into." When *im–*, meaning "into," is added to a base word, the new word means "into" something.
- Write on the board the following words for review: *inactive, inability, imprison, implant.* Guide students to identify the base word and prefix in each word and explain how the prefix changes the base word's meaning.
- Have students add the prefix *in–* to the following review words: *correct, capable.* Have them add the prefix *im–* to the following review words: *migrate, peril*. Have students explain how the prefix change the words' meaning. Invite them to check the words' meanings in a print or online dictionary.

Theme

Step 1 Connect and Teach

Project or display Anchor Chart 9: **Theme**.

Remind students that many stories and dramas have a **theme**. Review the definition of *theme* and the examples on the Anchor Chart. Then make the following points:

- The theme is often not stated in the story. Readers have to use clues from the story to figure out the theme. Draw attention to the questions that help to suggest the author's theme or message.
- A theme is different from the **topic** of a story. As needed, explain that the topic is the person or thing the story is about. Use a familiar story, such as *The Tortoise and the Hare* to show how its theme (overconfidence can lead to failure) differs from its topic (a race between two animals).
- Tell students they will practice identifying the theme to gain a deeper understanding of the tale/fable *Gigi and the Wishing Ring*.

Online

ANCHOR CHART 9: Theme Online Ed

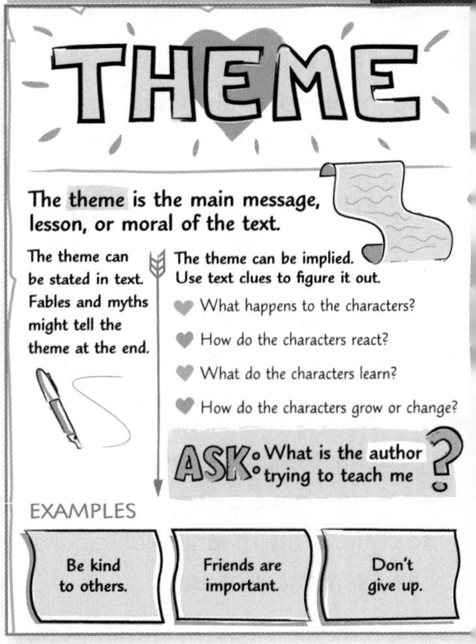
THEME
The theme is the main message, lesson, or moral of the text.
The theme can be stated in text. Fables and myths might tell the theme at the end.
The theme can be implied. Use text clues to figure it out.
What happens to the characters?
How do the characters react?
What do the characters learn?
How do the characters grow or change?
ASK: What is the author trying to teach me?
EXAMPLES
Be kind to others.
Friends are important.
Don't give up.

LEARNING OBJECTIVES

- Identify the author's message or theme.
- Distinguish theme from topic.
- **Language** State the difference between theme and topic.

MATERIALS Online Ed

Anchor Chart 9 *Theme*
Printable *Anchor Chart 9: Theme*
Teaching Pal *Book 1, pp. 324–341*
myBook *Book 1, Gigi and the Wishing Ring, pp. 324–341*
Know It, Show It *p. 90*

INSTRUCTIONAL VOCABULARY

- **moral** the lesson in a story
- **theme** the big idea, moral, or lesson of a piece of writing
- **topic** the person or thing a text is about

SPANISH COGNATES

- **moral** *moral*
- **theme** *tema*

LEARNING MINDSET

Self-Reflection

Reflect Review paragraphs 189–191 on page 338 of *Gigi and the Wishing Ring*. *How does Gigi reflect on his actions? What lesson does he learn? Gigi lies to Maliarda and she lies to him. Do you think Gigi will make the same mistake again?* Remind students that it isn't always easy to reflect on our work because we often find mistakes. But, like Gigi, we learn lessons from reflecting. Reflection gives us a chance to improve and avoid making the same mistakes again.

Go to Your Teaching Pal

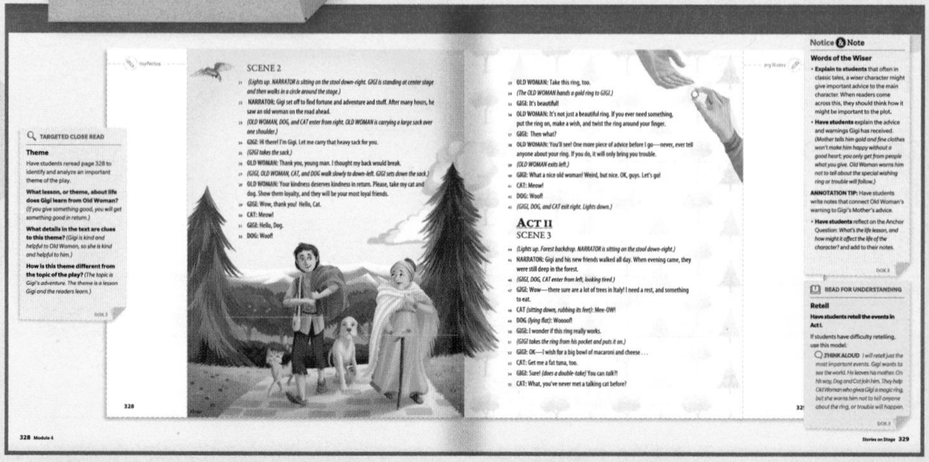

Online Ed

ANNOTATE IT!

Students may use the annotation tools in their eBook.

Step 2 Apply to Text

In your Teaching Pal, use the purple **TARGETED CLOSE READ** prompts on pages 328 and 338 to guide students to apply the Theme skill to *Gigi and the Wishing Ring* and to find evidence to support their responses. Use the **CLOSE READING** routine. Students may refer to the questions on Know It, Show It page 90 as you discuss them.

- Read aloud the first two questions on Teaching Pal page 328. Then have students reread *my*Book page 328 and determine the theme and the clues that suggest it. *(If you give something good, you will get something good in return; Gigi is kind and helpful to the old woman. So she is kind and helpful to him.)*
- Then read the last question on Teaching Pal page 328. Discuss how the theme differs from the topic. *(The topic is Gigi's adventure. The theme is a lesson Gigi and the readers learn.)*
- Have students turn to page 338. Use the prompts to identify and analyze the theme. Refer back to the Anchor Chart to support the discussion. Students may add sticky notes to the chart to note other examples of themes they identify in *Gigi and the Wishing Ring*.

Step 3 Engage and Respond

INDEPENDENT PRACTICE: Reading

- Ask students to work in pairs to choose another story they have read and identify the topic and theme of that text.
- Have partners identify the evidence in the text that suggests the theme. Remind students that the theme may *not* be stated, so they will need to look for clues in the story.
- Have partners use the **COLLABORATIVE DISCUSSION** routine to discuss how they found the theme by using evidence in the text.
- You may wish to have students complete the reading activity during daily small-group time.
- You may wish to have students complete the Know It, Show It page 90 during daily small-group time.

ENGLISH LEARNER SUPPORT: Facilitate Language Connections

For Spanish-speaking students, point out that the English words *theme* and *topic* translate to the same word in Spanish: *tema*. Explain that in English, the words' meanings are different. Have students explain the difference between theme and topic.

LINK TO SMALL-GROUP INSTRUCTION

REINFORCE THEME Review and extend the skill as needed during small-group time to support students' need for differentiation. *See the lesson on p. T321.*

Options for Differentiation

As the class engages in independent and collaborative work, meet with Guided Reading Groups or differentiate instruction based on student need.

GUIDED READING GROUPS

Match Students to Books + Instruction

- Choose just-right books based on level, skill, topic, or genre.

L → M → N → O → P → Q

Leveled Readers

- Deliver instruction with each book's **Take and Teach Lesson**, choosing appropriate sessions based on need.

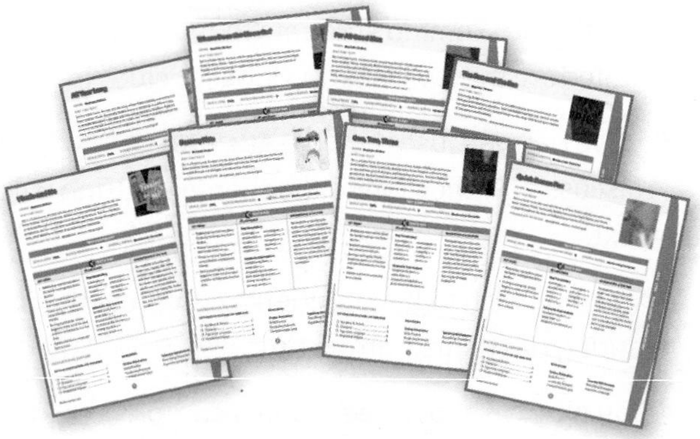

- Check comprehension, reinforce instruction, and extend learning with suggested supporting activities.

ENGLISH LEARNER SUPPORT

Recount Information

- Use **Tabletop Minilessons: English Language Development 11.3 (Collaborative Problem Solving)** to reinforce and practice the language skill.

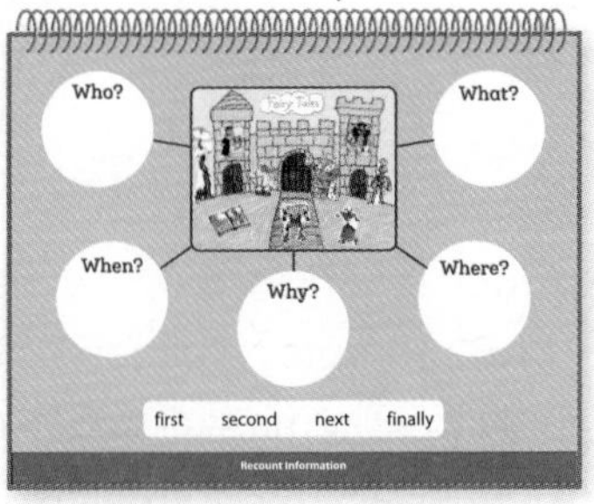

Tabletop Minilessons: English Language Development

- Then use the following text-based prompts with *Gigi and the Wishing Ring* to guide application of the language skill. Begin with the prompt at the student's identified language proficiency level. As students progress, use lighter supports to encourage increased language proficiency.

SUBSTANTIAL
Read aloud a scene from the drama with students, and then have students recount the story by acting out the key events and dialogue they remember. Allow them to use gestures and English words they know.

MODERATE
Assign individuals to be characters from a scene. Have them take turns retelling parts of the scene from that character's point of view, making sure to include key information and events. They can use sentence frames such as: *First, I _____. Then I _____. In the end, I _____.*

LIGHT
Have the group act out a scene from the drama. Remind them to include all characters from the scene, as well as the key events and details.

REINFORCE THEME

Demonstrate

- Use **Tabletop Minilessons: Reading Card 9** to remind students that the **topic** is who or what a drama is about, while the **theme** is the big idea, moral, or lesson in the drama.
- Model filling out Printable: Reading Graphic Organizer 9 to identify theme in *Gigi and the Wishing Ring.*

Apply to Independent Reading

- Now have students identify theme in an appropriate book or drama they are reading independently. Customize these prompts to the texts students choose.
  - » *What is the topic of the drama?*
  - » *Was the theme directly stated, or did you have to figure it out?*
  - » *What clues did you use to figure out the theme?*
- Have students complete Printable: Reading Graphic Organizer 9 for their independent reading book.

THEME
The theme is the main message, lesson, or moral of the text.
The theme can be stated in text. Fables and myths might tell the theme at the end.
The theme can be implied. Use text clues to figure it out.
What happens to the characters?
How do the characters react?
What do the characters learn?
How do the characters grow or chang
ASK: What is the author trying to teach me
EXAMPLES
Be kind to others.
Friends are important.
Don't give up.
Gigi and the Wishing Ring

Tabletop Minilessons: Reading

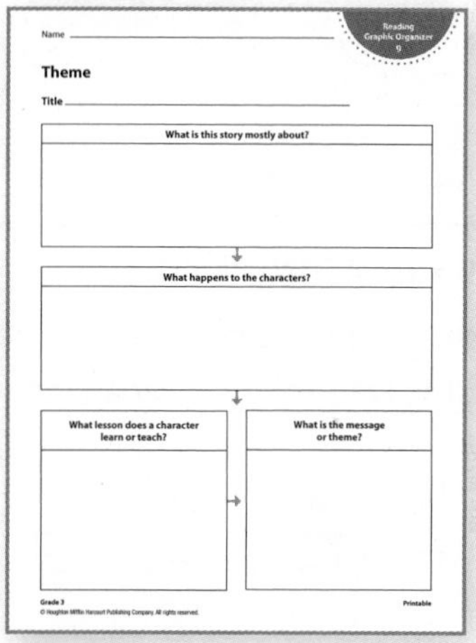

Printable: Reading Graphic Organizer 9

SCAFFOLD AND EXTEND

ALMOST THERE → READY FOR MORE

- Help students differentiate between topic and theme. Guide them to find both in their reading.
- Prompt students to identify the topic and theme, and explain how they identified both.
- Have students explain what differentiates topic from theme in general, and then state examples from their own reading.

EL ENGLISH LEARNER SUPPORT

SUBSTANTIAL

Ask *either/or* questions such as: *Is the topic ______ or ______? Is the theme ______ or ______?*

MODERATE

Guide students to identify topic and theme. Then use sentence frames: *The topic is ______. The theme is ______.*

LIGHT

Encourage students to elaborate on their answers to the questions.

Options for Independent and Collaborative Work

While you meet with small groups, have other students engage in literacy activities that reinforce the lesson's learning objectives. Choose from these options.

Independent Reading

Student Choice Library

Rigby
LEVELED LIBRARY

APPLY READING SKILL

Theme Students complete Printable: Reading Graphic Organizer 9 for an independent reading book.

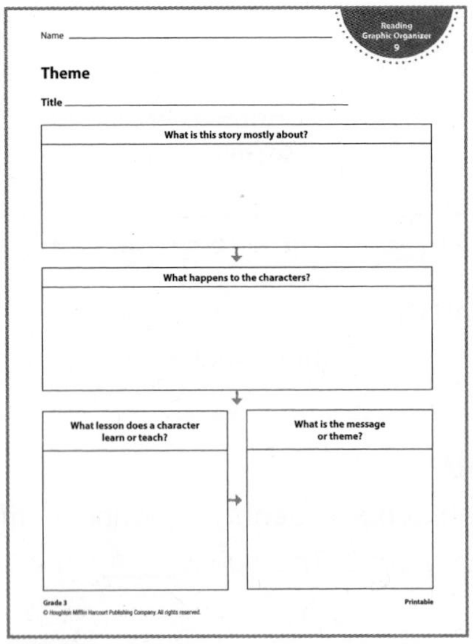

Printable: Reading Graphic Organizer 9

APPLY LANGUAGE SKILL

Recount Information Students complete Printable: Language Graphic Organizer 11 for an independent reading book.

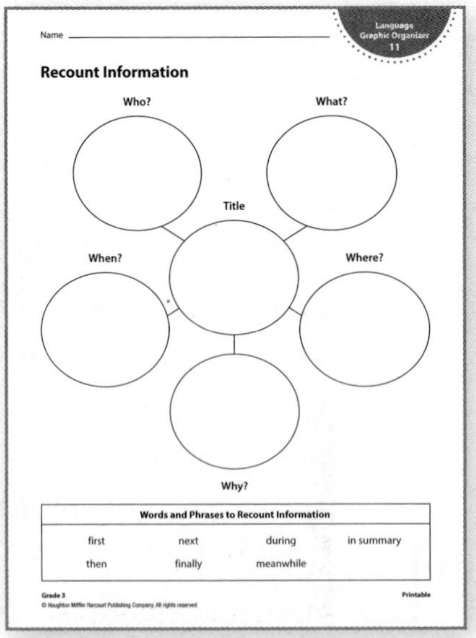

Printable: Language Graphic Organizer 11

Literacy Centers

See pp. T274–T275.

- READING CENTER
- VOCABULARY CENTER
- DIGITAL STATION
- WRITING CENTER
- PROJECT CENTER

Reading

Students read to identify the theme. *See Engage and Respond, p. T319.*

Additional Skills Practice

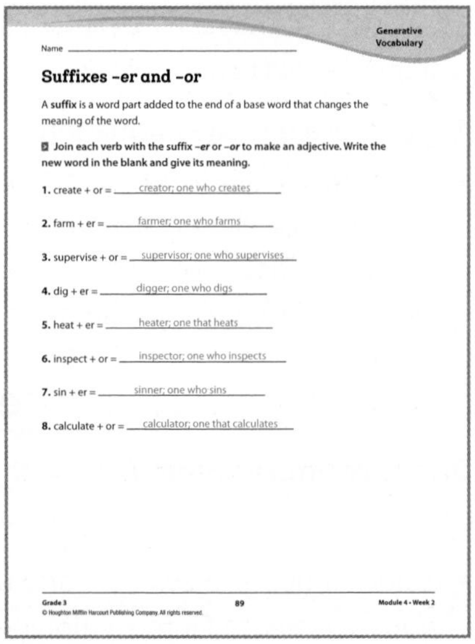

Name ______________________

Generative Vocabulary

Suffixes -er and -or

A **suffix** is a word part added to the end of a base word that changes the meaning of the word.

Join each verb with the suffix *-er* or *-or* to make an adjective. Write the new word in the blank and give its meaning.

1. create + or = creator; one who creates
2. farm + er = farmer; one who farms
3. supervise + or = supervisor; one who supervises
4. dig + er = digger; one who digs
5. heat + er = heater; one that heats
6. inspect + or = inspector; one who inspects
7. sin + er = sinner; one who sins
8. calculate + or = calculator; one that calculates

Grade 3 89 Module 4 • Week 2

Know It, Show It, p. 89

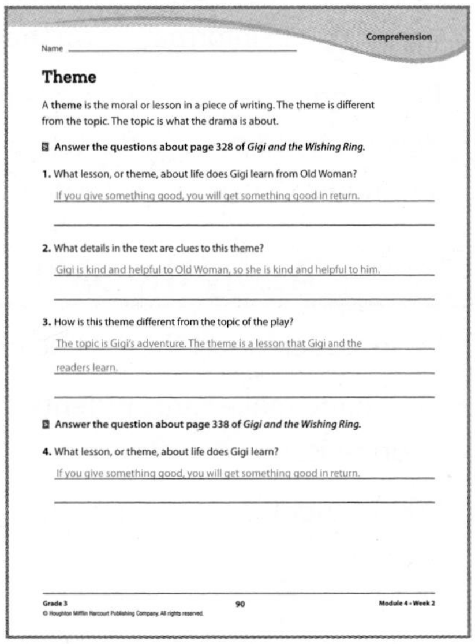

Name ______________________

Comprehension

Theme

A **theme** is the moral or lesson in a piece of writing. The theme is different from the topic. The topic is what the drama is about.

Answer the questions about page 328 of *Gigi and the Wishing Ring*.

1. What lesson, or theme, about life does Gigi learn from Old Woman?
   If you give something good, you will get something good in return.
2. What details in the text are clues to this theme?
   Gigi is kind and helpful to Old Woman, so she is kind and helpful to him.
3. How is this theme different from the topic of the play?
   The topic is Gigi's adventure. The theme is a lesson that Gigi and the readers learn.

Answer the question about page 338 of *Gigi and the Wishing Ring*.

4. What lesson, or theme, about life does Gigi learn?
   If you give something good, you will get something good in return.

Grade 3 90 Module 4 • Week 2

Know It, Show It, p. 90

Wrap-Up

Share Time

At the end of the Reading Workshop, have students reflect on their learning by sharing how they applied **theme** or another area of focus during independent work time. Choose from these options:

- Use the **SOLO CHAIR** routine. Select a reader each day to come to the front of the class and tell what he or she learned from the reading by using a skill or strategy.
- **THINK-PAIR-SHARE** Students share their thinking with a partner. Select a few pairs each day to share with the whole class.
- **RETURN TO ANCHOR CHART** Have students add sticky notes about their independent reading to the Theme Anchor Chart. Call on a few students to explain what they added and why.

Online Ed

ANCHOR CHART 9: Theme

COMMUNICATION

Evaluate and Organize Information

LEARNING OBJECTIVES

- Determine relevance of information for research.
- Organize information for research to demonstrate understanding.
- **Language** Comprehend content to determine relevance to a topic.

MATERIALS Online Ed

computer with internet access, informational books and articles, notecards

INSTRUCTIONAL VOCABULARY

- **brainstorm** to think of a lot of ideas quickly before thinking about them more carefully later
- **evaluate** to decide what is most important to know
- **research** to study and find out about a subject

Step 1 Introduce the Skill

Evaluate Information Tell students that when they do research they should evaluate the information they gathered to determine how it is relevant it is to their research question.

- Provide some examples of sources. Tell students they will look for relevant information that can help them answer the Essential Question: *Why might some stories be told better as plays?*
- Model evaluating information. Read aloud a source title then preview the headings and illustrations. Say: *I want to evaluate, or see how relevant this information is to my research. I'll ask, "Does this help to answer my research question?"* Discuss how the information in the source answers or doesn't answer the Essential Question. Guide students to decide whether or not it is relevant.

Step 2 Guided Practice

Organize Information Explain that research notes are used to write reports. Organizing research notes before writing will help students organize their writing.

- Guide students to evaluate and take notes on a relevant source. They should write one piece of information per notecard.
- Point out that students' notecards can be organized into categories according to the type of information on the card.
- Brainstorm categories that relate to the Essential Question, such as "what makes a good play" and "story elements." Write them on the board. Model sorting several notes. Then guide students to begin sorting their own notes.

Step 3 Apply the Skill

- Have students sort their notecards to reflect an organizational scheme.
- Monitor to make sure students' organization reflects an understanding of the information.
- When students have finished, organize them into small groups to share their categories.

ENGLISH LEARNER SUPPORT: Develop Keywords

SUBSTANTIAL

List categories for students. Have them repeat the words with you. Students may use words or phrases for notes. Help them sort notes into their categories.

MODERATE

Guide students to sort their notes and explain using the sentence frame: *This information goes in [name of organizational category] because* ______.

LIGHT

Prompt students to generate additional categories to sort information. Have volunteers explain why they sorted their information as they did.

Synthesize Topic Knowledge

LEARNING OBJECTIVES

- Recognize and describe the features of a drama.
- Synthesize knowledge gained from the week's texts.
- **Language** Compare subjects from two selections using sentence frames for support.

MATERIALS Online Ed

myBook *Book 1, pp. 300–301, 324–339*

Display and Engage *Knowledge Map 4.5*

Genre Focus

- Review with students the characteristics of a drama. Explain that a drama is written to be performed on stage. Key features include a cast of characters, dialogue, and stage directions. Like a story, a drama has characters, setting, and plot with a beginning, middle, and end. A drama may be divided into acts and scenes, which are like chapters in a book.
- Discuss with students the drama they encountered this week. Tell them that *Gigi and the Wishing Ring* is an example of a classic drama.
- Ask students to name the features of a drama that appear in the selection, and how these features help them to understand the story and help them to picture it being performed on a stage.

Knowledge Focus

- Project Display and Engage: Knowledge Map 4.10. Have students turn to *myBook* page 324.
- Tell students to think about what makes *Gigi and the Wishing Ring* a good story to tell as a play. *(It has fantasy elements that can be shown visually on stage; it has a strong main character and supporting characters.)*
- Then work with students to add information from *Gigi and the Wishing Ring* to the Knowledge Map.

DISPLAY AND ENGAGE: Knowledge Map 4.10 Online Ed

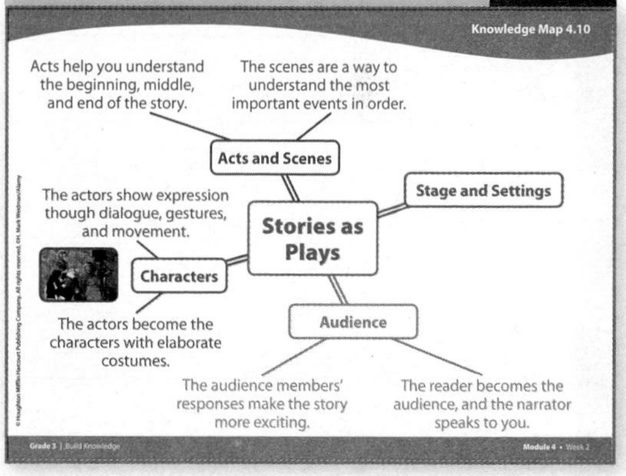

- Have students discuss their Knowledge Maps and their responses to the Essential Question: *Why might some stories be better told as plays?*
- Tell students that they will return to the Knowledge Map for the Week 3 Make Connections activity.

ENGLISH LEARNER SUPPORT: Facilitate Discussion

SUBSTANTIAL

Use these frames to help students to connect the reading to the Essential Question: *A play has* _____. Gigi and the Wishing Ring *also has* _____.

MODERATE

Prompt students to connect the reading to the Essential Question. Gigi and the Wishing Ring *is better performed as a play because* _____.

LIGHT

Ask students to connect the reading to the Essential Question. Ask: *What makes* Gigi and the Wishing Ring *a good story for a play?*

Notes

MODULE 4 Week 3

LANGUAGE ARTS CONNECTION: Drama

Stories on Stage

Essential Question Why might some stories be better told as plays?

Essential Skills

VOCABULARY

- Critical Vocabulary: *drowsy, hesitation, burden, reassuring, greedily, unnoticed*
- Vocabulary Strategy: Spiral Review: Multiple Meaning Words
- Generative Vocabulary: Latin Roots *aud, vis;* Spiral Review: Suffixes *-er/-or* "one who..."

READING WORKSHOP

- Monitor and Clarify
- Elements of Drama
- Literary Elements
- Theme

FOUNDATIONAL SKILLS

- Decoding: Vowel *au, aw, al, o*
- Spelling: Vowel Sound in *talk*
- Fluency: Reading Rate

COMMUNICATION

- Speaking and Listening: Oral Instructions
- Make Connections

WRITING WORKSHOP

- Narrative Writing: Story
- Writing Quotations

LEARNING MINDSET: Self-Reflection

THIS WEEK'S SELECTIONS

myBOOK

DRAMA/MYTH
Two Bear Cubs

Rigby
LEVELED LIBRARY

WEEK 3

Week at a Glance

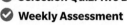

Suggested Daily Times

- VOCABULARY/ SYNTHESIZE AND CONNECT 10–15 minutes
- READING WORKSHOP 60–85 minutes
- FOUNDATIONAL SKILLS 15–30 minutes
- COMMUNICATION 15–30 minutes
- WRITING WORKSHOP 30–45 minutes

This Week's Words

BIG IDEA WORDS

audition *rehearse* *ability* *actor*

CRITICAL VOCABULARY WORDS

drowsy	*hesitation*	*burden*
reassuring	*greedily*	*unnoticed*

HIGH-FREQUENCY WORDS

whether *simple* *divided*

INSTRUCTIONAL VOCABULARY

clarify	*monitor*	*act*
cast of characters	*dialogue*	*drama*
scene	*script*	*stage direction*
conflict	*event*	*literary elements*
plot	*resolution*	*moral*
theme	*topic*	

Assessment Options

Online Ed

- **Selection Quiz: *Two Bear Cubs***
- **Weekly Assessment**
  - Comprehension
  - Generative Vocabulary: Latin roots *aud, vis*
  - Grammar: Writing Quotations

Intervention

For students needing strategic intervention, choose from daily small-group options for differentiation. Access online Foundational Skills and Word Study Studio for additional support.

LESSON 11

VOCABULARY

Academic Vocabulary, pp. T334–T335

- Introduce Critical Vocabulary: *drowsy, hesitation, burden, reassuring, greedily, unnoticed*

READING WORKSHOP

Two Bear Cubs Teaching Pal

GENRE Drama/Myth

Shared Reading: MINILESSON, pp. T336–T337

- Connect and Teach: Monitor and Clarify
- Apply to Text: ***Two Bear Cubs***
- Engage and Respond: Speaking and Listening

SMALL-GROUP INSTRUCTION

Options for Differentiation

- Guided Reading Groups, p. T338
- English Learner Support: Cause and Effect, p. T338
- Reinforce Monitor and Clarify, p. T339

Options for Independent and Collaborative Work, pp. T340–T341

FOUNDATIONAL SKILLS

Decoding, pp. T342–T343

- Vowel *au, aw, al, o*

Spelling, p. T344

- Vowel Sound in *talk*

Fluency, p. T345

- Reading Rate

WRITING WORKSHOP

Narrative Writing: Story, p. W62

- Revising III: Adding Dialogue

Grammar, p. W330

- Quotation Marks

LESSON 12

VOCABULARY

Academic Vocabulary, p. T346

- Review Critical Vocabulary: *drowsy, hesitation, burden, reassuring, greedily, unnoticed*

Vocabulary Strategy, p. 347

- Spiral Review: Suffixes *–er/–or* "one who…"

READING WORKSHOP

Two Bear Cubs ic Teaching Pal

GENRE Drama/Myth

Shared Reading: MINILESSON, pp. T348–T349

- Connect and Teach: Elements of Drama
- Apply to Text: ***Two Bear Cubs***
- Engage and Respond: Write a Character Study

SMALL-GROUP INSTRUCTION

Options for Differentiation

- Guided Reading Groups, p. T350
- English Learner Support: Cause and Effect, p. T350
- Reinforce Elements of Drama, p. T351

Options for Independent and Collaborative Work, pp. T352–T353

COMMUNICATION

Project Checkpoint: Practice and Present, pp. T17, T331

WRITING WORKSHOP

Narrative Writing: Story, p. W63

- Editing I: Grammar and Mechanics

Grammar, p. W331

- Capitalizing and Punctuating Quotations

LESSON 13

VOCABULARY

Generative Vocabulary, pp. T354–T355
- Latin roots *aud, vis*
- Spiral Review: Suffixes *-er / -or* "one who"

READING WORKSHOP

Two Bear Cubs
GENRE Drama/Myth
Teaching Pal
Shared Reading: MINILESSON, pp. T356–T357
- Connect and Teach: Literary Elements
- Apply to Text: ***Two Bear Cubs***
- Engage and Respond: Writing

SMALL-GROUP INSTRUCTION

Options for Differentiation
- Guided Reading Groups, p. T358
- English Learner Support: Cause and Effect, p. T358
- Reinforce Literary Elements, p. T359

Options for Independent and Collaborative Work, pp. T360–T361

FOUNDATIONAL SKILLS

Decoding, pp. T362–T363
- Vowel *au, aw, al, o*

WRITING WORKSHOP

Narrative Writing: Story, p. W64
- Editing II: Peer Proofreading

Grammar, p. W332
- Commas in Quotations

LESSON 14

VOCABULARY

Academic Vocabulary, pp. T364–T365
- Vocabulary Spiral Review

READING WORKSHOP

Two Bear Cubs
GENRE Drama/Myth
Teaching Pal
Shared Reading: MINILESSON, pp. T366–T367
- Connect and Teach: Theme
- Apply to Text: ***Two Bear Cubs***
- Engage and Respond: Writing

SMALL-GROUP INSTRUCTION

Options for Differentiation
- Guided Reading Groups, p. T368
- English Learner Support: Cause and Effect, p. T368
- Reinforce Theme, p. T369

Options for Independent and Collaborative Work, pp. T370–T371

COMMUNICATION

Speaking and Listening, p. T372
- Oral Instructions

Make Connections, p. T373
- Synthesize Topic Knowledge

WRITING WORKSHOP

Narrative Writing: Story, p. W65
- Publishing

Grammar, p. W273
- Review Verb Tenses

LESSON 15

SYNTHESIZE AND CONNECT

Module Wrap-Up, pp. T374–T375
- Synthesize Knowledge
- Make Connections

READING WORKSHOP

Performance Task, pp. T376–T377
Teaching Pal
- Writing to a Prompt

SMALL-GROUP INSTRUCTION

Options for Differentiation
- Guided Reading Groups, p. T378
- English Learner Support: Cause and Effect, p. T378

Options for Independent and Collaborative Work, p. T379

COMMUNICATION

Project Checkpoint: Project Presentation, pp. T117, T380
- Write a Play

WRITING WORKSHOP

Narrative Writing: Story, p. W66
- Sharing

Grammar, p. W334
- Connect to Writing: Using Quotations

Literacy Centers

- **While you meet with small groups, have students work independently in Literacy Centers. Familiarize students with the week's activities and post a daily rotation schedule.**
- **Have students complete Printable: Exit Ticket for each activity so you can monitor their work.**

READING CENTER

Readers' Theater

- Preview Printable: **Readers' Theater 4**, "A Tale with a Twist," and assign parts to mixed-ability groups of five students.
- The part of Carlos is ideal for struggling readers, and the part of Carrie can be read by a proficient reader.

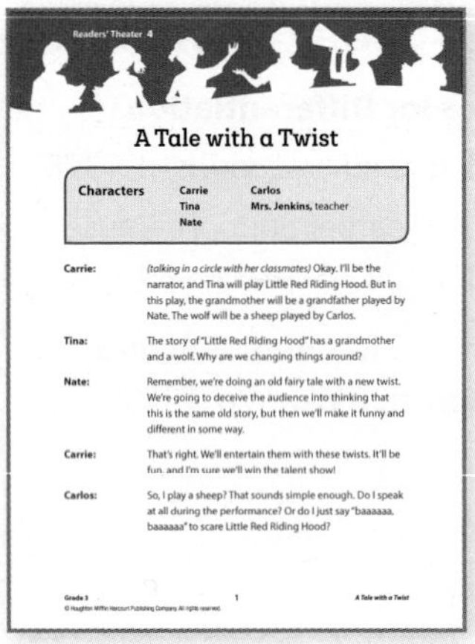
Readers' Theater 4

A Tale with a Twist

Characters	Carrie	Carlos
	Tina	Mrs. Jenkins, teacher
	Nate	

Carrie: *(talking in a circle with her classmates)* Okay. I'll be the narrator, and Tina will play Little Red Riding Hood. But in this play, the grandmother will be a grandfather played by Nate. The wolf will be a sheep played by Carlos.

Tina: The story of "Little Red Riding Hood" has a grandmother and a wolf. Why are we changing things around?

Nate: Remember, we're doing an old fairy tale with a new twist. We're going to deceive the audience into thinking that this is the same old story, but then we'll make it funny and different in some way.

Carrie: That's right. We'll entertain them with these twists. It'll be fun, and I'm sure we'll win the talent show!

Carlos: So, I play a sheep? That sounds simple enough. Do I speak at all during the performance? Or do I just say "baaaaaa, baaaaaa" to scare Little Red Riding Hood?

Grade 3 1 *A Tale with a Twist*
© Houghton Mifflin Harcourt Publishing Company. All rights reserved.

Printable: Readers' Theater 4

Independent Reading

- Have students self-select or continue reading an independent reading book.
- Remind students to set a purpose for reading and to record their progress on their Printable: **Reading Log**.
- Have students use Printable: **Independent Reading** for fiction or nonfiction to note key ideas as they read.
- Display and review Anchor Chart 36: **Respond to Text**.
- You may want to choose from these additional options to have students interact with their books:
- **Mixed-Ability Groups** Students discuss their self-selected books, using the questions on the Reading Log.
- **Make a Bookmark** Students expand on their understanding by creating a bookmark representing an event from the book and explaining the significance to a classmate.

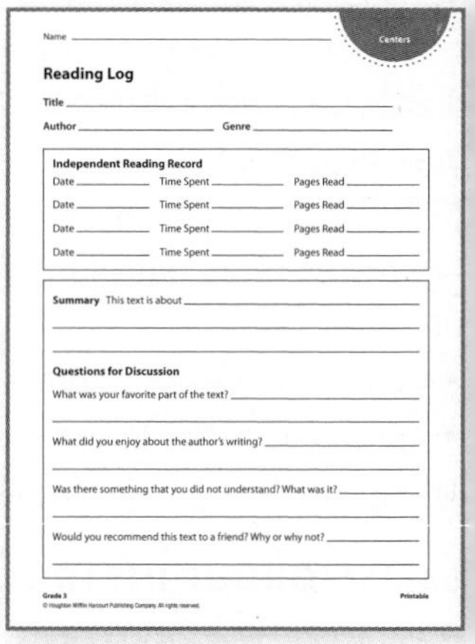
Name ______ Centers

Reading Log

Title ______

Author ______ Genre ______

Independent Reading Record

Date ______ Time Spent ______ Pages Read ______

Date ______ Time Spent ______ Pages Read ______

Date ______ Time Spent ______ Pages Read ______

Date ______ Time Spent ______ Pages Read ______

Summary This text is about ______

Questions for Discussion

What was your favorite part of the text? ______

What did you enjoy about the author's writing? ______

Was there something that you did not understand? What was it? ______

Would you recommend this text to a friend? Why or why not? ______

Grade 3 Printable
© Houghton Mifflin Harcourt Publishing Company. All rights reserved.

Printable: Reading Log

VOCABULARY CENTER

Super Six Words *(Use in Lessons 12–15.)*

- Have students use Printable: **Super Six Words** to list Big Idea Words and this week's Critical Vocabulary words that relate to the module topic.
- Then have students select six words from their lists that they think are most important, interesting, or new to them.
- Tell students to write a sentence for each selected word.
- Explain to students that they will come back to this list at the end of each week in the module.

Name ______ Centers

Super Six Words

1. Take a clean sheet of paper. Write your name at the top. Then write the module title.
2. Create four columns labeled Week 1, Week 2, Week 3, and Super Six.
3. Each week, list words about the topic from the texts you read in that week's column.
4. At the end of each week, choose and circle six words on your weekly list that you think are most important to the topic.
5. Write a sentence for each of those six words. Make sure your sentences show the meanings of the words.
6. At the end of the module, you will have eighteen words and sentences.
7. Now, choose six words from those eighteen words you think are most important to the topic. Write them in the Super Six column.
8. Use your Super Six words to write a summary of what you have learned about the module topic.

Grade 3 Printable
© Houghton Mifflin Harcourt Publishing Company. All rights reserved.

Printable: Super Six Words

DIGITAL STATION

Listener's Choice

- Have students listen to one of this week's selections, *Two Bear Cubs*, or a Leveled Reader of their choice.
- Tell them to add the title to their Printable: **Listening Log**, as well as listing the listening skills they used, a summary of the selection, and questions they have about the selection or book.

Keyboarding

- Have students practice keyboarding using Printable: **Keyboarding 4.3**.

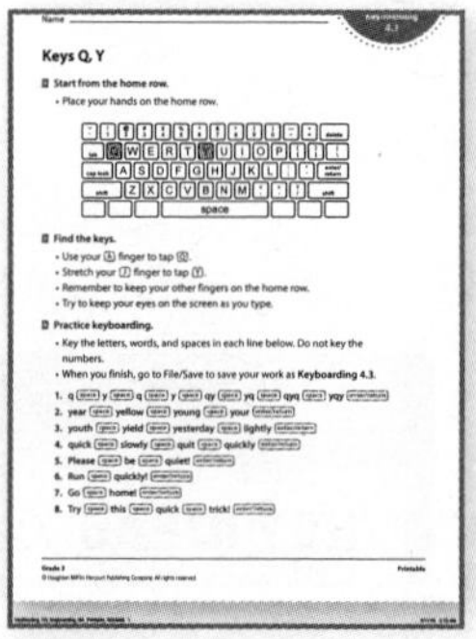

Printable: Keyboarding 4.3

WRITING CENTER

Write a Character Study *(Use in Lessons 14 and 15)*

- Have students use Printable: **Peer Conferencing Routine** to discuss their writing.
- Tell peers to use the tips on *my*Book page 359 as they review the work of others and offer feedback.

Writing Workshop

- Have students work on a piece of writing.
- Depending on where students are in their writing, they may use the time to prewrite, draft, revise, edit, or publish.
- Students may choose from among tasks such as these:
  - » Have peers proofread each other's writing for proper grammar, usage, and mechanics.
  - » Have peers practice presenting their writing to each other.

PROJECT CENTER

Project Checkpoint: Practice and Present

- Have students work in groups, using Printable: **Project 4.3** to guide them as they conclude the project. Groups should complete the following over the course of the week:
  - ☑ Practice their plays.
  - ☑ Deliver their plays, and demonstrate good listening skills when not presenting.
  - ☑ Discuss what they learned from the presentations.
  - ☑ Reflect with their group and independently on what went well during the experience and what could be improved.

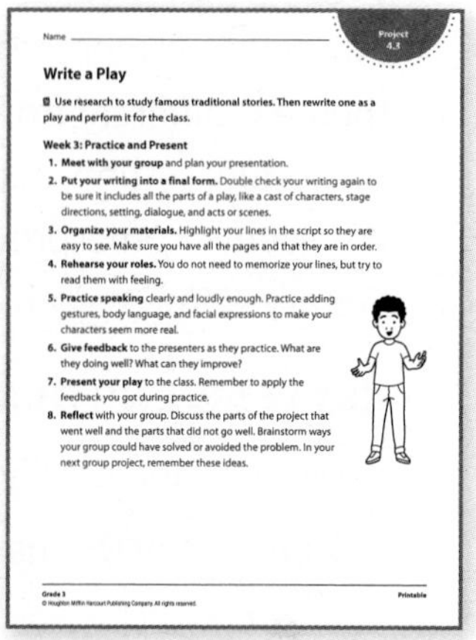

Printable: Project 4.3

Reading Remake

(Use in Lessons 12–15.)

- Have students complete the Make a Book Trailer activity on Printable: **Reading Remake 8**.
- Ask partners to explain to one another how their book trailer shows their understanding of the selection.

Printable: Reading Remake 8

Preview Lesson Texts

Build understanding of this week's texts so that you can best support students in making connections, understanding key ideas, and becoming lifelong readers.

Two Bear Cubs retold by Robert D. San Souci

GENRE Drama

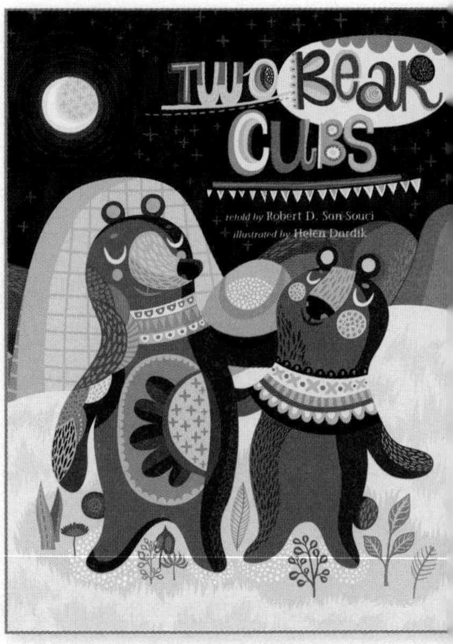

WHY THIS TEXT?

Students will identify the theme of this folktale-inspired drama and distinguish how a theme is different from a topic. As they read, they will be exposed to elements of drama (dialogue, setting, acts/scenes) and will monitor how the events in one scene build on the events from a previous scene. The selection will also provide examples of how literary elements can enhance this type of "performance" literature.

KEY LEARNING OBJECTIVES

- Monitor and Clarify
- Elements of Drama
- Literary Elements
- Theme

TEXT COMPLEXITY

OVERALL RATING Slightly Complex

This selection is clearly fantastical with a simple, linear chronology.

MAKE CONNECTIONS

BUILD KNOWLEDGE AND LANGUAGE

- **Language Arts Connection:** Drama

FOUNDATIONAL SKILLS

- **Decoding: Vowel *au, aw, al, o*:** *across, crawls, always, also, hawk*

WRITING WORKSHOP

- **Narrative Writing:** Story
- **Writing Quotations**
- **More Plural Nouns**

TEXT X-RAY

KEY IDEAS

Key Idea *p. 345*
A mother bear warns her cubs not to go "downriver" as strange things happen there.

Key Idea *p. 346*
The older cub convinces his reluctant sibling to go downriver with him. They nap on a stone that grows into a mountain.

Key Idea *p. 350*
Mother Bear and her animal friends attempt to rescue the cubs, but cannot ascend the slope.

Key Idea *p. 356*
A tiny measuring worm saves the cubs. Sometimes the small can be braver and more powerful than those who are bigger.

LANGUAGE

Metaphor
"the stone was the seed of a mountain" *p. 347* Ask students if they think a stone can grow like a plant. Remind them that seeds grow into plants, not stones. Explain that the author knows this as well, however his use of this metaphor adds to the fantastical aspects of the story.

Idiom
found his courage *p. 352*
Reinforce with students that courage is not an object that you can find/locate in the physical world. This idiomatic expression means that when someone is scared they can sometimes find bravery within themselves to help them face a frightening or difficult situation.

Introduce Critical Vocabulary

Step 1 Introduce the Words

LEARNING OBJECTIVES

- Identify real-life connections between words and their use.
- Use newly acquired vocabulary expressively.
- **Language** Answer questions and discuss meanings to develop vocabulary.

MATERIALS Online Ed

Display and Engage *Critical Vocabulary 4.11a, 4.11b*

Vocabulary Cards *4.20–4.25*

CRITICAL VOCABULARY

- **greedily (p. 346)**
- **hesitation (p. 346)**
- **burden (p. 349)**
- **unnoticed (p. 351)**
- **drowsy (p. 352)**
- **reassuring (p. 355)**

Project Display and Engage: **Critical Vocabulary 4.11a** and **4.11b**. Then use the **VOCABULARY** routine to introduce the Critical Vocabulary from *Two Bear Cubs*. You may wish to display the corresponding Vocabulary Card for each word as you discuss it.

1. Read aloud each word and have students repeat it.
2. Read aloud and discuss each word's student-friendly explanation.
3. Point out the example for the word. Have students suggest other examples.

Online Ed

DISPLAY AND ENGAGE:
Critical Vocabulary 4.11a and 4.11b

Critical Vocabulary 4.11A

Critical Vocabulary

1. **greedily** When you do something **greedily**, you take more than you need. *My cat greedily ate both her food and our dog's food!*
2. **hesitation** **Hesitation** is a pause that shows you are unsure about doing something. *Rostam showed some hesitation before he agreed to go skydiving.*
3. **burden** A **burden** is something that is heavy to carry. *This backpack has become a burden because I stuffed too many books in it.*
4. **unnoticed** If something is **unnoticed**, it is not seen by anyone. *The owl remained unnoticed because it was the same color as the tree trunk.*
5. **drowsy** A **drowsy** person is sleepy and not able to think clearly. *Emmy didn't get enough sleep, and now she is too drowsy to do her homework.*

TEACHER TIP

Encourage students to replace common words and phrases, such as *sleepy* and *cheering up*, with new vocabulary such as *drowsy* and *encouraging*.

ENGLISH LEARNER SUPPORT: Build Vocabulary

SUBSTANTIAL

Ask partners to act out being drowsy and carrying a burden.

MODERATE

Have students use this sentence frame to describe being drowsy. *When I am drowsy, I feel ______ and find it hard to ______.*

LIGHT

Ask pairs to share sentences describing a time when they were very drowsy but had to do something anyway.

Step 2 Guided Practice

Guide students to interact with the words by discussing questions such as these:

- *If you take something* ***greedily****, do you want a little or a lot of it? Explain.*
- *If you invite someone to a party and she reacts with* ***hesitation****, is she excited about going? Explain.*
- *When you have a* ***burden****, is it more useful to be smart or to be strong? Explain.*
- *If you want to be* ***unnoticed*** *at night, should you wear dark clothes or should you carry a bright flashlight? Explain.*
- *Does it help to be* ***drowsy*** *if you want to do a good job at something? Why or why not?*
- *When you are* ***reassuring*** *someone, are you helping them or asking for help? Explain.*

Ask students when they are most likely to act greedily or with hesitation, and when they might like to go unnoticed. Have students point out items in the room that would be the biggest burden to carry. Have students share the words they might use when reassuring someone. Ask them to name the time of day when they are most often drowsy.

Step 3 Apply

- Have students work independently to complete steps 3 and 4 on Vocabulary Cards 4.20–4.25.
- Have students use the **TURN AND TALK** routine to discuss with a partner the prompt on each Vocabulary Card.

greedily

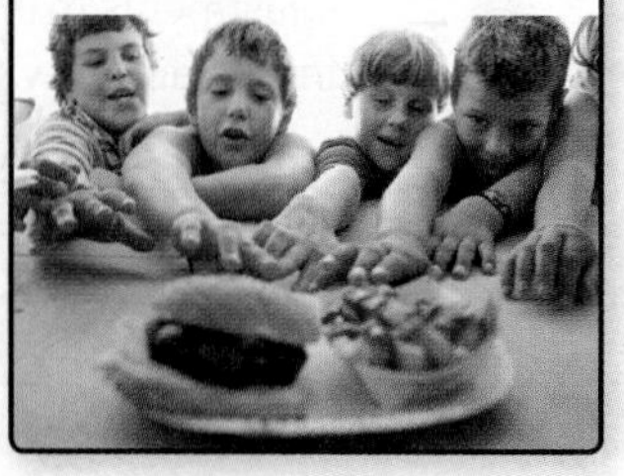

Vocabulary Cards

LEARNING MINDSET

Self-Reflection

Review Remind students that that it takes time and effort when using new skills. *Don't be afraid to try out new words in the classroom, and don't give up if you make a mistake! Every time you practice, you do better and better. Soon you'll be using new words confidently wherever you go!*

Monitor and Clarify

Step 1 Connect and Teach

LEARNING OBJECTIVES

- Monitor comprehension and make adjustments to improve understanding when needed.
- **Language** Articulate strategies for clarifying comprehension.

MATERIALS | Online Ed

Anchor Chart 2 *Monitor and Clarify*

Printable *Anchor Chart 2: Monitor and Clarify*

Teaching Pal *Book 1, pp. 342–359*

***my*Book** *Book 1, Two Bear Cubs, pp. 342–359*

Display and Engage *Build Background 4.11*

INSTRUCTIONAL VOCABULARY

- **clarify** to try to make clear what you don't understand in your reading
- **monitor** to check for understanding while reading

SPANISH COGNATES

- **clarify** *clarificar*
- **monitor** *monitor*

- Tell students that they are going to read a drama called *Two Bear Cubs* by Robert D. San Souci.
- Project or display Anchor Chart 2: Monitor and Clarify. Draw attention to the question at the top.
- Explain that good readers **monitor**, or pay close attention to, their understanding of a text. Point out that if they don't understand something, they stop to **clarify**, or make clear, whatever they didn't understand.
- Review and discuss each of the strategies a reader can use when a particular word is confusing or unfamiliar.
- Use a similar process to discuss how to address sections of text that are unclear after the first read.
- Tell students that they will practice monitoring and clarifying their understanding when they read *Two Bear Cubs.*

ANCHOR CHART 2: Monitor and Clarify | Online Ed

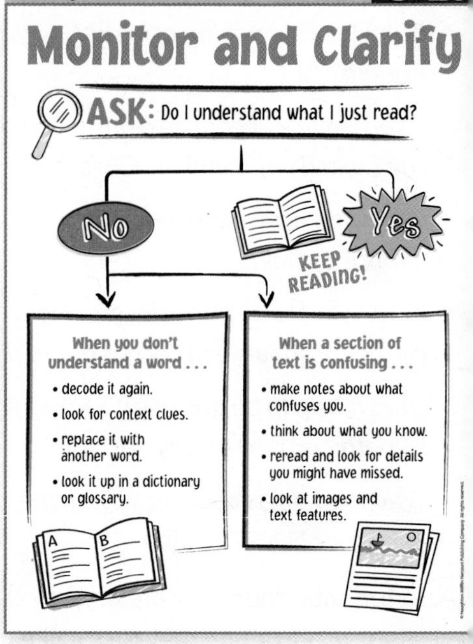

Notice & Note

Contrasts and Contradictions

- The Teaching Pal prompts in this lesson feature the **Notice & Note Signpost: Contrasts and Contradictions**
- As needed, refer to p. T208 to review the signpost with students.

ASSESSMENT OPTION

Assign the Selection Quiz to check comprehension of *Two Bear Cubs.*

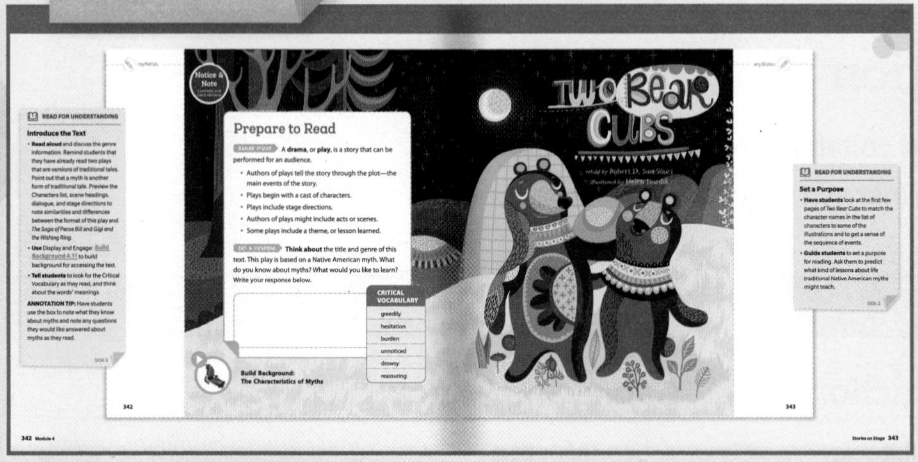

Online

ANNOTATE IT!

Ed

Students may use the annotation tools in their eBook.

Step 2 Apply to Text

In your Teaching Pal, pages 342–357, use the blue **READ FOR UNDERSTANDING** prompts and the red **Notice & Note** prompts to read *Two Bear Cubs* as students follow along and annotate their *my*Book.

- **Genre Study** Guide students through the genre information on page 342. Point out that this drama is an adaptation of myth/traditional tale.
- **Set a Purpose** Read the Set a Purpose section on page 342. Prompt students to set their own purpose for reading *Two Bear Cubs.*
- **Build Background** Project Display and Engage 4.11: Build Background and read the information aloud with students. Ask students what a myth called *Two Bear Cubs* might explain.
- **Read and Comprehend** Use the **READ FOR UNDERSTANDING** routine as you guide students to read the selection. Pause occasionally, using the prompts in your Teaching Pal to gauge students' understanding and to have them monitor and clarify their understanding. As students monitor and clarify their understanding of the text, have them refer back to the Anchor Chart to review the strategies they can use.
- Check students' understanding by asking them to retell the myth in their own words.

Step 3 Engage and Respond

INDEPENDENT PRACTICE: Speaking & Listening

- After reading, use the **COLLABORATIVE DISCUSSION** routine with the Collaborative Discussion questions on Teaching Pal and *my*Book page 357. Have students annotate their *my*Book with details from the text and visuals as evidence to explain their responses.
- Ask volunteers to read aloud the Speaking and Listening Tips. Remind students that as they listen, they should think about a polite way to connect their ideas to the speaker's ideas, even if they disagree.
- You may want to have students conduct their discussions during daily small-group time.

ENGLISH LEARNER SUPPORT: Support Comprehension

SUBSTANTIAL

Show me the word you don't know. Tell me what you can do to understand the word.

MODERATE

What can you do when you don't know a word? What strategy will you use first?

LIGHT

If I don't understand ______, I can try to______.

LINK TO SMALL-GROUP INSTRUCTION

REINFORCE MONITOR AND CLARIFY Review and extend the skill as needed during small-group time to support students' need for differentiation. *See the lesson on p. T339.*

Options for Differentiation

As the class engages in independent and collaborative work, meet with Guided Reading Groups or differentiate instruction based on student need.

GUIDED READING GROUPS

Match Students to Books + Instruction

- Choose just-right books based on level, skill, topic, or genre.

L M N O P Q

Leveled Readers

- Deliver instruction with each book's **Take and Teach Lesson**, choosing appropriate sessions based on need.

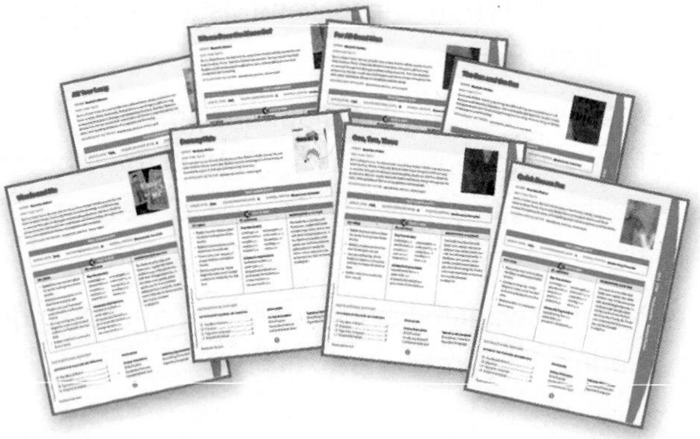

- Check comprehension, reinforce instruction, and extend learning with suggested supporting activities.

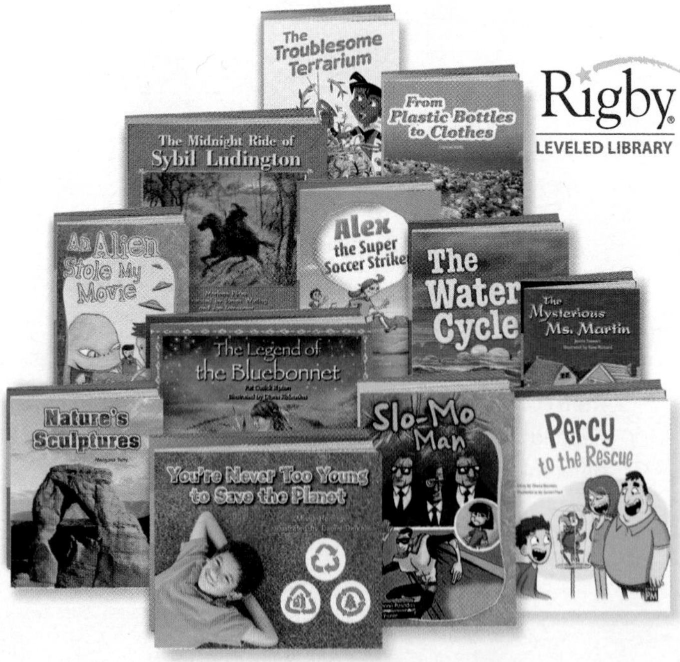

ENGLISH LEARNER SUPPORT

Cause and Effect

- Use **Tabletop Minilessons: English Language Development 12.1 (Listening)** to introduce and practice the language skill.

Tabletop Minilessons: English Language Development

- Then use the following text-based prompts with *Two Bear Cubs* to guide application of the language skill. Begin with the prompt at the student's identified language proficiency level. As students progress, use lighter supports to encourage increased language proficiency.

SUBSTANTIAL
Read aloud the first page of Scene 1. Tell students to raise their hand when they hear the reason why Mother Grizzly doesn't want her bear cubs to scare away the fish. Have them reply using the sentence frame: *If the bear cubs scare away the fish, then _____.*

MODERATE
Read aloud the first page of Scene 1. Ask: *Why doesn't Mother Grizzly want her cubs to scare away the fish? Why doesn't she want her cubs to go downriver?* Have them answer using sentence frames: *Mother Grizzly doesn't want her cubs to _____ because _____.*

LIGHT
After students listen to the first page of Scene 1, ask: *What does Mother Grizzly say the effect of the cubs splashing in the water will be? Why doesn't she want her cubs to go downriver?*

REINFORCE MONITOR AND CLARIFY

Demonstrate

- Use **Tabletop Minilessons: Reading Card 2** to remind students that when they **monitor** while they read, they pay close attention to their understanding. When they **clarify**, they pause as they read to check their understanding, and reread or look for context clues if there is something they don't understand.
- Model filling out Printable: Reading Graphic Organizer 2 to monitor and clarify in *Two Bear Cubs*.

Apply to Independent Reading

- Now have students use monitor and clarify in an appropriate book or article they are reading independently. Customize these prompts to the texts students choose.
  - » *Where in the text did you need to pause to check your understanding?*
  - » *What did you do to clarify your understanding of the text?*
  - » *How did monitoring and clarifying your reading help you to better understand what you read?*
- Have students complete Printable: Reading Graphic Organizer 2 for their independent reading book.

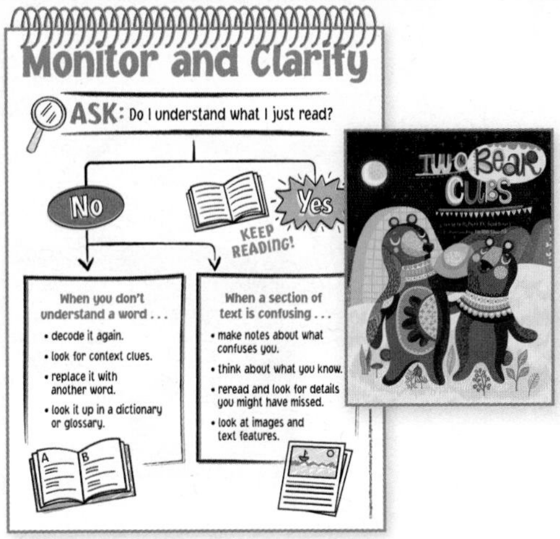

Tabletop Minilessons: Reading

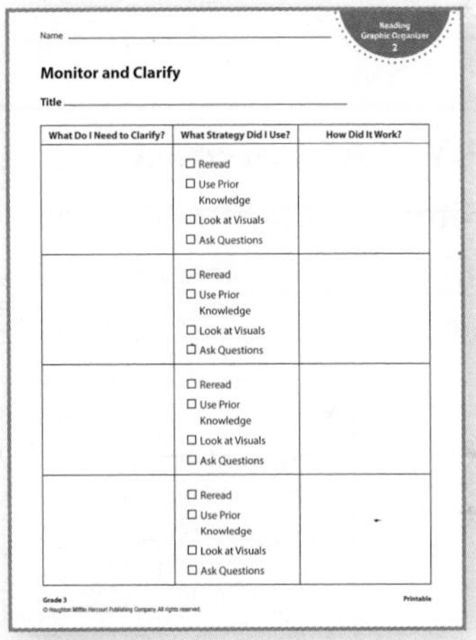

Printable: Reading Graphic Organizer 2

SCAFFOLD AND EXTEND

ALMOST THERE → READY FOR MORE

- Identify a section of text that is challenging for students and guide them to monitor and clarify.
- Prompt students to point out a section of text where they had to pause in their reading. Have them tell what they did to clarify it.
- Have students explain what kinds of monitoring and clarifying best helped them when they were reading.

EL ENGLISH LEARNER SUPPORT

SUBSTANTIAL

Say: *Do you understand this part of the text? Do you need to clarify it? Let's try _____ to clarify our understanding.*

MODERATE

Have students complete sentence frames such as: *I needed to pause to check my understanding when _____. I used _____ to clarify my understanding of the text.*

LIGHT

Ask: *Where in the text did you need to pause to check your understanding. What did you do to clarify your understanding?*

Options for Independent and Collaborative Work

While you meet with small groups, have other students engage in literacy activities that reinforce the lesson's learning objectives. Choose from these options.

Independent Reading

Student Choice Library

Rigby
LEVELED LIBRARY

APPLY READING SKILL

Monitor and Clarify Students complete Printable: Reading Graphic Organizer 2 for an independent reading book.

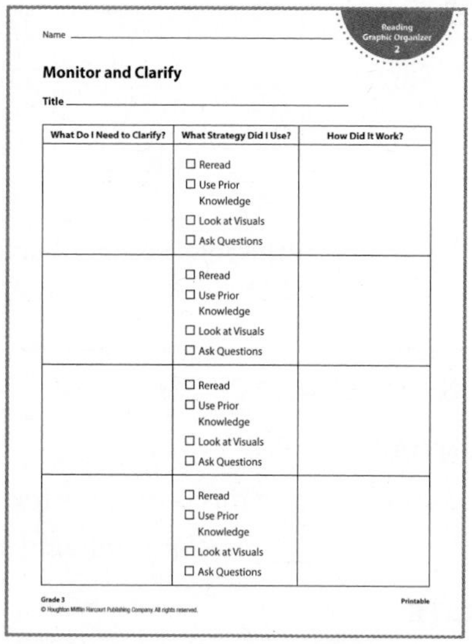
Reading Graphic Organizer 2

Name

Monitor and Clarify

Title

What Do I Need to Clarify?	What Strategy Did I Use?	How Did It Work?
	☐ Reread ☐ Use Prior Knowledge ☐ Look at Visuals ☐ Ask Questions	
	☐ Reread ☐ Use Prior Knowledge ☐ Look at Visuals ☐ Ask Questions	
	☐ Reread ☐ Use Prior Knowledge ☐ Look at Visuals ☐ Ask Questions	
	☐ Reread ☐ Use Prior Knowledge ☐ Look at Visuals ☐ Ask Questions	

Grade 3 Printable
© Houghton Mifflin Harcourt Publishing Company. All rights reserved.

Printable: Reading Graphic Organizer 2

APPLY LANGUAGE SKILL

Cause and Effect Students complete Printable: Language Graphic Organizer 3 for an independent reading book.

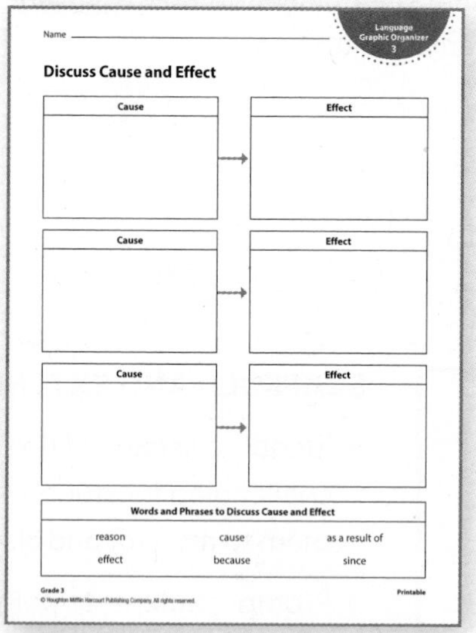
Language Graphic Organizer 3

Name

Discuss Cause and Effect

Cause		Effect
	→	

Cause		Effect
	→	

Cause		Effect
	→	

Words and Phrases to Discuss Cause and Effect

reason	cause	as a result of
effect	because	since

Grade 3 Printable
© Houghton Mifflin Harcourt Publishing Company. All rights reserved.

Printable: Language Graphic Organizer 3

Notice & Note

Contrasts and Contradictions

When students encounter this signpost in their independent historical fiction reading, encourage them to ask and answer the Anchor Question: *Why would the character feel/act this way?*

Literacy Centers

See pp. T330–T331.

- READING CENTER
- VOCABULARY CENTER
- DIGITAL STATION
- WRITING CENTER
- PROJECT CENTER

Speaking and Listening

Partners discuss the Collaborative Discussion questions. *See Engage and Respond, p. T337.*

Additional Skills Practice

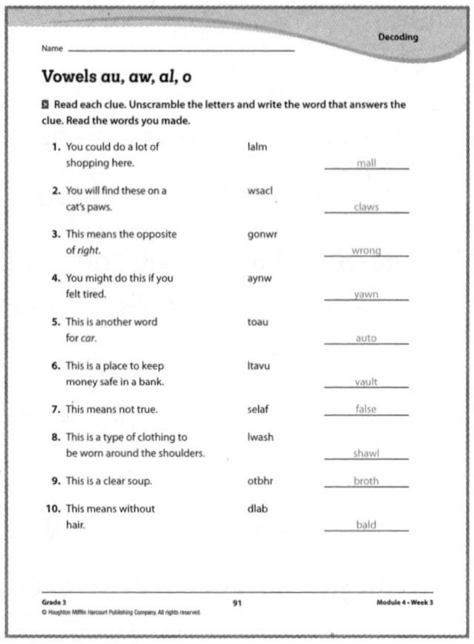
Decoding

Name ______

Vowels *au, aw, al, o*

Read each clue. Unscramble the letters and write the word that answers the clue. Read the words you made.

1.	You could do a lot of shopping here.	lalm	mall
2.	You will find these on a cat's paws.	wsacl	claws
3.	This means the opposite of *right*.	gonwr	wrong
4.	You might do this if you felt tired.	aynw	yawn
5.	This is another word for *car*.	toau	auto
6.	This is a place to keep money safe in a bank.	ltavu	vault
7.	This means not true.	selaf	false
8.	This is a type of clothing to be worn around the shoulders.	lwash	shawl
9.	This is a clear soup.	otbhr	broth
10.	This means without hair.	dlab	bald

Grade 3 91 Module 4 • Week 3
© Houghton Mifflin Harcourt Publishing Company. All rights reserved.

Know It, Show It, p. 91

Wrap-Up

Share Time

At the end of the Reading Workshop, have students reflect on their learning by sharing how they applied **monitor and clarify** or another area of focus during independent work time. Choose from these options:

- Use the **SOLO CHAIR** routine. Select a reader each day to come to the front of the class and tell what he or she learned from the text by using a skill or strategy.
- **THINK-PAIR-SHARE** Students share their thinking with a partner. Select a few pairs each day to share with the whole class.
- **RETURN TO ANCHOR CHART** Have students add sticky notes about their independent reading to the Monitor and Clarify Anchor Chart. Call on a few students to explain what they added and why.

Online Ed

ANCHOR CHART 2: Monitor and Clarify

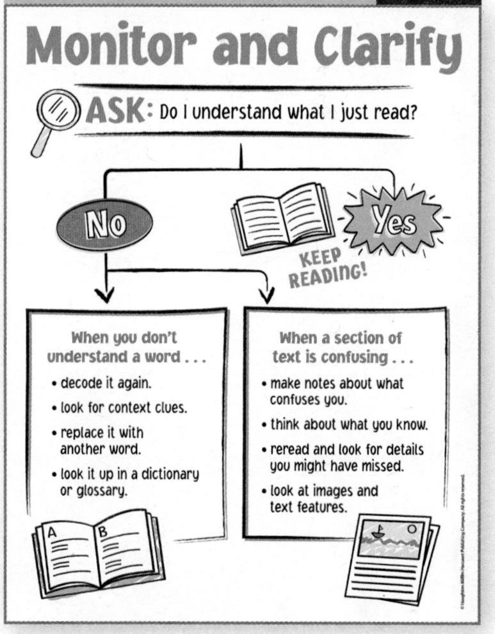

Vowels *au, aw, al, o*

Step 1 Introduce the Skill

LEARNING OBJECTIVES

- Decode and read words with vowels *au, aw, al,* and *o*.
- Spell and write words with vowels *au, aw, al,* and *o*.
- **Language** Read words with vowels *au, aw, al,* and *o* and understand their meanings.

MATERIALS **Online Ed**

Display and Engage *Decoding 4.11*
Know It, Show It *p. 91*

Vowels *au* and *aw* Display and read aloud the words *cause* and *saw*, emphasizing the vowel sound /aw/ in each word.

- Underline *au* in *cause* and *aw* in *paw*. Explain that *au* and *aw* are vowel teams. In these words, they stand for the /aw/ sound. Tell students that *w* is sometimes part of a vowel team.
- Display the words *pause, straw,* and *yawn*. Underline *au* or *aw* in each word. Note that the letters *au* and *aw* stand for the /aw/ sound in all of these words.
- Guide students to read the words aloud.

Vowels *al* and *o* Display and read aloud the words *walk* and *lost*, emphasizing the vowel sound /aw/ in each word.

- Underline *al* in *walk* and *o* in *lost*. Note that in these words, *al* and *o* stand for the /aw/ sound. Explain that in *walk,* the letter *l* is silent.
- Display the words *tall, long,* and *moss*. Underline *al* or *o* in each word. Note that the letters *al* and *o* stand for the /aw/ sound in all of these words.
- Guide students to read the words aloud.

au	aw	al	o
sauce	lawn	ball	song
taught	shawl	fall	moth
fault	gnaw	chalk	boss

- Remind students that they have learned multiple ways to spell the /aw/ sound. Point out the spelling patterns in the top row.
- Then read aloud the example words in each column, emphasizing the vowel sound in each while underlining the letters that stand for the sound.

ENGLISH LEARNER SUPPORT: Support Word Meaning

SUBSTANTIAL
Ensure that students understand the meaning of each Blend and Read word by sharing pictures or gestures.

MODERATE
Guide students to understand the meanings of the Blend and Read words that are homophones: *pause/paws, haul/hall.*

LIGHT
Challenge partners to use each of the Blend and Read homophones (*pause/paws, haul/hall*) in a sentence to demonstrate their understanding of its meaning.

Step 2 Guided Practice

- Project Display and Engage: **Decoding 4.11**.
- Have students read the Blend and Read lines aloud. Provide feedback as needed.
- At the end of each line, prompt a conversation about the words: *How are the vowel sounds the same? How are the spellings the same or different?*
- Have partners reread the Blend and Read lines and quiz each other on the spellings for the /aw/ sound.

Online Ed

DISPLAY AND ENGAGE: Decoding 4.11

Decoding 4.11

Blend and Read

Vowels *au, aw, al, o*

The vowels *au, aw, al,* and *o* stand for the /aw/ sound. The letter *W* is sometimes part of a vowel team. The *l* in *al* is silent.

1	pause (au)	hawk (aw)	soft (o)	paws (aw)	walk (al)
2	ball (al)	lost (o)	draw (aw)	toss (o)	haul (au)
3	gauze (au)	call (al)	off (o)	thaw (aw)	fault (au)
4	moth (o)	claw (aw)	hall (al)	jaw (aw)	taught (au)
5	caught (au)	cost (o)	halt (al)	fawn (aw)	launch (au)

6 All (al) will applaud (au) for the singer if she sings the song (o) without a flaw (aw).

Grade 3 | Foundational Skills — Module 4 • Week 3

Step 3 Apply

INDEPENDENT PRACTICE

- Have students work in small groups or with partners to complete Know It, Show It page 91.
- Encourage students to share with each other the strategies they use to decode words with vowels *au, aw, al,* and *o*.

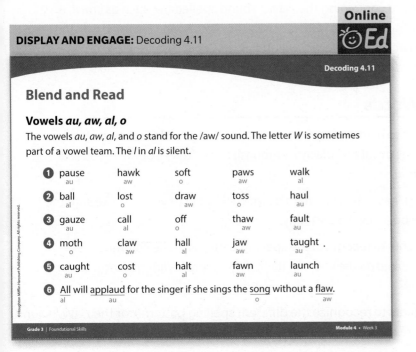

CORRECT & REDIRECT

If students have trouble decoding words with vowels *au, aw, al,* and *o*, use the model below.

- **Correct** the error. *The letters* au, aw, al, *and* o *can be pronounced /aw/.*
- **Model** how to decode the word *gauze*. */gōōz/. That does not sound right. Since I know the letters* au *can stand for /aw/, I'll try that sound: /gôz/,* gauze. *That sounds right.*
- **Guide** students to decode the words *thaw* and *golf*.
- **Check** students' understanding by displaying the word *halt*. *What spelling pattern helps you decode this word?*
- **Reinforce** by repeating the process with the word *taught*.

Spelling the /aw/ Sound

LEARNING OBJECTIVES

- Learn spelling patterns for the vowels *au, aw, al,* and *o*.
- **Language** Spell words with the vowels *au, aw, al,* and *o* and understand their meanings.

MATERIALS | **Online** Ed

Anchor Chart 37 *Cursive Handwriting*

Printables *Anchor Chart 37: Cursive Handwriting, Dictation Sentences 4.11, Spelling Word Cards 4.11, Proofreading 4.11*

Optional *Use Printable: Dictation Sentences 4.11 to administer a pretest.*

SPELLING WORDS

BASIC

1. **talk**
2. **cross**
3. **awful**
4. **law**
5. **cloth**
6. **cost**
7. **crawl**
8. **chalk**
9. **also**
10. **raw**
11. **salt**
12. **wall**
13. **lawn**
14. **always**

REVIEW

15. **thousand**
16. **powder**
17. **blouse**
18. **frown**

CHALLENGE

19. **squawk**
20. **haunt**
21. **stalk**
22. **sauce**

Introduce the Spelling Words

- Before working with the basic and challenge words, you might want to revisit the review words. These also appear in Printable: Dictation Sentences 4.11. Display one of the Spelling Anchor Chart Printables, as appropriate.
- Cut out and display the spelling word cards from Printable: Spelling Word Cards 4.11. Read each word aloud and discuss its meaning as needed.
- Tell students that you are going to work together to sort the words into categories based on the spelling of the /aw/ sound. Read aloud the words *talk, cross,* and *law,* and display those cards as column headings.
- Hold up a word containing the /aw/ sound spelled *aw,* such as *crawl*, and model your thinking: *The word is* crawl. *The /aw/ sound is spelled* aw. *And I see the column head* law, *which has the same /aw/ sound and spelling pattern. So I'll place the word in that column.*

Sort the Words

- Ask students to help you sort the remaining word cards. For multisyllabic words such as *awful* and *always*, emphasize the /aw/ sound as you read the word aloud.
- After sorting, have students read down each list with you to make sure the words have been sorted correctly.
- Guide students to recognize the spelling patterns in the columns. Ask: *What vowel sound do the words in this column share? What spelling pattern do they share?*
- Guide students to recognize the different spelling patterns for the /aw/ sound. Ask: *What are the different spelling patterns for the /aw/ sound?* (*au, aw, al, o*)

Handwriting/Keyboarding

- Display and review Anchor Chart 37: Cursive Handwriting.
- Have students practice handwriting or keyboarding by writing or typing the spelling words. As needed, use the handwriting models from the resources section of this Teacher's Guide.

ENGLISH LEARNER SUPPORT: Support Word Meaning

ALL LEVELS Make sure students understand the meaning of the spelling words and dictation sentences. If necessary, use visuals or gestures as support. For Spanish-speaking students, point out the Spanish cognates *costo* for *cost* and *sal* for *salt*. After you've reinforced word meanings, have students practice reading the spelling words aloud.

LINK TO SMALL-GROUP INSTRUCTION

REINFORCE FOUNDATIONAL SKILLS For spelling practice for the remainder of the week: Display this week's spelling words for reference and have students work with Printable: Proofreading 4.11. Remind students to check the spelling words they use in the writing section to confirm they have spelled the words correctly. Have students use the Spelling Anchor Chart Printables to reinforce spelling knowledge.

Reading Rate

Introduce the Skill

LEARNING OBJECTIVES

- Read orally at an appropriate rate.
- Read aloud grade-level text with fluency and accuracy.
- Apply decoding skills when reading connected text.
- **Language** Comprehend texts using teacher support.

MATERIALS

Online Ed

Printable *Fluency 4.11*
Word Cards *3.41–3.43*

DECODING → FLUENCY CONNECTION

The passage on Printable: Fluency 4.11 includes words that contain this week's decoding element. Use the passage to monitor whether students can accurately and fluently read these grade-level words.

HIGH-FREQUENCY WORDS

- **whether**
- **divided**
- **simple**

- Explain that good readers adjust their reading rate based on what they are reading. When good readers read for fun, their rate is usually faster than when they read for information.
- Distribute Printable: Fluency 4.11 to students, and project it for whole-group discussion. Tell students that you will demonstrate how to read the passage at an appropriate rate.

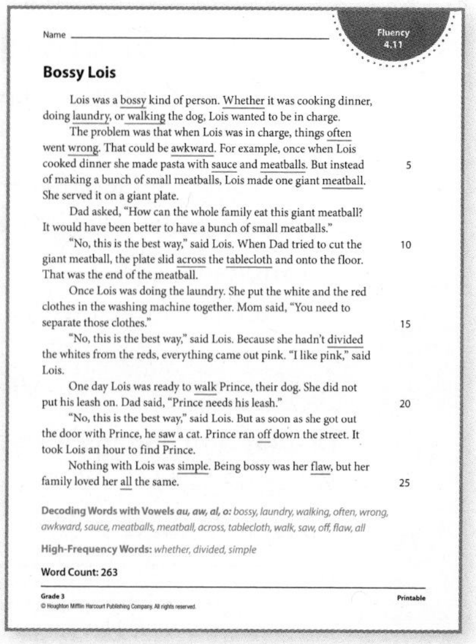

Name ____________

Fluency 4.11

Bossy Lois

Lois was a bossy kind of person. Whether it was cooking dinner, doing laundry, or walking the dog, Lois wanted to be in charge.

The problem was that when Lois was in charge, things often went wrong. That could be awkward. For example, once when Lois cooked dinner she made pasta with sauce and meatballs. But instead of making a bunch of small meatballs, Lois made one giant meatball. She served it on a giant plate.

Dad asked, "How can the whole family eat this giant meatball? It would have been better to have a bunch of small meatballs."

"No, this is the best way," said Lois. When Dad tried to cut the giant meatball, the plate slid across the tablecloth and onto the floor. That was the end of the meatball.

Once Lois was doing the laundry. She put the white and the red clothes in the washing machine together. Mom said, "You need to separate those clothes."

"No, this is the best way," said Lois. Because she hadn't divided the whites from the reds, everything came out pink. "I like pink," said Lois.

One day Lois was ready to walk Prince, their dog. She did not put his leash on. Dad said, "Prince needs his leash."

"No, this is the best way," said Lois. But as soon as she got out the door with Prince, he saw a cat. Prince ran off down the street. It took Lois an hour to find Prince.

Nothing with Lois was simple. Being bossy was her flaw, but her family loved her all the same.

Decoding Words with Vowels *au, aw, al, o*: *bossy, laundry, walking, often, wrong, awkward, sauce, meatballs, meatball, across, tablecloth, walk, saw, off, flaw, all*

High-Frequency Words: *whether, divided, simple*

Word Count: 263

Grade 3 Printable

Printable: Fluency 4.11

- Read aloud the first paragraph slowly, taking long pauses at the commas. Point out that this reading rate is too slow. Explain that because the passage is fiction, you can speed up your rate in order to enjoy the story. Model reading at an appropriate rate. Discuss with students that reading at an appropriate rate allows readers to gain better understanding and more enjoyment from the reading experience. After you read the entire passage, point out how you used the vowel spellings *au, aw, al,* and *o* to decode the words *laundry, awkward, meatballs,* and *bossy*.
- After you finish reading the passage, have students read it aloud with you, using the **CHORAL READING** routine.

Apply

- Have students work in pairs or small groups using the **PARTNER READING** routine to read aloud the passage.
- Monitor students for reading rate. Note especially how students handle the more challenging words, such as *awkward, separate,* and *flaw,* and provide support, as needed.

HIGH-FREQUENCY WORDS

Point out the high-frequency words in the passage on Printable: Fluency 4.11. Remind students that high-frequency words appear often in texts they read. Students can learn to recognize them, rather than decode them, so that they can read more fluently.

Print and distribute Printables: Word Cards 3.41–3.43, which feature this week's high-frequency words, and have students work independently or in pairs to read and complete the activities for each word. For struggling readers, walk through the notes for one or two words before they continue working with a partner.

ENGLISH LEARNER SUPPORT: Support Comprehension

ALL LEVELS As you model reading fluently, have students raise their hand when they hear a word they do not recognize. Work with students to decode the word and practice saying it aloud. Discuss the word's meaning, using gestures or pictures for support if needed. Then have students read the entire sentence chorally. Provide corrective feedback, as needed.

Review Critical Vocabulary

Step 1 Reinforce Vocabulary

- Project Display and Engage: Critical Vocabulary 4.11 to review and discuss the Critical Vocabulary, student-friendly explanations, and examples of the words. Have students take turns using the words in sentences.

Step 2 Guided Practice

- Have student partners take turns answering questions about the Critical Vocabulary words. Provide questions such as the following for students to ask one another, and invite them to create their own questions as well. As needed, direct students to Display and Engage 4.11 for the word meanings.

1. If someone behaves greedily at dinner, what might they do?
2. What might make you react with hesitation?
3. When your backpack feels like a burden, what can you do?
4. Is it easy for a giraffe to be unnoticed? Why?
5. At what time of day do you start to feel drowsy?
6. If someone is worried, how can you be reassuring?

Step 3 Apply

INDEPENDENT PRACTICE

- Have students work in small groups or independently. Tell them to complete Know It, Show It page 92. For the last item on the page, tell students to include clues to each word's meaning in their sentences. Have groups share their sentences. Ask listeners to identify the context clue in each sentence.
- You may wish to have students complete the Know It, Show It page during small-group time.

LEARNING OBJECTIVES

- Review and extend understanding of word meanings.
- Use context to determine the meanings of unfamiliar words.
- **Language** Use newly acquired vocabulary expressively.

MATERIALS

Online Ed

Display and Engage *Critical Vocabulary 4.11*

Know It, Show It *p. 92*

CRITICAL VOCABULARY

- **greedily**
- **hesitation**
- **burden**
- **unnoticed**
- **drowsy**
- **reassuring**

ENGLISH LEARNER SUPPORT: Support Discussion

Use tiered supports as needed to help students as they answer questions about the Critical Vocabulary.

SUBSTANTIAL

Show me what you might do if you were acting greedily.

MODERATE

If someone is behaving greedily, they are _____.

LIGHT

Have students give examples of people acting greedily.

Multiple-Meaning Words

LEARNING OBJECTIVES

- Use context to determine the relevant meanings of multiple-meaning words and use the words in context sentences.
- Use print and digital reference materials to clarify meanings.
- **Language** Identify and use multiple-meaning words using strategic learning techniques.

MATERIALS Online Ed

Display and Engage *Vocabulary Strategy 4.12a, 4.12b, 4.12c*

INSTRUCTIONAL VOCABULARY

- **multiple-meaning words** words that are spelled the same but have more than one meaning

Step 1 Review the Strategy

Project Display and Engage: Vocabulary Strategy 4.12a, 4.12b, and 4.12c. Read aloud the two paragraphs.

Online

DISPLAY AND ENGAGE: Vocabulary Strategy 4.12a, 4.12b, and 4.12c

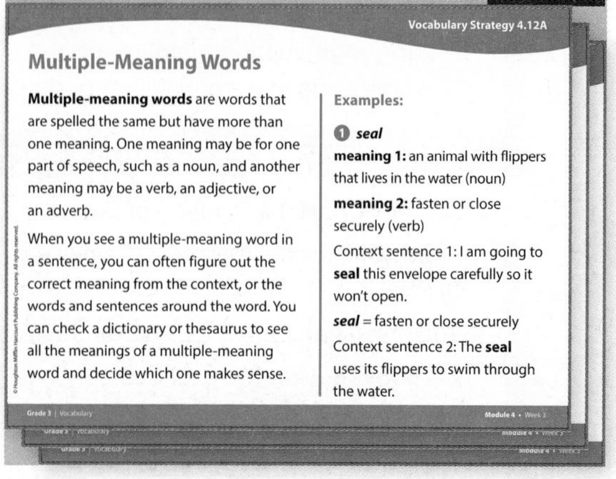
Vocabulary Strategy 4.12A

Multiple-Meaning Words

Multiple-meaning words are words that are spelled the same but have more than one meaning. One meaning may be for one part of speech, such as a noun, and another meaning may be a verb, an adjective, or an adverb.

When you see a multiple-meaning word in a sentence, you can often figure out the correct meaning from the context, or the words and sentences around the word. You can check a dictionary or thesaurus to see all the meanings of a multiple-meaning word and decide which one makes sense.

Examples:

1 ***seal***

meaning 1: an animal with flippers that lives in the water (noun)

meaning 2: fasten or close securely (verb)

Context sentence 1: I am going to **seal** this envelope carefully so it won't open.

seal = fasten or close securely

Context sentence 2: The **seal** uses its flippers to swim through the water.

Grade 3 | Vocabulary — Module 4 • Week 3

- Review that multiple-meaning words are words that are spelled the same but have different meanings, and that context clues can help identify meaning.
- Use the first example to model using context clues to find the meaning of *seal* in a sentence and writing a context sentence using a second meaning. Seal *can be a noun naming an animal with flippers that lives in the water, or it can be a verb that means "to fasten or close securely." I can tell* seal *is used as a verb in the context sentence. The sentence also says, "so it won't open." That clue tells me* seal *means "to fasten or close securely." If I want to write a context sentence using* seal *to mean "an animal", I'll use the clue words* swim *and* flippers.

Step 2 Guided Practice

- Have students read the definitions for the multiple-meaning word *stick*. Ask them to identify the word's meaning as used in the context sentence and then write a context sentence using the second meaning.
- Ask students to identify the context clues and how they reveal the word meaning.

Step 3 Apply the Strategy

INDEPENDENT PRACTICE

- Have students work independently or in pairs to find these multiple-meaning words in *Two Bear Cubs*: *stage, play, rock, saw*. Have them use context to determine and write the word's meaning. They can use a reference source as needed.
- Next, tell students to write a second meaning for each word, again using a reference source as needed. Then have them write a context sentence for this meaning.
- Have students exchange sentences with a partner, identify the meaning of each multiple-meaning word, and identify the context clues.

ENGLISH LEARNER SUPPORT: Understand and Use Multiple-Meaning Words

SUBSTANTIAL
Invite students to use gestures or oral sentences to show different meanings of *play*. Offer guidance as needed.

MODERATE
Supply sentence frames to help students write context sentences: *A word related to play is _____. I can use that as a context clue.*

LIGHT
Ask students to explain how they decided which context clues to use to show the correct meaning of *play* in their sentence.

Elements of Drama

Step 1 Connect and Teach

LEARNING OBJECTIVES

- Identify and discuss elements of drama.
- **Language** Identify elements of drama using terms *prologue* and *scene.*

MATERIALS

Online Ed

Anchor Chart 14 *Elements of Drama*

Printable *Anchor Chart 14: Elements of Drama*

Teaching Pal *Book 1, pp. 342–359*

myBook *Book 1, Two Bear Cubs, pp. 342–359*

Know It, Show It *p. 94*

INSTRUCTIONAL VOCABULARY

- **act** a chapter in a play that contains more than one scene
- **cast of characters** the characters in a drama or play
- **dialogue** the words that characters say aloud to one another
- **drama** a story acted out by actors
- **scene** actions of a play in one setting
- **script** text of a play including dialogue and stage directions
- **stage direction** information that tells actors where to move, how to look or speak, or information about the set

SPANISH COGNATES

- **act** *acto*
- **scene** *escena*

- Remind students that a **drama,** or play, is a story performed by actors on a stage.
- Project or display the Anchor Chart 14: Elements of Drama.
- Review that dramas have characters, dialogue, and settings, just like stories. However, dramas are written in a **script** form.
- Use the Anchor Chart to review the features of a script: **cast of characters, dialogue,** and **stage directions**. Point out that a script is organized in **acts** and **scenes**.
- Explain that *Two Bear Cubs* has a **prologue,** or introduction. Point out that the events in each scene that follows build on the prologue and earlier scenes.
- Tell students they will identify the elements of a drama to gain a deeper understanding of *Two Bear Cubs.*

Online Ed

ANCHOR CHART 14: Elements of Drama

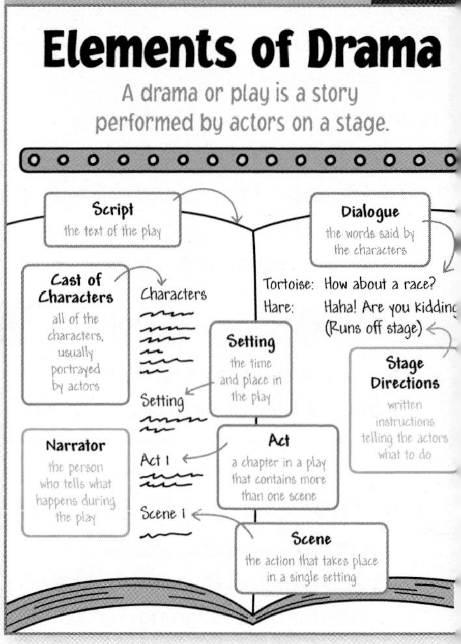
Elements of Drama
A drama or play is a story performed by actors on a stage.
Script
the text of the play
Dialogue
the words said by the characters
Cast of Characters
all of the characters, usually portrayed by actors
Characters
Tortoise: How about a race?
Hare: Haha! Are you
(Runs off stage)
Setting
the time and place in the play
Setting
Stage Directions
written instructions telling the actors what to do
Narrator
the person who tells what happens during the play
Act 1
Act
a chapter in a play that contains more than one scene
Scene 1
Scene
the action that takes place in a single setting

Go to Your
Teaching Pal

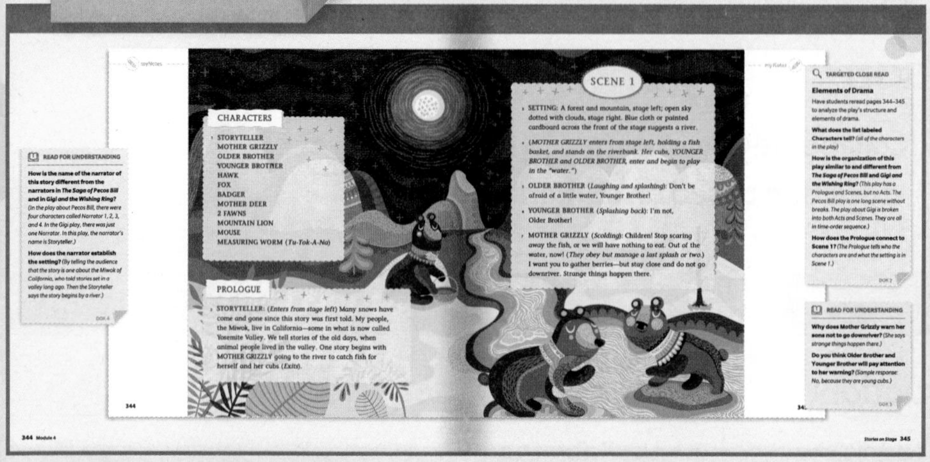

READ FOR UNDERSTANDING

How is the name of the narrator of this story different from the narrators in *The Saga of Pecos Bill* and in *Gigi and the Wishing Ring*? *(In the play about Pecos Bill, there were four characters called Narrator 1, 2, 3, and 4. In the Gigi play, there was just one Narrator. In this play, the narrator's name is Storyteller.)*

How does the narrator establish the setting? *(By telling the audience that the story is one about the Miwok of California, who told stories set in a valley long ago. Then the Storyteller says the story begins by a river.)*

DOK 4

CHARACTERS

STORYTELLER
MOTHER GRIZZLY
OLDER BROTHER
YOUNGER BROTHER
HAWK
FOX
BADGER
MOTHER DEER
2 FAWNS
MOUNTAIN LION
MOUSE
MEASURING WORM (*Tu-Tok-A-Na*)

PROLOGUE

STORYTELLER: (*Enters from stage left*) Many snows have come and gone since this story was first told. My people, the Miwok, live in California—some in what is now called Yosemite Valley. We tell stories of the old days, when animal people lived in the valley. One story begins with MOTHER GRIZZLY going to the river to catch fish for herself and her cubs (*Exits*).

SCENE 1

SETTING: A forest and mountain, stage left; open sky dotted with clouds, stage right. Blue cloth or painted cardboard across the front of the stage suggests a river.

(*MOTHER GRIZZLY enters from stage left, holding a fish basket, and stands on the riverbank. Her cubs, YOUNGER BROTHER and OLDER BROTHER, enter and begin to play in the "water."*)

OLDER BROTHER (*Laughing and splashing*): Don't be afraid of a little water, Younger Brother!

YOUNGER BROTHER (*Splashing back*): I'm not, Older Brother!

MOTHER GRIZZLY (*Scolding*): Children! Stop scaring away the fish, or we will have nothing to eat. Out of the water, now! (*They obey but manage a last splash or two.*) I want you to gather berries—but stay close and do not go downriver. Strange things happen there.

TARGETED CLOSE READ

Elements of Drama

Have students reread pages 344–345 to analyze the play's structure and elements of drama.

What does the list labeled Characters tell? *(all of the characters in the play)*

How is the organization of this play similar to and different from *The Saga of Pecos Bill* and *Gigi and the Wishing Ring*? *(This play has a Prologue and Scenes, but no Acts. The Pecos Bill play is one long scene without breaks. The play about Gigi is broken into both Acts and Scenes. They are all in time-order sequence.)*

How does the Prologue connect to Scene 1? *(The Prologue tells who the characters are and what the setting is in Scene 1.)*

DOK 2

READ FOR UNDERSTANDING

Why does Mother Grizzly warn her sons not to go downriver? *(She says strange things happen there.)*

Do you think Older Brother and Younger Brother will pay attention to her warning? *(Sample response: No, because they are young cubs.)*

DOK 3

344 Module 4

Stories on Stage 345

Online Ed

ANNOTATE IT!

Students may use the annotation tools in their eBook.

Step 2 Apply to Text

In your Teaching Pal, use the purple **TARGETED CLOSE READ** prompts on page 345 to guide students to apply the Elements of Drama skill to *Two Bear Cubs* and to find evidence to support their responses. Use the **CLOSE READING** routine. Students may refer to the questions on Know It, Show It page 94 as you discuss them.

- Read aloud the first question on Teaching Pal page 345. Then have students re-read *my*Book pages 344–345 to identify and discuss the cast of characters. *(all of the characters in the play)*
- Then read the last two questions on Teaching Pal page 345 to discuss the plays' organization and how the Prologue prepares readers for Scene 1. *(This play has a Prologue and Scenes, but no Acts. The Pecos Bill play is one long scene without breaks. The play about Gigi is broken into both Acts and Scenes. They are all in time order sequence. The Prologue tells who the characters are and what the setting is in Scene 1.)*
- Refer back to the Anchor Chart to support the discussion. Students may add sticky notes to the chart to note the elements of drama they identify in *Two Bear Cubs*.

Step 3 Engage and Respond

INDEPENDENT PRACTICE: Writing

- **Write a Character Study** Turn to pages 358–359 in your Teaching Pal. Have students turn to pages 358–359 in their *my*Book. Use the **WRITING RESPONSE** routine.
- Read the directions with students and use the Teaching Pal prompts to guide them as they plan and complete their character studies.
- Provide time for students to share their character studies with small groups.
- You may want to have students complete their writing during daily small-group time.
- You may want to have students complete Know It, Show It page 94 during daily small-group time.

ENGLISH LEARNER SUPPORT: Support Comprehension

SUBSTANTIAL

Point to the part of the Prologue that connects to Scene 1. What do the bears do in Scene 1?

MODERATE

Which part of the Prologue connects to Scene 1? How does the Prologue help you understand Scene 1?

LIGHT

Have partners use academic vocabulary such as *prologue* and *scene* to explain and analyze elements of drama.

LINK TO SMALL-GROUP INSTRUCTION

REINFORCE ELEMENTS OF DRAMA Review and extend the skill as needed during small-group time to support students' need for differentiation. *See the lesson on p. T351.*

Options for Differentiation

As the class engages in independent and collaborative work, meet with Guided Reading Groups or differentiate instruction based on student need.

GUIDED READING GROUPS

Match Students to Books + Instruction

- Choose just-right books based on level, skill, topic, or genre.

L → M → N → O → P → Q

Leveled Readers

- Deliver instruction with each book's **Take and Teach Lesson**, choosing appropriate sessions based on need.

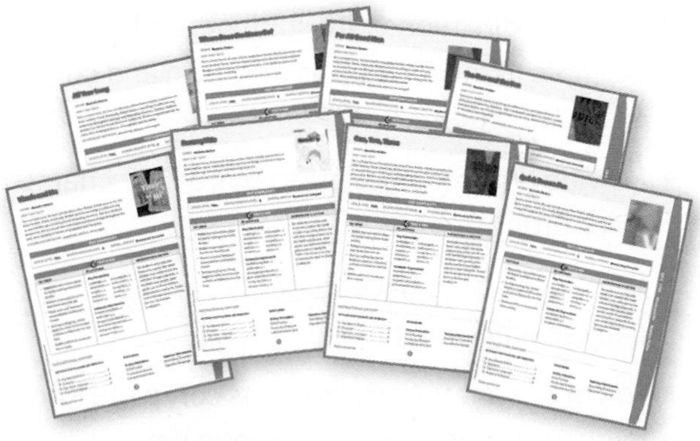

- Check comprehension, reinforce instruction, and extend learning with suggested supporting activities.

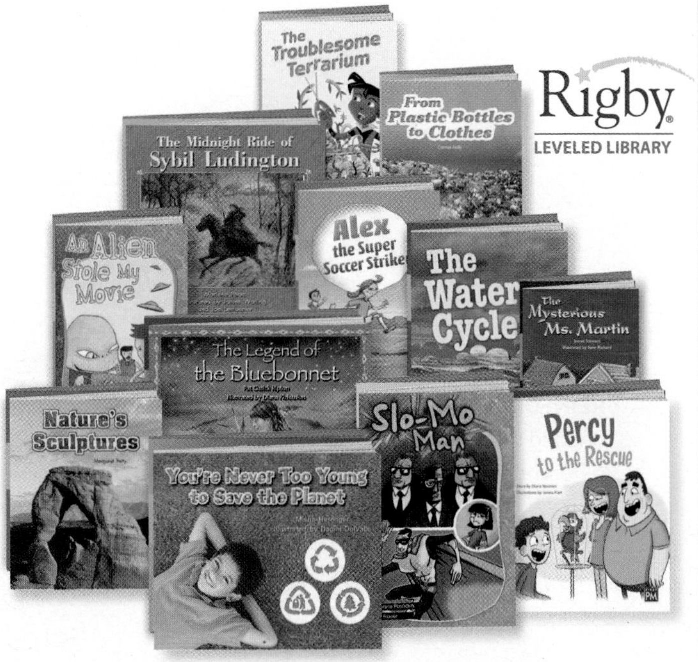

EL ENGLISH LEARNER SUPPORT

Cause and Effect

- Use **Tabletop Minilessons: English Language Development 12.1 (Speaking)** to reinforce and practice the language skill.

Tabletop Minilessons: English Language Development

- Then use the following text-based prompts with *Two Bear Cubs* to guide application of the language skill. Begin with the prompt at the student's identified language proficiency level. As students progress, use lighter supports to encourage increased language proficiency.

SUBSTANTIAL
Have students orally complete cause-and-effect sentence frames about Scene 1 such as: *A full belly and the hot sun causes the bear cubs to feel* _____. Allow them to complete the frames by pointing to illustrations and using their home language as needed.

MODERATE
Facilitate an oral dialogue about Scene 1 using question-and-answer stems such as: *What causes _____? The cause of _____ is _____. What is the effect of _____? The effect of _____ is _____.*

LIGHT
Display cause-and-effect signal words *cause, effect, reason,* and *because*. Have students use the words to ask the group cause-and-effect questions about Scene 1. Students should answer orally, using text evidence.

REINFORCE ELEMENTS OF DRAMA

Demonstrate

- Use **Tabletop Minilessons: Reading Card 14** to remind students that a **drama**, or play, is a story performed by actors on a stage. It is written in the form of a **script**, which may be divided into **acts**, like chapters, and scenes, which are smaller parts of acts. A **cast of characters** tells who the characters are in the play. The drama may begin with a **prologue**, or introduction. **Dialogue** is the words the characters speak. **Stage directions** tell what the characters do onstage.
- Model filling out Printable: Reading Graphic Organizer 14 to identify elements of drama in *Two Bear Cubs*.

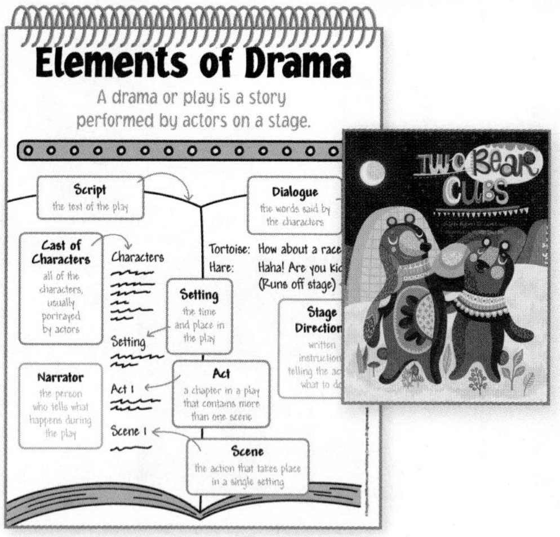
Elements of Drama
A drama or play is a story performed by actors on a stage.
Script
the text of the play
Dialogue
the words said by the characters
Cast of Characters
all of the characters, usually portrayed by actors
Characters
Tortoise: How about a race
Hare: Haha! Are you kid
(Runs off stage)
Setting
the time and place in the play
Stage Direction
Narrator
the person who tells what happens during the play
Act 1
Act
a chapter in a play that contains more than one scene
Scene 1
Scene
the action that takes place in a single setting
TWO BEAR CUBS

Tabletop Minilessons: Reading

Apply to Independent Reading

- Now have students identify the elements of drama in an appropriate play that they are reading independently. Customize these prompts to the texts students choose.
  - » *Does the script have a prologue? Is it divided into acts and scenes?*
  - » *Who are the characters, and what is the setting?*
  - » *How do the dialogue and stage directions help you to understand the characters and events?*
- Have students complete Printable: Reading Graphic Organizer 14 for their independent reading book.

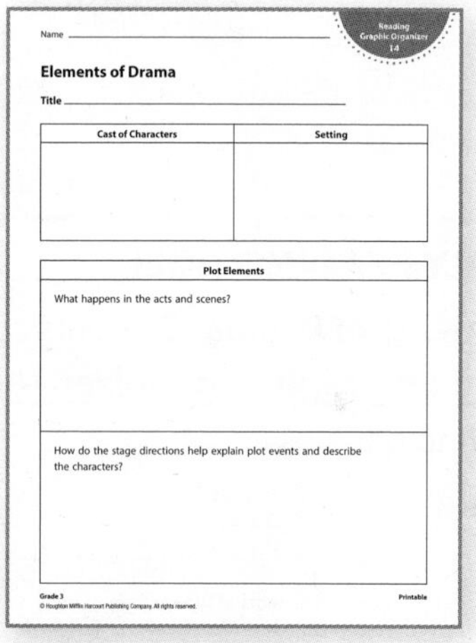
Name

Reading Graphic Organizer 14

Elements of Drama

Title

Cast of Characters	Setting

Plot Elements
What happens in the acts and scenes?
How do the stage directions help explain plot events and describe the characters?

Grade 3

Printable

Printable: Reading Graphic Organizer 14

ALMOST THERE

READY FOR MORE

SCAFFOLD AND EXTEND

- Guide students to locate each element of drama in their reading. Then prompt them to recall major events in the drama.
- Prompt students to identify the characters, setting, dialogue, and stage directions for each act or scene.
- Have students explain how changing one of the elements in the drama would change the story it tells.

EL ENGLISH LEARNER SUPPORT

SUBSTANTIAL

Point to an element of drama and ask *yes/no* questions such as: *Is this the cast of characters? Is this a line of dialogue?*

MODERATE

Supply sentence frames such as: *The setting of this act/scene is* ______. *The characters are* ______. *The events tell about* ______.

LIGHT

Encourage students to elaborate on their answers to the questions.

INDEPENDENT APPLICATION

Options for Independent and Collaborative Work

While you meet with small groups, have other students engage in literacy activities that reinforce the lesson's learning objectives. Choose from these options.

Independent Reading

Student Choice Library

Rigby
LEVELED LIBRARY

APPLY READING SKILL

Elements of Drama Students complete Printable: Reading Graphic Organizer 14 for an independent reading book.

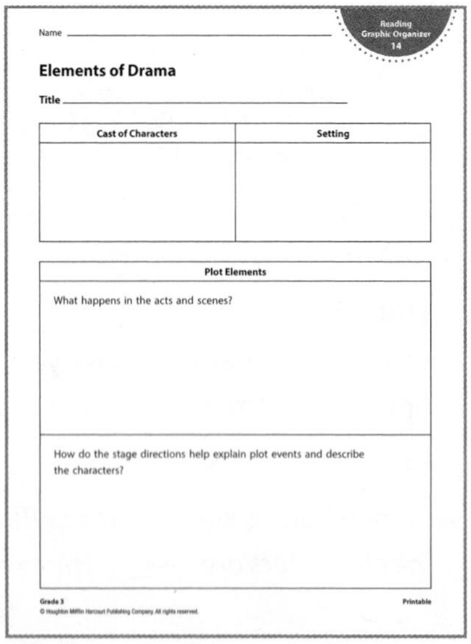
Name ______

Reading Graphic Organizer 14

Elements of Drama

Title ______

Cast of Characters	Setting

Plot Elements
What happens in the acts and scenes?
How do the stage directions help explain plot events and describe the characters?

Grade 3 Printable
© Houghton Mifflin Harcourt Publishing Company. All rights reserved.

Printable: Reading Graphic Organizer 14

APPLY LANGUAGE SKILL

Cause and Effect Students complete Printable: Language Graphic Organizer 3 for an independent reading book.

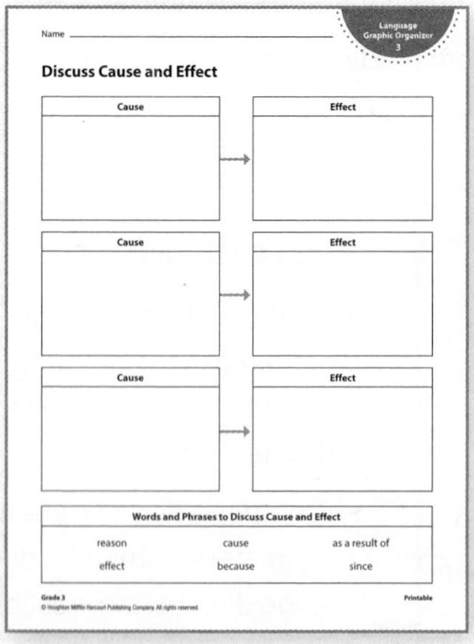
Name ______

Language Graphic Organizer 3

Discuss Cause and Effect

Cause		Effect
	→	
Cause		Effect
	→	
Cause		Effect
	→	

Words and Phrases to Discuss Cause and Effect		
reason	cause	as a result of
effect	because	since

Grade 3 Printable
© Houghton Mifflin Harcourt Publishing Company. All rights reserved.

Printable: Language Graphic Organizer 3

Literacy Centers

See pp. T330–T331.

- READING CENTER
- VOCABULARY CENTER
- DIGITAL STATION
- WRITING CENTER
- PROJECT CENTER

Writing

Students write a character study.

See Engage and Respond, p. T349.

Additional Skills Practice

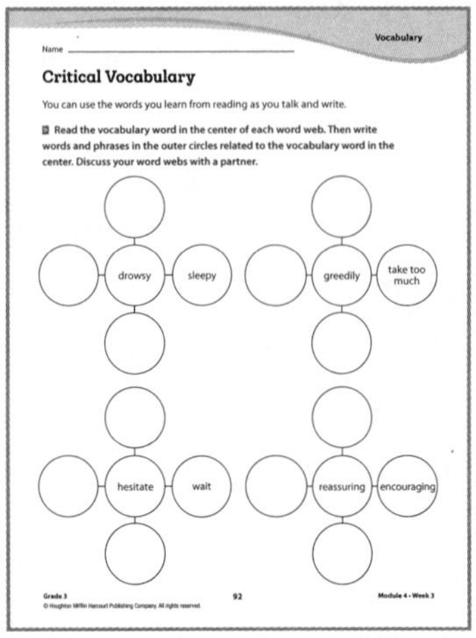
Name
Vocabulary
Critical Vocabulary
You can use the words you learn from reading as you talk and write.
Read the vocabulary word in the center of each word web. Then write words and phrases in the outer circles related to the vocabulary word in the center. Discuss your word webs with a partner.

drowsy
sleepy
greedily
take too much
hesitate
wait
reassuring
encouraging

Grade 3 92 Module 4 • Week 3

Know It, Show It, p. 92

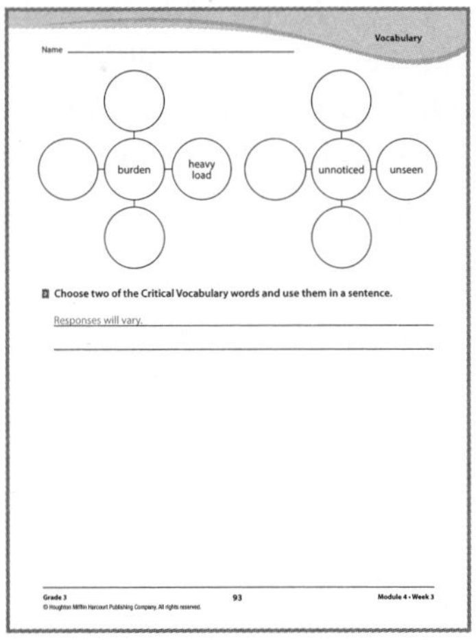
Name
Vocabulary

burden
heavy load
unnoticed
unseen

Choose two of the Critical Vocabulary words and use them in a sentence.
Responses will vary.

Grade 3 93 Module 4 • Week 3

Know It, Show It, p. 93

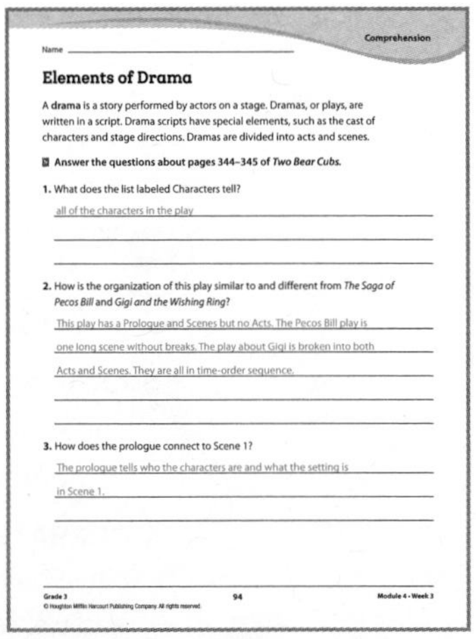
Name
Comprehension
Elements of Drama
A drama is a story performed by actors on a stage. Dramas, or plays, are written in a script. Drama scripts have special elements, such as the cast of characters and stage directions. Dramas are divided into acts and scenes.
Answer the questions about pages 344–345 of *Two Bear Cubs*.
1. What does the list labeled Characters tell?
all of the characters in the play
2. How is the organization of this play similar to and different from *The Saga of Pecos Bill* and *Gigi and the Wishing Ring*?
This play has a Prologue and Scenes but no Acts. The Pecos Bill play is one long scene without breaks. The play about Gigi is broken into both Acts and Scenes. They are all in time-order sequence.
3. How does the prologue connect to Scene 1?
The prologue tells who the characters are and what the setting is in Scene 1.
Grade 3 94 Module 4 • Week 3

Know It, Show It, p. 94

Wrap-Up

Share Time

At the end of the Reading Workshop, have students reflect on their learning by sharing how they applied **Elements of Drama** or another area of focus during independent work time. Choose from these options:

- Use the **SOLO CHAIR** routine. Select a reader each day to come to the front of the class and tell what he or she learned from the reading by using a skill or strategy.
- **THINK-PAIR-SHARE** Students share their thinking with a partner. Select a few pairs each day to share with the whole class.
- **RETURN TO ANCHOR CHART** Have students add sticky notes about their independent reading to the Elements of Drama Anchor Chart. Call on a few students to explain what they added and why.

Online Ed

ANCHOR CHART 14: Elements of Drama

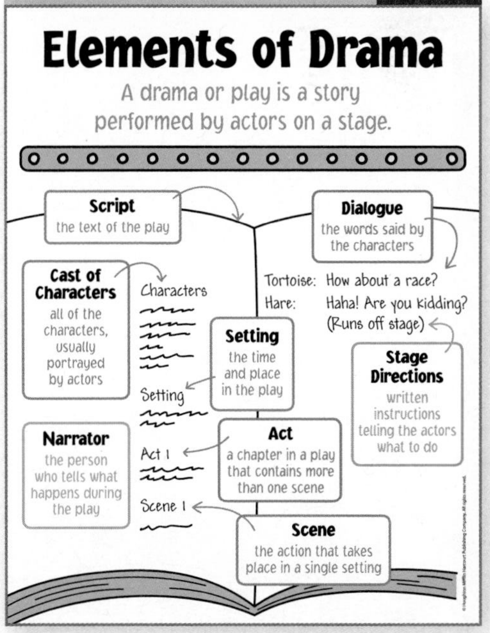
Elements of Drama
A drama or play is a story performed by actors on a stage.
Script
the text of the play
Dialogue
the words said by the characters
Cast of Characters
all of the characters, usually portrayed by actors
Characters
Tortoise: How about a race?
Hare: Haha! Are you kidding? (Runs off stage)
Setting
the time and place in the play
Stage Directions
written instructions telling the actors what to do
Setting
Narrator
the person who tells what happens during the play
Act
a chapter in a play that contains more than one scene
Act 1
Scene 1
Scene
the action that takes place in a single setting

Latin Roots *aud, vis*

Step 1 Introduce the Skill

LEARNING OBJECTIVES

- Determine the meaning of grade-level academic vocabulary with Latin roots.
- Use a dictionary or glossary to determine the meanings of unknown words.
- **Language** Discuss words with the Latin roots *aud* and *vis* to show understanding of the target roots.

MATERIALS Online Ed

Display and Engage *Generative Vocabulary 4.13*

Know It, Show It *p. 95*

INSTRUCTIONAL VOCABULARY

- **root** a basic word part, usually from Greek or Latin, that carries meaning

Project Display and Engage: Generative Vocabulary 4.13. Read aloud the paragraphs.

Online Ed

DISPLAY AND ENGAGE:
Generative Vocabulary 4.13

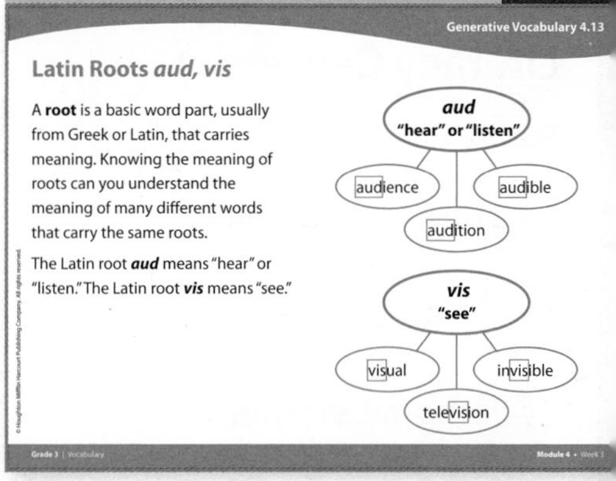

Generative Vocabulary 4.13
Latin Roots aud, vis
A root is a basic word part, usually from Greek or Latin, that carries meaning. Knowing the meaning of roots can you understand the meaning of many different words that carry the same roots.
The Latin root aud means "hear" or "listen." The Latin root vis means "see."
aud
"hear" or "listen"
audience
audible
audition
vis
"see"
visual
invisible
television

- Write the words *audience* and *vision* on the board and underline the roots *aud* and *vis*. Tell students that knowing the meaning of the roots *aud* and *vis* can help them understand the meaning of these and many other words with these roots.
- Then model how to use roots to determine the meaning of a word. *The Latin root* aud *means "hear" or "listen." This makes sense, because an* audience *listens to a performance. When I see the root* aud *in other words, I will know the words have something to do with hearing or listening. For example, the word* audition *contains the root* aud. *At an audition, people perform for others who are listening.*

  The Latin root vis *means "see."* Vision *is the ability to see. When I see the root* vis *in other words, I will know the words have something to do with seeing. For example, the word* television *contains the root* vis. *We turn on a television to see what is on the screen.*

ENGLISH LEARNER SUPPORT: Build Vocabulary

SUBSTANTIAL
Show familiar words with the roots *aud* and *vis*. Guide students to identify the root, and discuss each word's meaning with them.

MODERATE
Have pairs name as many words as they can with the roots *aud* and *vis*. Allow them to use reference sources as needed.

LIGHT
Have pairs say sentences using the lesson's *aud* and *vis* words.

Step 2 Guided Practice

- Display the words *auditorium* and *visualize*. Ask students to identify the root *aud* or *vis* in each word and make predictions about the meaning, based on their knowledge of the root.
- Then ask students to look up each word in a print or online dictionary to confirm their predictions. Have volunteers provide a definition of each word.

Step 3 Apply the Skill

INDEPENDENT PRACTICE

- Have students work in pairs to complete Know It, Show It page 95. Tell partners to read the instructions and have them complete the activity together.
- Then each student write a new sentence for each *aud* and *vis* word. Have partners read their sentences to one another to confirm the meaning of each word. Invite volunteers to read their sentences aloud.
- You may wish to have students complete the Know It, Show It page during small-group time.

Spiral Review

Suffixes *–er, –or* Remind students that a suffix is a word part added to the end of a base word that changes the meaning of the word.

- Review that the suffixes *–er* and *–or* can mean "one who" or "one that." Both suffixes change a verb into a noun. Remind students that a base word's spelling may change slightly when the suffix *–er* or *–or* is added. For base words ending in *e*, the *e* is dropped before the suffix is added. *For base words that end in a vowel followed by a consonant, the consonant is doubled before the suffix is added.*
- Write on the board the word *teller*. Guide students to identify the base word and the suffix in *teller* and explain how the suffix changes the base word's meaning. Then repeat the exercise with *narrator*.
- Have students add the suffix *–er* to the following words: *gather, taste*. Have them add the suffix *–or* to the following words: *invent, visit*. Have students explain how the suffixes change the words' meaning. Invite them to check the words' meanings in a print or online dictionary.

Literary Elements

Step 1 Connect and Teach

LEARNING OBJECTIVES

- Analyze plot, including conflict and resolution.
- Analyze how plot elements support the author's purpose.
- **Language** Describe a drama's plot using the words *conflict, problem,* and *resolution.*

MATERIALS | Online Ed

Anchor Chart 12 *Literary Elements*

Printable *Anchor Chart 12: Literary Elements*

Teaching Pal *Book 1, pp. 342–359*

myBook *Book 1, Two Bear Cubs, pp. 342–359*

Know It, Show It *p. 96*

INSTRUCTIONAL VOCABULARY

- **conflict** challenge or problem
- **event** occurrence in a story
- **literary elements** parts of a story (characters, setting, plot, and events)
- **plot** conflicts, events, and resolution that make up a story
- **resolution** how the conflict is solved

SPANISH COGNATES

- **conflict** *conflicto*
- **event** *evento*
- **literary** *literario*
- **resolution** *resolución*

Project or display Anchor Chart 12: Literary Elements.

Online Ed

ANCHOR CHART 12: Literary Elements

Literary Elements
Literary elements are the pieces that make up a story.
Characters:
the people and animals in a story
• What do they say and think?
• What do they do?
• What do other characters say and think about them?
Setting:
where and when the story takes place
• affects the plot because certain events happen in certain settings
• affects the plot by creating its mood
Plot:
Conflict
the main problem that the characters face
Resolution
how the conflict or problem is solved
Events:
things that happen in a story
• to change a character
• to affect the mood
• to build the plot

Remind students that both stories and dramas include characters, settings, plot, and events. These pieces of a story are called **literary elements.** Direct attention to the corresponding parts of the Anchor Chart as you make the following points:

- The **plot** of a story or drama has a sequence of **events** that happen. The events are what move the plot along.
- A plot also includes a **conflict,** or problem and a **resolution,** or solution.
- Authors plan a sequence of events that fits their purpose for writing. That purpose may be to tell a story in a funny way, to build suspense, or show how characters change.
- Tell students they will practice analyzing literary elements to gain a deeper understanding of the drama/myth *Two Bear Cubs.*

LEARNING MINDSET

Self-Reflection

Apply Point out that none of the other characters in the play believe that Measuring Worm can rescue the cubs, but he says he will try anyway. Explain that students can apply that kind of determination to their own learning: *When you reflect on your work, see your mistakes as a chance to do better next time. Then you can reflect on your accomplishments when you don't make that mistake again. Just like Measuring Worm, say, "I'll try."*

Go to Your Teaching Pal

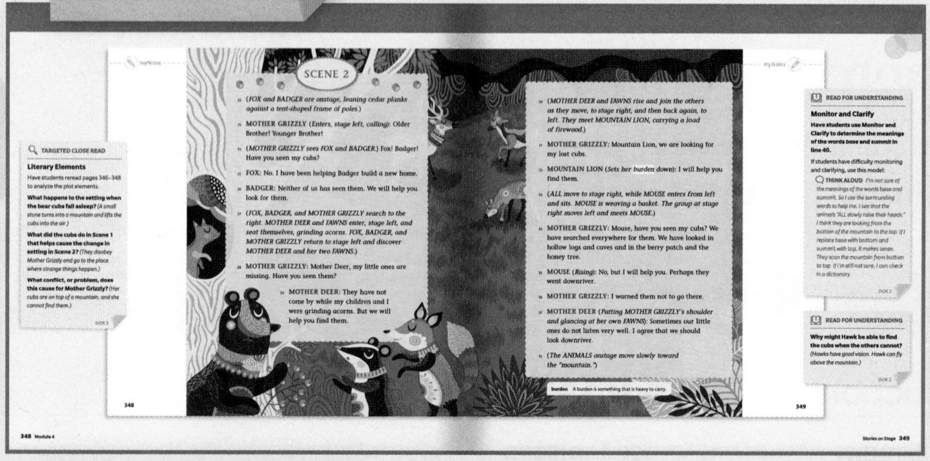

Online

ANNOTATE IT!

Students may use the annotation tools in their eBook.

Step 2 Apply to Text

In your **Teaching Pal**, use the purple **TARGETED CLOSE READ** prompts on pages 348 and 355 to guide students to apply the Literary Elements skill to *Two Bear Cubs* and to find evidence to support their responses. Use the **CLOSE READING** routine. Students may refer to the questions on Know It, Show It page 96 as you discuss them.

- Read aloud the first two questions on Teaching Pal page 348. Then have students reread *my*Book pages 346–348. Tell students to look for clues to the setting and how it changes. *(A small stone turns into a mountain and lifts the cubs into the air. They disobey Mother Grizzly and go to the place where strange things happen.)*
- Then read the last question on Teaching Pal page 348 to discuss the conflict. *(Her cubs are on top of a mountain, and she cannot find them.)*
- Have students turn to pages 353–355. Use the prompts to have them identify the plot's resolution and how it comes about. Refer back to the Anchor Chart to support the discussion. Students may add sticky notes to the chart to note literary elements they identify in *Two Bear Cubs*.
- Extend the conversation by having students determine the central message citing text evidence.

Step 3 Engage and Respond

INDEPENDENT PRACTICE: Writing

Assign scenes from the play to partners, making sure that all the scenes in the drama are covered. Tell students they will write about what happens in their scene in a paragraph. Remind them to include all key events related to the conflict and resolution of the plot. Use the **WRITING RESPONSE** routine.

- Have partners review their paragraph to determine if any key details are missing. Students should add details to their story scenes as needed.
- Ask for volunteers who wrote about each of the three scenes. Have students read their writing aloud, in order, and discuss how the sequence of events moves the plot forward.
- You may want to have students complete their writing during daily small-group time.
- You may want to have students complete the Know It, Show It page 96 during daily small-group time.

EL ENGLISH LEARNER SUPPORT: Support Comprehension

SUBSTANTIAL
Have students use illustrations for support. Supply sentence frames.
The cubs' problem is _____. _____ solves the problem.

MODERATE
_____ has a conflict because _____. There is a resolution when _____.

LIGHT
Have students explain the multiple problems in the drama and the resolution. Encourage them to add details to their explanations.

LINK TO SMALL-GROUP INSTRUCTION

REINFORCE LITERARY ELEMENTS Review and extend the skill as needed during small-group time to support students' need for differentiation. *See the lesson on p. T359.*

Options for Differentiation

As the class engages in independent and collaborative work, meet with Guided Reading Groups or differentiate instruction based on student need.

GUIDED READING GROUPS

Match Students to Books + Instruction

- Choose just-right books based on level, skill, topic, or genre.

L M N O P Q

Leveled Readers

- Deliver instruction with each book's **Take and Teach Lesson**, choosing appropriate sessions based on need.

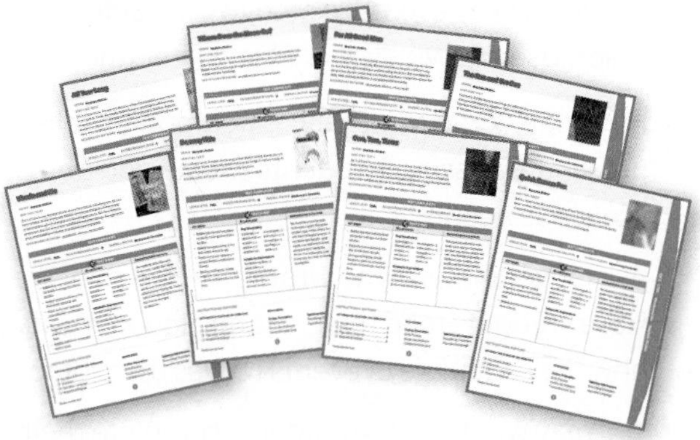

- Check comprehension, reinforce instruction, and extend learning with suggested supporting activities.

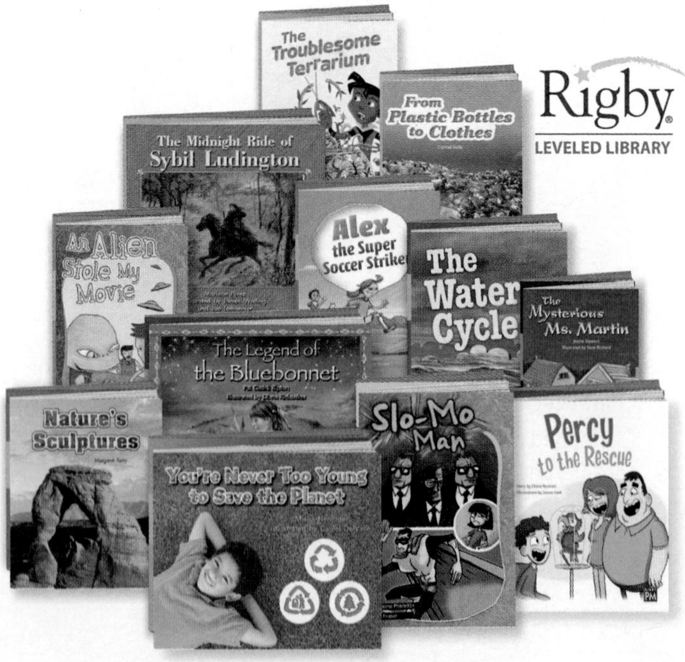

Rigby LEVELED LIBRARY

ENGLISH LEARNER SUPPORT

Cause and Effect

- Use **Tabletop Minilessons: English Language Development 12.2 (Reading)** to reinforce and practice the language skill.

Tabletop Minilessons: English Language Development

- Then use the following text-based prompts with *Two Bear Cubs* to guide application of the language skill. Begin with the prompt at the student's identified language proficiency level. As students progress, use lighter supports to encourage increased language proficiency.

SUBSTANTIAL

Choral read paragraph 46. Point to each animal's name in the paragraph and ask, *What happened to [animal's name] when it tried to climb the mountain?* Guide students to point to and read words to complete: *When [animal's name] tried to climb the mountain, it* ______.

MODERATE

Ask: *What caused each animal to fail to reach the cubs on the mountain?* Have students read and find examples in paragraph 46 to answer the question using the frame: *[Animal's name] failed to climb the mountain because* ______.

LIGHT

Have students read Scene 2 to find the answers to the following questions: *What did Mother Bear do to cause the other animals to help her find her cubs? What caused each animal to fail to reach the cubs on the mountain?*

REINFORCE LITERARY ELEMENTS

Demonstrate

- Use **Tabletop Minilessons: Reading Card 12** to remind students that all stories have certain **literary elements** that are the same. The **plot** of a story or drama has a sequence of **events** that move the plot along and serve the author's purpose for writing. A plot often begins with a **conflict**, or problem, and ends with a **resolution**, or solution.
- Model filling out Printable: Reading Graphic Organizer 12 to identify literary elements in *Two Bear Cubs.*

Apply to Independent Reading

- Now have students identify literary elements in an appropriate book or article they are reading independently. Customize these prompts to the texts students choose.
  - » *Who are the characters?*
  - » *What is the setting?*
  - » *What are the main story events, and how are they affected by characters and setting?*
- Have students complete Printable: Reading Graphic Organizer 12 for their independent reading book.

Literary Elements
Literary elements are the pieces that make up a story.
Characters:
the people and animals in a story
• What do they say and think?
• What do they do?
• What do other characters say and think about them?
Setting:
where and when the story takes place
Plot:
Conflict
the main problem that the characters face
Resolution
how the conflict or problem is solved
Events:
things that happen in a story
• to change a character
• to affect the mood
• to build the plot
Two Bear Cubs

Tabletop Minilessons: Reading

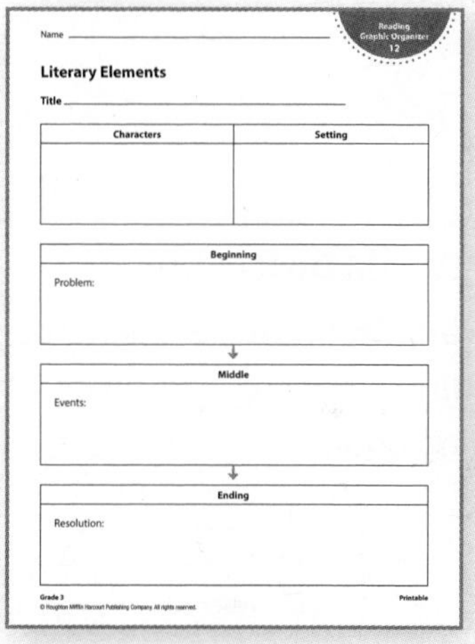

Printable: Reading Graphic Organizer 12

SCAFFOLD AND EXTEND

ALMOST THERE

READY FOR MORE

- Prompt students to identify characters, setting, conflict, and resolution. Guide them to retell plot events in sequence.
- Have students identify the characters, setting, conflict, and resolution, and then retell plot events in sequence.
- Have students explain how plot elements serve the author's purpose for writing.

EL ENGLISH LEARNER SUPPORT

SUBSTANTIAL

Support students in completing the sentence frames: *The characters are _____. The conflict/resolution is _____.*

MODERATE

Give students a bank of sequence words such as *first, next, then,* and *last,* and have them use them to retell plot events.

LIGHT

Have students retell plot events with a partner. Encourage them to use sequence words.

Options for Independent and Collaborative Work

While you meet with small groups, have other students engage in literacy activities that reinforce the lesson's learning objectives. Choose from these options.

Independent Reading

Student Choice Library

Rigby
LEVELED LIBRARY

APPLY READING SKILL

Literary Elements Students complete Printable: Reading Graphic Organizer 12 for an independent reading book.

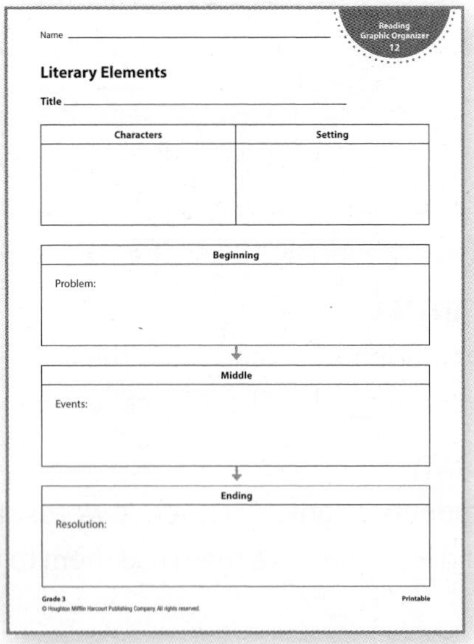
Name
Reading Graphic Organizer 12
Literary Elements
Title

Characters	Setting

Beginning
Problem:

Middle
Events:

Ending
Resolution:

Grade 3 Printable
© Houghton Mifflin Harcourt Publishing Company. All rights reserved.

Printable: Reading Graphic Organizer 12

APPLY LANGUAGE SKILL

Cause and Effect Students complete Printable: Language Graphic Organizer 3 for an independent reading book.

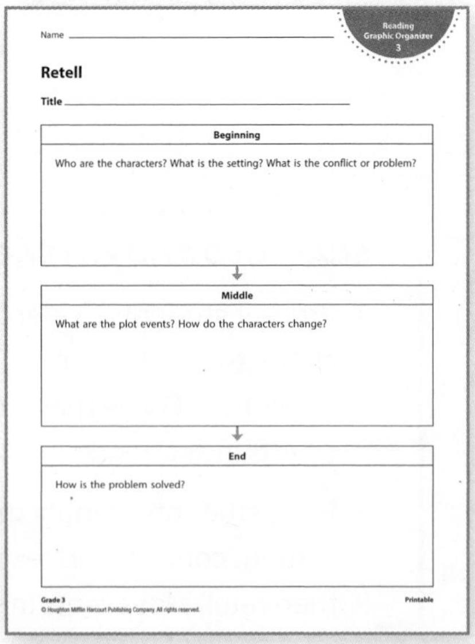
Name
Reading Graphic Organizer 3
Retell
Title

Beginning
Who are the characters? What is the setting? What is the conflict or problem?

Middle
What are the plot events? How do the characters change?

End
How is the problem solved?

Grade 3 Printable
© Houghton Mifflin Harcourt Publishing Company. All rights reserved.

Printable: Language Graphic Organizer 3

Literacy Centers

See pp. T330–T331.

- READING CENTER
- VOCABULARY CENTER
- DIGITAL STATION
- WRITING CENTER
- PROJECT CENTER

Writing

Students write a paragraph about a scene from a play. *See Engage and Respond, p. T357.*

Additional Skills Practice

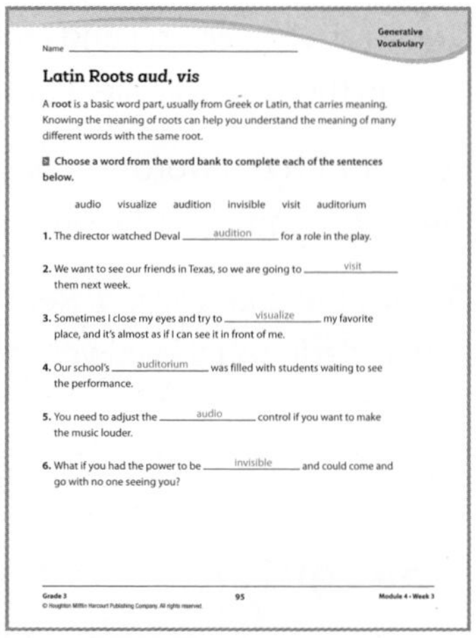
Generative Vocabulary

Name

Latin Roots aud, vis

A **root** is a basic word part, usually from Greek or Latin, that carries meaning. Knowing the meaning of roots can help you understand the meaning of many different words with the same root.

Choose a word from the word bank to complete each of the sentences below.

audio visualize audition invisible visit auditorium

1. The director watched Deval __audition__ for a role in the play.
2. We want to see our friends in Texas, so we are going to __visit__ them next week.
3. Sometimes I close my eyes and try to __visualize__ my favorite place, and it's almost as if I can see it in front of me.
4. Our school's __auditorium__ was filled with students waiting to see the performance.
5. You need to adjust the __audio__ control if you want to make the music louder.
6. What if you had the power to be __invisible__ and could come and go with no one seeing you?

Grade 3 95 Module 4 • Week 3

Know It, Show It, p. 95

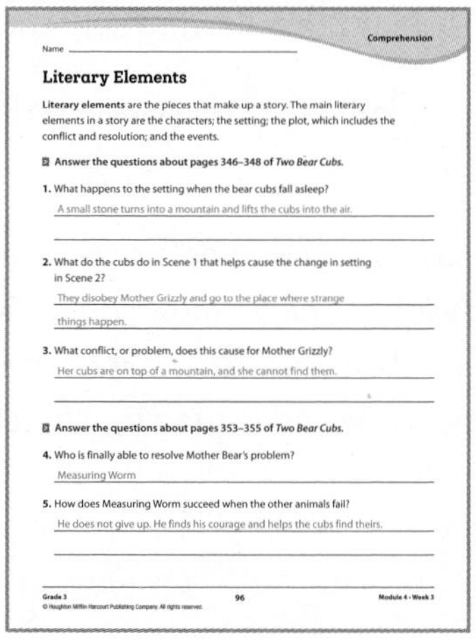
Comprehension

Name

Literary Elements

Literary elements are the pieces that make up a story. The main literary elements in a story are the characters; the setting; the plot, which includes the conflict and resolution; and the events.

Answer the questions about pages 346–348 of *Two Bear Cubs*.

1. What happens to the setting when the bear cubs fall asleep?
A small stone turns into a mountain and lifts the cubs into the air.
2. What do the cubs do in Scene 1 that helps cause the change in setting in Scene 2?
They disobey Mother Grizzly and go to the place where strange things happen.
3. What conflict, or problem, does this cause for Mother Grizzly?
Her cubs are on top of a mountain, and she cannot find them.

Answer the questions about pages 353–355 of *Two Bear Cubs*.

4. Who is finally able to resolve Mother Bear's problem?
Measuring Worm
5. How does Measuring Worm succeed when the other animals fail?
He does not give up. He finds his courage and helps the cubs find theirs.

Grade 3 96 Module 4 • Week 3

Know It, Show It, p. 96

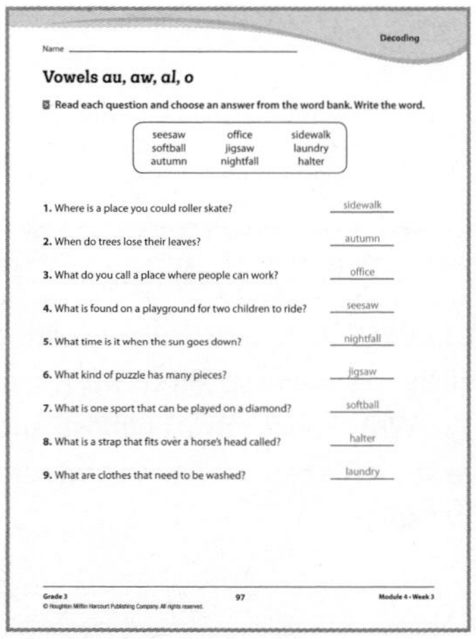
Decoding

Name

Vowels au, aw, al, o

Read each question and choose an answer from the word bank. Write the word.

seesaw office sidewalk softball jigsaw laundry autumn nightfall halter

1. Where is a place you could roller skate? sidewalk
2. When do trees lose their leaves? autumn
3. What do you call a place where people can work? office
4. What is found on a playground for two children to ride? seesaw
5. What time is it when the sun goes down? nightfall
6. What kind of puzzle has many pieces? jigsaw
7. What is one sport that can be played on a diamond? softball
8. What is a strap that fits over a horse's head called? halter
9. What are clothes that need to be washed? laundry

Grade 3 97 Module 4 • Week 3

Know It, Show It, p. 97

Wrap-Up

Share Time

At the end of the Reading Workshop, have students reflect on their learning by sharing how they applied **literary elements** or another area of focus during independent work time. Choose from these options:

- Use the **SOLO CHAIR** routine. Select a reader each day to come to the front of the class and tell what he or she learned from the reading by using a skill or strategy.
- **THINK-PAIR-SHARE** Students share their thinking with a partner. Select a few pairs each day to share with the whole class.
- **RETURN TO ANCHOR CHART** Have students add sticky notes about their independent reading to the Literary Elements Anchor Chart. Call on a few students to explain what they added and why.

Online

ANCHOR CHART 12: Literary Elements

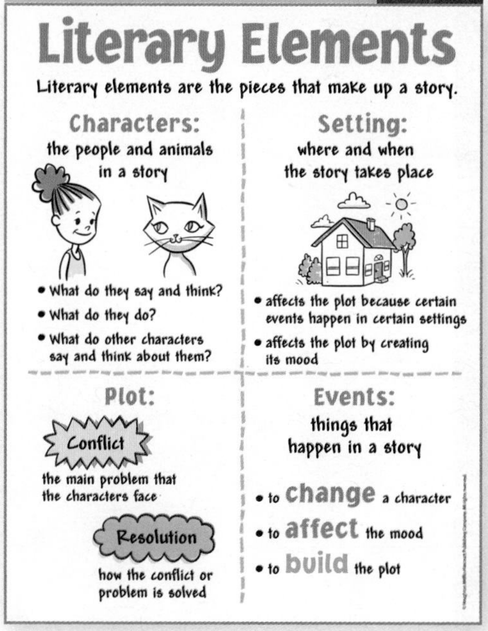

Vowels *au, aw, al, o*

Step 1 Reinforce the Skill

LEARNING OBJECTIVES

- Decode and read with vowels *au, aw, al,* and *o*.
- Recognize spelling patterns for vowels *au, aw, al,* and *o*.
- **Language** Articulate sounds for vowels *au, aw, al,* and *o* and read words containing those sounds.

MATERIALS	Online Ed

Display and Engage *Decoding 4.13*
Know It, Show It *p. 97*

Vowels *au, aw, al, o* Remind students that they have learned the sounds and spellings of the vowels *au, aw, al,* and *o*.

- **Transition to Longer Words** Display the word *coffee*. Explain that students can divide longer words into syllables to make them easier to decode and read.
- Draw a line between *f* and *f* in *coffee*. Say each syllable: /kôf/ /fē/. Underline the *o* in the first syllable. Point out that the /aw/ sound is in the first syllable.
- Repeat with the words *author, drawback,* and *already.* Guide students to read the words and identify the /aw/ sound spelled *au, aw,* and *al*.
- Display the chart below. Read each word aloud, emphasizing the /aw/ sound and underlining the vowel spelling in each word.

au	aw	al	o
daughter	strawberry	falter	strongest

- Display the following sentence and underline the word *falter*.

The horse may falter, or hesitate, if the rider doesn't have control.

Say: *Let's say I didn't recognize the word* falter. *I see the vowel spelling* al *in the first syllable, which I know can stand for the /aw/ sound. I'll use that to help me sound out the word: /fôl/ /tər/,* falter. *It sounds like a word I've heard, and the context helps me understand that falter means "to hesitate."*

ENGLISH LEARNER SUPPORT: Utilize Language Transfer

ALL LEVELS In Spanish, vowel sounds tend to be spelled consistently. Point out that in English, the vowel spellings *au, aw, al,* and *o* can all stand for the same sound in English, /aw/. Write *sauce, awful, almost,* and *off*. Say each word, emphasize the /aw/ sound, and have students repeat. Ask volunteers to underline the letters in each word that stand for the /aw/ sound.

Step 2 Guided Practice

- Project Display and Engage: **Decoding 4.13**.
- Have students read the Blend and Read lines aloud. Provide feedback as needed. At the end of each line, prompt a conversation about the words: *How are the vowel sounds the same? How are the spellings the same or different?*
- Have partners reread the Blend and Read lines and quiz each other on the spellings for the /aw/ sound.

Online Ed

DISPLAY AND ENGAGE: Decoding 4.13

Decoding 4.13

Blend and Read

Vowels *au, aw, al, o*

1	recall (al)	drawback (aw)	often (o)	because (au)	meatball (al)
2	belong (o)	offer (o)	almost (al)	applause (au)	softness (o)
3	frosty (o)	auction (au)	although (al)	scrawny (aw)	install (al)
4	caution (au)	sprawling (aw)	audio (au)	glossy (o)	saucer (au)
5	awning (aw)	officer (o)	faucet (au)	crawfish (aw)	walkway (al)

6 The director gave a small (al) bow and waved awkwardly (aw) at the audience (au).

7 The inventor designed an awesome (aw) new pinball (al) machine.

Grade 3 | Foundational Skills Module 4 • Week 3

Step 3 Apply

INDEPENDENT PRACTICE

- Have students work in small groups or with partners to complete Know It, Show It page 97.
- Encourage students to share with each other the strategies they use to decode words with vowel diphthongs.

CORRECT & REDIRECT

If students have trouble decoding words with vowels *au, aw, al,* and *o,* use the model below.

- **Correct** the error. *The letters* au, aw, al, *and* o *can be pronounced /aw/.*
- **Model** how to decode the word *caution. /kă/ /shən/. That doesn't sound like a word I know. I see the letters* au *in the first syllable, so I'll try the /aw/ sound: /kô/ /shən/,* caution. Caution *is a word I know.*
- **Guide** students to decode the words *scrawny* and *glossy*.
- **Check** students' understanding by displaying the word *install. What spelling pattern helps you decode this word?*
- **Reinforce** by repeating the process with *faucet*.

Vocabulary Spiral Review

Step 1 Review Vocabulary

LEARNING OBJECTIVES

- Review vocabulary.
- Identify real-life connections between words and their use.
- Play a guessing game to enhance vocabulary knowledge.
- **Language** Discuss target vocabulary words and expand vocabulary knowledge by playing a guessing game.

MATERIALS Online Ed

- **Display and Engage** *3.6, 3.8, 3.11*
- **Vocabulary Cards** *3.11, 3.12, 3.13, 3.14, 3.15, 3.16, 3.18, 3.20, 3.21*

- Tell students they will review some of the Critical Vocabulary they have learned so far this year and complete an activity based on those words.
- Project Display and Engage: Critical Vocabulary 3.6, Critical Vocabulary 3.8, and Critical Vocabulary 3.11 to remind students of the Module 3, Week 2 and Week 3 Critical Vocabulary words and their meanings.

Online Ed

DISPLAY AND ENGAGE: Critical Vocabulary 3.6, 3.8 and 3.11

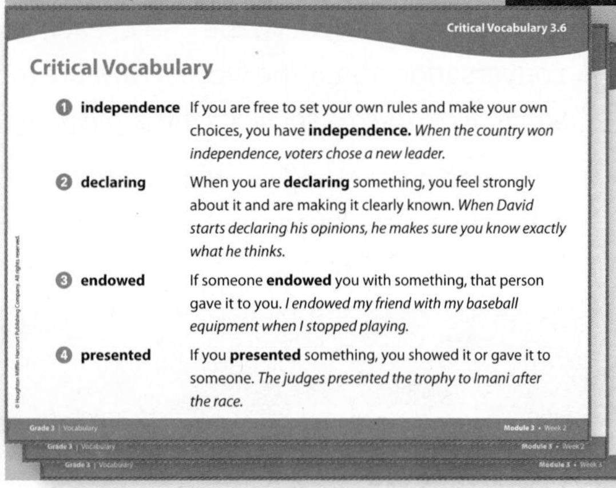
Critical Vocabulary 3.6

Critical Vocabulary

1. **independence** If you are free to set your own rules and make your own choices, you have **independence.** *When the country won independence, voters chose a new leader.*
2. **declaring** When you are **declaring** something, you feel strongly about it and are making it clearly known. *When David starts declaring his opinions, he makes sure you know exactly what he thinks.*
3. **endowed** If someone **endowed** you with something, that person gave it to you. *I endowed my friend with my baseball equipment when I stopped playing.*
4. **presented** If you **presented** something, you showed it or gave it to someone. *The judges presented the trophy to Imani after the race.*

Grade 3 | Vocabulary Module 3 • Week 2

- After reviewing the meanings, call out words and have volunteers take turns using the words in sentences of their own. If students are having trouble creating sentences, have them give synonyms or antonyms for the word.
- Continue until all students have had a chance to work with one or more of the words.

Step 2 Guided Practice

- Use Vocabulary Cards 3.11, 3.12, 3.13, 3.14, 3.15, 3.16, 3.18, 3.20, and 3.21 to remind students of the meanings of the words *declaring, endowed, presented, broad, hoisted, monument, torch,* and *sculptor.*
- Tell students they will play a guessing game with the words. One student will act out a word, and other students will guess the word. Explain that they will need to recall the words' meanings to tell which word is being acted out.
- To demonstrate, act out the meaning of *gritty* by running your hand across a rough object or rubbing your fingers together to indicate something rough textured. Have students identify the word that matches this action. Then ask a volunteer to use the word in a sentence that describes your actions.
- As needed, demonstrate the activity again with another word.

Step 3 Apply the Skill

- Tell students they will act out the remaining words in groups.
- Divide the class into groups of four to six students. Provide each group with index cards, each containing one of the vocabulary words. (Or you can have students create the cards themselves.)
- Ask a volunteer to be the first "actor." He or she should pick a card and act out that word. The rest of the group should try to identify which word the student is acting out. After someone guesses the word, he or she should use it in a sentence describing what the actor was doing.

EL **ENGLISH LEARNER SUPPORT: Act Out Word Meanings**

SUBSTANTIAL
Review the Vocabulary Cards with students to ensure understanding. Let students try out ideas for acting out the words, and offer suggestions as needed. Encourage students to work in pairs when they are the "actors."

MODERATE
Pair students with English-fluent partners to act out and guess words.

LIGHT
Have partners brainstorm ideas for acting out the words, writing down ideas in advance of the game.

TEACHER TIP

Encourage students to notice when they hear people using any of the Critical Vocabulary words in everyday conversation. Have them make notes about where, when, and how the words where used and share them with the class.

Theme

Step 1 Connect and Teach

LEARNING OBJECTIVES

- Identify theme.
- Distinguish *theme* from *topic*.
- **Language** Articulate the theme of a drama.

MATERIALS — Online Ed

Anchor Chart 9 *Theme*
Printable *Anchor Chart 9: Theme*
Teaching Pal *Book 1, pp. 342–359*
myBook *Book 1, Two Bear Cubs, pp. 342–359*
Know It, Show It *p. 98*

INSTRUCTIONAL VOCABULARY

- **moral** the lesson in a story
- **theme** the big idea, moral, or lesson of a piece of writing
- **topic** the person or thing a text is about

SPANISH COGNATES

- **moral** *moral*
- **theme** *tema*

Project or display Anchor Chart 9: **Theme**.

Remind students that many stories and dramas have a **theme**, or lesson. Review the definition of *theme* and the examples on the Anchor Chart. Then make the following points:

- The theme is different from the **topic** of the story. The theme is the lesson or message the author wants to share with readers. It is often a lesson about life. The **topic** is the person or thing the story is about.
- The theme is sometimes written directly in the story, but most often it is not. Readers use clues from the story to figure out the theme.
- Questions, such as those shown on the Anchor Chart, will help students figure out the theme.
- Tell students they will practice identifying the theme to gain a deeper understanding of *Two Bear Cubs.*

Online Ed

ANCHOR CHART 9: Theme

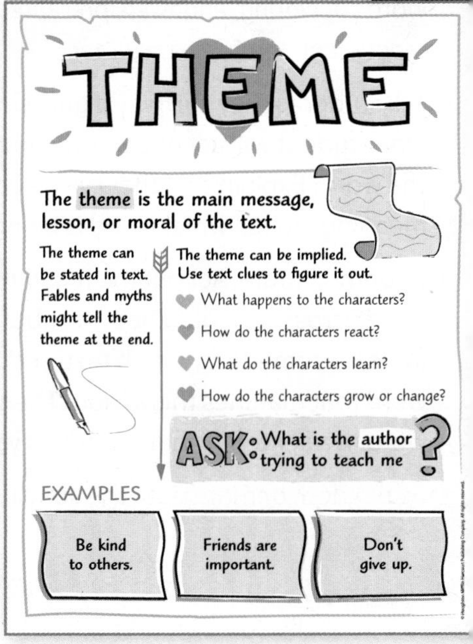
THEME
The theme is the main message, lesson, or moral of the text.
The theme can be stated in text. Fables and myths might tell the theme at the end.
The theme can be implied. Use text clues to figure it out.
What happens to the characters?
How do the characters react?
What do the characters learn?
How do the characters grow or change?
ASK: What is the author trying to teach me?
EXAMPLES
Be kind to others.
Friends are important.
Don't give up.

LEARNING MINDSET

Self-Reflection

Reflect Review paragraphs 76–79 on page 356 of *Two Bear Cubs. What mistakes did the cubs make? How do they feel? Do you think they will make the same mistake again?* Point out that facing up to mistakes can be difficult, but it's one of the best ways to learn and improve.

Go to Your Teaching Pal

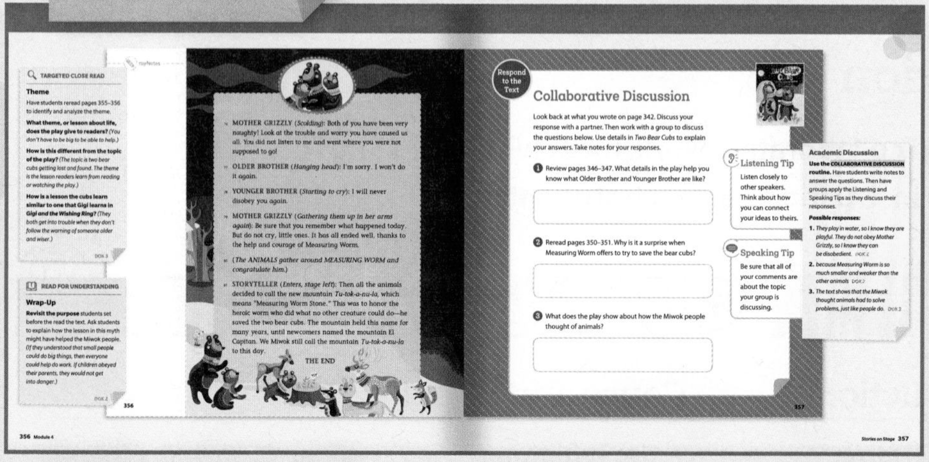

Online Ed

ANNOTATE IT!

Students may use the annotation tools in their eBook.

Step 2 Apply to Text

In your **Teaching Pal**, use the purple **TARGETED CLOSE READ** prompts on page 356 to guide students to apply the Theme skill to *Two Bear Cubs* and to find evidence to support their responses. Use the **CLOSE READING** routine. Students may refer to the questions on Know It, Show It page 98 as you discuss them.

- Read aloud the first two questions on Teaching Pal page 356. Then have students reread *my*Book pages 355–356 to identify the theme and differentiate it from the topic. *(You don't have to be big to be able to help. The topic is two bear cubs getting lost and found. The theme is the lesson readers learn from reading or watching the play.)*
- Then read the last question on Teaching Pal page 356. Discuss how this play's theme compares to that of *Gigi and the Wishing Ring*. *(They both get into trouble when they don't follow the warning of someone older and wiser.)*
- Refer back to the Anchor Chart to support the discussion. Students may add sticky notes to the chart to note other examples of support for the theme they identify in *Two Bear Cubs*.

Step 3 Engage and Respond

INDEPENDENT PRACTICE: Writing

- Have students work in pairs to draft or outline a new version of the story. Explain that their new story should have the same characters but share a different theme or lesson. Use the **WRITING RESPONSE** routine.
- Have partners discuss possible themes and how their story could reveal it. Students may find it helpful to fill in a story map or other graphic organizer to plot out their story.
- Invite volunteers to share their stories with the class or with small groups.
- You may wish to have students complete the writing activity during daily small-group time.
- You may wish to have students complete the Know It, Show It page 98 during daily small-group time.

ENGLISH LEARNER SUPPORT: Facilitate Discussion

SUBSTANTIAL

Is the story about fishing or getting lost? Do the animals learn a lesson?

MODERATE

What is the story about? What lesson do the animals learn?

LIGHT

How do the animals change their thinking? What is the play's theme?

LINK TO SMALL-GROUP INSTRUCTION

REINFORCE THEME Review and extend the skill as needed during small-group time to support students' need for differentiation. *See the lesson on p. T369.*

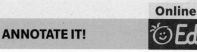

Options for Differentiation

As the class engages in independent and collaborative work, meet with Guided Reading Groups or differentiate instruction based on student need.

GUIDED READING GROUPS

Match Students to Books + Instruction

- Choose just-right books based on level, skill, topic, or genre.

L M N O P Q

Leveled Readers

- Deliver instruction with each book's **Take and Teach Lesson**, choosing appropriate sessions based on need.

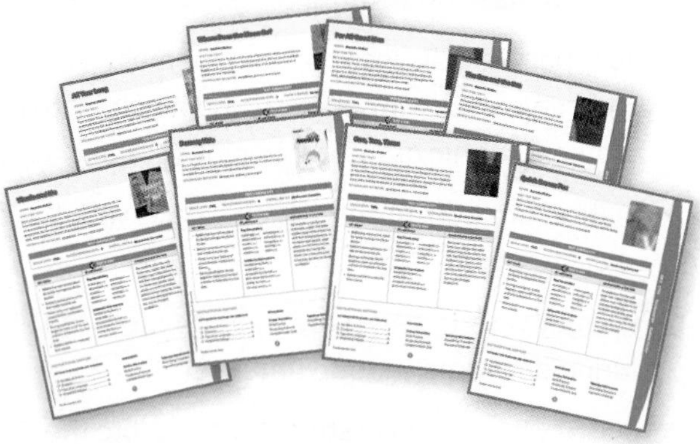

- Check comprehension, reinforce instruction, and extend learning with suggested supporting activities.

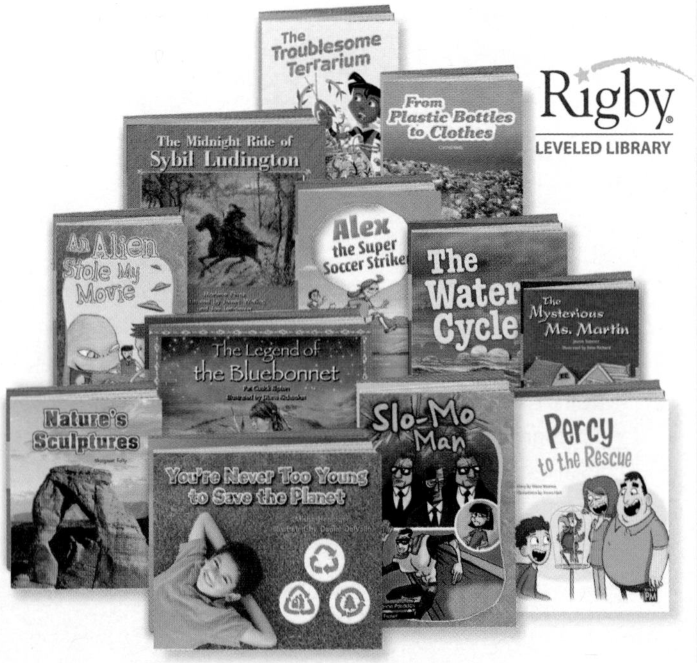

ENGLISH LEARNER SUPPORT

Cause and Effect

- Use **Tabletop Minilessons: English Language Development 12.2 (Writing)** to reinforce and practice the language skill.

Franco rolls around in the grass **because** his back is itchy. "Franco, now you are dirty," says Rumi. "This is a good **reason** for a bath." She scrubs him with soap and washes the soap off. Then Franco shakes and twists his body, **causing** the water to go all over Rumi. "Franco!" cries Rumi. "Now I am wet!"
Cause and Effect

Tabletop Minilessons: English Language Development

- Then use the following text-based prompts with *Two Bear Cubs* to guide application of the language skill. Begin with the prompt at the student's identified language proficiency level. As students progress, use lighter supports to encourage increased language proficiency.

SUBSTANTIAL

In paragraph 76 of Scene 3, Mother Grizzly says to the cubs, "Look at the trouble and worry you have caused us all!" Have students draw a label a picture that shows how the cubs caused trouble and worry.

MODERATE

Direct students to the last page of Scene 3. Have them write answers to the following questions using the frames: *Who caused trouble and worry? ______ caused trouble and worry. Whose help and courage caused the story to end well? The help and courage of ______ caused the story to end well.*

LIGHT

Direct students to Scene 3. Have them write answers to the following questions using complete sentences: *How did the two cubs cause trouble and worry? How did Measuring Worm's help affect the story's outcome?*

REINFORCE THEME

Demonstrate

- Use **Tabletop Minilessons: Reading Card 9** to remind students that the **topic** is who or what a drama is about, while the **theme** is the big idea, moral, or lesson in the drama.
- Model filling out Printable: Reading Graphic Organizer 9 to identify theme in *Gigi and the Wishing Ring*.

Apply to Independent Reading

- Now have students identify theme in an appropriate book or drama they are reading independently. Customize these prompts to the texts students choose.
  - » *What is the topic of the drama?*
  - » *Was the theme directly stated, or did you have to figure it out?*
  - » *What clues did you use to figure out the theme?*
- Have students complete Printable: Reading Graphic Organizer 9 for their independent reading book.

THEME
The theme is the main message, lesson, or moral of the text.
The theme can be stated in text. Fables and myths might tell the theme at the end.
The theme can be implied. Use text clues to figure it out.
What happens to the characters?
How do the characters react?
What do the characters learn?
ASK: What is the author trying to teach me
EXAMPLES
Be kind to others.
Friends are important.
Don't give up.
Two Bear Cubs

Tabletop Minilessons: Reading

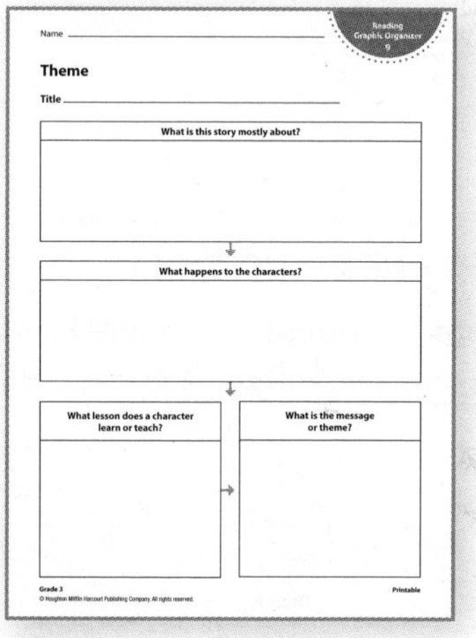
Theme
What is this story mostly about?
What happens to the characters?
What lesson does a character learn or teach?
What is the message or theme?

Printable: Reading Graphic Organizer 9

ALMOST THERE

READY FOR MORE

SCAFFOLD AND EXTEND

- Help students differentiate between topic and theme. Guide them to find both in their reading.
- Prompt students to identify the topic and theme, and explain how they identified both.
- Have students explain what differentiates topic from theme in general, and then state examples from their own reading.

EL ENGLISH LEARNER SUPPORT

SUBSTANTIAL

Ask *either/or* questions such as: *Is the topic ______ or ______? Is the theme ______ or ______?*

MODERATE

Guide students to identify topic and theme. Then use sentence frames: *The topic is ______. The theme is ______.*

LIGHT

Encourage students to elaborate on their answers to the questions.

Options for Independent and Collaborative Work

While you meet with small groups, have other students engage in literacy activities that reinforce the lesson's learning objectives. Choose from these options.

Independent Reading

Student Choice Library

Rigby
LEVELED LIBRARY

APPLY READING SKILL

Theme Students complete Printable: Reading Graphic Organizer 9 for an independent reading book.

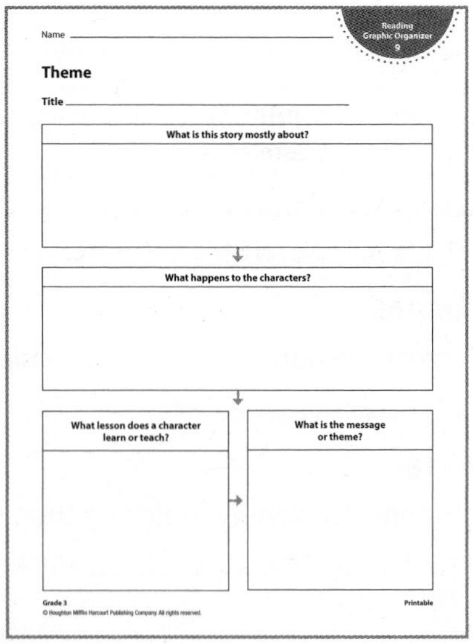
Name
Reading Graphic Organizer 9
Theme
Title
What is this story mostly about?
What happens to the characters?
What lesson does a character learn or teach?
What is the message or theme?
Grade 3
Printable

Printable: Reading Graphic Organizer 9

APPLY LANGUAGE SKILL

Cause and Effect Students complete Printable: Language Graphic Organizer 3 for an independent reading book.

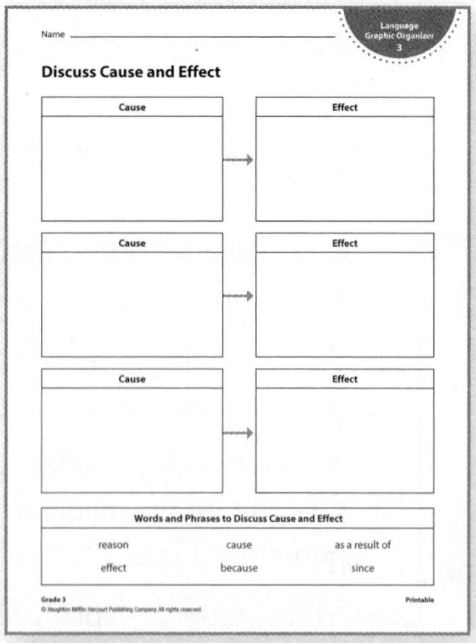
Name
Language Graphic Organizer 3
Discuss Cause and Effect

Cause	Effect

Words and Phrases to Discuss Cause and Effect		
reason	cause	as a result of
effect	because	since

Grade 3
Printable

Printable: Language Graphic Organizer 3

Literacy Centers

See pp. T330–T331.

- READING CENTER
- VOCABULARY CENTER
- DIGITAL STATION
- WRITING CENTER
- PROJECT CENTER

Writing

Partners draft a story outline. *See Engage and Respond, p. T367.*

Additional Skills Practice

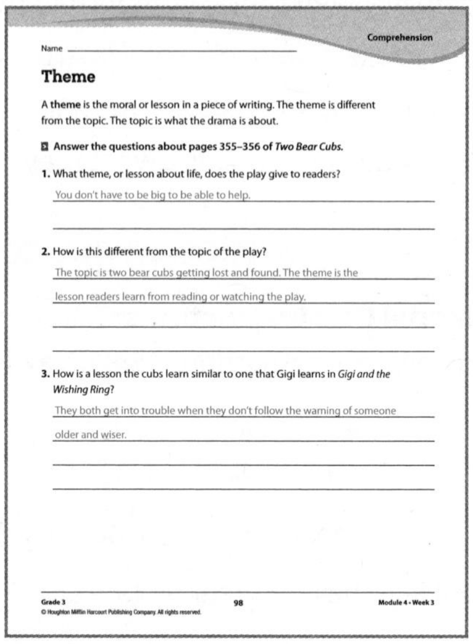
Name ______ Comprehension

Theme

A **theme** is the moral or lesson in a piece of writing. The theme is different from the topic. The topic is what the drama is about.

Answer the questions about pages 355–356 of *Two Bear Cubs*.

1. What theme, or lesson about life, does the play give to readers?
You don't have to be big to be able to help.

2. How is this different from the topic of the play?
The topic is two bear cubs getting lost and found. The theme is the lesson readers learn from reading or watching the play.

3. How is a lesson the cubs learn similar to one that Gigi learns in *Gigi and the Wishing Ring*?
They both get into trouble when they don't follow the warning of someone older and wiser.

Grade 3 98 Module 4 • Week 3
© Houghton Mifflin Harcourt Publishing Company. All rights reserved.

Know It, Show It, p. 98

Wrap-Up

Share Time

At the end of the Reading Workshop, have students reflect on their learning by sharing how they applied **theme** or another area of focus during independent work time. Choose from these options:

- Use the **SOLO CHAIR** routine. Select a reader each day to come to the front of the class and tell what he or she learned from the reading by using a skill or strategy.
- **THINK-PAIR-SHARE** Students share their thinking with a partner. Select a few pairs each day to share with the whole class.
- **RETURN TO ANCHOR CHART** Have students add sticky notes about their independent reading book to the Theme Anchor Chart. Call on a few students to explain what they added.

Online Ed

ANCHOR CHART 9: Theme

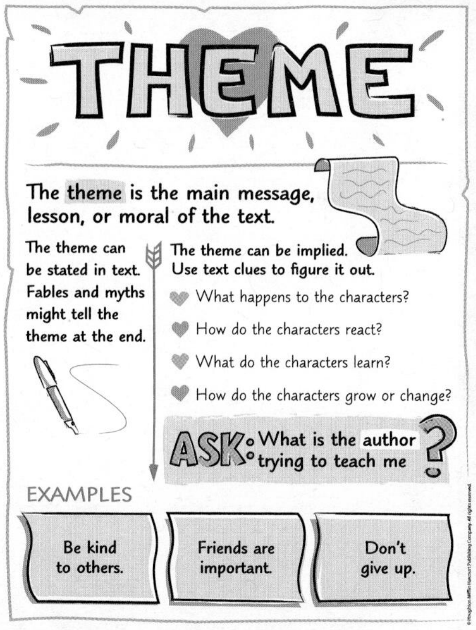
THEME
The theme is the main message, lesson, or moral of the text.
The theme can be stated in text. Fables and myths might tell the theme at the end.
The theme can be implied. Use text clues to figure it out.
What happens to the characters?
How do the characters react?
What do the characters learn?
How do the characters grow or change?
ASK: What is the author trying to teach me?
EXAMPLES
Be kind to others.
Friends are important.
Don't give up.

Oral Instructions

Step 1 Introduce the Skill

Explain Oral Instructions Explain that oral instructions are directions that are spoken. They give steps for how to make or do something.

- Display and review Anchor Chart 34: Following and Giving Instructions.
- Instructions include steps that must be followed in an orderly way.
- Speakers must give oral instructions simply, clearly, and slowly.
- Tell students that they must listen actively to oral instructions. They should restate, or say again, what they heard to clarify errors and help them remember.

Step 2 Guided Practice

Model Oral Instructions Tell students you will show them how to give and follow oral instructions. Set up a divider between you and a volunteer.

- On your side of the divider, draw a simple drawing on a piece of paper or make a simple six-block construction with different colored blocks.
- Model how to give instructions. Emphasize clear, simple steps in precise order.
- Help the volunteer restate and follow the instructions by modeling as needed.

Step 3 Apply the Skill

Give and Follow Oral Instructions Have partners give and follow instructions.

- Repeat the exercise with the divider and drawing or blocks. Have students take turns giving and following instructions.
- Monitor to make sure speakers are speaking clearly and logically, and followers are listening attentively and repeating what they hear,
- When students have finished, have them share what was easy and what was challenging about giving and following oral instructions.

LEARNING OBJECTIVES

- Follow oral instructions
- Write instructions.
- **Language** Use sequence words to write instructions.

MATERIALS Online Ed

Anchor Chart 34 *Following and Giving Instructions*

Printable *Anchor Chart 34: Following and Giving Instructions*

INSTRUCTIONAL VOCABULARY

- **instructions** directions for how to do something
- **sequence** an order of events (beginning, middle, end)

ENGLISH LEARNER SUPPORT: Develop Keywords

SUBSTANTIAL

Allow students to use gestures while giving instructions, as well as ordinal number sentence frames such as: *First _____. Second _____. Third _____.*

MODERATE

Provide students with a list of ordinal numbers (*first, second, third, fourth,* and so on), and have them use it to help them give instructions.

LIGHT

Monitor students as they give and follow instructions. Ask: *Did your instructions follow a logical order? Was there a clearer way you could have said that?*

Synthesize Topic Knowledge

Genre Focus

- Review with students the characteristics of a drama. Explain that a drama is written to be performed on stage. Key features include a cast of characters, dialogue, and stage directions. Like a story, a drama has characters, setting, and plot with a beginning, middle, and end. A drama may be divided into acts and scenes, which are like chapters in a book.
- Discuss with students that the selection, *Two Bear Cubs,* is an example of a drama.
- Ask students to name the features of a drama that appear in the selection, and how these features help them to understand the story and help them to picture it being performed on a stage.

LEARNING OBJECTIVES

- Recognize and describe the features of a drama.
- Synthesize knowledge gained from the week's texts.
- **Language** Articulate what has been learned about the essential question from their reading.

MATERIALS Online Ed

myBook *Book 1, pp. 300–301, 342–357*

Display and Engage *Knowledge Map 4.14*

Knowledge Focus

- Project Display and Engage: Knowledge Map 4.14. Have students turn to *my*Book page 305.
- Tell students to think about what makes *Two Bear Cubs* a good story to perform as a play. *(There are many different kinds of animal characters to play; The growing mountain would be interesting to show on the stage; There is a good message at the end.)*
- Then work with students to add information from *Two Bear Cubs* to the Knowledge Map.

Online Ed

DISPLAY AND ENGAGE:
Knowledge Map 4.14

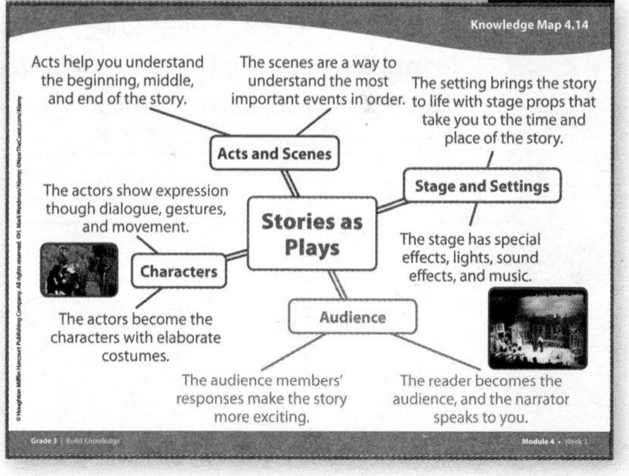

- Have students discuss their completed Knowledge Maps and synthesize what they learned by connecting it to the Essential Question: *Why might some stories be better told as plays?*

ENGLISH LEARNER SUPPORT: Facilitate Discussion

SUBSTANTIAL

Use these frames to help students to connect the reading to the Essential Question: *A play has* _____. Gigi and the Wishing Ring *also has* _____.

MODERATE

Prompt students to connect the reading to the Essential Question. Gigi and the Wishing Ring *is better performed as a play because* _____.

LIGHT

Ask students to connect the reading to the Essential Question. Ask: *What makes* Gigi and the Wishing Ring *a good story for a play?*

Synthesize Knowledge

Revisit Vocabulary Network and Knowledge Map

LEARNING OBJECTIVES

- Synthesize information from multiple selections.
- Discuss vocabulary about a topic.
- Evaluate and reflect on module selections.
- Make connections between and to module selections.
- **Language** Articulate ideas and opinions about module selections.

MATERIALS

Online Ed

myBook *Book 1, pp. 296–363*

Display and Engage *Knowledge Map 4.14*

Anchor Chart 8 *Synthesize*

Anchor Chart 30 *Make Connections*

Printables *Anchor Chart 8: Synthesize; Anchor Chart 30: Make Connections; Reading Graphic Organizer 8; Selection Review*

- Project or display Anchor Chart 8: Synthesize. Read it with students.
- Tell students that they will synthesize what they learned in *Stories on Stage*. Have students page through the selections in *my*Book Module 4.
- Next, have students revisit the vocabulary network they completed on *my*Book pages 298–299. Draw the web on the board or on chart paper, and invite volunteers to write words they added. Discuss how the words relate to dramas, or plays. Ask volunteers to use the words in oral sentences.
- Then have students turn to *my*Book pages 300–301 to review the knowledge map they built throughout the module. Project Display and Engage: Knowledge Map 4.14. Discuss with students the ideas and concepts in the knowledge map, and invite students to add ideas of their own.

Online Ed

ANCHOR CHART 8: Synthesize

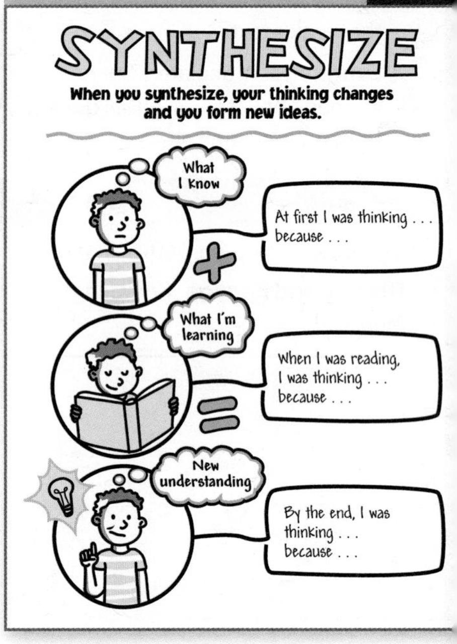
SYNTHESIZE
When you synthesize, your thinking changes and you form new ideas.
What I know
At first I was thinking . . . because . . .
What I'm learning
When I was reading, I was thinking . . . because . . .
New understanding
By the end, I was thinking . . . because . . .

Apply Module Knowledge

- Ask students to use Printable: Reading Graphic Organizer 8 to note evidence from the selections and information from the knowledge map as they discuss and respond to the questions below. Encourage students to use the vocabulary network entries in their responses.
  - » *What new information did you learn about dramas, or plays, in this module?*
  - » *How has this information changed your thinking about dramas?*
  - » *What else would you like to find out about the topic?*

ENGLISH LEARNER SUPPORT: Facilitate Discussion

SUBSTANTIAL

Use sentence frames such as *I learned that plays* _____. *I want to learn about* _____.

MODERATE

Use sentence frames such as *I read about* _____ *and learned that plays* _____. *I still want to know* _____.

LIGHT

Use sentence frames such as *I was surprised to learn that plays* _____. *This makes me want to find out* _____.

Make Connections

Reflect on Module Selections

- Project or display Anchor Chart 30: **Make Connections** or begin one of your own. Tell students that good readers find ways to make connections to the texts they read.

Online

ANCHOR CHART 30: Make Connections

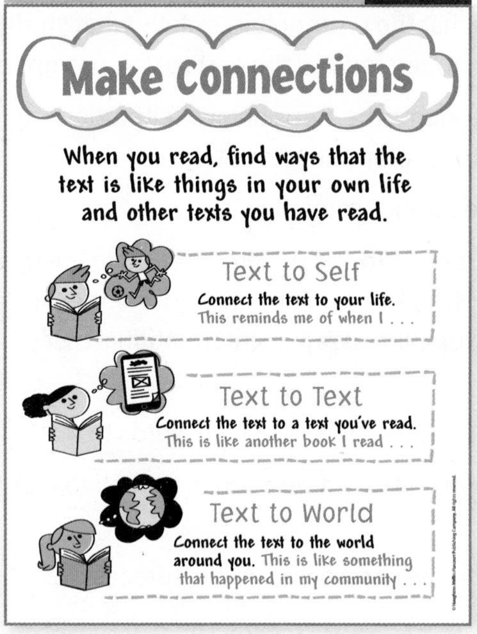

Make Connections
When you read, find ways that the text is like things in your own life and other texts you have read.
Text to Self
Connect the text to your life.
This reminds me of when I . . .
Text to Text
Connect the text to a text you've read.
This is like another book I read . . .
Text to World
Connect the text to the world around you. This is like something that happened in my community . . .

- As you point to the corresponding parts of the Anchor Chart, explain to students that they can connect what they read to their personal experiences, to ideas in other texts, and to society, or the world around them.
- Further the discussion by asking about specific connections. For example, ask *How were themes in each tale or story alike? How were they different?*
- Then have students turn to *my*Book pages 296–297. Read the module title, quote, and essential question aloud. Have students discuss the module as a whole, explaining how the selections they read connect to one another, as well as to the module topic, quote, and essential question.

Evaluate Module Selections

- Have students turn to the Table of Contents on *my*Book page 8. Ask students to rate each selection in Module 4, based on how much they enjoyed it, learned from it, or would recommend it to others.
- Have students mark each selection in the Table of Contents with 1–4 stars, based on these ratings: four stars = loved it, three stars = liked it, two stars = it was OK, and one star = did not like it.
- Have students turn to a partner and share their selection ratings.
- **Write a Review** Have students work independently to complete Printable: **Selection Review** to write a review of their favorite selection in this module.
- Point out and explain the section of the review where students will make connections to their favorite selection.

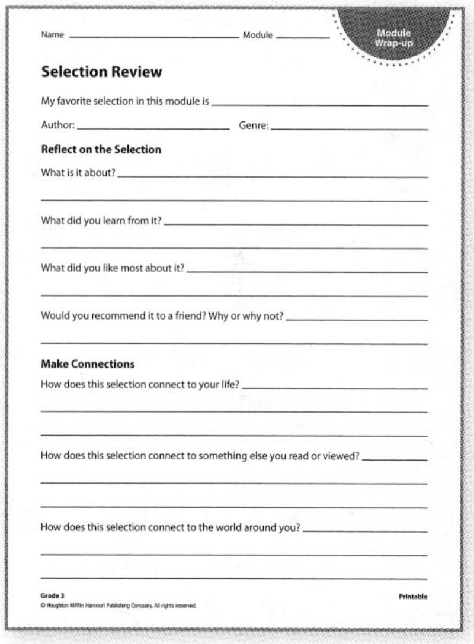
Name ______ Module ______
Module Wrap-up

Selection Review

My favorite selection in this module is ______

Author: ______ Genre: ______

Reflect on the Selection

What is it about? ______

What did you learn from it? ______

What did you like most about it? ______

Would you recommend it to a friend? Why or why not? ______

Make Connections

How does this selection connect to your life? ______

How does this selection connect to something else you read or viewed? ______

How does this selection connect to the world around you? ______

Grade 3 Printable

Printable: Selection Review

- **Discuss Reviews** Pair students who reviewed the same selection and students who reviewed different selections to discuss their reviews. What did they both like? Why is that selection their favorite? Can their partner be persuaded to like the other selection? Encourage students to state their opinions and offer reasons and support. Then gather the class to discuss overall results. Encourage volunteers to share their reviews with the class.

LEARNING MINDSET

Self-Reflection

Reflect Provide sentence frames to encourage students to tell about a time they reflected on their work in this module. *I looked back at my ____. When I looked back at my work, I noticed ____. I decided to ____.*

ENGLISH LEARNER SUPPORT: Elicit Participation

SUBSTANTIAL
Ask students to rate their favorite selection using these frames: *I liked ____. I gave this selection ____ stars. My favorite part was ____.*

MODERATE
Prompt students to use sentence frames to evaluate the selection. *This selection was my favorite/least favorite because ____.*

LIGHT
Have students share what they learned from their favorite selection. Provide sentence frames, such as *When I read ____, I learned ____.*

Performance Task

Step 1 Discuss Writing to a Prompt

LEARNING OBJECTIVES

- Learn and apply strategies for writing to a prompt.
- Write a story that includes key literary elements: character, setting, events, and plot, including a problem and solution.
- Gather ideas from sources to use in writing.
- Follow the steps of the writing process: plan, draft, revise and edit, and publish.
- **Language** Write a story, demonstrating an understanding of key literary elements.

MATERIALS Online Ed

Anchor Chart 37 *Cursive Handwriting*
Printable *Anchor Chart 37: Cursive Handwriting*
Teaching Pal *Book 1, pp. 360–363*
***my*Book** *Book 1, pp. 360–363*

INSTRUCTIONAL VOCABULARY

- **character** a person or animal in a story
- **event** something that happens in a story
- **plot** the conflict, events, and resolution that make up a story's structure
- **problem** something in a story that creates a challenge for the characters
- **setting** where and when a story takes place

- Point out the Prompt label on *my*Book page 360. Tell students that many writing tasks they will encounter begin with a prompt that explains the task.
- Tell students that the prompt tells exactly what students have to do and that it is important to understand all the parts of the prompt before beginning to write.
- Share with students the steps below. Tell students to follow these steps when responding to writing task prompts.
  1. Read the prompt carefully.
  2. Ask yourself, "What is the prompt asking me to do? What am I supposed to write?" Make sure you understand whether you are being asked to write a story, an opinion essay, an informational essay, or some other kind of writing.
  3. Restate the prompt in your own words to make sure you understand it.
  4. Decide which selection(s) you may need to look back at to use in your writing.
  5. Complete the parts of the writing process: plan, draft, revise and edit, and publish.
- Display and read aloud the prompt on *my*Book page 360. Use the Think Aloud below to model how to break apart the prompt and note key words in it.

THINK ALOUD *The first sentence of the prompt asks me to think about the problems and challenges that the characters faced in the texts I read. The next two sentences tell me to write a story that could be performed as a play. The story should be about a character who faces a problem or challenge.*

The next sentence tells me to use the texts and video for ideas about how the characters work out their problems. I will look back at the texts to see how the characters solve the challenges they face. I will think about this as I write my story.

ENGLISH LEARNER SUPPORT: Support Comprehension

SUBSTANTIAL
Have students work with more proficient peers. Tell them to highlight key words in the prompt and use their home language to clarify the task.

MODERATE
Provide sentence frames: *I will write a _____. It should tell about _____.*

LIGHT
Provide sentence frames: *I will write a _____ about _____. The character(s) will _____. At the end _____.*

Go to Your
Teaching Pal

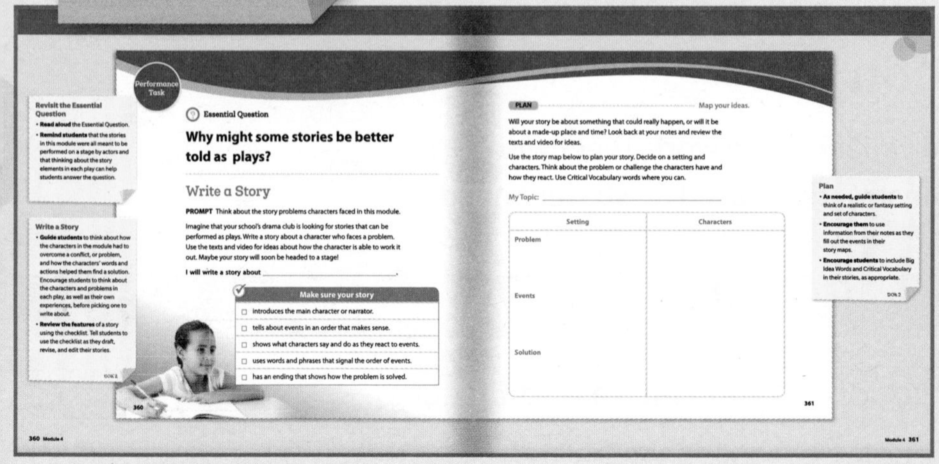

Revisit the Essential Question
- **Read aloud** the Essential Question.
- **Remind students** that the stories in this module were all meant to be performed on a stage by actors and that thinking about the story elements in each play can help students answer the question.

Write a Story
- **Guide students** to think about how the characters in the module had to overcome a conflict, or problem, and how the characters' words and actions helped them find a solution. Encourage students to think about the characters and problems in each play, as well as their own experiences, before picking one to write about.
- **Review the features** of a story using the checklist. Tell students to use the checklist as they draft, revise, and edit their stories.

DOK 2

Performance Task

Essential Question

Why might some stories be better told as plays?

Write a Story

PROMPT Think about the story problems characters faced in this module.

Imagine that your school's drama club is looking for stories that can be performed as plays. Write a story about a character who faces a problem. Use the texts and video for ideas about how the character is able to work it out. Maybe your story will soon be headed to a stage!

I will write a story about ______________.

Make sure your story
- ☐ introduces the main character or narrator.
- ☐ tells about events in an order that makes sense.
- ☐ shows what characters say and do as they react to events.
- ☐ uses words and phrases that signal the order of events.
- ☐ has an ending that shows how the problem is solved.

360

360 Module 4

PLAN — Map your ideas.

Will your story be about something that could really happen, or will it be about a made-up place and time? Look back at your notes and review the texts and video for ideas.

Use the story map below to plan your story. Decide on a setting and characters. Think about the problem or challenge the characters have and how they react. Use Critical Vocabulary words where you can.

My Topic: ______________

Setting	Characters
Problem	
Events	
Solution	

361

Plan
- **As needed, guide students** to think of a realistic or fantasy setting and set of characters.
- **Encourage them** to use information from their notes as they fill out the events in their story maps.
- **Encourage students** to include Big Idea Words and Critical Vocabulary in their stories, as appropriate.

DOK 2

Module 4 361

Online

ANNOTATE IT!

Students may use the annotation tools in their eBook.

Step 2 Apply

WRITING PROCESS

In your **Teaching Pal**, use the yellow prompts to guide students as they complete the steps of the writing process.

- Read through the checklist on page 360 with students. Tell them that as they write, they should return to this checklist to make sure their story reflects everything in it.
- Before filling in their story map for the Plan step, tell students to think about the genre of their story. Will it be realistic fiction, with characters and events that could be real, or fantasy, with a made-up place and time? Point out that the answer to that question will help students plan their stories and make decisions about the characters, setting, and plot. Remind students that the information they write in their story map should be a detailed plan for their story.
- As students draft their stories, tell them to introduce the characters and the problem at the beginning of the story. Tell students to write the events in a clear order. Remind them that in the middle of the story, the characters' words and actions should show how they work through the problem.
- For the ending, pose these questions: *How do the characters finally solve their problem? What do the characters say and do that shows they have solved the problem?*
- Review the rubric on page 363 with students. As partners confer to revise and edit, remind them to listen to each other's comments carefully and to find one positive thing to say about their partner's work before offering suggestions for improvement.
- Have students use the rubric to self-evaluate their work.

Step 3 Publish

- After students have created a final copy, discuss each method of sharing the story. Ask students which one they would prefer and why. Then offer these additional options.
- Create a comic strip of the story.
- Include the story in a classroom anthology of stories.
- Display and Review Anchor Chart 37: Cursive Handwriting.

ENGLISH LEARNER SUPPORT: Scaffold Writing

SUBSTANTIAL

Have students talk through story ideas. Allow them to draw and/or use their home language as they plan with you or more proficient peers.

MODERATE

Ask questions to help students plan: *Who are the characters? Where are they? What is the problem? How do they solve the problem? How does the story end?*

LIGHT

Encourage students to plan for dialogue that shows how characters solve the problem. Review how to correctly punctuate dialogue.

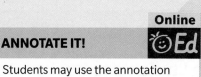

Options for Differentiation

As the class engages in independent and collaborative work, meet with Guided Reading Groups or differentiate instruction based on student need.

GUIDED READING GROUPS

Match Students to Books + Instruction

- Choose just-right books based on level, skill, topic, or genre.

L M N O P Q

Leveled Readers

- Deliver instruction with each book's **Take and Teach Lesson**, choosing appropriate sessions based on need.

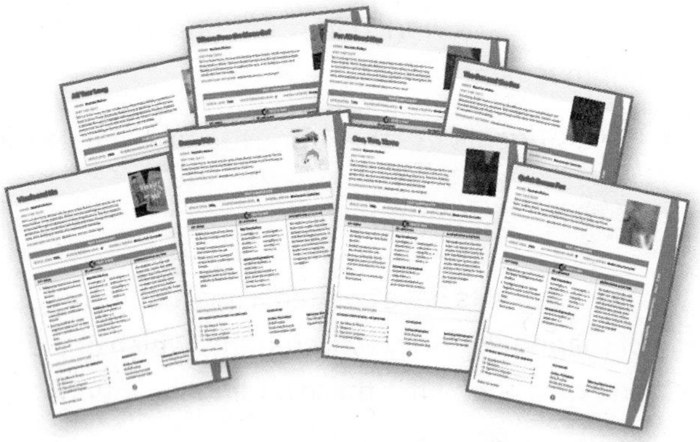

- Check comprehension, reinforce instruction, and extend learning with suggested supporting activities.

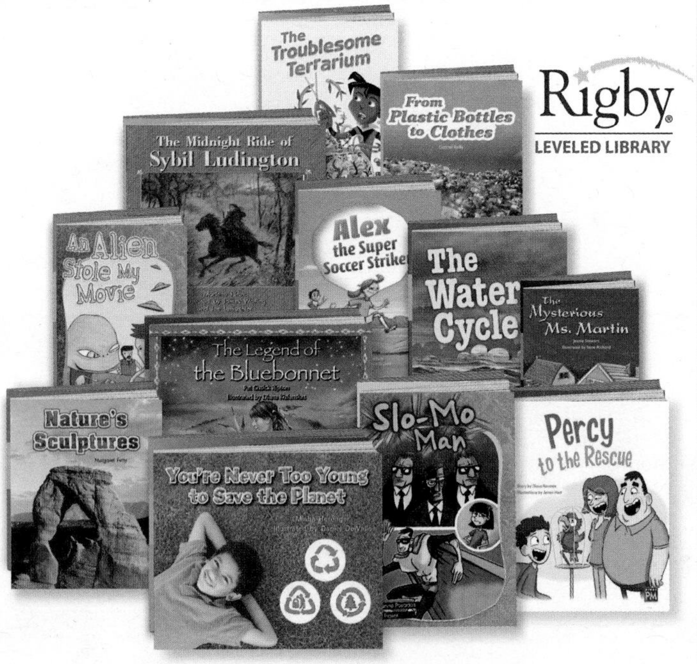

ENGLISH LEARNER SUPPORT

Cause and Effect

- Use **Tabletop Minilessons: English Language Development 12.3 (Collaborative Problem Solving)** to reinforce and practice the language skill.

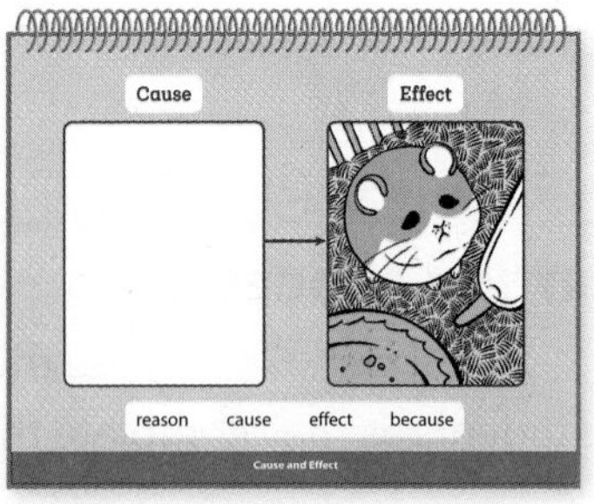

Tabletop Minilessons: English Language Development

- Then use the following prompts to guide application of the language skill to students' understanding of the module topic. Begin with the prompt at the student's identified language proficiency level. As students progress, use lighter supports to encourage increased language proficiency.

SUBSTANTIAL
Have students fold a piece of paper in half and label the two sides *Cause* and *Effect*. Ask them to illustrate a cause-and-effect scenario, and then share it with the group.

MODERATE
Guide students to fill in a cause-and-effect chart for a cause-and-effect scenario. Then have them explain it to a partner using sentence frames such as: _____ *caused* _____. *The effect of* _____ *was* _____.

LIGHT
Encourage partners to use the words *cause* and *effect* to discuss a cause-and-effect scenario.

Options for Independent and Collaborative Work

While you meet with small groups, have other students engage in literacy activities that reinforce the lesson's learning objectives. Choose from these options.

Independent Reading

Student Choice Library

Rigby
LEVELED LIBRARY

APPLY READING SKILL

Synthesize Students complete Printable: Reading Graphic Organizer 8 for an independent reading book.

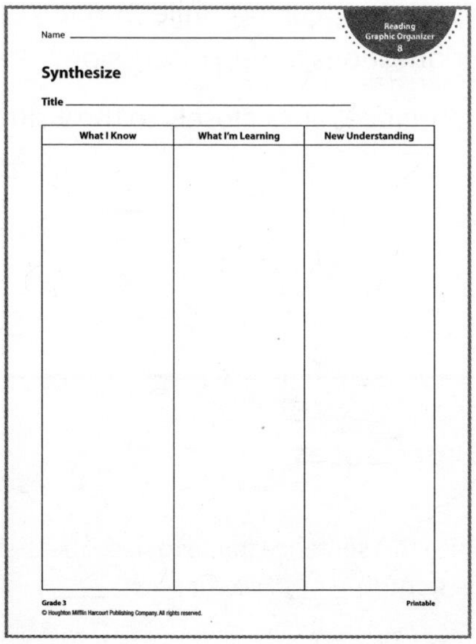

Name
Reading Graphic Organizer 8

Synthesize

Title

What I Know	What I'm Learning	New Understanding

Grade 3
© Houghton Mifflin Harcourt Publishing Company. All rights reserved.
Printable

Printable: Reading Graphic Organizer 8

APPLY LANGUAGE SKILL

Cause and Effect Students complete Printable: Language Graphic Organizer 3 for an independent reading book.

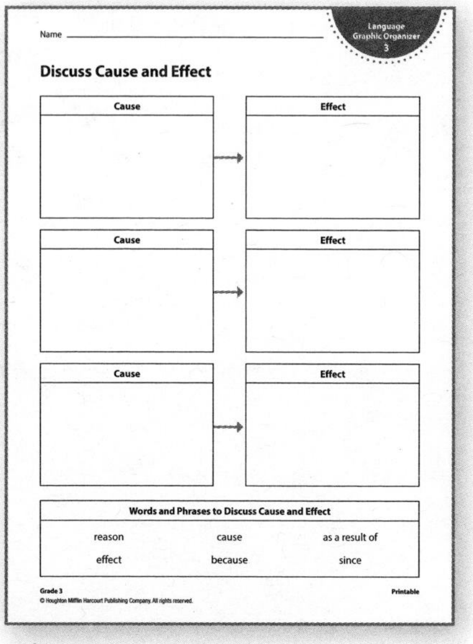

Name
Language Graphic Organizer 3

Discuss Cause and Effect

Cause	Effect

Cause	Effect

Cause	Effect

Words and Phrases to Discuss Cause and Effect		
reason	cause	as a result of
effect	because	since

Grade 3
© Houghton Mifflin Harcourt Publishing Company. All rights reserved.
Printable

Printable: Language Graphic Organizer 3

Write a Play

Practice and Present

Prepare and Rehearse Allow students time to organize their presentation materials and rehearse their roles with their groups.

Deliver Presentations Give each group a designated timeframe in which to present their projects. You may want to invite family members and other students.

- Remind audience members to listen attentively and be polite to the presenters. Encourage listeners to take notes and to ask questions at the end.
- Briefly discuss each presentation. Provide feedback questions such as these: *What did this group do well? What might your group have done differently?*

Reflect and Celebrate Establish a time for students to reflect on the project and on what they've learned, and to celebrate their achievements.

- After the groups have presented, have students discuss as a whole class what they learned about plays.
- Have each student write a sentence or two about their favorite part of the project and what they learned from it.
- You may want to compile each group's script into a folder or portfolio for the class to keep and share.

Assess

- ☑ **Speaking and Listening** Do students speak clearly and with emotion appropriate to the scene? Do students demonstrate active listening skills? Do students work collaboratively?
- ☑ **Writing** Are students' scripts complete and accurate summaries of the traditional story they are retelling? Do they appeal to an appropriate audience?
- ☑ **Collaboration** Do students take turns speaking while working on their project? Do they ask and answer questions during discussion?
- ☑ **Presentation** Do student performances stick closely to the written script?

LEARNING OBJECTIVES

- Present a project.
- Listen actively and provide feedback during discussion.
- Self-assess project work using a rubric.
- **Language** Have students react to presentations.

MATERIALS — Online Ed

Printable *Project 4.3 Project Rubric*

Classroom materials

research notes and project materials

copies of play

pen or pencil

prop and costumes, if desired

SUGGESTED PACING

Students worked on their projects in groups during Small Group or during a designated time for project work, using the pacing below as a general guide.

WEEK 1 Introduce and Research

WEEK 2 Write and Create

WEEK 3 Practice and Present/Assess

ENGLISH LEARNER SUPPORT: Describe Experiences

SUBSTANTIAL

Have students finish this sentence frame to describe their experience: *This group told the story of _____. I liked it when _____.*

MODERATE

Have audience members generate original language to summarize the beginning, middle, and end of the play they just watched.

LIGHT

Ask students to tell how this play is different from the version of the story they have heard before.

Resources

Online Ed

FIND ADDITIONAL RESOURCES

Scope and Sequence

Word Lists

- Big Idea Words, Critical Vocabulary, Instructional Vocabulary
- High-Frequency Words

Glossary of Professional Terms

Differentiated Spelling Instruction: Placement Support and Differentiated Lists

Language Differences

- Alphabet
- Phonological Differences
- Grammatical Differences

Professional Learning

Access these professional resources to learn more about the research foundations for *Into Reading.*

Armbruster, Bonnie B., Fran Lehr, and Jean Osborn. *Put Reading First: The Research Building Blocks for Teaching Children to Read: Kindergarten Through Grade 3*, Edited by C. Ralph Adler. Maryland: National Institute for Literacy at ED Pubs, 2001.

Beck, Isabel. L., Margaret. G. McKeown and Linda Kucan. *Bringing Words to Life: Robust Vocabulary Instruction*. Guilford Press, 2013.

Blachowicz, Camille L. Z., and Peter Fisher. "Vocabulary Lessons." *Educational Leadership* 61, no. 6 (2004): 66–69.

Darling-Hammond, Linda. (2014). *Next Generation Assessment: Moving Beyond the Bubble Test to Support 21st Century Learning*, Chapter 1. John Wiley & Sons.

Darling-Hammond, Linda, Brigid Barron, P. David Pearson, Alan H. Schoenfeld, Elizabeth. K Stage, Timothy D. Zimmerman, Gina N. Cervetti, and Jennifer. L. Tilson *Powerful Learning: What We Know About Teaching for Understanding*. John Wiley & Sons, 2015.

Ehri, Linnea C., and Julie Rosenthal. "The Spellings of Words: A Neglected Facilitator of Vocabulary Learning." *Journal of Literacy Research* 39, no. 4 (2007): 389–409.

Fisher, Douglas, and Nancy Frey. *Better Learning Through Structured Teaching: A Framework for the Gradual Release of Responsibility*. 2nd ed. Virginia: ASCD, 2014.

Fisher, Douglas. and Nancy Frey. "Content Area Vocabulary Learning." *The Reading Teacher,* 67, no.8 (2014): 594–599.

Graham, Steve, and Michael Hebert. "Writing to Read: A Meta-Analysis of the Impact of Writing and Writing Instruction on Reading." *Harvard Educational Review* 81, no. 4 (2011): 710–744.

Green, Tamara. M. *The Greek & Latin Roots of English*. Rowman & Littlefield, 2014.

Lyster, Roy, Kazuya Saito, and Masatoshi Sato. "Oral Corrective Feedback in Second Language Classrooms." *Language Teaching* 46, no. 1 (2013): 1–40.

Ness, Molly. K. "Reading comprehension strategies in secondary content area classrooms: Teacher use of and attitudes towards reading comprehension instruction." *Reading Horizons*, 55, no.1 (2016): 58–84.

Neuman, Susan B., Tanya Kaefer, and Ashley Pinkham. "Building Background Knowledge." *The Reading Teacher* 68, no. 2 (2014): 145–148.

Partnership for Assessment of Readiness for College and Careers. *PARCC model content frameworks: English language arts/literacy grades 3–11*. 2011. Retrieved from www.parcconline.org/sites/parcc/files/PARCCMCFELALiteracyAugust2012_FINAL.pdf

Xiaoyan, L. "A reflection on morphology and generative vocabulary." *Business* 21 (2014): 301.

Credits

Module 3

iv (tl) ©Heinemann Educational Publishing; iv (tcl) ©Anthony Rathbun/Houghton Mifflin Harcourt; iv (cl) ©George Brainard/ Houghton Mifflin Harcourt; iv (bcl) ©Josh Edelson/Houghton Mifflin Harcourt; iv (bl) ©Danny Moloshok/Houghton Mifflin Harcourt; iv (tr) ©Andrew Collings Photography; iv (tcr) ©Kellie Henricksen; iv (cr) ©Heinemann Educational Publishing; iv (bcr) ©Tom Smedes/ Houghton Mifflin Harcourt; iv (br) ©John Amis/Houghton Mifflin Harcourt; v (cl) ©Andres Leighton/Houghton Mifflin Harcourt; v (tr) ©Scott Eisen/Houghton Mifflin Harcourt; v (tl) ©F. Isabel Campoy; v (tcr) ©Jill Eggleton QSO; v (tcl) ©Josh Edelson/Houghton Mifflin Harcourt; xiii (br) ©Heinemann Educational Publishing; xiii (br) ©Heinemann Educational Publishing; xvi hands (bl) ©WAYHOME studio/Shutterstock; xvi ipad (bl) ©Alexey Boldin/Shutterstock; xvii (br) ©michaeljung/Shutterstock; xxiii (cl) ©image 100/Corbis; xxxvi ©Donald Iain Smith/Moment/Getty Images; xxxvii ©Erik Isakson/ Getty Images; T1 people looking up ©Joel Carillet/iStock/Getty Images Plus/Getty Images, fireworks ©Bailey-Cooper Photography/ Alamy; T4 ©Songquan Deng/Shutterstock, ©Michael Steden/ Shutterstock; T6 ©Songquan Deng/Shutterstock, ©Michael Steden/Shutterstock; T8 (tcr) ©Steve Debenport/Getty Images; T8 (tcl) ©monkeybusinessimages/iStockphoto/Getty Images; T8 (bcl) ©Christopher Futcher/Getty Images; T8 (bcr) ©Jupiterimages/ Banana Stock/Alamy; T9 (br) ©Houghton Mifflin Harcourt; T10 (tcl) ©Monkey Business Images/Shutterstock; T10 (tcr) ©Alamy; T10 (bcr) ©Darrin Henry/Shutterstock; T10 (bcl) ©Alamy; T11 (br) ©Syda Productions/Shutterstock; T15 (cr) ©Ron Thomas/iStock/ Getty Images; T21 people looking up ©Joel Carillet/iStock/Getty Images Plus/Getty Images, fireworks ©Bailey-Cooper Photography/ Alamy; T21 (bl) ©Ron Thomas/iStock/Getty Images; T28 ©Songquan Deng/Shutterstock, ©Michael Steden/Shutterstock; T49 (tr) ©Ron Thomas/iStock/Getty Images; T81 people looking up ©Joel Carillet/iStock/Getty Images Plus/Getty Images, fireworks ©Bailey-Cooper Photography/Alamy; T137 people looking up ©Joel Carillet/iStock/Getty Images Plus/Getty Images, fireworks ©Bailey-Cooper Photography/Alamy; ipad with screenshot (all) ©MrAesthetics/Shutterstock; learning mindset head outline (all) ©Carla Francesca Castagno/Dreamstime

Module 4

iv (tl) ©Heinemann Educational Publishing; iv (tcl) ©Anthony Rathbun/Houghton Mifflin Harcourt; iv (cl) ©George Brainard/ Houghton Mifflin Harcourt; iv (bcl) ©Josh Edelson/Houghton Mifflin Harcourt; iv (bl) ©Danny Moloshok/Houghton Mifflin Harcourt; iv (tr) ©Andrew Collings Photography; iv (tcr) ©Kellie Henricksen; iv (cr) ©Heinemann Educational Publishing; iv (bcr) ©Tom Smedes/ Houghton Mifflin Harcourt; iv (br) ©John Amis/Houghton Mifflin Harcourt; v (cl) ©Andres Leighton/Houghton Mifflin Harcourt; v (tr) ©Scott Eisen/Houghton Mifflin Harcourt; v (tl) ©F. Isabel Campoy; v (tcr) ©Jill Eggleton QSO; v (tcl) ©Josh Edelson/Houghton Mifflin Harcourt; xiii (br) ©Heinemann Educational Publishing; xiii (br) ©Heinemann Educational Publishing; xvi hands (bl) ©WAYHOME studio/Shutterstock; xvi ipad (bl) ©Alexey Boldin/Shutterstock; xvii (br) ©michaeljung/Shutterstock; xxiii (cl) ©image 100/Corbis; xxxvi ©Donald Iain Smith/Moment/Getty Images; xxxvii ©Erik Isakson/Getty Images; T191 ballerina looking down ©Marco Kesseler/Alamy, mouse costume ©aerogondo/Adobe Stock; T194 (tr) ©Stanislav Rishnyak/Alamy; T196 (tl) ©Stanislav Rishnyak/ Alamy; T198 (tcr) ©Steve Debenport/Getty Images; T198 (tcl) ©monkeybusinessimages/iStockphoto/Getty Images; T198 (bcl) ©Christopher Futcher/Getty Images; T198 (bcr) ©Jupiterimages/ Banana Stock/Alamy; T199 (br) ©Houghton Mifflin Harcourt; T200 (tcl) ©Monkey Business Images/Shutterstock; T200 (tcr) ©Alamy; T200 (bcr) ©Darrin Henry/Shutterstock; T200 (bcl) ©Alamy; T201 (br) ©Syda Productions/Shutterstock; T211 (bl) ©Narcis Parfenti/ Shutterstock; T211 ballerina looking down ©Marco Kesseler/Alamy, mouse costume ©aerogondo/Adobe Stock; T218 (b) ©Stanislav Rishnyak/Alamy; T239 (tr) ©Narcis Parfenti/Shutterstock; T271 ballerina looking down ©Marco Kesseler/Alamy, mouse costume ©aerogondo/Adobe Stock; T327 ballerina looking down ©Marco Kesseler/Alamy, mouse costume ©aerogondo/Adobe Stock; ipad with screenshot (all) ©MrAesthetics/Shutterstock; learning mindset head outline (all) ©Carla Francesca Castagno/Dreamstime

Acknowledgments

"The Lion King's Friend" by Barbara Hall from Appleseeds magazine, 2005. Text copyright © 2005 by Cricket Media. Reprinted by permission of Cricket Media. All Cricket Media material is copyrighted by Carus Publishing d/b/a Cricket Media, and/or various authors and illustrators. Any commercial use or distribution of material without permission is strictly prohibited. Please visit http://www.cricketmedia.com/info/licensing2 for licensing and http://www.cricketmedia.com for subscriptions.

"Patriotic Tunes" by Kathiann M. Kowalski from Cobblestone magazine, 2013. Text copyright © 2013 by Cricket Media. Reprinted by permission of Cricket Media. All Cricket Media material is copyrighted by Carus Publishing d/b/a Cricket Media, and/or various authors and illustrators. Any commercial use or distribution of material without permission is strictly prohibited. Please visit http://www.cricketmedia.com/info/licensing2 for licensing and http://www.cricketmedia.com for subscriptions.

Handwriting

Individual students have various levels of handwriting skills, but they all have the desire to communicate effectively. To write correctly, they must be familiar with concepts of

- directionality (top-to-bottom and left-to-right)
- size (tall, short)
- open and closed letters
- capital and lowercase letters
- manuscript vs. cursive letters
- letter and word spacing
- punctuation

Explain Stroke and Letter Formation

Tell students that most manuscript letters are formed with a continuous stroke, so students will not often pick up their pencils when writing a single letter. Explain that when they begin to use cursive handwriting, students will have to lift their pencils from the paper less frequently and will be able to write more fluently. Provide students with a copy of the manuscript and cursive handwriting models on pages R6–R8 for future reference.

Teach Writing Position

Establishing the correct posture, pen or pencil grip, and paper position for writing will help prevent handwriting problems.

Posture Tell students to sit with both feet on the floor and with hips to the back of the chair. They can lean forward slightly but should not slouch. Ask them to make sure their writing surface is smooth and flat. It should be at a height that allows their upper arms to be perpendicular to the surface and their elbows to be under their shoulders.

Reinforce Directionality

Confirm that students understand directionality: regardless of whether the print or write in cursive, they must work from left to right and top to bottom.

Writing Instrument Have students use an adult-sized number-two lead pencil for their writing assignments. Explain that as they become proficient in the use of cursive handwriting, they can use pens to write final drafts.

Paper Position and Pencil Grip Explain to students that as they write in cursive, the position of the paper plays an important role. The paper should be slanted along the line of the student's writing arm, and the student should use his or her nonwriting hand to hold the paper in place. Tell them to hold their pencils or pens about one inch from the tip.

Then ask students to assume their writing position. Check each student's position, providing adjustments as necessary.

Develop Handwriting

The best instruction builds on what students already know and can do. Given the wide range in students' handwriting abilities, a variety of approaches may be needed. Use the following activities as you choose to provide regular handwriting practice to students of all proficiency levels.

Online
Ed
ANCHOR CHART 37:
Cursive Handwriting
Cursive Handwriting
In cursive handwriting, the letters in each word are connected.
This is cursive handwriting.
Practice connecting the letters. Be sure the connecting lines are not too short or too long.
Look at my cursive writing!
a b c d e f g
Think about the size and shape of each letter. Practice forming each letter neatly and correctly.

Write in Cursive Project or display Anchor Chart 37: Cursive Handwriting. Point out the characteristics of cursive writing and the differences from the manuscript alphabet, as needed. Then duplicate for each student the model of the cursive alphabet on page R6. Have students trace each lowercase and uppercase letter. Then have students write each letter in both lowercase and uppercase on a separate sheet of lined paper.

Slant Letters Correctly Tell students that most cursive letters slant very slightly to the right. Have them practice writing the lowercase alphabet. Tell them to check that they have slanted their letters correctly by drawing a faint vertical line through the middle of each letter. If they have correctly slanted each letter, the lines will all be parallel to each other.

Letter Spacing Explain to students that when writing in cursive, they should leave an equal amount of space between each letter in a word. Tell students that if they leave too little or too much space between letters, their writing will be difficult to read. Write the following words on the board and have students write them on a sheet of lined paper: *batch*, *reject*, *vanish*, *sloppy*, *rhythm*.

Word Spacing Tell students that it is important to leave the correct amount of space between each word in a sentence. Tell students to leave a space about the width of a pencil between words. Demonstrate how to do this. Then have students practice letter and word spacing by writing phrases that describe the weather, such as *hot and dry*.

Join Uppercase and Lowercase Letters Tell students that when writing most proper nouns in cursive, they must join an uppercase and a lowercase letter. Have students practice joining uppercase and lowercase letters by writing the following state names: *Alabama, California, Florida, New York*. Then explain that some uppercase letters, such as *D, P, T, V,* and *W,* do not join with a lowercase letter. Have students practice writing the following proper nouns, making sure not to join the first and second letter: *Dallas, Phoenix, Texas, Virginia, Washington.*

Answer Questions Have students practice writing sentences by answering "how" questions about things they see and do on a daily basis. For example, you might ask, *How do you get to school?* Tell students to write their answers in complete sentences and use their best cursive writing.

Write Sentences Have students write five original sentences about their daily routines. Remind them to slant their letters correctly and to leave the correct amount of space between the letters in each word and between the words in a sentence. Have them trade papers with a classmate and give feedback on the legibility of their partner's cursive writing.

Write a Paragraph Have students write an original paragraph about a favorite book, sport, or other activity. Remind them to use the correct posture for writing, paying special attention to leaving appropriate spacing between letters in a word and between words in a sentence.

Assess Handwriting

To assess students' handwriting skills, review samples of their written work. Note whether they use correct letter formation and appropriate size and spacing. Note whether students follow the conventions of print, such as correct capitalization and punctuation. When writing messages, notes, and letters, or when publishing their writing, students should write legibly in cursive, leaving appropriate spacing between letters and words to make the work readable for their audience.

HANDWRITING Cursive Alphabet

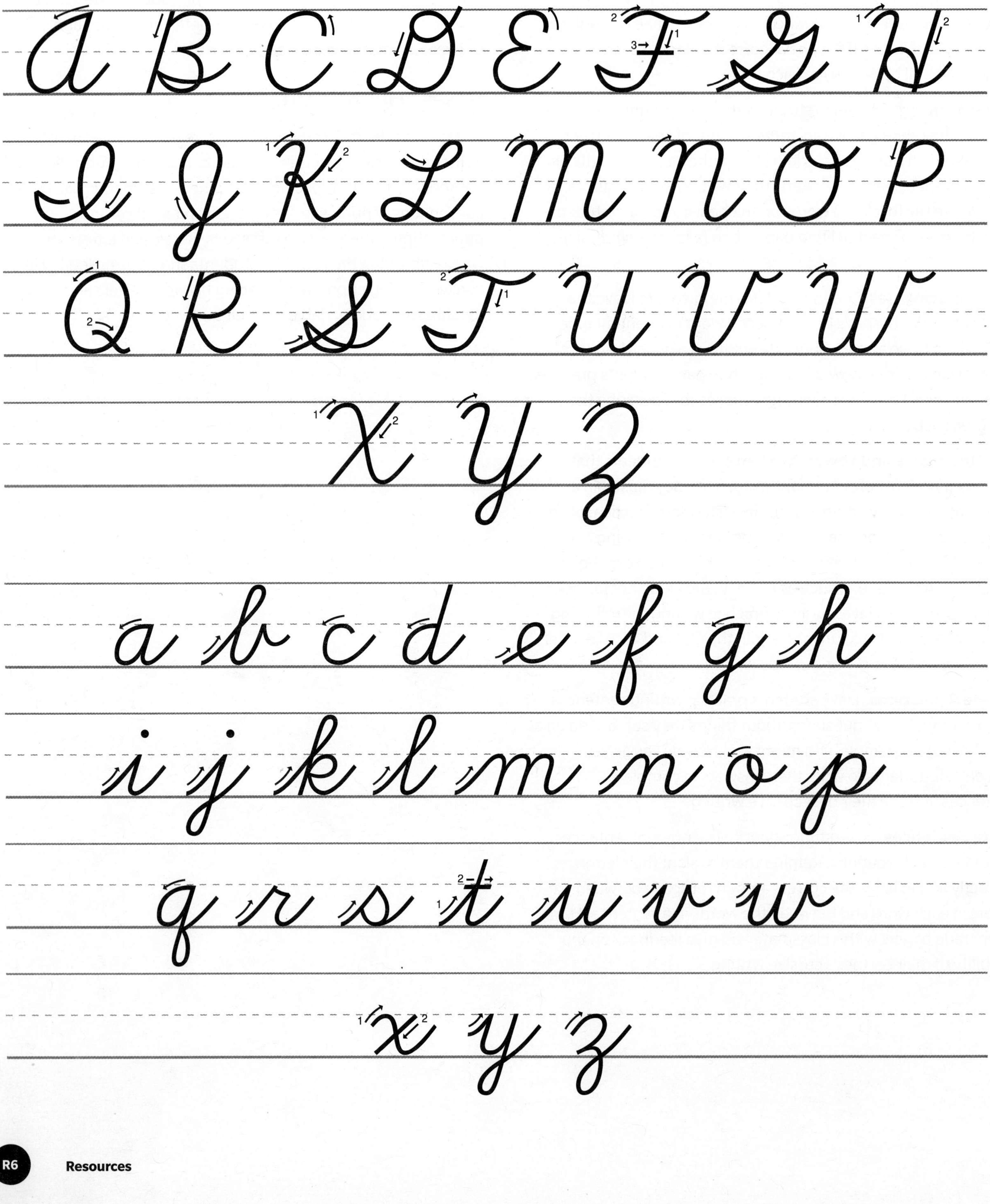

HANDWRITING Manuscript Alphabet

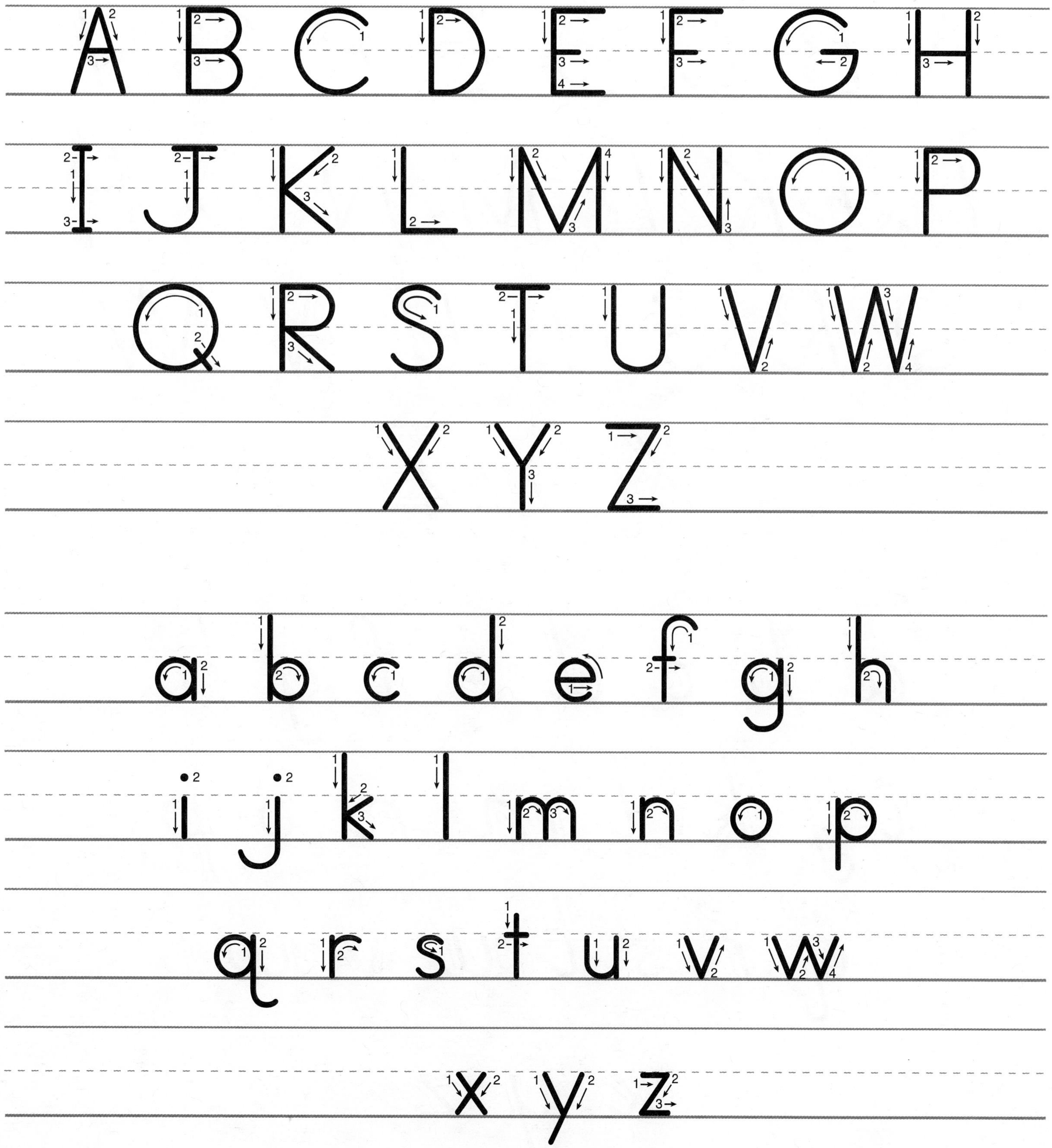

CONTINUOUS STROKE Manuscript Alphabet

Collaborative Discussion

SCORE of 2	• The student engages effectively in collaborative discussions, building on others' ideas and expressing her or his own clearly. • The student comes to discussions prepared, having read or studied required material. The student explicitly draws on that preparation and other information known about the topic to explore ideas under discussion. • The student follows agreed-upon rules for discussions and carries out assigned roles. • The student asks and answers questions to check understanding and clarify information and makes pertinent comments that contribute to the discussion and link to the remarks of others. • The student reviews the key ideas expressed and explains her or his own ideas and understanding in light of the discussion.
SCORE of 1	• The student somewhat engages in collaborative discussions, sometimes building on others' ideas and expressing her or his own. • The student comes to some discussions prepared, having read or studied required material. The student draws on that preparation and other information known about the topic to explore ideas under discussion. • The student mostly follows agreed-upon rules for discussions and carries out assigned roles with some prompting. • The student asks and answers some questions and may make comments that contribute to the discussion. • The student reviews the ideas expressed and sometimes explains her or his own ideas and understanding in light of the discussion.
SCORE of 0	• The student does not engage in discussions and does not build on others' ideas or express her or his own. • The student does not come to discussions prepared. • The student does not follow agreed-upon rules for discussions or carry out assigned roles. • The student does not pose or respond to questions to follow up on information or make comments that contribute to the conversation.

Response Writing

SCORE of 2	• Response provides a **complete and correct** explanation of, or answer to, the question. • Response includes clear and specific explanations, interpretations, and opinions of the text based on effective comprehension, inference, analysis, evaluation, and/or comparison. • Response is supported with details from the text.
SCORE of 1	• Response provides a **partially complete and correct** explanation of, or answer to, the question. • Response attempts to include explanations, interpretations, and opinions of the text, but they may be unclear or unsubstantiated, and they show limitation in comprehension, inference, analysis, evaluation, and/or comparison. • Response is supported with limited details (in quantity or quality) from the text.
SCORE of 0	• Response is incorrect, irrelevant, or not provided.

PERFORMANCE TASK • Narrative Writing

	SCORE				
	4	**3**	**2**	**1**	**NS**
PURPOSE/ORGANIZATION	The narrative is clear, focused, and well organized throughout. • Contains an effective and complete plot • Develops strong setting, narrator/characters • Includes a variety of transitions to connect ideas • Contains a logical sequence of events • Includes an effective introduction and conclusion	The narrative's organization is adequately maintained, and the focus is generally clear. • Plot is mostly effective/may contain small flaws • Develops setting, narrator/characters • Adequate use of transitions to connect ideas • Contains an adequate sequence of events • Includes adequate introduction and conclusion	The narrative is somewhat organized and may be unclear in some parts. Plot may be inconsistent. • Minimal development of setting, narrator/characters • Contains inconsistent use of transitions to connect ideas • Sequence of events is weak or unclear • Introduction and conclusion need improvement	The narrative's focus and organization are not clear. • Little or no plot • Little or no development of setting, narrator/characters • Contains few or inappropriate transitions and weak connections among ideas • Sequence of events is not organized • Introduction and/or conclusion may be missing	• not intelligible • not written in English • not on topic • contains text copied from source • does not address the purpose for writing
DEVELOPMENT/ELABORATION	The narrative includes effective elaboration using details, dialogue, and description. • Characters, setting, experiences, and events are well developed • Links to sources may enrich the narrative • Writer uses a variety of narrative techniques that strengthen the story or illustrate the experience • Contains effective sensory, concrete, and figurative language • Style is appropriate and effective	The narrative includes adequate elaboration using details, dialogue, and description. • Characters, setting, experiences, and events are adequately developed • Links to sources may contribute to the narrative • Writer uses a variety of narrative techniques that generally move the story forward and illustrate the experience • Contains adequate sensory, concrete, and figurative language • Style is mostly appropriate	The narrative includes partial or ineffective elaboration using unclear or inconsistent details, dialogue, and description. • Characters, setting, experiences, and events lack consistent development • Links to sources may be unsuccessful but do not detract from the narrative • Writer uses inconsistent or weak narrative techniques • Contains weak sensory, concrete, and figurative language • Style is inconsistent or inappropriate	The narrative provides little or no elaboration using few or no details, dialogue, and description. • Very little development of characters, setting, experiences, and events • Links to sources, if present, may interfere with the narrative • Writer's use of narrative techniques are minimal and may be incorrect • Little or no sensory, concrete, and figurative language • Little or no evidence of style	• not intelligible • not written in English • not on topic • contains text copied from source • does not address the purpose for writing

	2	**1**	**0**	**NS**
CONVENTIONS	The narrative demonstrates adequate command of conventions. • Consistent use of correct sentence structures, punctuation, capitalization, grammar, and spelling	The narrative demonstrates partial command of conventions. • Limited use of correct sentence structures, punctuation, capitalization, grammar, and spelling	The narrative demonstrates little or no command of conventions. • Rare use of correct sentence structures, punctuation, capitalization, grammar, and spelling	• not intelligible • not written in English • not on topic • contains text copied from source

PERFORMANCE TASK • Informative/Explanatory Writing

	SCORE				
	4	**3**	**2**	**1**	**NS**
PURPOSE/ORGANIZATION	The response is clear, focused, and well organized throughout. • Main or central idea is clear, focused, and effective for task, audience, and purpose • Includes a variety of transitions to relate ideas • Contains a logical sequence of ideas with strong relationships between them • Includes an effective introduction and conclusion	The response's organization is adequately maintained, and the focus is generally clear. • Main or central idea is clear, mostly focused, and mostly effective for task, audience, and purpose • Includes some variety of transitions to relate ideas • Contains an adequate sequence of ideas with adequate relationships between them • Includes an adequate introduction and conclusion	The response is somewhat focused but may be unclear in parts. Organization may be inconsistent. • Main or central idea may be somewhat unclear, lack focus, or be ineffective for task, audience, and purpose • Includes little variety of transitions to relate ideas • Sequence of ideas may be weak or unclear • Introduction and conclusion need improvement	The response's focus and organization are not clear. • Main or central idea may be confusing; response may be inappropriate for task, audience, and purpose • Includes few or no transitions to relate ideas • Sequence of ideas is unorganized; may include off-topic ideas • Introduction and/or conclusion may be missing	• not intelligible • not written in English • not on topic • contains text copied from source • does not address the purpose for writing
EVIDENCE/ELABORATION	The response presents strong support for the main and supporting ideas with effective use of evidence from sources, facts, and details, elaborating with specific and effective language. • Evidence from sources is integrated and relevant and supports key ideas • Writer uses a variety of elaborative techniques • Vocabulary is clear and appropriate for task, audience, and purpose • Style is appropriate and effective	The response presents adequate support for the main and supporting ideas with evidence from sources, facts, and details, adequately elaborating with a mix of specific and general language. • Evidence from sources is integrated and relevant and adequately supports key ideas • Writer uses some elaborative techniques • Vocabulary is mostly appropriate for task, audience, and purpose • Style is generally appropriate and effective	The response presents inconsistent support for the main and supporting ideas with limited evidence from sources, facts, and details. Elaboration is inconsistent with simple language. • Evidence from sources may be poorly integrated or irrelevant or only loosely supports key ideas • Writer uses few elaborative techniques • Vocabulary is somewhat inappropriate for task, audience, and purpose • Style is largely ineffective	The response presents little support for the main and supporting ideas with little or no evidence from sources, facts, or details. Elaboration is inadequate or absent. • Evidence from sources, if present, may be irrelevant with little support for key ideas • Writer uses few or no elaborative techniques • Vocabulary is inappropriate for task, audience, and purpose • Style is weak or absent	• not intelligible • not written in English • not on topic • contains text copied from source • does not address the purpose for writing

	2	**1**	**0**	**NS**
CONVENTIONS	The response demonstrates adequate command of conventions. • Consistent use of correct sentence structures, punctuation, capitalization, grammar, and spelling	The response demonstrates partial command of conventions. • Limited use of correct sentence structures, punctuation, capitalization, grammar, and spelling	The response demonstrates little or no command of conventions. • Rare use of correct sentence structures, punctuation, capitalization, grammar, and spelling	• not intelligible • not written in English • not on topic • contains text copied from source

PERFORMANCE TASK • Opinion Writing

	SCORE				
	4	**3**	**2**	**1**	**NS**
PURPOSE/ ORGANIZATION	The response is clear, focused, and well organized throughout. • Opinion is clear, focused, and effective for task, audience, and purpose • Includes a variety of transitions to relate ideas • Contains a logical sequence of ideas with strong relationships between them • Includes an effective introduction and conclusion	The response's organization is adequately maintained, and the focus is generally clear. • Opinion is clear, mostly focused, and mostly effective for task, audience, and purpose • Includes some variety of transitions to relate ideas • Contains an adequate sequence of ideas with adequate relationships between them • Includes an adequate introduction and conclusion	The response is somewhat focused but may be unclear in parts. Organization may be inconsistent. • Opinion may be somewhat unclear, lack focus, or be ineffective for task, audience, and purpose • Includes little variety of transitions to relate ideas • Sequence of ideas may be weak or unclear • Introduction and conclusion need improvement	The response's focus and organization are not clear. • Opinion may be confusing; response may be inappropriate for task, audience, and purpose • Includes few or no transitions to relate ideas • Sequence of ideas is unorganized; may include off-topic ideas • Introduction and/or conclusion may be missing	• not intelligible • not written in English • not on topic • contains text copied from source • does not address the purpose for writing
EVIDENCE/ELABORATION	The response presents strong support for the opinion with effective use of evidence from sources, facts, and details, elaborating with specific and effective language. • Evidence from sources is integrated and relevant and supports key ideas • Writer uses a variety of elaborative techniques • Vocabulary is clear and appropriate for task, audience, and purpose • Style is appropriate and effective	The response presents adequate support for the opinion with evidence from sources, facts, and details, adequately elaborating with a mix of specific and general language. • Evidence from sources is integrated and relevant and somewhat supports key ideas • Writer uses some elaborative techniques • Vocabulary is mostly appropriate for task, audience, and purpose • Style is generally appropriate and effective	The response presents inconsistent support for the opinion with limited evidence from sources, facts, and details. Elaboration is inconsistent and uses simple language. • Evidence from sources may be poorly integrated or irrelevant or only loosely supports key ideas • Writer uses few elaborative techniques • Vocabulary is somewhat inappropriate for task, audience, and purpose • Style is largely ineffective	The response presents little support for the opinion with little or no evidence from sources, facts, or details. Elaboration is inadequate or absent. • Evidence from sources, if present, may be irrelevant, with little support for key ideas • Writer uses few or no elaborative techniques • Vocabulary is inappropriate for task, audience, and purpose • Style is weak or absent	• not intelligible • not written in English • not on topic • contains text copied from source • does not address the purpose for writing

	2	**1**	**0**	**NS**
CONVENTIONS	The response demonstrates adequate command of conventions. • Consistent use of correct sentence structures, punctuation, capitalization, grammar, and spelling	The response demonstrates partial command of conventions. • Limited use of correct sentence structures, punctuation, capitalization, grammar, and spelling	The response demonstrates little or no command of conventions. • Rare use of correct sentence structures, punctuation, capitalization, grammar, and spelling	• not intelligible • not written in English • not on topic • contains text copied from source

Inquiry and Research Project

	SCORE			
	4	3	2	1
COLLABORATION	• Students made valuable contributions to each task within the project. • Students provided constructive feedback and input during preparation steps and check-ins. • Discussions were polite and productive. • Group members demonstrated clear understanding of the role of collaboration in project success.	• Students somewhat contributed to each task within the project. • Students provided some useful feedback and input during preparation steps and check-ins. • Discussions were polite but got off-track. • Group members demonstrated a basic understanding of the role of collaboration in project success.	• Students made partial contributions to tasks within the project. • Students had trouble providing useful feedback and input during preparation steps and check-ins. • Discussions led to disagreements or were frequently off-topic. • Group members made little effort to collaborate.	• Students made few or no contributions to tasks within the project. • Students were unable to provide useful feedback and input during display steps and check-ins. • Discussions did not take place, or students had trouble interacting with each other. • Group members did not work as a team.
RESEARCH AND TEXT EVIDENCE	• Information is organized in a clear and logical way. • Students chose a variety of reliable print and digital resources. • Research is carefully documented. • Text evidence is used successfully throughout the project.	• Information is mostly organized in a clear and logical way. • Students chose a few reliable print and digital resources. • Research is documented but disorganized or unclear. • Text evidence is used well in some parts of the project.	• Information is somewhat organized. • Students chose only print or only digital resources. • Research is not documented. • Text evidence is weak or used in a limited way.	• Information has little to no organization. • There is no evidence of the use of reliable sources. • Research was limited or not conducted. • Text evidence has not been used.
CONTENT	• Content maintains a clear focus throughout. • Written portions of the project are well thought out and answer the project question thoroughly. • Visuals are useful and enhance the product. • The project is error-free.	• Content is focused but may stray at times. • Written portions of the project are well thought out and mostly address the project question. • Visuals are somewhat useful. • The project contains some errors.	• Content is unfocused in some areas. • Written portions of the project provide some information but lack purpose. • Visuals are not useful. • All parts of the project contain minimal errors	• Content is haphazard throughout. • Written portions of the project are unclear and do not address the project question. • Visuals or multimedia are not present. • The project contains major errors.
PRESENTATION	• The presentation is dynamic and engaging. • Information is shared in an effective way. • The presentation is well organized. • Students are able to give thoughtful answers to audience questions.	• The presentation is engaging and effective. • The display has parts that could be better organized. • Students are able to answer most questions from the audience.	• The presentation is helpful but not very engaging. • Information is shared but confusing at times. • The display lacks clear organization. • Students struggle to answer questions about their display.	• The presentation is off-topic and irrelevant or confusing. • The display is disorganized. • Students are unable to answer questions about their display.

HMH Into Reading™ Teacher's Guide Index

The Index for the separate Writing Workshop Teacher's Guide can be found beginning on page R56.

A

HMH Into Reading™ Teacher's Guide Index

B

C

HMH Into Reading™ Teacher's Guide Index

HMH Into Reading™ Teacher's Guide Index

D

HMH Into Reading™ Teacher's Guide Index

E

HMH Into Reading™ Teacher's Guide Index

G

HMH Into Reading™ Teacher's Guide Index

HMH Into Reading™ Teacher's Guide Index

H

I

HMH Into Reading™ Teacher's Guide Index

K

L

HMH Into Reading™ Teacher's Guide Index

HMH Into Reading™ Teacher's Guide Index

HMH Into Reading™ Teacher's Guide Index

M

N

HMH Into Reading™ Teacher's Guide Index

HMH Into Reading™ Teacher's Guide Index

HMH Into Reading™ Teacher's Guide Index

S

HMH Into Reading™ Teacher's Guide Index

HMH Into Reading™ Teacher's Guide Index

T

HMH Into Reading™ Teacher's Guide Index

V

HMH Into Reading™ Teacher's Guide Index

HMH Into Reading™ Teacher's Guide Index

W

Writing Workshop Teacher's Guide Index

The Index for the *HMH Into Reading*™ Teacher's Guide can be found beginning on page R14.

A

B

Writing Workshop Teacher's Guide Index

Writing Workshop Teacher's Guide Index

E

Writing Workshop Teacher's Guide Index

F

G

Writing Workshop Teacher's Guide Index

Writing Workshop Teacher's Guide Index

Writing Workshop Teacher's Guide Index

Writing Workshop Teacher's Guide Index

Writing Workshop Teacher's Guide Index

S

U

V

Writing Workshop Teacher's Guide Index